THE QUANTIFIED WORKER

The information revolution has ushered in a data-driven reorganization of the workplace. Big Data and artificial intelligence (AI) are used to surveil workers and shift risk. Workplace wellness programs appraise our health. Personality job tests calibrate our mental state. The monitoring of social media and the surveillance of the workplace measure our social behavior. With rich historical sources and contemporary examples, *The Quantified Worker* explores how the workforce science of today goes far beyond increasing efficiency and threatens to erase individual personhood. With exhaustive detail, Ifeoma Ajunwa shows how different forms of worker quantification are enabled, facilitated, and driven by technological advances. Timely and eye-opening, *The Quantified Worker* advocates for changes in the law that will mitigate the ill effects of the modern workplace.

Ifeoma Ajunwa is a 2021–2022 Fulbright scholar, an award-winning tenured law professor at the University of North Carolina School of Law, and adjunct professor at the Kenan-Flagler Business School. She is the founding director of the Artificial Intelligence Decision-Making Research Program and a faculty associate at the Berkman Klein Centre at Harvard University.

D1617545

The Quantified Worker

LAW AND TECHNOLOGY IN THE MODERN WORKPLACE

IFEOMA AJUNWA

University of North Carolina School of Law

CAMBRIDGE
UNIVERSITY PRESS

Shaftesbury Road, Cambridge CB2 8EA, United Kingdom

One Liberty Plaza, 20th Floor, New York, NY 10006, USA

477 Williamstown Road, Port Melbourne, VIC 3207, Australia

314–321, 3rd Floor, Plot 3, Splendor Forum, Jasola District Centre, New Delhi – 110025, India

103 Penang Road, #05–06/07, Visioncrest Commercial, Singapore 238467

Cambridge University Press is part of Cambridge University Press & Assessment, a department of the University of Cambridge.

We share the University's mission to contribute to society through the pursuit of education, learning and research at the highest international levels of excellence.

www.cambridge.org
Information on this title: www.cambridge.org/9781107186033

DOI: 10.1017/9781316888681

First published 2023

A catalogue record for this publication is available from the British Library.

A Cataloging-in-Publication data record for this book is available from the Library of Congress.

ISBN 978-1-107-18603-3 Hardback
ISBN 978-1-316-63695-4 Paperback

For Papa and Mama.
Also for J., A., and A., you are my anchor and my sails.

Contents

Figures

Acknowledgments

This book was six years in the making. Long hours seated or standing at a writing desk, tapping out words. Squeezing in hours of writing in the morning, afternoon, or late night. It was tiring, mentally and physically taxing. There were euphoric moments of having landed on the *mot juste*, having carved the clear paragraph that cuts clean, but also the deepest pits of despair when doubts set in.

There were so many people I met on the way, who in one way or another propped me up; puffed me up when I became deflated; gave me sustenance, both physical and spiritual; and in big and small ways helped me to keep on keeping on. I am tremendously grateful to all the people who have helped this book to come to fruition. I have a great fear that I will inevitably forget to name someone here, so I ask in advance, please forgive me, and please know that even if I forgot you here, I didn't forget in my heart.

First and foremost, a huge thanks to Matt Gallaway, my editor at Cambridge University Press. I was a still newish assistant professor of law and I had not even dared dream that I would write an academic book when he first approached me, after reading one of my articles. You believed, and because of you, I did too. Thanks also to my second editor at Cambridge University Press, Jadyn Fauconier-Herry. Many thanks also to Alice Marwick who designed the book cover – you understood the concept I had in mind, and it's a thrill to see it come to life.

Thanks to my mentors: Dr. Danielle Allen, Dr. Nancy Baym, Dr. Ruha Benjamin, Dr. Yochai Benkler, Dr. danah boyd, Dr. Lolita Buckner-Inniss, Anupam Chandler, Danielle Keats Citron, Julie Cohen, Dr. Kate Crawford, Dr. Veena Dubal, Cynthia Estlund, Andrew Ferguson, Dr. Mary Gray, Michele Goodwin, Martha Minow, Brishen Rogers, Frank Pasquale, Jason Schultz, Dan Solove, Dr. Angela Onwuachi-Willig, and Jonathan Zittrain. Your book writing successes inspired me. A special thanks to Dr. Josh Whitford, my dissertation advisor, who once said to me, "You know, you're already an academic?" Yes, I believe it now.

Thanks to the research assistants who have worked with me on this book: Julie Cannon Syjah Harris, Minjae Kim Kylie O'Donnell, Jake Schindler, Elisabeth

Tidwell, and Kayleigh Yerdon, and my copy editor, Barbara Smith-Mandell. Thank you for your tireless work.

To my writing group friends: Dr. Brooke Erin Duffy, Dr. Filiz Garip, Maggie Gardner, Tashara Leak, Ngozi Okidegbe, and Franita Tolson, thank you for your companionship, the tea, and the laughter.

To all my Lutie sisters, and especially Erika George, Taja-Nia Henderson, Osamudia James, Tamara Lawson, Catherine Smith, Peggy Smith, Erika Wilson, and so many others. Your excellence is my example.

A heartfelt thank you to others who believed in me, encouraged me, and supported me in tremendous ways throughout this book writing journey: Ashley Adaji, Dr. Deji Adeleke, Adewale Adeleke, Grace Ajunwa, Mario Barnes, Peace Bosah, Dr. Melissa Ajunwa Bohonos, Dr. Darren Bush, Samantha Oluchi Etchie, Alero Etchie, Arlene Ford, Corey Ford, Jeff Ford Dr. Joel Ford, Sue Glueck, Carissa Byrne Hessick, Sajni Jobanputra, Anne Klinefelter, Kathy Miller Dr. Steven Nuñez, Leigh Osofsky, Daniel Oyolu, Dr. Adaeze Ugwoke, and Dr. Chibuzo Ukonu.

Finally, a big thank you to all my family members, both in the U.S. and in Nigeria – I would not be who I am without you.

I am grateful also for generous funding from the National Science Foundation, the Fulbright Program, the Robert Wood Johnson Foundation, Cornell University Social Science Research Center, and Microsoft.

Introduction

The quantified worker is awakened by an electronic device she wears on her wrist. First it is a gentle vibration, then the sensation gradually increases in intensity. The device tracks information on her sleeping habits – when she went to sleep, how long she slept, even whether it was fitful or peaceful sleep. An elevated heart rate – perhaps from vigorous nocturnal activity or perhaps merely a disturbing nightmare – is also noted. Once she is out of bed, the device counts her steps. In the mirror she brushes her teeth vigorously – she hopes that counts for exercise. Because the quantified worker is part of a workplace wellness program, all the information from her electronic device is dispatched to the program and, in return, her employer pays her health insurance premium. To continue with the program, the quantified worker must also exercise for 30 minutes every day; she earns redeemable points each time she goes to a gym because she has a card with an embedded chip that keeps electronic tabs on her gym visits. As part of her wellness program, the quantified worker must also keep a food diary. She is expected to photograph each meal and list the ingredients on an app on her phone. At the beginning of the program, the quantified worker submitted to genetic testing. The result: a genetic profile for the quantified worker outlining her propensity for certain diseases and extrapolating what diet she must follow to maintain optimal health. As part of the wellness program, the quantified worker was encouraged to download a health application on her phone. On this app, she is expected to track all her prescription medications and also her menstrual cycle. There is also an option for tracking ovulation cycles.[1]

For the quantified worker, it is not only her body that is quantified, it is also her mind. To apply for the job, the quantified worker had to run the gauntlet of automated hiring platforms. She acquiesced to platform authoritarianism as the platforms demanded information to shape how she would be presented as a candidate

---

[1] In 2016, a *Wall Street Journal* investigation found that bosses were using outside firms to track prescription medicine use and to deploy that data to predict which employers were sick or trying to get pregnant. See Rachel Emma Silverman, "Bosses Tap Outside Firms to Predict Which Workers Might Get Sick," *Wall Street Journal*, Feb. 17, 2016.

and how she could eventually be sorted. Part of the application compelled the quantified worker to take a personality job test. She answered questions such as "How often do you smile per day?" and "Do you find yourself feeling sad for no reason?" Then the quantified worker sat for a video interview. In the comfort of her own home, she sat alone in a room, eyes rigidly fixed straight ahead on her laptop camera. She was careful to never show too much of the whites of her eyes, a sure sign of aggression. Instead, she kept her gaze just slightly narrowed, never looking right and most definitely not left. She stared straight at the camera, making eye contact with the machine. Her friends have told her she tends to speak with her hands, elucidating her points with fluid hand flourishes, so she kept her hands gripped on a pencil on the desk in front of her – like an anchor or deadweight. It is true that this made her feel like she was attempting to speak with a muzzle on, but no matter, she would appear confident to the machine evaluating her. She sat ramrod straight. After all, good posture is a proxy for good character. She reminded herself not to shift in her chair – you don't want the AI thinking you are shifty, untrustworthy.

Once the quantified worker is hired, mechanical managers become her immediate supervisors. Whether she is hired to an office job where she wears a lapel pin that tracks her movements around the office and might record snippets of conversation, or whether she works a factory job requiring physical exertion where she must wear a safety exoskeleton that can detect whether she is indeed lifting with her knees, her mechanical managers silently and perpetually record her every move. If she works in an office with sensitive information, she might wear a badge with a radio-frequency identification (RFID) allowing her entrance to certain rooms and excluding her from others – for extra convenience, an RFID chip might be inserted under her skin, thereby taking the term *embedded manager* to new heights. If she works in an office, there are cameras everywhere except the bathroom – a code to unlock the bathroom door already documents who enters and for how long. As she sits and types at her computer, her keystrokes are logged. The websites she visits on her computer are logged. And for the hypervigilant employer, there is no need to stand over her shoulder to peer at her computer screen – a program will take a screenshot of her computer screen at whatever interval is required. Her email communications are also tracked. Is she perhaps disgruntled from all the surveillance? Is she planning to leave the company? A program will track her visits and behavior on LinkedIn and will alert her human manager if she proves to be a significant flight risk. Her social media accounts also are surveilled. Any criticism of her employer is flagged: Such action may reflect on her advancement in the company or could lead to dismissal.

If this sounds to you like a dystopian future, you are half correct. This is not the future. It is the current plight of workers. Most workers are now caught up in what scholars such as Shoshanna Zuboff have identified as "surveillance capitalism," their every move tracked and monitored in service of profit-making. When William Whyte published *The Organization Man* in the fall of 1956, it carried a warning that large American corporations were systemically eroding the individuality of their workers. Furthermore, Whyte warned, this suppression of individuality would be detrimental, not just to the individual, but also to the corporation itself because of the concomitant loss of creativity and innovation. In addition to Whyte's warning, other books such as *Windows on the Workplace* (1942) and *The Electronic Sweatshop* (1988) have raised questions about the deleterious effects of work technology on worker rights. With this book, I argue that technological advances have ushered in a new era in the workplace – the era of the quantified worker. This new era brings with it new legal challenges, both for the organization and for the worker.

I first started contemplating the quantified worker when I was a graduate student at Columbia University. At that time, as research for my dissertation, I was interviewing formerly incarcerated individuals who were seeking to re-enter society and the workplace. A common refrain emerged from the interviews: "I hate computers." At first, I thought this had to do with computer illiteracy. Many of these individuals had gone to prison in the early 1990s before personal computing had become widespread. I thought their frustration stemmed from their unfamiliarity with digital systems and the internet. But it was something more insidious. These individuals felt themselves shut out by "computers." In seeking to re-enter the workplace, they had confronted automated hiring platforms as gatekeepers. Gaps in their employment history or truthfully checking the box for "Have you been convicted of a crime?" or even merely "Have you ever been arrested?" was enough to get their application "red-lighted" and trashed – never to be considered by a human manager.

The individuals I interviewed were part of re-entry organizations, meaning that they were all actively seeking to re-enter society. They attended anger management classes, interviewing skills classes, and other courses meant to broker the social and cultural capital they needed to re-enter society. They were taught how to dress for an interview, how to firmly shake hands, how to make eye contact and convey confidence. How to speak professionally. How to explain their past criminal circumstances. How to relay the truth of their incarceration in a manner that would make them sympathetic to the hiring manager. But after hundreds of electronic applications that seemed to disappear into the internet chasm, they were starting to realize that none of that mattered. Unlike a human manager, artificial intelligence (AI) in the form of automated hiring lacks discretion. It is an unfeeling and implacable gatekeeper.

The Quantified Worker carries a warning – it rings the alarm bell that American workers are increasingly quantified in a manner and to a degree that had been hitherto unknown in history. The quantification of workers is not new; it is as old as the valuation of Roman slaves or the counting of bushels of cotton picked by African slaves in the Americas. What sets this new era of worker quantification apart is that the quantification is now aided by technological advances grouped under the catch-all term of *artificial intelligence*. These new technologies perform automated decision-making with machine learning algorithms, often ignoring the gestalt of the worker in favor of numbers on a screen. The zeitgeist of this new era of quantification is that it is simultaneously nebulous and impactful; the intangibles of human behavior and genetic predilection concretized as numbers to manage risk and profit for the firm.

First and foremost, this book is meant to serve as an eye-opening account of the impact of technology in the workplace – it is meant to spur academic discourse and further empirical exploration of the issues raised. Second, it is poised to answer this question: What should the law do? Given that the pervasive quantification of workers erodes worker personhood and belies the democratic ideal, how should the law respond? Thus, this is also a legally informed book that grapples with the complex legal questions raised by the introduction of AI technologies in the workplace. This book is also historically informed in that it reaches into the past to trace the development of worker subjugation through quantification as the most recent iteration of scientific management.

An important caveat is that the book's scope is constrained to mapping law and technology issues present within the traditional employer–employee relationship. As such this book does not squarely address the gig economy and other important instances of platform or solely online work. For that, I would point to works by Mary Gray and Siddharth Suri (*Ghost Work*), Niels Van Dorn, and Veena Dubal, among others.

This book puts forth a theory of worker quantification and parses its legal implications for worker voice and worker domination. In doing so, the book describes the breadth of worker quantification as facilitated, and often obfuscated, by modern-day technologies deployed in the workplace. In Part I The Ideology of Worker Quantification, Chapter 1 explains how worker quantification sprang from Taylorism and its practiced form, scientific management. Worker quantification is not merely about maximizing profit, but is preoccupied with worker control. Chapter 2 traces the historical responses to quantification in the form of Taylorism and lays out the socio-legal issues raised by scientific management.

Part II, The Mechanical Managers, documents the rise of mechanical managers in which the work of hiring, monitoring, and evaluating workers is increasingly being delegated to AI technologies. Chapter 3 focuses on automated hiring systems and platforms, and how bias may become baked into these systems. In this chapter, I examine the question of legal responsibility for preventing discrimination in hiring decisions based on AI and algorithms. Chapter 4 analyzes personality tests used in hiring, showing how such tests may violate medical privacy laws and allow for proxy discrimination against neuro-atypical candidates or individuals with mental illness. Chapter 5 moves on to automated video interviews, demonstrating the significant shortcomings of the pseudo-sciences of facial analysis and emotional recognition, and connects these new technologies to the pseudo-science of phrenology. I explain how reliance on these tools promotes discrimination against various protected groups, and how current laws are limited in their ability to address these problems. Chapter 6, on worker surveillance, explains the history of workplace surveillance and how the theories behind this practice ignore workers' rights to privacy and dignity in the workplace. Chapter 7 discusses the newest iteration of workplace wellness programs and how they may allow for genetic discrimination. Chapter 8 discusses the greater quantification of health (through surveillance) in the Covid era and how this might present new legal opportunities for health discrimination.

In Part III, Quantified Discrimination, I examine the ways in which technology used in the service of worker quantification can both facilitate and obfuscate discrimination on several axes. This is particularly troublesome for its potential to undo the gains for equal opportunity brought about by the Civil Rights Act of 1964 and other anti-discrimination laws. Chapter 9 focuses on wearable technologies as techno-solutions to employer concerns about maximizing profits and minimizing risks. In exploring how wearable technologies blur the line between work and non-work time, I discuss the legal questions of data ownership and control, the misuse and abuse of wearable tech, and the loss of worker privacy and autonomy. Chapter 10 delves into the long-standing issue of quantified racism in the workplace, revealing that workers are not equally quantified and that existing metrics of quantification bear the taint of racial prejudice.

Part IV, Business Ethics and New Legal Frameworks, examines ethical issues at the heart of worker quantification, and looks forward to propose new ethical and legal frameworks for tackling the issue of worker quantification. Chapter 11 discusses the ethical dimensions of worker quantification and relies on the legal philosopher John Rawls to argue for a new approach to the adoption of work technologies. In Chapter 12, I put forth proposals for legal frameworks that are more in line with the current capabilities of work technologies and will therefore be more adept at ensuring that workplace technologies do not contribute to worker domination.

We tend to think of a singular future of work. However, this tendency is a product of techno-fatalism – the belief that we must acquiesce to the unsavory unintended consequences of technology in exchange for reaping its benefits. Yet, many different futures of work are possible. Thus, in my conclusion, I imagine a future where data can be harnessed in the service of worker power. I contemplate how unions of the future could work together with organizations and corporations to transform the data in "data-driven workplaces" from driving whip to collaborative knowledge. Finally, I note that techno-solutionism can never be the full answer. Neither can we rely on business ethics as a self-policing measure for organizations. Technological innovation has served as a Trojan horse for surveillance technologies, and the law must act as a true bulwark against the rising inequality introduced by these technologies. In practice, this means the implementation of targeted laws and regulations that are intelligently tailored to address the discriminatory potential of our new mechanical managers.

PART I

The Ideology of Worker Quantification

1

The Rise of Scientific Management

The majority of these men believe that the fundamental interests of employees and employers are necessarily antagonistic. Scientific management, on the contrary, has for its very foundation the firm conviction that the true interests of the two are one and the same; that prosperity for the employer cannot exist through a long term of years unless it is accompanied by prosperity for the employee, and vice versa; and that it is possible to give the workman what he most wants – high wages – and the employer what he wants – a low labor cost – for his manufactures.

–Fredrick Winslow Taylor, *The Principles of Scientific Management*

The information revolution has ushered in a data-driven reorganization of the workplace, where Big Data, and the machine learning algorithms that can run them, are deployed to make meaning out of a mountain of minutiae of workers' actions and behaviors. As a 2013 *New York Times* article noted, "today, every e-mail, instant message, phone call, line of written code and mouse-click leaves a digital signal. These patterns can now be inexpensively collected and mined for insights into how people work and communicate, potentially opening doors to more efficiency and innovation within companies."[1] While some may refer to this new data-preoccupied "workforce science"[2] or "people analytics"[3] as a boon to workplace efficiency,[4] others see instead a digital panopticon.[5] Although debates about worker surveillance and employer attempts to measure worker efficiency are not new controversies, what is novel is the manner and degree to which workers are now being quantified. Given recent technological developments such as the mass collection of data

[1] Steven Lohr, "Big Data, Trying to Build Better Workers," *New York Times*, Apr. 20, 2013.
[2] See Alec Levenson and Gillian Pillans, *Strategic Workforce Analytics*, Corporate Research Forum Report, Nov. 2017.
[3] See Jean Paul Isson and Jesse S. Harriot, *People Analytics in the Era of Big Data* (Hoboken, NJ: Wiley, 2016).
[4] Peter Cappelli, *The Future of the Office* (Philadelphia: Wharton School Press, 2021).
[5] Olivia Solon, "Big Brother Isn't Just Watching: Workplace Surveillance Can Track Your Every Move," *The Guardian*, Nov. 6, 2017.

(dubbed "Big Data") and the computerized algorithms that may perform rapid analyses on those data while also creating *de novo* models for analysis (machine learning algorithms), the characteristics, skills, and outputs of the contemporary worker have become *quantified* in a manner and to a degree previously unseen in history. This quantification in turn is changing the very nature of work, blurring boundaries between work and nonwork and raising new legal questions about employee privacy, worker power and autonomy, and the limits of employer control over the worker.

It is a given that new technology is constitutive, that is, new technology changes the way we view the world and can, in fact, constitute the world and social relations anew. However, it is often overlooked that technology and ideology are co-constitutive. In other words, technology only exists insofar as it is conceived as part of an ideology and is used in service of that ideology. Thus, technology is never neutral: Embedded in both its design and use cases are theories of what is and what ought to be. For example, Jayaweera and Amunugama make the distinction between inventions (as a priori neutral objects) and technology as objects or processes arising out of "a particular meeting of economic, social, and political circumstances which automatically guarantee its exploitation and conversion into an instrument of economic and social power."[6] Technology does not spring from the ether and does not exist in a vacuum. Rather, it sprouts in a political economy steeped in history. Technology is both a product and response to the socio-political zeitgeist of its time. Thus, technology is both made available and shaped by extant legal frameworks. Co-constitutively, new legal frameworks are in turn prompted by new technology use cases.

Jürgen Habermas, a sociologist of critical theory and technology, warned that technology only *appears* to be autonomous from societal ideology, but that this is far from reality.[7] As Dutton subsequently noted, emerging technologies have the tendency to "reinforce" the interests of the holders of power in organizations; thus, without legal interventions, new technologies arrive poised to automate the bias of the power elite.[8] Furthermore, technology is not limited to merely fulfilling a job task or work purpose; rather, the function of any given technology will morph to coincide with the organizational characteristics of the organization in which it is used. In turn, technology will also have its own organizational effects that impact the work environment and lives of workers. Robey found that computer technology within stable organizational environments is deployed to further centralize control, while the same technology within unstable organizational environments is used to

---

[6] Neville Jayaweera and Sarath Amunugama, *Rethinking Development Communication* (Singapore: Asian Mass Communication Research and Information Centre, 1987).

[7] Jürgen Habermas, *Theory and Practice*, trans. John Viertel (Boston: Beacon Press, 1971). See also Jürgen Habermas, *Knowledge and Human Interests*, trans. Jeremy J. Shapiro (Boston: Beacon Press, 1971).

[8] Susan E. Jackson and Jane E. Dutton, "Discerning Threats and Opportunities," *Administrative Quarterly* 33, no. 3 (1988): 370–87; Jane E. Dutton and Jane Webster, "Patterns of Interest Around Issues," *Academy of Management Journal* 31, no. 3 (1988): 663–75.

further decentralize functions.[9] This is readily apparent today in a comparison of the use of artificial intelligence (AI) technologies in the gig economy versus traditional workplaces. Work technologies of today come imprinted with ideologies about worker power, or the lack thereof. Today's work technologies reinforce attitudes and beliefs about how far the employer is entitled to seek control over workers.[10] Furthermore, they bring to high relief the gray areas in the law concerning protections for workers and their rights. The end result is a pressing societal imperative to reach a consensus on new legal regimes and social choices necessary to maintain fundamental societal values of democracy and liberty.

The mention of social choice is to underscore that this book is decidedly anti-technological determinism or, to acknowledge its most recent iteration, anti-techno-fatalism. Veblen posits work technology as always in full control:

> The machine throws out anthropomorphic habits of thought. It compels the adaptation of the workman to his work, rather than the adaption of the worker ... the machine process gives no insight into questions of good or evil, merit or demerit, except in point of material causation, nor into the foundations or the constraining force of law and order ...[11]

To accept Veblen's description as a foregone fact is both techno-determinist and techno-fatalistic. To see it as what it is – a description of one possible future of technology – is techno-realist. As Held notes, "technocratic consciousness fulfils the ideological function of legitimating the pursuit of particular interests. It conceals behind a façade of objectivity the interests of classes and groups that actually determine the function, direction, and pace of technological and social developments."[12] Hill concurs in his assessment and argues against attributing power solely to the potential of technology. Furthermore, he notes, "Social, economic, and political negotiations are involved in bringing particular technological systems into existence."[13] The law plays a large part by legitimizing or delegitimizing specific use cases for technology: It allows or disallows the continued existence of certain types of technologies and signals ahead for what new technology may be brought into existence.

Legal scholars, more so than others, have started to buck the passivity of techno-fatalism. From Frank Pasquale's *The Black Box Society*, in which he calls for the regulation of the shadowy data brokers that have mushroomed as a result of the

[9] Daniel Robey, "Computers and Management Structure: Some Empirical Findings Re-examined," *Human Relations* 30, no. 11 (1977): 963–76.

[10] See A. Rodder, "Technologies of Control: The Construction of the Modern Worker" (MS thesis, University of Oslo, 2016).

[11] Thorstein Veblen, *The Theory of Business Enterprise* (New Brunswick, NJ: Transaction Books, 1904), 310–11.

[12] David Held, *Introduction to Critical Theory: Horkheimer to Habermas* (Berkeley: University of California Press, 1980), 264–65.

[13] Stephen Hill, *The Tragedy of Technology: Human Liberation versus Domination in the Late Twentieth Century* (London: Pluto Press, 1988), 6.

information revolution,[14] to Julie Cohen's *Between Truth and Power*, which highlights the configurability of networked information technologies as battlegrounds for well-resourced parties to shape their development, to scholars like James Grimmelmann who maintains that algorithmic subjects "deserve a better explanation than 'the computer said so'," legal scholars exhort us to ask questions about the undesirable effects of technology on society and whether these effects should be accepted as inevitable.[15]

1.1 THE THEORY OF WORKER QUANTIFICATION

My theory of worker quantification hinges on the observation that AI technologies have been deployed to work concurrently and cumulatively to quantify not just worker productivity, but also all aspects of worker behavior. Whereas the concept of scientific management was focused on quantifying the work, chipping work into concrete and minute tasks that could be both quantified and standardized for great efficiency gains, the workforce science of today, as an iteration of scientific management, goes far beyond that. Now, it is not merely the job task that is being quantified, but it is also the worker's health through workplace wellness programs, the worker's mental state through personality job tests, and the worker's social behavior through workplace surveillance and the monitoring of social media.[16] To be sure, worker quantification is enabled, facilitated, and driven by technological advances, but the impulse toward worker quantification also derives from the ideologies that came before those technological advances.

1.2 NOT ANTI-TECHNOLOGY; RATHER, PRO-REGULATION

One common response to critiques of new technology is the accusation of Luddism. Yet, as some have observed, this accusation misdiagnoses the problem. As early as 1984, political scientist Raphael Kaplinsky contended, "The problem lies not with the technology but in a form of social organization which misuses its potential to produce frighteningly destructive weapons, inappropriate products and undesirable work processes."[17] As Keith Grint and Steve

---

[14] Frank Pasquale, *The Black Box Society: The Secret Algorithms that Control Money and Information* (Cambridge, MA: Harvard University Press, 2015).

[15] James Grimmelmann and Daniel Westreich, "Incomprehensible Discrimination," *California Law Review Online* 7, no. 1 (2017): 164.

[16] See Indy Wijngaards et al., "Worker Well-Being: What It Is, and How It Should Be Measured," *Applied Research in Quality of Life* 17 (2021): 795–832; Fred Oswald, "Can a Personality Test Determine if You're a Good Fit for a Job?" *Speaking of Psychology* (blog), interview with Fred Oswald, PhD, episode 150, July 2021, www.apa.org/research/action/speaking-of-psychology/personality-tests; Kathryn Zickuhr, *Workplace Surveillance Is Becoming the New Normal for U.S. Workers*, Report, Washington Center for Equitable Growth, Aug. 18, 2021.

[17] Raphael Kaplinsky, *Automation: The Technology and Society* (London: Addison-Wesley Longman Ltd., 1984).

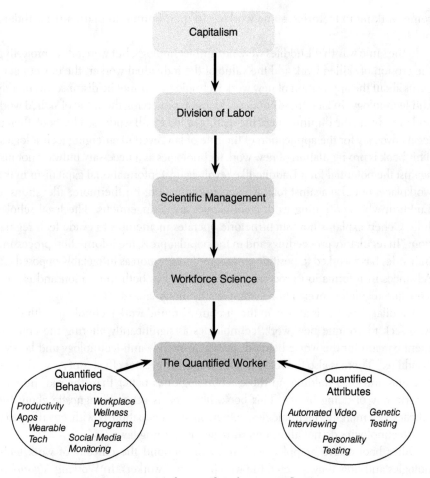

FIGURE 1.1 A theory of worker quantification

Woolgar illuminate in their 1997 *The Machine at Work*, the Luddites were not anti-technology; rather, they were actively protesting against a social reorganization of work that would devalue their artisanal skill and threaten their livelihood. A symbolic perspective of Luddism "suggests that the machine was merely a metaphor for a cultural revolution that the Luddites more or less recognized as inherently destructive of all that they held dear: the pre-industrial moral economy was about to be ripped apart by *laissez-faire* capitalism."[18] The conclusion is that the Luddites were "not so much against machinery as against the power of the machinery ... the real conflict of the time is the struggle of various classes,

[18] Keith Grint and Steve Woolgar, *The Machine at Work: Technology, Work, and Organization* (Cambridge: Polity Press, 1997), 49.

some working in factories, some working in their homes, to maintain a standard of life."[19]

In the same way that Luddites were not anti-technology, but were rather protesting the erosion of skilled work and the value of the individual worker, the current concerns about the application of new work technologies cannot be dismissed as merely anti-technology. In fact, these concerns focus on preserving the value of skilled work and preventing the diminution of the quality of life for all workers. This book then is legal advocacy for the application of the rule of law, even to emerging technologies. This book is pro-regulation of new work technologies as a necessary bulwark not just against the potential for a Luddite-like revolt against informational capitalism in the workplace, but also against total worker subordination. Furthermore, allegations of Luddism when critiquing work technologies are disingenuous. The legal scholar Julie Cohen explains how such rhetoric operates in attempts to evade tech regulation: "In regulatory proceedings and in the popular press, the information processing industries have worked to position privacy and innovation as intractably opposed .... Advances in information processing are privileged as both innovation and expression, and regulatory oversight is systematically marginalized."[20]

A similar dynamic is at play in the discourse around work technology, with those who seek to critique new work technologies as significantly altering the employment bargain for the worse being dismissed as merely anti-technology and labeled "Luddite." There is also the retort of presuming the greater efficacy of AI work technologies and thus holding up those technologies as better than the old, human-centric way of doing things. This book, however, is generally agnostic about the efficacy of emerging technologies; rather, its preoccupation is with ensuring that new technologies do not allow end runs against existing laws.

Other books have grappled with questions around the efficacy of work technologies and how they affected the workplace and workers. In *Working Algorithm: Software Automation and the Future of Work*, Benjamin Shestakofsky examines, in great detail, the pros and cons of automation in the workplace. Shestakofsky conducted a nineteen-month study at a software firm and observed how, when the company went through shifts in priorities, employees and employers also shifted their methods of working to accommodate technological advancements. Shestakofsky's research challenged a received wisdom that new work technologies can or are meant to replace traditional labor; rather he found that technology at the software firm was implemented to complement human labor and that managers actually attempted to reconfigure the workplace to achieve this purpose.[21]

[19]   Grint and Woolgar, *The Machine at Work*, 15 (quoting Hammond and Hammond, *The Village Laborer*).
[20]   Julie E. Cohen, "The Surveillance-Innovation Complex: The Irony of the Participatory Turn," in *The Participatory Condition of the Digital Age*, ed. Darin Barney et al. (Minneapolis: University of Minnesota Press, 2016), 218.
[21]   Benjamin J. Shestakofsky, "Working Algorithm, Software Automation and the Future of Work," *Work and Occupations* 44, no. 4 (2017): 376–423.

In *Algorithms at Work: The New Contested Terrains of Control*, Katherine C. Kellogg, Melissa A. Valentine, and Angèle Christin apply Richard Edwards's theory of "contested terrain" to examine how new technologies are revamping the workplace. Contested terrain describes the conflict between capital and labor and how systems of control are designed by employers to surmount this conflict.[22] Kellogg, Valentine, and Christin explain how algorithms operate in the workplace through six main mechanisms — restricting, recommending, recording, rating, replacing, and rewarding — that allow managers to "maximize the value of labor."[23] While the authors note that algorithmic control is more comprehensive than previously observed and may indeed eliminate the demand for direct supervisors and managers, they also note that the shift to rational control may drive the need for more job categories in developing algorithms for the workplace. But even the hopeful conclusion that new jobs will be created by algorithmic restructuring of the workplace cannot overshadow the reality of automation discontent, seen in the authors' description of the rise of "algoactivism" — the phenomenon of workers resisting algorithmic control. The authors also raise legal and ethical concerns related to new technologies in the workplace. Notably, the authors cite the lack of legal policies that could "protect employee privacy, limit managerial surveillance, prevent discrimination, and reclassify independent contractors as employees," and call for the "reconceptualization of workers' privacy rights" to clearly define context-specific norms given the rapid changes wrought by emerging work technologies in the workplace.[24]

Similarly, in *Future Work*, Jeffrey M. Hirsch explores the real and potential impacts of modern technology on the workplace, examining the nature of emerging technologies and their implications for law and policy. He focuses on four fields of innovation: artificial intelligence, X Reality (an "inclusive [term] for altered-reality environments"), automation, and surveillance technologies.[25] According to Hirsch, the practical hazard these advancements pose comes from the "combination of various technologies" to create a "blended workplace" of humans and machines.[26] Hirsch suggests that the impact of new technology on the labor market will be a change in the nature of work as opposed to a net loss of jobs. He also focuses on the liabilities new technologies can pose in the workplace, noting, for example, that increased worker monitoring requires a serious reconsideration of privacy laws and regulations to protect workers.[27] Ultimately, Hirsch concludes that new legislation

---

[22] Richard Edwards, *Contested Terrain: The Transformation of the Workplace in the Twentieth Century* (New York: Basic Books, 1979).

[23] Katherine C. Kellogg, Melissa A. Valentine, and Angèle Christin, "Algorithms at Work: The New Contested Terrain of Control," *Academy of Management Annals* 14, no. 1 (2020): 366–410.

[24] Kellogg, Valentine, and Christin, "Algorithms at Work," 394.

[25] Jeffrey M. Hirsch, "Future Work," *University of Illinois Law Review* 2020 (2020): 913.

[26] Hirsch, "Future Work," 915.

[27] Hirsch, "Future Work," 937.

is necessary to keep pace with how emerging technologies are transforming organizational control, that is the mantle taken up in this book.

1.3 THE HISTORICAL QUANTIFICATION OF WORKERS AND THE PROTESTANT WORK ETHIC

The quantification of workers is not new. From the Roman Empire before the Christian era to the transatlantic slave trade, to the Industrial Revolution, human beings have increasingly become quantified both as the labor they produce and as liabilities. In the Roman Empire, the military constituted a critical labor force that provided for the empire's rise and extended reign, and central to military management was timekeeping. The Romans used both the sundial and klepsydra to measure the hours. The klepsydra, a bowl from which water emptied at a predetermined rate, was used to divide the night into four separate, three-hour-long shifts. Clerks used the same technology to log the daily arrivals and departures of soldiers, messengers, and packages of a given camp. Romans even used time markers to record soldier movements as a unit. In this way, the quantification of military activities through time was aided by a rigid military structure that further quantified labor within a hierarchy according to rank.[28]

Quantification was likewise applied to solider pay, which was determined by a fixed scale that accounted for the individual's rank within a given legion and was distributed in equal annual installments with standardized deductions for food, armor, and supplies.[29] Each legion's base camp featured a savings bank, headed by the legion's standard bearer, that meticulously recorded the credits, debits, and deductions of all soldiers within the legion, keeping "individual statements of account … for each man."[30] Thus, the quantification of soldiers into standardized numerical units allowed for meticulous record-keeping and oversight that gave leaders the means to efficiently manage vast operations despite technological resources that seem limited by modern standards.

While the Roman Empire quantified labor for military efficiency, the transatlantic slave trade saw humans quantified as commodities for profit. Slavery provided an essential labor force in Roman times, but Roman slavery was far less standardized and featured many different paths to both enslavement and freedom.[31] The transatlantic slave trade, however, was built upon quantification. In her book *Saltwater Slavery*, Stephanie Smallwood parses this quantification in depth. Examining the ledgers of the Royal African Company (RAC), Smallwood describes the requirement

[28] George Cupcea, "Timekeeping in the Roman Army," *The Classical Quarterly* 67, no. 2 (2017): 597–606.

[29] Cupcea, "Timekeeping in the Roman Army"; W. R. Davies, "Peace-Time Routine in the Roman Army" (PhD thesis, Durham University, 1967), chap. 4.

[30] Davies, "Peace-time Routine in the Roman Army," 223.

[31] See Keith Bradley, *Slavery and Society at Rome* (Cambridge: Cambridge University Press, 1994).

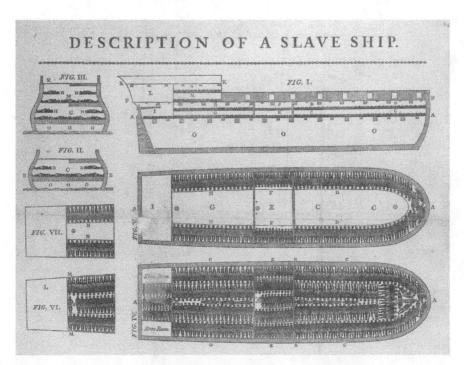

FIGURE 1.2 Diagram of the English slave ship *Brookes* (active 1782–1804), from Thomas Clarkson, *The History of the Rise, Progress, and Accomplishment of the Abolition of the African Slave-Trade by the British Parliament* (London, 1808). Courtesy of The British Library, www.bl.uk/learning/timeline/item106661.html.

that ships departing Africa acquire "'full complements'" of slaves before being permitted to set sail, which in practice meant that slavers packed ships past capacity to ensure a profitable voyage once the survivors made it to the American slave market. Smallwood describes the commodification of slaves as traders sought to quantify how much the Africans could endure so that they could maximize their profits. The widely distributed diagram of the British slave ship *Brookes* (see Figure 1.2) demonstrated how traders sought to maximize space by tightly packing humans into spaces with a mere 10 inches of clearance; another widely published diagram showed a Brazilian slave ship that allowed an average of 23 inches of space per man and 13 inches of space per woman. Quantification was further required by the Board of Trade in London, which sought data concerning how many slaves were transported, delivered, and sold to check for efficiency.[32] Ship manifests document such data, listing the name, sex, age, height, race, and owner of each slave entering a New World port.

[32] Stephanie E. Smallwood, *Saltwater Slavery: A Middle Passage from Africa to American Diaspora* (Cambridge, MA: Harvard University Press, 2008).

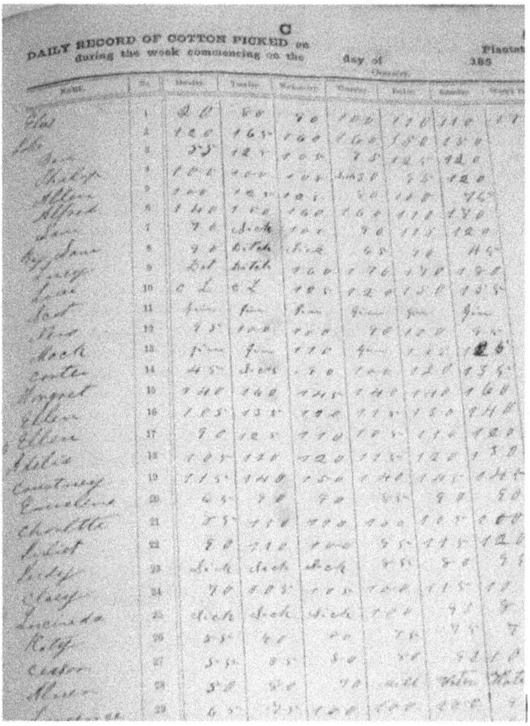

FIGURE 1.3 Sample entry in Affleck's *Cotton Plantation Record and Account Book*. (courtesy of Buffalo and Lake Erie County Public Library, Grosvenor Rare Book Room, posted May 29, 2012, https://grorarebookroom.wordpress.com/2012/05/29/cotton-plantation-record-and-account-book/)

For those who survived the Middle Passage, quantification and dehumanization only heightened. An article about the ledger of slave trader William James Smith notes that it records the first names of all the people Smith bought and sold over a five-year period, accompanied by his expenses, such as clothing, meals, and travel expenses; the price he got for their sale; and his net gain.[33] In her book *Accounting for Slavery*, Caitlin Rosenthal further examines the quantification that occurred on plantations, describing complex hierarchies of plantation management that allowed owners to profit from economies of scale.[34] Thomas Affleck's *Cotton Plantation Record and Account Book* (see Figure 1.3) is a key example of technological advancements in quantification. First published in 1847, this best-selling accounting manual featured blank spreadsheets used to track each slave's productivity and conduct yearly reviews of gross profits, expenses, and worker performance. Arguably most

[33] Rebecca Onion, "Tracking a Slave Trader through His Expense Reports," *Slate*, Apr. 7, 2014.
[34] Caitlin Rosenthal, *Accounting for Slavery: Masters and Management* (Cambridge, MA: Harvard University Press, 2018).

emblematic of the complete dehumanization and commodification of enslaved individuals was Affleck's method for calculating the depreciation of slave labor, accounting for age, sex, ability, and "temperament."[35] Rosenthal argues that such methods of management directly correlate with the systems of labor management seen during the nineteenth century.[36]

Indeed, the Industrial Revolution largely saw historical systems of quantification intersect with technological innovation, amplifying the amount of labor that managers could extract from workers. Advancements in transportation technologies (such as construction of canals and railroads), communication technologies (such as the telegraph), and the financialization of credit resulted in the market revolution. The market revolution saw small-scale home production of goods shift to the factory setting as expanded markets made large-scale production both possible and profitable.[37] However, this new method of production required new technologies and methods of management which, too, quantified workers in new ways. While the Romans relied on systems of time management to structure military movements, the Industrial Revolution necessitated systems of time management to schedule when employees should report for work in order to maximize production hours. Timekeeping technologies became more precise, largely thanks to the chronometer, and factory clocks were developed to measure worker shifts. In 1888, Willard Bundy created time-recording devices that allowed employers to track hours worked by their employees.[38] However, shift work was not the only measure by which workers were quantified.

The factory setting fundamentally changed the nature of work, in turn increasing the significance of quantification in employee management. Specialization and division of labor – as proposed by Adam Smith in his capitalist manifesto *The Wealth of Nations* – was at the heart of factory production. Specialization saw work broken down into increasingly smaller tasks that required less skill and allowed for more gains in efficiency. As factories became exponentially larger, management became increasingly important to more closely coordinate the smaller tasks required to develop a finished product. In 1881, Frederick Winslow Taylor used the stopwatch to conduct his first time study on worker productivity, giving birth to the new field of scientific management that sought to quantify work processes to optimize efficiency. Taylor advocated for "piecework production," which paid employees for each unit they produced. Employees who produced more would be paid proportionally more. Taylor believed that by quantifying production, he could

---

[35] Matthew Desmond, "In Order to Understand the Brutality of American Capitalism, You Have to Start on the Plantation," *New York Times Magazine*, Aug. 14, 2019.

[36] Rosenthal, *Accounting for Slavery*.

[37] David S. Bright et al., *Principles of Management* (OpenStax, 2019), 61–63, https://opentextbc.ca/principlesofmanagementopenstax/.

[38] Alun C. Davies, "The Industrial Revolution and Time Keeping," *Open University*, Aug. 30, 2019, www.open.edu/openlearn/history-the-arts/history/history-science-technology-and-medicine/history-technology/the-industrial-revolution-and-time; Rhett DePauw, "A Brief History of Time Management," *Exaktime*, Oct. 11, 2017, www.exaktime.com/blog/brief-history-time-management/.

motivate workers to produce more and could prevent worker unionization against management.[39] Thus quantification of production not only increased production, but also served as a mechanism to manage and control human capital.

But how did the quest for maximum productivity as the highest ideal gain such a hold on society through Taylorism? The Protestant work ethic has been acknowledged as a key underpinning of capitalism, a theory Max Weber advanced in his 1905 *The Protestant Ethic and the Spirit of Capitalism*. Weber and others argued that capitalist ideology stems from the Calvinist belief in predestination, the idea that only a handful of individuals are predestined for paradise or guaranteed heavenly eternity, while all others face some form of eternal damnation. Given that there was no objective measure of who was predestined for heaven, Protestants sought to evidence their salvation through earthly means. The mark of predestination thus became simple: material success. To embrace this ideology meant a dogged and single-minded pursuit of material wealth, especially as achieved through industry and maximum productivity. Protestantism shunned both hedonism and previous iterations of Christianity that admonished the accumulation of earthly goods, giving way to a work ethic that encouraged "fruitful use of God-given resources" and systematic, organized lifestyles. Eventually, Weber argues, the underpinnings of the Protestant ethic diverged from religion and found new life in a reason-based capitalism that has gone on to dominate global markets. Some critics have argued against the historical accuracy of some of Weber's assertions. For example, Joseph Schumpeter has provided evidence to show that capitalism started in Italy, a predominantly Catholic country, and not in the more Calvinist parts of Europe, as Weber presumes.[40] The extent to which Weber's theory resonates in economic rationality remains in question; nonetheless, attributes that Weber assigns to the Protestant ethic can be found as cultural markers of capitalism today.

1.4 TAYLORISM AS RHETORIC, SCIENTIFIC MANAGEMENT AS PRACTICE

In his 1911 *Principles of Scientific Management*, Taylor underscored a major presumption of his new theory for worker organization: the notion that employers and employees can overcome their historical antagonism in the pursuit of increased productivity, which would lead to shared prosperity. The measure of productivity espoused by Taylor is simply a ratio of quantitative product output over time spent on the task; the modern concept of profits still derives from this notion. Taylor introduced his system as a solution to the "evils" that prevent the attainment of maximum prosperity, notably, overcoming worker resistance to producing maximum

---

[39] Bright et al., *Principles of Management*, 63–68.
[40] Francis Fukuyama, "The Calvinist Manifesto," *New York Times*, Mar. 13, 2005; Joseph A. Schumpeter, *History of Economic Analysis* (1954; repr., London: Routledge, 1994), 74–75.

output every day. Taylor explains the three reasons why workers resist as the belief that efficiency in production would result in fewer jobs, the lack of trust that management would pay wages that represent output, and an attachment to outdated rule-of-thumb methods. Soldiering – the systematic identification of the maximum wage available for the minimum amount or slowest work possible – results from workers noticing that when their productivity reaches a certain level, day rates are capped and piece rates are dropped. Under this system, there is a clear maximum earning potential that does not always correlate with effort. Taylor's solution was to systematically move knowledge and decision-making to managers, alleviating these pressures on the workers so that they would focus on completing tasks as directed and in incentivized time frames.[41] Essentially, the worker should receive a bonus for complying with the time limit and productivity parameters of the task.

Taylor wrote a series of essays and presentations leading up to the publication of *The Principles of Scientific Management,* many of which centered on various experiments to demonstrate how systematically collected data could influence managerial task design.[42] One of his most notable experiments focused on improving the efficiency of loading pig iron for distribution. He claimed his changes to the process benefited both the employer by increasing the amount of pig iron loaded in a tighter time frame, and the employee through piece rate–based wages.

However, two management historians, Charles D. Wrege and Richard M. Hodgetts, recently returned to the data provided by Taylor's observing assistants and cross-referenced efficiency with weather conditions to evaluate his claims of improving worker motivation and efficiency. They found that, even given inconsistencies in which piece rate workers chose to work which days and regardless of weather, most of the workers returned primarily to the old day-rate system, presumably due to overwork and fatigue. They also argue that Taylor's claim that he achieved a cost per ton loaded of $0.05 would have been impossible because of the level of incentive required to coax workers back to his piece-rate system.[43] However, in spite of lack of evidentiary support, Taylor's concepts and different variations of scientific management have persevered for over a century. However, not all of those variations hew true to Taylor's original theories.

Theoretically, Taylorism operates on the principle that streamlining tasks based on methodologically collected data, choosing the best-suited workers for each task, and implementing incentive structures that make the most of individual performance will

[41] Frederick Winslow Taylor, *The Principles of Scientific Management* (New York: Harper & Row, 1911), 1, 2, 7, 17; Harry J. Van Buren III, "Fairness and the Main Management Theories of the Twentieth Century: A Historical Review, 1900–1965," *Journal of Business Ethics* 82, no. 3 (2008): 633–44.

[42] Charles D. Wrege and Richard M. Hodgetts, "Frederick W. Taylor's 1899 Pig Iron Observations: Examining Fact, Fiction, and Lessons for the New Millennium," *Academy of Management Journal* 43, no. 6 (2020): 1283–88. Wrege and Hodgetts evaluate the data provided by Taylor's assistants, the regional weather, and the costs of gondolas to demonstrate Taylor's embellishment of efficiency via piece work.

[43] Wrege and Hodgetts, "Frederick W. Taylor's 1899 Pig Iron Observations," 1283–88.

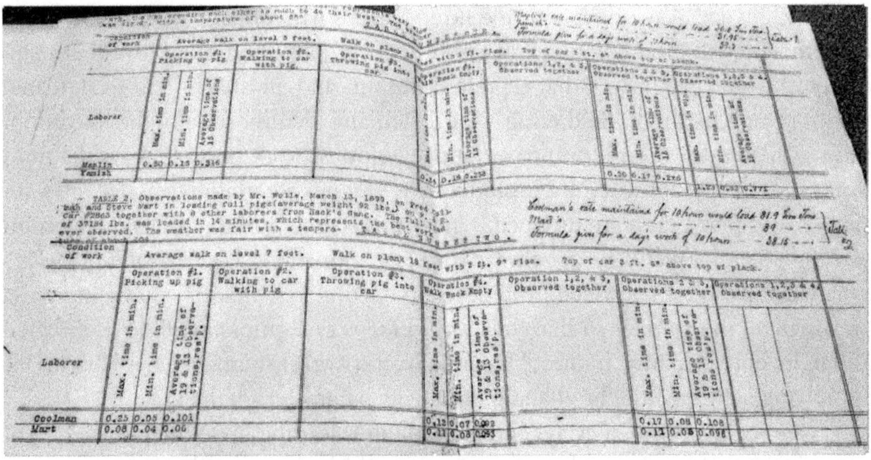

FIGURE 1.4 Data sheet from the pig iron experiments. Table 2 (at the bottom) describes the full weight (37,184 lb) of the pig iron loaded by a team of ten laborers in 14 minutes. Even more notable is the comment "which represents the best work ever observed." Archival material courtesy of the Kheel Center, Cornell University.

optimize the prosperity derived from the system by employers and employees alike. In formalizing this approach, Taylor also indicated that an important factor to consider was that the worker would benefit from a split cognitive load. This meant that whereas the worker formerly had to identify his own strengths, choose a task, and learn that task efficiently, under scientific management, all the planning shifted to the manager,[44] and the worker simply followed instructions. Although Taylorism emphasizes distributive justice as part of scientific management, in practice the benefits to the employees are often deprioritized in favor of maximum prosperity to the employer. Much of the criticism facing this approach to management has dealt with this disproportionate allocation of incentives and the assumption of a "right to manage," which is granted in terms of obligation to serve the owners and by virtue of their superior knowledge.[45] Immediate responses to Taylor's article in *American Magazine* expressed fears about the impact this approach to management and work would have on global society.

An excerpt from a letter from H. L. Holmes to *American Magazine* in April 1911 describes the worry surrounding this system:

> The business men's profits would be greatly increased by his system no doubt; his employees would each be more efficient and productive, therefore he would need fewer of them; these few would wear out faster, and the masses of the people would be out of employment. What kind of nation would ours be, composed of a few

[44] See Taylor, *Principles of Scientific Management*, 15, 17. Page 15 lists the "new duties" given to managers under scientific management.
[45] Van Buren, "Fairness and the Main Management Theories of the Twentieth Century," 634, 641.

inordinately rich men, a number of scientifically efficient workers putting in every amount of their time at highly productive labor, and throngs of forcibly idle men with nothing? Is the condition of humanity nothing, beside the gains of capital?

Then of course, if this system prevails, the speeding will go on all over the world. A few wealthy men, a number of overworked men and masses of idle, penniless men cannot buy up the immense output of products. Where will the market be found? I should like an answer to these questions.[46]

Echoes of these fears could be heard in the latter portion of the twentieth century as manufacturing jobs in the United States began to be outsourced to other, cheaper labor markets, and again in the early portion of the twenty-first century when an array of administrative tasks made their way to cheaper markets as well.

Administrative theorists believe that organizational structure is the key to efficiency. Henri Fayol and Lyndall F. Urick published works in the 1940s arguing that the ideal organizational structure could be applied across industry contexts to benefit the maximum number and types of organizations.[47] This theory stresses the necessity of management: Managers are expected to dictate the tasks and procedures, and employees are presumed to desire and require this high level of direction. The administrative perspective prioritizes the "right to manage" well above organizational justice that benefits employees.[48]

Contrary to its connotative meaning, bureaucratic theory[49] was one of the only early theories of management to emphasize organizational justice. In this system, workers are controlled by the expectation that they will comply to uniform procedures. This neglects Taylor's emphasis on choosing the right man to train for each job; instead, it elevates the role of managers in designing tasks so that anyone, anywhere can be trained to the system and pick up the procedures. Van Buren describes the dispassionate procedural nature of decision-making and employee relations under bureaucratic theory as demonstrating nondiscriminatory values. The evidence to support this claim is that employees who occupy the same level within the hierarchy are expected to comply with identical procedures, which also ensures that clients receive the same type of service across employees, thereby reducing the influence of personal relationships and politics. However, for bureaucratic theory, the delineations between employees and managers are still very clear and there is no theoretical

[46] Letter from L. M. Holmes to *American Magazine*, Apr. 30, 1911, in response to Taylor's article on scientific management, Stevens Institute of Technology Digital Collections: Samuel C. Williams Library, Frederick Winslow Taylor Collection.
[47] See Henri Fayol, *General and Industrial Management* (London: Pitman & Sons, 1949); Lyndall F. Urick, *The Elements of Administration* (New York: Harper, 1944).
[48] Van Buren, "Fairness and the Main Management Theories of the Twentieth Century," 635–36.
[49] The seminal works on bureaucracy theory are Peter M. Blau, *The Dynamics of Bureaucracy: A Study of Interpersonal Relations in Two Government Agencies* (Chicago: University of Chicago Press, 1955); Michael Crozier, *The Bureaucratic Phenomenon* (London: Tavistock, 1964); and Max Weber, *The Theory of Social and Economic Organization*, trans. A. M. Henderson and Talcott Parsons, ed. Talcott Parsons (Oxford: Oxford University Press, 1947).

space for increased involvement from employees regarding how best to implement procedures or what level of remuneration should be associated with their work.[50]

Aside from bureaucratic theory, other theories of employee governance took a so-called humanist direction. The human relations approach[51] reconsidered the significance of understanding the needs of workers and their informal group identities. The major difference between this approach and scientific management is that informal groups were not demonized or strategized against; rather they were considered potential spaces for additional utilization and manipulation for the benefit of organizations. The criticism of this approach should be self-evident from the associated language. Employees were still not considered legitimate, participatory contributors to organizational goal determination;[52] however, this approach still sought to make them *feel* valued in this capacity.

The human resources perspective[53] emphasized the forgotten portion of theoretical scientific management: that employees should also prosper. This approach to management suggests that employees shouldn't be treated as though they don't wish to contribute, but instead should be treated in more egalitarian ways. Human resource advocates suggest that "soldiering" was a result of a perceived devaluation of workers' contribution, not by an innate desire to do as little as possible,[54] as Taylor had suggested in *The Principles of Scientific Management*.[55] This approach argues that paying employees fairly and considering their perspective on potential contributions will motivate them to work harder, which brings back the element of distributive justice that figures prominently in Taylor's writings.

1.5 SCIENTIFIC MANAGEMENT AS (MIS)APPLIED TAYLORISM

Although the terms *Taylorism* and *scientific management* are often used interchangeably, scientific management tends to rely on a selection of the most general efficiency principles that Taylor provided while neglecting his ostensible distributive

---

[50] Van Buren, "Fairness and the Main Management Theories of the Twentieth Century," 636.

[51] The seminal works on the human relations approach are Fritz Jules Roethlisberger and William J. Dickson, *Management and the Worker: An Account of a Research Program Conducted by the Western Electric Company, Hawthorne Works, Chicago* (Cambridge, MA: Harvard University Press, 1939); Fritz Jules Roethlisberger, *Management and Morale* (Cambridge, MA: Harvard University Press, 1941); Elton Mayo, *The Social Problems of an Industrial Civilization* (Cambridge, MA: Harvard University, Graduate School of Business Administration, 1945); William H. Whyte, *Money and Motivation: Analysis of Incentives in Industry* (New York: Harper & Row, 1955); and William H. Whyte, *The Organization Man* (New York: Simon & Schuster, 1956).

[52] Van Buren, "Fairness and the Main Management Theories of the Twentieth Century," 637.

[53] The seminal works on the human resources perspective are Chris Argyris, *Personality and the Organization: The Conflict between the System and the Individual* (New York: Harper, 1957); Douglas McGregor, *The Human Side of Enterprise* (New York: McGraw Hill, 1960); Victor H. Vroom, *Work and Motivation* (New York: Wiley, 1964); and Frederick Herzberg, *Work and the Nature of Man* (Cleveland: World Publishing Co., 1966).

[54] Van Buren, "Fairness and the Main Management Theories of the Twentieth Century," 637.

[55] Taylor, *Principles of Scientific Management*, 6.

justice goals. The shift from the regional industrial space of Taylorism to the global organizational space of scientific management was catalyzed by a case between the eastern railroads and the Interstate Commerce Commission.[56] Primarily from 1910 to 1911, Justice Brandeis and Frederick Taylor corresponded frequently by letter, with Brandeis seeking support from Taylor for his push to regulate trade, primarily targeting the rail companies.[57] In response to this request, Taylor provided a list of eighteen effects scientific management could achieve, including happiness, honesty, morality, cooperation, loyalty, and health. The scientific management effect of happiness can be achieved in two ways, first by "correcting misfits of man and job" and second by "discovery and removal of special causes of grouch." Honesty comes from "making bluffing difficult, unsafe, and undesirable" through inspection and surveillance. Morality was supposed to be achieved by removing degrading work and by setting a pace too fast for moral wavering. Taylor's examples of immoral work included a group of children who worked nude inside a textile bleaching operation; the chemicals had dyed their skin such that they looked like "Indians." A second example was working with human urine to clean books. Under scientific management, a cheap chemical would replace the urine because "we don't ask anybody to do anything we cannot and will not do ourselves."[58] The short form list did not contain direct advice on how scientific management leads to health among workers – Taylor simply concludes that it does.

Interestingly, Taylor draws a connection between the cleanliness and organization of "hard workers" handling white flat sheet stock in a printing establishment and the fact that they do not chew tobacco, comparing them with the chewing, messy glue workers a few floors below. Based on this connection, he suggests not hiring workers who chew because they may be less organized and less apt for scientific working conditions.[59] Today, smokers face similar presumptions about their ability to work without breaks and to remain healthy when compared to a nonsmoking applicant or worker.[60] Taylor's embrace of temperance led him to advise against hiring drinkers; today, many young people have been warned not to share evidence

[56] Robert Kanigel, "Taylor-Made: How the World's First Efficiency Expert Refashioned Modern Life in His Own Image," *The Sciences* 37 (May 1997): 21.

[57] Letter from Louis D. Brandeis, Esq., to Frederick Winslow Taylor, Esq., Oct. 26, 1910, Stevens Institute of Technology Digital Collections: Samuel C. Williams Library, Frederick Winslow Taylor Collection.

[58] Memorandum from Frederick Winslow Taylor, Esq., to Louis D. Brandeis, Esq., Nov. 1910, Stevens Institute of Technology Digital Collections: Samuel C. Williams Library, Frederick Winslow Taylor Collection.

[59] Memorandum from Frederick Winslow Taylor, Esq., to Louis D. Brandeis, Esq., Nov. 1910, Stevens Institute of Technology Digital Collections: Samuel C. Williams Library, Frederick Winslow Taylor Collection.

[60] See generally Mary Elizabeth Dallas, "Smokers Cost Employers More than Nonsmokers," *WebMD: Health Day News*, June 4, 2013, www.webmd.com/smoking-cessation/news/20130604/smokers-cost-employers-thousands-more-than-nonsmokers. This study showed less productivity for a sample of smokers than nonsmokers, although this study may reflect an existing presumption of a smoking employee's work ability.

on social media when they imbibe, for fear of losing job opportunities. This preoccupation with personal choices of workers is now facilitated by machine learning
and algorithmic decision making.

In terms of application, concentration, and faithfulness, Taylor depends on nor-
malizing the level of output expected so that a worker can expect to be shamed
by his workmates for slowing down the overall process. Thus, he says, it becomes
unnecessary to block off views of lovely gardens because the workers will train themselves and each other not to spend too much time looking.[61] Today surveillance
technologies designed to constantly track keystrokes, phone calls, and website visits function similarly, in that workers train themselves to hew to certain expected
behavior, as they know that their activities are being monitored.

In another letter to Brandeis, Taylor describes how the workers in the scientific
management shops did not participate in a sympathetic strike when half or more of
other shops participated.[62] He suggests these figures are proof that the system instills
faithfulness among workers. Furthermore, Taylor describes a democratized workplace where eventually there is no line between worker and manager, to the point
the manager will function as more of a "helper" to the worker.[63] In reality, this ideal
has been for the most part ignored in the application of scientific management.

With greater skill and versatility, great workers were expected to master their factory line,[64] and Taylorism assumed that doing very well at a particular task type will
translate to doing the same thing well in slightly different contexts. This is one of the
patterns used in today's machine learning models. Essentially, these models help
firms figure out who the "best man for the job" already was, and to find another one
like him to handle similar tasks.[65]

Louis D. Brandeis, in his defense of the set rate, declared Frederick W. Taylor
a genius for his efficiency techniques. When former Commerce secretary and efficiency enthusiast Herbert Hoover was elected to the presidency in 1928, scientific
management officially ruled the nation in symbol and in practice.[66] Today, the
principles of scientific management continue to influence the ways employees are

---

[61] Memorandum from Frederick Winslow Taylor, Esq., to Louis D. Brandeis, Esq., Nov. 1910, Stevens
Institute of Technology Digital Collections: Samuel C. Williams Library, Frederick Winslow Taylor
Collection.

[62] Letter from Frederick Winslow Taylor, Esq., to Louis D. Brandeis, Esq., Nov. 11, 1910, Stevens
Institute of Technology Digital Collections: Samuel C. Williams Library, Frederick Winslow Taylor
Collection.

[63] Memorandum from Frederick Winslow Taylor, Esq., to Louis D. Brandeis, Esq., Nov. 1910, Stevens
Institute of Technology Digital Collections: Samuel C. Williams Library, Frederick Winslow Taylor
Collection.

[64] Memorandum from Frederick Winslow Taylor, Esq., to Louis D. Brandeis, Esq., Nov. 1910, Stevens
Institute of Technology Digital Collections: Samuel C. Williams Library, Frederick Winslow Taylor
Collection.

[65] See Gideon Mann and Cathy O'Neal, "Hiring Algorithms Are Not Neutral," *Harvard Business
Review*, Dec. 9, 2016.

[66] Kanigel, "Taylor-Made," 18, 22.

selected for specific roles, even when machine learning–based algorithms appear to make those decisions.

Scientific management as applied Taylorism had already moved into office spaces, and even operating rooms, by the turn of the twentieth century. For example, in the 1910s, Frank B. Gilbreth, a Taylorized bricklayer turned scientific manager and motion study photographer, documented and directed the efficiency of a wide variety of work and home tasks together with his wife, Lillian. He incorporated specially designed timepieces and motion capture editing techniques to this effect.[67] Gilbreth thought the medical field would be the noblest adaptation of efficiency expertise. During one of his observations, he famously told a surgeon, "If you were laying brick for me you wouldn't last ten minutes."[68]

But proponents of scientific management often ignored certain aspects of Taylor's ideas or applied them incorrectly. Taylor emphasized that the worst-case scenario for scientific management would be managers applying techniques, like timing, without paying special attention to the underlying principles. Without the attentiveness to all four principles, Taylor warned, workers would likely reject attempts at conversion and have a higher propensity to organize against the manager.[69] Unfortunately, the application of Taylorist principles did often neglect to consider all four of his principles, including the idea of prosperity for workers. If you have ever heard someone begrudgingly refer to themselves as "just another cog in the machine," you have witnessed the resentment associated with common practice of Taylorism.

Fordism, particularly, ignored the portion of Taylor's doctrine devoted to choosing the very best men for each job task. Rather, Ford focused on the job tasks with the intent to break them down into minute tasks that could be done by anyone. Additionally, the detached nature of a mechanized line controlled by a distant manager did not improve employee/employer relations in the ways Taylor desired after his disheartening experience in the steel mills, where he had to "punish" his friends in order to make them comply with efficiency expectations.[70]

1.6 THE EMPLOYER AS DICTATOR

An important aspect of scientific management is how it affects the relationship between the employee and employer. In *Private Government*, Elizabeth Anderson identifies the events and ideological shifts that bridged Smith's liberal free market ideal and Marx's much colder perspective on the dangers of the free market economy.[71] Looking at the

---

[67] Kanigel, "Taylor-Made, 21.

[68] Kanigel, "Taylor-Made," 22.

[69] Taylor, *Principles of Scientific Management*, 1, 69–74.

[70] Carl H. A. Dassbach, "The Origins of Fordism: The Introduction of Mass Production and the Five-Dollar Wage." *Critical Sociology* 18, no. 1 (1991): 78, 88; Taylor, *Principles of Scientific Management*, 1, 24.

[71] Elizabeth Anderson, *Private Government: How Employers Rule Our Lives (and Why We Don't Talk about It)* (Princeton, NJ: Princeton University Press, 2017).

span of European history, most people were subject to the owners of the land they occupied, even to the extent that moonlighting wages were to be handed to the lord they served. Women were also subservient to male heads of households, who were ultimately subservient to the king. Anderson calls this the private government system, in which the people being ruled do not have any say in decisions about the rules they must follow. If we think about life at that point in history, it becomes easier to understand how a market without monopolies or guilds dictating when and where goods could be sold, as well as to and by whom, might be attractive to free market liberals/social and economic egalitarians. Smith and the Levellers believed that if people were allowed to feed their families by farming the land they occupied, they would have more incentive to care for the land; likewise, if after laboring as an apprentice a worker was able to open their own shop, they would have incentive to work to their best ability. These ideas came to the forefront after arguments that upper-class domination was required for society to function were disproven, primarily by the example of free men occupying woods and other less-regulated areas who were making livings for themselves quite happily.[72]

According to free market liberals/social and economic egalitarians, especially Thomas Paine, all people should be allowed to own property. Paine also outlined one of the first plans to alleviate poverty by collecting estate tax (land tax) and using that to fund education, which in turn would produce skilled laborers and societal contributors. He tried to reconcile this perspective with that of the free-market-supporting early nineteenth-century Republicans by suggesting that land was a common good and so-called landowners owed a rent to the community for benefiting from occupying that land. In this early, idealized free-market space, people would labor under a higher-skilled person until they had saved enough money from their fair wage to open their own small business. Tradespeople and business owners would be one and the same; additionally, they would not have the time or energy to manage and train more than ten or so people at a time, and having the owner working alongside the workers would not result in working conditions unamenable to an owner's own comfort. The Industrial Revolution changed these dynamics entirely – no longer did masters and workers share space, tasks, and libations, and the labor was markedly deskilled, with the intellectual components consumed by the supervisors. The workers were now subject to the tyranny of the stopwatch and the time clock. Low wages offered no hope of saving for a better life, and shops had been scaled up to a degree that made competing with them unfathomable to artisans.[73]

Discussions of surveillance and sanctions revolve around issues of privacy, which Anderson defines as being relative to or from a person. If something is private from a person, they have no right to know it, no stake in it, and no guidance in decisions related to it; the inverse is true when something is public. However, public and private spheres overlap where spaces may be private from one group but public to

---

[72] Anderson, *Private Government*, 1–37.
[73] Anderson, *Private Government*, 24–31, 35–37.

another, like a private club, for example. Additionally, it is not only a parliament or a congress that can constitute a government – anywhere with a systematic hierarchy has a government of some type. And any type of government deals with different types of freedom, whether negative freedom (no one is meddling with what you choose to do), positive freedom (resources provide access to many choices in actions), or republican freedom (free from domination).[74] A private government threatens all of these freedoms, but most of all republican and negative freedoms.

A prime example of this is Ford's Sociological Department, which was championed by some human relations historians as a way for workers to be identified as in need. Anderson suggests instead that its purpose was to identify employees who would be left out of the $5 per day wage deal for any of a number of personal violations, including not bathing properly. Anderson notes similarities with the present-day Affordable Care Act, wherein workers can be subject to penalties on their healthcare premium for non-compliance with company wellness programs.[75]

The idea that employers can impose a penalty for noncompliance points to an antagonistic relationship between employer and employee. Ronald Coase originated the theory of the firm; like scientific management, this theory suggests that antagonism between entrepreneur and laborer can be lessened through communication, especially regarding the entrepreneur's expectations of the worker. However, this is rarely the case in practice. At-will employment laws allow businesses to fire employees for any and no reason in most states, and the worker's only legal protections are very specific to discriminatory practices and safety regulations, and have nearly nothing to do with protecting the employee's private rights to do and say what they please when they are not at work. Anderson notes that while many firm theorists suggest that workers are not subservient to employers because they too can end the contract at any time for any reason, those theorists fail to address the fact that the employer bears fewer consequences in that scenario. She also comments on the tendency of these theorists and many libertarians to neglect the portion of work and life that follows the signing of the labor contract, simply relying on the freedom to sign or not as evidence of the ideal free market. The reality of the situation is that private governments housed in American workplaces enjoy the kinds of sanctioning powers that are far beyond the reach of democratic state governments.[76]

The most important driver of positive change in the workplace will be workers' voices. Traditionally this feat has been accomplished via labor unions and workplace democracy; however, the majority of workers today have not been union members, and workplace democracies are complicated by subjective assessments of the contributions of different employee types. Anderson recommends a return to the company union, which provides co-governance between employee and employer.

[74] Anderson, *Private Government*, 43–44, 46.
[75] Anderson, *Private Government*, 49–50.
[76] Anderson, *Private Government*, 52, 54–59, 63.

The company union structure has been successfully modeled in Europe, but was outlawed in the United States by the National Labor Relations Act of 1935.

Worker domination is enabled, achieved, and enforced through worker quantification. Thus, worker quantification is not merely an individual or solely economic problem, but is rather a political problem that is consequential for the maintenance of democracy. As technological advances offer more opportunities to quantify workers and further encroach on worker freedoms or erode worker personhood, we run the risk of rending the very fabric of democracy. Worker quantification is a problem because new technologies that allow for discrete discrimination in hiring can exclude entire segments of the population from the workplace, further widening the chasm of inequality. Even when a worker is hired, other emerging technologies that allow for near total control of the worker allow the employers to "own" the employee, erasing worker voice and self-determination not just in the workplace itself but also in their self-expression and political will.

As we consider how technology has assisted the employer in controlling workers, we must also look at how the law has played unwitting accomplice to the domination of workers. It has done this, first, through the law's traditional deference to the employers,[77] and second, through the law's conservatism – while businesses are adopting new technologies at breakneck speed and transforming the employment bargain, the law remains staid.

1.7 WORKERS' COMPENSATION LAWS AND LEGALIZED WORKER QUANTIFICATION

We must also consider that the law has (in)advertently contributed to worker quantification. Early workers' compensation laws were purported to benefit both the worker and the employer by limiting the worker's ability to sue for negligence and by standardizing compensation for workers who had been injured on the job. It was also expected that workplaces would become safer, given that the employer would now be responsible for compensating workers for their injuries. Workers' compensation legislation was enacted quickly around 1910 in the most progressive states, and most other states adopted the system by 1920. The federal courts deemed these regulations beyond their scope and so until the New Deal era, state workers' compensation programs operated autonomously.[78]

---

[77] For example, my 2020 law review article notes how, in modern America, the law's deference to the employer has resulted in nearly insurmountable legal hurdles to proving employment discrimination, particularly in regards to racial discrimination. Ifeoma Ajunwa, "The Paradox of Automation as Anti-Bias Intervention," *Cardozo Law Review* 41 (2020): 1671–742.

[78] Allard E. Dembe, "How Historical Factors Have Affected the Application of Worker's Compensation Data to Public Health," *Journal of Public Health Policy* 31, no. 2 (2010): 231; Nate Holdren, "Incentivizing Safety and Discrimination: Employment Risks under Workmen's Compensation in the Early Twentieth Century United States," *Enterprise and Society* 15, no. 1 (2014): 52.

Some early criticisms of these state systems came from statisticians who decried the lack of record-keeping related to industrial accidents. For example, in 1927 Lewis DeBlois of the National Bureau of Casualty & Surety Underwriters alleged that industry officials and scholars chose not to develop adequate ways of quantifying industrial accidents because they simply did not value the lives of workers. In the 1930s, the government began tracking limited types of workers' compensation data, primarily the monetary losses by firms and the amounts covered by different insurers. There still seemed to be a lack of interest in understanding what circumstances led to injury or loss of life on the job.[79]

To add insult to injury, the financial data quickly led many firms to adopt discriminatory hiring and firing practices. Married men became less attractive as employees because if they were debilitated or killed on the job (which was fairly common in this era), the family would receive more benefits over time compared to the simple funeral expense of a single man. Some industry leaders would argue that this was simply untrue, that these men were valued for their stability and their contribution of future workers.[80]

Additionally, older people and people with pre-existing conditions were also deemed less attractive as employees due to the potential severity of the impact of an injury.[81] A letter from the American Federation of Labor to its Central Bodies in 1929 requests union leaders to document instances of age discrimination. The form asked questions both about the nature of machines and work excluding those over forty-five years of age, and about the attribution of the cause of the exclusion, whether they believed it to be caused by group insurance, pension plans, or private company insurance.[82]

Workers with pre-existing conditions were also at risk of exclusion because workers' compensation law dictated that if a man with one eye lost that eye in a work accident, he would be compensated at the level of a man with two eyes who had lost them both, because obviously his ability to function was equally impacted by the injury.[83] The same would be true of a person with a missing limb.

Workers' compensation laws demanded that employers either demonstrate they had enough money in a fund to compensate the number of claims they might face in a year, or invest in private or state insurance policies to aggregate this risk across firms. Self-insurance was more common among very large companies like General Electric, Pullman, American Tobacco, and Standard Oil. In theory, this suggests

---

[79] Dembe, "How Historical Factors Have Affected the Application of Workers Compensation Data to Public Health," 233–34.

[80] Holdren, "Incentivizing Safety and Discrimination," 36.

[81] Holdren, "Incentivizing Safety and Discrimination," 37–38.

[82] Letter from Green, President of American Federation of Labor to Central Bodies, Mar. 1929, Correspondence of American Federation of Labor President William Green on Microfilm No. 5402, Cornell University Library: Kheel Center for Labor-Management Documentation and Archives.

[83] Holdren, "Incentivizing Safety and Discrimination," 38.

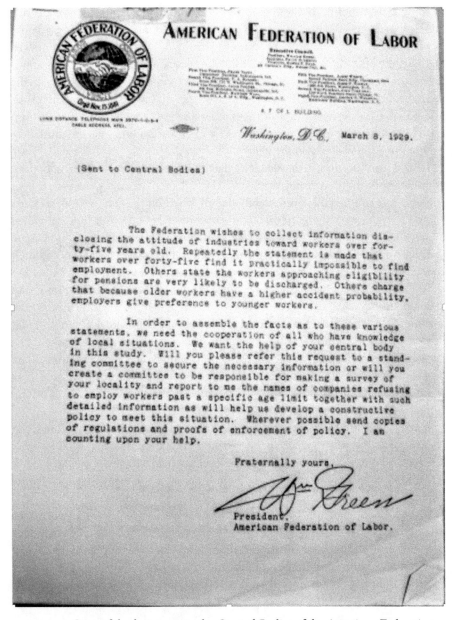

FIGURE 1.5 Copy of the letter sent to the Central Bodies of the American Federation of Labor in March 1929 with a request to report agism. Archival materials courtesy of Kheel Center, Cornell University.

that self-insurers would be the safest places to work because they would want to control these costs by improving workplace safety. In practice, however, companies could also cut costs by not employing workers in higher-risk pools. A superintendent

From

Union ....
Secretary ....
Address ....
City ....State ....

PROBLEMS OF OLDER WORKERS

(1) Are workers in your organization displaced who have reached
the age of 45 or over? ....

   (a) What machines have displaced the members of your union
and in what proportions? ....
Date of introduction of machines ....

   (b) Have these workers been able to find employment as op-
eratives of these machines or have new workers been employed and the old ones gone to new fields? ....
....
....

   (c) Have there been technical changes in methods of production other than new machines which have decreased the
number of workers necessary to produce a given quantity
or which have removed the need for some types of crafts-
manship? ....
....
....

(2) Are these displaced workers discriminated against when they
seek re-employment? ....

   (a) What companies refuse to employ workers 45 years and
over? ....
....

FIGURE 1.5 (continued)

for Pullman wrote that he had "been trying to work out some plan by which we would avoid getting cripples in the service." Meanwhile, insurance companies like Travelers published pamphlets claiming that any discriminatory practice was taking

2.

```
(b) Can you supply copies of rules or other evidences of
    this discrimination?
(3) Is discrimination against older workers due t.
    (a) to group insurance? ............................................
    ...................................................................
    (b) to pension plans? ..............................................
    ...................................................................
    (c) to compensation risks insured by private companies? ..
    ...................................................................
(4) Do you know of any efforts of placement or retraining to
    help displaced workers find ways to earn a living? ......
    ...................................................................
```

_____
Secretary

FIGURE 1.5 (continued)

place at the company level, and at their aggregate level, dismissing individuals with pre-existing health conditions or older age would be less meaningful financially. The insurance companies suggested that getting rid of self-insurance altogether was the best answer to ending this type of discrimination. Notably, these pamphlets were published in response to claims that adjusters would mention to managers that dismissing employees with varicose veins, missing limbs, or eyes would lower their rates in the future.[84]

Edward Phelps has argued that these discriminatory practices evinced pre-existing biases in firms. The laws merely provided an excuse for the exclusion of certain groups because of the discriminatory nature of costs associated with any insurance option (self, private, or state). In 1914, the Ohio Industrial Commission found it impossible to ascertain the number of people rejected due to physical impairment because only those who passed initial screening and were then rejected were documented. Many men were intimidated by the required screening physicals, and it was assumed that they stopped applying for fear of rejection, thus making it appear as though fewer people with disabilities were being denied employment.[85]

The practice of rewarding or penalizing for health has once again come to the forefront in part due to incentives in the Affordable Care Act for promoting employee health.[86] Penalizing people for their health status is not a novel practice; however, what might be the newest variation of the practice is the introduction of genetic testing. Some forms of genetic testing would allow employers to exclude people based on their potential for developing a debilitating illness in the future. This type of testing by employers would mean that someone with a higher potential of getting cancer in the future may never even have the opportunity to work toward their career goals. Current laws protecting people with disabilities do not have contingency or precedent for protecting people who have a higher potential of becoming disabled in the future but who are at present functionally unaffected.[87] The 2016 Genetic Information Non-Discrimination Act (GINA), likewise, does not provide full protection.[88]

1.8 TECHNOLOGIES OF CONTROL

Even before Taylorism, several varieties of early skill-saving technology (those types that take on the role of the skilled laborer) and machinery were designed primarily to increase efficiency, with the secondary role of controlling the bargaining power of skilled laborers and artisans. Innovations like the cropping frame, which mechanized the spinning of wool, allowed for the hiring of unskilled workers, including women and children, for a job once reserved for well-paid craftsman. The Luddites famously protested these types of innovations with eruptions of factory destruction in an effort to preserve their socioeconomic position throughout nineteenth-century

[84] Holdren, "Incentivizing Safety and Discrimination," 42–46, 53.
[85] Holdren, "Incentivizing Safety and Discrimination," 54, 58–59.
[86] Laura Anderko et al., "Promoting Prevention through the Affordable Care Act: Workplace Wellness," *Preventing Chronic Disease* 9 (2012): E175.
[87] Ifeoma Ajunwa, "Genetic Data and Civil Rights," *Harvard Civil Rights-Civil Liberties Law Review* 51, no. 1 (2016): 75–114.
[88] Ajunwa, "Genetic Data and Civil Rights."

England. Although skill-saving technology did reduce the prosperity of certain skilled laborers, at the same time it allowed new kinds of engineers and craftsman to grow and prosper.[89] The simultaneity of these technologically motivated shifts in worker demographics represents a component of unified growth theory.[90]

Taylor's *Principles of Scientific Management* dictates that workers should not be allowed to socialize as part of the prevention of soldiering. The system of control to prevent soldiering was primarily social, and it included rotating workers from group to group to avoid cohesiveness or group identity, and the assumption that providing proper instructions for each task would reduce the need for intragroup conversation.[91] Additionally, in developing these systems, stopwatches were regularly used to enforce breaks and work periods as well as to calculate efficiency. The rate of work was a key factor in the instructions designed for each task.

One of the best-known applications of Taylorism is in the form of the moving assembly lines of Henry Ford's factories. Predominantly starting around 1913, the assembly line functioned to maintain a high pace for each task phase. Instead of supervisors standing among the workers timing the completion of individual tasks, a single manager could enforce a time limit across an entire process. The line also allowed for the $5 per day wage increase because the tasks were so thoroughly broken down along the line that pay grades and piecework systems were no longer needed. The problems connected with these innovations, however, included incidentally creating a grander group identity than the identity associated with individual crafts and creating a system vulnerable to the sabotage of a single worker or small group.[92]

In a more recent application of Taylorism, in the late twentieth century, the bureaucratic perspective incorporated computer programming and analytics into employee control mechanisms. The goal was to limit the capabilities of machines, and in so doing, to fix the skills available to workers such that each worker would have to comply with the standard procedures for their position.[93]

The technocracy we see today ultimately descended from Taylor disciple Henry L. Gantt's fleeting attempts to establish an "aristocracy of the capable," prying rule from politicians and financiers and placing it into the hands of engineers and efficiency experts.[94] This approach to controlling workers assumes that those with the highest engineering and efficiency expertise should exercise control over all systems – labor, social, and political. As will be discussed in the rest of the book,

---

[89] Kevin Hjortshøj O'Rourke, "Luddites, the Industrial Revolution, and the Demographic Transition," *Journal of Economic Growth* 18, no. 4 (2013): 373, 374, 376.

[90] See Oded Galor and David N. Weil, "Population, Technology, and Growth: From Malthusian Stagnation to the Demographic Transition and Beyond," *American Economic Review* 90, no. 4 (2000): 806–28.

[91] Taylor, *Principles of Scientific Management*, 1, 41–42.

[92] Dassbach, "Origins of Fordism," 78–79, 89.

[93] Joan Greenbaum, *Windows on the Workplace: Technology, Jobs, and the Organization of Office Work*, 2nd ed. (New York: Monthly Review Press, 2004), 56–58.

[94] Kanigel, "Taylor-Made," 21.

we are now witnessing the introduction of new technologies of control in the work-place. From automated hiring platforms whose primary functions are to serve as culling systems, to wearable technology that monitors the worker's every move, to productivity applications that minutely quantify the labor output of the worker, today's worker is at the mercy of modern-day technologies of control which now quantify workers to a manner and to a degree that Taylor himself could never have envisioned.

2

Socio-Legal Responses to Scientific Management

Everything that is really great and inspiring is created by the individual who can labor in freedom.

–Albert Einstein

1799
The Combination Act of 1979
prohibits trade unions and collective bargaining

1842
Commonwealth v. Hunt

1880–90s
The Pinkerton Detectives involved in
strike-breaking and union-busting

1890
The Sherman Act

1892
Homestead Strike (=Homestead Steel Strike,
Pinkerton Rebellion, Homestead Massacre)

1893
• Employment of Pinkerton Detectives
Hearings
• Anti-Pinkerton Act signed into law
President Harrison

1893
Repeal Portion of the Acct of Mar. 3, 1893
(Anti-Pinkerton Act) Hearings

1901
Labor Organizations, Labor Disputes, and
Arbitration Hearings

1910 Bethlehem Steel Strike

FIGURE 2.1 Timeline of key socio-legal events preceding and resulting from the implementation of scientific management

1911
- *The Principles of Scientific Management* by Frederick Winslow Taylor published.

1911–12
- *The Taylor and Other Systems of Shop Management* (vol. 1–3) Hearings
- *Investigation of Taylor System and Shop Management Hearing*

1913
Employees of the Watertown Arsenal petitioned to abolish the practice of scientific management at their workplace.

1914
Ford's Five-Dollar Day

1915
Time Study and Premium Payments Hearings

1920s
The Rise of Fordism

1935
The Wagner Act Establishes the National Labor Relations Board

1936
Violations of free speech and assembly and interference with rights of labor

1936–37
Sit-down strikes

1938
Fair Labor Standards Act

1939
Oppressive Labor Practices Act Hearings

1940
NLRB v. Ford Motor Co., 114 F.2d 905
- Proposed Amendments to the NLRA Hearings

1941
Bethlehem Steel Co. v. NLRB, 120 F.2d 641
Ford Strike, Walkout (April, 1941) (Henry Ford signed C.I.O Contract)

1940s–60s
Mature Fordism

1942
NLRB v. Baldwin Locomotive Works, 128 F.2d 39

1945
Lochner v. New York

1947
The Taft-Hartley Act AKA the Labor Management Relations Act

1959
Investigation of Improper Activities in the Labor or Management Field Hearings

FIGURE 2.1 (continued)

1961
Impact of Automation on Employment Hearings

1966
Fafnir Bearing Co. v. NLRB, 362 F.2d 716

1969
Hamburg Shirt Corp. v. NLRB, 419 F.2d 1275

1970
Opinion of Justices, 358 Mass. 827

1972
Worker Alienation Hearings

1977
• *United States ex rel. Weinberger v. Equifax, Inc.* 557 F.2d 456
• Public Hearing on Record-Keeping Practices of Private Investigations Firms Hearings

1979
Pressures in Today's Workplace Hearings

1981
• *NLRB v. Crystal Springs Shirt Corp.*, 637 F.2d 399
• The Human Factor in Innovation and Productivity Hearings

2010
Lewis v. Smithfield Packing Co. 2010 U.S. Dist. LEXIS 87883

2011
McDonald v. Kellogg Co., 2011 U.S. Dist. LEXIS 11800

FIGURE 2.1 (continued)

In 1911, the U.S. House of Representatives passed House Resolution 90, which stated that "the Taylor system appears to be of such a character and nature as to be detrimental to the best interests of American workingmen." And because "one of the highest functions of any Government is to guard with zealous care the happiness and welfare of its great army of producers," the Committee on Labor was tasked with investigating this new system. The Special Committee on Taylor and Other Systems of Shop Management held hearings from April 1911 through February 1912, in which they questioned a cross-section of managers, foremen, and laborers, including a Mr. Alexander Crawford, a foreman and machinist.

MR. FITZGERALD: Do you think the stop-watch or the bonus system will ever be the means to elevating the laboring man in his position?
MR. CRAWFORD: I am not a believer in the stop-watch system.

MR. FITZGERALD: Just state to the committee why you do not believe in the stop-watch system.

MR. CRAWFORD: Because it looks to me that if a stop watch was placed in the hands of an irresponsible man he could it to the advantage of the man he was timing for one thing.

MR. FITZGERALD: You have no objection to the government's findings out or to any employer finding out, just how quickly the work could be done?

MR. CRAWFORD: Not at all. I have no objection to the Government doing anything reasonable or rational.

THE CHAIRMAN: You think in the general use of the stop watch for ascertaining the time, because the employer has the selection of the person who shall take the time, that that is one method that might be abused.

MR. CRAWFORD: Exactly.

MR. REDFIELD: Then it is not the watch you object to, but the man behind the watch?

MR. CRAWFORD: It is the application of it.

MR. REDFIELD: It is the way it is applied?

MR. CRAWFORD: Yes.

MR. JOHNSTON: Mr. Crawford, I should judge from your statement just made that you believe that the lash of the stop watch or of the pencil faddist is equally as bad as the lash of the whip?

MR. CRAWFORD: Yes, in a way, I believe a self-respecting workman will feel the lash of a stop watch just as the slaves felt the lash of the whip.[1]

These hearings reveal that prior to the rise of scientific management, there were already disputes about the management and control of workers, going back to the beginning of America's Second Industrial Revolution around 1870. This period was also the time of the Gilded Age, an era of both immense wealth and abject poverty. Technological developments offered new economic opportunities, but industrial work was characterized by low wages, dangerous working conditions, long hours, and no compensation for injuries.[2] Starting with the Second Industrial Revolution and the management practices it ushered in, and through the rise of scientific management and Fordism, this chapter traces the socio-legal responses to scientific management as it was practiced (or abused) by American firms (see Figure 2.1).

2.1 LEGAL CLIMATE PRIOR TO SCIENTIFIC MANAGEMENT

Prior to the advent of scientific management, the legal climate in America reflected the increasing tension between management and workers. The Industrial Revolution had brought factory work and a division of labor that not only required quality

---

[1] Testimony of Mr. Alexander Crawford [foreman and machinist], in U.S. House of Representatives, *The Taylor and other Systems of Shop Management: Hearings before the Committee on Labor* ... Vol. 1 (Washington DC: Government Printing Office, 1911), 419 (emphasis added).

[2] American Social Project, *Who Built America?* Vol. 2, *Since 1877* (New York: Worth Publishing, 2000), 33–37.

control and managerial oversight, but also increasingly subjected workers to poor working conditions. As small family-centered workshops gave way to factory workplaces, more and more workers were shifted into unskilled positions and became much less familiar with their employers. Unlike the older apprentice relationship, where youngsters lived with a family and worked alongside a master to learn their trade, in a factory setting, work time was clearly separated from family time, and employees were treated less like people and more like machines. While this could have been purely a result of the large number of employees working in such massive factories – where it may have simply been impossible for an employer to foster close relationships with all of his employees – the diminished familiarity also erased the employers' sense of personal responsibility towards employees.[3]

The ill effects of the Industrial Revolution were first seen in England before they diffused to the United States, where industrialization happened later. In an 1832 account from England, an observer reported that "it is truly lamentable to behold so many thousands of men who formerly earned 20 to 30 shillings per week, now compelled to live on 5s, 4s, or even less."[4] The economic and personal pressures of industrialization meant that factory owners would reduce wages to cover increased costs of materials and improve their own profit margin, and a standard workday might be fourteen to sixteen hours long, with little time off.[5] When workers responded to these poor conditions by trying to organize, the British Parliament passed the Combination Acts, which made it illegal for workers to unionize or join together for the sake of asking for better working conditions.[6] Though the acts were repealed only twenty-five years after their passage, this response to early workplace monitoring and poor working conditions can certainly indicate the lack of respect for the workforce that existed during the Industrial Revolution, a sentiment that carried over to attempts to stop workers from organizing in America.[7]

2.1.1 *The Pinkertons*

In 1855, Scottish immigrant Allan Pinkerton, a police detective, and his partner, Edward Rucker, formed the North-Western Police Agency – later known as the Pinkerton National Detective Agency – to provide private "police" services.[8]

---

[3] American Social Project, *Who Built America?* Vol. 1, To 1877, 371–75, 379, 385.

[4] E. P. Thompson, *Making of the English Working Class* (New York: Vintage Books, 1963), 284.

[5] Thompson, *Making of the English Working Class*.

[6] John Orth, "English Combination Acts of the Eighteenth Century," *Law and History Review*, 5, no. 1 (1987): 175–211, https://doi.org/10.2307/743940.

[7] Orth, "English Combination Acts," 175–211. See also *Commonwealth v. Hunt*.

[8] Frank Morn, *The Eye That Never Sleeps: A History of the Pinkerton National Detective Agency* (Bloomington: Indiana University Press, 1982). See also J. A. Zumoff, "Politics and the 1920s Writings of Dashiell Hammett," *American Studies* 52, no. 1 (2012): 79–80.

With employer control over workers largely unregulated, companies deployed the Pinkertons, as they came to be known, for a variety of tasks – particularly those related to infiltrating and busting unions, enforcing company rules, and monitoring workers deemed a threat to the interests of employers.[9] When it became common for businesses to employ the Pinkertons, as well as other groups and individuals, to disrupt or harass labor organizers, particularly during labor disputes in the 1880s and early 1890s,[10] the Pinkertons became "synonymous with anti-labor repression" due to their "union-busting and strike-breaking." Anti-labor repression became a significant part of their detective work as they spied on workers, sabotaged and disrupted trade unions, defended strike-breakers, and attacked striking workers. There was probably "no major strike in [the period between the 1870s and the end of the First World War] which the Pinkertons were not involved in brutalizing the labor movement."[11]

As such anti-union activities became prevalent, public hostility against private investigation agencies grew,[12] and in May 1892 the U.S. Congress launched investigations into the employers' reliance on mercenaries to counter workers in labor disputes.[13] Deeming that the Pinkerton detectives had "been employed unlawfully by railroad corporations engaged in the transportation of the United States mail and interstate commerce," Congress convened the "Investigation of the Employment of Pinkerton Detectives in Connection with the Labor Troubles at Homestead, Pa." to learn about "the character of their employment by corporations ..., the number so employed, and whether such employment had provoked breaches of peace or caused the destruction of property."[14] In the hearings, Robert A. Pinkerton testified that for the Homestead incident, the agency had provided 310 men with "about 250 rifles, about 300 pistols, and ammunition and night clubs ... known as watchmen's sticks or police batons." Pinkerton also testified that the agency's principal business was providing private detectives and supplying watchmen for businesses, residences, and events, but acknowledged that the agency had also built up the business of furnishing watchmen or guards for companies and trains in case of strikes, riots, and labor troubles, and for banks and private property.[15]

[9] Morn, *Eye That Never Sleeps*.
[10] 5 U.S.C.S. § 3108 (generally).
[11] Zumoff, "Politics and the 1920s Writings of Dashiell Hammett," 79. See Robert Michael Smith, *From Blackjacks to Briefcases: A History of Commercialized Strikebreaking and Unionbusting in the United States* (Athens: Ohio University Press, 2003).
[12] Jeremiah K. Geffe, "License to Sniff: The Need to Regulate Privately Owned Drug-Sniffing Dogs," *Journal of Gender, Race, and Justice* 19, no. 1 (2016): 174.
[13] Joshua S. Press, "Crying Havoc over the Outsourcing of Soldiers and Democracy's Slipping Grip on the Dogs of War," *Northwestern University Law Review* 103 (2008): 115.
[14] U.S. House of Representatives, *Investigation of the Employment of Pinkerton Detectives ...* (Washington DC: Government Printing Office, 1892), 1. See "Riot at Homestead," *Chicago Tribune*, July 6, 1892, https://chicagotribune.newspapers.com/search/?ymd=1892-07-06.
[15] Testimony of Robert A. Pinkerton, in U.S. House, *Investigation of the Employment of Pinkerton Detectives*, 190, 195–96.

In the hearings, the committee heard from many witnesses, including employers, employees, sheriffs, labor organizers, and those related to the Pinkerton Detective Agency. Henry Clay Frick, chairman of the Carnegie Steel Company, opined about past labor strikes against Carnegie Steel and the difficulties the company had in managing workers, especially in light of the recent dispute over wage cuts and the failure of collective bargaining. He particularly expressed his doubt of the sheriff's power to protect company property, stating that it was "necessary for [them] to secure [their] own watchmen to assist the sheriff."[16]

Hugh O'Donnell, a member of W. T. Robers Lodge, No. 125, of the National Amalgamated Association of Iron and Steel Workers, indicated that workers looked upon the Pinkertons as "armed invaders, men who [were] thoroughly antagonistic to all laboring interests and allies of the capitalists" and that workers were opposed to them because they were concerned that the company would employ non-union men to run the works if the Pinkertons got possession of the property of the company.[17] In addition, T. V. Powderly, a General Master Workman of the Knights of Labor, condemned the methods of the Pinkertons as irritating to workers and disrupting to the peace because he believed them to be related to injustice and violations of the law.[18] However, Robert Pinkerton claimed that "the men employed by us in the strike work are selected with great care" and that there was no instance where any of their watchmen had been convicted of a crime. They also testified that the agency seldom permitted the watchmen to carry arms, and even so, it was only when they were authorized to do so by the legal authorities or deputy sheriffs.[19]

The committee concluded that employing Pinkerton watchmen or guards "in case of strikes and labor troubles has grown very largely out of the sloth and dilatoriness of the civil authorities to render efficient and prompt protection to persons and property in such cases" and that such employment without the consent of the state was "calculated to produce irritation among the strikers, frequently resulting in hostile demonstrations and bloodshed."[20] The committee disapproved of the use of private guards for property protection, but blamed the resort to private guards on the inadequacy of public police protection. And the committee found that Congress had "no right to intermeddle with the private contracts and acts of the companies engaged in transportation between them and their employees" despite its power

---

[16] Testimony of Henry Clay Frick, in U.S. House, *Investigation of the Employment of Pinkerton Detectives*, 31–32.

[17] Testimony of Hugh O'Donnell, in U.S. House, *Investigation of the Employment of Pinkerton Detectives*, 97.

[18] Testimony of T. V. Powderly, in U.S. House, *Investigation of the Employment of Pinkerton Detectives*, 219–47, esp. 221–24.

[19] Statement of Messrs. Pinkerton, in U.S. House, *Investigation of the Employment of Pinkerton Detectives*, 221.

[20] U.S. House of Representatives, "Employment of Pinkerton Detectives," Report No. 2447, Feb. 7, 1893, xiv–xv, in *The Reports of Committees of the House of Representatives for the Second Session of the Fifty-Second Congress, 1892–93*. Washington DC: Government Printing Office, 1893.

FIGURE 2.2 Original logo of the Pinkerton's National Detective Agency, ca. 1850s (public domain)[21]

to "regulate, facilitate, and protect interstate commerce,"[22] and concluded that the states, not the federal government, should intervene in this issue.[23] A few states had already restricted the use of private guards, and more states did so after the congressional hearings; in addition, Congress enacted the Anti-Pinkerton Act of 1893, prohibiting "an individual employed by the Pinkerton Detective Agency, or similar organization" from being "employed by the Government of the United States or the government of the District of Columbia." The ban included services performed by such employees even when they are not of detective or investigative nature, and an organization is not considered "similar" to the Pinkertons unless it offers quasi-military armed forces for hire.[24]

Labor unrest, with company owners trying to enforce their control and workers struggling to exercise influence over their workplace, continued into the early twentieth century. And it was against that backdrop of legal dispute regarding the boundaries of employer control over workers that Taylor published *The Principles of Scientific Management* in 1911. In that same year the practice of scientific management was subjected to congressional investigation.

2.2 PRE-TAYLORISM: EMERGING LABOR POLICY

Although the nature of work has changed over the centuries, the tension between the interests of those who provide labor and those who profit from it has proved a historical constant. A poignant example is found in the turbulent history of the British Combination Acts, legislation passed in 1799 and 1899 which criminally punished any laborer "who combined with another to gain an increase in wages or a decrease

---

[21] Editors of Encyclopedia. "Pinkerton National Detective Agency." *Encyclopedia Brittanica*, Sep. 25, 2017, www.britannica.com/topic/Pinkerton-National-Detective-Agency.
[22] U.S. House, "Employment of Pinkerton Detectives," Report No. 2447, xv–xvi.
[23] See David A. Sklansky, "The Private Police," *UCLA Law Review* 46, no. 4 (1999): 1215.
[24] 5 U.S.C.S. § 3108 (organizations subject to section); 48 CFR 37.109.

in hours," who encouraged work stoppages, or who "objected to working with any other workman."[25] These acts banned any and all collective action for trade workers, but were rooted in previous anti-union legislation directed at individual trades.[26]

The first British Combination Act, resulting from the London tailors' strike of 1720, banned strikes, voided all agreements that increased wages or reduced hours, and created legally fixed hours and wages, granting judges the power to alter these limits. Combination could also be prosecuted under common-law conspiracy doctrines, which prohibited an "agreement between two or more persons to commit an unlawful act or to accomplish a lawful end by unlawful means,"[27] regardless of what the parties had conspired about. A 1726 act, passed in response to a weavers' strike, banned collective action, but also banned employers from paying workers in goods rather than wages.[28] Yet the balance of labor laws still weighed largely in employers' favor.

This bias is seen in the Silkmakers Act of 1773, the Hatters Act of 1777, and the Papermakers Act of 1796, which included minor concessions to labor, but continued to criminalize collective action by various trade groups. William Wilberforce proposed a ban on all combination in the country, which he viewed as "a general disease in our society."[29] Prime Minister William Pitt championed Wilberforce's suggestion, and a new bill was introduced in 1799 which prohibited any contract made by workmen to advance wages, reduce hours, decrease the quantity of work, influence hiring and employment, or influence productivity.[30] Responding to criticisms that the act was vague and to countrywide worker protests, in 1800 the act was repealed and replaced by new legislation that made minimal changes to statutory language, but also banned combination among employers to reduce wages, add or alter work hours, or increase the quantity of work. While the latter was a concession to labor's interests, penalties for violations of the law were considerably less steep for employers than for workers. Notably, the 1800 act also called for arbitration of all disputes concerning workplace issues.[31]

These acts were largely rooted in a public fear stemming from the recent French Revolution's Reign of Terror, together with the long-held British tradition of government paternalism and the sentiment that laborers ought to work for reasonable wages and the government should provide for those who could not find work.[32] Ruling class fear of a working class uprising like that in France led them to see

---

[25] Orth, "English Combination Acts," 175–211.

[26] Orth, "English Combination Acts," 195.

[27] Orth, "English Combination Acts," 175–211.

[28] Orth, "English Combination Acts," 182–83, 186.

[29] Wilberforce, quoted in Orth, "English Combination Acts," 195.

[30] Orth, "English Combination Acts," 196–97.

[31] Orth, "English Combination Acts," 202, 204.

[32] William Frank Shawl, "The Repeal of the Combination Acts, 1824–1825" (MA thesis, Montana State University, 1954), 29.

combination by employers as a minor offense, while viewing combination by workers as a political crime. The fear that workers' discontent could give rise to another revolution was merged with the employers' aversion to high wages to create a strong anti-union sentiment.[33]

Ultimately, in 1824, the laws were repealed following parliamentary consensus that they "had failed in their object [and] had also dangerously antagonized the working class." By this point the Industrial Revolution was well underway and spreading, governing class sentiment began to shift to a more market-centered approach as put forth by Adam Smith's *Wealth of Nations,* and even employers began to think wages should be set by the market rather than through government intervention.[34] Thus, the rise and fall of the Combination Acts can largely be attributed to the prevailing social, economic, and political attitudes of the time.

While new legislation in 1825 granted workers more rights than Combination Acts past, common-law conspiracy remained a powerful tool to enjoin collective activity, and under British common law in the nineteenth century, courts generally found that conspiracy was illegal even if "the matter about which they conspired might have been lawful for them ... to do, if they had not conspired to do it."[35] While the general Combination Acts were enacted after American independence, much of the U.S. legal system relied upon British common law. Thus, while the United States had no formal law prohibiting union activity in the early nineteenth century, courts were undecided as to whether such activity was nonetheless illegal conspiracy under common law. It was this issue of criminal conspiracy which the Supreme Court of Massachusetts took up in *Commonwealth v. Hunt* (1842).

When the Industrial Revolution created a consolidated labor force, some workers turned to collective action to advocate for better wages, conditions, or working hours. The early nineteenth-century courts largely ruled against labor in deciding whether laborers exercising their collective bargaining power were committing criminal conspiracy. These cases relied heavily on the precedent of English common law in general; in particular, the common-law holding that combination to raise wages was an illegal conspiracy as applied to the U.S. courts was at the heart of many debates. While some cases, such as *Commonwealth v. Pullis* (1806), found that under common law, combination to increase wages was illegal, other decisions, such as *People v. Melvin* (1811), held that combination itself was not illegal, but the means workers used to achieve that end were.[36] Ultimately, it was *Commonwealth v. Hunt* that set the standard for interpreting how and if common law applies to combination.

[33] Shawl, "Repeal of the Combination Acts," 31.
[34] Shawl, "Repeal of the Combination Acts," 58 (quote), 95.
[35] *R. v. Journeyman-Taylors of Cambridge,* 8 Mod. 10–11, 88 Eng. Rep. 9 (K.B. 1721), quoted in Orth, "English Combination Acts," 183.
[36] Bill Nahill, "*Commonwealth v. Hunt,*" *American Legal History,* Mar. 12, 2013.

The facts of *Hunt* concern the combination of the Boston Journeymen Bootmaker's Society, who were indicted for conspiracy on the grounds that they unlawfully combined to create a closed shop policy that would prohibit non-Society members from gaining employment alongside them "to the great damage and oppression" of their employers and non-Society workers. Particularly, the charging party held that Society members "did compel" employer Issac B. Wait to fire journeyman Jeremiah Horne, who refused to abide by Society rules.[37] In 1840, the defendants were found guilty at criminal trial after the judge instructed the jury that the Society was an illegal conspiracy as a matter of law, and that a guilty verdict was appropriate if the individuals on trial were found to have participated in that conspiracy. Defendant's counsel disagreed, arguing that the Society was not a conspiracy, as they did not plan or intend "to do a criminal act, or to do any lawful act by criminal means."[38] The case was appealed to resolve this matter of law.

The court found that while common-law conspiracy doctrine was in force in Massachusetts, it did not apply in this case. The court defines conspiracy as "a combination of two or more persons, by some concerted action, to accomplish some criminal or unlawful purpose, or to accomplish some purpose, not in itself criminal or unlawful, by criminal or unlawful means," and clarified that the government can independently decide what constitutes "criminal activity" to implicate a conspiracy charge.[39] Although England had anti-combination and wage-setting laws on the books, the United States did not adopt such laws upon declaring independence. The appellate court found that the Society's purpose "to induce all those engaged in the same occupation to become members of it ... is not unlawful," and stated that while such a combination could give members "power" to commit unlawful acts, there is no proof that the Society combined for this purpose. Further, there was no evidence that "the objects of this association ... were obtained by criminal means." The court affirmed workers' rights to "work for whom they please, or not to work, if they prefer"; as such, it is not a criminal act to collectively refuse to work out of respect for their own interests. Because the act of combining was not unlawful, and there was no evidence that the act was a violation of any contract between the workers and employer, the court found that there was no conspiracy. The trial court decision was therefore reversed on the grounds that no illegal purpose or illegal means to conspire were asserted.[40]

Hunt was a landmark decision because it ruled that combination was not inherently illegal; in fact, Chief Justice Shaw explicitly stated that individuals can combine for "useful and honorable purposes."[41] This marks a serious diversion from

---

[37] Charges of the indictment, quoted in *Commonwealth v. Hunt*, 45 Mass. 111, 1842 Mass. LEXIS 111, at **1 and **3.

[38] *Commonwealth v. Hunt*, 45 Mass. 111, 1842 Mass. LEXIS 111, at **5.

[39] *Commonwealth v. Hunt*, 45 Mass. 111 (1842), 123, 122.

[40] *Commonwealth v. Hunt*, 45 Mass. 111 (1842), 129–30, 136.

[41] *Commonwealth v. Hunt*, 45 Mass. 111(1842), 129.

English tradition and thus a distinct moment in U.S. labor history. As noted above, combination in England was viewed negatively in both formal law and public opinion. While the Combination Acts ultimately failed, their failure was rooted in issues of public wage-setting and a fear of uprising rather than in a major change in sentiment towards combination. The *Hunt* case explicitly states that the United States did not *de facto* adopt England's views on combination; it was first up to the U.S. legislature to decide what activity was illegal.

For a time, *Hunt* reigned as precedential in conspiracy cases. However, by the 1860s, it seems that courts had resumed their pre-*Hunt* tendencies to rule in favor of employers against the interests of unions. A New Jersey case in 1867 with "virtually identical facts" claimed to distinguish *Hunt*; that was the last year that *Hunt* was cited as controlling precedent in a labor law case.[42] This shift coincides with the Second Industrial Revolution (also known as the Technological Revolution) sweeping the United States. The nature of work was changing in the decades leading up to 1840; it was in a state of "constant flux," as described by Jeff Hirsch in his seminal article "Future Work." While Hirsch discusses the means by which new technologies may alter employer–worker relationships in the present day, parallels can be drawn to this early period of labor history.[43] As technological advancements in the second half of the nineteenth century altered production capacity in the United States, so too did the relationship between employer and employee shift. In 1846, the first sewing machine was patented, revolutionizing the clothing industry, and by 1869, the transcontinental railroad was complete, expanding the scope of markets and capital; the telephone, the lightbulb, and electricity all followed.[44] By the late nineteenth century, the nature of production had changed entirely in response to these advances. The factory system expanded exponentially, division of labor and unskilled work became the status quo, and the semi-skilled journeymen at issue in *Hunt* were effectively obsolete at a large scale. As the nature of work changed, the government tried to formulate a response to nurture yet manage the rapid growth of American industry. In 1890, the government, primarily concerned with monopoly power, passed the Sherman Act, which outlaws "every contract, combination or conspiracy in restraint of trade."[45] From 1890 until it was amended in 1914, this law effectively banned all labor union activity in the United States.

The Sherman Act marks a significant, if nuanced, turning point in U.S. labor policy. It was around this time that Frederick Taylor began his first studies in time management; however, his time management system was not yet complete or widely known. Thus, the Sherman Act must be analyzed as a pre-Taylorism policy

---

[42] Walter Nelles, "*Commonwealth v. Hunt*," *Columbia Law Review* 32, no. 7 (1932): 1165.

[43] Hirsch, "Future Work," 890.

[44] Emma Griffin, *Liberty's Dawn: A People's History of the Industrial Revolution* (New Haven, CT: Yale University Press, 2014).

[45] Federal Trade Commission, "The Antitrust Laws," in *Guide to Antitrust Laws*, www.ftc.gov/tips-advice/competition-guidance/guide-antitrust-laws/antitrust-laws (accessed Jan. 4, 2021).

born from other factors of the Industrial Revolution. While post-Taylorism labor policy largely concerns the relationship between labor and industry, the Sherman Act was similar to the Combination Acts in that it focused on the relationship between industry and the greater economy. Just as England sought to regulate competition through combination laws that prohibited payment in the form of goods or commodities, the United States sought policy that would limit the proliferation of harmful monopolies brought about by advances in industry.[46] Or at least that was the rhetoric advanced to justify the Sherman Act. The claimed intent of the act largely concerned monopoly power and big corporations, yet the observed impact was almost entirely felt by laborers who sought to organize. Parsing out what the Sherman Act says about labor relations in the United States at the time it was passed thus requires careful deduction.

In the 1880s, states found themselves lacking the constitutional authority to regulate monopolies, and certain minor political parties, such as the Grangers, spoke adamantly against the issue; however, the two major parties at the time were generally unconcerned with checking monopoly power. Leading up to the 1888 presidential election, the Republican Party was singled out for their weak platform concerning anti-trust legislation. In what the *New York Times* viewed as an attempt to save face, prominent Republican John Sherman of Ohio introduced the issue of tariff measures to control competition before the Senate. Republicans sought to largely code discussion around trusts in terms of tariff reform; as such, the first bill Sherman introduced before Congress concerned tariffs. The issue of labor was noticeably absent until Democratic senator James George of Mississippi, in a lengthy speech denouncing the legislation, asserted that there was a strong "likelihood that combinations of farmers and laborers formed to combat the trusts would themselves fall within the punitive provisions of the bill." While George's suspicions proved to be prophetic, his concerns were never directly addressed. Sherman did concede "that it was difficult to identify the line between lawful and unlawful combinations"; however, he believed the issue should be left to the courts and enforcement pursued by the Justice Department. George attempted to include amendments that would provide legal remedies to protect farmers and laborers against trusts, but his amendments failed and his concerns again went unanswered. Politically, Democrats and Republicans alike seemed to have lost interest in the bill. Politicians and the media apparently agreed that it was "worthless" legislation that would not effectively regulate trusts, but it was passed regardless with little fanfare, thanks to Republican momentum.[47]

Indeed, the act did not prove effective in regulating the trusts it claimed as the center of concern. Even when it was evident the legislation was failing, Sherman

---

[46]   Peter R. Dickson and Philippa K. Wells, "The Dubious Origins of the Sherman Antitrust Act: The Mouse That Roared," *Journal of Public Policy and Marketing* 20, no. 1 (2001): 6.

[47]   Dickson and Wells, "Dubious Origins of the Sherman Antitrust Act," 7–11, quotes at 9.

never proposed any new amendments and the Justice Department was not allocated funds to enforce the act until 1903. The act did, however, prove incredibly harmful to labor interests. Of the first six cases brought by the Justice Department under the Sherman Act, four were against labor unions. Many had foreseen this outcome, yet stunningly, a proposed amendment to exclude labor unions from the legislation's reach was passed by the Senate but "'mysteriously' ignored by the Judiciary Committee that drafted the final legislation."[48] It was not until 1914, with the passage of the Clayton Act, that labor unions were excluded from the reach of the Sherman Act.

There is little direct discussion concerning labor and the passage of the act to understand how it was intended to impact their combination activities. While certain senators suggested that labor's right to combine should be protected – a sentiment in line with the *Hunt* decision – they did not go so far as to actually protect them. The first case that declared labor unions illegal under the act, *U.S. v. Workingmen's Amalgamated Council of New Orleans*, came in 1893; what's further telling is that action to protect workers against this supposedly unintended consequence did not come for another eleven years. Inferences can certainly be drawn from this record of inaction and historical context. It is evident from media coverage and stated positions that the Republican Party was, at the very least, sympathetic to trusts and industrial corporations.[49] The extent to which this bill harmed labor combination suggests, therefore, that enjoining combination was, at best, not adverse to the interests of trusts and, at worst, significantly aligned with corporate interests.

The Sherman Act, therefore, reflects a period of U.S. labor history where corporate interests reigned supreme; labor and political policy were largely defined by "laissez-faire economics" that saw government support corporate interests through both hands-off governance and favorable policies. As the Industrial Revolution allowed monopolies to flourish, these monopolies bolstered production and the U.S. economy at the expense of labor and the common man. This was a trade that both corporations and government were apparently willing to make. Exploiting and controlling workers by suppressing their bargaining power was the method of choice for maximizing production. As the nineteenth century turned over to the twentieth, however, a new era of politics began. The Progressive Era, spanning from 1896 to 1916, saw government reject the exploitation and unfair competition of the nineteenth century with the belief that reforms centered in social scientific principles were the solution to the ills of society.[50] It was under the ideologies of this regime that Taylorism would flourish.

---

[48] Dickson and Wells, "Dubious Origins of the Sherman Antitrust Act," 11.
[49] Dickson and Wells, "Dubious Origins of the Sherman Antitrust Act," 8–9.
[50] Thomas C. Leonard, "Progressive Era Origins of the Regulatory State and the Economist as Expert," *History of Political Economy* 47, no. 5 (2015): 50.

2.3 HEARINGS ON TAYLORISM AND SHOP MANAGEMENT

By 1911, the U.S. government had been experimenting with and had partially installed the "Taylor system" (as scientific management was then known) at U.S. arsenals and navy yards. Critics of the system claimed it was detrimental to the best interests of both government service and the workers. As the system had been in partial operation for a considerable time, Congress decided to investigate the Taylor system's "applicability to Government works, its effects on the health and pay of employees, its effect on wages and labor cost, and [other matters that may] give a thorough understanding of the results of the installation of this system."[51] The published transcripts of the hearings comprise nearly two thousand pages in three volumes, covering hearings held from October 1911 through February 1912, and included workers at the Watertown Arsenal (in Massachusetts) and the Brooklyn Navy Yard.

The workers and their representatives expressed the same genre of concerns related to the unfairness of the Taylorist systems of management, which they saw as setting impossible work standards. John O'Leary, representative of "the molders employed in the Government yards in the Boston industrial district," objected to the introduction and extension of the Taylor system or any similar system, because it required always working at a very high speed, "sometimes to the limit of human endurance," for less money, and argued that the same methods could not be equally applied to all types of molding work.[52] Joseph Hicklin, an iron molder at the Watertown Arsenal, described how the time allowed to make a mold was suddenly changed from twenty-four hours to fourteen hours and expressed workers' dismay at the constant monitoring by other men standing over them all the time.[53]

In hearings held in January 1912, the witnesses particularly discussed the use of the stopwatch in selecting the fastest man working. Based on Taylor's claim that workers could not get a proper amount of efficiency by using ordinary piecework (i.e., work paid for based on the amount of production) and his advice on employing the fastest man, the Rock Island Arsenal was trying to introduce a new shop management system that was a similar but modified version of the one installed at the Watertown Arsenal.[54] The hearings also included many letters sent by workers to General Crozier, chief of the Ordnance Department. The workers indicated that "the force at the arsenal [was] almost demoralized by [the] practice of timing every moment of the men with a stop watch," which was "an un-American system, one calculated to anger

---

[51]   U.S. House, *Taylor and Other Systems of Shop Management*, 1:3.
[52]   Testimony of Mr. John R. O'Leary [International Molders' Union of North America], in U.S. House, *Taylor and Other Systems of Shop Management*, 1:3–4, 6.
[53]   Testimony of Mr. Joseph Hicklin [iron molder, Watertown Arsenal], in U.S. House, *Taylor and Other System of Shop Management*, 1:143–48, 176–200.
[54]   See U.S. House of Representatives, *Taylor and Other Systems of Shop Management* ..., Vol. 2 (Washington DC: Government Printing Office, 1912), 1088–89.

self-respecting employees."[55] According to the workers, it was "un-American, humiliating, and an insult to the honesty and fair dealing and self-respect of an American mechanic to have a man standing over him with a watch." Also, the system "did not give the operator credit for the necessary nonproductive movements or time required to do a day's work." In addition, they claimed that the system "caused a cut in wages" as piece prices had been established so low under the timer system to the point where it was less than common laborers were getting in the vicinity, and they gave a table of prices as evidence. However, F. E. Hobbs, lieutenant colonel from the Ordnance Department, responded to the letter, denying each claim in detail.[56]

Many witnesses who testified at the hearings focused on what they found to be the objectionable features of Taylorism. H. F. Winkler, a toolmaker at Rock Island Arsenal, described the stopwatch as a "miserable feature" of the Taylor system. Another feature was making the task of a workman "so severe that only one out of every five can stand under it." In addition, he described that there was "no place for a worker who could not hold up to the worker who had the highest end of the work" and explained that these features were from Taylor's book, *Scientific Shop Management*.[57] Other workers concurred with Winkler's opinion. A. A. Gustafson (a toolmaker) indicated that workers would not oppose the Taylor system for its efficiency, but were protesting against it because of some of its features.[58] According to F. S. Leonard (an inspector), due to the bonus system, "men lost confidence in one another and [stood] ready to cut one another's throats in the shop."[59] And Hugo F. Leuders (a metal worker) stated that the men had no objection to a system at work but that the stop watch is "one thing that they do not care for."[60]

In the hearings, Taylor claimed that one of the very essential features of the system was "that a task must never be given to a man that would overwork him in any way," but Leonard responded that he had understood it in reverse that "the task must be put on him to get the most out of him." As a response, Taylor read a section of his book, explaining his reference to men well suited to their jobs as the definition of the best men. Yet, workers expressed their fear that under the bonus system, the task would be made so hard that it would be very difficult for the majority of the men to keep up and that they might lose employment because they could not keep up with the pace.[61]

55 U.S. House, *Taylor and Other Systems of Shop Management*, 2:838–45, 1161–62 (quotes at 838).
56 U.S. House, *Taylor and Other Systems of Shop Management*, 2:839–45 (quotes at 840).
57 Testimony of H. F. Winkler [toolmaker, Rock Island Arsenal], U.S. House, *Taylor and Other Systems of Shop Management*, 2:883, 887, 888 (quotes at 887, 888).
58 Testimony of A. A. Gustafson [toolmaker, Rock Island Arsenal], in U.S. House, *Taylor and Other Systems of Shop Management*, 2:920–21.
59 Testimony of F. S. Leonard [inspector, Rock Island Arsenal], in U.S. House, *Taylor and Other Systems of Shop Management*, 2:923–24.
60 Testimony of Hugo F. Leuders [metal worker, Rock Island Arsenal], in U.S. House, *Taylor and Other Systems of Shop Management*, 2:1000.
61 Testimony of F. S. Leonard, in U.S. House, *Taylor and Other Systems of Shop Management*, 2:927, 928.

In the hearings overall, the witnesses discussed features of the system being introduced and whether the new system should be considered as the Taylor system.[62]
One of the features of the Taylor system workers opposed was that it "seemed as a
scientific scheme to exploit labor," as they pointed out that Taylor stated in his book
that the system would not let workers make too much money.[63] Furthermore, Paul
G. Linter (a machinist) stated that he objected to having the Taylor system because
"the relentless speeding up of workers beyond their endurance" and the elimination
of the mechanic[64] would affect working conditions. Lastly, the hearing contained
not only the opinions of workers and others in support of the system,[65] but also infor-
mative tables, such as the Decisions of the Chief of Ordniance Affecting the Status
of Employees at the Rock Island Arsenal.[66]

The hearings held in January and February of 1912 included the testimony of
Frederick Winslow Taylor.[67] Taylor explained that he did not intend people to associate the system with his name. In developing different parts of the system, he had
originally designated the name *piece rate system* because the prominent feature of
the system was a radically different type of piecework, but after learning that it was a
comparatively unimportant element, he named the system *task system* based on the
idea of setting a measured standard of work for each man to do each day. However,
since the word *task* held the connotation of a system treating men with severity and
not according to justice, as it was intended, Taylor decided on the term *scientific
management* for the system he had developed.[68]

In his testimony, Taylor emphasized that he planned to carry on his work on
scientific management because such work would be in service to workers under the
system. According to Taylor, the essence of scientific management was the mental evolution of both workers and management, with the desired end result being
that both sides would direct their focus away from the division of the surplus as
the all-important matter and turn their attention toward increasing the size of the
surplus so it becomes so large that it is unnecessary for management and workers to
quarrel over how it should be divided.[69] Thus the system would make workers and

---

[62] Testimony of George Patterson [master mechanic, Rock Island Arsenal], in U.S. House, *Taylor and
Other Systems of Shop Management*, 2:956–83.

[63] Testimony of Roy Kelly [metal polisher, Rock Island Arsenal], in U.S. House, *Taylor and Other
Systems of Shop Management*, 2:1007, 1008.

[64] Testimony of Paul G. Linter [machinist, Rock Island Arsenal], in U.S. House, *Taylor and Other
Systems of Shop Management*, 2:1067 (quote), 1070.

[65] See Testimony of Major D. M. King [Ordnance Department, Rock Island Arsenal], in U.S. House,
Taylor and Other Systems of Shop Management, 2:1092–111.

[66] U.S. House, *Taylor and Other Systems of Shop Management*, 2:1167–70.

[67] See U.S. House of Representatives, *The Taylor and Other Systems of Shop Management: Hearings …*
Vol. 3 (Washington DC: Government Printing Service, 1912), 1377–1508.

[68] Testimony of Frederick Winslow Taylor, in U.S. House, *Taylor and Other Systems of Shop
Management*, 3:1378.

[69] See Testimony of F. W. Taylor, in U.S. House, *Taylor and Other Systems of Shop Management*,
3:1388.

management friends who share mutual interests.[70] According to Taylor, in the end scientific management would enable all to live better because workers would be paid more when the system was properly applied.[71]

Taylor thought it was natural for workers to be suspicious of their employers,[72] but he believed that his system was a kinder style of management for the workers. Taylor's testimony was preoccupied with justifying scientific management and with proving the efficacy of scientific management with evidence.[73] For example, with a pig iron handle example, he described that scientific management would allow exact and precise scientific investigation and knowledge to replace the old "I believe so" and "I guess so." He defined the system as "kindness" and "teaching."[74]

In addition, Taylor described the development and evolution of scientific management by explaining scientific experiments he had conducted for accurate motion and time study[75] and by defining "soldiering" (taking the most time to do the least work).[76] He also refuted skepticism regarding the scientific management system. First, Taylor claimed that there was not a single case in which fewer workers were employed after the implementation of scientific management.[77] Second, he stated that there was technically no "speeding up" that occurred under scientific management; it was merely the elimination of waste movements or soldiering and substitution of the best way.[78] Moreover, Taylor argued that workers objected to the stopwatch not because it made them nervous; rather, it was because the stopwatch made employers knowledgeable about how long tasks took, thus making it more difficult for workers to soldier.[79] Taylor illustrated his points with an exemplar of scientific management implementation at the American Locomotive Works and contrasted that example with that of Harrington Emerson. Taylor argued that Emerson had abandoned the very essence of scientific management, which was bringing mental change on the side of the workers, for the speed-up of the process.[80]

It is important to note, however, that even in his testimony, Taylor compared "first-class" workers to "first-class" horses and argued that scientific management had no place for those that were not "first-class," or those "who can work and won't

[70] Testimony of F. W. Taylor, in U.S. House, *Taylor and Other Systems of Shop Management*, 3:1434.
[71] See Testimony of F. W. Taylor, in U.S. House, *Taylor and Other Systems of Shop Management*, 3:1389–93.
[72] U.S. House, *Taylor and Other Systems of Shop Management*, 3:1392.
[73] See Testimony of F. W. Taylor, in U.S. House, *Taylor and Other Systems of Shop Management*, 3:1394–1410.
[74] Testimony of F. W. Taylor, in U.S. House, *Taylor and Other Systems of Shop Management*, 3:1399, 1403.
[75] Testimony of F. W. Taylor, in U.S. House, *Taylor and Other Systems of Shop Management*, 3:1415.
[76] Testimony of F. W. Taylor, in U.S. House, *Taylor and Other Systems of Shop Management*, 3:1429–31.
[77] Testimony of F. W. Taylor, in U.S. House, *Taylor and Other Systems of Shop Management*, 3:1438.
[78] Testimony of F. W. Taylor, in U.S. House, *Taylor and Other Systems of Shop Management*, 3:1411.
[79] Testimony of F. W. Taylor, in U.S. House, *Taylor and Other Systems of Shop Management*, 3:1499.
[80] Testimony of F. W. Taylor, in U.S. House, *Taylor and Other Systems of Shop* Management, 3:1491–92.

work."[81] Also, Taylor regarded the time a worker stops to think as time that was not productive and explained that this should be the reason for using a stopwatch.[82] When Taylor claimed that a worker under scientific management had the recourse of leaving the workplace, the chairman of the hearing contended that the employee would be placed at a greater disadvantage by quitting his employment than the employer would be by having the worker quit.[83] Yet, Taylor said that the need for scientific management seemed to be growing immensely and argued that labor unions should look upon scientific management as their best friend.[84]

Other witnesses included workers and managers of the Navy Department, Washington Navy Yard, Norfolk Navy Yard, Charlestown Navy Yard, Tabor Manufacturing Co., American Locomotive Co., and other companies, and they offered their support of the Taylor system based on their experiences. For example, Hudson W. Reed, a worker who was in charge of the time-study desk, gave testimony that everything under the Taylor system was done to lighten the burdens of the workers because it eliminated dangerous and disagreeable features connected with the operation.[85] Carl G. Barth, the industrial engineer famous for his association with Frederick Taylor, was also in support of Taylorism and helped introduce the system in many factories, such as the Link Belt Co. and the Tabor Co.; he described the system as reducing workers' mistakes.[86]

At the hearings, several lawmakers and labor leaders testified against Taylor's scientific management system. For instance, Harry J. Ruesskamp noted that if a man did not constantly work at his maximum capacity (which he described as being a "drone"), he was discharged. He believed that it was not the people in power, but the system itself that created bad conditions and harsh treatments on workers.[87] Representative Irvin S. Pepper (D–Iowa) emphasized points of contention in the Taylorist system, including the replacing of skilled mechanics by laborers and lowering of the wages, the relentless speeding up of workers to the extent that only a small portion of them could manage the pace, the use of the stopwatch, the system of promotion based on the contest principle, the bonus and differential rate systems for fixing compensation and the piecework system for ascertaining a day's work, the system of discipline, and the principle that workers must be dealt with individually

---

[81] Testimony of F. W. Taylor, in U.S. House, *Taylor and Other Systems of Shop Management*, 3:1455, 1456.

[82] Testimony of F. W. Taylor, in U.S. House, *Taylor and Other Systems of Shop Management*, 3:1496–97.

[83] See Testimony of F. W. Taylor, in U.S. House, *Taylor and Other Systems of Shop Management*, 3:1474.

[84] See Testimony of F. W. Taylor, in U.S. House, *Taylor and Other Systems of Shop Management*, 3:1507–8.

[85] Testimony of Hudson W. Reed [Tabor Manufacturing], in U.S. *House, Taylor and Other Systems of Shop Management*, 3:1510.

[86] See Testimony of Carl G. Barth, in U.S. House, *Taylor and Other Systems of Shop Management*, 3:1550.

[87] Testimony of Harry J. Ruesskamp [machinist], U.S. House, *Taylor and Other Systems of Shop Management*, 3:1817–19.

even regarding issues affecting more than one worker. According to Pepper, although Taylor had explained that the standard for the highest rate of speed was the speed at which the worker would be happy and thrive, workers could not be honest about their experiences when they received payment from employers. The system thus resulted in a great number of men being thrown out of employment.[88]

Regarding the lowering of wages and the undue speeding of men, N. P. Alifas, a man representing 1,500 workers at the Rock Island Arsenal, cited portions from Taylor's book which noted that only men well fitted for the work would be selected and argued that Taylor's aim had been to dispose of inefficient workers who could not maintain a high pace – Taylor's scientific management measured efficiency by the product of one's labor and if a man could not attain the maximum speed, he would be thrown away.[89] In addition, Samuel Gompers, president of the American Federation of Labor and Congress of Industrial Organizations (AFL), indicated that any organization among the workers under the Taylor system was practically impossible and that the system eliminated independence and self-assertion for workers. Gompers also asked for an investigation of an accident in which a number of workers were killed and some sustained burn injuries when a plug was released from a tank in the Midvale Steel Co., in order to ascertain whether there was a connection between that accident and the Taylor system. Gompers also expressed his belief that the Taylor system was detrimental to workers; the system produced wealth but people who did piecework had less control over their time than those who worked by the day.[90]

James O'Connell, president of the International Association of Machinists, also described his concern about the system. He indicated how Frederick Taylor described the system as "using strong men with big physical bodies but taking their heads off" and asserted that the system "stunted higher standard of manhood" in the United States. According to him, it was a "joke" to believe that the system benefitted labor or would lead workers to receive more money. Furthermore, the Taylor system did not permit collective bargaining at all, and piecework was in no way related to fairness because management, as well as the speedier and the stronger workers, set the standard of price and pace.[91]

It is clear from the testimony of workers, managers, owners, and Taylor himself that how a person viewed the system of scientific management depended largely on the person's place in the system and hierarchy, and that the new system had effects that went far beyond its goal of improving efficiency, raising existential questions

---

[88] U.S. House, *Investigation of Taylor System of Shop Management*, 1:4, 8.

[89] Statement of N. P. Alifas [Rock Island Arsenal], in U.S. House, *Investigation of Taylor System of Shop Management*, 11–15.

[90] Statement of Samuel Gompers [president AFL], in U.S. House, *Investigation of Taylor System of Shop Management*, 22, 26, 30.

[91] Statement of James O'Connell [international president, International Association of Machinists], U.S. House, *Investigation of Taylor System of Shop Management*, 35–36, 37–38.

about the role and value of workers in American society. The congressional investigation into the application of Taylorism in the workplace was a significant milestone in the evolution of labor policy.

2.4 POST-TAYLORISM LABOR LAW

Following his departure from Bethlehem Steel in 1901, Frederick Taylor went to work spreading his management system nationwide. His methodology resonated with Progressive leaders who sought reform that would protect the worker against the exploitation of industry. They viewed his "science"-based work system as a potential protection against irrational corporate actors. Progressives did not turn to Taylorism alone, however; they also sought to pass legislation that would protect workers outright. At issue in the landmark case *Lochner v. New York* (1905) was a progressive New York state law that capped maximum hours for bakers at sixty hours per week. The Supreme Court found that this law directly "interferes with the right of contract between the employer and employees" as protected by the Fourteenth Amendment, and thus declared it unconstitutional.[92]

In their analysis, the Court stated that "the right to purchase or sell labor is part of the liberty protected" by the Fourteenth Amendment provision for "life, liberty, [and] property." The state of New York justified their law as valid under the police powers traditionally understood to be within the purview of the states; that is, the right to make laws that concern the "safety health, morals, and general welfare of the public."[93] The Court sought to distinguish when the exercise of police powers seem to interfere with constitutional protections, which should prevail, and argued that *Lochner* is distinct from other cases where states exercised their police powers to limit hours of workers in other professions and circumstances. The primary issue the Court considered in *Lochner* was whether the maximum hours law for bakers constitutes "unreasonable, unnecessary and arbitrary interference with the right of the individual to his personal liberty or to enter into those contracts in relation to labor which may seem to him appropriate or necessary for the support of himself and his family."[94] The Court asserted that because bakers are capable of asserting their own interests, the law does not implicate a public health issue nor a health issue for the individual bakers. As such, "the act is not … a health law" but rather "an illegal interference" into an individual's right to contract. The Court went so far as to question the true "motives" under which the New York law and similar legislation was passed, as it believed "it is apparent that the public health or welfare bears but the most remote relation to the law."[95]

[92] *Lochner v. New York*, 198 U.S. 45 (1905), 52, 53.
[93] *Lochner v. New York*, 198 U.S. 45 (1905), 53.
[94] *Lochner v. New York*, 198 U.S. 45 (1905), 54–56, quote at 56.
[95] *Lochner v. New York*, 198 U.S. 45 (1905), 55–59, quotes at 61, 64.

Lochner's opinionated holding was strongly admonished in a dissent by Justice John Marshall Harlan, joined by Justices White and Day, and a separate dissent by Justice Holmes. Harlan's dissent significantly argued that "[i]f the end which the legislature seeks to accomplish be one to which its power extends, and if the means employed to that end, although not the wisest or best, are yet not plainly and palpably unauthorized by law, then the court cannot interfere ... The burden of proof ... is upon those who assert it to be unconstitutional."[96] While Harlan's dissent would inform labor law many years down the line,[97] Holmes's dissent is memorable for his simple assertion that "this case is decided upon an economic theory which a large part of the country does not entertain."[98] Indeed, in this statement, Holmes touched upon the dissonance between the Progressive movement and what would come to be known as the *Lochner* era. From the Sherman Act in 1890 until after the Wagner Act in 1937, courts adopted a "broad interpretation of due process that protected economic rights," protecting laissez-faire economics at the expense of Progressive reform aimed to protect workers' rights.[99]

Taylorism, however, grew out of laissez-faire economics. At its core, it was a method of worker control designed to improve production outcomes for industrial corporations. Thus, what is remarkable about the Progressive era is that unions, government, and corporations alike all initially supported its tenets. Progressives believed that scientific management had the power to revolutionize economics, offering "efficiency, workplace harmony, and social justice, all realized via the expert application of science."[100] Viewing science as always leading to rational and just outcomes, Progressives idealized Taylorism as a vehicle for positive social change and efficiency. Industrial corporations, too, believed in the virtues of Taylorism as a tool for productivity and efficiency but shunned Progressive attempts to impose restrictions on the workplace through labor protection laws. Indeed, Progressive idealization of Taylorism was likely misled. Taylor focused on the complete consolidation of power in management: He devised his system to take control back from workers who were halting production with threats of strikes or slowdowns.[101] In a system designed to vest power in corporations, Progressive reforms as seen in *Lochner*, which would necessarily limit corporate power, had no place. Ultimately, the *Lochner* court upheld Taylorism in its true form by allowing corporations to continue to manage nearly every aspect of worker life. This was true to Taylor's intent as evidenced by his 1911 claim that "In the past ... the man has been first, in the future,

[96] *Lochner v. New York*, 198 U.S. 45 (1905), 68.

[97] *Lochner v. New York* [summary], Oyez, www.oyez.org/cases/1900-1940/198us45 (accessed Jan. 4, 2021).

[98] *Lochner v. New York*, 198 U.S. 45, 75 (1905).

[99] "Lochner Era," Cornell Law School, Legal Information Institute, www.law.cornell.edu/wex/lochner_era (accessed Jan. 4, 2020).

[100] Leonard, "Progressive Era Origins of the Regulatory State and the Economist as Expert," 64.

[101] John Zerzan, "Unionism and Taylorism: Labor Cooperation with the 'Modernization' of Production," *Fifth Estate* 278 (Nov. 1976), www.fifthestate.org/archive/278-november-1976/unionism-and-taylorism/.

the system must be first."[102] Allowing the system to be first meant denying the worker protections challenged in *Lochner*.

Examining the history of labor relations as a whole up to this point, a clear pattern starts to emerge. Government is likely to take the side of whoever controls the means of production, as that is the class that holds the power to influence the economy and important decision-making. Government is, however, also interested in maintaining a sense of law and order. England's Combination Acts saw the government make minor concessions to prevent labor uprisings, while suppressing labor's voice. In *Hunt*, the court found that labor unions are not inherently illegal, as they may serve a valid purpose, but left the door open for combination laws to be enacted and collective action weakened. The *Hunt* court was considering a labor force that was rapidly consolidating and seeking work in a shifting economic landscape; in the years that followed, production became more advanced and the nature of work became more rigid and clearly defined. Labor combination, therefore, began to pose a serious threat to an economy poised to boom. The Sherman Act – whatever its intent – effectively squashed the threat of labor combination and in the years to come, Taylorism and the principles of scientific management justified its enforcement. The dominant Taylorist philosophy was that unionization that threatened to harm production should be avoided at all costs. Indeed, as Taylor preached, unionization would not be necessary if the principles of scientific management yielded a perfect system of labor for all, as many believed they would. Attempts to interfere with Taylorism through labor protection laws were likely met with extreme resistance by the *Lochner* court for this reason: The free market as guided by Taylorism would result in maximum production, which outside intervention would threaten.

Eventually, of course, labor – whose interests were never truly represented under Taylorism – fought back. During the *Lochner* era, tensions between labor and management intensified. The National Guard intervened nearly five hundred times between 1875 and 1910 to squash labor unrest. In 1919, one of the largest strikes in history was organized by steel workers nationwide.[103] Seeking to assuage the threat of railway strikes, a bipartisan Railroad Labor Board was established in 1920, and the Railroad Labor Act was amended in 1926, requiring railways to recognize collective bargaining, providing for arbitration, and prohibiting employers and workers alike from interfering with one another's rights. This legislation set the groundwork for the Wagner Act of 1935, which established the National Labor Relations Board and legally protected private sector employees' right to organize and take collective action.[104]

---

[102] Leonard, "Progressive Era Origins of the Regulatory State and the Economist as Expert," 64.

[103] Joshua Freeman, "The History of Labor in the U.S.," U.S. Dept. of State: FPC Briefing, June 17, 2020, https://2017-2021.state.gov/briefings-foreign-press-centers/the-history-of-labor-in-the-u-s/index.html; "1919 Steel Strike," *Encyclopedia of Cleveland History*, https://case.edu/ech/articles/n/1919-steel-strike (accessed Jan. 5, 2021).

[104] Ralph S. Rice, "The Wagner Act: Its Legislative History and Its Relation to National Defense," *Ohio State Law Journal* 8, no. 1 (1941): 22.

The Wagner Act came on the heels of the Great Depression in the novel New Deal era of government. From 1920 to 1932, the United States experienced twelve straight years of Republican leadership, defined by a big-business-centric platform. Two-term president Calvin Coolidge was quoted as saying "Business is America's business."[105] During this time, unionization fell while Taylorism became largely accepted as fact in the new world order. To quote James Gross in his 2002 article "Worker Rights as Human Rights: Wagner Act Values and Moral Choices," "Unions had no place in the … Scientific Management approach that imposed tight control over workers whose obedience was secured by the use of financial and disciplinary 'incentives.'"[106] What began as a mission to improve efficiency and bolster production processes developed into an ideology that swept the nation. The pursuit of efficiency permeated every aspect of life, from department stores to managing the home. In 1929, however, these systems of production came crashing down as the U.S. economy fell into the greatest economic collapse it had ever seen. In 1933, President Roosevelt passed the National Industrial Recovery Act (NIRA) in an attempt to revive the nation, including a provision for labor that banned yellow-dog contracts (contracts in which workers agree not to remain or become members of a union), created wage-hour laws, and protected their right to collective bargaining. The government's motive was economic, supposedly including this provision to ensure "it [would be] impossible for the industrialist to take advantage of the employees while the nation followed the road to industrial recovery."[107] Increasing and securing wages was an essential piece of the government's recovery strategy. Consolidation of power in scientific management was at this point adverse to the greater structure of the American economy.

The NIRA's labor provision went largely unenforced, a serious issue in the eyes of Congress and the nation. The government enacted a public resolution to amend enforcement, which also ultimately proved fruitless. The Wagner Act, or NLRA, was ultimately introduced to "cure the deficiencies of the Recovery Act['s]" labor failures. NLRA advocates asserted lack of action by the Justice Department, delays in board elections influenced by employers, company "unions," and lack of enforcement power as primary problems with the NIRA that rendered it ineffective. There was an implied consensus that the NLRA was necessary to remedy the NIRA, and congressional debate was "principally [concerned] with the scope and effect of the proposed bill." After the NIRA was declared unconstitutional, congressional debate turned to ensuring the NLRA legislation was constitutionally grounded. When Senator Wagner introduced the bill, he cited unequal wealth distribution, "technological obsolescence," and the failure of the NIRA as causal factors necessitating the legislation. The finalized act asserted the right of employees "to form, join, or assist a union"

---

[105] "Economic Boom," in *The USA: A Nation of Contrasts 1910–1929*, BBC: Bitesize, www.bbc.co.uk/bitesize/guides/zw9wb82/revision/2 (accessed Jan. 5, 2021).

[106] James A. Gross, "Worker Rights as Human Rights: Wagner Act Values and Moral Choices," *Journal of Labor and Employment Law* 4, no. 3 (2002): 489.

[107] Rice, "The Wagner Act," 26–27.

and "the right to engage in concerted activities for mutual aid or protection." It further forced employers to recognize a union in their workplace. Congress included a list of enumerated activities that constitute unfair labor practices, in addition to creating the National Labor Relations Board (NLRB) to enforce the act.[108]

Significantly, concerning the act, Congress repeatedly discussed the "partiality of the Act toward the employee without compensating privileges granted to the employer."[109] This was a break from the century-old labor policy tradition, dating back to the British Combination Acts, of siding with the employer. Yet the NLRA was not a break from Taylorism and the ideology of scientific management. As Taylorism became ingrained in the very understanding of work that all Americans unconsciously subscribed to, so it ironically influenced even the language of the NLRA. In describing "supervisors," the NLRA "refers to the use of 'independent judgment' by supervisors reflecting the Tayloristic [*sic*] view that the execution of work should be separated from its conception." The NLRA implies that employees are aligned with means of production and employers and managers are "aligned with capital." The act's decision to include a somewhat "arbitrar[y]" division of employees versus supervisors at all is further indicative of Taylorism's influence.[110] While the NLRA was a win for labor, it is obvious that the tenets of Taylorism had by this point transcended productivity on the factory floor to fundamentally alter the nature of modern work.

Labor rights legislation, activism, and progress along these attenuated lines continued until World War II. In 1937, the Supreme Court ended the *Lochner* era with their decision in *West Coast Hotel Co. v. Parrish*, which ruled that a minimum wage law for women was valid, overruling in the process precedent that relied on the right-to-contract arguments definitive of *Lochner* and other anti-labor cases.[111] Congress responded by passing the Fair Labor Standards Act in 1938, establishing minimum wage laws, a defined forty-hour work week, and paid overtime as legal obligations. These victories for labor were, however, ultimately short lived. The military–industrial complex and wartime economy largely pulled the United States out of the remnants of the Depression and unions were experiencing a golden age for labor. Unions engaged in a "war-time no strike pledge" that calmed tensions between workers and employers. Following the war, the tides began to change. A new Red Scare, the threat of union power, and a period of heavy strike activity created a political climate fueled by anti-union sentiment.[112] When the no-strike clause ended, labor

---

[108] Rice, "The Wagner Act," 32–34, 36–39; SHRM, *What Is the Function of the National Labor Relations Act (NLRA)?*

[109] Rice, "The Wagner Act," 42.

[110] Marion Crain, "Building Solidarity through Expansion of NLRA Coverage: A Blueprint for Worker Empowerment." *Minneapolis Law Review* 74, no. 1 (1990): 986.

[111] *West Coast Hotel Co. v. Parrish*, 300 U.S. 379 (1936).

[112] Freeman, "History of Labor in the U.S."; C. M. Lewis, "Labor Has Opposed Taft-Hartley for Decades: Here's Why It's Time to Repeal It," *Strike Wave*, Apr. 3, 2019, www.thestrikewave.com/original-content/2019/4/3/labor-has-opposed-taft-hartley-for-decades-heres-why-its-time-to-repeal-it.

"went on the offensive," giving way to "the biggest strike wave in American history" in the fight for better wages and a voice in the workplace.[113] Employers were opposed to the NLRA and many refused to comply with Board decisions; some companies refused to comply with the law at all until it was deemed constitutional by the 5–4 decision in *National Labor Relations Board v. Jones & Loughlin Steel Corporation* in 1937. In 1946, the Republican Party gained control of Congress for the first time since the New Deal era began in 1931. Branding themselves as the "conservative 'old guard,'" a group of first-term Republicans set to work eradicating New Deal legislation. They first set their sights on the Wagner Act, looking to limit the "economic power potential" that combination afforded labor. Their revision, the Taft-Hartley Act of 1947, was a critical blow to labor that substantially weakened the NLRA.[114]

Section 7 of the NLRA, which protected employees' right to unionize, was weakened under the Taft-Hartley Act by new language which stated employees had the right to not participate in a union unless as a condition of employment. The act added six new unfair labor practices to the NLRA's enumerated list to "protect employees' rights from these unfair practices by unions." Unions were not allowed to create closed shops, were required to adhere to "good faith bargaining" restrictions, and were prohibited from influencing employers to discriminate against employees who choose not to unionize; the act also enjoined secondary boycotts. Unions further were "prohibited from charging excessive dues or initiation fees and from 'featherbedding,' or causing an employer to pay for work not performed." The law also made changes concerning free speech and bargaining unit representation, and added new election procedures.[115] Collectively, these provisions crushed the power of the NLRA and discouraged unionization.

Much like the NLRA, Taft-Hartley espoused Taylorist ideology in its treatment of workers versus supervisors. Taft-Hartley decidedly excluded supervisors' unions from NLRA protection, stating explicitly that "[t]he term 'employee' … shall not include … any individual employed as a supervisor."[116] While supervisors can still organize under Section 14(a) of the act, their activities are not protected by the act and therefore they cannot compel management to bargain with them, among other exceptions. Congressional conversation concerning the provision centered around "management's need for faithful agents" and the potential that supervisors' unions could be unduly influenced by employee unions, threatening "the workplace hierarchy."[117] These concerns squarely reflect the Taylorist view that

[113] Lewis, "Labor Has Opposed Taft-Hartley for Decades."

[114] Lewis, "Labor Has Opposed Taft-Hartley for Decades"; Steven Wagner, "How Did the Taft-Hartley Act Come About?" *History News Network* (George Washington University), https://historynewsnetwork.org/article/1036 (accessed Jan. 6, 2020).

[115] NLRB, "1947 Taft-Hartley Substantive Provisions," www.nlrb.gov/about-nlrb/who-we-are/our-history/1947-taft-hartley-substantive-provisions (accessed Jan. 6, 2021).

[116] Quoted in Crain, "Building Solidarity through Expansion of NLRA Coverage," 972.

[117] Crain, "Building Solidarity through Expansion of NLRA Coverage," 973.

managerial oversight and impartiality were necessary to administer production in the most efficient way. If supervisors could be influenced by common workers, the workplace would not properly function. In enforcing this rule, the NLRB came to the conclusion that "managerial employees were not covered under the act for any reason" on the grounds that Congress intentionally excluded "employees who exercised a significant degree of authority over the rank and file."[118] Thus, the division between laborers and supervisors that Taylorism imagined was explicitly encoded in law and, in many ways, so was the "adversarial tension" that came along with it.[119] As the Taft-Hartley Act was never repealed, this tension persists to the present day.

The evolution of Taylorism from a novel technology to the very basis of the employer–employee relationship provides a potentially important parallel for the modern AI revolution. As a management practice, Taylorism is rooted in worker suppression and maximum production. Modern work, much like iterations past, takes this dynamic for granted – as inherent to the nature of work. However, new technologies have again shifted the landscape of the workplace, taking this dynamic to new extremes. For example, as examined by Jeff Hirsch in "Future Work," new automation technologies are marrying the science of robotics with human labor to increase production capacity.[120] Just as Taylorism did not replace human labor, but rather augmented it to the detriment of workers, so, too, do new technologies hold the potential for the same effect. Historically, lawmakers sought to capture the total value of these innovations through legislation such as the Sherman Act, which effectively curbed worker power to unionize. While lawmakers recognized the struggles of workers, it was years before they took action to correct the imbalance. In the modern day, similar patterns are emerging as technology pushes employers towards the new work arrangements of the gig economy. While many recognize that "our current workplace regulatory regime is ill-equipped to handle many of these current issues," little action has been taken to remedy the injustice.[121] It took decades to remedy the harm done by the laissez-faire government of the late nineteenth century and the Taylorist regime of the Progressive era. In the case of Taylorism, new technology was adopted at such a rapid pace that it became ubiquitous before society realized its full detrimental effects. This ideology of rapid adoption of technology for workplaces (move fast, and break things) still persists to the present day. History might indicate either that the law, which moves at a more glacial speed, must speed up or that the law must impose a slower pace of adoption of new technologies for the workplace. In considering how the law might approach technology in the modern workplace, it is helpful to consider legal cases and congressional

---

[118] Crain, "Building Solidarity through Expansion of NLRA Coverage," 975.
[119] Crain, "Building Solidarity through Expansion of NLRA Coverage," 987.
[120] Hirsch, "Future Work," 908.
[121] Hirsch, "Future Work," 915.

hearings in the decades after the imposition of scientific management, particularly ones related to wage and hour issues and management control.

2.4.1 *The NLRB and the Ford Motor Company*

In Senate hearings on proposed amendments to the NLRA, convened in 1940 as a continuation of hearings started in May 1939, a number of witnesses examined NLRB administration of the NLRA and sought ways to improve labor–management relations by sharing opinions on the Wagner Act and amendments. As part of his statement, R. J. Thomas, president of the United Automobile Workers of America, discussed historic business practices of Ford, including their wage policies and the Sociological Department.

Ford's five-dollar-a-day rate, which started in 1914, was the highest rate being paid in the automobile industry at that time. However, the minimum did not apply to all Ford workers, and those who did receive the five-dollar-a-day rate had to submit to what critics characterized as "un-American paternalism and snooping."[122] For instance, Ford Motor workers had to satisfy Ford's Sociological Department by demonstrating that they intended to lead model lives according to Henry Ford's ideas of virtue.

At the time of the hearings, the starting rate for all Ford employees was six dollars for an eight-hour day, and the average wage for all Ford production employees, including the highly skilled workers, was between eighty-three and eighty-five cents an hour (which comes to $6.64 to $6.80 for an eight-hour day).[123] This was 7.5 to 9.5 cents less than the average wage for auto workers in the United States. Ford's maximum daily wage was $8.50 for an eight-hour day, and only a very small group of highly skilled workers were paid by this rate, which was still less than the rate in other plants in the industry. Thus, although Henry Ford claimed to pay the "highest wage" in the auto industry, he was in fact paying less than the average wage for the industry to the majority of his workers.

Thomas also offered a summary written by Carl Raushenbush on Fordism. In 1913, the labor turnover at Ford Motor was 400 percent. The company used more machinery because of its belt methods, and to get the most out of its investment, Ford had to use the machines at the maximum rate. The faster pace of work became harder for employees to stand and the company needed more men who could bear the strain. Therefore, it was necessary for Ford to offer five dollars per day and an eight-hour day. The new wage plan was presented as profit sharing – the unskilled

---

[122] Statement of R. J. Thomas [president of UAW], in U.S. House of Representatives, *Proposed Amendments to the National Labor Relations Act: Hearings ...* Vol. 9 (Washington DC: Government Printing Office, 1940), 2376.

[123] Statement of R. J. Thomas [president of UAW], in U.S. House, *Proposed Amendments to the National Labor Relations Act*, 9:2377.

worker who had previously received $2.34 was encouraged to think of the remaining $2.66 of the $5.00 wage as his share of the profits, but his overtime rate was based on the original rate. In addition, not all workers received the new rate. A married man not supporting his family, all women workers, and single men under age twenty-two without anyone to support were excluded from the new rate, and Ford intended to keep the number of workers at the minimum wage by rehiring those at the minimum wage after a layoff.

Ford's Sociological Department took part in this approach by conducting investigations on the employees to discover whether they were living what the company considered to be wholesome lives and to create model people. In reality, the department functioned as a "huge spy department"[124] and kept the workers continually in fear of being discharged and blacklisted for joining unions. The Sociological Department and later service department[125] at Ford Motor Co. practiced not only espionage but also violence. For instance, newspapermen and other non-unionists had testified about the merciless beating of members of the UAW by the Ford service men at the Ford gates in Dearborn in 1937, and two Ford service men broke into the home of a worker. Labor Board cases and civil suits arose against Ford regarding the beatings and similar occurrences.

In *NLRB v. Ford Motor Co.* (1940), the Ford Motor Co. cross-petitioned to review the NLRB's order and additional collateral relief after the NLRB applied for judicial enforcement of its order regarding the company's unfair labor practices against workforce unionization. After Henry Ford publicly announced his anti-union attitude, the company had used violence and job actions to prevent unionization of the workforce.[126] The decision (revised version) of the Board comprised revised findings of fact and an order that commanded Ford to cease and desist from interfering with its employees in the exercise of their rights guaranteed in Section 7 of the NLRA, but Ford Motor Co. petitioned to challenge the validity of the order, alleging an erroneous background for the unfair labor practices.[127]

During the riot of May 26, 1937, a number of officers of the union and others, including employees of the company, were brutally assaulted by Ford service men while they were attempting to distribute union literature. The riot took place amid the industrial turmoil that began when a national wave of sit-down strikes followed the sit-down strikes in the General Motors and Chrysler plants in 1936 and 1937. Because of that, Ford contended that the Board was not considering the situation in which

---

[124] Statement of R. J. Thomas [president of UAW], in U.S. House, *Proposed Amendments to the National Labor Relations Act*, 9:2302.

[125] See Georgios Loizides, "Deconstructing Fordism: Legacies of the Ford Sociological Department" (PhD diss., Western Michigan University, 2004), 25, 145, 148.

[126] See Gilbert King, "How the Ford Motor Company Won the Battle and Lost Ground," *Smithsonian Magazine*, Apr. 30, 2013, www.smithsonianmag.com/history/how-the-ford-motor-company-won-a-battle-and-lost-ground-45814533/.

[127] *NLRB v. Ford Motor Co.*, 114 F.2d 905, 907–8 (6th Cir. 1940).

the employer had to take strong actions to protect its plants. However, the court concluded that the company's preparation to prevent the seizure of its property was more than adequate, considering that most of the union organizers were women. Also, credible evidence, including newspaper interviews, proved that the head of Ford's service department knew that the union's purpose was to distribute literature and that it would be met with violence by other workers, but the department would not take any action to prevent the violence. Therefore, it was found that the assaults upon the union organizers were an unfair labor practice and remedial measures should be enforced. Regarding other claims of unfair labor practices related to, for instance, the dissemination of employer propaganda and reinstatement of discharged employees, the court continued, set aside and denied, or amended the Board orders.[128]

2.4.2 *Notable Cases after* NLRB v. Ford

After the *Ford* case, a number of notable cases in the twentieth century would set precedents that changed the role of technology in the limitless surveillance of employees. In 1970, the Supreme Judicial Court of Massachusetts responded to the Massachusetts House of Representatives' question concerning the constitutionality of proposed legislation to limit employers' use of electronic surveillance that was intended to conduct time and motion studies, a practice of scientific management. The proposed legislation, House No. 5719 of 1970, would prohibit employers of manufacturing establishments and factories from operating any monitoring device for the purpose of a time or motion study of any employee without their express consent, and unless the employee had first been notified that the device was in operation. The bill defined a time and motion study as "any study of an employee at work to observe, analyze and measure his operations at or away from his machine or job in relation to his productivity, speed of operations, or method of work."[129]

Four justices stated that "although the title of the bill, [An Act Prohibiting the Operation of Any Device by an Employer to Monitor Certain Activities of His Employees], shows that the Legislature intended to protect the right of privacy of employees, the bill is all inclusive and goes far beyond its intent." They considered it unconstitutional because it swept too broadly. Two other justices agreed with this and also with another justice that "the Legislature could enact a bill which by its provisions would protect an employee's private and personal deportment and yet preserve the rights of an employer so as to pass Constitutional muster." The justices referred to *Connally v. General Constr. Co.* and their opinions on the previously proposed bill to support their answer.[130] Also, they stated that the act would not be

---

[128] *NLRB v. Ford Motor Co.*, 114 F.2d, 910, 911, 916 (6th Cir. 1940).

[129] Opinion of Justices, 358 Mass. 827, 828 (1970).

[130] See *Connally v. General Constr. Co.*, 269 U.S. 385, 391 (1926); and Opinion of the Justices, 356 Mass. 756, 758 (1969).

a denial of equal protection under the law because it applied only to manufacturing establishments and factories, as they were the most common places that used time and motion studies. Justice Spiegel dissented in part by asserting that the proposed bill was not overbroad and that it fell within the categories of general welfare and public safety areas. Yet, in the end, the court held that the proposed legislation was unconstitutional. This ruling reverberates today in the carte blanche that the employer has to electronically surveil employees in many states.

The case of *Fafnir Bearing Co. v. NLRB* dealt with many features of scientific management, such as the piece rate system and time studies.[131] In this case, the Second Circuit Court worked on cross-petitions regarding enforcement of an NLRB order directing the Fafnir Bearing Co. to allow the International Union, United Automobile, Aerospace, and Agricultural Implement Workers of America, Local 133, UAW, AFL-CIO to conduct independent time studies at the company's plant to determine whether the union should accept certain proposed piece rates or proceed to arbitration. According to the contract executed in 1962, employees were paid based on a "piece rate system," which was designed to provide them with an incentive to maximize their productivity. Also, a time study was conducted to determine how many units per hour an average employee working at a normal pace could produce. This figure being the "standard," those who produced less than or equal to the standard received a minimum wage, but those with greater production could increase their rate. However, there was no accurate method for setting standards, and there had been many company–union grievances in relation to this,[132] particularly regarding Section 8.4[133] and Subsection 8(a)(4)[134] of their agreement.

The union had filed numerous grievances by 1963 claiming that certain piecework prices did not conform to Section 8.4 of the agreement. At the third stage of the grievance procedure, after two unsuccessful steps, the union requested all time study data the company used to set the piece rates. Questioning the data supplied, the union requested permission to conduct its own time study to verify the proposed rates and consider the final step of the grievance machinery. The company refused

---

[131] *Fafnir Bearing Co. v. NLRB*, 362 F.2d 716 (2d Cir. 1966).

[132] See *Fafnir Bearing Co. v. NLRB*, 362 F.2d 716, 718 (2d Cir. 1966). Considering that the company had established over 10,000 new piecework prices each year, the number of grievances to which they gave rise was relatively modest. In 1961, there were 86 piece rate grievances; in 1962, there were 47; and in the first half of 1963, there were 33.

[133] *Fafnir Bearing Co. v. NLRB*, 362 F.2d 716, 718 (2d Cir. 1966). Section 8.4 of the governing agreement stated that piecework price "shall be set so that the average qualified operator working under normal job conditions and applying normal incentive efforts shall be able, after a reasonable trial period, to earn 5% above the standard earning rate of his labor grade (as indicated in the schedule installed by the parties."

[134] *Fafnir Bearing Co. v. NLRB*, 362 F.2d 716, 718 (2d Cir. 1966). Subsection 8(a)(4) allowed a piece rate revision only when "there had been a measurable change on accumulation of changes over a period of time in material, method or processes not previously taken into account in setting the price."

because they believed such study was unnecessary, the agreement did not authorize independent time studies, and the union's rights were protected with the arbitrator being able to conduct his own studies. When the union filed a charge with the Board, the Board decided that Sections 8(a)(1) and 8(a)(5) of the act were violated when the company refused to allow an independent time study.

The company claimed that the decision was directly contrary to this court's holding in *NLRB v. Otis Elevator Co.*[135] However, according to the court, this case was different, since Otis rejected the union's request for whatever data the company had in its possession and data could have been obtained by interviewing the members of the union. In the case of *Fafnir*, the union was in need of a "live" time study because piecework prices were established by a rate-setter based on the combination of subjective and objective factors. For instance, the rate-setter could adjust the actual timing of the job upward or downward and add an allowance based on his judgment for worker fatigue and delay. The court believed that the Board properly determined that the union's need to conduct the studies outweighed the company's interests in closing its doors. Therefore, authorizing independent time studies only when they were essential for the union to function intelligently on behalf of employees and when such studies would not unduly disrupt the productive operations of the company, the court enforced the order of the Board.

In *Lewis v. Smithfield Packing Co.*, the plaintiffs asserted claims under the Fair Labor Standards Act (FLSA) that their employer, Smithfield Packing Company, Inc., failed to compensate them for the time spent engaged in donning and doffing protective equipment and related activities. They sought unpaid back wages, unpaid benefits, liquidated damages, attorneys' fees, and other relief.[136] Fernandez, a registered professional engineer and certified professional ergonomist, was hired by the employer to conduct a time and motion study at Smithfield's Tar Heel facility. The time and motion study provided evidence of the time it took production employees to don, doff, wash, and dip various items, and to walk between different points in the facility. As part of the methodology called elemental analysis, he broke down each activity of employees into short elements and measured the time for each separately. He also used the Worker-Factor system, which provided a standardized walking rate and multiplied the rate by the distance employees walked, to measure walking times of the workers. In his report, after conducting a number of site visits, studying videotapes, and considering measurements and observations made, Fernandez offered opinions on the time it took employees to perform the identified activities.[137]

[135] *NLRB v. Otis Elevator Co.*, 208 F.2d 176 (2d Cir. 1953). The court held that the company's obligation under the NLRA to bargain collectively in good faith did not require any duty upon the company to open its plant for the union to conduct new time studies to obtain new data on which to formulate new standards.

[136] *Lewis v. Smithfield Packing Co.*, 2010 U.S. Dist. LEXIS 87883, 4–5 (E.D.N.C. 2010).

[137] *Lewis v. Smithfield Packing Co.*, 2010 U.S. Dist. LEXIS 87883, 9–11 (E.D.N.C. 2010).

The plaintiffs contended that Fernandez's opinions did not meet the relevance and reliability of requirements for admissibility[138] by arguing that the "continuous workday rule"[139] should be applied. However, the court held that Fernandez's testimony was reliable and relevant and that he was qualified.[140] In *Hosler v. Smithfield Packing Co.*, the court agreed with the Memorandum and Recommendation (M&R) filed in the previous case that Fernandez appeared more than qualified to provide expert testimony, his opinions concerned issues central to plaintiffs' FLSA claims, and his elemental analysis methodology was a reliable scientific methodology, and denied plaintiffs' motion to exclude his opinions as well.[141]

2.4.3 Surveillance of Workers and the Anti-Pinkerton Act

United States ex rel. Weinberger v. Equifax, Inc. (557 F.2d 456 (5th Cir. 1977)), which dealt with worker surveillance, has been widely cited in relation to defining organizations "similar" to the Pinkerton Detective Agency as intended by the Anti-Pinkerton Act of 1893. Weinberger sought a declaratory judgment that government use of Equifax, Inc., which was collecting and providing information on prospective government employees, violated the Anti-Pinkerton Act (5 U.S.C. § 3108 [1970]) because the company did not confine itself to examining files and public records, but used investigative techniques similar to those employed by detective agencies. He also alleged that Equifax's billing of the government for services performed violated the False Claims Act (31 U.S.C. § 231–32 [1970]).

The court considered the Anti-Pinkerton Act's legislative history to examine Weinberger's claim. The legislative history revealed that an organization was similar to the Pinkerton Detective Agency only if it offered for hire mercenary, quasi-military forces as strike-breakers and armed guards, a finding supported by the Senate report[142] investigating the Homestead incident and Representative Holman's statement.[143]

---

[138] *Lewis v. Smithfield Packing Co.*, 2010 U.S. Dist. LEXIS 87883, 5–9 (E.D.N.C. 2010), regarding the standard for admission of expert testimony.

[139] *Lewis v. Smithfield Packing Co.*, 2010 U.S. Dist. LEXIS 87883, 12 (E.D.N.C. 2010): "[T]he rule provides that the periods of time between the commencement of an employee's first principal activity of the workday and the completion of his last principal activity must be included in the computation of hours worked."

[140] *Lewis v. Smithfield Packing Co.*, 2010 U.S. Dist. LEXIS 87883, 13–18 (E.D.N.C. 2010).

[141] See *Hosler v. Smithfield Packing Co.*, 2010 U.S. Dist. LEXIS 101776, 3–4 (E.D.N.C. 2010).

[142] *United States v. Equifax, Inc.*, 557 F.2d 456, 462 (5th Cir. 1977). The Senate report clearly distinguished between types of detective agencies: "Some of them confine their operations to detective business, others furnish patrolmen to protect private property during the night, acting in harmony with the police force, while a few of them add to that kind of work the business of supplying armed men on occasions of strikes …"

[143] *United States v. Equifax, Inc.*, 557 F.2d 456, 462–3 (5th Cir. 1977), stating that the act "not only prohibited the employment of the Pinkerton force or any similar quasi-military organization by any officer of the Government or the District of Columbia, but it prohibited the employment of such force by any individual, firm, or corporation having contracts with the United States."

Therefore, the court concluded that because the plaintiff failed to allege that Equifax provided an armed guard, using Equifax was not regarded as illegal under the Anti-Pinkerton Act. The significance of this case is that, in the present day, employers continue to conduct credit and investigative background checks on prospective job applicants and may lawfully base the decision to extend employment opportunities on the results of those checks.

In *Bethlehem Steel Co. v. NLRB* (120 F.2d 641 [D.C. Cir. 1941]), the court held that the employer's hiring of labor spies to report on union growth was prohibited support. The Steel Workers Organizing Committee (SWOC), a union affiliated with the Congress of Industrial Organizations (CLO), filed unfair labor practice charges with the NLRB against Bethlehem Steel Corporation and its subsidiary Bethlehem Steel Company, claiming they had employed detectives to obtain information about union activities by surveilling workers, and had violated employees' rights guaranteed by Section 7 of the NLRA.[144] The company employed Pinkertons who spied on workers and then informed the company of union sentiment and activity at the company plants.[145] The court regarded employing spies to report on the growth of a new union as part of the support of a company union and interference with independent organization. The court also indicated that specifically how the spies' information was used and whether employees had knowledge about the surveillance did not have to be proven.[146]

The court held that the employer committed unfair labor practices within the meaning of the act, stating that Section 8(2) of the NLRA prohibited both financial and non-financial support that interfered in activities of labor organization or unionization, and therefore Bethlehem Steel Company's hiring of Pinkertons to report on new union growth was prohibited support under the act. In addition, regarding the company's payments to Johnstown Mayor to ensure his continued hostility to SWOC and the formation of a "Citizens' Committee,"[147] the court decided that the employer's payments to a local elected official who expressed anti-union sentiments during a labor strike was illegal under the act because such payments were intended for continued hostility to the union and created a biased city administration. The court's finding in favor of the workers confirmed that the company's actions had constituted an illegal interference with the workers' right to organize.

Viewed from one vantage, the Pinkertons were the antithesis of the Luddites, who were fighting to preserve artisanship and worker dignity. The Pinkertons had brutally retaliated against striking steel mill workers in Homestead at the behest of corporate leaders. The outcry associated with these corporate soldiers for hire led

---

[144] *Bethlehem Steel Co. v. NLRB*, 120 F.2d 641, 644 (D.C. Cir. 1941).
[145] See *Bethlehem Steel Co. v. NLRB*, 120 F.2d 641, 646 (D.C. Cir. 1941).
[146] *Bethlehem Steel Co. v. NLRB*, 120 F.2d 641, 647 (D.C. Cir. 1941).
[147] See *Bethlehem Steel Co. v. NLRB*, 120 F.2d 641, 646 (D.C. Cir. 1941).

to a variety of state legislation and the Anti-Pinkerton Act of 1893.[148] If we conceive of technology as the practical application of knowledge and accept the idea that surveillance influences productivity, then the Pinkertons were a special kind of controlling technology.

Although the New Deal in the 1930s included protections for collective bargaining to enhance worker conditions, wages, and so forth, it did not specify these labor goals.[149] The Wagner Act sought to outlaw unions at the company level in favor of outside unions, which were to be funded without the aid of management[150] and was a substantial part of the National Labor Relations Act of 1935. Taylorist conflict arose when it came time to determine if foremen should have the right to unionize.[151] Although initially the decision read that they were technically employees and so should have that right, the dynamics between workers and employers that resulted from Taylorist practices facilitated the Taft-Hartley Act, which rescinded protections for collective bargaining by supervisory, confidential, and managerial employees. Marion Crain argues that this kind of designation does more to secure current hierarchies than it does to progress labor laws and promote the core tenets of the Wagner Act, which she summarizes as industrial peace, empowerment of workers, and industrial democracy.[152]

In sum, although it seemed that the Wagner Act meant to emphasize several of the idealized principles of scientific management, it instead prolonged the problematic, practical applications of Taylor's vision. Thus, it is worth highlighting that some of the labor laws intended to help workers, like the Wagner Act, have had unintended consequences that, in certain contexts, harm workers. Therefore, any proposed new regulation to address the quantification of workers must pay careful attention to the history of labor and employment law to prevent history from repeating itself to the disadvantage of workers.

---

[148] See Pub. L. No. 89-554, 80 Stat. 416. (1966) (codified at 5 U.S.C. § 3108). "An individual employed by the Pinkerton Detective Agency, or similar organization, may not be employed by the Government of the United States or the government of the District of Columbia."

[149] Herbert Hovencamp, "Labor Conspiracies in American Law, 1880–1930," *Texas Law Review* 66, no. 1 (1988): 919–65.

[150] Mark Barenberg, "The Political Economy of The Wagner Act: Power, Symbol, and Workplace Cooperation," *Harvard Law Review* 106, no. 7 (1993): 1381–1496.

[151] Crain, "Building Solidarity through Expansion of NLRA Coverage."

[152] Crain, "Building Solidarity through Expansion of NLRA Coverage."

PART II

The Mechanical Managers

3

Automated Hiring and Discrimination*

Our system allows you to clone your best, most reliable people.
           –David Scarborugh, Unicru's Chief Scientist (2002)

The quantification of workers is perhaps most evident in the work of automated hiring platforms, which have been deputized as mechanical managers of employment opportunity. Beyond merely serving as a hiring tool, automated hiring platforms also concretize and quantify theories and presuppositions about what or who makes a good worker. Presuppositions that members of a particular ethnic or racial group or a particular gender are suited for or are superior for certain types of work abound. Recently, we have seen the resurgence of racial, ethnic, and cultural theories for success such as the "bourgeois norms" or "bourgeois cultural hegemony" espoused by law professors Amy Wax and Larry Alexander; the theory of Jewish brilliance aided by a tradition of religious inquiry and also religious persecution offered by the columnist Bret Stephens; and finally, the "Triple Package" proposition by law professors Amy Chua and Ned Rubenfeld, who argue that certain ethnic and racial groups in the United States (notably Mormons, Nigerians, and Jews) possess immutable characteristics such as "a superiority complex," a "sense of insecurity," and greater "impulse control" that enable their success.[1]

While there have been various articles debunking these theories of suitability for work or noting the lack of both methodological rigor and social scientific

---

* Parts of this chapter appear in different form in my previously published law review articles, "The Paradox of Automation as Anti-Bias Intervention," *Cardozo Law Review* 41 (2020): 1671–1742; and "The Auditing Imperative for Automated Hiring," *Harvard Journal of Law & Technology* 34, no. 2 (2021): 621–700.

[1] Amy Wax and Larry Alexander, "Opinion: Paying the Price for Breakdown of the Country's Bourgeois Culture," *Philadelphia Inquirer*, Aug. 9, 2017; Bret Stephens, "Opinion: The Secrets of Jewish Genius," *New York Times*, Dec. 27, 2019; Amy Chua and Jed Rubenfeld, *The Triple Package: How Three Unlikely Traits Explain the Rise and Fall of Cultural Groups in America* (New York: Penguin, 2014).

evidence to support them,[2] what is most important is that these theories go against the grain of current American law (the Civil Rights Act of 1964), which mandates equal opportunity in employment regardless of race or ethnicity. The history of the United States is one of the subjugation of the labor of certain minority racial groups, most notably those of African descent. Although the Emancipation Proclamation (1863) was a *de jure* end to slavery, both formal slavery and informal slavery in the form of sharecropping and forced labor persisted well into the twentieth century.[3] Post-slavery, Jim Crow laws also served to deny equal opportunity in employment to racial minorities. Women (of all races) were also denied equal opportunity in employment due to theories of the inferior intelligence of women and their unsuitability to work outside the home.[4]

3.1 THE PARADOX OF AUTOMATED DECISION-MAKING FOR HIRING

Given the long established history of human bias in hiring, it is not surprising that organizations are increasingly turning to automated hiring as a solution. Consider that nearly all Global 500 companies use algorithmic tools for recruitment and hiring.[5] Yet a 2017 study conducted by Aaron Smith and Monica Anderson of the Pew Research Center found that most Americans underestimate the diffusion of these automated hiring platforms in the workplace. Markedly, the study revealed that fewer than half of Americans are familiar with the concept of computer programs that can review job applications without human involvement. In fact, 57 percent of Americans say that they have heard nothing at all about automated hiring platforms in the past. Only 9 percent of respondents reported to have heard "a lot" about the technology.[6]

Remarkably, 76 percent of Americans stated that they would not want to apply for jobs that rely on computer programs to make hiring decisions. One twenty-two-year-old woman wrote that "a computer cannot measure the emotional intelligence or intangible assets that many humans have." Another stated, "I do believe

---

[2] See Angela Onwauchi-Willig and Jacob Willig-Onwuachi, "A House Divided: The Invisibility of the Multiracial Family," *Harvard Civil Rights-Civil Liberties Law Review* 44, no. 1 (2009): 231–53; and Devon W. Carbado, "Racial Naturalization," *American Quarterly* 57, no. 3 (2005): 633–58.

[3] Douglas A. Blackmon, *Slavery by Another Name: The Re-Enslavement of Black Americans from the Civil War to World War II* (New York: Doubleday, 2008).

[4] See, e.g., Cynthia Starnes, "Divorce and the Displaced Homemaker: A Discourse on Playing with Dolls, Partnership Buyouts and Dissociation Under No-Fault," *University of Chicago Law Review* 60, no. 1 (1993): 67–139; Jill Elaine Hasday, "The Principle and Practice of Women's 'Full Citizenship': A Case Study of Sex-Segregated Public Education," *Michigan Law Review* 101, no. 3 (2002): 755–810.

[5] Linda Barber, "E-Recruitment Developments," Institute for Employment Studies, HR Network Paper MP63, Mar. 2006, www.employment-studies.co.uk/system/files/resources/files/mp63.pdf

[6] Aaron Smith and Monica Anderson, *Automation in Everyday Life*, Pew Research Center, Oct. 4, 2017, quote at 50, http://assets.pewresearch.org/wp-content/uploads/sites/14/2017/10/03151500/PI_2017.10.04_Automation_FINAL.pdf.

hiring people requires a fair amount of judgment and intuition that is not well automated." On the other side of this spectrum, 22 percent of individuals reported that they would want to apply for jobs that use a computer program to make hiring decisions. The most common rationale for this response was the belief that software would be less biased than human reviewers.[7] Taken in its entirety, Smith and Anderson's study reveals apprehensions about algorithm-based hiring decisions. Whether these misgivings are rooted in privacy concerns or reflect concerns regarding the effectiveness of the hiring algorithms' software, the increasing trend towards the use of hiring algorithms in the workplace necessitates regulatory action to ensure that algorithmic-derived employment decisions are in line with anti-discrimination laws.

White-collar and white-shoe firms are also increasingly turning to hiring automation.[8] In 2016, the investment firm Goldman Sachs announced a key change to its process for hiring summer interns and first-year analysts. Candidates now have their resumes scanned – ostensibly by machine learning algorithms in search of keywords and experiences that have been pre-judged to be "good barometers of a person's success at Goldman." Bridgewater, the world's largest hedge fund, has taken the automation gambit the furthest; it is seeking to build an algorithmic model that would automate all management, including hiring, firing, and other managerial decision-making processes.[9] Although in many respects the algorithmic turn to hiring is purportedly driven by a desire for fairness and efficiency – for example, Goldman Sachs's hiring changes were prompted by a desire for a more diverse candidate pool[10] – these machine learning algorithms may have the unintended effects of perpetuating systemic biases or could have a disparate impact on protected categories.[11]

The trend towards automated hiring presents a legal paradox. Although the adoption of automation decision-making is often an intervention against unlawful discrimination,[12] there is evidence that algorithmic decision-making processes may

---

[7] Smith and Anderson, *Automation in Everyday Life*, quotes at 51, 52, 53.

[8] See, e.g., Richard Feloni, "Consumer-Goods Giant Unilever Has Been Hiring Employees Using Brain Games and Artificial Intelligence – and It's a Huge Success," *Business Insider*, June 28, 2017; Louis Efron, "How A.I Is About to Disrupt Corporate Recruiting," *Forbes*, July 12, 2016.

[9] Rob Copeland and Bradley Hope, "The World's Largest Hedge Fund Is Building an Algorithmic Model from Its Employees' Brains," *Wall Street Journal*, Dec. 22, 2016.

[10] Mary Thompson, "Goldman Sachs Is Making a Change to the Way It Hires," *CNBC*, June 23, 2016.

[11] See Harry Surden, "Machine Learning and Law," *Washington Law Review* 89, no. 1 (2013): 87–115 (on gaps in the law in regards to machine learning algorithms); Solon Barocas and Andrew Selbst, "Big Data's Disparate Impact," *California Law Review* 104, no. 3 (2016): 671–732 (on disparate impact associated with algorithmic decision-making).

[12] "Advocates applaud the removal of human beings and their flaws from the assessment process." Algorithms or automated systems are often seen as fair because they are "claimed to rate all individuals in the same way, thus averting discrimination." Danielle Keats Citron and Frank Pasquale, "The Scored Society: Due Process for Automated Predictions," *Washington Law Review* 89, no. 1 (2014): 4.

work as end runs around anti-discrimination laws such as Title VII of the Civil Rights Act of 1964 (42 U.S.C. §§ 2000e–2000e-17 (2018)) and could instead serve to replicate, amplify, and also obfuscate discrimination on a large scale.[13] I term this phenomenon "the paradox of automation as anti-bias intervention."

A co-author and I conducted an empirical study of work algorithms that involved a critical discourse analysis and affordance critique of the advertised features and rhetoric behind automated hiring systems as gleaned through 135 archival texts, tracing the timeline of the development of hiring platforms from 1990 to 2006.[14] That study concluded that while one purported *raison d'etre* and advertised purpose of automated hiring systems was to reduce hirer bias – "replacing messy human decisions with a neutral technical process" – the reality remained that "algorithmic specification of 'fit' can itself become a vehicle for bias."[15] Early adopters of auto-mated hiring decision-making tend to fall into the rhetoric found in the scholarship on automated decision-making, which limits its focus to technical definitions of fair-ness. Yet, even ostensibly neutral variables could still (in)advertently serve as proxies for protected variables, thus resulting in a disparate impact on protected classes, though the algorithmic processes are technically fair.[16] To compound the problem, adverse results as part of automated decision-making are often then framed as a tech-nical problem, with the corollary view that some form of techno-solutionist method is needed to fix the problem. Yet, as I will demonstrate, bias in automated decision-making is a legal problem rather than a technical one.

Another feature of the paradox of automation as anti-bias intervention in hir-ing is to reify automated decision-making. Proponents of automated decision-making in hiring argue that despite its flaws, automated decision-making evinces less bias and is thus preferable to human decision-making. In "Want Less-Biased Decisions? Use Algorithms," Alex Miller challenges many scholars' concern that "algorithms are often opaque, biased, and unaccountable tools being wielded in

---

[13] See, e.g., Ajunwa, "Paradox of Automation as Anti-Bias Intervention," 1673; Barocas and Selbst, "Big Data's Disparate Impact," 720; Pasquale, *The Black Box Society* (on legal issues associated with the non-transparent use of algorithmic decision-making in several societal spheres); Andrew Tutt, "An FDA for Algorithms," *Administrative Law Review* 69, no. 1 (2017): 87 ("This new family of algorithms holds enormous promise, but also poses new and unusual dangers."). See also Virginia Eubanks, *Automating Inequality: How High-Tech Tools Profile, Police, and Punish the Poor* (New York: St. Martin's Press, 2018); Safiya Umoja Noble, *Algorithms of Oppression: How Search Engines Reinforce Racism* (New York: New York University Press, 2018); Cathy O'Neil, *Weapons of Math Destruction: How Big Data Increases Inequality and Threatens Democracy* (New York: Crown Publishing, 2016); cf. Sandra G. Mayson, "Bias In, Bias Out," *Yale Law Journal* 128, no. 8 (2019): 2122–473 (arguing that the problem of disparate impact in predictive risk algorithms lies not in the algorithmic system but in the nature of prediction itself).

[14] Ifeoma Ajunwa and Daniel Greene, "Platforms at Work: Automated Hiring Platforms and Other New Intermediaries in the Organization of Work," *Work and Labor in the Digital Age* 33 (2019): 72.

[15] Ajunwa and Greene, "Platforms at Work," 79 ("From a diversity perspective, artificial intelligence can be very beneficial because it's blind to things like color, age, sexual orientation."). See also Jeff Meredith et al., "AI Identifying Steady Workers," *Chicago Tribune*, July 16, 2001.

[16] See generally Barocas and Selbst, "Big Data's Disparate Impact."

the interests of institutional power." He notes that although these critiques have helped people to avoid abusing algorithms, there is a pattern among the critiques, "which is that they rarely ask how well the systems they analyze would operate without algorithms."[17]

Miller cites multiple studies of algorithmic decision-making to support the notion that "[a]lgorithms are less biased and more accurate than the humans they are replacing." For instance, one study found that a job-screening algorithm "actually favored 'nontraditional' candidates" much more than human screeners did, "exhibit[ing] significantly less bias against candidates that were underrepresented at the firm." Other studies of algorithms related to credit applications, criminal justice, public resource allocations, and corporate governance all concluded that using algorithms results in less bias and greater accuracy compared to humans.[18]

In each of the examples he provides, Miller concedes that the algorithm programmers "trained their algorithms on past data that is surely biased by historical prejudices." Miller asserts, however, that while this fact might be alarming to many, "the humans [algorithms] are replacing are significantly more biased." He argues that a number of psychological and other studies of judgment and decision have demonstrated that "humans are remarkably bad judges of quality in a wide range of contexts." Thus, since humans are significantly bad at making decisions, "replacing them with algorithms both increased accuracy and reduced institutional biases." Miller refers to this as a "[p]areto improvement, where one policy beats out the alternative on every outcome [people] care about." He also emphasizes that there is no trade-off between productivity and fairness when using algorithms because "[a]lgorithms deliver more-efficient and more-equitable outcomes." Miller thus insists that it is worthwhile to "accept that – in some instances – algorithms will be part of the solution for reducing institutional biases" because the perils of human bias are far worse.[19]

Similarly, legal scholar Professor Stephanie Bornstein, in her article "Antidiscriminatory Algorithms," emphasizes the original intent of technology, which is "to improve upon human decision-making by suppressing biases to make the most efficient and least discriminatory decisions." Professor Bornstein notes that "[a]lgorithmic decision-making offers unprecedented potential to reduce the stereotypes and implicit biases that often infect human decisions."[20] However, Professor Bornstein acknowledges that despite the promise of algorithms to reduce bias in decision-making, there are concerns about algorithmic discrimination and the risk of reproducing existing inequality because the effectiveness of algorithms and decision-making greatly relies on what data is used and how.

---

[17] Alex P. Miller, "Want Less-Biased Decisions? Use Algorithms," *Harvard Business Review*, July 26, 2018 (emphasis omitted).
[18] Miller, "Want Less-Biased Decisions? Use Algorithms" (emphasis omitted).
[19] Miller, "Want Less-Biased Decisions? Use Algorithms" (emphasis omitted).
[20] Stephanie Bornstein, "Antidiscriminatory Algorithms," *Alabama Law Review* 70, no. 2 (2018): 521–23.

Yet Professor Bornstein believes that if algorithms are handled properly, they can still "suppress, interrupt, or remove protected class stereotypes from decisions."[21]

3.2 THE FALSE BINARY OF AUTOMATED DECISION-MAKING VERSUS HUMAN DECISION-MAKING

The aim of this book is not to serve as final arbiter of whether automated hiring decision-making is better than non-automated decision-making. The book is squarely preoccupied with examining the actual effects of automated decision-making and in thinking through necessary regulation for such systems. I deploy the term *algorithmic capture* to describe the combined effect of the belief that algorithms are more efficient and fairer[22] *and* the abdication of human accountability for undesirable outcomes as a result of employing machine learning algorithms as part of a decision-making process. Thus, although automated hiring platforms could have the potential to ameliorate employment discrimination, *this can only be the case* when they are properly regulated.

In response to the presupposed contest between automated decision-making and human decision-making in hiring, here are two points. It is true that human managers hold biases that are reflected in employment decisions unfavorable for protected classes. However, the impact of one biased human manager is constrained in comparison to the potential adverse reach of algorithms that could be used to exclude millions of job applicants from viewing a job advertisement or to sort thousands of resumes. The phenomenon of concern here is that given the "volume, velocity, and variety"[23] of data used in automated hiring, any bias in the system will be multiplied and magnified, greatly dwarfing the impact of any prejudice held by any one human manager. Second, to argue for or against automated decision-making versus human decision-making is to prop up a false binary. This ignores the social fact that the two can never be wholly disentangled and willfully elides all the many ways in which the human hand remains present in all automated decision-making. For automated decision-making, there is *always ex ante* human input when human decision-making directly dictates the design of the automated decision-making system, including deciding what variables should be considered and deciding how those variables should be measured. There is also the possibility for bias to be injected via *ex post* human input when determining how the results are interpreted. Thus, despite some of the proven benefits of automated hiring, there remains the potential for misuse resulting from present opportunities to introduce human bias

---

[21] Bornstein, "Antidiscriminatory Algorithms," 570.
[22] Danah Boyd and Kate Crawford, "Critical Questions for Big Data: Provocations for a Cultural, Technological, and Scholarly Phenomenon," *Information, Communication & Society* 15, no. 5 (2012): 663 (noting the aura of efficiency associated with big data-driven algorithms).
[23] David Gewirtz, "Volume, Velocity, and Variety: Understanding the Three V's of Big Data," *ZDNet*, Mar. 21, 2018, www.zdnet.com/article/volume-velocity-and-variety-understanding-the-three-vs-of-big-data.

at any stage of the automated hiring process – from design to implementation, and finally, to the interpretation of results.

Understanding the persistence of human judgment in automated decision-making prompts a reckoning of the current lacuna of its regulation. Although there are several types of algorithmic hiring systems, I see them as falling into two groups: (1) what I term "off-the-shelf" algorithms that employers can purchase or license and (2) what I term "bespoke" algorithms that employers can have a software developer create to their custom specifications. While I would concede that intent and liability might be analyzed differently for the employer depending on the type of algorithm in question, ultimately differences in hiring algorithms are less important than the fact that although AI in the form of machine learning algorithms has automated many work functions previously thought reserved for human judgment,[24] there have been scant new regulations to ensure that these new technological developments will conform to the normative ideal of equal economic opportunity for all, which is the bedrock of our democratic society.

The automation of the hiring process represents a particularly important technological trend and one that requires greater legal attention given its potential for employment discrimination. Whereas at one time, an applicant could rely on their interpersonal skills to make a favorable first impression on the hiring manager, these days the hiring algorithm is the initial hurdle to clear to gain employment.[25] This is particularly true for the U.S. low-wage and hourly workforce, as a co-author and I found through a survey of the top twenty private employers in the Fortune 500 list (comprised of mostly retail companies). That survey indicated that job applications for such retail jobs must be submitted online, where they will first be sorted by automated hiring platforms powered by algorithms.[26] And, as we saw in the examples of Goldman Sachs and Bridgewater discussed above, white-collar and white-shoe firms are also automating their hiring process, and even other management processes.

Thus, automated hiring represents an ecosystem in which, if left unchecked, a closed loop system forms – with algorithmically driven advertisement determining which applicants will send in their resumes, and automated sorting of resumes

---

[24] See Harry Surden, "Computable Contracts," *University of California at Davis Law Review* 46, no. 1 (2012): 646 (on how computer algorithms have difficulty deciphering language changes that are readily comprehensible to humans). But see, e.g., Erin Winick, "Lawyer-Bots Are Shaking Up Jobs," *MIT Technology Review*, Dec. 12, 2017; Carl Benedikt Frey and Michael A. Osborne, "The Future of Employment: How Susceptible Are Jobs to Computerisation?" *Technological Forecasting and Social Change* 114 (2017): 268 ("While computerisation has been historically confined to routine tasks involving explicit rule-based activities … algorithms for big data are now rapidly entering domains reliant upon pattern recognition and can readily substitute for labour in a wide range of non-routine cognitive tasks."). See also Eric Siegel, *Predictive Analytics: The Power to Predict Who Will Click, Buy, Lie, or Die* (Hoboken, NJ: Wiley, 2013).

[25] See Barber, "E-Recruitment Development," 3 (noting that nearly all Global 500 companies use e-recruitment and hire screening algorithmic tools).

[26] Ajunwa and Greene, "Platforms at Work," 90–91.

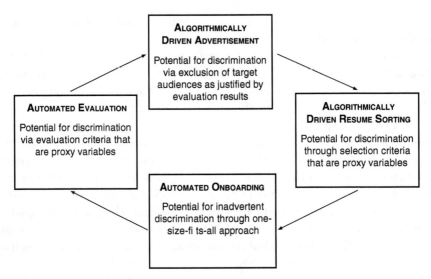

FIGURE 3.1 "The Paradox of Automation as Anti-Bias Intervention" (first published *Cardozo Law Review* 41, no. 5 (2020): 1694)[27]

leading to automated onboarding and eventual automated evaluation of employees, with the results of that evaluation being looped back into criteria for job advertisement and applicant selection.

As algorithmic technological advances present us with unprecedented legal challenges,[28] the use of machine learning algorithms in decision-making hiring processes represents a particularly sensitive legal issue because of the potential to create or exacerbate economic inequality. Yet, even with headline-making cases of bias, the issue of how to govern algorithmic systems remains a thorny one. In her article "Law for the Platform Economy," Professor Julie Cohen notes that much of the conduct of platforms is simply "intractable using conventional regulatory methodologies." For instance, "to enforce existing antidiscrimination laws effectively, the various agencies with enforcement authority need the ability to detect and prove discrimination, yet that task is increasingly difficult when decisions about lending, employment, and housing are made via complex algorithms used to detect patterns in masses of data and the data itself reflects preexisting patterns of inequality."[29]

---

[27] Ajunwa, Ifeoma. "The Paradox of Automation as Anti-Bias Intervention." *Cardozo Law Review* 41, no. 5 (2020): 1671–742.

[28] Kevin Ashley et al., "Legal Reasoning and Artificial Intelligence: How Computers 'Think' Like Lawyers," *University of Chicago Law School Roundtable* 8, no. 1 (2001): 19 (arguing that legal challenges exist precisely because even with computing advancements that allow computers to perform non-routine cognitive tasks, as noted by legal scholar Cass Sunstein, "at the present state of the art artificial intelligence cannot engage in analogical reasoning or legal reasoning"). And see note 13 above.

[29] Julie E. Cohen, "Law for the Platform Economy," *University of California at Davis Law Review* 51, no. 1 (2017): 189–90.

Professor Cohen concludes that these phenomena combine to constitute a space "devoid of protections for vital human freedoms, even as the activities conducted in that space become more and more fundamental to the exercise of those freedoms."[30]

Using Professor Anupam Chander's analogy of "baby-proofing" to the concept of "future-proofing," Cohen asks the question "Does the idea of 'future-proofing' law refer to a need to protect the … future from the … legal system? Or, does it refer to a need to protect … rule of law from the … future?" and responds that neither alone is quite accurate. This is because the law and technological development are co-constitutive. Professor Cohen argues that "legal institutions should change to meet the demands of the times, and so it is only logical that the ascendancy of platforms should produce new legal relationships and new institutional settlements." She reinforces that it is time to pay attention to the best paths for institutional evolution and the "extent to which legal institutions should bend to the service of emergent economic power."[31]

I echo Professor Cohen's sentiments here, particularly in cautioning against a techno-correctionist view of algorithmic bias. This techno-correctionist view tends to focus on technical fairness in lieu of examining assumptions undergirding automated decision-making and how these assumptions may run contrary to the legal principle of equal opportunity.

3.3 QUANTIFICATION OF LABOR MARKET DISCRIMINATION

One argument is that the underlying principles of automated hiring are not democratic at all. Rather, there is evidence that the impetus of automated hiring systems was not to ameliorate discrimination, but that automated hiring systems exist as a rational means to quantify and mechanize labor market discrimination. Recall the study of automated hiring systems discussed earlier, where a co-author and I determined that the stated purpose of reducing hirer bias belied the reality that the concept of "fit" programmed into the algorithm could "itself become a vehicle for bias." As part of our study, we found that Unicru's instruction manuals for users of its hiring platforms encouraged them to "clone your best people," identifying "best people" as existing high-performing employees per company records. This recommended process would be sure to replicate any existing inequalities in the demographics of current employees.

The design and the charge of automated hiring systems are thus informed by historical attitudes and past decisions about who is a good worker. Another example: In October 2019, Amazon made headlines when it discontinued use of "a secret AI recruiting tool that showed bias against women." The algorithmic hiring system had been in use since 2014 and was deployed to rate job candidates based on a range of

---

[30] Cohen, "Law for the Platform Economy," 199.
[31] Cohen, "Law for the Platform Economy," 203, 204.

one to five stars. Unfortunately, by 2015 a troubling pattern had emerged: The algorithmic system was downgrading resumes that it judged to be women candidates based on factors such as a reference to names of all-women's colleges or having the word *women's* on the resume. One explanation for this unintended outcome was the training data derived from resumes submitted to the company over a ten-year period. Most of those resumes were from men, which was a direct reflection of the gender disparity currently existing in the tech industry.[32]

Thus, this story reflects a fundamental issue with the design of algorithmic systems, which is that they are matching systems – their primary function is to match what already exists. To illustrate, most of us are familiar with the irritation of buying a product online and then having advertisements for that same product stalk every web page henceforth. But the advertisement algorithm is operating on limited logic: Your click on a link for raincoats signaled your interest in raincoats. So all the algorithm knows is you are interested in raincoats; it doesn't necessarily know that after that one click, you bought the raincoat and therefore no longer have an interest in viewing advertisements for them.

This matching design logic of algorithmic systems becomes a greater problem in the context of hiring algorithms. As a co-author and I revealed in our study of the history of the development of such systems, the advertised *function* of early algorithmic hiring systems was to replicate existing workers. Thus, if there were already existing race, gender, or other disparities in who is considered the model employee, the algorithmic hiring systems would replicate this. This socio-technical phenomenon in which ostensibly neutral hiring algorithms will nonetheless replicate bias is what I term the paradox of automation as anti-bias intervention. When automated hiring systems are used as an intervention for correcting existing bias, unless deliberate care is taken, the automated hiring may then merely reflect existing bias, thereby exacerbating the problem rather than ameliorating bias.[33]

3.3.1 *Algorithmic Matches Miss Qualified Candidates*

Another problem with hiring algorithms is that they are still not sophisticated enough to replace the discernment of human managers – this lack of nuance can also result in unintended adverse outcomes. Consider the case of one student I interviewed at Cornell University. This student, who was in the computer science PhD program, told me of an encounter at a hiring fair. A certain company's representative was lauding the student's resume as ideal and exactly what the company was looking for. The representative expressed surprise that the student had not yet applied for a job

---

[32] Jeffrey Dastin, "Amazon Scraps Secret AI Recruiting Tool That Showed Bias against Women," *Reuters*, Oct. 19, 2018, www.reuters.com/article/us-amazon-com-jobs-automation-insight/amazon-scraps-secret-ai-recruiting-tool-that-showed-bias-against-women-idUSKCN1MK08G.

[33] Ajunwa, "Paradox of Automation as Anti-Bias Intervention," 1696–99.

with their company, and exhorted the student to apply. The student's reply: "I've already applied twice. And your company rejected me both times." The representative was perplexed and decided to investigate. Soon the student got an email from the company: The culprit for the rejections was their automated hiring platform. They had programmed it to accept candidates with a BS in computer science, so in parsing resumes, the automated hiring platform had rejected the student's resume because it listed a BA in computer science, even though the student was currently in a computer science PhD program at an Ivy League university and thus would be considered more than qualified. In seeking to quantify applicants' qualifications, the programmers of the algorithm had drawn too tight a net, thereby resulting in the algorithmic system not catching all qualified candidates.

3.3.2 *Hidden Biases behind "Neutral" Factors*

There is yet a third genre of problems associated with automated hiring – and this is related to a problem akin to data laundering.[34] As some legal scholars have previously found, automated systems might serve to mask deliberately unlawful discrimination given that humans are still responsible for choosing factors to be deployed by the algorithmic system in making decisions.[35] This leaves room for a choice of factors that, in actuality, are merely proxies[36] for legally forbidden immutable characteristics such as race, gender, or disability. There are several ways these proxies might enter into automated hiring. One known example is the use of zip codes for resume parsing. Several automated hiring systems use zip codes as a variable for sorting.[37] There are several ways this can be accomplished. One is to program only one specific zip code for resume parsing, typically, the zip code of where the work site is located. The logic here is that doing so reduces length and time for transportation, thereby helping to ensure that the chosen candidate would arrive to work on time. Another method is to select a handful of zip codes that would be considered acceptable for the candidates to live in. The justification given for this approach is typically the same logic as the first: The select zip codes are within a certain mile radius of the workplace, say five or ten miles, and the objective is to deter tardiness and absenteeism. While zip codes might be seen as a useful and neutral factor for determining appropriate candidates, the problem is that this is a variable that bears societal noise.[38] Zip codes in the United States correlate closely to race as a testament to

[34] Ifeoma Ajunwa, "Automated Employment Discrimination," *Harvard Journal of Law and Technology* 34, no. 2 (2021): 674–78.

[35] Baracos and Selbst, "Big Data's Disparate Impact," 674.

[36] Baracos and Selbst, "Big Data's Disparate Impact," 726–27.

[37] See Vivian Giang, "The Potential Hidden Bias in Automated Hiring Systems," *Fast Company*, May 8, 2018, www.fastcompany.com/40566971/the-potential-hidden-bias-in-automated-hiring-systems.

[38] See Michael Feldman et al., "Certifying and Removing Disparate Impact," *2015 ACM SIGKDD Conference on Knowledge Discovery and Data Mining* no. 3 (2015): 1–28. I attribute this phrase *societal*

historical residential segregation practices.[39] Therefore, the use of zip codes as a hiring independent variable may not so much ensure worker attendance (particularly given the existence of personal cars and public transportation), as it may work to exclude racial minorities.[40]

To further illustrate the use of proxies, consider what I call "the story of Jareds." A corporation planning to adopt an automated hiring system tasked an employment law attorney to perform an audit on the automated hiring system. The attorney asked the question "Given a set of training resumes, what two factors would your system consider as the most important for choosing a candidate?" After reviewing the training resumes, the system's answer was that (1) the candidate is named Jared and (2) the candidate played high school lacrosse. While this result is risible, given that there seems to be no direct causal connection between these two factors and job performance, an examination of why these two factors proved important reveals something more troubling. There are several studies demonstrating that it is often possible to predict a candidate's race from their first name.[41] Using Social Security Administration (SSA) data, the website MyNameStats.com provides statistics for the distribution of names within any ethnic or racial group and also the frequency with which the name is assigned to a specific gender. At first glance, I would have presupposed that most people would consider the name Jared to belong to someone who identifies as male. This is confirmed by SSA statistical data, showing that the name Jared is used as a male name 100 percent of the time. Also, at first blush, I would assume that the name Jared belonged to a white person. This is also proven correct by statistical information. According to SSA data, the statistical distribution of the name Jared is 81.3 percent for the white race category – meaning there is an above average probability that a candidate named Jared is white.[42]

noise as part of algorithmic systems to Sorelle Friedler, who noted that discriminatory aspects in automated hiring systems are "noise" because they often serve to obscure the true goal of automated hiring, which is to find the best candidate.

[39] See, e.g., Juan F. Perea, "Doctrines of Delusion: How the History of the G.I. Bill and Other Inconvenient Truths Undermine the Supreme Court's Affirmative Action Jurisprudence," *University of Pittsburgh Law Review* 75, no. 1 (2014): 583–651 (education and housing benefits were administered by "universities, private banks, realtors, and white homeowners' associations, all of whom discriminated openly and pervasively against blacks"); Onwuachi-Willig and Willig-Onwuachi, "A House Divided," 245–46 (noting persistent and insidious housing discrimination and segregation in the United States); Sarah Ludwig, "Credit Scores in America Perpetuate Racial Injustice: Here's How," *The Guardian*, Oct. 13, 2015 (high scores are enabled by the intergenerational transfer of wealth historically denied to generations of African Americans).

[40] See Baracos and Selbst, "Big Data's Disparate Impact," 692.

[41] Marianne Bertrand and Sendhill Mullainathan, "Are Emily and Greg More Employable than Lakisha and Jamal? A Field Experiment on Labor Market Discrimination," *American Economic Review* 94, no. 4 (2004): 991–1013, esp. 1008; see also Miranda Bogen, "All the Ways Hiring Algorithms Can Introduce Bias," *Harvard Business Review*, May 6, 2019.

[42] MyNameStats.com, "First Names: JARED," www.mynamestats.com/First-Names/J/JA/JARED/index.html (last visited May 9, 2022).

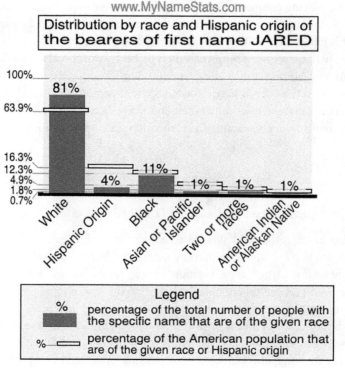

FIGURE 3.2 Distribution by race and Hispanic origin of the bearers of the first name Jared, using data from MyNameStats.com

These statistics show that the name Jared is a proxy variable for two characteristics: "white" and "male." Thus, what the importance of the name Jared as a factor for picking candidates reveals is an affinity for white male applicants in this particular workplace. But what about high school lacrosse? Is there a legal reason for using this as a determining factor? The first thought is that high school lacrosse is a team sport. For a job that requires teamwork, it is logical for an automated hiring system to search for some indicia that a candidate has experience being a good team player. An applicant that has played team sports can make that claim. But there exists a plethora of other high school team sports, and several of them are more common than lacrosse. Two that immediately come to mind are football and basketball. So why did the algorithmic system not reveal either of those as an important variable? Why high school lacrosse? As it turns out, high school lacrosse, unlike, say, football or basketball, is one of the least diverse sports in America. In 2018, only 18 percent of Division I men's lacrosse players were racial minorities. And only about 2.8 percent of Division I men's lacrosse players are Black, per NCAA statistics. Furthermore, lacrosse is considered one of the most expensive sports to play in the United States, with an average cost for a family running just short of $8,000 – just the minimum to purchase playing equipment is $800, then there are camps ranging from $225 to $1,000.[43] So the picture one gets from this is that a high school lacrosse player is not only highly likely to be white, but is also highly likely to have a high socio-economic status family background. This reveals then that the algorithmic system is favoring applicants who are not only white and male, but who also come from privileged backgrounds. As the story of Jareds illustrates, the capability for automated hiring to be used in the service of discrimination is boundless. Below I share several examples of the mechanisms of effectuating discrimination via automated hiring systems.

3.3.3 *Mechanisms of Discrimination*

3.3.3.1 Race Discrimination Disguised as "Cultural Fit"

Automated hiring is the distillation of a nebulous concept, "cultural fit," into hard and fast rules that are then deployed by automated hiring platforms to quantify a worker's fit for any particular job position. Our empirical study found that although one advertised purpose of automated hiring systems was to reduce hirer bias, the unique variables of top performers – ostensibly those who had already proven themselves to be culturally fit for the organization – would form the data fed to the hiring machine. The problem is that some of those variables may violate the intent of Title VII to allow for equal employment opportunity for protected classes. This problem is further exacerbated by how machine learning algorithms work. As matching systems, they do not treat "cultural fit" as an abstract concept, but rather attempt to wrestle it into concrete strict rules, thus creating the ludicrous scenario wherein a hiring system might conclude that bearing the name Jared makes one especially well qualified for a position.[44]

To achieve culling, employers study a number of qualities about candidates – from their resumes to their past employment experiences – to assess their "cultural fit" within the prospective company.[45] Cultural fit is defined as "the likelihood that a job candidate will be able to conform and adapt to the core values and collective behaviors that make up an organization."[46] For example, the 2016 "JobVite Recruiter Nation Report" states that "60% of recruiters rate culture fit of highest importance when making a hiring decision." This shows that recruiters considered cultural fit as

---

[43] Matt Liberman, "Inside the Lack of Racial Diversity in Lacrosse," *The Daily Orange* [Syracuse University], Apr. 22, 2019, http://dailyorange.com/2019/04/inside-lack-racial-diversity-lacrosse/.

[44] See Dave Gershgorn, "Companies Are on the Hook if Their Hiring Algorithms Are Biased," *Quartz*, Oct. 23, 2018, https://qz.com/1427621/companies-are-on-the-hook-if-their-hiring-algorithms-are-biased.

[45] See Laura Morgan Roberts and Darryl D. Roberts, "Testing the Limits of Antidiscrimination Law: The Business, Legal, and Ethical Ramifications of Cultural Profiling at Work," *Duke Journal of Gender Law & Policy* 14, no. 1 (2007): 371.

[46] Francesca Sales, "What Is Cultural Fit?" *Tech Target: SearchCIO*, last updated Sept. 2014, https://searchcio.techtarget.com/definition/Cultural-fit.

more significant than cover letters (26 percent), prestige of college (21 percent), and GPA (19 percent). Cultural fit of a candidate is topped only by previous job experience (67 percent).[47] When judging whether a candidate is a cultural fit, 83 percent of recruiters consider communication style most important.

While scholars are largely in agreement about the need for resumes and descriptions of past experiences, many are at odds with the notion of cultural fit.[48] In many regards, the determination of a candidate's cultural fit is subjective. Some studies report that assessing cultural fit comes down to an employer's "gut feeling."[49] Some respondents have concluded that a candidate might be a good fit if "[t]hey work well with others" – which seems to be something that is difficult to predict without ever seeing a candidate work with other people.[50] To this end, some scholars have promoted the idea that corporate culture can be learned because nearly every company that hires a new employee has a period of "socialization" or social training.[51] Other studies have also shown that interviewers are not even significantly adept at assessing applicants' personal characteristics from interviews.[52]

On the other hand, some researchers have argued that assessing cultural fit is important because "employee alignment to company culture influences worker satisfaction, engagement and retention," which can ultimately help the corporation to succeed.[53] Furthermore, a study of thirty-eight interviewers who were in the process of making hiring decisions found that interviewers can actually assess cultural fit "with significant degrees of accuracy" and that this factor is often "the best predictor of hiring recommendations."[54] Given both arguments, it is clear that there can be both positive and negative implications of trying to assess a candidate's cultural fit – but cultural fit can be a useful criterion for hiring only as long as an employer can make an accurate determination of such fit.

[47] Jobvite, "Jobvite Recruiter Nation Report 2016: The Annual Recruiting Survey," www.jobvite.com/wp-content/uploads/2016/09/RecruiterNation2016.pdf [https://perma.cc/KSC4-PV3Q].

[48] See, e.g., Christine Sgarlata Chung, "From Lily Bart to the Boom-Boom Room: How Wall Street's Social and Cultural Response to Women Has Shaped Securities Regulation," *Harvard Journal of Law & Gender* 33, no. 1 (2010): 175–245 (arguing that cultural fit within the finance industry is imperfect, as bias has been historically ingrained).

[49] Lauren Brown, "'Gut Feeling' Still the Most Common Deciding Factor in Hiring, Survey Shows," *People Management*, July 11, 2018, www.peoplemanagement.co.uk/news/articles/gut-feeling-most-common-deciding-factor-in-hiring-survey-shows [https://perma.cc/DZV4-SYEC].

[50] Jeff Pruitt, "3 Ways to Know if an Employee Is a Culture Fit," *Inc.*, Aug. 12, 2016, www.inc.com/jeff-pruitt/3-ways-to-know-if-an-employee-is-a-culture-fit.html [https://perma.cc/9BEC-JCBH].

[51] Richard Pascale, "The Paradox of 'Corporate Culture': Reconciling Ourselves to Socialization," *California Management Review* 27, no. 2 (1985): 26–47.

[52] Richard D. Arvey and James E. Campion, "The Employment Interview: A Summary and Review of Recent Research," *Personnel Psychology Journal* 35, no. 2 (1982): 281–322.

[53] Lauren Dixon, "The Pros and Cons of Hiring for 'Cultural Fit,'" *Chief Learning Officer: Talent Economy*, Dec. 6, 2017, www.chieflearningofficer.com/2017/12/06/pros-cons-hiring-cultural-fit [https://perma.cc/NWW2-8TQE].

[54] Daniel M. Cable and Timothy A. Judge, "Interviewers' Perceptions of Person–Organization Fit and Organizational Selection Decisions," *Journal of Applied Psychology* 82, no. 4 (1997): 546–61.

The problem is that, as employment law scholars such as Professor Natasha Martin have noted, "workplace decision-makers may gain awareness of the lack of cultural fit only after some time has passed." This means that even if an individual is hired, it is likely that the decision-maker's view of the worker will change over time with greater exposure. Professor Martin notes that "[t]his social construction of identity bears on selection of individuals when organizations make decisions based on cultural fit. By aligning employees with environmental factors, employers focus less on the candidate's skill set, and more on the intangibles that make uncovering discriminatory motive more difficult." For instance, cultural fit qualifications, such as "relish change," "possess passion for exceptional quality," "confront risks," or "think creatively" have an "amorphous quality because they are generalized and undefined with respect to any particular job task or role." Therefore, the ultimate decisions can rest merely on gut feelings such as "I just like that candidate" or "He just feels right." Even though choosing an individual based on seemingly aligned values may look like a good business decision, the problem with cultural fit in the selection process lies in the "imperceptibility of such characteristics, and the conscious and unconscious layering of meaning on such abstract terms by the decision-maker."[55] As Professor Charles Lawrence notes in *Unconscious Racism*, where an "employer perceives the white candidate as 'more articulate,' 'more collegial,' 'more thoughtful,' or 'more charismatic[,]' [h]e is unaware of the learned stereotype that influenced his decision."[56]

In sum, the problem with cultural fit is about the "perception of who belongs." Employers try to select candidates who match their "culturally consistent selection criteria," and in the fast-paced workplace, an employer has to make decisions with incomplete information about each candidate. Later, the same employee "might be deemed unfit in cultural terms … because he failed to attune to the organization's culture." In this situation, "[p]eople of color and other workplace minorities are often encouraged to assimilate, mask their true identity or ethnic salience, for example, to adapt to an organization's culture."[57] Citing to the work of Professors Devon Carbado and Mitu Gulati,[58] Martin explains that "[a]s long as the worker's difference is innocuous and unobtrusive, then the worker benefits from efforts to belong" and "once the employee fails to sufficiently cover, he may be deemed inconsistent with the organization and no longer befitting of inclusion."[59] Professors Carbado and Gulati have also argued that the "extra" identity work that women and

---

55 Natasha T. Martin, "Immunity for Hire: How the Same-Actor Doctrine Sustains Discrimination in the Contemporary Workplace," *Connecticut Law Review* 40, no. 4. (2008): 1156, 1158, 1159.
56 Charles R. Lawrence III, "The Id, the Ego, and Equal Protection: Reckoning with Unconscious Racism," *Stanford Law Review* 39, no. 2 (1987): 343.
57 Martin, "Immunity for Hire."
58 See Devon W. Carbado and Mitu Gulati, "Working Identity," *Cornell Law Review* 85, no. 5 (2000): 1262; Carbado, "Racial Naturalization," 655.
59 Martin, "Immunity for Hire," 1160.

minorities are forced to do to conform to workplace perceptions of "cultural fit" is a form of employment discrimination.[60]

Courts, however, have consistently sided with defendants in contestations of cultural fit as a criterion for hiring and firing. One notorious case is *Natay v. Murray Sch. Dist.*, in which the courts sided with the employer when deciding the cultural fit of an employee. The plaintiff, hired by the school district as a provisional teacher, was the only Native American in the group of forty-seven recently hired provisional teachers and on the school faculty. The plaintiff described her treatment at the school as discriminatory from the start; the principal snubbed her at the first staff meeting, disciplined her but not another teacher, and came late to her scheduled evaluations. In addition, the principal told Natay at one point that she was "geographically, racially, culturally, and socially out of place" at the school, and her contract was not renewed after unfavorable evaluations. The school district superintendent decided that the plaintiff was "not an excellent teacher and not someone [he] would want Murray School District to hire on a long-term basis." Natay had an informal conference with the superintendent, but her arguments did not change the decision. Of the district's provisional teachers hired for that school year, only Natay's contract was not renewed, and on her last day of work, the principal made another racially derogatory comment to her.[61] Natay brought a discriminatory discharge claim in federal district court, and the court entered summary judgment in favor of the employer. She appealed.

In the Tenth Circuit, the court reviewed the district court's grant of summary judgment, using the same standards, as well as the evidence and reasonable inferences drawn from the evidence. It stated that although the plaintiff proved that the principal showed discriminatory actions, she lacked evidence showing that the superintendent, the ultimate decision-maker, had a discriminatory reason not to renew her contract. Based on the "cat's paw" doctrine, she did not prove that the "manager who discharged the plaintiff merely acted as a rubber stamp, or the 'cat's paw,' for a subordinate employee's prejudice," regardless of the manager's discriminatory intent. Also, the court used the *McDonnell Douglas* burden-shifting framework, deciding that the plaintiff satisfied the prima facie case and succeeded in shifting the burden to the school district. Although the plaintiff claimed that the superintendent's investigation of her performance was inadequate because he never sat in her classroom to observe her, the court stood on the side of the superintendent, whose affidavit detailed other steps in his investigation and decision to not renew the contract due to her ineffectiveness. Thus, the court concluded that the plaintiff's showing did not reasonably give rise to an inference that the employer's reasons were pretextual and affirmed the decision of the district court.[62]

---

[60] See Carbado and Gulati, "Working Identity," 1262.
[61] *Natay v. Murray Sch. Dist.*, 119 Fed. Appx. 259, 260, 261 (10th Cir. 2005).
[62] *Natay v. Murray Sch. Dist.*, 119 Fed. Appx. 259, 262 (10th Cir. 2005).

Despite the uncritical acceptance of the law that determining cultural fit is a permissible or even necessary criterion for job selection, several studies now demonstrate that confirming "cultural fitness" is not always essential for job success. One such study conducted by business professors at Stanford and Berkeley found that the capacity to change and a person's flexibility – that is, high "enculturability" – were more important than pre-existing cultural fit in regard to long-term success.[63] According to the authors of the study,

> Our results suggest that firms should place less emphasis on screening for cultural fit, … [a]s other work has shown, matching on cultural fit often favors applicants from particular socioeconomic backgrounds, leading to a reduction in workplace diversity. Instead, our work points to the value of screening on enculturability.[64]

The researchers propose three enculturability questions that employers might consider regarding potential candidates: "1. To what extent do candidates seek out diverse cultural environments? 2. How rapidly do they adjust to these new environments? 3. How do they balance adapting to the new culture while staying true to themselves?"[65]

Given these new research findings, more companies are abandoning "cultural fit" as a factor for hiring. For example, in a bid to create a more inclusive hiring process, Facebook outlawed the term *culture fit* as interview feedback, instead "requiring interviewers to provide specific feedback that supported their position."[66] Facebook also took steps to "proactively identify unconscious bias" in their interview process and "developed a 'managing unconscious bias' training program."[67]

Other companies now embrace "hiring for values fit" as a method to decrease unconscious bias in interviewing. For example, Atlassian, an Australia-based company, redesigned its interview process: "[V]alues fit interviewers are carefully selected and given training on topics like structured interviewing and unconscious bias." The interview is structured with a set of behavioral questions to assess whether a candidate would thrive in an environment with their company values. As one of Atlassian's chief officers explains, "Focusing on 'values fit' ensures we hire people who share our sense of purpose and guiding principles, while actively looking for those with diverse viewpoints, backgrounds, and skill sets. We're trying to build a healthy and balanced culture, not a cult."[68] This approach has borne positive results

---

[63] Amir Goldberg et al., "Fitting In or Standing Out? The Tradeoffs of Structural and Cultural Embeddedness," *American Sociological Review* 81, no. 6 (2016): 1208–11.

[64] Amir Goldberg and Sameer B. Srivastava, "Should You Hire for Cultural Fit or Adaptability?" *re:Work*, Dec. 6, 2016, https://rework.withgooogle.com/glob/hire-for-cultural-fit-or-adaptability/

[65] Rich Lyons, "Lose Those Cultural Fit Tests: Instead Screen New Hires for 'Enculturability,'" *Forbes*, June 7, 2017.

[66] Lars Schmidt, "The End of Culture Fit," *Forbes*, Mar. 21, 2017.

[67] Schmidt, "End of Culture Fit"; Sheryl Sandberg, "Managing Unconscious Bias," *Meta Newsroom*, July 28, 2015, https://newsroom.fb.com/news/2015/07/managing-unconscious-bias [https://perma.cc/A2KG-H5AZ].

[68] Schmidt, "End of Culture Fit"; Atlassian, "Company Values," www.atlassian.com/company/values [https://perma.cc/WS37-QL4Q] (last visited Mar. 2, 2020).

for Atlassian. In 2015, 10 percent of their technical workforce identified as female. In 2016, 17 percent of recent hires were women, and women held 14 percent of all technical roles. Similarly, in 2015, their U.S.-based team had 23 percent of employees identifying as people of color. In 2016, people of color comprised 32 percent of their new hires.[69]

3.3.4 *Age Discrimination through Proxy Variables and Design*

There are several ways that automated hiring systems can enable, facilitate, and obscure discrimination. This is especially apparent for instances of age discrimination on platforms. First, it undeniable that age discrimination is rife in American society. In 2007, while giving a speech at Stanford University, the tech mogul Mark Zuckerberg opined, "I want to stress the importance of being young and technical … Young people are just smarter."[70] It is this sort of casual ageism that led the comedian Bill Maher to note that "ageism is the last acceptable prejudice in America."[71] Dr. Bill Thomas, author of *What Are Old People For?*, shares a similar sentiment: "Aging is the last form of bigotry you can speak of in public."[72]

Although the Age Discrimination in Employment Act (ADEA), which prohibits age discrimination in hiring practices for employees and applicants who are forty years old or older,[73] became law in 1967, age discrimination remains very much a part of American working life. This is most apparent in the tech industry. In 2014, Noam Scheiber published a devastating expose of the extent of ageism in Silicon Valley, finding that many tech workers, even some in their twenties, had undergone plastic surgery in a bid to maintain the preternatural youthful appearance they had deemed necessary for job retention.[74] In 2018, investigators from *ProPublica* discovered that IBM may have engaged in systemic age discrimination. The investigators concluded that the tech company had "eliminated more than 20,000 American employees ages 40 and over, about 60 percent of its estimated total U.S. job cuts" between the years 2013 and 2018, and noted that "in the words of one confidential planning document," the company's strategy was designed to "correct [the] seniority mix."[75]

---

[69] Schmidt, "The End of Culture Fit"; Atlassian, "Building Equitable, Balanced Teams and a Sense of Belonging," www.atlassian.com/belonging [https://perma.cc/3949-T3ZN] (last visited Mar. 2, 2020).

[70] Andrew S. Ross, "In Silicon Valley, Age Can Be a Curse," *SF Gate*, Aug. 20, 2013, www.sfgate.com/bu~siness/bottomline/article/In-Silicon-Valley-age-can-be-a-curse-4742365.php.

[71] Greg Gilman, "Bill Maher Rips 'Shallow' American Culture for Allowing 'Ageism' to Impact Politics," *The Wrap*, Nov. 9, 2014, https://perma.cc/U4M3-YHC6.

[72] See Nicole Karlis, "Time to Rethink How We Talk about Older People," *Salon*, Mar. 31, 2018, www.salon.com/2018/03/31/time-to-rethink-how-we-talk-about-the-elderly/.

[73] 29 U.S.C. §§ 621; 631(a)-b) (2012). But note that some jurisdictions have passed laws to include workers under age forty.

[74] Noam Scheiber, "The Brutal Ageism of Tech," *The New Republic*, Mar. 23, 2014.

[75] Peter Gosselin and Ariana Tobin, "Cutting 'Old Heads' at IBM," *ProPublica*, Mar. 22, 2018.

Several legal scholars have tackled the issue of age discrimination in employment, with many noting the limitations of the ADEA in effectively curtailing age
discrimination.[76] Although the ADEA prohibits employers and employment agencies from age discrimination in advertising, recruiting, and hiring for jobs, and from
sending or publishing employment ads that discriminate or indicate a preference
or limitation based on age,[77] the ADEA now also requires proof that age was a "but
for" factor for the adverse employment decision. This means that, as affirmed by the
Supreme Court in the case of *Gross v. FBL*, the plaintiff has to prove "by a prepon-
derance of the evidence, that age was the 'but-for' cause of the challenged adverse
employment action." This was a departure from the previous standard that age only
had to be a "motivating factor."[78] Thus, *Gross* has made it much more difficult for
plaintiffs to prove ADEA cases.[79]

Scholars have noted that the Supreme Court's majority ruling in *Gross* overruled
a twenty-year precedent to the detriment of labor and employment law plaintiffs.
Furthermore, the "casual, one-paragraph redefinition [in *Gross*] of what it means
for an action to be taken 'because of' a protected characteristic may well have consequences beyond the age discrimination context," as the decision moves claims
under the ADEA away from the Title VII standard of establishing discrimination
(which can be proven by establishing a protected characteristic was a "motivating
factor" in the adverse employment action).[80]

The current standard of proof for making age discrimination claims has also ham-
pered ADEA plaintiffs from making mixed-motive claims. Mixed-motive claims are
those in which plaintiffs argue that a protected characteristic was a motivating or
substantial factor in an adverse employment action, even if other motivating factors
used could have been lawful.[81] Ultimately, this means that significantly fewer cases

---

[76] See, e.g., Laurie A. McCann, "The Age Discrimination in Employment Act at 50: When Will It
Become a 'Real' Civil Rights Statute?" *ABA Journal of Law and Employment Law* 33, no. 1 (2017):
94–95; Pnina Alon-Shenker, "Legal Barriers to Age Discrimination in Hiring Complaints," *Dalhousie
University Law Journal* 39, no. 1 (2016): 313; Debra Lyn Bassett, "Silencing Our Elders," *Nevada Law
Review* 15, no. 2 (2015): 527; Michael Harper, "Reforming the Age Discrimination in Employment Act:
Proposals and Prospects," *Employee Rights and Employment Policy* 16, no. 1 (2012): 13–49; Jamie Darin
Prenkert, "Bizarro Statutory Stare Decisis," *Berkeley Journal of Employment and Labor Law* 28, no. 1
(2007): 217–68; Aida Marie Alaka, "Corporate Reorganizations, Job Layoffs, and Age Discrimination:
Has *Smith v. City of Jackson* Substantially Expanded the Rights of Older Workers under the ADEA?"
Albany Law Review 70, no. 1 (2006): 143–80; Michael Evan Gold, "Disparate Impact under the Age
Discrimination in Employment Act of 1967," *Berkeley Journal of Employment and Labor Law* 25,
no. 1 (2004): 1–86; Judith D. Fischer, "Public Policy and the Tyranny of the Bottom Line in the
Termination of Older Workers," *South Carolina Law Review* 53, no. 2 (2002): 211–47.

[77] 29 U.S.C. § 623(a), (b), (e) (2012).

[78] *Gross v. FBL Fin. Servs.*, 557 U.S. 167 (2009), at 175–77, 180.

[79] Michael L. Foreman, "*Gross v. FBL Financial Services* – Oh So Gross!" *University of Memphis Law
Review* 40, no. 4 (2010): 688.

[80] Melissa Hart, "Procedural Extremism: The Supreme Court's 2008–2009 Labor and Employment
Cases," *Employee Rights and Employment Policy Journal* 13, no. 1 (2009): 265, 269, 270.

[81] Hart, "Procedural Extremism," 265–66, 271.

of age discrimination can be proven under the ADEA because many employers might have used lawful considerations in addition to a plaintiff's age when making employment decisions.

Courts have also begun to defer to employers to show that they addressed "reasonable factors other than age" in their contested employment decisions. For example, in the 2016 case *Villarreal v. RJ Reynolds Tobacco*, plaintiff Richard Villarreal applied for a territory sales manager job at Reynolds Tobacco via an online platform. He was forty-nine years old at the time he sent his application. After applying, Villarreal was never contacted, and he did not follow up with Reynolds. However, several years later, he learned that the company's internal hiring guidelines described "targeted candidates" as those "2–3 years out of college" and directed reviewers to "stay away from" applicants whose resumes showed that they had been "in sales for 8–10 years." After hearing about these internal guidelines, Villarreal filed suit alleging a violation of the ADEA.[82]

In *Villarreal*, the majority effectively stated that, although Reynolds Tobacco had used discriminatory guidelines internally, Mr. Villarreal could not prove age discrimination because he did not diligently follow up regarding his application decision. Thus, the employment decision could have been made for a number of factors other than Villarreal's age.[83] The *Villarreal* decision indicates the court's deference to the employer to show that a decision was made for "reasonable factors other than age."[84] Reynolds, as defendant to any age discrimination claim, did not have to show its decision was not discriminatory; it simply had to show that its decision could have been for other factors related to Villarreal's application.[85] Effectively, the decision in *Gross*, in which plaintiffs must show age was the "but for" factor in an adverse employment decision,[86] coupled with that in *Villarreal*, in which employers must simply show age was not the sole factor in their decisions,[87] have now made ADEA violations very difficult to prove.

Given the limitations of the ADEA, several studies show that age discrimination in hiring has been exacerbated by automated hiring.[88] An audit study by the Federal Reserve Bank of America using 40,000 fictitious resumes showed evidence of age bias among several low-skilled job categories such as sales, administrators, and janitors. The study showed that for male applicants over age forty, there was a 30 percent decrease in call-back rate. But older women applicants fared even worse, with a 47 percent decrease in call-back rate for administrative jobs.[89] Another investigative

---

[82] *Villarreal v. R.J. Reynolds Tobacco Co.*, 839 F.3d 958, 961 (11th Cir. 2016).

[83] See *Villarreal v. R.J. Reynolds Tobacco Co.*, 839 F.3d 958, 970–72.

[84] See 29 U.S.C. § 623(f)(1).

[85] See *Villareal v. R.J. Reynolds Tobacco Co.*, 839 F.3d 958, 970.

[86] See *Gross v. FBL Fin. Servs.*, 557 U.S. 167 (2009).

[87] See *Villareal*, 839 F.3d at 967.

[88] See Austin O'Connor, "Bias towards Older Workers on the Rise as Age Discrimination Goes Online," *Milwaukee Independent*, Jan. 10, 2018.

[89] David Neumark, Ian Burn, and Patrick Button, "Age Discrimination and Hiring of Older Workers," *FRBSF Economic Letter*, Feb. 27, 2017, www.frbsf.org/economic-research/publications/economic-letter/2017/february/age-discrimination-and-hiring-older-workers/.

study by ProPublica concluded that Facebook ad targeting had allowed several employers to target applicants by age and thus resulted in the exclusion of several applicants over age forty. For instance, in one targeted ad for "part-time package handlers," the investigative study concludes that Facebook enabled United Parcel Service (UPS) to run an advertisement that targeted only individuals between the ages of eighteen and twenty-four. In another job advertisement, the study found that State Farm had targeted an audience of only nineteen- to thirty-five-year-olds.[90]

One mechanism for age discrimination through automated hiring platform is the design features that enable advertisement practices that serve to redline, cull, or dissuade older job applicants. One method for achieving these discriminatory ends is the use of proxies for age in advertising language. A significant legal problem, however, is that it has gotten more difficult over time for plaintiffs to make a case that language used in advertising is discriminatory on the basis of age. In the 1975 case of *Hodgson v. Approved Personnel Services*, the Fourth Circuit found that the use of the phrase *recent graduate* in job advertisement was not "merely informational" but rather was in violation of the ADEA because it was meant to dissuade older applicants.[91] Yet, in the 1996 case of *Boyd v. City of Wilmington*, the Eastern District Court of North Carolina found that an advertisement indicating that "candidates for MPA or MSIR degrees were preferred" was not discriminatory under the ADEA. The Court noted that although the language referred to newly created degrees (which ostensibly are more likely to be held by younger applicants), the plaintiff had failed to prove the "discriminatory intent" of the employer.[92]

Although proving age discrimination through advertisement verbiage has gotten more difficult under the ADEA, some state laws have noted the discriminatory effect of certain phrasing for job advertisements. For example, in the 2008 case of *Reid v. Google*, a worker in California sued his former employer, Google, with a claim of age discrimination in violation of the California Fair Employment and Housing Law (FEHA). Google terminated Reid for a lack of "cultural fit" and in his performance review it noted that "[a]dapting to Google culture is the primary task for the first year ... [which includes] ... [y]ounger contributors, inexperienced first line managers, and the super fast pace." Reid also alleged that, perhaps as a result of the described culture placing importance on youth and speed, his colleagues often made disparaging remarks about his age and speed of work and seemed to doubt the relevance of his opinions. The California Supreme Court ruled for Reid, with a finding that "stray remarks" may be considered evidence of age discrimination.[93]

---

[90] Julia Angwin, Noam Schelber, and Ariana Tobin, "Facebook Job Ads Raise Concerns about Age Discrimination," *New York Times*, Dec. 20, 2017.

[91] *Hodgson v. Approved Personnel Serv., Inc.*, 529 F. 2d 760, 766 (4th Cir. 1975).

[92] *Boyd v. City of Wilmington*, 943 F. Supp. 585, 587, 590–92 (E.D.N.C. 1996).

[93] See *Reid v. Google, Inc.*, 50 Cal. 4th 512, 516, 517–19, 543–46 (2008).

Other advertisement language pitched at culture fit such as "digital native" has also been found to be a pretext for age discrimination.[94]

Another mechanism through which age discrimination could be achieved in automated hiring is the targeting of job advertisements. Prior to the digital age, newspapers were the primary medium for job advertisement. This meant that any reader could pick up a newspaper and view all the job advertisements in that paper, even the ones that explicitly attempted to exclude said reader. Although the advent of the internet was heralded as a democratizing event for humankind, the truth is that recent technological advancements allow for even more targeted, and also more discreet, segregation of opportunities than previously imagined. Consider, for example, the now-defunct Facebook Affinity Groups. These groups were derived from Facebook users of different demographics, and advertisers were then afforded the choice to target their ads to particular Affinity Groups. One complaint filed against Facebook notes that with these Affinity Groups, clients or advertises could chose to "refine" their target audience and thus limit their advertisements to certain types of applicants. The complaint also alleges that, to the benefit of age discrimination, these Affinity Groups allowed employers to restrict their advertisements to specific age bands, such as to prospective applicants between the ages of "18 and 38."[95] It is worth underscoring that by eliminating older applicants from even viewing advertisements, employers effectively shrink their applicant pools to younger workers,[96] which is a violation of the ADEA.

Automated hiring platforms afford yet another mechanism for age discrimination, and this is through the digital redlining of older workers into job positions (such as part-time jobs) that are inferior to those offered to younger workers. One notable example was Indeed.com, which at one point had a specific category entitled "Part Time Jobs, Senior Citizen Jobs." Linking part-time jobs with senior citizen jobs in this way is discriminatory because of the impression that these are the only types of jobs suitable to senior citizens. It is also a form of redlining because, while Indeed .com touted itself as listing 16 million jobs worldwide, there were only 158,000 positions available under the "Part Time Jobs, Senior Citizen Jobs" category, potentially leaving a user of the site with the impression that a vast majority of the job positions were reserved for younger workers. At one point a mere 0.9 percent of jobs on Indeed .com were advertised specifically to older workers, despite the fact that those workers are a much larger percentage of the working population, which should raise concerns regarding how job websites, as part of automated hiring platforms, can enable age discrimination. It is also worth noting that Indeed.com is not the only website

[94] See Jessica Sink and Richard A. Bales, "Born in the Bandwidth: 'Digital Native' as Pretext for Age Discrimination," *ABA Journal of Labor and Employment Law* 31, no. 3 (2016): 521–23; Vivian Giang, "This Is the Latest Way Employers Mask Age Bias, Lawyers Say," *Fortune*, May 4, 2015.

[95] Class Action Complaint & Demand for Jury Trial, *Commc'ns Workers of Am. v. T-Mobile, Inc.*, No. 17-cv-07232 (Dec. 20, 2017) [https://perma.cc/9FHQ-UACR] (lawsuit was settled with Facebook agreeing to discontinue the Affinity Groups).

[96] Bob Sullivan, "Online Job Sites May Block Older Workers," *CNBC*, Mar. 13, 2017.

accused of the digital redlining of older workers. Monster.com was also shown to have a special home page for older workers, titled "Careers at 50+."[97] With the help of these categories, automated hiring systems effectuate age discrimination through digital redlining, which nudges older applicants to jobs under the aforementioned genre of categories while dissuading them from applying to other available jobs.

Perhaps the most insidious mechanism for discrimination on automated hiring platforms is what is called "platform authoritarianism," which is the socio-technical phenomenon in which a lack of choice as to whether to use a platform is coupled with a demand to engage with that platform "solely on its dictated terms, without regard for established laws and business ethics."[98] Platform authoritarianism is effectuated by design choices for hiring platform user interfaces that constrain user choice regarding what information must be entered into the system. One notable example: In a complaint filed with the office of the Illinois Attorney General, a seventy-year-old man alleged that he had been unable to use an online resume building tool (a part of an automated hiring system) because of built-in age restrictions. Note that some online hiring platforms have user interfaces that include drop-down menus that start in the 1980s, which has the effect of screening out those who graduated earlier or have had longer job tenure. Some even go as far to explicitly ask for birth dates and to block that question from being skipped.[99] The resulting investigation from the Illinois man's complaint found that, at the time, several hiring platforms such as Monster.com, Ladders.com, Indeed.com, and several others had varying age cut-offs built into their interface that served to limit the age of applicants.[100]

Another recurring issue with automated hiring is a lack of proof, particularly when proxies can stand in for protected characteristics such as age. These proxies can then be used for age discrimination without leaving proof that there was age-related data collected by the automated hiring. This was possibly the case in *Gladden v. Bolden*. Gladden, a fifty-three-year-old man, applied for a job at NASA, which used the online platform RESUMIX to sort through applicants resumes. Gladden, who is also African American, claimed that the system discriminated based on age and race by keeping his resume from being reviewed by a human manager, although he was qualified for the position. However, the District Court granted summary judgement, finding that the RESUMIX system did not collect data having to do with age. The court did not require the company to turn over the data of all the applicants, since they were able to show that age was not a factor used by RESUMIX based on the fact that there was no explicit demand to input age. This decision was affirmed on appeal by the D.C. Circuit.[101]

---

[97] Sullivan, "Online Job Sites May Block Older Workers,"

[98] Ifeoma Ajunwa, "Facebook Users Aren't the Reason Facebook Is in Trouble Now," *Washington Post*, Mar. 23, 2018.

[99] See O'Connor, "Bias towards Older Workers on the Rise as Age Discrimination Goes Online."

[100] Ina Jaffe, "Older Workers Find Age Discrimination Built Right into Some Job Websites," *NPR: All Things Considered*, Mar. 28, 2017.

[101] *Gladden v. Bolden*, 802 F. Supp. 2d 209 (D.D.C. 2011).

Given the potential for proxies to stand in for age data, the required showing by the ADEA that age must be the sole "but for" factor for employment denial has proven to be a persistent stumbling block for plaintiffs filing complaints alleging age discrimination in automated hiring systems. In the 2012 case of *Cramblet v. McHugh*, Cramblett filed a claim that he was denied several job positions because of his age. A computer algorithm weeded out resumes from all applicants during the first round of resume review, and Cramblett claimed that the system sought to exclude resumes of older applicants. However, the court noted that there was no evidence that the algorithm based its decision in any way on age. While Cramblett claimed that certain skills on a resume are based on age and thus would affect the manner in which the system ranks candidates, the court concluded that this was not enough to show that age was the reason Cramblett was not hired, as required by the ADEA.[102]

3.4 AUTOMATED HIRING AS LEGALLY ACCEPTED GATEKEEPER

When it comes to litigation to redress employment discrimination via automated hiring, an American legal tradition of deference to the employer plus the particular problematic features of automated hiring present several obstacles. First, depending on the level of automation in the hiring process, it becomes difficult to determine intent to discriminate as required for finding liability under the disparate treatment cause of action under Title VII.[103] Second, when bringing suit under the disparate impact cause of action, the design features of automated hiring systems, as well as trade secret claims that may arise, impede the plaintiff's ability to provide the statistical proof required to establish a prima facie case. And third, litigation remedies in employment anti-discrimination law do not address privacy and discrimination issues associated with the collection of personal and biometric data from job candidates, as enabled by automated video interviewing. For these reasons, I argue that employment law, with its emphasis on litigation as redress for employment discrimination, is limited in its capacity to address the full spectrum of identified problems with automated hiring.

Automated hiring brings to high relief the deference accorded to employers vis-à-vis the employment bargain.[104] In an empirical legal study, Professors Clermont and Schwab found:

> Employment discrimination plaintiffs ... manage many fewer happy resolutions early in litigation, and so they have to proceed toward trial more often. They win

---

[102] *Cramblett v. McHugh*, No. 3:10-CV-54-PK, 2012 WL 7681280 (D. Or. Nov. 19, 2012).
[103] Charles Sullivan, "Employing AI," *Villanova Law Review* 63, no. 3 (2018): 398 (arguing the legal difficulties of assigning intent to a machine learning automated hiring system, when the machine, learning from previous decisions, can write its own new models to follow).
[104] Perhaps the most emblematic example of the American legal system's deference to employers is the case of *Lochner v. New York*, 198 U.S. 45 (1905), which held that any limit on the number of hours (in excess of sixty hours) that employees of a bakery could work was unconstitutional. Although that particular decision has since been overturned, there is a wealth of scholarship noting the continued

a lower proportion of cases during pretrial and at trial. Then, more of their successful cases are appealed. On appeal, they have a harder time upholding their successes and reversing adverse outcomes.[105]

Likewise, after Professor Wendy Parker conducted an empirical study of 659 cases alleging racial discrimination in employment, she concluded that judges operate under the assumption that those types of claims are generally without merit.[106] For cases alleging implicit bias, Professor Franita Tolson has also noted that courts will find in favor of the employee in only the most extreme cases because the courts have "statutory concerns and ... [believe] that they are not qualified to resolve these claims."[107] Professor Selmi echoes these conclusions and observes,

> When it comes to race cases, which are generally the most difficult claim for a plaintiff to succeed on, courts often seem mired in a belief that the claims are generally unmeritorious, brought by whining plaintiffs who have been given too many, not too few, breaks along the way. These biases, as well as others, inevitably influence courts' treatment of discrimination cases, and help explain why the cases are so difficult to win.[108]

In addition to this legal deference in contested cases of employment discrimination, employers exercise a great deal of latitude in choosing which job applicants they hire and fire.[109] This is especially true of at-will jurisdictions, where employees can be hired and fired based on a vast list of criteria determined by the employer. In her

deference to employers. See Cynthia L. Estlund, "The Ossification of American Labor Law," *Columbia Law Review* 102, no. 6 (2002): 1527 (noting that the "ossification of labor law" is due, in part, to a lack of "democratic renewal"); Franita Tolson, "The Boundaries of Litigating Unconscious Discrimination: Firm-Based Remedies in Response to a Hostile Judiciary," *Delaware Journal of Corporate Law* 33. no. 2 (2008): 379 (courts want to avoid turning Title VII into a rule by which employers could be held liable for "perceived slights" towards employees). See also Kevin M. Clermont and Stewart J. Schwab, "How Employment Discrimination Plaintiffs Fare in Federal Court," *Journal of Empirical Legal Studies* 1, no. 2 (2004): 429–58 (claiming that employment discrimination plaintiffs, unlike many other plaintiffs, have always done substantially worse in judge trials than in jury trials); Michael J. Zimmer, "The New Discrimination Law: Price Waterhouse Is Dead, Whither McDonnell Douglas?" *Emory Law Journal* 53, no. 2 (2004): 1944 ("The 5.8 percent reversal rate of defendant trial victories is smaller in employment discrimination cases than any other category of cases except prisoner habeas corpus trials."). See also Ruth Colker, "The Americans with Disabilities Act: A Windfall for Defendants," *Harvard Civil Rights-Civil Liberties Law Review* 34, no. 1 (1999): 100 (in reported decisions from 1992 to 1998, defendants prevailed in more than 93 percent of the cases decided at the trial court level and were more likely to be affirmed on appeal); Theodore Eisenberg, "Litigation Models and Trial Outcomes in Civil Rights and Prisoner Cases," *Georgetown Law Journal* 77, no. 4 (1989): 1577 (only claims filed by prisoners have a lower success rate than claims filed by employment discrimination plaintiffs).
[105] Clermont and Schwab, "How Employment Discrimination Plaintiffs Fare in Federal Court," 429.
[106] Wendy Parker, "Lessons in Losing: Race Discrimination in Employment," *Notre Dame Law Review* 81, no. 3 (2006): 893.
[107] See Tolson, "Boundaries of Litigating Unconscious Discrimination," 378.
[108] Michael Selmi, "Why Are Employment Discrimination Cases So Hard to Win?" *Louisiana Law Review* 61, no. 3 (2001): 556–57.
[109] Clyde W. Summers, "Employment at Will in the United States: The Divine Right of Employers," *University of Pennsylvania Journal of Labor and Employment Law* 3, no. 1 (2000): 65–86.

article "Discrimination at Will: Job Security Protections and Equal Employment Opportunity in Conflict," Professor Julie Suk notes that employment discrimination scholars have argued that "employment at will seriously undermines the effectiveness of employment discrimination law in bringing about race and gender equality in the workplace."[110] Other legal scholars have articulated exactly why this is the case as they note that the job protections present in antidiscrimination law might dissuade employers from hiring job applicants from protected groups. In her book *Working Together*, Professor Estlund argues that employers have perverse disincentives to hire racial minorities when Title VII operates in the context of employment at will[111] because of the risk of incurring expenses in a Title VII suit. As Professors Ian Ayres and Peter Siegelman put it, "protection against discriminatory firing acts as a kind of tax on hiring those to whom it is extended."[112] Furthermore, employment at will as a norm "affects the burdens of production and proof under the *McDonnell Douglas* framework when individual Title VII cases are litigated, often to the detriment of plaintiffs."[113] This imbalance of power in favor of the employer is tilted even further by automated hiring platforms.

---

[110] Julie C. Suk, "Discrimination at Will: Job Security Protections and Equal Employment Opportunity in Conflict," *Stanford Law Review* 60, no. 1 (2007): 81.
[111] Cynthia Estlund, *Working Together: How Workplace Bonds Strengthen a Diverse Democracy* (Oxford: Oxford University Press, 2003), 152. And see Suk, "Discrimination at Will," 83.
[112] Ian Ayres and Peter Siegelman, "The Q-Word as Red Herring: Why Disparate Impact Liability Does Not Induce Hiring Quotas," *Texas Law Review* 74, no. 1 (1996): 1489.
[113] Suk, "Discrimination at Will," 81.

4

Personality Job Tests

Hiring the right people takes time, the right questions and a healthy dose of curiosity. What do you think is the most important factor when building your team? For us, it's personality.

–Richard Branson

Dad, I had an almost perfect SAT, and I was at Vanderbilt a few years ago. If I can't get a part-time minimum-wage job, how broken am I?

–Kyle Behm

The plaintive *cri de coeur* above came from Kyle Behm. While on break from college after being diagnosed with bipolar disorder, Mr. Behm was denied employment at several supermarkets.[1] The one factor the businesses had in common: They all used personality job tests.

Personality job tests are often deployed as part of automated hiring systems and represent yet another vehicle for the quantification of workers. In 2014, a study found that personality tests were being used to assess the personality, skills, cognitive abilities, and other traits of 60 to 70 percent of prospective workers in the United States, a 30 to 40 percent increase from 2009. In 2014, Hogan Assessments estimated that workplace personality testing had become a $500-million-a-year business and was growing by 10 to 15 percent a year.[2]

Personality job testing was first introduced in 1919 by the U.S. Army in the form of the Woodworth Personal Data Sheet. That test was deployed to screen potential recruits and rule out those who were determined to have a propensity towards shell shock.[3] Personality tests as part of job applications were temporarily put to a stop in 1965, after two organizational psychologists conducted a study showing that

[1] Cathy O'Neil, "Personality Tests Are Failing American Workers," *Bloomberg*, Jan. 18, 2018.
[2] Lauren Weber and Elizabeth Dwoskin, "Are Workplace Personality Tests Fair?" *Wall Street Journal*, Sept. 29, 2014.
[3] Robert M. Kaplan and Dennis P. Saccuzzo, *Psychological Testing: Principles, Applications, and Issues*, 8th ed. (Belmont, CA: Wadsworth Cengage, 2012).

personality tests were an invalid basis for making employment decisions. Robert M. Guion and Richard F. Gottier examined twelve years of research on the validity of personality tests and noted several flaws in the tests, notably regarding the theories linking personality characteristics to jobs as well as the actual efficacy of the personality tests. Measurements of the consistency and strength of relationships between personality characteristics and work-related outcomes were called into question.[4] Other research studies have concluded that personality accounts for only about 5 percent of employee job success, while the other 95 percent of performance has nothing to do with personality.[5] Furthermore, although 80 percent of Fortune 500 companies use personality assessments for employee selection, only 14 percent are said to have data indicating positive business impacts of such testing.[6]

4.1 GUIDELINES FOR PERSONALITY JOB TESTS

The Equal Employment Opportunity Commission (EEOC) provides the Uniform Guidelines on Employment Selection Procedures (UGESP), which govern the use of employment tests. These guidelines require that every employer maintain records of the impact that its pre-employment tests and other employee selection procedures have on persons in a protected class.[7] They also require that if an employer's records show its selection process has an adverse disparate impact on members of a group in a protected class, the employer should separately analyze for adverse impacts from each of the various components of the selection process, which could include personality tests.[8] Furthermore, a selection process or individual component such as a personality test that has an adverse impact could be deemed discriminatory unless it is "validated" in accordance with UGSEP. There are three kinds of validity that are required: content validity, criterion-related validity, and construct validity.[9]

First, content validity is when a job analysis defines a job in terms of the important behaviors, tasks, or knowledge required for successful performance, and the assessment or test is a representative sample of those behaviors, tasks, or knowledge (e.g., a typing or mathematics test, or an exam for certified public accountants). The UGESP state that to demonstrate the content validity of a selection procedure, its user should show that the behaviors measured in the selection procedure are a representative sample of the behaviors required of the job in question, or that the

4   Robert M. Guion and Richard F. Gottier, "Validity of Personality Measures in Personnel Selection," *Personnel Psychology* 18, no. 2 (1965): 160.
5   H. Beau Baez, "Personality Test in Employment Selection: Use with Caution," *Cornell HR Review*, Jan. 26, 2013.
6   Whitney Martin, "The Problem with Using Personality Tests for Hiring," *Harvard Business Review*, Aug. 27, 2014.
7   29 C.F.R. § 1607.4(A).
8   29 C.F.R. § 1607.4(C).
9   29 C.F.R. § 1607.14.

selection procedure provides a representative sample of the work product of the job in question.[10]

Next, criterion-related validity relates to a test's ability to predict how well a person will perform on the job. Tests, or predictors, are then devised and used to measure different job dimensions of the criterion variables. "Tests" may include having a college degree, scoring a required number of words per minute on a typing test, having a number of years of experience, and so on. These predictors are then validated against the criteria used to measure job performance, such as supervisor appraisals, attendance, and quality of work performed. There are two different approaches to measuring criterion-related validity. One is an assessment of concurrent validity, where the employer tests current employees and compares scores with job performance ratings, so that the test scores and performance measures are available at the same time. The other is an assessment of predictive validity, where the employer compares applicants' test results with their subsequent job performance.[11]

Finally, construct validity refers to the extent to which a selection device measures a particular "construct" that, according to a job analysis, underlies the successful performance of the job in question.[12] Typical constructs include intelligence, honesty, dependability, and so on. These constructs are largely what is being tested by personality job tests – and because they are theoretical constructs, they raise legal questions as to both their validity and legality vis-à-vis anti-discrimination laws.

Although personality tests fell out of favor in the 1960s, there was a resurgence of personality job tests following the ban of polygraph testing for employment screening in 1988.[13] This resurgence is not without controversy: In 2012 and 2013, Kroger and six other companies were accused of discrimination against people with mental illness through their use of personality tests.[14] The complaints were brought by corporate lawyer Roland Behm on behalf of his son, Kyle.

According to the complaints, Kyle applied online for hourly jobs at Finish Line Inc., Home Depot, Kroger, Lowe's, PetSmart, Walgreens, and Yum Brands Inc., and was required to take the same personality test for each application. Despite having held similar positions in the past, Kyle was turned down for every position he applied for. However, Kyle's story was unique – unlike many applicants who never hear back after sending in job applications, Kyle was told by a Kroger employee that he scored "red" because the test had determined that Kyle might ignore customers if he was feeling upset.[15]

---

[10]   29 C.F.R. § 1607.14
[11]   29 C.F.R. § 1607.14
[12]   29 C.F.R. § 1607.14
[13]   Yvonne Koontz Sening, "Heads or Tails: The Employee Polygraph Protection Act," *Catholic University Law Review* 39, no. 1 (1989): 235–68.
[14]   Weber and Dwoskin, "Are Workplace Personality Tests Fair?"
[15]   Weber and Dwoskin, "Are Workplace Personality Tests Fair?"

In addition to this information he received from the Kroger employee, Kyle recognized some of the questions from the Kroger test as identical to ones on a mental health examination he had taken before being diagnosed with bipolar disorder (a diagnosis rendered about eighteen months before his job rejections).[16] For these reasons, Kyle suspected that the tests he had taken for these jobs had ruled him out on the basis of his bipolar disorder, though he had never told them of his diagnosis and was not legally required to do so.[17] Kyle's case was ultimately settled out of court.

Though that settlement was not made public, some companies appear to have been inspired by it to change their hiring practices. For example, Lowe's said it has changed its online application process to ensure that people with mental disabilities could have fairer consideration for opportunities.[18] Yet, a large number of companies are still offering similar tests, which could exclude a large portion of the U.S. population – especially workers such as Kyle, who have mental health conditions.[19]

Although the use of personality tests for employment continues to be lawful, the use of tests that tend to exclude certain portions of the population are not. In the 1984 case *Larry P. v. Riles*, the Ninth Circuit Court of Appeals reviewed a holding from the District Court for the Northern District of California, in which the District Court found that a school's use of IQ tests violated federal statutes and equal protection clauses of the U.S. and California Constitutions. The IQ tests had been used to determine students' placement in special education classes and were both racially and culturally biased. The IQ tests in question were used to place children into several groups: (1) the "trainable mentally retarded," a group of children with severe learning disabilities who could not benefit from schooling; (2) the "educable mentally retarded," a group of children who were considered incapable of being educated through the regular program, but who could benefit from special educational facilities; and (3) the children who could be placed in the regular program. In addition, there were two categories of students who, with help, could be returned to the regular school program even if they showed low IQ test scores: (4) "culturally disadvantaged minors," children with cultural or economic disadvantages "with potential for successfully completing a regular educational program" and (5) "educationally handicapped minors," students with marked learning or behavioral disorders who were capable of returning to a regular school program but who could not currently benefit from the regular schooling program.[20]

The District Court found that from 1968 until trial in 1977, Black children were significantly overrepresented in the "educable mentally retarded" (EMR) group at such a rate that was not likely to have occurred by chance, because of their lower

[16] O'Neil, "Personality Tests Are Failing American Workers. "
[17] Weber and Dwoskin, "Are Workplace Personality Tests Fair?"
[18] O'Neil, "Personality Tests Are Failing American Workers."
[19] Weber and Dwoskin, "Are Workplace Personality Tests Fair?"
[20] *Larry P. v. Riles*, 793 F.2d 969, 972 (9th Cir. 1984).

scores on the IQ tests. Then it found that the EMR group was "not designed to help students learn the necessary skills to return to the regular instructional program," but rather to teach "social adjustment" and "economic usefulness."[21] In fact, the students placed in EMR classes were provided with instruction that de-emphasized academic skills, so the students would naturally fall farther and farther behind children in the regular classes.[22] The program meant that an overrepresented portion of Black children were being placed into classes that would stunt their development because of their responses to an IQ test that had been developed on an all-white population.

On review, the Ninth Circuit confirmed that these tests violated the Rehabilitation Act of 1973, which states that "no otherwise qualified handicapped individual in the United States … shall solely by reason of his handicap, be … subjected to discrimination under any program or activity receiving Federal financial assistance."[23] The tests also violated the Education for All Handicapped Children Act, which provides that a state qualifying for federal assistance must establish "procedures to assure that testing and evaluation materials and procedures utilized for the purposes of evaluation and placement of handicapped children will be selected and administered so as not to be racially or culturally discriminatory."[24] Further, because they had a discriminatory impact on Black schoolchildren, the tests violated Title VII of the Civil Rights Act of 1964, which prohibits federal funding where individuals are subjected to discrimination based on their race.[25]

Under the Title VII framework, the school could escape liability by demonstrating that this disproportionate impact was required by educational necessity. To demonstrate this, the school argued that the EMR classes could present a benefit for Black children. However, the Ninth Circuit found this argument unconvincing, as the District Court had already suggested that EMR classes were "dead-end" classes that de-emphasize academic skills. Next, the school argued that even if the impact of the tests was adverse, it was not caused by discriminatory criteria (the IQ tests), but by these other non-discriminatory factors: (1) the placement was based on a number of evaluation tools, not solely the IQ tests; (2) the tests were validated for Black schoolchildren and therefore accurately reflected mental retardation in Black children; and (3) Black children have a higher percentage of mental retardation than white children. Naturally, the Ninth Circuit found these arguments to be equally unconvincing, as the school district could not prove that the scores were representative for Black children, since the tests had been developed primarily on white children. Yet, the Ninth Circuit reversed the District Court as to its holding of intentional discrimination under the Fourteenth Amendment because

[21] *Larry P. v. Riles,* 495 F. Supp. 926, 941 (N.D. CA 1979).
[22] *Larry P. v. Riles,* 495 F. Supp. 926, 941 (N.D. CA 1979).
[23] 29 U.S.C. § 794.
[24] 20 U.S.C. § 1412(5)(C).
[25] *Larry P. v. Riles,* 793 F.2d.

the pervasiveness of a discriminatory effect, without more evidence, could not be equated to discriminatory intent. Still, in so holding, the court made clear that IQ tests for schoolchildren must be shown to accurately place all students.[26]

In the case of personality tests, there is evidence that they are discriminatory to women, racial/ethnic monitories, and people with mental illness or cognitive disorders. First, if it is accepted that certain personality traits predominate in specific population groups (perhaps due to enculturation), then optimizing a given test for certain traits versus others may have adverse impacts on specific groups. For example, women (due to enculturation) may be statistically more likely than men to score high for traits such as nurturing or deferential and less likely to score high for traits such as assertive or controlling. Members of various races or nationalities may be statistically more or less likely to score particularly high for traits such as humility or confidence, risk aversion, risk-taking, conflict avoidance, cooperation, or independence.[27] The problems with determining personality traits as part of the job search are twofold: (1) whether any of these traits are causally related to job performance in the given position and (2) whether the test in question is *actually* able to measure these traits.

Since personality tests have become part of the job selection process, some studies have found them to favor white applicants. For example, one study of a major retailer's 1,363-store rollout of a Unicru personality test found significant gaps between the scores of Black and Latino applicants, compared to those of white applicants (nearly 55 percent of white candidates scored "green" compared to only about 47 percent of Black candidates).[28] In another case, Leprino Foods was accused of discriminatory hiring practices based on its pre-employment test, WorkKeys, which was used to select hires for on-call laborer positions. WorkKeys tested applicants' skills in mathematics, locating information, and observation; however, these skills were not critical to the entry-level tasks performed by on-call laborers, such as inspecting products, monitoring equipment, and maintaining sanitation at the facility. Because the company was unable to show that the test was related to the positions being offered, it entered into a consent decree mandating payment of back wages, interest, and benefits to 253 rejected African American, Latino, and Asian workers. It also agreed to discontinue use of the pre-employment test and hire at least thirteen of the original applicants.[29] In a similar case, the EEOC investigated Target for deploying pre-employment tests that disproportionately screened out applicants for

[26] *Larry P. v. Riles*, 793 F.2d.

[27] Julie Furr Youngman, "The Use and Abuse of Pre-Employment Personality Tests," *Business Horizons* 60, no. 3 (2017): 261–69.

[28] David H. Autor and David Scarborough, "Does Job Testing Harm Minority Workers? Evidence from Retail Establishments," *Quarterly Journal of Economics* 123, no. 1 (2008): 219–77.

[29] U.S. Dept. of Labor, "US Labor Department Settles Charges of Hiring Discrimination with Federal Contractor Leprino Foods," *U.S. Department of Labor Newsroom*, July 19, 2012, www.dol.gov/newsroom/releases/ofccp/ofccp20120719.

upper-level positions based on race and sex. The EEOC also found that an assessment performed by psychologists during Target's hiring process qualified as a pre-employment offer medical examination, which is verboten under the Americans with Disabilities Act (ADA). Target settled, agreeing to pay a $2.8 million fine and discontinue its use of the tests.[30]

In addition to racial discrimination, personality tests have also been shown to be a discriminatory tool to exclude applicants with mental illness. For example, in one study, JobsFirstNYC found that questions about emotional instability and depression were common in the personality tests they reviewed. In one of those tests used by CVS, candidates were asked to disclose whether they agreed or disagreed with statements such as "1) You change from happy to sad without any reason; 2) You get angry more often than nervous; 3) Your moods are steady from day to day."[31] After the ACLU of Rhode Island filed a complaint with the state's Commission for Human Rights, the Commission found "probable cause" that CVS's inclusion of these statements violated the ADA.[32]

Other than people with mental illness, neuro-atypical candidates are also at a disadvantage when confronted with personality tests. People on the autism spectrum may express emotion differently in writing in comparison to people who are neuro-typical, resulting in incorrect classifications about their emotional state or personality. Plus, applicants who have dyslexia may find it difficult to handle personality tests that require written communication.[33]

To complicate the issue further, applicants suffering from cognitive disorders might have a wide array of traits associated with those cognitive disorders that are reliably linked to personality tests. The irony is that some of those traits may actually work well for certain job positions, but most job personality tests are not sophisticated enough to make those distinctions and will simply eliminate the candidate. This is confirmed by a study which demonstrated that common traits of attention-deficit/hyperactivity disorder (ADHD) could be linked to certain personality traits commonly used in Five-Factor Model personality tests (such as Myers–Briggs). Specifically, the study found that although inattention (which is common with ADHD) is negatively associated with conscientiousness, hyperactivity (which is also common with ADHD) is consistent with extroversion, a trait desired by employers.[34]

30 EEOC, "Target Corporation to Pay $2.8 Million to Resolve EEOC Discrimination Finding," *U.S. EEOC Newsroom*, Aug. 24, 2015, www.eeoc.gov/newsroom/target-corporation-pay-28-million-resolve-eeoc-discrimination-finding.

31 ACLU RI, "ACLU and CVS/Pharmacy Resolve Discrimination Complaint," *ACLU of R. I. News*, July 19, 2011, www.riaclu.org/news/post/aclu-and-cvs-pharmacy-resolve-discrimination-complaint.

32 ACLU RI, "ACLU and CVS/Pharmacy Resolve Discrimination Complaint."

33 Anhong Guo et al., "Toward Fairness in AI for People with Disabilities: A Research Roadmap," *ACM SIGACCESS Accessibility and Computing* 125 (Oct. 2019): 1, https://doi.org/10.1145/3386296.3386298.

34 Laura E. Knouse et al., "Adult ADHD Symptoms and a Five Factor Model Traits in a Clinical Sample: A Structural Equation Modeling Approach," *Journal of Nervous Mental Disease* 20, no. 10 (Oct. 2014): 848–54.

4.1.1 *The Five-Factor Model of Personality*

The Five-Factor Model of personality, also known as the Big-Five Model, is a theory of personality that is currently widely accepted and deployed by psychologists to assess an individual's personality type. The Five-Factor Model uses five core personality traits to determine the personality makeup of an individual: conscientiousness, agreeableness, neuroticism, openness, and extroversion. The core personality traits used in the Five-Factor Model are not binary, meaning that their existence does not boil down to "yes" or "no" answers. The answers an individual gives while taking a Five-Factor Model personality test place that individual at a specific point on a sliding-scale spectrum which determines how much of each of the core personality traits that individual possesses. Where an individual lands on each personality trait's sliding scale is meant to help psychiatrists predict how they are likely to behave in various situations.[35]

For example, within the Five-Factor Model, the personality trait of conscientiousness is operationalized to determine how an individual might regulate their impulses and participate in goal-oriented activities. An individual's level of self-control, inhibition, and continuity of behavior are all examined to determine a level of conscientiousness that is meant to predict if that individual could be described as someone who is organized, disciplined, and careful, among other similar attributes. Under this model, someone who is determined to have problems controlling their impulses can be described as someone who may have problems completing tasks and/or reaching goals.[36]

The personality trait of agreeableness seeks to predict how an individual may interact with others in various settings. An individual's ability to trust others and how much they care about being accepted or liked are examined to determine a level of agreeableness, which is meant to predict if that individual can be expected to want to help others, work in groups, and/or generally be a likeable team player. Someone who scores low on the agreeableness scale can be described as someone that tends to be uncooperative, unsympathetic, and even manipulative under the Five-Factor Model.[37]

An individual's level of neuroticism is measured to determine how they view the world, and how they may react to troubling events or difficulties that occur in their lives. Those who are determined to have higher levels of neuroticism are considered to be less emotionally stable than those who are determined to have lower levels of neuroticism. Someone who scores low on the neuroticism scale is considered to be more calm and secure in themselves and the world around

---

[35] Robert R. McCrae and Oliver P. John, "An Introduction to the Five-Factor Model and Its Applications," *Journal of Personality* 60, no. 2 (1992): 175–215. http://psych.colorado.edu/~carey/courses/psyc5112/readings/psnbig5_mccrae03.pdf.

[36] McCrae and John, "Introduction to the Five-Factor Model and Its Applications."

[37] McCrae and John, "Introduction to the Five-Factor Model and Its Applications."

them, and generally have higher self-esteem than someone who is assigned a higher score.[38]

Next, the Five-Factor Model examines an individual's openness. Someone who scores high on the scale of openness is considered more creative, unconventional, and apt to try new things. Conversely, if an individual scores low on the scale of openness, then they are considered to be more predictable, traditional, and resistant to change.

The last personality trait that is examined by the Five-Factor Model is extroversion. An individual who is determined to have a high level of extroversion is considered to be someone who is outgoing, enjoys social interaction, and is more likely to seek excitement. Someone who is found to have a low level of extroversion is considered to be more reserved, likely enjoys being alone, and is less likely to enjoy being the center of attention.

The Five-Factor Model was developed in the 1980s and became a popular tool for employers and recruiters to use in identifying and hiring new employees in the 1990s through the present day. The most popular personality test that is based on the Five-Factor Model is the Meyers–Briggs test. Proponents of the model believe that the trait of conscientiousness is consistently linked to job performance. One conclusion is that individuals who are found to have higher levels of conscientiousness perform better at their jobs, while those with lower levels of conscientiousness are found to perform worse.[39]

Opponents of the use of the Five-Factor Model in hiring point to the lack of evidence that all the personality factors are connected to job performance or competency. They argue that pre-employment personality tests based on the Five-Factor Model go too far in examining the mindset of job applicants, as exemplified by the fact that the results of these assessments can be easily linked to mental health disorders.[40] This is a credible concern given that the Five-Factor Model is also deployed to assist mental health professionals in diagnosing mental health disorders.

4.1.2 *The Five-Factor Model's Relation to the DSM-5*

The American Psychiatric Association (APA) officially adopted the Five-Factor Model's method and incorporated it into the fifth edition of the *Diagnostic and Statistical Manual of Mental Disorders* (DSM-5), published in 2013. The DSM seeks to classify mental disorders through the use of consistent methods and standard criteria, and is the primary authority psychiatrists use in diagnosing mental

---

[38] McCrae and John, "Introduction to the Five-Factor Model and Its Applications."
[39] Robert E. Gibby and Michael J. Zickar, "A History of the Early Days of Personality Testing in American Industry: An Obsession with Adjustment," *History of Psychology* 11, no. 3 (2008): 164, 178, www.researchgate.net/publication/23562101_A_history_of_the_early_days_of_personality_testing_in_American_industry_An_obsession_with_adjustment.
[40] Youngman, "Use and Abuse of Pre-Employment Personality Tests."

health disorders in the United States. Since the first edition was published in 1952, each new edition of the DSM has sought to improve the diagnosis and treatment of individuals facing potential mental disorders, steadily adding, removing, and revising mental disorders based on the latest research.[41]

The APA's backing of the Five-Factor Model represented a clear break from the previous "categorical" approach to diagnosing mental disorders. The categorical model diagnoses mental disorders by determining if an individual has symptoms or characteristics that are typical of the disorder examined, assuming that each mental health disorder either occurs or does not – either an individual has the mental health disorder or they do not. This approach made for wide-ranging diagnosis categories that cast a wide net across many individuals suffering different levels of mental health impairment. In contrast, the Five-Factor Model is presented as a "dimensional" model that allows for a range of levels quantifying each personality trait.[42]

The DSM's adoption of the Five-Factor Model was meant to assist mental health professionals in determining both the existence of a mental health disorder and also its severity. The DSM-5 updated the diagnostic methods that are to be applied by mental health professionals by expanding and changing the criteria used in determining the existence and severity of many mental health disorders. This approach aims to give a more accurate and detailed diagnosis for individuals suffering from mental health issues in an attempt to more effectively treat them. Prior to the adoption of the Five-Factor Model, all previous versions of the *Diagnostic and Statistical Manual of Mental Disorders* published by the APA were based on the categorical model.[43]

Since the Five-Factor Model was "codified" by the APA in the DSM-5 manual, personality testing businesses have boomed. It is estimated that approximately 80 percent of Fortune 500 companies currently use pre-employment personality testing of some kind during the application process – and most of that testing is based on the Five-Factor Model. This demonstrates how mammoth the personality testing industry has become. However, companies deploying pre-employment assessments based on the Five-Factor Model should take caution, as the EEOC now has a special enforcement focus against employers who are alleged to systemically discriminate and/or screen out certain types of applicants.[44]

---

[41] APA, *Diagnostic and Statistical Manual of Mental Disorders* (DSM-5) (Washington DC: American Psychological Association, 2015). See APA, "DSM History," www.psychiatry.org/psychiatrists/practice/dsm/history-of-the-dsm (accessed May 10, 2021).

[42] Melissa Potuzak et al., "Categorical vs Dimensional Classifications of Psychotic Disorders," *Comprehensive Psychiatry* 53, no. 8 (2012): 1118–29.

[43] See, e.g., APA, "Highlights of Changes from DSM-IV-TR to DSM-5," https://psychiatry.msu.edu/_files/docs/Changes-From-DSM-IV-TR-to-DSM-5.pdf (accessed May 10, 2021).

[44] See EEOC, "Systemic Enforcement at the EEOC," www.eeoc.gov/systemic-enforcement-eeoc (accessed May 10, 2021).

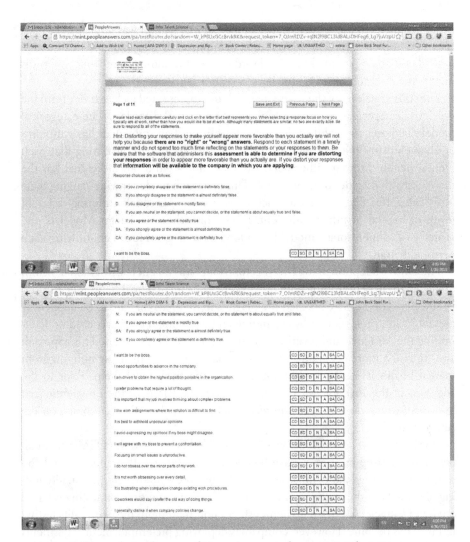

FIGURE 4.1 Screenshots of page 1 of Kroger's pre-employment test that states instructions and includes questions to measure the applicant's agreeableness

4.1.3 *The Five Factor Model and Kroger's Pre-Employment Personality Test*

This section reviews the Kroger pre-employment personality test that Kyle Behm took, with screenshots taken by his father and attorney Roland Behm on April 30, 2015.[45] As Figure 4.1 shows, this test follows the Five-Factor Model wherein test takers are asked to give answers that range from strongly agree to strongly disagree with regard to the statement made in the question.

---

[45] These screenshots are reproduced here with the permission of Roland Behm who took them.

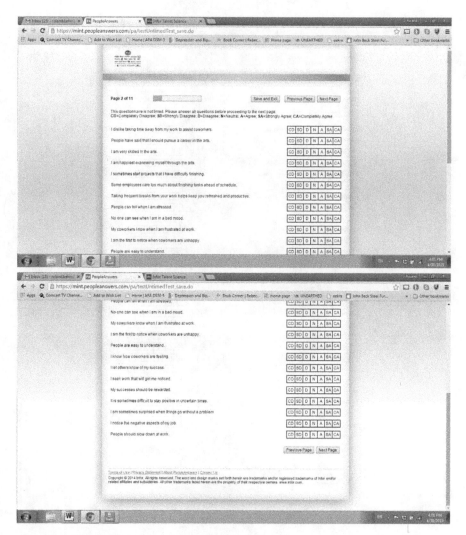

FIGURE 4.2 Screenshots of page 2 of Kroger's pre-employment test questions that measure levels of openness and neuroticism

The first page of the Kroger pre-employment personality test asked questions mostly related to how much ambition and submissiveness an applicant has, including how they would react to authority and conflict, while examining the applicant's drive for success. The trait of conscientiousness is examined by including questions relating to self-discipline, achievement striving, and deliberation. Questions relating to the applicant's compliance and submission to authority fall into the personality trait of agreeableness as examined by the Five-Factor Model.

Figure 4.2 shows the second page of the test. Here the applicant is asked about their artistic abilities, their ability to control their outward emotions, and their need

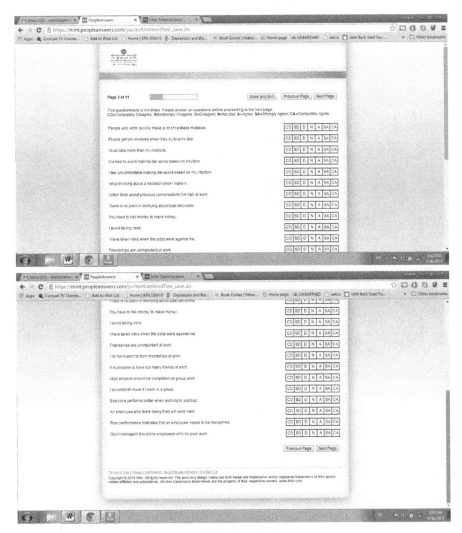

FIGURE 4.3 Screenshots of page 3 of Kroger's pre-employment test, with questions to measure neuroticism through an applicant's level of self-consciousness, impulsiveness, anxiety, and vulnerability

for celebration and acceptance from others. Along with more questions digging into his ability to be productive, Kyle was asked questions to measure his levels of openness and neuroticism. These questions start to pry more into the applicant's mental makeup, and this is where this exam starts to show itself as more than just a personality test.

Next, on page 3 (Figure 4.3), the applicant is asked questions related to their decision-making, their risk-taking, and how much they dwell on decisions they have made. Also, the applicant is asked questions to measure how they would interact

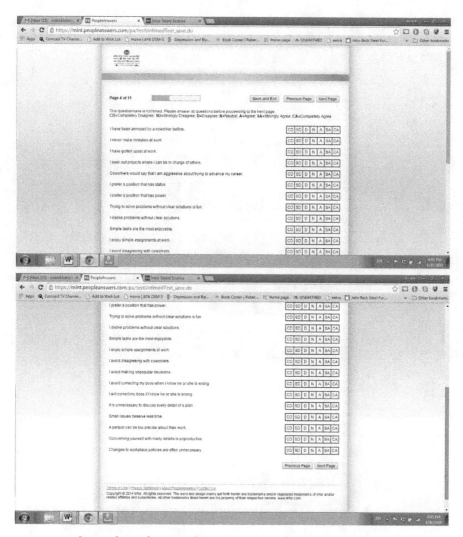

FIGURE 4.4 Screenshots of page 4 of Kroger's pre-employment test, with questions to examine neuroticism and extroversion

socially with co-workers. These questions measure the applicant's level of self-consciousness, impulsiveness, anxiety, and vulnerability. All of these traits fall under the personality trait of neuroticism as measured by the Five-Factor Model. The applicant is also questioned about discipline and the threat of being fired as a form of motivation to perform at work.

On the next page (Figure 4.4), Kroger asks the applicant about how easily annoyed they can be at work, their levels of openness, and their assertiveness and ambition to gain higher levels of status and power. Here, the applicant's levels of neuroticism

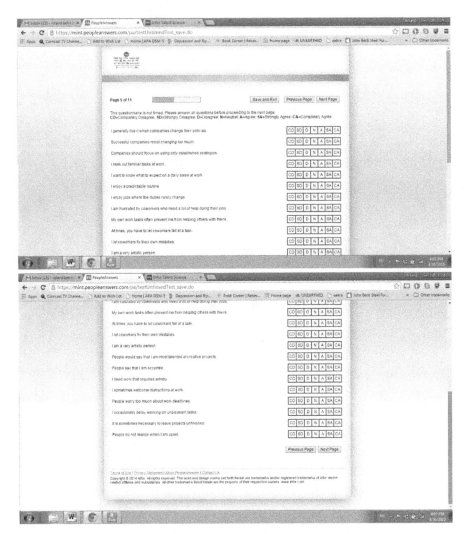

FIGURE 4.5 Screenshots of page 5 of Kroger's pre-employment test, with questions that examine openness and agreeableness, along with conscientiousness

and extroversion are being examined through the Five-Factor Model. Again, the test is showing itself as much more than just a personality test.

The fifth page of Kroger's pre-employment personality test (see Figure 4.5) asks the applicant questions about their ability and willingness to adapt to change, their desire to help co-workers, and their perceived artistic abilities. The applicant's levels of openness and agreeableness are examined with these questions. The applicant's conscientiousness is also again examined with questions relating to their ability to meet deadlines and how important they perceive deadlines to be.

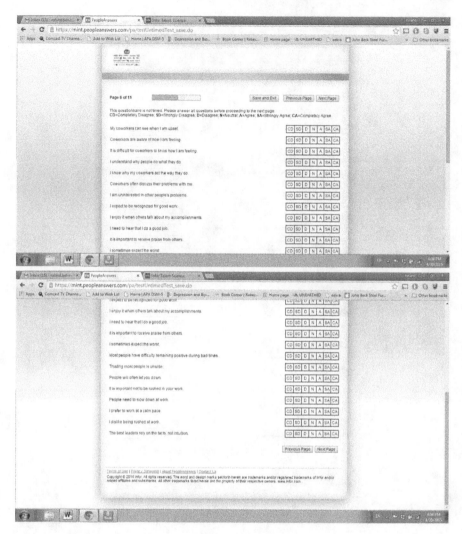

FIGURE 4.6 Screenshots of page 6 of Kroger's pre-employment test, with questions that examine openness and agreeableness, along with conscientiousness

On page six of Kroger's pre-employment personality test (see Figure 4.6), Kyle was asked questions about his ability to control his emotions at work, his interest in interacting with co-workers, and his need for praise at work. His levels of neuroticism and extroversion are measured in these questions according to the Five-Factor Model. His trust in others is also examined, along with how deliberate he would be with work-related tasks. Only the questions relating to deliberation measure the trait of conscientiousness.

On the seventh page of Kroger's pre-employment personality test (Figure 4.7), Kyle was asked questions about how much he follows his instincts and intuition,

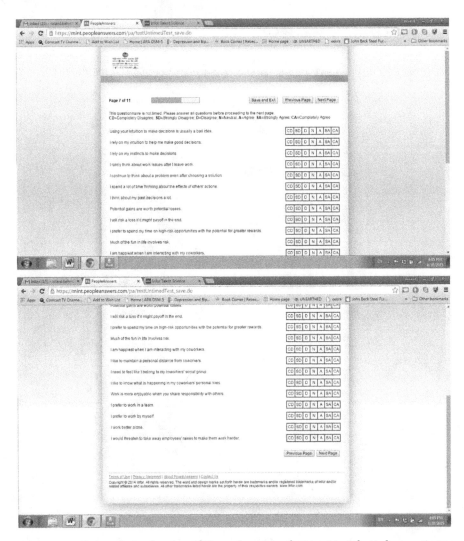

FIGURE 4.7 Screenshots of page 7 of Kroger's pre-employment test that asks questions that examine openness and neuroticism

how likely he is to take risks, and how much he dwells on decisions he has made. He is also asked questions about his need for social interaction and acceptance. Kyle's personality traits for openness and neuroticism are further examined by these questions as outlined by the Five-Factor Model.

On page eight, Kroger asks the applicant about their need for power and acceptance at work, their ability to submit to authority, and how detail oriented they might be (see Figure 4.8). The applicant is asked about how challenged they want to be at work, along with their ability to accept change. The applicant's

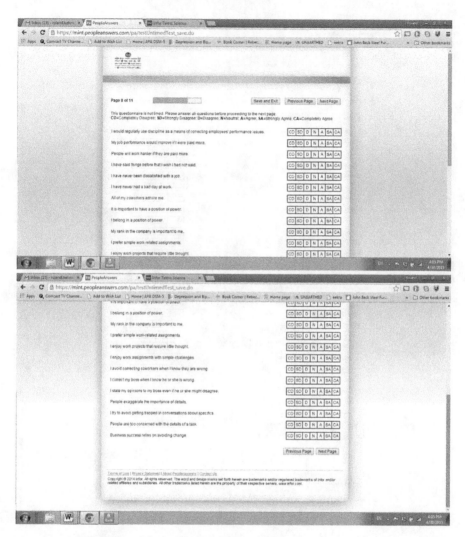

FIGURE 4.8 Screenshots of page 8 of Kroger's pre-employment test that asks questions that examine an applicant's conscientiousness as well as extroversion and neuroticism

conscientiousness is further examined here, along with their levels of extroversion and neuroticism.

On the ninth page of Kroger's pre-employment personality test (see Figure 4.9), the applicant is again asked about their desire for routine and creativity, and how important it is for tasks to completed on time. The applicant is also asked their opinion on how much help co-workers deserve to have in the workplace. Again, the applicant's ability to control their emotions at work is measured by the questions towards the end of page nine. The personality traits of openness,

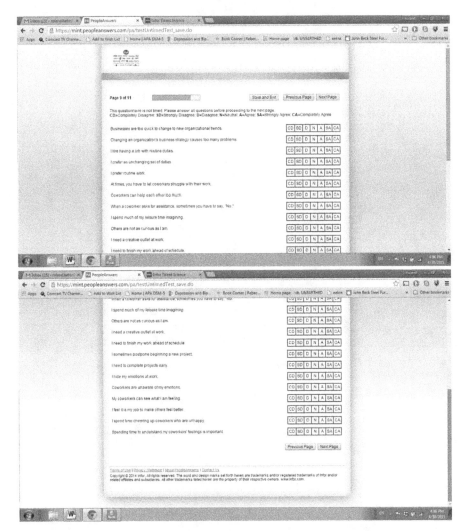

FIGURE 4.9 Screenshot of page 9 of Kroger's pre-employment test that asks questions that measure openness, neuroticism, and conscientiousness

neuroticism, and conscientiousness are measured in these questions through the Five-Factor Model.

On page ten of the Kroger pre-employment exam (see Figure 4.10), Kyle's ability to trust others was measured, along with how much recognition he desires for successes at work. In an effort to measure his decision-making process, he was asked questions related to how much he follows his intuition and how much he likes to take risks. Again, his levels of agreeableness were being measured, along with the traits of neuroticism and extroversion as outlined by the Five-Factor Model.

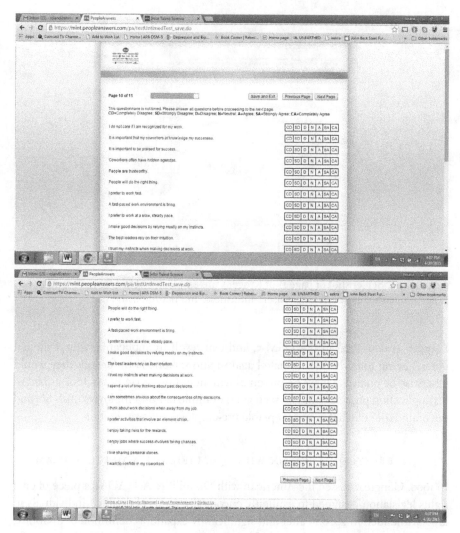

FIGURE 4.10 Screenshots of page 10 of Kroger's pre-employment test, asking questions to measure the applicant's agreeableness, neuroticism, and extroversion

On the final page of Kroger's pre-employment exam (see Figure 4.11), Kyle was asked a combination of questions that examined his need for social interaction, his motivations, and his ability to control stress. In the final question, he was also asked about his self-confidence. His levels of extroversion, conscientiousness, and neuroticism again were examined through the use of the Five-Factor Model.

As you can see, the entire pre-employment exam tests personality characteristics following the Five-Factor Model of personality testing. The answers given on this test could be deployed by a mental health professional to diagnose a mental health

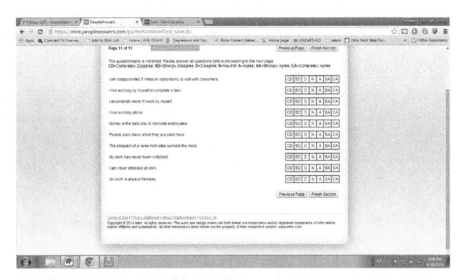

FIGURE 4.11 Screenshot of page 11 of Kroger's pre-employment test that asks questions to again measure extroversion, conscientiousness, and neuroticism

disorder as described in the DSM-5, and can result in applicants (with a mental illness) being unfairly discriminated against and screened out for jobs they would otherwise be qualified for. The pre-employment test that Kyle Behm took as part of his application process could be seen as an example of how employers push beyond the boundaries of what is an acceptable pre-employment examination.

4.2 EEOC GUIDANCE ON WHAT QUALIFIES AS A MEDICAL EXAM

In 1990, Congress passed the American with Disabilities Act (ADA), a piece of civil rights legislation designed to explicitly encode the rights of disabled individuals in law.[46] Amended in 2008 to alter and significantly expand its definition of disability, the ADA applies to employers with fifteen or more employees and features specific protections for disabled individuals in various settings, including the job application process. The updated ADA Amendments Act of 2008 (ADAAA) overturned several Supreme Court decisions that Congress believed applied the definition of disability too narrowly, which had resulted in the failure to protect numerous classes of individuals suffering from various health conditions.[47] The ADA specifically

---

[46] ADA National Network, "What Is the Americans with Disabilities Act (ADA)?" www.adata.org/learn-about-ada (last visited Mar. 17, 2021).

[47] EEOC, "Notice Concerning the Americans with Disabilities Act (ADA) Amendments Act of 2008," Mar. 25, 2011, www.eeoc.gov/statutes/notice-concerning-americans-disabilities-act-ada-amendments-act-2008. See also, EEOC, "Fact Sheet: Disability Discrimination," Jan. 15, 1997, www.eeoc.gov/laws/guidance/fact-sheet-disability-discrimination.

regulates pre-employment assessments, prohibiting the use of "qualification standards, employment tests, or other selection criteria that screen out or tend to screen out an individual with a disability or a class of individuals with disabilities" unless the assessment or criterion is proven to be a job-related business necessity.[48]

Beyond pre-employment assessments, the ADA also includes specific provisions concerning medical examinations. While an employer is permitted to "make pre-employment inquiries into the ability of an applicant to perform job-related functions," the ADA prohibits any medical examination or inquiry to determine an applicant's disability status unless it constitutes a job-related business necessity.[49] However, regardless of job-relatedness, the ADA prohibits an employer from requiring any medical exams before a conditional offer of employment is made.[50]

The EEOC is responsible for investigating allegations of workplace discrimination and enforcing federal laws such as the ADA.[51] As necessary, the EEOC publishes enforcement guidance on each form of discrimination prohibited by federal law to provide the EEOC's interpretation of each law.[52] The EEOC Enforcement Guidance on Disability-Related Inquires and Medical Examinations of employees under the ADA defines a medical exam as a test that "seeks information about an individual's physical or mental impairments or health."[53] A test that measures traits such as honesty, preferences, and habits is not considered a medical exam by the EEOC for the purposes of the ADA.[54]

The EEOC has outlined a seven-factor test to analyze and determine whether a test qualifies as a medical exam for purposes of the ADA, and noted that the existence of any one of the listed factors could be enough to deem a test or procedure as medical. The following factors should be examined to determine whether a pre-employment test is a medical exam:[55]

- Whether the test is administered by a healthcare professional
- Whether the test is interpreted by a healthcare professional
- Whether the test is designed to reveal an impairment of physical or mental health
- Whether the test is invasive

---

[48] 42 U.S.C. § 12112(b)(6).

[49] 42 U.S.C. § 12112(d)(2).

[50] EEOC, "Questions and Answers: Enforcement Guidance on Disability Related Inquiries and Medical Examinations under the Americans with Disabilities Act," July 27, 2000, www.eeoc.gov/laws/guidance/questions-and-answers-enforcement-guidance-disability-related-inquiries-and-medical.

[51] See EEOC, "Overview," www.eeoc.gov/overview (accessed May 10, 2021).

[52] See EEOC, "Enforcement Guidances and Related Documents," www.eeoc.gov/enforcement-guidances-and-related-documents (accessed May 10, 2021).

[53] EEOC, "Enforcement Guidance on Disability-Related Inquiries and Medical Examinations of Employees under the ADA," July 26, 2000, [hereafter "Enforcement Guidance"], www.eeoc.gov/laws/guidance/enforcement-guidance-disability-related-inquiries-and-medical-examinations-employees.

[54] EEOC, "Enforcement Guidance."

[55] EEOC, "Enforcement Guidance."

- Whether the test measures an employee's performance of a task or measures their physiological responses to performing the task
- Whether the test is normally given in a medical setting
- Whether medical equipment is used

In determining whether a pre-employment test is a medical exam, the EEOC further instructs that a medical exam is one that is likely to elicit information about a disability, which can provide a basis for discriminatory treatment.[56] Since there is not a blanket answer on what is or is not a medical exam for the purposes of the ADA, the courts must analyze each case individually to determine which tests violate the ADA's rule against pre-employment medical exams.

This analysis was used in the case of *Karraker v. Rent-a-Center*, where employees seeking a promotion were required to take the Minnesota Multiphasic Personality Inventory (MMPI), a personality test. The Seventh Circuit Court of Appeals found that the MMPI constituted a medical exam under the ADA because the test was "designed, at least in part, to reveal a mental illness and has the effect of hurting the employment prospects of one with a mental disability."[57] The MMPI, the defendants claimed, was just used to measure personality traits. The court found that along with measuring personality traits, the MMPI also measures an individual's level of depression, hypochondria, hysteria, paranoia, and mania, all of which can lead to a diagnosis of a psychiatric disorder.[58] The MMPI included questions asking test takers to answer true or false to statements such as:

- I see things or animals or people around me that others do not see.
- I commonly hear voices without knowing where they are coming from.
- At times I have fits of laughing and crying that I cannot control.
- My soul sometimes leaves my body.

How the answers to these questions would help a Rent-a-Center manager do their job more effectively remains unclear. Rent-a-Center argued that the MMPI merely tested a "state of mood" and conceded that the test taker might be more likely to score higher on the depression scale if they were simply having a bad day because they lost their keys that morning.[59]

The EEOC has taken action in several other cases where employers have been accused of violating Title VII of the Civil Rights Act of 1964 by allegedly administering pre-employment tests that seek to discriminate against applicants for reasons such as race, sex, or national origin. One such case involved national electronics retailer Best Buy. After a long investigation, the EEOC determined that over the course of a seven-year period, Best Buy's use of pre-employment

---

[56] EEOC, "Enforcement Guidance."
[57] *Karraker v. Rent-a-Center, Inc.*, 411 F.3d 831, 836 (7th Cir. 2005).
[58] *Karraker v. Rent-a-Center, Inc.*, 411 F.3d.
[59] *Karraker v. Rent-a-Center, Inc.*, 411 F.3d. at 836.

personality testing screened out and disadvantaged several applicants based on their race and national origin. Instead of litigating the issue, Best Buy and the EEOC resolved the case with Best Buy agreeing to discontinue the use of the assessments, while also agreeing to regular reporting of its hiring data to the EEOC for several years.[60]

The EEOC simultaneously announced the resolution of a separate but related case involving CVS pharmacy's pre-employment testing that the EEOC believed also screened out and impacted specific applicants based on their race and national origin. Through the EEOC's investigation, they determined that CVS used these pre-employment exams over the course of an eight-year period, starting in 2002 and ending in 2010. The EEOC appears to have made an identical agreement with CVS, where the company agreed to discontinue the use of the assessments while also improving its hiring process to prevent future discrimination. CVS also agreed to regularly submit reporting data to the EEOC for several years to confirm their adherence to their agreement with the EEOC.[61]

These cases illustrate that if an employer is using a pre-employment personality test of any kind, there is the potential for an EEOC investigation to be triggered by any complaints. An investigation may lead to potential action against the employer if the EEOC believes that the employer administered an improper test.

4.2.1 *Tests Based on Five-Factor Model Are Medical Exams*

Since 2013, the Five-Factor Model has been adopted and used by mental health professionals to diagnose mental health disorders. As discussed earlier, the APA adopted the Five-Factor Model's dimensional approach to determine not only whether a mental health disorder exists, but also how severe the disorder may be depending on the resulting levels of each personality trait measured by the Five-Factor Model – a clear break from the previous categorical approach used by previous editions of the DSM. This leaves the newest mental health diagnostic manual, DSM-5, and the ADA in conflict. When determining whether a pre-employment personality test is a medical exam, the EEOC and the court use a seven-factor test, as discussed previously. The third factor considered by this test asks "whether the test is designed to reveal an impairment of physical or mental health."[62] Since DSM-5 is now based on the Five-Factor Model, it is fair to say that *any* pre-employment personality test that is based on the Five-Factor Model should be *per se* considered a medical exam. This

---

[60] EEOC, "Best Buy and EEOC Reach Agreement to Resolve Discrimination Charge," *EEOC Newsroom*, July 6, 2018, www.eeoc.gov/newsroom/best-buy-and-eeoc-reach-agreement-resolve-discrimination-charge.

[61] EEOC, "CVS Caremark Corporation and EEOC Reach Agreement to Resolve Discrimination Charge," *EEOC Newsroom*, July 6, 2018, www.eeoc.gov/newsroom/cvs-caremark-corporation-and-eeoc-reach-agreement-resolve-discrimination-charge.

[62] *Karraker v. Rent-a-Center, Inc.*, 411 F.3d. at 835.

determination can be solely based on a consideration of the third factor of the seven-factor test from the ADA.[63]

Additionally, employers do not need to have actual or constructive knowledge of whether a job applicant actually has a diagnosed disability to be in violation of the rules of the ADA in a pre-employment personality test scenario. A job applicant's disability status has no bearing on whether a pre-employment exam violates the ADA.[64] The EEOC Enforcement Guidance makes it abundantly clear that the ADA's rules on inquiries and pre-employment exams apply to every potential and actual employee, regardless of disability.[65]

Note that this does not categorically preclude employers from giving pre-employment tests. It does mean, however, that a pre-employment test based on the very method that mental health professionals use to diagnose mental health disorders is, in itself, a medical exam. If this test is not a medical exam, then why would the American Psychiatric Association abandon methods and practices that were used in the first four editions of their diagnostic manual in favor of the method and approach used by the Five-Factor Model? The DSM-5 Task Force spent nearly six years examining research and information related to the Five-Factor Model while assembling the DSM-5, which adopted the Five Factor Model.[66]

Moreover, an employer's claim that a given test is not for a medical purpose does not prevent said test from being considered a medical exam, for the purposes of the ADA. Employers are not exempt from liability by feigning ignorance of their pre-employment personality tests' diagnostic abilities and medical application.[67] For example, the Sixth Circuit Court in *Kroll v. White Lake Ambulance Authority* explained the irrelevance of an employer's intent when administering pre-employment personality tests. The Court further discussed and used an EEOC-provided example found in its enforcement guidance to demonstrate what it considers to be an illegal pre-employment medical exam:

> A psychological test is designed to reveal mental illness, but a particular employer says it does not give the test to disclose mental illness (for example, the employer says it uses the test to disclose just tastes and habits). But, the test also is interpreted by a psychologist, and is routinely used in a clinical setting to provide evidence that can be used to diagnose mental health (for example, whether an applicant has paranoid tendencies, or is depressed). Under these facts, this test is a medical examination.[68]

[63] See *Karraker v. Rent-a-Center, Inc.*, 411 F.3d at 836.
[64] See, e.g., *Harrison v. Benchmark Elecs. Huntsville, Inc.*, 593 F.3d 1206, 1211–12 (11th Cir. 2010), *Murdock v. Washington*, 193 F.3d 510, 512 (7th Cir. 1999), *Fredenburg v. Contra Costa Cnty. Dep't of Health Servs.*, 172 F.3d 1176, 1182 (9th Cir. 1999), *Griffin v. Steeltek, Inc.*, 160 F.3d 591 (10th Cir. 1998).
[65] See EEOC, "Enforcement Guidance."
[66] See APA, "DSM History."
[67] EEOC, "Enforcement Guidance."
[68] *Kroll v. White Lake Ambulance Authority*, 691 F.3d 809, 816–817 (6th Cir. 2012).

Thus, the *Kroll* case dismissed the typical defenses that employers use when their pre-employment testing methods are questioned: a lack of intent to use the test as a medical exam and placing the blame on the personality testing company for selling them an assessment that potentially violates federal law.

This raises a question: If employers are prohibited from using tests like the Meyers–Briggs in pre-employment testing, what types of alternatives do they have? The answer to this can be found in personality trait research and analysis using the factors in the Five-Factor Model itself. Studies have shown that the trait of conscientiousness is "the most potent noncognitive predictor of occupational performance."[69] Conscientiousness is the one factor out of the Five-Factor Model that actually measures an individual's habits towards productivity and task completion through its assessment of an individual's impulse control. While other personality traits may have a causal link towards job performance, conscientiousness is the only trait measured in the Five-Factor Model that could reasonably determine an applicant's competence, tendency to procrastinate, and self-discipline, among other job-related characteristics.[70] Thus, a pre-employment personality test that only included questions related to conscientiousness could be a solution that satisfies both employers and the ADA. Looking solely at a job applicant's ability to control impulses that prevent job efficiency could allow employers to evaluate the applicant, without adding other questions that could amount to an illegal pre-employment medical exam.

4.3 EMPLOYERS' DUTIES IN RELATION TO CONFIDENTIAL MEDICAL INFORMATION

It is worth noting here another legal issue that might arise from pre-employment testing. Under the federal Medical Records Regulation, an employer is required to maintain information collected from a medical exam regarding an applicant, place that information in a separate file, and treat the information as a confidential medical record.[71] When a potential employee alerts an employer to the existence of a disability, the employer is required to follow federal laws to reasonably accommodate and not discriminate against the potential employee.[72] When people are diagnosed with a physical or mental disability, out of fear of being treated unfairly, they understandably may keep their medical diagnosis to themselves when they apply for jobs.

If the job applicant is required to take a pre-employment personality assessment, then the employer's duty to follow the requirements of the Medical Records Regulation can arise if the assessment is deemed to be an improper medical exam. If an employer is found to be in violation of the Medical Records Regulation for not

---

[69] Michael P. Wilmot and Deniz S. Ones, "A Century of Research on Conscientiousness at Work," *PNAS* 116, no. 46 (Nov. 12, 2019): 23004–23010, www.pnas.org/content/116/46/23004.short.

[70] Wilmot and Ones, "A Century of Research on Conscientiousness at Work."

[71] 29 C.F.R. § 1630.14(d)(4)(i).

[72] 29 C.F.R. § 1630.14(d)(5).

properly handling the confidential medical information regarding a job applicant, they can face significant sanctions and heavy fines. An employer can be sanctioned for a violation of the Medical Records Regulation whether they intended to give a medical exam or not.

4.4 PRE-EMPLOYMENT TESTING AND AUTISM SPECTRUM APPLICANTS

Besides applicants with mental illness, personality tests can also disadvantage individuals on the autism spectrum. In 2018, the EEOC filed suit against national discount and costume retailer Party City for refusing to hire an otherwise qualified employee who was on the autism spectrum and suffered from severe anxiety. The applicant had worked on building her self-confidence through help from Easter Seals of New Hampshire over a period of several years before she applied for a position at Party City. When the applicant applied for the job at Party City, she had already successfully worked in previous retail jobs and previously volunteered at a day care center. The applicant appeared at her interview accompanied by her job coach from Easter Seals, which proved to be a problem for the hiring manager. According to the EEOC, the hiring manager told the job coach that they had previously hired people who needed job coaches due to disabilities, but that the experiences at Party City with hiring people "like that" had not been successful.[73] The hiring manager then concluded the meeting by apparently telling the job coach in a patronizing manner "Thank you for bringing her here" while the applicant was still in the room.[74]

After refusing to hire the applicant, Party City hired six people in the following days, two of whom had no prior work history. Of the hires with no prior work experience, one was sixteen years old and the other was a recent high school graduate. The EEOC asserted that Party City violated the protections of the ADA by failing to provide reasonable accommodations to the qualified applicant to aid with her disability; in this case, the use of a job coach.[75] Party City ultimately settled its case with the EEOC, agreeing to pay $155,000, along with agreeing to improve its hiring policies and no longer refuse the use of a job coach as a reasonable accommodation.[76]

In another case, the EEOC filed suit against a Maryland company which failed to hire an individual once he disclosed that he was autistic. The company allegedly initially considered the applicant highly qualified for the lab technician job in question, "fast-track[ing] [the candidate's] participation in the hiring process"[77]

[73] EEOC, "EEOC Sues Party City for Disability Discrimination," *EEOC Newsroom*, Sept. 19, 2018, www.eeoc.gov/newsroom/eeoc-sues-party-city-disability-discrimination.
[74] EEOC, "Party City to Pay $155,000 to Settle EEOC Disability Discrimination Lawsuit," *EEOC Newsroom*, Apr. 22, 2019, www.eeoc.gov/newsroom/party-city-pay-155000-settle-eeoc-disability-discrimination-lawsuit.
[75] EEOC, "EEOC Sues Party City for Disability Discrimination."
[76] EEOC, "Party City to Pay $155,000 to Settle EEOC Disability Discrimination Lawsuit."
[77] EEOC, "Randstad US Sued by EEOC for Disability Discrimination," *EEOC Newsroom*, May 13, 2011, www.eeoc.gov/newsroom/randstad-us-sued-eeoc-disability-discrimination.

as a result. Once the applicant disclosed his disability, however, "he was told that the lab technician position had been put 'on hold.'"[78] Ultimately, the applicant was not hired and the company went on to fill the position with another recruit. The EEOC argued that this adverse employment decision was made in response to the applicant's autism disclosure, in violation of the ADA.[79]

In a recent EEOC enforcement action against a Subway restaurant franchise in Bloomington, Indiana, the agency argued that the franchise "violated federal law by rejecting a hard-of-hearing applicant because of his hearing and resultant speech impairments."[80] The franchise allegedly chose not to hire a hearing impaired candidate "because of his disability, citing a 'communication concern' due to the applicant's 'hearing' and 'speaking.'"[81] The EEOC argued that this adverse employment action constitutes disability discrimination that violates the ADA. This is a significant action by the EEOC because the agency has now declared that it does not simply allow employers to argue that an impairment materially disqualifies a disabled individual from a given job. While sandwich makers with specific ways of speaking may have been typical in the Subway franchise, or in the employer's view may have even been preferable, the EEOC effectively stated that such speaking patterns are not a legitimate consideration for job qualification such that the deaf individual may be disqualified.[82]

As Party City, Randstad US, and Subway learned, refusing to hire an applicant simply because of their disability and refusing to provide reasonable accommodations to the applicant are both violations of the protections of the ADA. In addition, individuals with disabilities are unfairly targeted in pre-employment exams that are based on the Five-Factor Model. For example, job applicants who are diagnosed as being on the autism spectrum face challenges in expressing emotions or picking up on social cues, resulting in any test misreading their mood or temperament. Pre-employment tests based on the Five-Factor Model may thus consistently return negative results for those on the autism spectrum and thus could be considered discrimination based on a disability.[83]

4.5 A COMPLIANT PRE-EMPLOYMENT TEST

The EEOC took action against CVS for using a pre-employment test during the application process that screened out applicants based on their race and national origin over an eight-year period. After the case was resolved, CVS pharmacy's pre-employment test took the form of a "virtual job tryout" that puts the applicant in the

---

[78] EEOC, "Randstad US Sued by EEOC for Disability Discrimination."

[79] EEOC, "Randstad US Sued by EEOC for Disability Discrimination."

[80] EEOC, "Subway Franchisee Sued by EEOC for Disability Discrimination," *EEOC Newsroom*, Sept. 23, 2020, www.eeoc.gov/newsroom/subway-franchisee-sued-eeoc-disability-discrimination.

[81] EEOC, "Subway Franchisee Sued by EEOC for Disability Discrimination."

[82] EEOC, "Subway Franchisee Sued by EEOC for Disability Discrimination."

[83] Guo, "Toward Fairness in AI for People with Disabilities: A Research Roadmap."

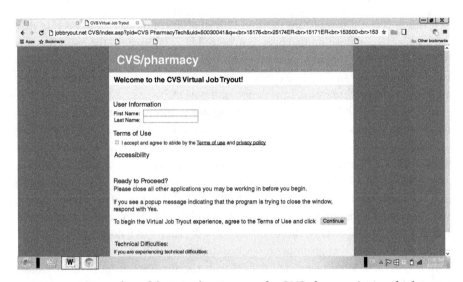

FIGURE 4.12 Screenshot of the introduction page for CVS pharmacy's virtual job tryout

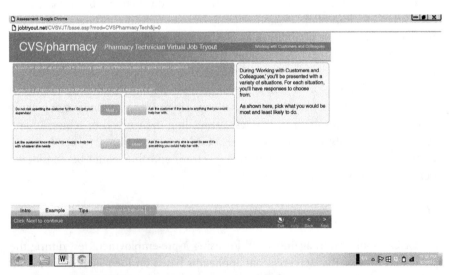

FIGURE 4.13 Screenshot of the first scenario in CVS's virtual job tryout that deals with a customer who is upset and wants to speak to a supervisor

role they are applying for and sees how they would respond to situations and questions that arise while working at CVS. Figures 4.12 through 4.24 show screenshots taken by Roland Behm on June 2, 2015, of the CVS pre-employment test administered post-EEOC enforcement. Figure 4.12 is simply the introduction page of the virtual job tryout.

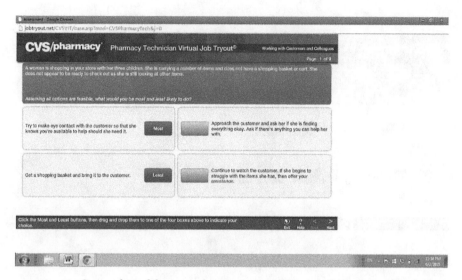

FIGURE 4.14 Screenshot of the second scenario in CVS's virtual job tryout that deals with encountering a customer who might need assistance

First, the applicant is put in the situation of dealing with a customer who is upset and wants to speak to a supervisor (see Figure 4.13). The applicant is asked to decide between four potential responses that would indicate what they are most and least likely to do in the scenario described. Next, the applicant is asked about what they would do if they were to encounter a customer who might need assistance (see Figure 4.14). The applicant's responses can be used by the employer to see how the applicant will handle situations that are likely to occur and to help determine if the applicant is an appropriate fit for the job.

Next, the applicant is put in two different situations where there are disagreements with a customer (Figures 4.15 and 4.16). The first conflict deals with a pricing issue and the second deals with a customer attempting to use a photocopied coupon that is not accepted by CVS. The applicant is then given another set of four options for each scenario relating to how they would respond to the situation. The answers to these questions could be important not just for pre-employment testing but also to train and coach an applicant on CVS's customer policies if they are hired.

In the next two questions (Figures 4.17 and 4.18), the applicant is presented with a scenario of dealing with a patient who is unhappy because of issues with their prescription medication. In the first, the applicant is tasked with dealing with a patient who is upset that their medication appears different. In the second question, the applicant is asked to deal with a patient who was prescribed a medicine that their insurance does not cover. Again, the applicant is given four options of how they would deal with each situation, and asked to select their most and least likely course of action.

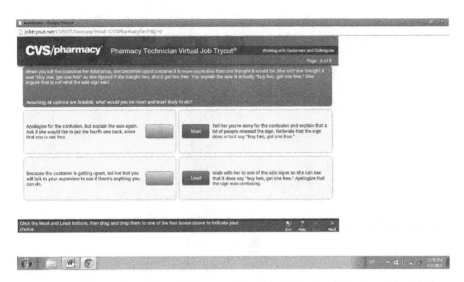

FIGURE 4.15 Screenshot of the third scenario in the CVS virtual job tryout that deals with a pricing issue

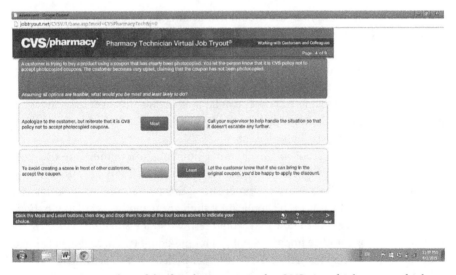

FIGURE 4.16 Screenshot of the fourth scenario in the CVS virtual job tryout, which concerns a customer attempting to use a coupon not accepted by CVS

The final two questions (Figures 4.19 and 4.20) from the CVS pre-employment exam deal with common situations that may arise with a CVS patient/customer. In the first, the applicant is asked how they would deal with a CVS patient who is having a problem with their prescription being refilled by their doctor. In the second,

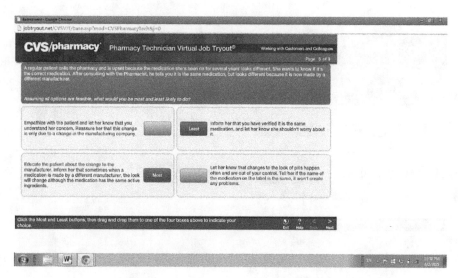

FIGURE 4.17 Screenshot of a scenario in the CVS virtual job tryout, where the applicant must deal with a patient upset that their medication appears different

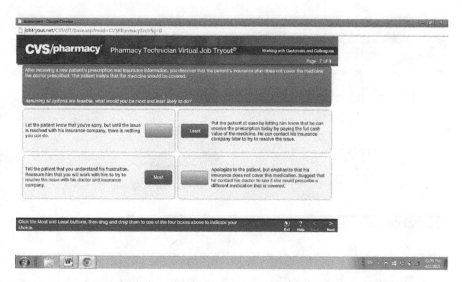

FIGURE 4.18 Screenshot of a scenario in the CVS virtual job tryout, where the applicant must deal with a patient who was prescribed a medicine that their insurance does not cover

the applicant is asked how they would assist a customer who needs help finding an over-the-counter medication. Again for each scenario, the applicant is given four options of how they would respond to each scenario.

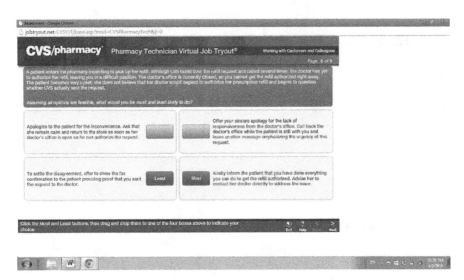

FIGURE 4.19 Screenshot a scenario in the CVS virtual job tryout, where the applicant must deal with a patient who is having a problem with their prescription being refilled by their doctor

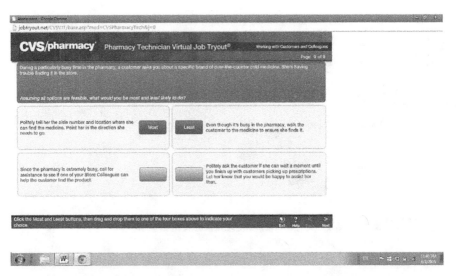

FIGURE 4.20 Screenshot of the last scenario in the CVS virtual job tryout, where the applicant is asked how they would assist a customer who needs help finding an over-the-counter medication

After a few more situational questions, the CVS virtual job tryout presents scenarios dealing with inventory issues. Figure 4.21 shows a scenario where the applicant is asked to determine if the inventory listed matches with the actual inventory for the items on hand, and Figure 4.22 shows what the correct answers are.

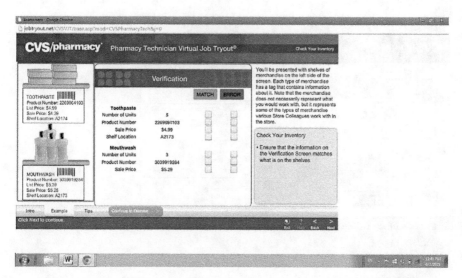

FIGURE 4.21 Screenshot of the first questions in the CVS virtual job tryout addressing inventory handling, where the applicant is asked to determine if the inventory listed matches with actual inventory for the items on hand

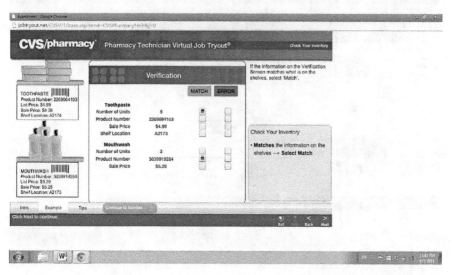

FIGURE 4.22 Screenshot of the answers to the first question regarding inventory handling, shown in Figure 4.21

Figure 4.23 shows a question from the CVS pharmacy technician virtual job tryout, where the applicant is given a slightly more complicated but similar inventory scenario. Here the applicant is asked to determine if the inventory listed below matches the actual inventory on hand related to quantity, price, item number, and

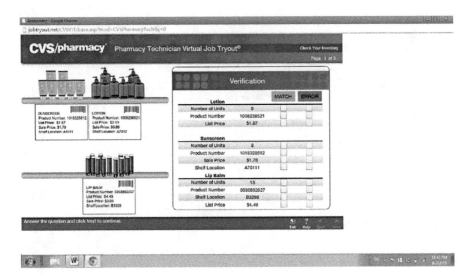

FIGURE 4.23 Screenshot of a question from the CVS virtual job tryout, where the applicant is asked to determine if the inventory listed matches actual inventory

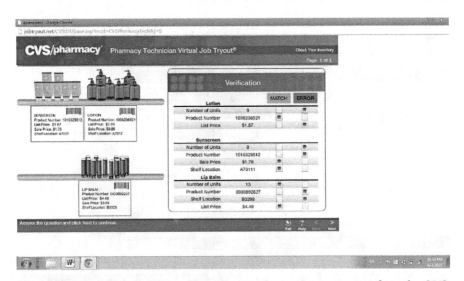

FIGURE 4.24 Screenshot of the correct answer to the inventory question from the CVS virtual job tryout, shown in Figure 4.23

shelf location. Figure 4.24 shows the correct answers. CVS can use the applicant's answers to determine their competency in math and ability to spot mistakes.

As you can see, the pre-employment exams administered by Kroger and CVS differ greatly. While the Kroger exam follows the popular Meyer–Briggs test that is based on the Five-Factor Model, CVS's virtual job tryout puts the applicant directly in the position they are seeking and determines how they would respond to various common situations. The pre-employment exam for CVS was not always this way. Pursuant to EEOC action, CVS overhauled its pre-employment testing process and focus. This new CVS test shows yet another way that companies can use pre-employment testing that is appropriate for the work being sought.[84] The CVS example shows that a company can change their pre-employment testing methods and still achieve the goal of finding capable and qualified employees for their company. The more a company ensures their pre-employment exam focuses solely on actual job-related issues, the less likely it is that the exam will be viewed as an improper medical exam.

Personality tests represent yet another vehicle to quantify workers. It is a given that employers have a vested interest in selecting workers whose personalities are well suited for their job tasks. However, there is a thin line between employers choosing appropriate workers versus discriminating against workers who express themselves differently, though they are still perfectly capable of completing the required job tasks. Personality tests that in actuality are medical examinations of mental health contravene legal protections for workers with disabilities. Previous cases have shown that employers cannot simply shift the legal blame to the vendors they employ to develop the test. To avoid potential legal action and enforcement by the EEOC, employers should not deploy pre-employment tests that are derived from the Five-Factor Model.

---

[84] ACLU of RI, "ACLU and CVS/Pharmacy Resolve Discrimination Complaint."

5

Automated Video Interviews[*]

We have to do all this song and dance for A.I., or a robot, or whatever it is before we even talk to an actual person – if that ever happens.

–Jade[1]

Automated video interviewing as the newest iteration of automated hiring represents the latest salvo in the war to quantify not just the output of the worker, but also the gestalt of the ideal worker. What is most remarkable about automated video interviewing is that it attempts to reach beyond the boundaries of the quantifiable and touch the ineffable – it seeks to quantify human emotions and affect. There is, however, a clear link between the current twenty-first-century use of automated video interviewing and the nineteenth- to twentieth-century practice of phrenology as a pseudo-science. Given the racist and eugenic origins of phrenology, the law should stand firmly against this new attempt to quantify workers through automated video interviews.

Jessica Clements, a job applicant with a visual impairment, had this to say about their automated video interview: "I couldn't read the questions, I had to zoom in. And when it flipped to the front-facing camera, it was actually really distracting."[2] Alex Huang, a job applicant who is not a native speaker of English, suspects he lost several job opportunities because automated video interviewing is prevalent in his job industry, financial services. He believes that although he speaks fluent English, automated interview video systems had trouble understanding his tone and syntax. He finally got his current job position by insisting on an interview conducted by a human rather than an AI system.[3] As AI-based video interviewing continues to grow

---

[*] This chapter has been adapted from the article "Automated Video Interviewing as the New Phrenology," *Berkeley Technology Law Journal* 36 (2022).

[1] Rachel Withers, "Should Robots Be Conducting Job Interviews?" *Slate*, Oct. 5, 2020, https://slate .com/technology/2020/10/artificial-intelligence-job-interviews.html.
[2] Alex Lee, "An AI to Stop Hiring Bias Could Be Bad News for Disabled People," *Wired*, Nov. 26, 2019, www.wired.co.uk/article/ai-hiring-bias-disabled-people.
[3] Alex Huang, Phone interview with author (Aug. 6, 2020).

as a prominent recruiting tool, it is critical to examine how such workplace tech-nologies could serve as end runs around employment anti-discrimination laws such as Title VII of the Civil Rights Act of 1964 (42 U.S.C. §§ 2000e–2000e-17) and the Americans with Disabilities Act (42 U.S.C. §§ 12101, et seq).

5.1 THE RISE OF AUTOMATED VIDEO INTERVIEWING

Video interviewing as a field began in the early 2000s with two companies: HireVue and Montage. According to VidCruiter CEO Sean Fahey, these companies "invented pre-recorded video interviewing, where people record at home while hiring manag-ers were doing something else."[4] In video interviewing's nascency, convenience was the driving force behind the technology. Employers would provide candidates with a set of standardized question; candidates would video record their answers to each question and send in a videotape, which employers could then review when making hiring decisions. This system meant that employers could better compare candi-dates and get multiple opinions, while saving money and time on recruiter travel.[5] Interview-focused hiring startups such as GreenJobInterview provided one of the first purpose-built, live video interview platforms before the age of Zoom.[6]

Since its inception, video interviewing has evolved. Asynchronous digital inter-views recorded and sent via the internet have now become standard practice, but a new step has been added before the interview is reviewed by a human decision maker. HireVue was one of the first companies to offer AI-based assessments.[7] HireVue's assessments traditionally used vocal and facial analysis technology, draw-ing on "[a] database of about 25,000 pieces of facial and linguistic information" to provide recruiters with a measure of a candidate's potential job performance. In 2019, the algorithms assessed factors such as "a candidate's tone of voice, their use of passive or active words, sentence length and the speed they talk," and facial expressions such as "brow furrowing, brow raising, the amount eyes widen or close, lip tightening, chin raising and smiling."[8] While, as of 2021, HireVue claimed it had discontinued use of its facial recognition technology, it continued to use lin-gual analysis and there is no formal ban or rule preventing the reimplementation of facial recognition technology.[9] More importantly, HireVue's marriage of AI and

---

[4] VidCruiter, "Where Did Video Hiring Come from and Where Is It Going?" https://vidcruiter.com/video-interviewing/history-of-video-interview/ (accessed Nov. 6, 2021).

[5] Mark Newman, *The HireVue Story*, Vimeo, Apr. 26, 2013, https://vimeo.com/64921188.

[6] VidCruiter, "Where Did Video Hiring Come from and Where Is It Going?"

[7] HireVue, "Our Science: Meet the IO Psychology Team," www.hirevue.com/our-science (accessed Apr. 22, 2021).

[8] Ivan Manokha, "How Using Facial Analysis in Job Interviews Could Reinforce Inequality," *PBS News Hour: Making Sen$e*, Oct. 7, 2019, www.pbs.org/newshour/economy/making-sense/how-using-facial-recognition-in-job-interviews-could-reinforce-inequality.

[9] Will Knight, "Job Screening Service Halts Facial Analysis of Applicants," *Wired*, Jan. 12, 2021, www.wired.com/story/job-screening-service-halts-facial-analysis-applicants/.

video interviewing has become entrenched as standard practice for recruitment. A 2020 study that analyzed the claims and practices of various algorithmic hiring companies found that one-third of the eighteen companies analyzed were employing video-based assessments.[10]

Companies are adopting the video interview at a fast rate. In 2011, a survey of 506 companies found that 47 percent were using video interviewing to speed up the hiring process, while another 22 percent responded they would consider video interviewing as a tool to recruit geographically diverse candidates.[11] A 2015 survey of 700 executives found that 50 percent were using video interviews to "narrow the candidate pool."[12] Significantly, these statistics report the state of video interviewing before AI-based assessments were introduced; recent reports suggest the industry has grown at an even faster pace since the integration of AI technology. As of 2018, 60 percent of organizations were using video interviews, a number that dramatically spiked in 2020 due to global shutdowns induced by the Covid-19 pandemic.[13] A 2020 Gartner HR survey reported 86 percent of respondents were turning to new virtual interview technology to facilitate remote hiring.[14] Data specific to industry leader HireVue shows that as of 2021, the platform was being used by 733 corporations, the majority of which employed more than 10,000 employees and touted more than $1 billion a year in revenue. Computer software, health care, retail, and financial services industries ranked among the top users of HireVue's services.[15] The incredible reach of HireVue's automated video hiring technology as a single platform warrants closer scrutiny. A serious consideration of AI-based video interview technology's potentially discriminatory effects is necessary given the rapid adoption and scale of video interviewing, alongside the unproven validity of its AI-based predictions.

Some evidence suggests that the corporate frenzy to join the bandwagon of technological hiring comes at the expense of candidates who have the most to lose. Even the average job candidate has decried a lack of autonomy and noted a sense of

[10]   Manish Raghavan et al., "Mitigating Bias in Algorithmic Hiring: Evaluating Claims and Practices," *FAT* '20: Proceedings of the 2020 Conf. on Fairness, Accountability, and Transparency* (Jan. 2020): 473.

[11]   Heather O'Neill, "Video Interviewing Cuts Costs, but Bias Worries Linger," *Workforce*, Oct. 5, 2011, www.workforce.com/news/video-interviewing-cuts-costs-but-bias-worries-linger.

[12]   Roy Maurer, "Use of Video for Recruiting Continues to Grow," *SHRM*, Aug. 21, 2015, www.shrm.org/resourcesandtools/hr-topics/talent-acquisition/pages/use-video-recruiting-grow.aspx.

[13]   Nilam Oswal, "The Latest Recruitment Technology Trends and How to Really Use Them," *PC World*, Feb. 9, 2018, www.pcworld.idg.com.au/article/633219/latest-recruitment-technology-trends-how-really-use-them/; Gartner, "Gartner HR Survey Shows 86% of Organizations Are Conducting Virtual Interviews to Hire Candidates during Coronavirus Pandemic," Gartner Newsroom, Press Release, Apr. 30, 2020, www.gartner.com/en/newsroom/press-releases/2020-04-30-gartner-hr-survey-shows-86—of-organizations-are-cond.

[14]   Gartner, "Gartner HR Survey Shows 86% of Organizations"

[15]   Enlyft, "Companies Using HireVue," https://enlyft.com/tech/products/hirevue#:~:text=We%20have%20data%20on%20733,and%20%3E1000M%20dollars%20in%20revenue (accessed Apr. 22, 2021).

despair when the hiring decision hinges on AI-based video interview technology. A group of candidates interviewed by the *Washington Post* shared that they found the video interview process "alienating and dehumanizing."[16] Some candidates have even begun to distinguish between video interviews and "real" interviews, which they believe are more likely to lead to meaningful hiring decisions. A college graduate speaking to *Slate* magazine described feeling disappointed when she realized her interview was a taping to be reviewed by "an A.I. thing" as opposed to a conversation with a real recruiter.[17] For some candidates, video interviews have come to represent part of the culling process of automated hiring rather than a meaningful opportunity to prove one's qualifications.[18]

For other candidates, the concern around video interview technology runs even deeper. Kat, a software engineering student also interviewed by *Slate*, noted that video interview technology made her "[feel] like [she] was not valued as a human." Also, as a Black woman, her concerns around dehumanization were exacerbated by her recognition that "A.I. is known to perpetuate bias against people of color or fail to recognize them at all." Her friends and other professionals encouraged her to decline video interviews that used AI, which she reported was her plan going forward.[19] Individuals with disabilities have received the same advice from disability advocates who believe video interview algorithms run the risk of unfairly screening out candidates with disabilities.[20]

Although HireVue and some other video interview platforms claim to mitigate bias in their hiring systems, concerns for race, disability, and other types of discrimination do not seem unfounded. Not all companies engage in algorithm de-biasing efforts, and for those that do, it is not clear that those mitigation efforts are effective at catching all manifestations of bias in hiring algorithms.[21] Given the ample evidence of AI-based hiring technologies perpetuating discrimination in the past, such as the case of Amazon's proprietary screening tool that systematically discriminated against women,[22] it is critical to identify the shortcomings of existing legislation in order to design a more protective regulatory regime for automated video interviewing.

---

[16] Drew Harwell, "A Face-Scanning Algorithm Increasingly Decides Whether You Deserve the Job," *Washington Post*, Nov. 6, 2019.

[17] Withers, "Should Robots Be Conducting Job Interviews?"

[18] Ifeoma Ajunwa, "The Auditing Imperative for Automated Hiring," *Harvard Journal of Law & Technology* 34, no. 2 (2021): 622–23.

[19] Withers, "Should Robots Be Conducting Job Interviews?"

[20] Jim Fruchterman and Joan Mellea, "Expanding Employment Success for People with Disabilities," *Benetech*, Nov. 2018, https://benetech.org/about/resources/expanding-employment-success-for-people-with-disabilities/.

[21] See Raghavan et al., "Mitigating Bias in Algorithmic Hiring," 477 (noting that simply using outcome based de-biasing to comply with the Title VII 4/5th rule may not effectively capture all forms of algorithmic discrimination).

[22] See Dastin, "Amazon Scraps Secret AI Recruiting Tool."

5.2 PHRENOLOGY AS POPULAR PSEUDO-SCIENCE

To fully apprehend the depth of the legal problems presented when companies seek to quantify workers via automated video interviews, we must consider the impetus and origins of the practice. The genesis for automated video interviewing is the premise that emotions or character may be surmised from the human face or facial expressions. Scholars like Kate Crawford have identified a "phrenological impulse," which is the desire to entertain assumptions about an individual's emotions and character merely from external appearances.[23] Yet, there remains no scientific consensus that artificial intelligence systems are capable of accurately interpreting human emotions from facial expressions. One recent psychological study, conducted in 2019, found no disprovable evidence that artificial intelligence could accurately ascertain a person's emotions solely from facial expressions.[24] Despite the lack of evidence to support the efficacy of automated video interviewing, this type of recruitment technology is still being marketed and deployed as part of hiring efforts.

5.2.1 *The Rise of Phrenology*

Phrenology was the brainchild of German physiologist Dr. Franz Joseph Gall. Gall, a relatively "handsome man" who himself had a "broad 'noble head,'" sought to transform the then somewhat informal field of psychology – the study of brain functions – into a true science.[25] Gall rejected the traditional philosophical grounds for understanding the human brain, instead turning to what he considered to be concrete scientific data to create a field that would come to be known as phrenology, based on his own scientific hypothesis for the inner workings of the mind. Gall's studies began with observing both animal and human behavior. He studied social structures, from "family life" to "jails and asylums," with the intention to identify the "fundamental faculties" of mankind through an analysis of objective data. At the center of Gall's theory was the cerebral localization hypothesis. Gall believed that the brain was divided into separate essential organs, each of which served a unique and essential function. These functions extended not only to essential intellectual skills but also to genetically coding for moral and emotional capabilities.[26]

[23] Kate Crawford, "Time to Regulate AI That Interprets Human Emotions," *Nature*, Apr. 6, 2021, www .nature.com/articles/d41586-021-00868-5; see also Kate Crawford, *Atlas of AI: Power, Politics, and the Planetary Costs of Artificial Intelligence* (New Haven, CT: Yale University Press, 2021).

[24] Lisa Feldman Barrett et al., "Emotional Expressions Reconsidered: Challenges to Inferring Emotions from Human Facial Movements," *Psychological Science in the Public Interest* 20, no. 1 (2019), https:// journals.sagepub.com/doi/10.1177/1529100619832930.

[25] Pierre Schlag, "Commentary: Law & Phrenology," *Harvard Law Review* 110, no. 4 (1997): 877–78 (quoting Nelson Sizer, *Forty Years in Phrenology* (1888), 380–81).

[26] Schlag, "Commentary: Law & Phrenology," 879 (quoting Robert M. Young, *Mind, Brain and Adaptation in the Nineteenth Century* (1990), 16).

Thus, according to Gall's hypothesis, one's individual behavior and intellect were directly related to the development and structure of one's physical brain anatomy. Gall rested his argument in part on an appeal to the specialization seen throughout nature: Just as eyes serve a specialized function, just as ears serve a predetermined purpose, it followed logically, for Gall, that different regions of the brain would follow suit. Gall based many of his "objective" scientific observations on anecdotal evidence. For example, Gall found that those who "learn by heart" always feature "large prominent eyes." Gall noticed a similar pattern with other physical traits as they corresponded to mental capacities. According to Gall, these observations soon led him to the "certainty that the difference in the form of heads is occasioned by the difference in the form of the brains." Also, these differences presented themselves by size. Any region of the brain that was more developed in an individual would be larger in size, and would also feature more prominently in outward appearance.[27]

Based upon his cerebral localization hypothesis, Gall conducted further pseudo-scientific tests to arrive at a construction of no less than "twenty-seven fundamental faculties" located in different regions of the skull that explained human behavior.[28] Gall relied on "empirical observation" of numerous individuals, relying heavily on correlation to associate some specific traits with particular regions of the brain. After identifying where in the brain they deemed particular faculties to reside, Gall and other phrenologists began to make value judgements concerning what each faculty meant for individual behavior and personality. Phrenologists took great care to isolate the supposed various faculties, describing what they believed to be the detailed nature of each region of the brain and each region's independent relationship to behavior. Building on Gall's work, Dr. Johann Spurzheim observed that the faculties identified by Gall could be further divided into feelings and intellect, with subdivisions therein that created a detailed hierarchy and organizational framework within which to interpret phrenological findings.[29]

Although the study of phrenology began in the late eighteenth century, it did not gain prominence until an 1815 article in the *Edinburgh Review*, a respected intellectual magazine of the time, condemned the newfound "science" as "utterly destitute of every qualification necessary for the conduct of a philosophical investigation."[30] Middle-class individuals fascinated by this new and previously unknown theory, however, began to follow phrenologists' findings despite backlash from the scientific community. In the eyes of the public at that time, Spurzheim had successfully

[27] Schlag, "Commentary: Law & Phrenology," 879, 880 (quoting Gall, *On the Functions of the Brain* (1835), 88–89).
[28] Schlag, "Commentary: Law & Phrenology," 881 (enumerating Gall's list of twenty-seven faculties as Amativeness, Philoprogenitiveness, Adhesiveness, Combativeness, Destructiveness, Secretiveness, Acquisitiveness, Self-Esteem, Love of Approbation, Cautiousness, Eventuality (and Individuality), Locality, Form, Vocabulary, Language, Coloring, Tune, Number, Constructiveness, Comparison, Causality, Wit, Ideality, Benevolence, Imitation, Veneration, and Firmness).
[29] Schlag, "Commentary: Law & Phrenology," 882, 883.
[30] John van Wyhe, "Ridiculing Phrenology: 'This Persecuted Science,'" *History of Phrenology on the Web*, www.historyofphrenology.org.uk/ridicule.htm (last updated 2011).

refuted the *Edinburgh Review* article, and in 1820, the first phrenological society was formed in Edinburgh, Scotland. Phrenology's popularity took off in a wave that swept from Britain to America. In 1838, the first meeting of the Phrenological Association convened, modeled on respected scientific associations that had excluded phrenology from their ranks. In phrenology, the "enthusiastic and the arrogant" found a "scientific" justification for personally held beliefs. The American "phrenological Fowlers" were a group of phrenology advocates who gave lectures, established institutions across the world, published new research, and even read heads for a fee. By 1844, the Fowlers' publishing house was distributing phrenological research and propaganda nationwide. Fowler philosophy, spearheaded by Lorenzo Niles Fowler and Samuel R. Wells, based their version of phrenology on the theories of George Combe. Though many original phrenologists viewed the Fowlers' brand of phrenology as a deviated form, it was this brand that embedded itself in American social and legal institutions, and that persisted despite scientific invalidation.[31]

5.2.2 *Phrenology in Law and Society in the Nineteenth to Twentieth Centuries*

Phrenology in America embedded itself in both the fashionable and legal societies of the nineteenth century. In 1873, writer Mark Twain underwent an anonymous phrenological examination wherein a phrenologist determined that Twain had no sense of humor. Interestingly, a few months later when Twain returned and publicly announced his well-known name, the phrenologist discovered Twain's skull did in fact house an impressive bump of humor.[32] While inconsistencies such as those identified during Twain's encounters were well known during the height of phrenology's popularity, public opinion far outweighed scientific criticisms. Phrenology was used in workplace evaluations and screening decisions, with George Combe himself stating he "would never employ a clerk who had not a large coronal region." Similar to many personality tests of the early twentieth century, phrenology was also used in some cases to determine an individual's suitability for a given career;[33] indeed, some employers would include particular phrenological profiles in their job solicitations.[34] In 1912, a phrenological evaluation of a seven-year-old suggested she was best suited for a career in medicine or teaching.[35]

---

[31] John van Wyhe, "Overview," *History of Phrenology on the Web*, www.historyofphrenology.org.uk/overview.htm (last updated 2011).

[32] Amanda C. Pustilnik, "Violence on the Brain: A Critique of Neuroscience in Criminal Law," *Wake Forest Law Review* 44 (2009): 191.

[33] Olivia Goldhill, "Centuries before Myers-Briggs, Workplace Personalities Were Assessed Using Skull Measurements," *Quartz at Work*, Dec. 29, 2017, https://qz.com/work/1168283/centuries-before-myers-briggs-workplace-personalities-were-assessed-using-phrenology/.

[34] Minna Scherlinder Morse, "Facing a Bumpy History," *Smithsonian Magazine*, Oct. 1997, www.smithsonianmag.com/history/facing-a-bumpy-history-144497373/.

[35] Goldhill, "Centuries before Myers-Briggs, Workplace Personalities Were Assessed Using Skull Measurements."

Phrenology also subtly made its way into the American legal system: It informed theories of criminal law reform, it was a method by which jurists evaluated an individual's culpability, and it was critically used as a "mitigating factor" during criminal sentencing. Phrenological evaluations were used to determine who might be at risk to commit a crime; some police departments used phrenology to typify criminals and arrest them, even in the absence of any evidence a crime had been committed. Even judges relied on phrenological evidence as fact in official judgments. In the 1853 murder trial *Farrer v. State*, the Ohio Supreme Court relied on phrenological evaluation to determine whether a housekeeper could be held liable for poisoning. The judge presiding over the case ruled that the housekeeper was "remarkably ugly"; thus it was evident that she was both "criminally insane" and subject to "murderous impulses." In 1840, a judge stated from the bench that "no man ... would dispute that the brain ... consists of distinct organs, each having a distinct function, and that power of function is influenced by organic size." Phrenology even influenced the M'Naghten test for insanity, which presupposes that an individual's "ability to know right from wrong" is distinct from any mental disease they may suffer. This distinction was erroneously rooted in phrenology's theory of separate, individually functioning mental organs, yet nevertheless persisted in case law all the way until 1966 – well after phrenology had fallen out of use.[36]

By the 1950s, the field of phrenology was all but dead. Its demise began nearly as soon as its success. In 1838, at the same time the first phrenological society was called to order, scientists already had evidence that the brain did not actually house enough separate regions to allow each major personality trait its own organ. In fact, evidence at that time increasingly suggested that many parts of the brain must work in tandem to function. Eventually, scientists also came to realize that brain size had little to no correlation to intelligence or efficiency.[37] Thus, for much of phrenology's rise there was growing evidence of its invalidity.

Despite these challenges, the practice of phrenology persevered for over a century. The practice remained embedded in social institutions and common thought. By 1888, the theory was so ingrained that the editors of *Encyclopedia Britannica*, in refuting the theory, felt the need to publish a seven-page essay on their reasoning.[38] Thus, it was not so much scientific evidence *alone* that finally led society to cast phrenology aside, as phrenology had never truly even been classified as a science. It was instead a combination of changing social theories and norms paired with scientific evidence that resulted in genuine change. Simply, phrenology became "unfashionable." As Freudian psychoanalysis gained popularity in the early 1900s, people began to cast aside the theory of fixed traits in favor of the more intriguing and mysterious

---

[36] Pustilnik, "Violence on the Brain," 192–94.
[37] Pustilnik, "Violence on the Brain," 194.
[38] Morse, "Facing a Bumpy History."

influence of the unconscious mind.[39] Although the field of phrenology itself was eventually associated with "zealous extremists," some of its influences lived on. In the early nineteenth century, the spirit of phrenology gave rise to the racially charged anthropological theory that Europeans were superior to other humans based on the shape and size of their skulls. Advocates for this spin-off movement included Paul Broca, who went on to found the Anthropological Society in Paris circa 1859.[40]

5.3 THE ROOTS OF AUTOMATED VIDEO INTERVIEWING IN PHRENOLOGY

Even as the pseudo-science of phrenology fell out of fashion, its influence did not fully dissipate. Rather, its core ideologies, motivations, and social implications evolved and assimilated into new, more fashionable theories. Phrenology is the fundamental belief that human behavior is innate, that is, that an individual is born with certain set behavioral tendencies and capabilities. Phrenology is thus predicated on the belief that human behavior is quantifiable. It presupposes that a limited number of traits exist, and the prevalence of such traits in an individual is directly proportional to their physical characteristics. Franz Gall had sought to create a system wherein individuals could be objectively measured through quantifiable observations. But Gall's methods were flawed, and his science was founded on judgments derived from normative comparisons and perceived value.[41] Although Gall's intent was to create an objective study of the human mind, the result was a theory that was at best pseudo-scientific, and at worst, a social tool used to reinforce a static social hierarchy and rationalize racialized class inequality.[42] These social implications did not disappear when phrenology fell out of use.

The ideological goal to quantify human behavior morphed into the well-respected field of psychology, which has experienced its own evolutions over the past century. Phrenology (1840s) lent its logic to the science of behaviorism (1920s), which sought to understand human motivation through observable behavior as opposed to observable physical features. Behaviorism was replaced by cognitive psychology (1950s), which shifted focus from observable external behavior to observable brain functions in order to understand human traits such as perception, memory, problem-solving, and intelligence. Although the scientific evidence has shifted and methods of scientific evidence have improved, there remain some parallels between phrenological theory and cognitive psychology's focus on the brain's inner structures.[43]

[39] Pustilnik, "Violence on the Brain," 194; van Wyhe, "Overview."
[40] van Wyhe, "Overview."
[41] Schlag, "Commentary: Law & Phrenology," 879.
[42] Goldhill, "Centuries before Myers-Briggs, Workplace Personalities Were Assessed Using Skull Measurements."
[43] Kendra Cherry, "The Origins of Psychology," *Very Well Mind*, June 25, 2020, www.verywellmind .com/a-brief-history-of-psychology-through-the-years-2795245.

Digital interview techniques have evolved into the present-day automated video interviewing systems that do not merely passively record a candidate's response, but are often the intermediate arbiters of the candidate's character and job suitability.[44] HireView, the most popular and widely used of these technologies,[45] has been using AI to enhance the video interview process since 2013, using measurements not unlike those used in phrenology.[46] By measuring a candidate's body language, tone, key words, and even facial expressions, HireView creates a single "'employability score'" that is ranked against other applicants.[47] While HireVue claims its technology removes bias from the hiring process by applying a single, objective algorithm to all candidates,[48] the fact remains that automated hiring technologies compare individuals to a concept of what is "normal."[49] Thus, some might consider HireVue's system an iteration of phrenology.

In the same way that phrenology "scientifically" assessed individuals based on normative, anecdotal observations, video interview technology such as that used by HireVue measures candidates' responses against a normative sample of individuals who are perceived to be successful at a given job. Companies such as HireVue collect "training data" in the form of interviews and performance records from existing high-performing employees at a given company. Using the training data, the traits exhibited by top performers are set as the rewarding variables that the automated systems will use to screen candidates. These traits are often nuanced – for example, better enunciation or simply leaning forward on the table could be a trait that correlates to successful salespeople at a given company, and thus it becomes a variable that the algorithm rewards.[50] This type of training data reflects one of the most basic logical fallacies – that correlation is not causation: The fact that a variable is correlated with job success does not necessarily mean that variable is causative of job success. Furthermore, depending on correlations for employment may undermine the equal opportunity principle. A candidate-screening technology developed by Amazon that ran on similar algorithmic principles was taken out of service when

[44] Richard Feloni, "I Tried the Software Thata Uses AI to Scan Applicants for Companies Like Goldman Sachs and Unilever Before Meeting Them – and It's Not as Creepy as It Sounds," *Business Insider*, Aug. 23, 2017, www.businessinsider.com/hirevue-ai-powered-job-interview-platform-2017-8 (containing information demonstrating that the hiring software does evaluate applicants).
[45] HireVue, "HireVue Ranked a Fastest Growing Company on Deloitte's 2018 Technology Fast 500," Press release, Nov. 15, 2018, www.hirevue.com/press-release/deloitte-2018-technology-fast-500-hirevue-ranked-fastest-growing-company.
[46] Feloni, "I Tried the Software That Uses AI to Scan Applicants."
[47] Angela Chen, "The AI Hiring Industry Is under Scrutiny – But It'll Be Hard to Fix," *MIT Technology Review*, Nov. 7, 2019, www.technologyreview.com/2019/11/07/75194/hirevue-ai-automated-hiring-discrimination-ftc-epic-bias/.
[48] Feloni, "I Tried the Software That Uses AI to Scan Applicants."
[49] Knight, "Job Screening Service Halts Facial Analysis of Applicants.
[50] Alex Engler, "For Some Employment Algorithms, Disability Discrimination by Default," Brookings Institute, Oct. 31, 2019, www.brookings.edu/blog/techtank/2019/10/31/for-some-employment-algorithms-disability-discrimination-by-default/.

it came to light that the technology disproportionately ranked men higher than women.[51] One reason for this was that the technology likely compared candidates to the traits commonly shared by existing top performers, and the top performers were overwhelmingly men. This is not because men were more competent, but simply because past biases in recruitment give men a historical advantage. As such, in this case, objective scientific measurement was, in reality, algorithmic processes that reflected back societal biases – just as the pseudo-science of phrenology had previously done.

Just as phrenology sought to quantify human character through observable physical traits, video interview technologies also seek to quantify and objectively understand human behavior as it relates to job success. An inherent underlying assumption of these technologies is that there truly do exist observable physical manifestations that give insight into the character and behavioral traits that define a successful individual. Video interviewing technology is purportedly motivated by objectivity, yet it ranks candidates based on judgments rooted in normative comparisons. The algorithms of the video interviewing are trained to search for certain traits deemed to be valuable, but these normative conclusions are based on samples of existing employees, and these samples are neither random nor representative. Yet, video interviewing technology has been uncritically embraced by society much in the same way that phrenology was. HireVue alone boasted more than 600 clients in 2017, many of them multinational corporations such as Unilever, Goldman Sachs, and Under Armour.[52] Unfortunately, akin to phrenological thinkers of the eighteenth century, early adopters of automated video interviewing have largely failed to consider the scientifically shaky foundations undergirding the video interviewing technologies they rely on.

5.4 DISCRIMINATORY EFFECTS OF FACIAL AND EMOTION ANALYSIS

Although companies such as HireVue claim to no longer use facial recognition,[53] there have been no independent audits to substantiate such claims.[54] Thus, it remains urgent to understand and redress the racial impact of both the facial and emotion analysis used for automated video interviews. In *Mitigating Bias in Algorithmic*

---

[51] Dastin, "Amazon Scraps Secret AI Recruiting Tool."
[52] Feloni, "I Tried the Software That Uses AI to Scan Applicants."
[53] HireVue, "HireVue Leads the Industry with Commitment to Transparent and Ethical Use of AI in Hiring," Press Release, Jan. 12, 2021, www.hirevue.com/press-release/hirevue-leads-the-industry-with-commitment-to-transparent-and-ethical-use-of-ai-in-hiring ("Independently, early in 2020, HireVue proactively removed the visual analysis component from all of its new assessments. HireVue's internal research demonstrated that recent advances in natural language processing had significantly increased the predictive power of language. With these advances, visual analysis no longer significantly added value to assessments.").
[54] Ajunwa, "Auditing Imperative for Automated Hiring," 672 (noting that HireVue's audit was conducted by a company that HireVue had hired and, after the audit was completed, there were still "many questions [left] unanswered").

Hiring: Evaluating Claims and Practices, Raghavan et al. point to "[a] wave of studies [which have] shown that several commercially available facial analysis techniques suffer from disparities in error rates across gender and racial lines."[55] In 2018, Joy Buolamwini and Timnit Gebru examined the performance of facial analysis algorithms across four "intersectional subgroups" of males or females featuring lighter or darker skin. Buolamwini and Gebru found that algorithms designed to identify gender performed better on male faces as opposed to female (the algorithms did not take transgender individuals into account) and light faces as opposed to dark; of all groups, darker-skinned females were misclassified the most often.[56] This troubling finding suggests that the facial analysis software employed by video interview algorithms may be less accurate when identifying job candidates of color and women of all races.

This finding is further corroborated by Lauren Rhue, who found that the emotion analysis feature of two facial recognition algorithms "interprets emotions differently based on the person's race." One recognition software interpreted Black individuals as angrier than whites regardless of whether the individual was smiling; the other platform viewed Black individuals as more contemptuous than white people when their face featured an "ambiguous" expression, though "[a]s the players' smile widen[ed], the disparity disappear[ed]."[57] Thus, not only is facial recognition technology less accurate at identifying women and people with darker skin tones, but it is also less accurate at interpreting emotions expressed by individuals with such skin tones. Given video interviewing's reliance on facial and emotion recognition technology, this disparity is incredibly troubling. Thus, by building algorithms to rely on this inaccurate technology, video interview platforms are nearly guaranteeing discriminatory results.

For AI scholar Luke Stark, these discriminatory outcomes are not merely a by-product of a flawed design; rather, the racialization of the human face is integral to the mission of facial analysis. By "attach[ing] numerical values to the human face," humans are necessarily being quantified and judged by classifiable visual signs – race foremost of all. Thus, for Stark, facial recognition technologies "both create and reinforce discredited categorizations around gender and race." It is this observation that leads Stark to boldly claim that "facial recognition is the plutonium of AI ... anathema to the health of human society, and [something that should be] heavily restricted as [a] result."[58] Legal scholars like Woodrow Hartzog have also called for a wide ban on facial recognition technologies.[59]

---

[55] Raghavan et al., "Mitigating Bias in Algorithmic Hiring," 475.

[56] Joy Buolamwini and Timnit Gebru, "Gender Shades: Intersectional Accuracy Disparities in Commercial Gender Classification," *Proceedings of Machine Learning Research* 81 (2018): 2, 8.

[57] Lauren Rhue, "Racial Influence on Automated Perceptions of Emotions," Paper, Nov. 9, 2018, SSRN, https://dx.doi.org/10.2139/ssrn.3281765

[58] See Luke Stark, "Facial Recognition Is the Plutonium of AI," *XRDS: Crossroads* 25, no. 3 (2019): 52–53.

[59] See Evan Selinger and Woodrow Hartzog, "The Inconsentability of Facial Surveillance," *Loyola Law Review* 66, no. 1 (2019): 105; see also CLIC Faculty, "Professor Woodrow Hartzog Calls for a Ban on Facial Recognition Technology in New Publication," *Northeastern: Clic,* Apr. 14, 2020, www.northeastern.edu/clic/2020/04/.

Interviews are the gateway to work and to earning a livelihood, a fundamental human right.[60] Incorporating facial and emotion recognition technology into the interview process means the interview process could become tainted by racialized bias. To date, millions of video interviews that rely on facial and emotion analysis have been conducted.[61] Although some platforms have claimed to have discontinued the use of facial recognition technology,[62] many automated systems still claim to act as emotion recognition systems.

5.5 THE PSEUDO-SCIENCE OF EMOTION RECOGNITION

As a recent report on the background, uses, and ethical issues that underlie the use of emotion recognition technologies in China's authoritarian state notes, "Two fundamental assumptions undergird emotion recognition technologies: that it is possible to gauge a person's inner emotions from their external expressions, and that such inner emotions are both discrete [i.e., quantifiable] and uniformly expressed across the world."[63] These core principles have historical precedent. In an examination of modern emotion recognition technology, Rich Firth-Godbehere asserts that the roots of universal-emotion theories trace all the way back to the Greek philosopher Aristotle and seventeenth-century artist Charles Le Brun, early forefathers of the controversial and since-discredited racist field of physiognomy. In the late nineteenth century, Charles Darwin sought to marry theories of universal emotions with the science of his day. In 1872 Darwin published *The Expression of the Emotions in Man and Animals*, an offshoot of evolutionary theory that suggested "some kind of common evolutionary ancestor" explained the parallels between "some instinctual actions" expressed by both animals and humans.[64] However, it was not Darwin but mid-twentieth-century psychologist Paul Ekman whose research would lay the groundwork for emotion recognition AI.

In the 1960s, Ekman laid the groundwork for basic emotion theory (BET). Ekman developed two primary theories.[65] First, working in conjunction with scientists Silvan Tomkins and Wallace Friesen, Ekman theorized that there are "six basic emotions: happiness, anger, sadness, disgust, surprise, and fear."[66] Conducting

---

[60] See G.A. Res. 217 (III) A, Universal Declaration of Human Rights, art. 23(1) (Dec. 10, 1948) ("Everyone has the right to work, to free choice of employment, to just and favourable conditions of work and to protection against unemployment.").

[61] See Manokha, "How Using Facial Analysis in Job Interviews Could Reinforce Inequality" (discussing HireVue's 2019 claim that their algorithm assessed such nuanced traits as "brow furrowing, brow raising, the amount eyes widen or close, lip tightening, chin raising and smiling."); see also Maurer, "Use of Video for Recruiting Continues to Grow."

[62] See Maurer, "Use of Video for Recruiting Continues to Grow."

[63] Article 19, "Emotional Entanglement: China's Emotion Recognition Market and Its Implications for Human Rights," [Report], Jan. 2021, 15.

[64] Rich Firth-Godbehere, "Silicon Valley Thinks Everyone Feels the Same Six Emotions," *NEXT*, Sep. 5, 2018, https://howwegettonext.com/silicon-valley-thinks-everyone-feels-the-same-six-emotions-38354a0ef3d7.

[65] Article 19, "Emotional Entanglement," 15.

[66] Firth-Godbehere, "Silicon Valley Thinks Everyone Feels the Same Six Emotions."

studies with a remote civilization in Papua New Guinea, Ekman concluded that these emotions are consistent "across cultures." Ekman's second theory concerned "micro-expressions": He believed that not only are basic emotions universal, but also that minute expressions, which "occur briefly in response to stimuli, are signs of 'involuntary emotional leakage [which] exposes a person's true emotions.'"[67]

According to AI scholar Kate Crawford, this is the pseudo-science underlying the emotion recognition AI of today. Crawford argues that the marriage of Ekman's theories with computer science was one of convenience: "[T]he six emotions Ekman described fit perfectly into the model of the emerging field of computer vision." Ekman's theory was attractive because it allowed emotions to be quantified, and in turn, allowed the quantification of emotions to be "standardized and automated at scale."[68] However, this union wholly ignored the mounting questions regarding the validity and accuracy of Ekman's theories.

By the early twentieth century, scientists had already begun to suspect that theories of universal emotion expression were inaccurate.[69] Anthropologist Margaret Mead was an early skeptic. While researching the people of a remote Samoan island in the 1920s, Mead concluded "that fundamental human experiences – including emotions – varied from culture to culture." Ekman's New Guinea studies appeared to challenge Mead's conclusions, but his research methods were called into question when a later researcher discovered that the subjects of Ekman's study had in actuality previously interacted with Western researchers, which called into question the extent to which they were truly culturally isolated.[70] Furthermore, Ekman's use of translators and photographs of exaggerated faces has further called into question the accuracy of his findings, as more recent research shows that emotions are harder to recognize when they are less exaggerated.[71] Given Ekman's flawed methodology, it is not clear that his findings actually challenge Mead's earlier conclusions concerning cultural emotional differences.

Ekman's theory of micro-expressions has also been proven "to be both unreliable (due to [the] brevity and infrequency [of micro-expressions]) and discriminatory."[72] This finding is particularly discrediting for video interviewing technology, which is known to rely on facial analysis that examines minute facial movements.[73]

---

[67] Article 19, "Emotional Entanglement," 15.

[68] Crawford, "Time to Regulate AI That Interprets Human Emotions."

[69] See, generally, Lisa Feldman Barrett, "Are Emotions Natural Kinds?" *Perspectives on Psychological Science* 1, no. 1 (2006): 28 (the author conducted several studies disproving the universality of facial expressions as representing emotions).

[70] Firth-Godbehere, "Silicon Valley Thinks Everyone Feels the Same Six Emotions."

[71] Firth-Godbehere, "Silicon Valley Thinks Everyone Feels the Same Six Emotions" (citing James Russell, "Language, Emotion, and Facial Expression," Copernicus Center for Interdisciplinary Studies/YouTube, Nov. 26, 2011, www.youtube.com/watch?v=oS1ZtvrgDLM).

[72] Article 19, "Emotional Entanglement," 16 (citing Andrea Korte, "Facial Recognition Technology Cannot Read Emotions, Scientists Say," AAAS, Feb. 16, 2020, www.aaas.org/news/facial-recognition-technology-cannot-read-emotions-scientists-say).

[73] See Manokha, "How Using Facial Analysis in Job Interviews Could Reinforce Inequality" (discussing video interview platform HireVue's facial analysis technology, which formerly considered facial

Another study found that facial expressions and the universal emotions that supposedly underlie them are "only weakly associated" at best.[74] Furthermore, in perhaps one of the more compelling recent studies, "Emotional Expressions Reconsidered: Challenges to Inferring Emotion from Human Facial Movements," Lisa Feldman Barrett et al. "systematic[ally] review" evidence concerning emotion recognition to ultimately conclude that "how people communicate anger, disgust, fear, happiness, sadness, and surprise varies substantially across cultures, situations, and even across people within a single situation." As Barrett et al. note, emotion recognition literature is lacking context-specific studies of facial expressions. They propose that the unknowns around facial recognition technology should cause scientists to "step back from what we think we know about reading emotions in faces."[75] This warning should also be heeded by automated video interview system creators. Essentially, the work of Barrett et al. invalidates automated video interview technology not merely on the basis of biased algorithms or biased training data but also on the premise that the entire field of science on which automated video interviewing is based is misleading and underdeveloped. According to the authors,

> [T]ech companies may well be asking a question that is fundamentally wrong. Efforts to simply "read out" people's internal states from an analysis of their facial movements alone, without considering various aspects of context, are at best incomplete and at worst entirely lack validity, no matter how sophisticated the computational algorithms.[76]

5.6 THE LIMITS OF CURRENT LEGISLATION

Given the deeply flawed science behind automated video interviewing and the growing evidence that its use may perpetuate racial and other biases in hiring, one question remains: What legal protections, if any, are afforded the job candidate who is obligated to use automated video interviews as part of their job search?

5.6.1 *Title VII*

Title VII of the Civil Rights Act of 1964 "prohibits employers from discriminating against employees and applicants for employment on the bases of race, color, religion, national origin, and sex."[77] Video interviewing algorithms may run afoul of

---

movements such as "brow furrowing, brow raising, the amount eyes widen or close, lip tightening, chin raising and smiling.").

[74] Article 19, "Emotional Entanglement," 16 (citing J. I. Durán, R. Reisenzein, and J. M. Fernández-Dols, *Coherence between Emotions and Facial Expressions* (2017)).

[75] Barrett et al., "Emotional Expressions Reconsidered," 1, 48, 51.

[76] Barrett et al., "Emotional Expressions Reconsidered," 48.

[77] Jennifer Issacs, "Proving Title VII Discrimination in 2019," ABA, www.americanbar.org/groups/young_lawyers/projects/no-limits/proving-title-vii-discrimination-in-2019/ (accessed Mar. 12, 2021).

Title VII if algorithmic decision-making is found to discriminate against candidates across any of these protected classes. For example, algorithms relying on biased or incomplete training data may produce discriminatory hiring decisions that penalize those who do not reflect the white, male majority that historically has been advantaged in the workplace.

A Title VII claim brought against a discriminatory video interview algorithm would likely follow the path of a disparate impact claim as opposed to disparate treatment. Intent is essential to disparate treatment claims, and it would be particularly difficult to prove intent when the machine acts as an opaque intermediary between employers and candidates.[78] Intent may be especially difficult to prove in cases where video interview tools take steps to screen out bias on the basis of protected classes. Even if an applicant could prove intent and harm under disparate treatment theory, an employer may still then claim a legitimate, nondiscriminatory alternative reason for its action.[79] Plausible alternatives include a significant correlation between the tool in question and job performance.[80]

Unfortunately, disparate impact theory does not offer much better protection. In McKenzie Raub's Title VII analysis of video interview algorithms in "Bots, Bias and Big Data: Artificial Intelligence, Algorithmic Bias and Disparate Impact Liability," she suggests that plaintiffs may have issues establishing a prima facie case under disparate impact theory "when the discrimination is the result of incomplete, incorrect, or non-representative data ... [or data that] fails to represent groups in accurate proportions." According to Raub, statistically proving discrimination as required for a prima facie case could be particularly complicated considering that "segments of protected classes could be excluded from employment opportunities because of a lack of access to the required technology to participate in the hiring practices that use artificial intelligence."[81] Applying this insight specifically to video hiring, a minority applicant opt-out bias may mean that individuals who try to bring an adverse impact claim do not have enough peers who have used the technology to effectively prove their discrimination was statistical rather than circumstantial. Thus, although a discriminatory video interview algorithm may in fact have an adverse impact, a lack of aggregated evidence may make it difficult for applicants to establish a case for protection under Title VII.

---

[78] See Bornstein, "Antidiscriminatory Algorithms," 524 ("Worse still, current scholarship suggests, the apparent neutrality of algorithms and the 'black box' nature of machine learning make this hiring trend a new way of doing business that could be unreachable by existing antidiscrimination law."); McKenzie Raub, "Bots, Bias and Big Data: Artificial Intelligence, Algorithmic Bias and Disparate Impact Liability in Hiring Practices," *Arkansas Law Review* 71, no. 2 (2018): 550 n.174.

[79] See Jennifer Jolly-Ryan, "Have a Job to Get a Job: Disparate Treatment and Disparate Impact of the 'Currently Employed' Requirement," *Michigan Journal of Race & Law* 18, no. 1 (2012): 201.

[80] See Sullivan, "Employing AI," 420–21 (2018); Sandra F. Sperino, "Disparate Impact of Negative Impact: Future of Non-Intentional Discrimination Claims Brought by the Elderly," *Elder Law Journal* 13, no. 2 (2005): 358.

[81] Raub, "Bots, Bias and Big Data," 547–48.

Notably, other scholars take a slightly different approach on this issue than Raub by placing the onus on employers to prevent algorithmic discrimination.[82] As those scholars argue, "employment antidiscrimination law imposes an affirmative duty of care on employers to ensure that they are avoiding practices that would constrain equal opportunity in employment." Calling on the work of other legal scholars, I have argued that this duty, emanating from Title VII protections, creates an "auditing imperative" for video interviewing.[83] Such an imperative would require employers to proactively audit their algorithms for any instance of bias, which would in turn "enable litigation by generating data to serve as statistical evidence of disparate impact or by discovering practices that could be considered *discrimination per se*."[84] An auditing imperative could therefore aid plaintiffs in bringing an effective prima facie case under Title VII.

However, even if a job applicant can prove a prima facie case, it may be relatively easy for an employer to establish that their criteria for the algorithmic models in question are job related and constitute a business necessity. Establishing a business necessity reason for the hiring practice can serve as an affirmative defense for employment discrimination.[85] As previously noted, for issues concerning artificial intelligence, the primary question "seems to be 'whether ... the target variable ... is job related' ... [and] actually predictive of the job related trait." Video interview algorithms "are prognostic by nature," created for the sole purpose of identifying job-related traits.[86] Relying on biased input data – where a target variable is perhaps positively correlated with both successful job performance and historical discrimination – means that an employer may meet its burden to prove that a model correlates to job performance even if the model has a discriminatory impact.

The open question concerning an employer's burden of proof is if that burden extends beyond proving mere statistical correlation to job performance; that is, as others have asked, does an employer have to go as far as to "[show] that no problems exist with the data or model construction that are biasing the results"?[87] Legal scholar Pauline Kim suggests that Title VII could be interpreted to apply this higher burden;[88] however, many other scholars suggest it is unlikely the court would

[82] Ajunwa, "Auditing Imperative for Automated Hiring," 626–27 (referencing the work of other legal scholars such as Richard Thompson Ford, James Grimmelmann, Robert Post, David Benjamin Oppenheimer, and Noah Zatz).
[83] Ajunwa, "Auditing Imperative for Automated Hiring," 625.
[84] Ajunwa, "Auditing Imperative for Automated Hiring," 674.
[85] 42 U.S.C. § 2000e-2(k)(1)(A)(i) ("[A plaintiff] demonstrates that a respondent uses a particular employment practice that causes a disparate impact on the basis of [a protected characteristic] and the respondent fails to demonstrate that the challenged practice is job related for the position in question and consistent with its business necessity.").
[86] Raub, "Bots, Bias and Big Data," 549–50.
[87] Raub, "Bots, Bias and Big Data," 551 (quoting Pauline T. Kim, "Data-Driven Discrimination at Work," *William & Mary Law Review* 58, no. 3 (2017): 912).
[88] Kim, "Data-Driven Discrimination at Work," 921.

require such proof under existing case law.[89] A plaintiff would need open access to an algorithm to parse out these insights – and such access would almost certainly be impossible to obtain.[90] As Professor Sandra Sperino notes, employers are "reluctant to produce this information voluntarily," resulting in an informational asymmetry that disadvantages plaintiffs in the litigation process.[91]

This power imbalance continues to play out even for plaintiffs who succeed to the next step in the litigatory process, when the claimant has the opportunity to prove that a less discriminatory alternative employment practice exists after an employer has made its case. As Raub points out, "[i]f an employer fails to effectively disclose or defend the validity of its algorithm and data collection … the plaintiff is hamstrung."[92] That is, a claimant cannot effectively defend themself against a model they cannot examine or understand. James Grimmelman and Daniel Westreich come to a similar conclusion in "Incomprehensible Discrimination," wherein they examine the legal implications of a hiring model that is positively correlated with job performance yet yields a discriminatory impact. Grimmelman and Westreich find that it may be hard for a claimant to "improve on an algorithm it did not create and does not understand"; thus, the claimant would likely fail to offer the sort of "concrete and less discriminatory alternative" necessary to prevail under current Title VII case law. Grimmelman and Westreich propose, like Pauline T. Kim, a heightened standard to prove business necessity, which would "[require an employer] to show not just that its model's scores are … *correlated* with job performance but *explain* it."[93] Unfortunately, this proposed heightened standard has not been adopted as the standard interpretation of an employer's burden under Title VII.

For example, accent discrimination is a very credible threat when employers are using automated video interviewing, yet plaintiffs bringing accent discrimination claims rarely prevail in court. Many video interview algorithms employ vocal analysis; in fact, a recent audit of HireVue's algorithms suggests that accent discrimination may already be present in the company's assessment outcomes.[94] Title VII case law suggests that there is a path for candidates to bring such accent discrimination claims under Title VII's "national origin" protection clause.[95] Under Title VII, an employer

---

[89] See Grimmelmann and Westreich, "Incomprehensible Discrimination," 168–69 (stating that an employer would theoretically meet its burden of proof "by showing an 'undisputed statistically and practically significant correlation'" between an algorithms outcome and a measure of job performance); see also Barocas and Selbst, "Big Data's Disparate Impact," 702–5 (highlighting that courts employ a varying standard of job-relatedness and business necessity, generally accepting some finding that an outcome is predictive of job-performance as satisfying an employer's burden).

[90] Raub, "Bots, Bias and Big Data," 550.

[91] Sperino, "Disparate Impact of Negative Impact," 361.

[92] Raub, "Bots, Bias and Big Data," 552.

[93] Grimmelmann and Westreich, "Incomprehensible Discrimination," 164, 169, 170.

[94] Jeremy Kahn, "HireVue Drops Facial Monitoring Amid A. I. Algorithm Audit," *Fortune*, Jan. 19, 2021, https://fortune.com/2021/01/19/hirevue-drops-facial-monitoring-amid-a-i-algorithm-audit/.

[95] Mari J. Matsuda, "Voices of America: Accent, Antidiscrimination Law, and a Jurisprudence for the Last Reconstruction," *Yale Law Journal* 100, no. 5 (1991): 1332.

may consider an employee's accent when making a hiring decision only "if [the] accent materially interferes with being able to do the job."[96] As judges have ruled, the mere presence of an accent alone does not automatically mean there is material interference. In *Fragante v. Honolulu*, the Ninth Circuit distinguishes between discriminating against someone because an accent is present and discriminating on the grounds that an accent makes communication difficult. An employer may make a hiring decision based only on the "effect" of a candidate's accent.[97] Further, a manager's subjective dislike or preference concerning an accent is likely not enough to prove material interference. In *EEOC v. Brown and Brown Chevrolet, Inc.*, the EEOC charged that a car dealership's failure to promote a salesman on the grounds that he should "speak 'more like an American'" was a Title VII violation.[98] Algorithms that discriminate on the basis of accent would need to prove that the accent in question is a relevant factor in determining job performance. It is not clear that mere correlation between that trait and previous high performers is enough to meet this burden.

Yet, despite the potential for candidates to find protection under Title VII for instances of accent discrimination, the likelihood of prevailing remains low because employers are likely to mount a successful business necessity defense. As Mari Matsuda identifies in "Voices of America: Accent, Antidiscrimination Law, and a Jurisprudence for the Last Reconstruction," in practice, "[t]he fact that communication is an important element of job performance ... tends to trump this prohibition against discrimination, such that it is impossible to explain when or why plaintiffs will ever win in accent cases. In fact, they almost never do." According to Matsuda, the issue is that Title VII prohibits discrimination on the basis of a protected class but allows discrimination on the basis of "job ability." For accent discrimination, this means that when employers argue that accent is inextricably linked to job-related communication skills, they can effectively evade Title VII liability. Matsuda summarizes the issue succinctly: "[I]n every accent case the employer will raise the [customers] 'can't understand [the employee or job candidate]' defense, and in almost every reported case, the courts have accepted it."[99] For video interview algorithms that show evidence of accent discrimination, this means that employers may effectively evade liability by claiming that the discrimination in question was a valid result of the algorithm's assessment of communication skills. Claiming the algorithm found that the applicant's accent impeded effective communication with the AI in question may be enough for employers to prevail.

---

[96] EEOC, "Fact Sheet: Immigrants' Employment Rights under Federal Anti-Discrimination Laws," EEOC, Apr. 27, 2010, www.eeoc.gov/laws/guidance/fact-sheet-immigrants-employment-rights-under-federal-anti-discrimination-laws.

[97] *Fragante v. Honolulu*, 888 F.2d 591, 599 (9th Cir. 1989).

[98] David Woodfill, "Brown & Brown Settles Suit over Nigerian Accent," *East Valley Tribune*, Oct. 7, 2011, www.eastvalleytribune.com/news/brown-brown-settles-suit-over-nigerian-accent/article_f41851cd-f3ab-537b-9d60-74127f44a6ba.html.

[99] Matsuda, "Voices of America," 1332, 1348, 1350.

Overcoming the employer's business necessity defense against a Title VII suit is incredibly difficult. Indeed, on the whole, Title VII places too great of a burden on plaintiffs and thus fails to offer any substantive protection in the age of machine learning and video interviewing. Although there are mounting calls from some scholars to reconsider the mandates and burdens of Title VII in ways more favorable to plaintiffs, the current judicial interpretation of Title VII ultimately renders it inadequate to fully address the unlawfully discriminatory impact of video interviewing.

5.6.2 *The Americans with Disabilities Act*

Although the American with Disabilities Act could provide some protection for disabled applicants, the heightened burden of proof for ADA cases now established by *Murray*[100] means that proving discrimination on the basis of a disability for job applicants may be difficult. In 1990, Congress passed the ADA, a piece of civil rights legislation designed to explicitly encode the rights of disabled individuals in law.[101] Amended in 2008 to alter and significantly expand the definition of disability under the act, the ADA applies to employers with fifteen or more employees and features specific protections for disabled individuals in various settings, including the job application process.[102] The ADA specifically regulates pre-employment assessments, prohibiting the use of "qualification standards, employment tests or other selection criteria that screen out or tend to screen out an individual with a disability or a class of individuals with disabilities" unless the assessment or criterion is proven to be a job-related business necessity.[103] As video interview algorithms serve as a form of assessment, they may therefore implicate the ADA if they are found to screen out applicants on the basis of their ability status. Employers must take care that their assessment algorithms allow employees with impairments concerning "sensory, manual, or speaking skills … [to achieve] results [which] accurately reflect the skills, aptitude, or whatever other factor of such applicant or employee that such test purports to measure." Failure to do so constitutes discrimination under the ADA.[104]

Beyond pre-employment assessments, the ADA also includes specific provisions concerning medical examinations. While an employer is permitted to "make preemployment inquiries into the ability of an applicant to perform job-related functions,"

---

[100] See *Murray v. Mayo Clinic*, 934 F.3d 1101, 1105 (9th Cir. 2019), *cert. denied*, 140 S. Ct. 2720 (2020) ("Because *Head's* reasoning is clearly irreconcilable with *Gross* and *Nassar*, we overrule *Head's* holding that a plaintiff bringing a discrimination claim under Title I of the ADA need show only that a disability was a motivating factor of the adverse employment action. We hold instead that an ADA discrimination plaintiff bringing a claim under 42 U.S.C. § 12112 must show that the adverse employment action would not have occurred *but for* the disability." [emphasis added]).

[101] ADA National Network, "What Is the Americans with Disabilities Act (ADA)?"

[102] EEOC, "Notice Concerning the Americans with Disabilities Act (ADA) Amendments Act of 2008"; EEOC, "Fact Sheet: Disability Discrimination."

[103] Americans with Disabilities Act of 1990, 42 U.S.C. § 12112(b)(6) (1990).

[104] 42 U.S.C. § 12112(b)(7).

the act prohibits any medical examination or inquiry to determine an applicant's disability status, be it in kind or severity, unless it constitutes a job-related business necessity.[105] Regardless of job-relatedness, the act prohibits an employer from requiring any medical examinations before a conditional offer of employment is made.[106] According to Melson-Silimon et al., in "Personality Testing and the Americans with Disabilities Act," criteria for determining if a pre-employment assessment constitutes a medical examination includes the following:

> [T]he test (a) was administered by a healthcare/medical professional; (b) was interpreted by a healthcare or medical professional; (c) was originally designed to reveal an impairment or an applicant's current mental or physical health; (d) was invasive; (e) measured a physiological response (e.g., heart rate) to a (job-related) physical task; (f) is typically used in a medical setting; or (g) involved the use of medical equipment.[107]

Significantly, ADA provisions concerning medical examinations extend to "psychological tests that are designed to identify a mental disorder or impairment." The EEOC effectively distinguishes between prohibited psychological tests that constitute a medical examination and other forms of psychological tests; it states there are some permissible tests for pre-offer employment screening under the ADA, "includ[ing] measures of honesty, preferences, and habits."[108]

The EEOC has taken action in numerous cases since the ADA went into effect. When and how it chooses to enforce the ADA may offer significant guidance for interpreting how it may approach enforcement in terms of video interview algorithms. Take, for example, *EEOC v. Subway Inc.* filed in Indiana.[109] The agency argued that the franchise "violated federal law by rejecting a hard-of-hearing applicant because of his hearing and resultant speech impairments." The franchise allegedly chose not to hire an impaired candidate "because of his disability, citing a 'communication concern' due to the applicant's 'hearing' and 'speaking.'" The EEOC argued that this adverse employment action constituted disability discrimination that violates the ADA.[110] This enforcement action is significant, as it shows that the EEOC does not simply allow employers to argue that an impairment materially disqualifies a disabled individual from a given job. While sandwich makers

[105] 42 U.S.C. §§ 12112(d)(2)(B), (d)(4)(A).

[106] EEOC, "Questions and Answers: Enforcement Guidance on Disability Related Inquiries and Medical Examinations under the Americans with Disabilities Act," EEOC, July 17, 2000.

[107] Arturia Melson-Silimon et al., "Personality Testing and the Americans with Disabilities Act: Cause for Concern as Normal and Abnormal Personality Models Are Integrated," *Industrial and Organizational Psychology* 12, no. 2 (2019): 121 (citing EEOC, "Enforcement Guidance on Disability-Related Inquiries and Medical Examinations of Employees under the ADA," July 26, 2000).

[108] Melson-Silimon et al., "Personality Testing and the Americans with Disabilities Act.

[109] See EEOC, "Subway Franchisee to Pay $28,700 to Settle EEOC Disability Discrimination Suit," *EEOC Newsroom*, Press Release, Mar. 26, 2021, www.eeoc.gov/newsroom/subway-franchisee-pay-28700-settle-eeoc-disability-discrimination-suit.

[110] EEOC, "Subway Franchisee Sued by EEOC for Disability Discrimination."

with specific ways of speaking may have been typical in the Subway franchise, or in the employer's view may have even been preferable, the EEOC effectively stated that such speaking patterns are not a legitimate consideration for job qualification such that the deaf individual may be disqualified. Thus, video interview algorithms that consider certain speaking patterns in making an employment decision may directly violate the ADA.

In *EEOC v. Ranstad US, LP*[111] the EEOC filed suit against a Maryland company that failed to hire an individual once he disclosed that he was autistic. The company allegedly initially considered the applicant highly qualified for the lab technician job in question, "fast-track[ing] [the candidate's] participation in the hiring process" as result. Once the applicant disclosed his disability, however, "he was told that the lab technician position had been put 'on hold.'" Ultimately, the applicant was not hired and the company went on to fill the position with another recruit. The EEOC argued that this adverse employment decision was made in response to the applicant's autism disclosure, in violation of the ADA.[112] The case was settled with Randstad agreeing to pay $60,000.[113] In the context of video interview assessments, this case is significant because it suggests that employers may be liable for discrimination on the basis of a hidden disability once it is revealed through the hiring process. Given the invasive nature of data-based insights, a video interview algorithm may effectively disclose and penalize disability without an individual ever consenting to such disclosure. Such penalty would directly violate the ADA without a candidate ever even knowing the disclosure occurred.

Although automated video interviewing is still a relatively new practice, there is some case law concerning the legality of personality testing under the ADA. This case law provides compelling, if not controlling, precedent for certain video interview algorithms that also test for personality traits. HireVue, for example, states that its assessments are designed to produce "excellent insight into attributes like social intelligence (interpersonal skills), communication skills, *personality traits*, and overall job aptitude."[114] Given the vague yet potentially invasive nature of the insights video interview algorithms produce concerning an individual's personality, it is valuable to consider how case law has treated personality testing under the ADA when evaluating protections for video interview candidates.

To the extent that automated video interviewing systems are also personality tests, *Thompson v. Borg-Warner Protective Services Corp* (1996) helped establish that they do not necessarily violate the ADA's medical examination clause in all instances. The

---

[111] *EEOC v. Randstad*, Civil Action No. 1:11-cv-01303-WDQ).

[112] EEOC, "Randstad US Sued by EEOC for Disability Discrimination."

[113] EEOC, "Randstad US, LP to Pay 60,000 to Settle EEOC Disability Bias Suit," *EEOC Newsroom*, May 10, 2102, www.eeoc.gov/newsroom/randstad-us-lp-pay-60000-settle-eeoc-disability-bias-suit.

[114] Patricia Barnes, "Artificial Intelligence Poses New Threat to Equal Employment Opportunity," *Forbes*, Nov. 10, 2019 (emphasis added), www.forbes.com/sites/patriciagbarnes/2019/11/10/artificial-intelligence-poses-new-threat-to-equal-employment-opportunity/?sh=6e0a33036488.

court found that plaintiff Bog-Warner's use of a personality test called PASS-III to screen security guard applicants was legal, directly applying the factors laid out by the EEOC's guidance to determine that PASS-III was not a medical exam for ADA purposes. By distinguishing between prohibited pre-offer medical exams and pre-employment assessments that provided "information surrounding an applicant's character or personality traits, and their fit for the job," the court effectively found that personality tests may be permitted by the ADA in some forms.[115] Video interview assessments must therefore meet more specific criteria to invoke the ADA's medical examination protection.

The Seventh Circuit Court of Appeals decision in *Karraker v. Rent-a-Center* (2005) sheds insight on what an assessment that violates the ADA's medical examination clause may look like. In *Karraker*, the court found that Rent-a-Center's use of the MMPI as one of many variables in their pre-promotion test constituted discrimination under the ADA because "although applicant responses were not interpreted by a medical professional, the use of the MMPI would still be likely to identify and 'weed out' individuals with personality disorders who are protected under the ADA."[116] The court found that the MMPI was at least partly designed to identify mental illness and thus constituted a medical examination.[117] Applied to video interview algorithms, this case shows that algorithms need not be interpreted by a doctor to violate the ADA; they need only be proven to be designed even in part to reveal mental impairments. Based on *Karraker's* precedent, any video interview algorithm that incorporated the MMPI or a similar medical assessment in its design may violate the ADA. However, given the opaque nature of algorithms, proving such integration would be nearly impossible. What's more, the MMPI is a more obvious example of an assessment designed to reveal mental impairments, given its use as a medical diagnostic tool. It is not clear how courts would apply this precedent to proprietary algorithmic insights which *de facto* reveal impairments by coding for particular traits that are proxies for disability.

Even if courts did find automated video interviewing to constitute an illegal medical assessment under the ADA, job candidates may still struggle to prevail on their claims. In *Barnes v. Cochran*, the court found that a pre-employment psychological evaluation *did* violate the ADA's ban on pre-offer medical evaluation, applying the EEOC's seven-factor guidance to the case. However, the court nonetheless ruled in favor of the employer, arguing that the plaintiff did not meet their burden of proof to show that "employment was denied for discriminatory reasons," thus mooting the ADA violation. According to Melson-Silimon et al., "[t]his decision highlights the burden plaintiffs face when suing on the grounds of disability-based discrimination; specifically, any legitimate justification articulated by the defendant for an adverse employment decision must be proven by the plaintiff to be a pretext for

---

[115] Melson-Silimon et al., "Personality Testing and the Americans with Disabilities Act," 122–23.

[116] Melson-Silimon et al., "Personality Testing and the Americans with Disabilities Act" (quoting *Karraker v. Rent-a-Center, Inc.*, 411 F.3d 831, 837 (7th Cir. 2005)).

[117] Abdi Tinwalla and J. Richard Ciccone, "ADA and Medical Examinations," *Journal of the American Academy of Psychiatry and Law* 34, no. 2 (2006): 256.

discrimination."[118] Given that employment algorithms consider thousands of different data points, it may be nearly impossible to prove that the disability in question was the deciding factor in the algorithm's ultimate employment recommendation. This is an issue not limited to medical examination cases, but central to all ADA claims brought against video interview algorithms.

Critically, the ADA was modeled in part as parallel legislation to the Civil Rights Act of 1964. Title I of the ADA specifically and intentionally mirrors Title VII, down to EEOC enforcement power granted over both statutes.[119] Applying the ADA to video interviewing thus faces many of the same challenges seen in a Title VII case. ADA claims follow a litigation structure similar to Title VII claims, though they largely fall under disparate treatment theories rather than disparate impact theories. This means an applicant would need to prove that an employer would not have made the adverse employment decision in question but for the individual's disability. Thus, it is not enough for a claimant to provide evidence that a video interview algorithm constituted a prohibited pre-offer medical examination or could have screened out candidates with disabilities.[120] The candidate must still prove that in their specific case, the fact that the interviewing algorithm screened them out on the basis of a disability was the causative reason for why they did not get a job offer. Satisfying such a burden of proof would require a deep insight into the algorithm in question, a level of access the job applicant would almost certainly be denied. Prevailing on an ADA claim would therefore prove a serious challenge in the face of the opaque nature of hiring algorithms given that first, many applicants are prevented from examining the hiring algorithms, and second, the black box nature of some algorithms makes it difficult to ascertain how exactly the discrimination happened.[121]

5.6.3 *Privacy Law Protections for Job Applicants*

Given the limited reach of anti-discrimination laws in addressing employment discrimination in automated video interviewing systems, it is important to consider other legal mechanisms or regimes for doing so. Automated video interviewing systems pose great privacy risks because, as a necessary means to quantifying the veracity and character of job applicants, they capture a treasure trove of biometric data. The question then becomes: Are there any extant privacy laws that can provide some legal protection to job applicants?

---

[118] Melson-Silimon et al., "Personality Testing and the Americans with Disabilities Act," 123.

[119] Robert D. Dinerstein, "The Americans with Disabilities Act of 1990: Progeny of the Civil Rights Act of 1964," *Human Rights Magazine* 31, no. 3 (July 1, 2004), www.americanbar.org/groups/crsj/publications/human_rights_magazine_home/human_rights_vol31_2004/summer2004/irr_hr_summer04_disable/.

[120] Third Circuit Model Jury Instruction for Employment Claims under the Americans with Disabilities Act (Apr. 2019), www.ca3.uscourts.gov/sites/ca3/files/9_Chap_9_2019_April.pdf.

[121] Joshua A. Kroll et al., "Accountable Algorithms," *University of Pennsylvania Law Review* 165, no. (2017): 636.

5.6.3.1 Notice and Consent

In the United States, federal information privacy law and policy generally follows a framework known as "notice-and-consent." Legal scholar Daniel Susser explains the origins of this framework in *Notice after Notice-and-Consent*, as he examines common criticisms of the policy. Notice-and-consent grew out of a 1973 project by the U.S. Department of Health, Education, and Welfare (HEW) to mitigate "the threat to individual privacy posed by the government's move toward computerized record-keeping." HEW's response was to establish the Fair Information Practice Principles (FIPPs) to guide regulation and policymaking around information privacy.[122] Critically, the FIPPs are only guidance; they do not in and of themselves have the weight of law.[123] Rather, they "encourage" compliance through the threat of "Federal Trade Commission (FTC) enforcement actions" on the basis of "'unfair and deceptive' trade practices." Thus, the value of the FIPPs is heavily dependent on how the FTC conceptualizes and enforces them. The FTC updated the FIPPs in 2000 "as guidance for designing commercial privacy policies."[124] The revised FIPPs offer four recommendations concerning Notice, Choice, Access, and Security, stating that:

- Notice – Websites would be required to provide consumers clear and conspicuous notice of their information practices, including what information they collect, how they collect it (e.g., directly or through non-obvious means such as cookies), how they use it, how they provide choice, access, and security to consumers, whether they disclose the information collected to other entities, and whether other entities are collecting information through the site.
- Choice – Websites would be required to offer consumers choices as to how their personal identifying information is used beyond the use for which the information was provided …
- Access – Websites would be required to offer consumers reasonable access to the information a website has collected about them, including a reasonable opportunity to review information and to correct inaccuracies or delete information.
- Security – Websites would be required to take reasonable steps to protect the security of the information they collect from consumers.[125]

---

[122] Daniel Susser, "Notice after Notice-and-Consent: Why Privacy Disclosures Are Valuable Even if Consent Frameworks Aren't," *Journal of Information Policy* 9 (2019): 37, 39–40.

[123] See U.S. GAO, "In-Car Location-Based Services," GAO-14-81, Appendix I: Objectives, Scope, and Methodology 23, 25 n.4 (2013) ("FIPPs are widely accepted principles for protecting the privacy and security of personal information. They were first proposed in 1973 by a U.S. government advisory committee. FIPPs are not precise legal requirements. Rather, they provide a framework of principles for balancing the need for privacy with other interests.").

[124] Susser, "Notice after Notice-and-Consent," 41.

[125] FTC, "Privacy Online: Fair Information Practices in the Electronic Marketplace," Report to Congress, May 2000, 36–37, www.ftc.gov/sites/default/files/documents/reports/privacy-online-fair-information-practices-electronic-marketplace-federal-trade-commission-report/privacy2000.pdf.

These principles gave rise to the notice-and-consent regime. Susser purports that the FIPP revisions are significant given their "procedural" nature; because the FTC "drop[ped] the substantive concerns about data reliability and purpose specificity" that were central to the original FIPPs, the resulting notice-and-consent framework essentially allows employers to use consumer information as they see fit, so long as consumers knowingly agree. According to Susser, this "free-market approach to privacy" has been panned by critics for (1) not truly providing consumers "real options to choose from"; (2) allowing businesses to exploit "information asymmetries" at the expense of the uninformed consumer; (3) proving to be an unfeasible method for "engag[ing] with a huge number of information actors" in the modern day; (4) forcing consumers to "make onetime decisions" about particular pieces of data without knowing the long-term "aggregate" effects of that data; and (5) ignoring the "social interests" inherent to data, instead vesting all decision-making authority with consumers. Susser, calling on various other critics, including Joel Reidenberg, Solon Barocas, and Helen Nissenbaum, ultimately declares "[n]otice-and-consent … to be a failed regulatory model."[126] He joins other scholars in proposing an alternative model for regulating information privacy in the age of Big Data, explored in more detail below.

The failures of the notice-and-consent framework are especially salient in the context of algorithm-based video interviewing. Consenting to give up one's data rights in the video interview process may not feel like much of a choice when employment is at stake; companies may not offer, or advertise that they offer, any meaningful alternative method of job candidate evaluation. As such, the nature of the hiring process means candidates may consent by default. Furthermore, it is important to consider when and how employers provide notice disclosures to candidates. Some video interview vendors only act as "data processer[s]"; that is, *employers* – not the software company itself – retain the rights to control data candidates provide.[127] Thus, a candidate cannot simply turn to a vendor's website to understand how their data will be used. They instead must seek out an employer's privacy policy directly.

This poses two potential issues. First, how employers choose to provide a privacy notice may influence consenting; if the disclosure occurs right before a candidate starts an interview, it is likely that the applicant may see consent as part of the bargain for the opportunity of an interview. Second, delegating data control to employers means that a candidate's privacy rights are directly tied to the power asymmetry of the pre-employment relationship. Candidates may be less likely to ask questions or request data access from an employer for fear of risking their job

---

[126] Susser, "Notice after Notice-and-Consent," at 41–47.
[127] HireVue, "HireVue Privacy Notice" ("If you are a job candidate ('Candidate') or employee ('Employee') using our Services on behalf of one of our customers who are engaging us to provide the Services to them (the 'Potential Employers'), we are collecting and processing your personal information on behalf of the Potential Employers. In such cases, we are acting as a data processor and are collecting and processing your personal information on their behalf and in accordance with their instructions.").

opportunity. Furthermore, candidates who engage with the same video interview software for interviews across multiple companies may not realize that their privacy rights are changing with each successive interview. As such, they may only read the first disclosure and consent to all successive disclosures under the assumption that the substance is the same. This potential confusion is significant given the serious privacy issues inherent to video interviewing, which I discuss in more detail below. Above all, as identified by Susser, notice-and-consent's procedural protections do not address any of the substantive privacy issues that candidates face. If an employer chooses to share the highly sensitive, aggregated data insights they mined from a candidate's interview with other businesses or potential employers, it is not clear what substantive rights over their data notice-and-consent would give a candidate if they had already signed an initial, broad consent agreement.

5.6.3.2 Privacy in State Law

Given the massive gaps left by federal privacy law, some states have taken steps to protect against the threat of employers harnessing the power of Big Data. For example, in 2019 Illinois passed the Artificial Intelligence Video Interview Act (AIVIA), specifically designed to govern privacy risks associated with video inter-view assessments. This law, dubbed "the first of its kind in the US,"[128] includes five main requirements employers using AI video technology, such as HireVue, must adhere to. First, employers are required to "notify the applicant, in advance, that the organization is using the technology to analyze video interviews." The law further mandates that employers "[e]xplain to the applicant 'how the [AI] works' and what general characteristics the technology uses to evaluate applicants."[129] This clear call for transparency is helpful. However, many video technology companies do not publish adequate information on the workings of their products.[130] Thus, the effects of this part of the law may take one of two paths: Either AI video providers will be forced to publish more information about their algorithms *or* the standard for meet-ing this transparency mandate will be effectively so low as to render it meaningless. Beyond transparency, the law requires that employers "[o]btain, in advance, the applicant's consent to use the technology." The law also features provisions for data protection. It imposes limits on "the distribution and sharing of the video," granting access "to only those persons 'whose expertise or technology' is necessary to evaluate

---

[128] Rebecca Heilweil, "Illinois Says You Should Know if AI Is Grading Your Online Job Interviews," *Vox*, Jan. 1, 2020, www.vox.com/recode/2020/1/1/21043000/artificial-intelligence-job-applications-illinios-video-interivew-act.

[129] Matthew Jedreski et al., "Illinois Becomes First State to Regulate Employers' Use of Artificial Intelligence to Evaluate Video Interviews," Davis Wright Tremaine LLP, Sept. 3, 2019, www.dwt.com/blogs/artificial-intelligence-law-advisor/2019/09/illinois-becomes-first-state-to-regulate-employers.

[130] See generally Kroll et al., "Accountable Algorithms," 636 (arguing that many algorithmic systems are "black box" systems with little explanation of their workings).

the applicant." Further, candidates are given some control over what happens to the video after their assessment. Employers are required to "destroy the video (and all backup copies) within 30 days" of the applicant requesting its destruction.[131]

The law firm David Wright Tremaine, LLP (DWT), identifies a few key issues with the Illinois law. Chiefly, it fails to define "'artificial intelligence' and 'artificial intelligence analysis'" along with other "key terms." This ambiguity may mean that certain AI uses by employers, such as "to track data about its candidates," may not be covered. Further, ambiguity in the transparency part of the law may, as suggested above, pose serious problems for its effective use. DWT notes that the law does not go in depth to specify or define "how much detail about the AI technology an employer must provide when 'explaining how artificial intelligence works' to an applicant" or what "'characteristics' of the AI employers must disclose."[132] Therefore, employers may be permitted to use broad, cursory statements such as "AI will assess a candidate's performance"[133] to satisfy this requirement, statements that do not serve the true spirit of transparency. There is further no requirement that candidate consent be expressly written. DWT notes, further, that the law "does not include a private right of action or any explicit penalties," which could raise serious issues in enforcing its provisions. As for data destruction, DWT points out that it is not clear if "data that an employer extracts or derives from the video interviews … is subject to the destruction duty under the law." If such data is not protected by the AIVIA, then the extent to which the act allows candidates control over their interview data is potentially limited. Lastly, DWT points out that "there is no guidance on what it means for a job to be 'based in' Illinois, and the statute is silent as to whether employees may refuse to consider applicants who refuse to consent."[134]

Ultimately, AIVIA is a step in the right direction, as it touches on the serious concerns of transparency and data rights. However, the primary, overarching issue with the act is a lack of specificity. Failing to define key terms, to expand on essential provisions, or to stipulate any enforcement mechanism means that the effective impact of transparency and data rights measures is limited and that employers who wish to evade the law may do so. Further, while some employers may surely make a good faith effort to comply, many employers are not themselves privy to how the AI they use truly works. Companies such as HireVue closely guard their algorithms and technologies to protect their market share, to the detriment of clients and candidates alike. In order to push AI video interview companies to be more transparent, the law must put in place effective penalties such that employers would not choose to use the technology unless AI companies provided enough information. Effective legislation must hold enough weight to impact all stakeholders in the AI

[131] Jedreski et al., "Illinois Becomes First State to Regulate Employers' Use of Artificial Intelligence."
[132] Jedreski et al., "Illinois Becomes First State to Regulate Employers' Use of Artificial Intelligence."
[133] Ajunwa, "Auditing Imperative for Automated Hiring," 644.
[134] Jedreski et al., "Illinois Becomes First State to Regulate Employers' Use of Artificial Intelligence."

video interview universe. Again, it is important to reiterate that Illinois is "at the forefront of regulating technology and personal data."[135] AIVIA should be commended
as first-of-its-kind legislation that is shedding light on critical issues of public interest.
It simply needs to go further to counterbalance the immense power the AI sphere
currently holds. Regardless, AIVIA acts as a model for other states to specifically
protect consent and disclosure data rights around video interviewing. Given that
federal protections may not apply, such specific legislation is an important first step
in protecting applicant data.

Another Illinois law, the Biometric Information Privacy Act (BIPA), passed in
2008, offers more substantive protections around the specific issue of biometric privacy. Key BIPA provisions around biometric data collection and use by businesses
include "informed consent," "a limited right to disclosure," "protection obligations
and retention guidelines," "prohibit[ions on] profiting from biometric data," "a
private right of action for individuals harmed by BIPA violations," and provisions
for "statutory damages." Given that video interview assessments varyingly consider
vocal and facial expressions, assessments may actually qualify for BIPA protections,
as biometric data refers to "the measurement and statistical analysis of an individual's physical and behavioral characteristics," including "voice prints," "fac[ial] …
features," and "gestures … [and] voice."[136] While BIPA is primarily procedural in
nature – again adhering to the federal notice-and-consent framework – it does afford
candidates the right to sue and provide protections concerning third-party access to
sensitive biometric data. This is important considering the serious potential harm
that may come to candidates if sensitive biometric interview data is sold to third
parties, not in the least limited to the threat of deep fakes. BIPA therefore fills a
gap as it encodes specific kinds of information privacy in law, though it stops short
of prohibiting the collection of such information altogether. Unfortunately, while
other states, including Texas and Washington, have passed similar laws, these states
appear to offer even more limited protections than Illinois.[137] Therefore, while offering a partially useful model, BIPA does not constitute or represent sweeping biometric privacy protections at the state level.

[135] Jedreski et al., "Illinois Becomes First State to Regulate Employers' Use of Artificial Intelligence."
[136] Jackson Lewis, "Illinois Biometric Information Privacy Act FAQs [2021]," www.jacksonlewis.com/
sites/default/files/docs/IllinoisBIPAFAQs.pdf.
[137] See Fischer Phillips, "Collection of Biometric Data Raises Privacy Concerns for Employees and
Compliance Issues for Employers," *Fisher Phillips Insights*, Mar. 15, 2018, www.fisherphillips.com/
Employment-Privacy-Blog/collection-of-biometric-data-raises-privacy-concerns; see also Capture of
Use of Biometric Identifier Act, 50 Tex. Bus. & Com. Code Ann. § 503.001 (resembling BIPA by
requiring that, prior to being authorized to collect biometric identifiers, organization must obtain
informed consent, that need not be in writing, from individuals but, differing from Illinois state law by
only allowing the Texas attorney general to enforce the law, as the law does not provide a private right
of action); H.B. 1493, 2017 Sess., 65th Leg. (Wash. 1999) (limiting the definition of "biometric data" so
that it likely excludes the facial recognition technology social media and photo storage websites use to
automatically tag users in digital photographs and applying the law only to those biometric identifiers
"enrolled" in a commercial database).

Some states have gone beyond specific privacy applications, instead creating more broad privacy protections to govern information exchanges at large. The California Consumer Privacy Rights Act (CCPA), passed in 2020, offers one such example.[138] CCPA gives consumers specific, enumerated rights over their data:

1. Right to correct inaccurate information ...
2. Right to have personal information collected subject to data minimization and purpose limitations ...
3. Right to receive notice from businesses planning on using sensitive personal information and ask them to stop ...
4. Right to access information ... [and]
5. Right to opt out of sharing information with third parties.[139]

As of January 1, 2021, CCPA protections were extended to California job applicants.[140] While the CCPA largely follows notice-and-consent frameworks, it takes significant steps towards giving consumers and employees meaningful control over their data by allowing individuals to opt out of data sharing and certain uses of their data over its life span.

Given the new nature of the law, it's difficult to measure its practical effects; reports suggest that the law's rollout has resulted in a mix of "firms ... disclosing too little data – or far too much." Companies such as Uber and Lyft have been selective as to what data they choose to disclose and what they choose to retain. One Los Angeles man who tried to access his data reported that "[e]veryone seems to be ... see[ing] what they can get away with ... I hate to say it, but I think the companies are going to win."[141] Compliance concern is real. Even if a state creates an all-encompassing information privacy law that extends to consumers and job applicants alike, ensuring that companies actually comply with the law is a massive regulatory task that state-level agencies may struggle to keep up with. This reality makes the need for federal regulation with comprehensive enforcement mechanisms all the more critical.

On the whole, state laws offer some information privacy protections for citizens of certain states who fall within certain categories. However, essentially no federal or state law offers any affirmative declaration of the data rights of job applicants. Notice-and-consent guidance has resulted in a serious gap in substantive protections. These patchwork state protections ultimately do not provide comprehensive protections.

---

[138] Privacy Rights Clearinghouse, "California Privacy Rights Act: An Overview," Dec. 10, 2020, https://privacyrights.org/resources/california-privacy-rights-act-overview.

[139] Privacy Rights Clearinghouse, "California Privacy Rights Act."

[140] AB-25 (Cal. 2019. California Consumer Privacy Act of 2018, https://leginfo.legislature.ca.gov/faces/billTextClient.xhtml?bill_id=201920200AB25.

[141] Greg Bensinger, "So Far, under California's New Privacy Law, Firms Are Disclosing Too Little Data – or Far Too Much," *Washington Post*, Jan. 21, 2020, www.washingtonpost.com/technology/2020/01/21/ccpa-transparency/.

5.6.3.3 The Role of the Fair Credit Reporting Act

The Fair Credit Reporting ACT (FCRA) is a 1970 law enacted "to regulate the credit reporting industry because of concerns about the fairness and accuracy of credit reports";[142] however, in recent years, legal scholars, and even the FTC itself, have suggested that its consumer privacy protections may extend to businesses using consumer data and data-based insights.[143] Thus, it is important to consider what, if any, privacy protections the FCRA may offer to video interview candidates.

The FCRA governs "compan[ies] ... collecting and sharing third-party data that is used or expected to be used as a factor in determining eligibility for credit, insurance, employment, or other purpose[s] authorized under the FCRA."[144] These companies are considered "consumer reporting agencies" (CRAs) under the FCRA, formally defined as

> any person which, for monetary fees, dues, or on a cooperative nonprofit basis, regularly engages in whole or in part in the practice of assembling or evaluating consumer credit information or other information on consumers for the purpose of furnishing consumer reports to third parties.[145]

Legal scholars Pauline T. Kim and Erika Hanson note that "entities that assemble and evaluate information for non-commercial uses as well as entities that assemble information about the entity's own interactions with its customers" are not considered CRAs.[146] Therefore, employers likely could not qualify as CRAs because interview reports would be for internal, non-commercial use; however, external video interview vendors who provide assessments to employers may qualify as CRAs. Thus, from the outset, it seems that video interview vendors may be governed by the FCRA to the extent that the data collected during a video interview is: (1) for commercial use and (2) considered a consumer report. Kim and Hanson refer to

---

[142] Pauline T. Kim and Erika Hanson, "People Analytics and the Regulation of Information under the Fair Credit Reporting Act," *St. Louis University Law Journal* 61, no. 117 (2016): 20.

[143] See Kim and Hanson, "People Analytics and the Regulation of Information under the Fair Credit Reporting Act," 28; see also Ajunwa, "Auditing Imperative for Automated Hiring," 655; Karen Sanzaro, "Big Data: FTC Issues Report Cautioning That Use of Big Data May Violate Federal Consumer Protection Laws or Raise Ethical Considerations," Alston and Bird: Privacy, Cyber, & Data Strategy Blog, Jan. 19, 2016, www.alstonprivacy.com/big-data-ftc-issues-report-cautioning-that-use-of-big-data-may-violate-federal-consumer-protection-laws-or-raise-ethical-considerations/ (summarizing the FTC warning that companies using Big Data may be subject to the FCRA, references FTC enforcement actions against a firm that used consumer data for "eligibility determinations" without complying to FCRA).

[144] Chi Chi Wu, "Data Gatherers Evading the FCRA May Find Themselves Still in Hot Water," National Consumer Law Center, June 14, 2019, https://library.nclc.org/data-gatherers-evading-fcra-may-find-themselves-still-hot-water.

[145] Wu, "Data Gatherers Evading the FCRA May Find Themselves Still in Hot Water" (quoting 15 U.S.C. § 1681a(f)).

[146] Kim and Hanson, "People Analytics and the Regulation of Information under the Fair Credit Reporting Act," 21–22.

a three-prong framework that courts have developed to determine if "information constitutes a consumer report under the law":

1) the information was communicated by the consumer reporting agency; 2) it bears on the "consumer's credit worthiness, character, general reputation, personal characteristics, or mode of living"; and 3) it was "used or expected to be used or collected in whole or in part for one of the enumerated purposes.[147]

All "elements" must be "satisfie[d]" to constitute a consumer report.[148] Also expressly excluded from "consumer reports" are "report[s] containing information solely as to transactions or experiences between the consumer and the person making the report."[149] It seems plausible that video interviews may fall within this exclusion: The only consumer-specific data that interview assessments consider is collected from the interaction between the candidate and the algorithm. However, the algorithms *do* consider thousands of external data points about other individuals.[150] While this is not information about the consumer, it is information used to make judgments and assumptions about the consumer that are not limited to the "transactions or experiences between the consumer" and reporter.[151] The question would be to what extent this external information is actually "contain[ed]" within the report.[152]

Thus, it seems possible that video interviews, where vendors collect candidate data to determine a candidate's "character" or "personal characteristics" (among other things) for the purposes of employment eligibility could qualify as consumer reports under the FCRA.[153] Therefore, video interview vendors would likely qualify as CRAs. As I explored in a 2020 law review article, "The Paradox of Automation," applying FCRA frameworks to hiring algorithms "may enable the job applicant to discover if the employer had access to discriminatory information or even to establish a pattern of discriminatory information furnished to the employer for protected groups, thus perhaps assisting in a disparate impact cause of action." As CRAs, vendors would be required "to 'follow reasonable procedures to assure the maximum possible accuracy of [their] files,'"[154] including allowing "consumers to review information in their files without charge, investigat[e] alleged inaccuracies, and provid[e] information to consumers about their rights." Employers, as the entity using the consumer report, would be required to

---

[147] Kim and Hanson, "People Analytics and the Regulation of Information under the Fair Credit Reporting Act," 22 (quoting *Ernst v. Dish Network, LLC*, 49 F. Supp. 3d 377, 381 (S.D.N.Y. 2014) (citing cases from the U.S. Courts of Appeals)).

[148] Kim and Hanson, "People Analytics and the Regulation of Information under the Fair Credit Reporting Act," 22.

[149] 15 U.S.C. § 1681a(d).

[150] 15 U.S.C. § 1681 Part II(b)(3).

[151] 15 U.S.C. § 1681(a)(d)(2)(i).

[152] 15 U.S.C. § 1681(a)(d)(2)(i).

[153] 15 U.S.C. § 1681a(e).

[154] Ajunwa, "Paradox of Automation as Anti-Bias Intervention," 1735, 1740.

provide a clear, conspicuous, and stand-alone disclosure [to applicants] that a consumer report may be obtained for employment purposes; they would be required to request written authorization from the applicant or employee for procurement of the report; and certify to the consumer reporting agency its compliance with the requirements of the statute and that it will not violate any equal employment opportunity law.[155]

Furthermore, the FCRA would require that an employer "provide notice before rejecting a job application … or taking any other adverse employment action" in addition to "provid[ing the applicant] a copy of the consumer report relied upon and a description of the individual's rights under the FCRA," which include "an opportunity to review the report and attempt to correct any mistakes." After rejecting the applicant, the employer would further have to follow through with several more procedural steps, including providing information about the CRA who provided the report and "notice of the individual's rights to dispute the accuracy or completeness of the report and to receive an additional copy of the report if requested within sixty days." Failure to comply would result in FTC enforcement action.[156]

As Kim and Hanson note, the protections afforded by the FCRA are "procedural." Indeed, the FCRA does not offer job applicants any substantive right to privacy and does not limit "the *types* of information that can be collected or reported."[157] However, if video interviews were considered consumer reports under the FCRA, it seems possible that FCRA protections may ameliorate some problems inherent to video interviewing. Particularly, given the opaque nature of algorithms, disclosures concerning the reasoning for an adverse employment action on the basis of the interview may provide valuable "insight as to how [candidates] are evaluated" and could help "society … regain some measure of checks over the information that is used to 'screen' candidates as part of the automated hiring trend."[158]

---

[155] Kim and Hanson, "People Analytics and the Regulation of Information under the Fair Credit Reporting Act," 22–23.
[156] Kim and Hanson, "People Analytics and the Regulation of Information under the Fair Credit Reporting Act."
[157] Kim and Hanson, "People Analytics and the Regulation of Information under the Fair Credit Reporting Act," 25.
[158] Ajunwa, "Paradox of Automation as Anti-Bias Intervention," 1741.

6

The Unbounded Workplace and Worker Surveillance

A watched pot never boils.

–Poor Richard (pseud. Benjamin Franklin)

It is "un-American, humiliating, and an insult to the honesty and fair dealing and self-respect of an American mechanic to have a man standing over him with a watch."

–Colonel F. E. Hobbs, *The Taylor and Other Systems of Shop Management*

The quantification of workers necessitates the careful monitoring or surveillance of their activities. Though the monitoring of workers is not a new concept, the Taylorist revolution and its accompanying technological advances have transformed both the nature and degree of surveillance for workers. While technological innovations permitted an expansion of the workplace beyond the bounded confines of a physical workplace, Taylorist concerns with "soldiering" and quantifying worker productivity introduced both the necessity and the desire for greater worker surveillance. In the present moment, mechanical managers in the form of productivity applications and wearable applications have been delegated the task of surveilling workers. The practice of Taylorism as scientific management meant the splintering of work into discrete tasks, enabling both the de-skilling of labor and a temporal fix for accounting for worker productivity. Scientific management, as applied Taylorism, required the surveillance of workers to standardize the time expected to complete job tasks – recall the image of Taylor and subsequent managers stalking the factory floor with a notebook and stopwatch, while peering over the shoulders of factory workers. Three things have worked in conjunction to stoke the demand for worker surveillance: the standardization of work time under Taylorism; the freeing of work from a bounded space; and, ultimately, the quest for productivity maximization as the paramount goal of scientific management. Thus, worker surveillance is inextricable from all past and current iterations of scientific management as a capitalist imaginary for workplace relations.

Scientific management requires worker surveillance to achieve its goals, and, in turn, the data from worker surveillance dictates the goals of scientific management.

Thus, scientific management both creates the necessity for worker surveillance and is sustained by it. Worker surveillance as part of scientific management creates a closed loop system – it is a chimera eating its own tail. Of interest to the law is how this closed loop system can engender inequality. The greater worker surveillance requisite for and encouraged by scientific management could widen the gulf of inequality by exacting greater control over workers through the vast amount of data accumulated from what Julie Cohen has termed "the Surveillance-Industrial complex." This surveillance also threatens to decimate the work/non-work divide. As the data from worker surveillance gives greater power to managers to drive productivity, it also feeds the appetite for more data. The question now is how the law should address this avarice for worker data. Given technological advances that have produced mechanical managers capable of indefatigable and perpetual surveillance, what should be meaningful delineations of the legal limits of worker surveillance? To answer this requires a reconsideration of the reasonable expectation of privacy for workers, and in turn, what sort of worker surveillance may be deemed (in)congruous with democratic notions of personhood and human dignity. When a worker's labor can be quantified to the minutiae, is the current law able to serve as a meaningful mediator against a data-driven subjugation of workers?

6.1 THEORIES OF WORKPLACE SURVEILLANCE AND THE PLIGHT OF WORKERS

When prompted to consider the concept of surveillance, many will recall an Orwellian dystopian society firmly under government control, inundated with video cameras at every corner, and "Big Brother–style" information monitoring and control. Indeed, in his acclaimed 1949 novel *Nineteen Eighty-Four*, George Orwell provides a terrifying vision of total surveillance featuring a protagonist, Winston Smith, who works in the Records Department of the state's Ministry of Truth. Smith's primary job task is to falsify records for the state – or to rewrite them so that they are "accurate" according to the totalitarian government of Oceana. In describing Smith's work conditions, Orwell provides detailed descriptions of hovering guards and *telescreens* – camera equivalents that track a worker's every move, in and out of the workplace. The reality of work life in modern-day America is not far off from this Orwellian dystopia.[1] But this is far truer for private employers than for governmental employers. For governmental employees, the Fourth Amendment, which circumscribes governmental surveillance action, provides some check on the extent to which government employees may be surveilled. For privately employed workers, there is no such federally mandated check. Not only does current federal law allow for unchecked worker surveillance in the private workplace, but worker surveillance has also begun to encroach on the home, which was previously seen as the wholly

[1]   John Broich, "2017 Isn't '1984' – It's Stranger than Orwell Imagined," *The Independent*, Feb. 1, 2017.

separate domain of the worker. This phenomenon is due to socio-technical developments allowing for telecommuting, and other exigencies, such as the Covid-19 health crisis. As work becomes increasingly unbounded by physical space and time, unchecked surveillance threatens the total erosion of the personhood of the worker.

Michel Foucault's *Discipline and Punish* is a critical text in the canon of surveillance scholarship. Foucault sets out to discover why physical violence as a form of punishment was eventually phased out from 1750 to 1820 with the rise of prisons, which seek to punish the "soul" rather than the body. Foucault lays out three fundamental concepts governing punishment: power, knowledge, and body. Power, present in any social relationship, Foucault argues, is inextricably linked with knowledge of the object one is punishing. Foucault describes five primary techniques and principles of disciplinary power. Most compelling among these is Foucault's description of "Bentham's panopticon." The panopticon is a simple structure consisting of a circular building, surrounded by windowed cells that allow for constant surveillance. In this arrangement, Foucault argues, the observer exercises power not through its actual exercise, but from the *expectation* of its exercise. That is, the threat of "infinite examination" in the "panoptic machine" is enough to inspire desired behaviors in those being observed.[2] The Foucauldian panopticon metaphor became one of the most predominate theories of work technology.[3]

[2] Michael Foucault, *Discipline and Punish: The Birth of the Prison* (New York: Random House, 1977), 189, 217.

[3] See Foucault, *Discipline and Punish*; Michael Foucault, "The Subject and Power," *Critical Theory* 8, no. 4 (1983): 777; James R. Beniger, *The Control Revolution: Technological and Economic Origins of the Information Society* (Cambridge, MA: Harvard University Press, 1986); Shoshana Zuboff, *In the Age of the Smart Machine: The Future of Work and Power* (New York: Basic Books, 1988); Mark Poster, *The Mode of Information: Poststructuralism and Social Context* (Chicago: University of Chicago Press, 1990); David Lyon, "An Electronic Panopticon? A Sociological Critique of Surveillance Society," *Sociological Review* 41, no. 4 (1993): 653–78; David Lyon, *Electronic Eye: The Rise of Surveillance Society* (Minneapolis: University of Minnesota Press, 1994); Barbara Townley, "Foucault, Power/Knowledge, and Its Relevance for Human Resource Management," *Academy of Management Review* 18, no. 3 (1993): 518–45; Graham Sewell, "The Discipline of Teams: The Control of Team-Based Industrial Work through Electronic and Peer Surveillance," *Administrative Science Quarterly* 43, no. 2 (1998): 397–428; Michael Brocklehurst, "Power, Identity and New Technology Homework: Implications for 'New Forms' of Organizing," *Organizational Studies* 22, no. 3 (2001): 445–66; Siew Kien Sia et al., "Enterprise Resource Planning (ERP) as a Technology of Power: Empowerment or Panoptic Control?" *ACM SIGNIS Database: Database for Advances Information Systems* 33, no. 1 (2002): 23–37; Michael B. Elmes et al., "Panoptic Empowerment and Reflective Conformity in Enterprise Systems–Enabled Organizations," *Information and Organization* 15, no. 1 (2005): 1–37; Leslie P. Willcocks, "Foucault, Power/Knowledge and Information Systems: Reconstructing the Present," in *Social Theory and Philosophy for Information Systems*, ed. John Mingers and Leslie P. Willcocks (New York: John Wiley & Sons, 2004), 238–98; Leslie P. Willcocks, "Michel Foucault in the Social Study of ICTs: Critique and Reappraisal," *Social Science Computer Review* 24, no. 3 (2006): 264–95; Kaspar Villadsen, "Managing the Employee's Soul: Foucault Applied to Modern Management Technologies," *Cadernos EBAPE BR* 5, no. 1 (2007): 1–10; Martin DeSaulles and David Horner, "The Portable Panopticon: Morality and Mobile Technologies," *Journal of Information, Communication, and Ethics in Society* 9, no. 3 (2011): 206–16; Aurélie Leclercq-Vandelannoitte et al., "Mobile Information Systems and Organizational Control: Beyond the Panopticon Metaphor," *European Journal of Information Systems* 23, no. 5 (2014): 543–57.

DeSaulles and Horner extended the metaphor to mobile technology in the workplace, such as mobile phones, terming those artifacts portable panopticons.[4] However, as Leclercq-Vandelannoitte et al. show through their case studies of banking organizations in which consultants voluntarily incorporated the use of mobile technology, the panopticon metaphor, as an imposed system of control, is limited in its power to describe wearable work surveillance technology. Rather, although the panopticon concept is still relevant, wearable tech like mobile devices may now extend control beyond physical barriers or even bounded time. Surveillance has now progressed from a hierarchical space to a more lateral and expansive space, with the advantage of a reverse gaze.[5] The controller is rendered invisible at all times, and in fact, time and space have lost relevance as electronic devices allow for perpetual and intimate surveillance.

The dissimulated nature of surveillance is further illustrated by the work of Karen Levy and Solon Barocas, who describe a theory of surveillance that departs from the nature of the panopticon as fixed in time and space, and trained on the subject for control. Rather, from Levy and Barocas's research, we see a theory of "refractive surveillance" that enacts worker surveillance from the data collected on customers. The surveillance in this case is indirect: It is refracted from the electronic data collected from customer relations. In their article, Levy and Barocas investigate how retailers' collection of data facilitates new forms of managerial control over workers. From this, they gather that retail stores change employees' work in four main ways, based on the information they collect about shoppers. First, employers create more dynamic schedules for their employees based on customer trends. The authors explain that labor costs are often a huge operating expense for employers, so employers have an interest in optimizing employee schedules to match the flow of customers in the store at any given time. Effectively, where there are fewer customers, there should be fewer employees. Thus, by tracking customer traffic patterns, employers can discern how many employees should be scheduled at any given time.[6]

Next, employers have shifted the ways in which they evaluate employees. By way of the same kind of technology that allows employers to monitor customers' movements, employers can also track how employees move around their stores during their working hours, the ways in which employees interact with customers, and how many sales are associated with each employee's behavior. These evaluation mechanisms are appealing to employers who have generally struggled to find effective ways to measure and reward staff performance. Conversely, these evaluation mechanisms may place employees' actions under a microscope, and could ultimately hinder

---

4 DeSaulles and Horner, "The Portable Panopticon."
5 Karen Levy and Solon Barocas, "Refractive Surveillance: Monitoring Customers to Manage Workers," *International Journal of Communication* 12 (2018): 1166–88.
6 Levy and Barocas, "Refractive Surveillance," 1173.

employees' performance if employees' only goal is to be in the right place at the right time to make a sale.[7]

Levy and Barocas point to an externalization of worker knowledge based on consumer data. The authors refer to this point as an extension of "clienteling" – the process through which retail employees build and sustain personal relationships with their repeat customers over time, gradually learning more about those customers in order to help sell them more products. Yet, with more surveillance of customers, the personal information that customers share could become available to a wider range of sales associates. By shifting the availability of this knowledge, customer surveillance can have the impact of empowering associates who have less skill at creating personal relationships, and devaluing the skills of workers who go to great lengths to get to know customers. In doing so, customer surveillance could shift the way workplaces work, and could potentially de-skill workforces over time.[8] Customer surveillance, and the knowledge it provides, might enable customer self-service to replace workers. Self-service technology has surveillance capabilities that are improving day by day and could eventually reach the point where it can identify more about customers than sales representatives can independently. At such time, self-service technology might become a permanent alternative to live employees, based on its knowledge of customers alone.[9]

Even prior to advanced technological surveillance systems, others have theorized about how workplace surveillance moderates workplace relations. The sociologist Michael Burawoy was preoccupied with the power struggle between workers and employers. In his influential book *Manufacturing Consent: Changes in the Labor Process under Monopoly Capitalism*, he sought to answer this question: Why do workers work as hard as they do? Burawoy advances the concept of "making out," a "competitive game" wherein workers push back against the control management has over their labor. Burawoy observed that while workers work to meet quotas imposed by managers, they do so only in proportion to how it affects their wage. Most significantly, Burawoy found that while these practices are fairly constant between earlier studies, the social dynamic of the workplace has changed. Whereas before there was a spirit of workers united against the constant management presence, as management has become less visible, worker conflict has primarily turned inward against other workers. As worker classes now begin to clash from within, Burawoy concludes that, in fact, "Class struggle was not the gravedigger of capitalism but its savior."[10]

Surveillance technologies are what has enabled management to become less visible, yet more powerful. Surveillance technology that is laser focused on the

[7] Levy and Barocas, "Refractive Surveillance," 1176–77.
[8] Levy and Barocas, "Refractive Surveillance," 1178–80.
[9] Levy and Barocas, "Refractive Surveillance," 1180.
[10] Michael Burawoy, *Manufacturing Consent: Changes in the Labor Process under Monopoly Capitalism* (Chicago: University of Chicago Press, 1979), quote at 195.

productivity of individual workers serves to recreate much the same "speed-up" as the Taylorist workplaces described in Chapter 2, in which the productivity level of the fastest worker is set as a yardstick for others to follow. Thus, management no longer has a need to be present to exert control; finding the fastest worker and creating the imperative for all other workers to match their speed has become the coercive force in the workplace.

Shoshana Zuboff has written prolifically on the issue of technological surveillance in the twenty-first century. With her first major work, *In the Age of the Smart Machine: The Future of Work and Power*, Zuboff describes two possible directions of technological progress: "automating" or "informating." While automating would further reduce the value of humans and human nature, informating would result in technology filling gaps in the labor force, taking on menial work to allow humans to engage in more fulfilling and stimulating tasks. The distinction rests in the "electronic text," a reference to the role of new technologies that create progress in the workplace. Free access to the text would result in equality; managerial control over the text, as a form of panoptical surveillance, would result in exacerbated power imbalances. Zuboff largely views the difference between more managerial control (automating) and a more egalitarian workplace (informating) as the result of organizational choices rather than uncontrollable market forces.[11]

In her second book, *The Support Economy: Why Corporations Are Failing Individuals and the Next Episode of Capitalism*, Zuboff explores the concept of market forces through the lens of Chandler's managerial capitalism. Zuboff, along with her co-author James Maxmin, suggests that a new form of capitalism called "distributed capitalism" could overturn the existing economic order. The goal of distributed capitalism is to capture the value of the individual as independent of the firm, relying on new technologies to outsource operational functions such as payroll. Ultimately, however, this form of capitalism never came to be; rather, Zuboff argues, *surveillance capitalism* won out.[12]

In *The Age of Surveillance Capitalism* and the article "Big Other: Surveillance Capitalism and the Prospects of an Information Civilization," which serves as its ideological predecessor, Shoshana Zuboff presents the theory of surveillance capitalism. As a result of the "blurred" divisions between firms and populations, surveillance capitalism is a "fully new institutionalized logic of accumulation." It progresses as follows: Consumers use a service, generating data in the process, and the firm gathers the data and reinvests it back into the firm in order to improve services. However, users generate more data than the firm needs; Zuboff calls this excess data "behavioral surplus." Firms realized they could market this excess data to other firms, which would be able to use it for consumer advertising and targeting.

---

[11] Zuboff, *In the Age of the Smart Machine*.
[12] Shoshana Zuboff and James Maxmin, *The Support Economy: Why Corporations Are Failing Individuals and the Next Episode of Capitalism* (New York: Penguin Books, 2002).

Thus, the average user switched from consumer to raw material in the "dispossession cycle" as firms sought to extract as much data as possible. This form of capitalism, according to Zuboff, was a choice made by the "'information civilization' of the early 21st century" to turn to surveillance as capital as opposed to an alternative "advocacy-oriented system," which would have also been possible thanks to the "econom[ic] transparency" that "computer mediation" makes possible. Although Zuboff's theories are useful for describing the relation of firms to the data collected from consumers, the theories mostly overlook the problem of electronic data now extracted from workers as part of the employment bargain.

6.2 A THEORY OF CAPTURED CAPITAL

I argue that in addition to the human capital workers provide, employers in a data-driven workplace may also derive *captured capital* from workers. Captured capital refers to the data that is siphoned from workers both knowingly and unknowingly as part of the employment bargain. This is "captured" data because there is an element of coercion in how it is obtained. It is "capital" because it holds both inherent and exchange value. The inherent value of this data lies in the organizational insights corporations may glean from it to achieve higher efficiency and productivity. For example, data gained from the work habits and practical work innovations of workers holds value in that said data can be used for work analytics to gain greater profits for the employer and may even serve to power the automation of jobs. The exchange value of the data lies in the fact that it can be sold, sometimes for end uses that are rather distal from the understanding of the workers who generated the data. Health data derived from workplace wellness programs, for example, may legally be sold to third parties for profit.[13]

The work of the legal scholar Matthew Bodie tends to support an argument against employer exploitation of employee data without just compensation. First, Bodie notes that the problematic "master-servant" doctrine,[14] which holds employees as agents of their employers who owe traditional fiduciary duties, is increasingly seen as outdated. As Bodie argues, it seems one-sided to argue that employees owe fiduciary duties to employers without acknowledging any corresponding duties on the part of employers.[15] Other scholars argue that this doctrine puts employees at a distinct disadvantage vis-à-vis their employers. Catherine Fisk and Adam Barry note that "[t]he employer owes no duty of loyalty to the employee and is free to

---

[13] Ifeoma Ajunwa, "Workplace Wellness Programs Could Be Putting Your Health Data at Risk," *Harvard Business Review*, Jan. 19, 2017.

[14] Restatement (Second) of Agency § 2 (1958); Restatement (Third) of Agency § 7.07(3)(A) (2006).

[15] Other scholars have also noted this one-sided bargain. See Ken Matheny and Marion Crain, "Disloyal Workers and 'Un-American' Labor Law," *North Carolina Law Review* 82 (2004): 1726 ("Such duties are unidirectional: workers are required to be loyal to their employers, but employers owe no reciprocal duty of loyalty.").

pursue its self-interest by firing him to hire another for a lower wage or for better skills. Yet the employee's ability to pursue her own self-interest by seeking better opportunities is limited."[16] Some scholars have detailed what duties employers *should* owe to employers. For Margaux Hall, employers who make healthcare coverage decisions on behalf of employees are acting as fiduciaries and as such would owe fiduciary duties.[17] In my reading, such a fiduciary duty would include refraining from collecting or selling health data information without express informed consent.[18]

Similarly, scholars such as Scott Fast have argued that employers should owe a duty of confidentiality to their employees that is akin to that of other fiduciary relationships. The recognition of such a fiduciary duty means that employers would be liable for sharing confidential employee information to third parties.[19] This argument is promoted by the Restatement of Employment Law, which affirms that an employee has a protected privacy interest "in personal information related to the employee that is provided in confidence to the employer."[20] Kent Greenfield has also advocated for prohibiting fraud in the context of employment relationship – such a rule would be a legal corollary to Rule 10b-5, which forbids fraud in the sale of securities.[21]

As it stands, there is no bright-line law that delineates what data employers may extract from employees and how such data may be used. With the advent of data analytics as a Taylorist system of management that thrives on the quantification of workers, employees are captive audiences for data extraction. Workers' data is indiscriminately captured and also transferred without any meaningful consent. Such data may often include sensitive, personal information. While several legal scholars have written about the ethical and privacy issues sparked by the captured capital of workers,[22] there have been no new federal laws to address these issues.

---

[16] Catherine Fisk and Adam Barry, "Contingent Loyalty and Restricted Exit: Commentary on the Restatement of Employment Law," *Employee Rights & Employment Policy Journal* 16, no. 2 (2012): 419.

[17] Margaux J. Hall, "A Fiduciary Theory of Health Entitlements," *Cardozo Law Review* 35, no. 5 (2014): 1729–80.

[18] See also Ajunwa, "Genetic Testing Meets Big Data."

[19] Scott L. Fast, "Breach of Employee Confidentiality: Moving toward a Common-Law Tort Remedy," *University of Pennsylvania Law Review* 142, no. 1 (1993): 433 ("[C]ourts could provide a common-law remedy for disclosures to third parties in much the same way that they recognize the confidentiality of physician-patient or attorney-client relationships.").

[20] Restatement of Employment Law § 7.05(a) (2015).

[21] Kent Greenfield, "The Unjustified Absence of Federal Fraud Protection in the Labor Market," *Yale Law Journal* 107, no. 3 (1997): 785–86 (proposing a model rule based on the text of Rule 10b-5).

[22] See e.g., Ifeoma Ajunwa et al., "Limitless Worker Surveillance," *California Law Review* 105, no. 3 (2017): 736–76; Matthew T. Bodie et al., "The Law and Policy of People Analytics," *University of Colorado Law Review* 88, no. 4 (2017): 987–1002; Kim, "Data-Driven Discrimination at Work," 865–920; Kate Crawford and Jason Schultz, "Big Data and Due Process: Toward a Framework to Redress Predictive Privacy Harms," *Boston College Law Review* 55, no. 1 (2014): 94; Barocas and Selbst, "Big Data's Disparate Impact," 674.

6.3 THE RISE OF SURVEILLANCE IN THE AMERICAN WORKPLACE

Changes to the workplace during the Industrial Revolution laid the groundwork for modern workplace surveillance practices, primarily by weakening connections between employers and employees and worsening the working conditions of many employees. The Industrial Revolution was a period of unprecedented economic and technological growth that transformed business strategies. The two most important changes that came with the Industrial Revolution were an increase in manufacturing machinery and the demand for more laborers.[23] Unlike the domestic system of work that existed before the Industrial Revolution, which entailed only two or three people per workplace, Industrial Revolution–era factories held hundreds and even thousands of employees.[24] With this massive increase in the workforce, employers found themselves needing to process far more information regarding employee productivity, the number of employees needed to meet business demands, and the amount of money they needed to pay employees for their time.[25]

At the same time as these workplaces were vastly growing, workers were shifted largely into unskilled positions and they became much less familiar with their employers. Unlike the master and apprentice relationship that had existed before this time, employees were treated less like people and more like the cogs of factory machines. This was mostly a factor of the number of employees working in such massive factories at once – it became impossible for an employer to foster close relationships with all of his employees. In turn, this lack of familiarity also lessened the employer's sense of personal responsibility for the well-being of the employees. When workers did attempt to agitate for better conditions, the British Parliament passed the Combination Acts, which made it illegal for workers to unionize or join together.[26] Although the Combination Acts were repealed twenty-five years after their passage, this legal response to early workplace monitoring and poor working conditions during the Industrial Revolution translated into the mistreatment of workers in America.[27]

By 1867, the Federation of Organized Trades and Labor Unions – the predecessor of today's AFL-CIO – began trying to call for all workers to have eight-hour workdays. They established a deadline of May 1, 1886, a date by which they believed all workers should have shorter workdays. This, if nothing else, would help workers to be treated more fairly in the workplace, they argued. That 1886 deadline was

---

[23] Beniger, *The Control Revolution*.
[24] See C. N. Trueman, "Factories in the Industrial Revolution," *The History Learning Site*, Mar. 2015, www.historylearningsite.co.uk/britain-1700-to-1900/industrial-revolution/factories-in-the-industrial-revolution/.
[25] Beniger, *The Control Revolution*.
[26] Orth, "English Combination Acts," 175–211.
[27] See Bloy, "Repeal of the Combination Acts (1824)."

not achieved. Instead, the issue was met with violent riots, including an explosion at a rally at Haymarket Square in Chicago, which left seven police officers and four workers dead.[28] Thus, while poor working conditions brought about by the Industrial Revolution led to uprisings and worker agitation for fairer labor conditions, the laws of the time proved an impediment to those actions. Instead, during the Industrial Revolution, economic and technological changes in the workplace allowed employers to diminish the autonomy of workers and to drive higher levels of productivity. For this reason, it can be said that the Industrial Revolution planted the seed for more organized workplace monitoring and worker surveillance down the line.

6.3.1 *The Role of the Pinkerton Detectives*

Soon after the Pinkerton Detectives formed in the mid-1800s, Chicago residents were alarmed to see a large wooden sign overlooking the city, with a giant eye and the words "We Never Sleep" printed along the bottom. This eye, which quickly became known as the "eye that never sleeps," became a symbol of the Pinkerton detectives and their new brand of social surveillance. It is strange to imagine, but when Allan Pinkerton first started his group of detectives, there was no official police force in Chicago. Instead, the city used a volunteer-based system for law enforcement. But in the face of a changing socioeconomic structure, Pinkerton felt that the country needed a police system.[29] With this in mind, he created the detective base that became the hallmark for surveillance in the nineteenth and twentieth centuries.

The Pinkertons both embodied and disrupted the panopticon effect – employees could expect to feel surveilled at all times and became accustomed to the feeling of constant supervision.[30] One of Pinkerton's earliest major works was the commissioning of an extensive archive of mug shots of all criminals and suspects investigated by the agency, along with written reports on those people.[31] This was America's first true criminal database. Furthermore, the Pinkerton detectives were also brought in to serve as an intelligence agency during the Civil War.[32] Effectively, as the agency grew, it also widened its scope, taking on surveilling and policing jobs all over the country as needed.

---

[28] Louis Jacobson, "Does the 8-Hour Day and the 40-Hour Week Come from Henry Ford, or Labor Unions?" *PolitiFact*, Sept. 2015, www.politifact.com/truth-o-meter/statements/2015/sep/09/viral-image/does-8-hour-day-and-40-hour-come-henry-ford-or-lab/.

[29] Christopher Razckowski, "From Modernity's Detection to Modernist Detectives: Narrative Vision in the Work of Allan Pinkerton and Dashiell Hammett," *MFS Modern Fiction Studies* 49, no. 4 (2003): 629.

[30] Foucault, *Discipline and Punish*.

[31] Razckowski, "From Modernity's Detection to Modernist Detectives. "

[32] See Pinkerton.com, "Our History: Our Roots Trace back to 1850," Pinkerton website, 2018, www.pinkerton.com/our-difference/history.

One of the most memorable examples of Pinkerton work on behalf of employers is the Homestead Strike of 1892, when a large group of workers from Andrew Carnegie's steel mill went on strike, showing their refusal to cooperate with the plant manager's new production demands. On July 2, 1892, the workers were fired for their union activity and the remaining workers – more than four-fifths of Carnegie's over 3,800 total workers – voted overwhelmingly to join the strike in retaliation against the discharge of the unionized employees. At this time, the plant's manager sent for three hundred Pinkerton guards, who arrived at the scene on the night of July 6, many of them armed.[33] The *New York Times*'s account of the event, published on July 7, 1892, explains that one steelworker stepped out to face the Pinkerton fleet and was instantly shot dead. This gunshot began an over twelve-hour-long battle of strikers against union-busters that left at least ten dead and many others wounded. After the fighting, one Pinkerton man was quoted as saying, "When I came here, I did not understand the situation or I never would have come. I was told that I was to meet and deal with foreigners. I had no idea that I was to fight American citizens ... I appeal for your permission to leave and get myself out of this terrible affair." This shows just how little information the Pinkerton detectives truly had about their own impact on American workers.[34]

Ultimately, these types of incidences spread the impression that Pinkerton detectives could be deployed to bust unions, enforce company rules, and surveil workers deemed to be a threat.[35] In 1893, Congress passed the Anti-Pinkerton Act, which limited the government's ability to hire Pinkerton detectives or any similar surveillance organization. But while this was a victory for public sector employees, who no longer had to fear outside surveillance from private agencies on behalf of their employers, the act left private employers' use of such agencies unchecked.[36]

6.3.2 *Taylorism and the Demand for Surveillance*

In the earliest period, worker monitoring was conducted in a relatively unorganized fashion, usually beginning with managers walking around factory floors, ensuring that workers were not idling and were instead working to their maximum capacities. In fact, in many cases, workers could not use restrooms without the permission of their employers.[37] The notion of ensuring maximum working efficiency from workers through surveillance stems from the work of Frederik Winslow Taylor whose brainchild, *Principles*

---

[33] See History.com Editors, "The Homestead Strike," The History Channel Online, April 28, 2018, www.history.com/topics/homestead-strike.

[34] See "Mob Law at Homestead: Provoked by an Attack of Pinkerton Detectives," *New York Times*, July 7, 1892, https://timesmachine.nytimes.com/timesmachine/1892/07/07/104139908.pdf.

[35] Morn, *The Eye That Never Sleeps*.

[36] See Pub. L. No. 89-554, 80 Stat. 416 (1966).

[37] CB Media, "Factories during the Industrial Revolution," IndustrialRevolution.org, 2010, https://industrialrevolution.org.uk/factories-industrial-revolution/.

of Scientific Management, promoted the pursuit of maximum worker productivity and business profitability through the specialization and the tactical measuring of employee activity. In turn, this measuring required greater worker surveillance.

Taylor's monitoring was, like that of the Industrial Revolution, geared towards making workers as efficient as possible. One of his most well-known principles was the idea of the piece-rate system of pay for employees. Instead of typical pay-per-day schemes, Taylor suggested that men be paid based on a fixed rate for each unit of production that they could create in the standard time needed to create it. These times were carefully measured to set a basic standard for how long an employee needed to produce one unit of production. Next, Taylor introduced a *differential* rate system, by which an employee would be paid more if he could finish the same job at an even quicker rate than the standard – of course, also contingent upon the item's perfect quality. If the employee could produce the item quicker, he would be paid more than he could be paid at competing establishments – or so the theory went. Effectively, this system helped to combat the standard method of pay, by which employees were paid for their time and their piece-by-piece rate of pay diminished with each extra item they created. In other words, all employees would be paid regardless of their output standard system, but under Taylor's system workers were incentivized to work harder by the promise of possible rate increases.[38]

To effectuate Taylor's system required minute surveillance. For example, this meant monitoring workers' progress by using stopwatches as often as possible.[39] Employers were encouraged to hover over employees with notepads in hand in order to drive new "incentive."[40] By 1916, discussion of the Taylorist management style made it all the way to the floor of the U.S. House of Representatives, at which time Representative Clyde Tavenner of Illinois addressed the House, noting that "the tasks promoted by Taylor were purposely made so severe that not more than one out of five laborers, perhaps even a smaller percentage than that, could keep up."[41] He went on to question the need for stopwatches for employee monitoring purposes in the workplace – a notion that was discussed at least once after his 1916 plea[42] – but nothing ever came of the discussions.

[38] Frederick Winslow Taylor, "A Piece-Rate System," Paper presented to ASME, June 1895, http://wps .prenhall.com/wps/media/objects/107/109902/ch17_a3_d2.pdf.

[39] Kanigel, *Taylor-Made,* 7.

[40] See "Scientific Management," *The Economist,* Feb. 2009, www.economist.com/news/2009/02/09/ scientific-management.

[41] See Congressional Record – Digital Collection, CR-1916-0601, 1361, June 1916, https://advance.lexis .com/r/documentprovider/53-7k/attachment/data?attachmentid=V1,215,58122,CR-1916-06010APPFro m1To22,1&attachmenttype=PDF&attachmentname=1361&origination=&sequencenumber=&ishot doc=false&#page=22.

[42] See Congressional Record – Digital Collection, CR – 1916-0825, 1920, Aug. 1916, https://advance.lexis .com/r/documentprovider/53-7k/attachment/data?attachmentid=V1,215,58122,CR-1916-08250APPFro m1To74,1&attachmenttype=PDF&attachmentname=1920&origination=&sequencenumber=&ishot doc=false&#page=41.

In some cases, it was reported that early workplace monitoring under the Taylorist system even came to look like friendly competitions, such that employees might get into the spirit of competition and find increased motivation to produce goods. The goal of such competitions may have been to distract employees from the feeling that they were being heavily watched.[43] These "friendly competitions" should be recognized as the precursors to modern-day gamified surveillance. As Julie Cohen describes, the modern-day surveillance–industrial complex often takes on a participatory turn – but even more concerning is how "[t]he rhetorics of participation and innovation that characterize the participatory turn" alter the work by seeking to "position surveillance as an activity exempted from legal and social control." As Cohen describes so vividly, present-day gamified surveillance environments both invite participation and masquerade as play, functioning as "actions that perform the in-world rituals of gameplay," including "actions to unlock benefits or 'level up' one's membership."[44] In this way, the surveillance invokes team spirit, team play, while the remaining coercion is diffused and decentralized, all with the goal of deflecting legal scrutiny.

Although some scholars argue that Taylorism was indeed a way to bond management and labor towards a central goal – increasing both the resources and instruction given to workers so that they could more efficiently perform their jobs[45] – many workers laboring under Taylorist management systems disputed this characterization, as I discussed in Chapter 2. Justin Schwartz writes that "even firms with employee participation programs leave virtually all decision-making power in the hands of management." This, among other things, could lead to an inherent lack of efficiency, as employees towards the bottom typically have the most hands-on practical knowledge, but are given the least say in how problems should be handled.[46] Organizational theorists recognize this phenomenon – when workers are able to innovate and discover more efficient methods of work that diverge from the standardized work model – as "practical drift."[47] Thus, a lack of worker input into organizational decisions tends to create the same types of inefficiencies that the Taylorist management style tries to correct.[48]

The labor economist Stephen Marglin has noted that the "hallmark of traditional capital management is supervision and discipline." Furthermore, Marglin argues that the purpose of the supervision and discipline is to bolster the power of a company's managers. Marglin concludes that while neither supervision nor

[43] Nikil Saval, *Cubed: A Secret History of the Workplace* (New York: Doubleday, 2014), 42.
[44] Cohen, "The Surveillance-Innovation Complex," 207–11.
[45] Oren Levin-Waldman, "Taylorism, Efficiency, and the Minimum Wage: Implications for a High Road Economy," Global Institute for Sustainable Prosperity, Working Paper No. 105, Feb. 2015, p. 3.
[46] Justin Schwartz, "Voice without Say: Why Capital-Manage Firms Aren't (Genuinely) Participatory," *Fordham Journal of Corporate and Financial Law* 18, no. 4 (2013): 963–1020.
[47] Cohen, "The Surveillance-Innovation Complex.
[48] Schwartz, "Voice without Say," 989.

discipline is necessary for increased productivity or profitability, they do play a role in giving employers two things. The first is that employers can play a role in production that they would otherwise lack and the second is that, by taking on more responsibility, they can take a larger share of the resulting profits at the expense of labor.[49] With reference to Adam Smith's pin manufacturing theory – in which Smith argues that the specialization of worker roles even in jobs so small as a pin-making factory can help workers to increase productivity[50] – Marglin argues that the main goal was never to increase productivity as much as it was to create a process for organization that "guaranteed to the entrepreneur an essential role in the production process, as an integrator of the separate efforts of his workers into a marketable product."[51] Thus, Marglin concludes that Taylorist supervision really serves no positive purpose for employees, but instead only benefits employers' interest in managerial control.

The best illustration of surveillance of the early Taylorist era as a method for employee control was the invention of the panopticon factory. Originally constructed in the late 1700s as a twelve-story Russian prison, this panopticon-style architecture was extended into the factory space in the early 1900s.[52] The architectural style included a round building, with chambers for prisoners – or employees – lining the walls.[53] A tower in the center allowed for the strategic placement of security guards – or managers – in such a way that minimized who could see them but maximized their view of the prisoners.[54] Panopticon factories took root in late 1700s Russia,[55] and ultimately expanded to the United States around the late 1800s, in conjunction with Taylor's new management ideology. One example is the Worcester State Hospital, which claims to have been built in the panoptic style in order to allow more efficient observation of the wards, but which truly enabled managers to more effectively monitor workers. The building, which was built in 1876, was ultimately shut down in 1991, with many people citing its resemblance to prison complexes.[56] Although Jeremy Bentham has received credit for designing the panopticon, his brother Samuel Bentham was the true designer. The structure's

---

[49] Stephen Marglin, "What Do Bosses Do? Pt. II," *Review of Radical Political Economy* 7, no. 1 (1975): 33; Stephen Marglin, "What Do Bosses Do? The Origins and Function of Hierarchy in Capitalist Production," *Review of Radical Political Economy* 6, no. 2 (1974): 62, 94.

[50] See Gavin Kennedy, "Of Pins and Things," The Adam Smith Institute of Economics, May 28, 2012, www.adamsmith.org/blog/economics/of-pins-and-things.

[51] Marglin, "What Do Bosses Do?" (1974), 62.

[52] Robert Sprague, "From Taylorism to the Omnipticon: Expanding Employee Surveillance beyond the Workplace," *Journal of Computer & Information Law* 25, no. 1 (2007): 1–35.

[53] See "Panopticon," *A Dictionary of Sociology*, last updated May 18, 2018 (Encyclopedia.com, Oxford University Press), www.encyclopedia.com/literature-and-arts/art-and-architecture/architecture/panopticon

[54] Alex Rosenblat, Tamara Kneese, and Danah Boyd, *Workplace Surveillance*, Open Society Foundations: Data and Society Working Paper, October 8, 2014.

[55] Phillip Steadman, "Samuel Bentham's Panopticon," *Journal of Bentham Studies* 14, no. 1 (2012): 1–30.

[56] See Opacity, "Worcester State Hospital," Urban Ruins, 2018, https://opacity.us/site56_worcester_state_hospital.htm.

initial function was not to imprison; rather, it was meant to serve to instruct. Yet, like so many other technological tools, the panopticon experienced a mission creep that led to its use for surveillance.

6.3.3 *The Sociological Department and Surveillance under Fordism*

Following the rise of Taylorist management, Henry Ford became notorious for truly exerting full control over his workers' lives. Ford's management style was most touted for the five-dollar-per-day pay he granted his workers, an unheard-of amount prior to that time. Furthermore, in 1914, when most workers in the United States still lacked the guarantee of eight-hour workdays, the Ford Motor Company was one of the largest corporations to offer eight-hour shifts.[57] However, there were many overlooked contingencies that came along with this payment structure and limited workday. The five-dollar-a-day rate came with a large dose of worker surveillance. Not only did employees have to work at the company for at least six months before they could earn five dollars per day, but they also had to adhere to an entirely new set of social rules. For instance, Ford claimed that he wanted all of his workers to be "model Americans," so he created a specific department within the Ford Motor Company that was tasked with keeping employees "in line." The department, dubbed the Ford Sociological Department, started out with a team of fifty investigators and ultimately became a group of two hundred individuals who parsed through every aspect of Ford's employees' lives.[58]

In some instances, these Ford investigators would arrive, unannounced, at employees' homes to make sure they were being kept clean. They would check in on employees' children to ensure that the children were being kept in school. They would even pry into working families' spending habits, marital relationships, and alcohol consumption to make sure that anyone who received a Ford paycheck was "of acceptable standards."[59] These tactics have largely contributed to the widespread view that Ford was one of the best and worst employers of all time.[60]

To many, it seemed that Ford began to care more about his employees' home lives than about the company. In one case, *Dodge v. Ford Motor Co.*, the Supreme Court held that Ford was "required to operate the Ford Motor Company in the interests of its shareholders," rather than in a charitable manner, to benefit employees or customers. This seemingly contradicted Ford's own view of the company, as he was quoted as stating that his company's purpose was to "spread the benefits of the industrial system to the greatest number of people, to help them build up

[57] Jacobson, "Does the 8-Hour Day and the 40-Hour Week Come from Henry Ford, or Labor Unions?"

[58] Michael Ballaban, "When Henry Ford's Benevolent Secret Police Ruled His Workers," *Jalopnik*, Mar. 23, 2014, https://jalopnik.com/when-henry-fords-benevolent-secret-police-ruled-his-wo-1549625731.

[59] Ballaban, "When Henry Ford's Benevolent Secret Police Ruled His Workers."

[60] David Lewis, *The Public Image of Henry Ford: An American Folk Hero and His Company* (Detroit: Wayne State University Press, 1975).

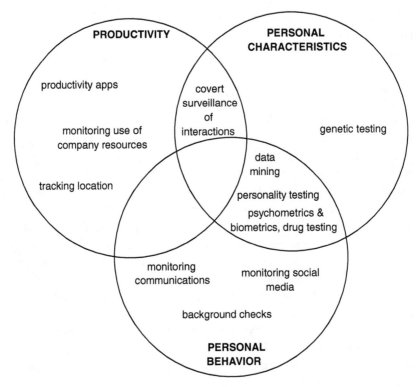

FIGURE 6.1 Categories of worker surveillance

their lives and homes."[61] Ultimately, Ford's motives were not merely altruistic. Ford noted that "if I can make men my employees, I never have to fear for my business. Everything I do to help them ultimately benefits me."[62]

Although Taylorism's primary focus had been on monitoring time spent on job tasks, the reality is that with applied Taylorism, first as scientific management and then in its iteration as part of Fordism, worker surveillance became more expansive and came to encompass far more behaviors than merely the time and manner of accomplishing the job tasks. These days, in the data-driven workplace, the purview of worker surveillance runs the gamut of quantifying the physical and emotional labor of the worker, and beyond. As shown in Figure 6.1, there are several categories of worker surveillance accomplished with the aid of a range of technologies. While some of these technologies are trained on directly verifying worker productivity, other technologies hone in on other worker characteristics that may also indirectly affect productivity. For example, technologies intent on monitoring productivity will directly document physical work output by logging keystrokes, verifying that

[61]   *Dodge v. Ford Motor Co.*, 204 Mich. 459, 505 (1919).
[62]   Sarah Terrill Bushnell, *The Truth About Henry Ford* (Chicago: Reilly & Lee Co., 1922), 204.

jobs tasks are completed or that benchmarks have been met in a timely fashion. Other technologies such as swipe cards, closed-circuit television (CCTV), geo-positioning services (GPS), and radio frequency identification (RFID) chips (sometimes embedded under the skin) help managers establish the location of workers at all times, thus monitoring for productivity and any potential behavioral misconduct. Beyond surveillance for productivity and prevention of misconduct, the emotional labor of the worker is now also under scrutiny as customer relationship management (CRM) tools allow customers to rate the emotional performance of workers.

Moving beyond merely ensuring productivity, there is the genre of worker surveillance meant to quantify and manage risk. A first case of this is represented by the biometric checks meant to verify identity, the background checks meant to confirm qualifications, and the criminal and credit records searches meant to check for past malfeasance. Then there is the category of worker surveillance meant to manage health risks. Even before the Covid-19 crisis, the health status and behaviors of workers had already come under scrutiny. Wellness programs allowed employers to manage the risk of healthcare costs by surveilling workers' exercise and eating habits. Some wellness programs have even begun to offer genetic testing. The coronavirus pandemic brought with it the public health concern of monitoring workers' infection status. Thus, in addition to self-reported health tracking, workers are now also monitored via thermal scans checking for fever and frequent testing on the job.

6.4 AN OVERVIEW OF WORKER SURVEILLANCE TODAY

Employee monitoring includes internet usage monitoring, GPS monitoring, key-logging, email monitoring, social media monitoring, audio recordings, videotaping, off-duty conduct monitoring, and monitoring of company devices.[63] A 2017 article noted that "GPS tracking, commonly available in company-owned vehicles, now extends to company-issued phones and even, on occasion, ID badges."[64] Problems can arise because "GPS tracking doesn't necessarily end when an employee's shift does. If a worker is allowed to take a company vehicle home at night or over the weekend, it might continue sending its location. And a tracking app on a mobile phone can keep broadcasting an employee's location during his or her off hours"; additionally, "a spokesperson for TSheets [a time-tracking software company] said the app's location-tracking feature automatically shuts off when employees clock out for the day, but that if the employee forgets to clock out, the app will continue sending the phone's location."[65] Other surveillance techniques include "taking photos of workers' computer screens at random, counting keystrokes and mouse clicks and

---

[63] Donna Ballman, "10 New (and Legal) Ways Your Employer Is Spying on You," *Business Insider*, Sept. 29, 2013.

[64] Robert Hackett, "Psst, Your Company Is Watching You Now," *Fortune*, Mar. 13, 2017.

[65] Kaveh Waddell, "Why Bosses Can Track Their Employees 24/7," *The Atlantic*, Jan. 6, 2017.

snapping photos of [workers] at their computers. [Employers are] plying sophisticated technology to instantaneously detect anger, raised voices or children crying in the background on workers' home-office calls. Others are using Darwinian routing systems that keep calls coming so fast workers have no time to go to the bathroom."[66]

6.4.1 *More Technology, More Surveillance*

The trend towards more surveillance in the workplace has increased in line with technological advancements such as leaps in computing ability. From 1999 to 2003, employers who admitted to electronically monitoring their employees jumped from 67 to 92 percent. Methods of monitoring largely included reviewing internet activity and email messages.[67] A 2007 survey by the American Management Association in collaboration with the ePolicy Institute found that 45 percent of employers tracked content, keystrokes, and time spent at the keyboard, while 43 percent monitored employee email use.[68] From 2007 to 2010, U.S. market use of employee surveillance technology rose by 43 percent.[69] This trend towards expanding surveillance has persisted: Experts estimate that by 2023, the employee monitoring solution industry may be worth as much as US$4 billion.[70] Increasingly, employers are turning to alternative monitoring methods, including monitoring workspace usage and aggregating data for insights into employee behavior.[71] From 2015 to 2018, the number of organizations employing alternative methods jumped from 30 percent to over 50 percent.[72] These findings are supported by a 2018 Accenture Strategy report, which found that 62 percent of businesses are using new technologies to collect employee data.[73] These statistics suggest that not only are U.S. industries tending towards more surveillance, but also new kinds of surveillance may be used to monitor employees in increasingly unsuspected, invasive ways.

---

[66] Sue Shellenbarger, "Work at Home? Your Employer May Be Watching," *Wall Street Journal*, July 30, 2008.

[67] Michael Workman, "A Field Study of Corporate Employee Monitoring: Attitudes, Absenteeism, and the Moderating Influences of Procedural Justice Perceptions," *Information and Organization* 19, no. 4 (2009): 219.

[68] AMA, "The Latest on Workplace Monitoring and Surveillance," American Management Association, April 8, 2019, www.amanet.org/articles/the-latest-on-workplace-monitoring-and-surveillance/.

[69] Phoebe V. Moore, "Electronic Performance Monitoring," Phoebevmoore blog, Oct. 29, 2019, https://phoebevmoore.wordpress.com/2019/10/29/electronic-performance-monitoring/.

[70] Jemimah Suemo, "2019 Employee Monitoring Software Industry Trends," *Worktime*, Oct. 21, 2019, www.worktime.com/2019-employee-monitoring-software-industry-trends.

[71] Brian Kropp, "5 Changes HR Leaders Can Expect to Manage in 2019," *Gartner: Insights*, Jan. 24, 2019, www.gartner.com/smarterwithgartner/5-changes-hr-leaders-can-expect-to-manage-in-2019/.

[72] Brian Kropp, "The Future of Employee Monitoring," *Gartner: Insights*, May 3, 2019, www.gartner.com/smarterwithgartner/the-future-of-employee-monitoring/.

[73] Tourang Nazari, "More Responsible Use of Workforce Data Required to Strengthen Employee Trust and Unlock Growth, According to Accenture Report," *Accenture Newsroom*, Jan. 21, 2019, https://newsroom.accenture.com/news/more-responsible-use-of-workforce-data-required-to-strengthen-employee-trust-and-unlock-growth-according-to-accenture-report.htm.

6.4.2 Surveillance for Productivity

Productivity surveillance may constitute a range of activities, from installing simple site-blocking software[74] to remotely accessing an employee's microphone and webcam.[75] The majority of productivity surveillance falls under the umbrella of "activity monitoring."[76] Activity monitoring – surveilling how an employee spends their time during work hours – is often enhanced by software that tracks idle time, records keystrokes, or even periodically screenshots an employee's computer. Most productivity services, such as Hubstaff, use data collected from employee surveillance to run productivity analytics reports. Hubstaff reports include total time and activities recorded by all employees in a given period, as well as statistics on idle time, application usage, and productivity trends over time.[77] Other companies are more direct. Prodoscore, a "productivity intelligence" company, tracks every employee activity across multiple platforms, compiling the data into a single daily score that is ranked against other employees.[78] While such services allow employers to identify productive performers and behaviors, they also may be used to weed out inefficient workers. WorkTime, another popular activity monitoring technology, offers a report of "top Facebook users" that employers may use to see which employees are wasting time.[79]

Other companies go well beyond invasive computer monitoring to evaluate and improve productivity. Some trucking companies now install electronic logging devices on their fleets to track driver efficiency on the road, with potentially dangerous consequences such as encouraging drivers to forgo rest breaks.[80] In 2018, Amazon developed a patented wristband designed to increase task efficiency by influencing warehouse workers' movements through vibrations on the wrist,[81] and Walmart patented a technology that uses audio surveillance to detect sounds of checkout scanners or bag movement in order to measure if employees are performing their jobs efficiently.[82] Humanyze, an MIT startup, created wearable badges that audio surveil for conversation partners, frequency, tone, and more, creating a data web of social

---

[74] AMA, "The Latest on Workplace Monitoring and Surveillance."

[75] Clever Control, *Frequently Asked Questions*, https://clevercontrol.com/faq (last visited Oct. 2, 2020).

[76] Bennett Cyphers and Karen Gullo, "Inside the Invasive, Secretive 'Bossware' Tracking Worker," Electronic Frontier Foundation, Deeplinks Blog, June 30, 2020, www.eff.org/deeplinks/2020/06/inside-invasive-secretive-bossware-tracking-workers.

[77] Hubstaff, "Time Reporting," https://hubstaff.com/time-report (last visited Oct. 2, 2020).

[78] Justin Bariso, "This Company's Approach to Remote Work Is the Worst I've Ever Seen," *Inc.*, Sept. 16, 2020, www.inc.com/justin-bariso/this-companys-approach-to-remote-work-is-worst-ive-ever-seen-emotional-intelligence.html.

[79] Sue Shellenbarger, "'Working from Home' without Slacking Off," *Wall Street Journal*, July 11, 2012.

[80] Chandra Steele, "The Quantified Employee: How Companies Use Tech to Track Workers," *PC Mag*, Feb. 14, 2020.

[81] Olivia Solon, "Amazon Patents Wristband That Tracks Warehouse Workers' Movements," *The Guardian*, Jan. 31, 2018.

[82] Ellen Shang, "Employee Privacy in the US Is at Stake as Corporate Surveillance Technology Monitors Workers' Every Move," *CNBC*, Apr. 15, 2019.

interactions that companies may use to distinguish productive behavior.[83] Some of these technologies are still in startup, or have yet to be rolled out to the workforce; however, they indicate a few important trends in the field of productivity surveillance. First, the more advanced technology becomes, the more invasive it tends to be, but employers are willing to trade employee privacy for the sake of productivity and improved profits. Second, large corporations are not limited to the surveillance technologies available at market. Resource-laden companies such as Walmart, Amazon, and PwC have all developed their own surveillance software specific to company needs. This raises issues of disclosure, as companies are not necessarily legally obligated to inform employees of when or how they are being monitored.[84]

6.4.3 *Surveillance for Behavior*

While surveillance software has been optimized for productivity tracking, it may also be used to monitor behavior. Surveillance can range from seeing if an individual is active on Skype or Microsoft to full implementation of specific technologies.[85] The bossware technologies described above, which allow activity monitoring, screen capture, keystroke logging, and even GPS tracking, collect data that employers may use to ensure employees are following workplace procedures.[86] These technologies seek to ameliorate a "common fear among bosses" that remote work leads to a greater shirking of work responsibilities.[87] Use of these technologies is growing: As of 2007, only 3 percent of employers were using GPS location tracking to monitor employee cell phones,[88] a number that jumped to 7 percent by 2018.[89] Examples of basic employee behavioral surveillance include installing video cameras,[90] covertly monitoring emails,[91] and measuring employee use of different applications against their responsibilities.[92] Some software is specifically targeted at identifying insider threats, instances when employees may steal company information or data

---

[83] Chris Weller, "Employees at a Dozen Fortune 500 Companies Wear Digital Badges That Watch and Listen to Their Every Move," *Business Insider*, Oct. 20, 2016.

[84] Max Freedman, "Spying on Your Employees? Better Understand the Law First," *Business News Daily*, updated Dec. 23, 2020.

[85] Alex Hern, "Shirking from Home? Staff Feel the Heat as Bosses Ramp Up Remote Surveillance," *The Guardian*, Sept. 27, 2020.

[86] Cyphers and Gullo, "Inside the Invasive, Secretive 'Bossware' Tracking Worker."

[87] Lora Jones, "I Monitor My Staff with Software That Takes Screenshots," *BBC News*, Sept. 29, 2020.

[88] AMA, "The Latest on Workplace Monitoring and Surveillance."

[89] Tam Harbert, "Watching the Workers," *SHRM*, Mar. 16, 2019, www.shrm.org/hr-today/news/all-things-work/pages/watching-the-workers.aspx.

[90] Ellen R. Shell, "The Employer-Surveillance State," *The Atlantic*, Oct. 15, 2018 (TSA use of security cameras to monitor for employee infractions).

[91] Shirin Ghaffary and Jason Del Rey, "Amazon Employees Fear HR Is Targeting Minority and Activism Groups in Email Monitoring Program," *Vox*, Sept. 24, 2020.

[92] Shellenbarger, "'Working from Home' without Slacking Off" (reporting that a boss discovered that an employee was studying for her masters degree during work hours).

for personal use or gain. Insider threat software uses behavior analytics to monitor employees and flag activities or events that are known precursors to security violations.[93] Other technology – such as PwC's house-developed facial recognition software, which recognizes when an employee leaves their seat – is used to ensure that employees remain in front of their computers during business hours.[94] PwC claims this technology ensures compliance in industries with sensitive legal obligations surrounding employee behavior and hours reporting.

Surveillance for behavior, however, goes beyond ensuring that employees are simply following procedure. Cogito, an audio surveillance software built on the same technology as Siri and Alexa, is used in some call centers to monitor when employees or callers show signs of distress or fatigue in their voice.[95] When certain tones are detected, Cogito reminds employees of the appropriate way to respond or modify their behavior. In addition to guiding behavior into procedural compliance, some technology can identify when employee behavior suggests they are likely to quit. Two university professors developed an algorithm that takes into account turnover shocks and an individual's "job embeddedness," as measured by data such as tenure, skills, education, and employment history, to produce a TPI score, a single number that predicts the likelihood an individual will quit.[96] Another company developed a code that analyzed employees' LinkedIn feeds to determine employees likely to quit and alert the company to intervene as necessary.[97] Walmart and others actively employ similar technology to determine employees at risk for turnover.[98] Behavioral surveillance, as such, may serve as both a compliance mechanism and a predictive tool that companies may use to modify outcomes.

6.4.4 *Social Media Surveillance*

The advent of social media is a relatively new phenomenon. As such, employee surveillance of workers on social media raises new legal questions that were unconceived of during the promulgation of laws addressing worker rights in the workplace. One might argue that social media, as a new technology phenomenon primarily used by the younger generation, has ushered in new norms regarding privacy in the workplace. Some might argue also that these norms run contrary to the notion of a work versus

---

[93] Andy Green, "A Practical Software Approach to Insider Threats," *Varonis: Inside Out Security Blog*, June 17, 2020, www.varonis.com/blog/a-practical-software-approach-to-insider-threats/.

[94] Ashleigh Webber, "PwC Facial Recognition Tool Criticised for Home Working Privacy Invasion," *Personnel Today*, June 16, 2020, www.personneltoday.com/hr/pwc-facial-recognition-tool-criticised-for-home-working-privacy-invasion/.

[95] Tom Simonite, "This Call May Be Monitored for Tone and Emotion," *Wired*, Mar. 19, 2018.

[96] Brooks Holtom and David Allen, "Better Ways to Predict Who's Going to Quit," *Harvard Business Review*, Aug. 16, 2019.

[97] Anne Loehr, "How to Predict Which of Your Employees Are About to Quit," *Fast Co.*, Mar. 10, 2018.

[98] Rachel E. Silverman and Nikki Waller, "The Algorithm That Tells the Boss Who Might Quit," *Wall Street Journal*, Mar. 13, 2015.

non-work dividing line. The research, however, disproves this notion. In an empirical study, researchers found that a majority of the respondents agreed strongly with the notion of a separation between work and personal life. A 2012 study focused on the attitudes of millennial workers surveyed about 2,500 Canadian and American undergraduates, and found that "54% of those surveyed strongly or somewhat agreed that 'work life is completely separate from personal life, and what you do in one should not affect the other'" and "56% disagreed that 'knowing how a person behaves outside of work hours gives managers insight into whether that person is ready for a promotion.'"[99]

Although there are no federal laws that address the surveillance of workers on social media, many states have passed laws prohibiting employers from requiring employees, and sometimes job applicants, to provide employers with their social media information. Some states have also passed laws prohibiting employers from discriminating against employees who refuse to give employers access to their personal social media accounts. Figure 6.2 shows a list of states that have passed such legislation as of 2022, now twenty-six states in total. In considering these twenty-six states and their respective statutes, remember also that there are twenty-four states that have no such laws – in those states, employers might still be able to require employees to provide them with personal social media information. Similarly, employers nationwide are still able to track employees or use any information that is "public" on the internet, including the information that employees publish to their public social media accounts.

Arkansas   Ark. Code § 11-2-124 (2014).
An employer cannot require, request, suggest, or cause a current or prospective employee to disclose his username and password to his social media account or change the privacy settings to his account. Even if the employer inadvertently receives access to an employee's social media account, he may not use the information to access the employee's social media account. https://law.justia.com/codes/arkansas/2014/title-11/chapter-2/subchapter-1/section-11-2-124/#:~:text=1%20%2D%20General%20Provisions-,%C2%A7%2011%2D2%2D124%20%2D%20Social%20media%20accounts,of%20current%20and%20prospective%20employees.&text=(vii)%20Website%20profiles%20or%20locations.&text=(iv)%20Set%20up%20by%20an,name%2C%20logos%2C%20or%20tradem

FIGURE 6.2 Laws regarding employers' use of social media to track employees (2020)[100]

---

99 Patricia Sanchez Abril et al., "Blurred Boundaries: Social Media Privacy and the Twenty-First-Century Employee," *American Business Law Journal* 49, no. 1 (2012): 103 ("Approximately 2500 Canadian and American undergraduate students answered questions relating to their employment status, privacy expectations concerning employer access to their OSN [online social network] profiles, and the existence of and adherence to OSN workplace policies, among other things. These questions were close ended, as respondents chose from a list of various answer choices in multiple choice and Likert-scale format.").

100 List of states from American Bar Association, Section of Labor and Employment Law, "Employee Monitoring and Workplace Privacy Law," www.americanbar.org/content/dam/aba/events/labor_law/2016/04/tech/papers/monitoring_ella.authcheckdam.pdf, (last visited Nov. 24, 2020), as well as a state-wide survey. Relevant laws hyperlinked in the name of each state within the chart. In total, 26 states have passed laws to this effect. The remaining 24 have been left out of the chart.

California   Cal. Lab. Code § 980 (2012).
An employer shall not require or request an employee or applicant for employment to disclose his username and password, access personal social media in the presence of the employer, or divulge any personal social media. https://leginfo.legislature.ca.gov/faces/codes_displaySection.xhtml?lawCode=LAB&sectionNum=980

Colorado   Colo. Rev. Stat. § 8-2-127 (2013).
An employer may not suggest, request, or require that an employee or job applicant disclose any username, password, or service through the employee's or applicant's personal electronic communications device. An employer cannot compel an employee or applicant to add anyone to their contacts on a personal social media account, or change the privacy settings associated with their personal social media accounts. https://www.colorado.gov/pacific/sites/default/files/Social%20Media%20Act.pdf

Connecticut   Conn. Gen. Stat. § 31-40x (2016).
No employer shall request or require that an employee or applicant provide such employer with a username and password, password, or any other authentication means for accessing a personal online account; request or require that an employee or applicant authenticate or access a personal online account in the presence of such employer; require that an employee or applicant invite such employer to accept an invitation from the employer to join a group affiliated with any personal online account of the employee or applicant; discharge, discipline, discriminate against any employee who refuses to provide the employer with a username and password; fail or refuse to hire any applicant as a result of his or her refusal to provide such employer with a username and password. https://www.cga.ct.gov/current/pub/chap_557.htm#sec_31-40x

Delaware   19 Del. Code § 709A (2015).
An employer shall not require or request an employee or applicant to do any of the following: (1) Disclose a username or password for the purpose of enabling the employer to access personal social media; access personal social media in the presence of the employer; use personal social media as a condition of employment; divulge any personal social media, except as provided in subsection (d) of this section; add a person, including the employer, to the list of contacts associated with the employee's or applicant's personal social media, or invite or accept an invitation from any person, including the employer, to join a group associated with the employee's or applicant's personal social media; alter the settings on the employee's or applicant's personal social media that affect a third party's ability to view the contents of the personal social media. https://legis.delaware.gov/SessionLaws/Chapter?id=15700

Illinois   820 Ill. Comp. Stat. 55/10 (2014).
It is illegal for an employer to inquire in any way of a prospective employee, or his former employers, about the employee's username or password for a personal online account, or to demand access to the account. https://www.ilga.gov/legislation/ilcs/documents/082000550K10.htm#:~:text=(a)%20It%20shall%20be%20unlawful,Compensation%20Act%20or%20Workers'%20Occupational

Louisiana   La. Rev. Stat. § 51:1953 (2014).
An employer shall not do any of the following: (1) request or require an employee or applicant for employment to disclose any username, password, or other authentication information that allows access to the employee's or applicant's personal online account; (2) discharge, discipline, fail to hire, or otherwise penalize or threaten to penalize an employee or applicant for employment for failure to disclose any information specified in this Subsection. http://legis.la.gov/Legis/Law.aspx?d=919877

FIGURE 6.2 (continued)

Maine   26 M.R.S. § 616 (2015).
An employer may not: (1) require or coerce an employee or applicant to disclose, or request that an employee or applicant disclose, the password or any other means for accessing a personal social media account; (2) require or coerce an employee or applicant to access, or request that an employee or applicant access, a personal social media account in the presence of the employer or an agent of the employer; (3) require or coerce an employee or applicant to disclose any personal social media account information; (4) require or cause an employee or applicant to add anyone, including the employer or an agent of the employer, to the employee's or applicant's list of contacts associated with a personal social media account; (5) require or cause an employee or applicant to alter, or request that an employee or applicant alter, settings that affect a 3rd party's ability to view the contents of a personal social media account; (6) discharge, discipline, or otherwise penalize or threaten to discharge, discipline or otherwise penalize an employee for the employee's refusal to disclose or provide access to information as specified in subsection 1, 2 or 3 or for refusal to add anyone to the employee's list of contacts associated with a personal social media account as specified in subsection 4 or to alter the settings associated with a personal social media account as specified in subsection 5; (7) fail or refuse to hire an applicant as a result of the applicant's refusal to disclose or provide access to information specified in subsection 1, 2 or 3, or refusal to add anyone as specified in subsection 4 or to alter their settings as specified in subsection 5. https://legislature.maine.gov/legis/statutes/26/title26sec616.html

Maryland   Md. Lab. & Empl. Code § 3-712 (2013).
An employer may not request or require that an employee or applicant disclose any username, password, or other means for accessing a personal account or service through an electronic communications device. An employer may require an employee to disclose any username, password, or other means for accessing nonpersonal accounts or services that provide access to the employer's internal computer or information systems. https://codes.findlaw.com/md/labor-and-employment/#:~:text=(2)%20An%20employer%20may%20require,internal%20computer%20or%20information%20systems.&text=(ii)%20ask%20the%20Attorney%20General,of%20the%20applicant%20or%20employee

Michigan   Mich. Comp. Laws § 37.273 (2012).
An employer shall not request an employee or applicant for employment to grant access, allow observation of, or disclose information that allows access to or observation of the employee's or applicant's personal internet account. An employer shall not discharge, discipline, fail to hire, or otherwise penalize an employee or applicant for employment for failure to grant access to, allow observation of, or disclose information that allows access to or observation of the employee's or applicant's personal internet account. http://www.legislature.mi.gov/(S(tv3c5sfcmuui0hmjop55y5f2))/mileg.aspx?page=getObject&objectName=mcl-37-273

Montana   Mont. Code Ann. § 39-2-307 (2019).
An employer or employer's agent may not require or request an employee or applicant for employment to: (a) disclose a username or password for the purpose of allowing the employer or employer's agent to access a personal social media account of the employee or job applicant; (b) access personal social media in the presence of the employer or employer's agent; or (c) divulge any personal social media or information contained on personal social media. https://leg.mt.gov/bills/mca/title_0390/chapter_0020/part_0030/section_0070/0390-0020-0030-0070.html

FIGURE 6.2 (continued)

Nebraska   Neb. Rev. Stat. 48-3503 (2016).
No employer shall: (1) require or request that an employee or applicant provide or disclose any username or password or any other related account information in order to gain access to the employee's or applicant's personal internet account by way of an electronic communication device; (2) require or request that an employee or applicant log into a personal Internet account by way of an electronic communication device in the presence of the employer; (3) require an employee or applicant to add anyone, including the employer, to the list of contacts associated with the employee's or applicant's personal Internet account or require or otherwise coerce an employee or applicant to change the settings on the employee's or applicant's personal account; (4) take adverse action against, fail to hire, or otherwise penalize an employee or applicant for failure to provide or disclose any of the information or to take any of the actions specified in subdivisions (1) through (3) of this section. https://nebraskalegislature.gov/laws/statutes.php?statute=48-3503

Nevada   Nev. Rev. Stat. § 613.135 (2013).
It is unlawful for any employer to directly or indirectly require, request, suggest, or cause any employee or prospective employee to disclose the username, password, or any information that provides access to his or her personal social media account. It is not unlawful for an employer to require an employee to disclose the username, password, or any other information to an account or a service, other than a personal social media account, for the purpose of accessing the employer's own internal computer or information system. https://www.leg.state.nv.us/nrs/nrs-613.html#NRS613Sec135

New Hampshire   N.H. Rev. Stat. § 275:74 (2014).
No employer shall request or require that an employee or prospective employee disclose login information for accessing any personal account or service through an electronic communication device; no employer shall compel an employee or applicant to add anyone, including the employer or the employer's agent, to a list of contacts associated with an electronic mail account or personal account or require an employee or applicant to reduce the privacy settings associated with any electronic mail or personal account that would affect a third party's ability to view the contents of the account; no employer shall take or threaten to take disciplinary action against any employee for such employee's refusal to comply with a request or demand by the employer that violates this subdivision. http://www.gencourt.state.nh.us/rsa/html/XXIII/275/275-74.htm

New Jersey   N.J. Stat. § 34:6B-6 (2013).
No employer shall require or request a current or prospective employee to provide or disclose any username or password, or in any way provide the employer access to, a personal account through an electronic communications device. https://law.justia.com/codes/new-jersey/2018/title-34/chapter-6b/section-34-6b-6/#:~:text=Section%3A%2034%3A6B%2D6%3A%20Prohibited%20actions%20by%20employers.&text=No%20employer%20shall%20require%20or,through%20an%20electronic%20communications%20device

New Mexico   N.M. Stat. Ann. § 50-4-34 (2017).
It is unlawful for an employer to request or require a prospective employee to provide a password in order to gain access to the prospective employee's account or profile on a social networking website or to demand access in any manner to a prospective employee's account or profile on a social networking website. Nothing in this section shall limit an employer's right to: 1) have polices regarding workplace internet use, social networking use and electronic mail use; 2) monitor the usage of the employer's electronic equipment and

FIGURE 6.2 (continued)

the employer's electronic mail without requesting or requiring a prospective employee to provide a password in order to gain access to the prospective employee's account or profile on a social networking site. Nothing in this section shall prohibit an employer from obtaining information about a prospective employee that is in the public domain. https://law.justia.com/codes/new-mexico/2017/chapter-50/article-4/section-50-4-34/

Oklahoma   40 Okla. Stat. § 173.2 (2014).
No employer located in this state shall (1) require an employee or prospective employee or prospective employee to disclose a username and password or other means of authentication for accessing a personal online social media account through an electronic communications device; (2) require an employee or prospective employee to access the employee's or prospective employee's personal online social media account in the presence of the employer; (3) take retaliatory personnel action that materially and negatively affects the terms and conditions of employment against an employee solely for refusal to give the employer the username or password to the employee's personal online social media account; (4) refuse to hire a prospective employee solely as a result of the prospective employee's refusal to give this information. https://oksenate.gov/sites/default/files/2019-12/os40.pdf

Oregon   Or. Rev. Stat. § 659A.330 (2013).
It is an unlawful employment practice for an employer to require or request an employee or an applicant for employment to establish or maintain a personal social media account, or to disclose or to provide access through the employee's or applicant's username and password, password or other means of authentication that provides access to a personal social media account; require an employee or applicant to authorize the employer to advertise on the personal social media account of the employee or applicant; compel an employee or applicant for employment to add the employer or an employment agency to the employee or applicant's list of contacts associated with the social media website; compel the employee or applicant to access the personal account in the presence of the employer in a manner that enables the employer to view the contents of the account that are visible only when the account is accessed by the account holder's username and password, password, or other means of authentication. https://oregon.public.law/statutes/ors_659A.330

Rhode Island   R.I. Gen. Laws § 28-56-1 et. seq. (2014).
No employer shall (1) require, coerce, or request an employee or applicant to disclose the password or any other means for accessing a personal social media account; (2) require, coerce, or request an employee or applicant to access a personal social media account in the presence of the employer or representative; (3) require or coerce an employee or applicant to divulge any personal social media account information, except when reasonably believed to be relevant to an investigation of allegations of employee misconduct or workplace related violation of applicable laws and regulations. http://webserver.rilin.state.ri.us/Statutes/title28/28-56/INDEX.HTM

Tennessee   Tenn. Code Ann. § 50-1-1003 (2014)
An employer shall not (1) request or require an employee or applicant to disclose a password that allows access to the employee's or applicant's personal Internet account; (2) compel an employee or an applicant to add the employer or an employment agency to the employee's or applicant's list of contacts associated with a personal Internet account; (3) compel a n employee or an applicant to access a personal Internet account in the presence of the employer in a manner that enables the employer to observe the contents of the employee's or applicant's personal Internet account; (4) take adverse action, fail to hire, or otherwise penalize an employee or applicant because of a failure to disclose information or take an action specified in subdivisions (a)(1)–(3).

FIGURE 6.2 (continued)

https://advance.lexis.com/documentpage/?pdmfid=1000516&crid=1780cf97-87dc-4c22-9b48-
de21e4001119&pdistocdoscslideraccess=true&config=025054JABIOTJjNmIyNi0wYjI0LTRjZG
EtYWE5ZC0zNGFhOWNhMjFINDgKAFBvZENhdGFsb2cDFQ14bX2GfyBTaI9WcPX5&pddoc
fullpath=%2fshared%2fdocument%2fstatutes-legislation%2furn%3acontentItem%3a5
C9P-5X40-R03M-30DC-00008-00&pdcomponentid=234180&pdtocnodeidentifier=ABYAABAA
KAAD&ecomp=w53dkkk&prid=af4e4530-bc42-4a8a-92fb-45fff08de287

Utah   Utah Code Ann. § 34-48-201 (2013)
An employer may not do any of the following: (1) request an employee or an applicant for employment to disclose a username and password or a password that allows access to the employee's or applicant's personal Internet account; or (2) take adverse action, fail to hire, or otherwise penalize an employee or applicant for employment for failure to disclose information described in Subsection (1). https://le.utah.gov/xcode/Title34/Chapter48/34-48-S201.html

Vermont   21 V.S.A. § 495I (2018)
An employer shall not require, request, or coerce an employee or applicant to do any of the following: (1) disclose a username, password, or other means of authentication, or turn over an unlocked personal electronic device for the purpose of accessing the employee's or applicant's social media account; (2) access a social media account in the presence of the employer; (3) divulge or present any content from the employee's or applicant's social media account; (4) change the account or privacy settings of the employee's or applicant's social media account to increase third-party access to its contents. An employer shall not require or coerce an employee or applicant to add anyone, including the employer, to his or her list of contacts associated with a social media account. https://legislature.vermont.gov/statutes/section/21/005/00495l

Virginia   Va. Code § 40.1-28.7:5 (2015)
An employer shall not require a current or prospective employee to: (1) Disclose the username and password to the current or prospective employee's social media account; or (2) Add an employee, supervisor, or administrator to the list of contacts associated with the current or prospective employee's social media account. If an employer inadvertently receives an employee's username and password, or other login information associated with the employee's social media account through the use of an electronic device provided to the employee by the employer or a program that monitors an employer's network, the employer shall not be liable for having the information but shall not use the information to gain access to an employee's social media account. An employer shall not: (1) Take action against or threaten to discharge, discipline, or otherwise penalize a current employee for exercising his rights under this section; or (2) Fail or refuse to hire a prospective employee for exercising his rights under this section. https://law.lis.virginia.gov/vacode/40.1-28.7:5/

Washington   Wash. Rev. Code § 49.44.200 (2013).
An employer may not request, require, or otherwise coerce an employee or applicant to disclose login information for the employee's or applicant's personal social networking account; request, require, or otherwise coerce an employee or applicant to access his or her personal social networking account in the employer's presence in a manner that enables the employer to observe the contents of the account; compel or coerce an employee or applicant to add a person, including the employer, to the list of contacts associated with the employee's or applicant's personal social networking account; request, require or cause an employee or applicant to alter the settings on his or her personal social networking account that affect a third party's ability to view the contents of the account; or take adverse action against the employee or applicant because the employee or applicant refuses to disclose his or her login

FIGURE 6.2 (continued)

information, access his or her personal account in the employer's presence, add a person to the list of contacts, or alter the settings on his or her personal account. https://app.leg.wa .gov/rcw/default.aspx?cite=49.44.200

West Virginia   W.V. Code § 21-5H-1 (2016)
An employer shall not do any of the following: (1) Request, require or coerce an employee or a potential employee to disclose a username and password, password or any other authentication information that allows access to the employee or potential employee's personal account; (2) Request, require or coerce an employee or a potential employee to access the employee or the potential employee's personal account in the presence of the employer; or (3) Compel an employee or potential employee to add the employer or an employment agency to their list of contacts that enable the contacts to access a personal account. http://www.wvlegislature.gov/wvcode/ChapterEntire.cfm?chap=21& art=5H&section=1

Wisconsin   Wis. Stat. § 995.55(2) (2014)
No employer may: (1) request or require an employee or applicant for employment, as a condition of employment, to disclose access information for the personal Internet account of the employee or applicant or to otherwise grant access to or allow observation of that account; (2) discharge or otherwise discriminate against an employee for exercising the right under Subsection (1); (3) refuse to hire an applicant for employment because the applicant refused to disclose access information for, grant access to, or allow observation of the applicant's personal Internet account. https://docs.legis.wisconsin.gov/statutes/ statutes/995/55

FIGURE 6.2 (continued)

6.5 EMPLOYEE RIGHTS AGAINST SURVEILLANCE

Despite the rise of invasive technologies to monitor employees, "[p]rivacy litigation in response to employee monitoring has not yet become a tsunami,"[101] and this is in large part because "[l]ittle protection currently exists for the privacy interests of employees."[102] The *Wheeler v. Jackson Nat'l Life Ins. Co.* case illustrates the limited rights of workers to avoid intrusive surveillance on the job:

> JNL [the company] was free to closely monitor Wheeler [the employee] to deter-
> mine if he was working on the days for which he was being paid, and it was allowed
> to discuss those issues with Wheeler without later being guilty of harassment.
> Even if JNL distressed Wheeler personally by putting him under a "performance
> microscope" that was not typical for all JNL employees, it did not violate the law
> in doing so.[103]

[101] V. John Ella, "Employee Monitoring and Workplace Privacy Law," Paper presented at the 2016 National Symposium on Technology in Labor and Employment Law, ABA: Labor and Employment Law Section, www.americanbar.org/content/dam/aba/events/labor_law/2016/04/tech/papers/monitoring_ ella.authcheckdam.pdf (accessed Nov. 24, 2020).
[102] Lewis Maltby, "Electronic Monitoring in the Workplace: Common Law & Federal Statutory Protection," National Workrights Institute: Privacy, www.workrights.org/nwi_privacy_comp_ ElecMonitoringCommonLaw.html (accessed Nov. 14, 2020).
[103] *Wheeler v. Jackson Nat'l Life Ins. Co.*, 159 F. Supp. 3d 828, 860 (M.D. Tenn. 2016).

V. John Ella, however, in a paper presented at an ABA conference, provided a comprehensive review of cases and laws limiting employee monitoring:
One significant case in California:

In 2015, a plaintiff in California sued her former employer after she refused to use an app, called "Xora," on her smart phone which would allow her boss to track her whereabouts 24 hours a day, 7 days a week and she was subsequently fired. *Arias v. Intermex Wire Transfer, LLC*, No. S-1500-CV-284763 SPC, Cal. Super. Ct. Bakersfield, Co., May 5, 2015.[104] That case was later settled out of court.

With regard to state-specific regulations:

Connecticut and Delaware require employers to give notice to employees prior to monitoring their e-mail communications or Internet access. Connecticut Gen. Stat. § 31-48d, Del. Code § 19-7-705. Colorado and Tennessee require public entities to adopt a policy related to monitoring of public employees' e-mail. Colo. Rev. Stat. § 24-72-204.5, Tenn. Code § 10-7-512.

Some states, including Missouri, North Dakota and Wisconsin, have passed laws prohibiting employers from requiring that an employee have a microchip containing an RFID device planted in the employee's body. Mo. Rev. Stat. § 285-035-1; N.D. Cent. Code § 12.1-15-06; Wis. Stat. § 146.25.

Camera surveillance is generally allowed if employees do not have a reasonable expectation of privacy, such as when cameras are visible and in a public space. However, if "the cameras are hidden … the employer generally needs to demonstrate a legitimate business reason for the surveillance.

Connecticut law prohibits an employer from using "any electronic device to record or monitor employee activities in areas designated for health or personal comfort or for safeguarding of employee possessions, such as restrooms, locker rooms, or lounges." Conn. Gen. Stat. Sec. 31-48b. California, West Virginia, Rhode Island and Michigan have similar laws prohibiting video cameras in bathrooms or locker rooms.

Most states recognize a common law tort for invasion of privacy. E.g., *Lake v. Wal-Mart*, 582 N.W.2d 231 (Minn. 1998).[105]

Aside from those discussed in Ella's summary, there have been several recent complaints also focusing on workplace surveillance. In *Boumekpor v. Wal-Mart Stores East, LP*, for example, a complainant argued that he was discriminated against based on his race, and that his employer, Walmart, subjected him to enhanced video surveillance because of his race. However, in dismissing his motion for summary judgment in August 2020, the District Court for the District of Massachusetts noted that the plaintiff had not provided enough evidence to show that his race was a factor in Walmart's decision to initiate targeted video surveillance of him.[106]

---

[104] Ella, "Employee Monitoring and Workplace Privacy Law."
[105] Ella, "Employee Monitoring and Workplace Privacy Law."
[106] *Boumkepor v. Wal-Mart Stores East*, 2020 WL 4569587, 3:18-CV-30093-KAR (Aug. 7, 2020).

Contrastingly, courts have a very low tolerance for surveillance when it touches on protected concerted activity. In a July 2020 case, the Northern District of New York found that where an employer creates the impression that an employee's protected concerted activities are being surveilled, the employer is in violation of the National Labor Relations Act (NLRA), even if there is no actual surveillance taking place. In *Murphy*, the employer told one employee that the employer had video from surveillance cameras of the employee talking to people and giving them authorization cards. The court found that where an employee would reasonably assume from the statement that their union activities had been placed under surveillance, the employer has created an impression of surveillance and is in violation of the NLRA's Section 8(a)(1) prohibition against employers interfering with or coercing employees in the exercise of their Section 7 rights to unionize.[107]

In one case, *Lemon v. Williamson County Schools*, workplace surveillance also became part of a worker's claim of constructive discharge and wrongful termination by her employer. Lemon, a public schoolteacher, claimed that her employer had placed cameras in her classroom for the purpose of intimidating her and forcing her resignation, among other actions designed to encourage her to resign from her role. Although the trial court initially dismissed her claims based on an allegedly improper application of the doctrine of constructive discharge, as well as her failure to provide sufficient facts, the Court of Appeals of Tennessee reversed that decision, and remanded the case for further proceedings on that claim, suggesting that persistent camera surveillance could be used to show constructive discharge.[108]

However, one recent case in which employees are fighting for the use of video surveillance footage in litigation has also depicted the potential value of workplace surveillance in some situations. For example, in *Eugene Scalia v. KP Poultry, Inc.*, plaintiffs challenged the deletion of surveillance videos during litigation, arguing that the videos of the workplace would have proved that the employees worked overtime and were therefore entitled to more pay.[109] In this case, the District Court for the Central District of California recommended that the plaintiff's Motion for Spoliation Sanctions be granted in part, because of the deletion of this relevant surveillance footage.

In the absence of broader federal protections against surveillance, many states have started passing their own laws to protect individuals from being watched without their knowing. Some of these laws take the form of general protections of the public, while others focus more directly on workplaces. For example, Figure 6.3 details some state laws which provide general protections against worker surveillance.

---

[107] *Murphy v. NCRNC, LLC.*, 2020 L.R.R.M. BNA 278, XX (July 27, 2020).
[108] *Lemon v. Williamson County Schools*, 2019 WL 4598201, 1 (Sept. 23, 2019).
[109] *Eugene Scalia v. KP Poultry, Inc.*, No. CV 19-3546-TJH, 2020 WL 6694315 (Nov. 6, 2020).

California   Cal. Penal Code § 653n
West Virginia   W. Va. Code § 21-3-20
Rhode Island   RI Gen. Laws 1956 § 28-6.12-1 (2005)
Laws making it a crime to install surveillance mirrors (two-way mirrors) in a restroom, shower, fitting room, or locker room.

Connecticut   Conn. Gen. Stat. § 31-48b.
Laws prohibiting employers from operating surveillance equipment in areas designed for employee rest or comfort.

Missouri   Mo. Rev. Stat. § 285-035-1
North Dakota   N.D. Cent. Code § 12.1-15-06
Wisconsin   Wis. Stat. § 146.25
Laws prohibiting employers from requiring that an employee have a microchip containing a radio frequency identification device (RFID) planted in the employee's body.

FIGURE 6.3 General protections against worker surveillance

However, some of the statutes listed in Figure 6.3 have a narrower impact than meets the eye. As is clear, the first set of statutes (in California, West Virginia, and Rhode Island) makes it a crime to install two-way mirrors in public restrooms, showers, fitting rooms, and locker rooms – all of which are spaces that are considered "public" but retain a private dimension.[110] These statutes can have the impact of ensuring that employers are also not monitoring employees in these semi-private spaces, yet they are not aimed at employers directly. By contrast, Connecticut's law, described in the second section, narrows in on protecting workers and details that employers cannot operate surveillance equipment in any area that is designed for employee rest or comfort.[111] Though narrowly applied just to employees, the scope of this law is also broader than the first group of statutes, applying to a variety of surveillance equipment in a variety of potential locations.

Though the Connecticut statute seemingly provides broader protections for employees, this statute it is not without its problems. First, in 2010, the Supreme Court of Connecticut clarified that this statute does not create a private right of action for employees – instead, their recourse could be obtained solely through the labor commissioner after a violation had been determined through an administrative hearing.[112] Moreover, the statute similarly does not provide a mechanism by which an employee could report an employer to the labor commissioner for violating the statute.[113] This suggests that although the statute provides "protection" for employees, it is likely very difficult for employees to claim such protection when

[110] See Cal. Penal Code § 653n; W. Va. Code § 21-3-20; RI Gen. Laws 1956 § 28-6.12-1 (2005).
[111] Conn. Gen. Stat. § 31-48b (amend. 2012).
[112] See *Gerardi v. City of Bridgeport*, 294 Conn. 461, 461 (2010).
[113] *Gerardi v. City of Bridgeport*, 294 Conn. 461, 462 (2010).

their rights are being violated. Further, it is important to note how few states have passed similar protections for employees – a fact that further elucidates the need for workplace surveillance protections on a broader, potentially national, scale.

To date, one of the most widely adopted ideas for protection against surveillance comes in the form of state laws preventing the recording of private communications. In some states, this idea has expanded into the workplace as well, through a variety of state laws that protect against the recording of communications for the purpose of union activity or require that employers notify employees prior to recording. Figure 6.4 details the laws in each state that prohibit the recording of private communications and shows that employees are either given very narrow protections or otherwise excepted from the state's general protection altogether.

As Figure 6.4 shows, many state laws do not specifically prohibit workplace surveillance. As such, when there is no state law that specifically allows or prohibits surveillance, courts determine whether an employee's privacy has been violated by looking at two competing interests: the employer's need to conduct surveillance and the employee's reasonable expectation of privacy. An employee who is using the restroom has a very strong, and reasonable, expectation of privacy, while an employee working in the ordinary course of their job may have less such expectation.

6.6 WORKER SURVEILLANCE AND THE RIGHT TO UNIONIZE

In 1935, the National Labor Relations Act (NLRA; 29 U.S.C. §§ 151–69) was passed. While the act promised employees the right to engage in collective bargaining and attempted to minimize certain management practices that were harmful to workers, it also opened up the question of the limitations on an employer's surveillance practices with relation to employee unionization. First, since the act's enactment, courts have typically held that employers may not keep union meetings under surveillance. In an early case, *NLRB v. Pennsylvania Greyhound Lines*, an employer had started its own union for employees prior to the enactment of the NLRA. Then, after the NLRA was passed, employees of Pennsylvania Greyhound Lines began attempts to form an independent union. During the organizing process, the employer actively surveilled the union meetings with the goal of preventing an independent union from forming. Ultimately, the NLRB held that the employer had violated the employees' rights to organize by surveilling their unionization meetings and threatening their unionization process.[114]

---

[114] Information from XpertHR, *Recording Communications and Video Surveillance Laws by State* (2020). The information in this chart depicts general privacy laws that protect individuals from being recorded, as well as those specific to the employment context. For ease of reading, I have bolded all of the instances where the word "employee" or "employer" appears, to show which states have considered surveillance in the employment context specifically.

Federal

Recording Audio Communications: It is unlawful to intentionally intercept, endeavor to intercept, or procure another to intercept or endeavor to intercept, any wire, oral, or electronic communication.

Video Surveillance: It is unlawful to use video surveillance for any unlawful purpose under the National Labor Relations Act, including monitoring, or giving the impression of monitoring, **employee** union activity and protected concerted Section 7 activity.

Alabama

Recording Audio Communications: It is unlawful to overhear record, amplify or transmit any part of a private communication of others without the consent of at least one of the persons engaged in the communication.

Video Surveillance: It is unlawful to record any person in any place where that individual has a reasonable expectation of privacy without prior consent and for the purposes of sexual gratification.

Alaska

Recording Audio Communications: It is unlawful to use an eavesdropping device to hear or record all or any part of an oral conversation without the consent of a party to the conversation.

Video Surveillance: It is unlawful to view or produce pictures of a nude or partially nude person without consent.

Arizona

Recording Audio Communications: It is unlawful to intentionally intercept a wire, electronic or other communication without either being party to the communication or having the consent of at least one of the parties involved.

Video Surveillance: It is unlawful to photograph, videotape, film, digitally record or secretly view another person in situations that person has a reasonable expectation of privacy without consent unless the surveillance is for security purposes and notice is posted.

Arkansas

Recording Audio Communications: It is unlawful for a person to intercept a wire, landline, oral, telephonic or wireless communication and to record or possess a recording of such communication unless the person is one of the parties or one of the parties has given prior consent.

Video Surveillance: It is unlawful to use any camera or recording device to secretly view or videotape a person in a private area out of public view if that person has a reasonable expectation of privacy and has not provided consent.

California

Recording Audio Communications: It is unlawful to wiretap, eavesdrop or record confidential conversations without the knowledge and consent of all parties to the conversation.

Video Surveillance: It is unlawful to use a camera or other recording device to view or record individuals without their permission in a rest room, locker room or changing room or any other location where an individual has a reasonable expectation of privacy. **Employers** may be exempt if surveillance is conducted in areas of private business used to count currency or other negotiable instruments.

FIGURE 6.4 State laws on recording private communications[115]

[115] *NLRB v. Pennsylvania Greyhound Lines*, 303 U.S. 261 (1938).

Colorado

Recording Audio Communications: It is unlawful to record or intercept a telephone conversation or any electronic communication, without the consent of at least one party to the conversation. An **employer** may use wiretapping or eavesdropping devices on its own premises for security or business purposes, if reasonable notice of the use of such devices is given to the public.

Video Surveillance: It is unlawful to film another individual's private parts without that person's consent if that individual has a reasonable expectation of privacy.

Connecticut

Recording Audio Communications: It is unlawful to intentionally overhear or record a telephone conversation unless all parties consent to such recording.

Video Surveillance: It is unlawful operate any electronic surveillance device or system to record or monitor **employees** in areas designed for the health or personal comfort of the **employees**, such as rest rooms, locker rooms or lounges. **Employers** must provide written notice to **employees** who will be affected by electronic monitoring unless the information is collected for security purposes in common areas such as waiting rooms and building entrances, or if the **employer** believes that **employees** are engaged in unlawful conduct or the creation of a hostile work environment.

Delaware

Recording Audio Communications: It is unlawful to intercept a wire, oral or electronic communication unless one party to the communication has given prior consent. **Employers** that wish to monitor telephone calls, email or internet use of **employees** are required to provide notice in written or electronic form each time the **employee** accesses the **employer's** electronic resources. **Employers** may run maintenance and/ or protection processes that manage the type or volume of email, telephone voicemail or internet use of **employees**, so long as the processes do not monitor or intercept the email, telephone voicemail or internet usage of a particular **employee.**

Video Surveillance: It is unlawful to install a camera or other recording device in any private place without consent of the person or persons entitled to privacy there. It is also unlawful to use a hidden camera to record individuals dressing or undressing in a private place.

District of Columbia

Recording Audio Communications: It is unlawful to attempt to intercept, try to intercept or disclose or use information known to be the contents of intercepted wire or oral communications unless the person is a party to the communication or a party to the communication has consented to the interception.

Video Surveillance: It is unlawful to record anyone in a bathroom or other private place when nude or engaging in sexual activity, unless the recording is for security monitoring in any building. There must be signs prominently displayed informing persons that the entire premises or portions of it are under surveillance.

Florida

Recording Audio Communications: It is unlawful to intercept and disclose wire, oral or electronic communications without a person's consent.

Video Surveillance: Florida prohibits the audio recording of **employees** if they have a reasonable expectation of privacy or if an **employee** is dressing, undressing or privately exposing his or her body at a time and a place where the individual has an expectation of privacy. **Employers** should notify **employees** if they intend to videotape them.

FIGURE 6.4 (continued)

Georgia

Recording Audio Communications: It is unlawful to clandestinely overhear, transmit, or record the private conversation of another in a private place if not a party to the conversation.

Video Surveillance: It is unlawful for any person through the use of any device without the consent of all persons observed to observe, photograph or record another individual in a private place and out of public view unless an owner of real property is recording such activities for security purposes and in areas where there is no reasonable expectation of privacy.

Hawaii

Recording Audio Communications: It is unlawful to intentionally intercept any wire, electronic or oral communication through the use of a device unless one of the parties to the communication has given prior consent to the interception.

Video Surveillance: Employers may use security cameras or surveillance videos in common areas of the workplace, but there are restrictions. Security cameras or surveillance videos may not be used in a private place where an individual has an expectation of privacy such as restrooms, changing rooms, dressing rooms or other areas where the **employee** may be in a state of undress. Surveillance equipment that records audio may not be used without obtaining prior written consent from the **employees** involved in the audio recording.

Idaho

Recording Audio Communications: It is unlawful to record telephone or other conversations clandestinely unless at least one party to the conversation gives consent. **Employers** can monitor phone calls at customer service desks for the purpose of quality assurance, but both the customer and the **employee** must be notified of the monitoring. However, once an **employee** receives a personal call, the **employer** must stop recording as soon as it is clear that the call is of a personal nature.

Video Surveillance: Any video recording or monitoring by an **employer** is required to have a business purpose. If an **employer** is monitoring with video cameras, those cameras may record only video, not audio, without prior consent, and any monitoring of restrooms or locker rooms is prohibited.

Illinois

Recording Audio Communications: It is unlawful to eavesdrop and knowingly and intentionally use a device in a surreptitious manner to record, hear, intercept, retain or transcribe a private conversation (to which an individual is not a party) unless the individual does so with the consent of all the parties to the conversation. An exception is provided for **employers** engaged in telephone solicitation, marketing or opinion research, or bank or credit card administration if the information is used for service quality control, education, training or internal research.

Employers are required to provide **employees** with notice that monitoring of their telephone may occur and provide access to personal-only phone lines that are not subject to monitoring. **Employers** should limit monitoring to business- related calls and cease monitoring immediately and destroy any recording once the **employer** realizes a call is not business-related.

Employers should refrain from using information obtained through monitoring in legal proceedings or from providing the information to law enforcement or other third parties.

Video Surveillance: It is unlawful to videotape, photograph, or film another person without that person's consent in restrooms, locker rooms, changing rooms and other private areas without their consent.

FIGURE 6.4 (continued)

Indiana
Recording Audio Communications: N/A
Video Surveillance: It is unlawful to record an individual in areas where that individual has a reasonable expectation of privacy, such as a changing stall or restroom.

Iowa
Recording Audio Communications: It is unlawful for a person to intercept a wire, oral, or electronic communication by use of a mechanical, electronic or other device or disclose information that was illegally intercepted or request that others engage in the illegal interception of messages unless one of the parties provides consent prior to the recording. It is also unlawful to connect a listening device or tap into telephone or other communication wires or listen to, record or otherwise intercept conversations or communications of any kind unless one is a party to the communication.
Video Surveillance: It is unlawful to record an individual without their prior consent in any private place where that individual would have a reasonable expectation of privacy for the purpose of arousing or gratifying the sexual desire of another person.

Kansas
Recording Audio Communications: It is unlawful to record or intercept telephone or other wire communications without the consent of one party to the communication. It is also unlawful to intercept telegraphs, letters or other means of private communication. It is unlawful to enter into a private place with the intent of surreptitiously listening to private conversations or observing personal conduct.
Video Surveillance: It is unlawful to engage in video surveillance in a private place where one may reasonably expect to be safe from surveillance for the purpose of viewing a person's body or undergarments without the person's knowledge or consent.

Kentucky
Recording Audio Communications: It is unlawful to use any device to intentionally overhear, record, amplify or transmit any part of a wire or oral communication without the consent of at least one party.
Video Surveillance: Employers may generally photograph **employees** in the workplace for the purposes of improving safety, efficiency and productivity as long as the photographing does not constitute an invasion of the **employee's** privacy and the **employer's** sole purpose is related to the work environment. It is unlawful to use filming devices for the purpose of observing or viewing another person's sexual conduct or nudity, or in a place where the individual has a reasonable expectation of privacy.

Louisiana
Recording Audio Communications: It is unlawful to intercept or have someone intercept any wire or oral communications.
Video Surveillance: An **employer** may not engage in the unauthorized electronic surveillance of its **employees** with respect to wire or oral communications except when an **employee** has consented to electronic surveillance. It is unlawful to use a hidden camera to observe or record a person if the person has not consented or if the recording is for a lewd or lascivious purpose.

Maine
Recording Audio Communications: It is unlawful to intercept the contents of any wire or oral communications without the consent of the sender or receiver.
Video Surveillance: An **employer** may not engage in audio and video surveillance in private places, except where the general public or substantial groups of people have access, without the consent of persons entitled to privacy.

FIGURE 6.4 (continued)

It is unlawful to install or use in a private place, any device for observing, photographing, recording, amplifying or broadcasting sounds or events in that place without the consent of the person entitled to privacy. A private place is a place where one may reasonably expect to be safe from surveillance, including, but not limited to, changing or dressing rooms, bathrooms and similar places.

Maryland

Recording Audio Communications: It is unlawful to record a conversation without the consent of all the parties to the conversation. It is also unlawful to intercept transmitted material, including images and audio recordings, without consent. If a consumer business monitors telephone calls for quality control, not only is the **employee** required to consent, but the customer must consent as well. Consent is presumed if a party knows he or she is being recorded.

Video Surveillance: It is unlawful to use a hidden camera in a bathroom or dressing room or on private property for purposes of conducting deliberate, surreptitious observation of a person inside the private residence or in a private place with prurient intent.

Massachusetts

Recording Audio Communications: It is unlawful to engage in wiretapping, intercepting, assessing or electronically overhearing a conversation. without the consent of all parties to the conversation. An **employer** may record a telephone conversation between **employees** or between an **employee** and a third party in Massachusetts only if the **employer** is a party to the conversation and all parties to the conversation consent.
Eavesdropping on **employee** phone calls is permissible only if justified by business necessity. Once an employer determines that a communication is private, the **employer** is required to stop listening.

Video Surveillance: It is unlawful to engage in electronic surveillance of any person nude or partially nude where that person has a reasonable expectation of privacy.

Michigan

Recording Audio Communications: It is unlawful to use any device to eavesdrop upon a conversation without the consent of all parties. Case law states that a private conversation may be recorded so long as that person is a party to the conversation.

Video Surveillance: It is unlawful to install, place, or use in any private place any device for observing, recording, transmitting, photographing or eavesdropping upon the sounds or events in that place without the consent of the person or persons entitled to privacy in that place.
A private place is a place where a person may reasonably expect to be safe from casual or hostile intrusion or surveillance. It does not include a place to which the public or a substantial group of the public has access.

Minnesota

Recording Audio Communications: It is unlawful to intercept wire, electronic or oral communications or use any device to intercept oral communications or intentionally disclose the contents of any intercepted communication unless one person is party to the communication or one person provides prior consent.

Video Surveillance: Video cameras recording sound are subject to wiretapping restrictions. With regard to video surveillance, it will depend on whether the individual has a reasonable expectation of privacy. Surveillance in a parking garage or public area would likely be acceptable as opposed to surveillance in a private office or restroom, which would be an invasion of privacy.
It is unlawful to use any type of device for observing, photographing, recording, amplifying or broadcasting sounds or events through the window or other aperture of a sleeping room

FIGURE 6.4 (continued)

in a hotel, a tanning booth or any other place where a reasonable person would have an expectation of privacy and has exposed or is likely to expose his or her intimate parts or the clothing covering the immediate area of the intimate parts.

Mississippi
Recording Audio Communications: It is unlawful to secretly tape a conversation, whether the conversation is face-to-face or electronically transmitted. This law does not apply to a conversation intercepted by someone who is a party to it.
Video Surveillance: It is unlawful to secretly record another person with lewd, licentious or indecent intent without that individual's consent while the individual is in a restroom, fitting room or areas where the individual would have a reasonable expectation of privacy.

Missouri
Recording Audio Communications: It is unlawful to intercept a wire communication, record it or disclose its contents without the consent of one of the parties to the communication. It is also unlawful to use an electronic or mechanical device to intercept any oral communication when that device transmits communications by radio or interferes with the transmission of the communication.
Video Surveillance: It is unlawful to knowingly view, photograph or film another person, without that person's knowledge and consent while the person is in a state of undress in a place where he or she would have a reasonable expectation of privacy.

Montana
Recording Audio Communications: It is unlawful to record a conversation without the knowledge of all parties to the conversation that the conversation is subject to monitoring. It is unlawful to purposely intercept an electronic communication.
Video Surveillance: It is unlawful for an owner, manager or **employee** of a business or landlord to secretly record a person in private places within public establishments, like restrooms and changing rooms.

Nebraska
Recording Audio Communications: It is unlawful to intentionally intercept any wire, electronic or oral communication and disclose its contents unless one party to the communication consents.
Video Surveillance: It is unlawful to view or record, either by video, audio or electronic means, a person in a state of undress who would have a reasonable expectation of privacy, such as in a restroom, locker room or shower room without his or her prior consent.

Nevada
Recording Audio Communications: It is unlawful to surreptitiously record or intercept a wire or telephone communications or private conversation without the consent of all parties to the communication. There is an exception to this for emergency communications.
Video Surveillance: It is unlawful to use a hidden camera to photograph or record the private area of a person in a place where the person has a reasonable expectation of privacy, regardless of whether a person is in a public or private place.

New Hampshire
Recording Audio Communications: It is unlawful to intercept, disclose, or use the contents of any telecommunication or oral communication without the consent of all of the parties. **Employers** are not permitted to monitor **employee** telephone and email communications without prior consent.

FIGURE 6.4 (continued)

Video Surveillance: It is unlawful to install or use a device for the purpose of observing, photographing, recording, amplifying, broadcasting or transmitting images or sounds of the private body parts of a person including the genitalia, buttocks or female breasts, or a person's body underneath that person's clothing; any images or sounds in a private place or any images or sounds outside of a private place which would not ordinarily be audible or comprehensible outside the place without the consent of the person entitled to privacy.

A private place is a place a person may reasonably expect to be safe from surveillance, including public restrooms; locker rooms; the interior of one's dwelling place; or any place where a person's private body parts, including genitalia, buttocks or female breasts, may be exposed.

There is an exception for public or private entities that within the scope of their **employment** and upon suspicion attempt to capture sounds or images via monitoring and surveillance to obtain evidence of illegal activity, violation of rules and regulations, fraudulent conduct or a pattern of business practices adversely affecting health or safety.

New Jersey

Recording Audio Communications: It is unlawful to intercept a wire, electronic or oral communication, or disclose or use the contents of an interception or evidence derived from it, unless one is a party to the communication, or one party has given prior consent.

There is a business-extension exception that allows **employers** to monitor **employee** conversations provided that the service provider or subscriber furnished the intercepting equipment, and the **employee** used the equipment in the ordinary course of business.

Video Surveillance: N/A

New Mexico

Recording Audio Communications: It is unlawful to interfere with communications, which means knowingly and without lawful authority reading, interrupting, taking or copying any message, communication or report intended for another by telegraph or telephone without the consent of the sender or intended recipient. New Mexico's statute limiting the monitoring of audio communications does not prohibit the recording of an in-person or telephone conversation by one of the parties to the conversation.

Video Surveillance: It is considered a crime of video voyeurism and unlawful to use any mode of visual surveillance to record the intimate areas of another person without their knowledge and consent while the person is in the interior of any areas where the person would have a reasonable expectation of privacy or under circumstances in which the person would have a reasonable expectation of privacy either in a public or private space.

New York

Recording Audio Communications: It is unlawful to wiretap, intercept, access or electronically overhear a conversation without the consent of at least one of the parties to the conversation.

An **employer** may record a telephone conversation between **employees** or between an **employee** and a third party in New York if the **employer** is a party to the conversation or one of the **employees** involved in the conversation consents.

Video Surveillance: An **employer** is prohibited from conducting video surveillance in certain areas of the **employer's** premises without a court order and from videotaping **employees** surreptitiously in private spaces such as restrooms, locker rooms or dressing rooms when an individual has a reasonable expectation of privacy. This law does not apply to audio surveillance, and video surveillance is permitted in other public areas.

It is also unlawful to engage in surreptitious visual surveillance for the purpose of

FIGURE 6.4 (continued)

amusement, profit, abuse, sexual gratification or for no legitimate purpose in any place where a person has a reasonable expectation of privacy and without the person's knowledge and consent. There is an exception for surveillance via a security system when notice is posted and video surveillance devices are installed in an obvious manner.

North Carolina

Recording Audio Communications: It is unlawful to willfully intercept, use any device to intercept, disclose the contents of, or use the contents of any wire, oral or electronic communication without the consent of at least one party to the communication.

Video Surveillance: It is unlawful to record and disseminate photographic images still or moving obtained while secretly peeping into a private room to observe any person for the purposes of sexual gratification.

North Dakota

Recording Audio Communications: It is unlawful to intercept any wire or oral communication by an electronic, mechanical or other device or intentionally disclose or use the contents of any intercepted communication unless one of the parties to the communication provides prior consent.

Video Surveillance: It is unlawful to install or use any device for observing, photographing or recording in a private space such as a dressing room or changing room with the intent to intrude upon or interfere with the occupant.

Ohio

Recording Audio Communications: It is unlawful to intercept a wire, oral, or electronic communications unless the person is a party to the communication or one of the parties has given prior consent.

Video Surveillance: It is unlawful to secretly or surreptitiously videotape, film, photograph, or otherwise record another person under or through clothing for the purpose of viewing that person's body or undergarments.
It is also unlawful to trespass, eavesdrop, surreptitiously videotape, film, photograph, or record another nude person (and additionally spying or eavesdropping on nude minors) or otherwise surreptitiously invade another's privacy. **Employers** should not engage in video surveillance in sensitive areas like restrooms, locker rooms, lactation rooms set aside for breast milk pumping, or other changing areas.

Oklahoma

Recording Audio Communications: It is unlawful for a person to intercept, use or disclose any wire, oral or electronic communication without prior consent of at least one participant to the communication. An **employer** must obtain prior consent from at least one participant to any email or telephone communication it intends to monitor.

Video Surveillance: It is unlawful to use video surveillance equipment in a clandestine manner for any illegal, illegitimate, prurient, lewd or lascivious purpose in order to view a person in a private place where the person has a reasonable expectation of privacy or to capture images of the private areas of a person's body whether that person is in a private or public place.

Oregon

Recording Audio Communications: It is unlawful to monitor or record a telephone, wire, or oral communication without the consent of one party. It is unlawful to monitor or record a live conversation without the consent of all parties to the communication.

Video Surveillance: Video surveillance conducted in a reasonable and unobtrusive manner will not give rise to a viable claim for invasion of privacy.

FIGURE 6.4 (continued)

Pennsylvania

Recording Audio Communications: It is unlawful to intercept, disclose, or use any wire, electronic, or oral communication without consent of all participants.

Video Surveillance: Audio recording of **employees** without their consent is unlawful. The law is silent with regard to video recordings. It is unlawful to view, photograph or film another person in a state of full or partial nudity without consent, under circumstances in which that person has an expectation of privacy.

Rhode Island

Recording Audio Communications: It is unlawful to monitor or record wire communication except where the person recording is a party to the communication or one of the parties has provided prior consent.

Video Surveillance: Employers are prohibited from making an audio or video recording of an **employee** in a restroom, locker room, or room designated by an **employer** for **employees** to change their clothes, unless authorized by court order.

It is unlawful to install or use visual surveillance devices to record the intimate areas of another person for the purposes of sexual arousal or gratification without that person's knowledge and consent.

South Carolina

Recording Audio Communications: It is unlawful to use an electronic, mechanical or other device to intercept oral communications unless the individual is a party to the communication or when one of the parties to the communication has given prior consent.

Employers may therefore monitor or review the contents of **employee** telephone conversations or voicemail or may create audio recordings of **employees** with prior consent or with disclosure by a party to the communication.

Video Surveillance: It is unlawful to use video or audio equipment to invade the privacy of others. South Carolina law prohibits the surreptitious visual surveillance and the recording of another person for sexual gratification without her consent when that person is in a place where the person has a reasonable expectation of privacy. This law does not apply to security surveillance in businesses in order to decrease theft.

South Dakota

Recording Audio Communications: It is unlawful for anyone who is not a sender or receiver of a telephone or telegraph communication or one who is not present during such a conversation or discussion to intentionally and with an instrument or device overhear or record the communication or to aid, authorize, **employ**, procure or permit another individual to do so without the consent of either the sender or the receiver.

Video Surveillance: It is unlawful to install a surveillance device in any private place without the consent of anyone entitled to privacy there. A private place is defined as a place where one may reasonably expect to be safe from casual or hostile intrusion or surveillance, but does not include a place to which the public or a substantial group has access.

It is also unlawful to use or disseminate any visual recording or photographic device to photograph or visually record a person without clothing or under or through the clothing, for the purpose of viewing the body of, or the undergarments worn by, that other person, without the consent or knowledge of that other person, with the intent to self-gratify, to harass or to embarrass and invade the privacy of that other person when the other person has a reasonable expectation of privacy.

Tennessee

Recording Audio Communications: It is unlawful to intentionally intercept, any wire, oral or electronic communication, procure another to do so or use or disclose such communications without the consent of at least one of the parties to the communication.

FIGURE 6.4 (continued)

Video Surveillance: It is unlawful to observe another without consent and knowingly spy upon, observe or otherwise view an individual, when the individual is in a place where there is a reasonable expectation of privacy, without the prior effective consent of the individual if the viewing would offend or embarrass an ordinary person if the person knew the person was being viewed; and was for the purpose of sexual arousal or gratification of the viewer.

Texas

Recording Audio Communications: It is unlawful to intercept, attempt to intercept, or **employ** or obtain another to intercept or attempt to intercept a wire, oral or electronic communication or use or divulge information obtained by such interception without the consent of at least one party to the communication.

Video Surveillance: It is unlawful to videotape or record another person in a bathroom, private dressing room or any other location without his or her consent for the purpose of sexual gratification or to invade his or her privacy.

Utah

Recording Audio Communications: It is unlawful to intercept any wire, electronic or oral communication or use or disclose any intercepted wire, electronic or oral communication without the consent of a party to the communication.

Video Surveillance: It is unlawful to make audio or video recordings of individuals without their consent, unless one is a party to the communication.

It is unlawful to install a hidden camera or audio recorder to tape a person in a private place without consent. A private place is a place where one may reasonably expect to be safe from intrusion or surveillance.

Vermont

Recording Audio Communications: N/A

Video Surveillance: It is unlawful to view, film or record the intimate areas of another person without that person's knowledge and consent while the person is in a place where the person would have a reasonable expectation of privacy.

Virginia

Recording Audio Communications: It is unlawful to intercept or record wire, oral, or electronic communications or disclose or use such communications unless one party to the conversation consents.

Video Surveillance: It is unlawful to engage in video surveillance or record any person in any state of undress in a place of privacy such as a restroom, locker room or dressing room without that person's consent.

Washington

Recording Audio Communications: It is unlawful to intercept or record private communications transmitted by telephone, telegraph, radio or other device unless all parties to the communication consent.

Video Surveillance: It is unlawful to engage in surreptitious video surveillance or record another person for the purpose of arousing or gratifying the sexual desire in a place where the person recorded would have a reasonable expectation of privacy, except when such surveillance is conducted for security purposes or during an investigation. It is unlawful to record or transmit any private conversation recording while viewing or videotaping **employees.**

FIGURE 6.4 (continued)

West Virginia
Recording Audio Communications: It is unlawful to intercept or attempt to intercept any wire, oral or electronic communication except if the person performing the interception is a party to the communication or if one of the parties has provided prior consent.
Video Surveillance: It is unlawful for any **employer,** whether public or private, to operate any electronic surveillance device or system for the purpose of recording or monitoring the activities of the **employees** in areas designed for the health or personal comfort of the **employees** or for safeguarding of their possessions, such as rest rooms, shower rooms, locker rooms, dressing rooms and **employee** lounges.
It is unlawful to visually portray or video record another person with their knowledge while that person is in a state of undress and would have a reasonable expectation of privacy.

Wisconsin
Recording Audio Communications: It is unlawful to intercept or attempt to intercept any wire, oral or electronic communication or use or disclose any intercepted communication unless one of the parties to it provides consent.
Video Surveillance: It is unlawful to install or use a surveillance or recording device in any private place.
An **employer** that owns or operates a locker room must adopt a written policy that specifies who may enter and remain in the locker room to interview or seek information from any individual in the locker room, details recording devices that may be used in the locker room and the circumstances under which they may be used, reflects the privacy interests of individuals who use the locker room and provides that no person may use a cell phone to capture, record, or transfer a representation of another person, under certain circumstances, in the locker room.

Wyoming
Recording Audio Communications: It is unlawful to intercept any oral, wire, or electronic communication except when the person intercepting the communication is a party to the communication or when one of the parties has provided prior consent.
Video Surveillance: It is unlawful to surreptitiously capture an image by means of a camera, video camera or any other image recording device of another person without his or her consent in an enclosed area where that person would have a reasonable expectation of privacy, such as a restroom, bath, shower, or dressing or fitting room.

FIGURE 6.4 (continued)

Then, in *NLRB v. Gate City Cotton Mills,* employers took their union surveillance and dissuasion tactics a step further. In this case, an employee, James Jackson, was both surveilled and harassed after his employer learned that he had been engaging in union-organizing activity. In a drastic shift from Jackson's previously favorable treatment, his employer began to remind him of trivial mistakes that they had formerly overlooked and ensured that he did not leave his work at any time. After six months of such treatment, Jackson even became ill and took a leave from work for a period of several months to regain his mental health. However, such leave was not enough, as his employer continued by surveilling Jackson's home. Ultimately, the NLRB ruled that employers "may not, under the guise of merely exercising their right of free speech, pursue a course of conduct designed to restrain and coerce their employees in the exercise of rights in the Act" and found that constant surveillance as a response to pro-union conduct was violative of the NLRA.[116]

This case, and others of the sort, set the precedent that workers who were taking part in the collective bargaining process could not be the target of surveillance under the NLRA. Similarly, the NLRA had, decades earlier, limited the actions of the Pinkerton detectives, who had prided themselves on their "union busting" abilities. The act held that employers could not take anti-union measures to diminish the right of employees to engage in unionization, which includes the hiring of external entities for the purpose of minimizing union activity.

The laws, as they currently stand, however, offer workers limited protection from surveillance in the American workplace. Yet, this century has seen vast leaps in computing technology, allowing for much more invasive worker monitoring. The socio-technical phenomenon of the advanced technological monitoring of workers presents a crisis. We stand now at a crossroads leading to two very different futures of work. On one hand, employers could be granted carte blanche to deploy technologies to quantify the worker, including through pervasive and intrusive surveillance. On the other, the government could act to institute federal laws to ensure that worker personhood, dignity, and autonomy are not so eroded as to eradicate the very notion of democracy.

[116] *NLRB v. Gate City Cotton Mills*, 167 F.2d 647, 649 (1948).

7

Workplace Wellness Programs

In the meantime, we play the corporate wellness game. Earning points on an app is the only option many of us have to try to hang on a bit longer in the space where we can still perform the labor that will eventually make our continued employment impossible.

–Ann Larson, a grocery store employee discussing her time
using a workplace wellness app

1762
Jean-Jacque Rousseau's *Emile* argues that physical education is positively linked to strong moral character.

1857
The Church begins linking physical ability to character. Use of the term "Muscular Christianity" in Charles Kingsley's novel *Two Years Ago* links athleticism with morality and spirituality.

1869
The YMCA establishes its first Christian Men's Gym in New York City.

1881
Alexander Graham Bell studies deafness, concluding that deafness is hereditary and that congenitally deaf parents are more likely to produce deaf children. He suggests that negative traits can be mitigated by systematic reproduction.

1856–1863
Austrian scientist Gregor Johann Mendel studies the inheritance of traits between generations, using plants. He discovers that living things "inherit" traits from their parents.

1860–1910
Muscular Christianity grows in England and arises in America, and leads to many changes in the Catholic Church, as well as "worship" of strength and strong traits.

1869
Fredrich Miescher discovers a weak acid in the nuclei of white blood cells, today called DNA.

1883
Sir Francis Galton, cousin of Charles Darwin, first uses the term eugenics, believing that the human race can selectively breed individuals with "desired traits."

FIGURE 7.1 Timeline of key events preceding workplace wellness programs and genetic testing in the workplace

1880–1920
The United States becomes the first country to undertake government-mandated compulsory sterilization programs, for the purpose of curing genetic "defects" to "improve" Americans.

1905
English biologist William Bateson coins the term "genetics" in a letter to a fellow scientist.

1910s
The popularity of eugenics grows in America.

1910
American evolutionary biologist Thomas Hunt Morgan narrows in on genes, showing that they reside on chromosomes.

1911
American geneticist Alfred Sturtevant makes the first genetic map, showing that chromosomes contain linearly arranged genes.

1927
US Supreme Court legitimizes forced sterilization for the intellectually disabled in *Buck v. Bell.*

1939–1945
Popular opinion towards eugenics and sterilization becomes more negative in light of Nazi Germany and World War II.

1941
Edward Lawrie Tatum and George Wells Beadle show that genes code for proteins, a critical finding for the field of genetics.

1942
US Supreme Court rules against the sterilization of criminals where the equal protection clause of the constitution is violated. This meant the United States could not exempt white-collar criminals from sterilization, if it intended to sterilize criminals.

1944
The Avery-MacLeod-McCarty experiment isolates DNA as genetic material, allowing for the evolution of isolated genetic tests.

1950s
Employee Assistance Programs are introduced to promote the health and wellness of employees, focused on alcoholism and mental health issues.

1960s–70s
Federal workplaces increase drug testing due to findings of increased drug user in soldiers during the Vietnam War.

1970s
The occupational safety and health movement, as well as the worksite health promotion movement begin in the United States.

1975
UC Berkeley Board of Regents inherit a fund created with the goal of "improving the human race" through eugenics and begin training genetic counselors.

FIGURE 7.1 (continued)

1979
California repeals state law allowing forced sterilization of the "feeble-minded."

1979
Johnson & Johnson's *Live for Life* program begins, becoming the prototype for big corporate worksite wellness programs.

1982
US federal government survey finds that 1.6% of companies are using genetic testing for employment purposes.

1990s
US federal government launches an initiative called *Healthy People 2000* that proposes that 75% of employers with fifty or more workers should offer health promotion services as a benefit.

1990
Start of the Human Genome Project, which looks to sequence and map a human genome.

1996
The Health Insurance Portability and Accountability Act (HIPAA) passes, protecting Americans from the nonconsensual release and misuse of their genetic information.

1997
Survey by the American Management Association finds between 6 to 10% of employers are conducting genetic tests

1998
Ninth Circuit rules that subjecting employees to genetic testing without their consent violates their constitutional rights in *Lawrence Berkeley Laboratory.*

2000
US federal government launches *Healthy People 2010*, aiming for 75% of worksites to have a comprehensive health promotion plan including health education and screening programs.

2003
End of the Human Genome Project

2008
At least 500 documented cases of genetic discrimination in the workplace have already been made by this year.

2008
The Genetic Information Nondiscrimination Act is passed to protect Americans from being treated unfairly due to differences in their DNA.

2010
Affordable Care Act passes, promoting employer wellness program; maximum reward given to employers using a wellness program, contingent on employee health increasing from 20% to 30% of the cost of health coverage.

2011
California governor signs CalGINA into law, broadening antidiscrimination laws in California by protecting against genetic discrimination in housing, mortgage lending, education, and public accommodations.

2012
Jennifer Doudna and a team at UC Berkeley publish a paper about CRISPR-Cas9, a tool that allows scientists to cut DNA strands and edit genomes in human cells.

FIGURE 7.1 (continued)

2014	2014
EEOC v. Orion rules that a wellness plan could force workers who opted out to pay 100% of the premium for their health insurance, as well as a $50 monthly penalty. *EEOC v. Flambeau* holds that the ADA's "bona fide benefit plan" exception applies to workplace wellness plans. *EEOC v. Honeywell* holds that a wellness plan could include surcharges if an employee or their spouse does not complete tobacco screening.	Employers begin using Fitbits as part of workplace wellness programs, tracking employees' movement and health.[1]
2015	
AETNA workplace study is a pilot test for genetic testing in the workplace, testing employees for three genes and uses the information to help individuals navigate their health and wellness options.	**2018** 53% of small employers and 82% of large firms in the United States offer workplace wellness programs.
	2020 To date, forty-eight states and Washington, DC, have enacted laws prohibiting some types of genetic discrimination in the workplace.

FIGURE 7.1 (continued)

For centuries, humans have believed physical fitness to be linked to a better self. This notion can be traced to philosophers as far back as Plato, who believed that reproduction should be monitored and controlled by the state in order to constructively build a physically strong society. Plato lacked the scientific proof to conclusively show that parents with strong traits would pass those traits down to their children, yet his philosophy explains the infanticide of ancient civilizations such as Rome and Greece. In those cultures, strength was so highly valued that newborns would be inspected by the city elders, who would determine each child's fate based on their physical traits.[2]

The assumed connection between physical fitness and a better society became prominent again in the eighteenth and nineteenth centuries in England, when strength became linked to a person's morality. Effectively, physically fit people were seen as more trustworthy moral actors.[3] This idea was first articulated in publication in 1762, when Jean-Jacques Rousseau described physical education as important for the formation of moral character in his treatise *Emile: Or, on Education*. Rousseau's treatise also linked sports to Christianity for the first time, signaling that physical

[1] James A. Martin, "Pros and Cons of Using Fitness Trackers for Employee Wellness," *CIO*, Mar. 24, 2014, at www.cio.com/article/2377723/pros-and-cons-of-using-fitness-trackers-for-employee-wellness .html (last visited May 25, 2021).

[2] Sara Goering, "Eugenics," *Stanford Encyclopedia of Philosophy* (Fall 2014 edition), https://plato.stanford .edu/cgi-bin/encyclopedia/archinfo.cgi?entry=eugenics; "Infanticide in the Ancient World," in Early Church History, https://earlychurchhistory.org/medicine/infanticide-in-the-ancient-world/.

[3] See Charles Kingsley, *Health and Education* (New York: Macmillan, 1887), 86 (proffering the moral value of sports, stating that "games conduce, not merely to physical, but to moral health").

ability could be part of a larger exercise in morality.[4] Over the next century, the idea of physical ability would become more and more heavily ingrained in Christianity. By 1857, Charles Kingsley coined the term *Muscular Christianity*, preaching the spiritual value that individuals garner from exercise, and specifically from team sports.[5] By 1869, Muscular Christianity had spread to the United States, with the first faith-based Christian Men's Gym opening as part of a YMCA in New York City.[6]

7.1 THE RISE AND FALL OF EUGENICS

At the same time, scientists such as Gregor Johann Mendel were studying the inheritance of traits between generations. Mendel, who would later become one of the founding fathers of the study of genetics, deployed a plant-based study to find that the genes of a plant's reproduction were predictable, and that some traits were dominant over other traits.[7] From there, the study of genetic inheritance grew swiftly. In 1869, Fredrich Mieschler discovered a weak acid in the nuclei of white blood cells, which we now know as DNA.[8] By 1881, Alexander Graham Bell completed a study on deafness, concluding that it is hereditary and that congenitally deaf parents are more likely to produce deaf children. From this, he suggested, like Plato had, that negative traits could be mitigated by systematic reproduction.[9] With these developments, in 1883, Sir Francis Galton, a cousin of Charles Darwin, coined the term *eugenics* to describe the belief that the human race could scientifically breed individuals with "desired traits."[10]

The popularity of eugenics grew throughout Europe and the United States in the late nineteenth and early twentieth centuries. In 1890, the United States entered the Progressive Era, in which the nation started to reshape its social and economic relations. This period brought in new concerns about the children of the poor. Acting on these concerns, the United States became the first country to undertake government-mandated compulsory sterilization programs for the purposes of curing genetic "defects" in society.[11] The basis of these programs was the thought that mentally or physically ill people should not produce children, since they would only continue to replicate their "deficiencies" and those deficiencies would become

---

4 Nick Watson et al., "The Development of Muscular Christianity in Victorian Britain and Beyond," *Journal of Religion & Society* 7 (2005): 3.

5 See Jim Parry, Simon Robinson, and Nick Watson, *Sport and Spirituality: An Introduction* (New York: Routledge, 2007).

6 YMCA, "History: 1800–1860s," YMCA.net, www.ymca.net/history/1800-1860s.html (accessed May 25, 2021).

7 Benjamin A. Pierce, *Genetics: A Conceptual Approach*, 7th ed. (New York: Macmillan, 2020).

8 Peter Snustad and Michael Simmons, *Principles of Genetics*, 6th ed. (Hoboken, NJ: John Wiley & Sons, 2011), 210.

9 See Alexander Graham Bell, *Memoir upon the Formation of a Deaf Variety of the Human Race*, Paper Presented to the National Academy of Sciences at New Haven, Nov. 13, 1882 (1883).

10 See Sir Francis Galton, *Inquiries into Human Faculty and Its Development* (1883), (London: MacMillan, 1883).

11 Adam Cohen, *Imbeciles: The Supreme Court, American Eugenics, and the Sterilization of Carrie Buck* (New York: Penguin, 2016), 20.

burdens on society. Acting on this notion, legalized sterilizations were often performed on people in prisons, hospitals, and mental institutions.[12]

The first state to enact forced sterilization legislation was Indiana in 1907, although both Michigan and Pennsylvania had proposed compulsory sterilization laws as early as 1897. Other states followed in succession, but sterilization rates across the United States remained relatively low until the Supreme Court decided *Buck v. Bell* (47 S.Ct. 584) in 1927. In *Buck v. Bell*, the Supreme Court held that a Virginia treatment center for the intellectually disabled could forcibly sterilize patients, including Carrie Buck, who was a "feeble-minded white woman" committed to the institution. Following the Court's decision in *Buck*, over 62,000 people were forcibly sterilized throughout the United States, 61 percent of whom were women. The decision in *Buck v. Bell*, which is now regarded as one of the worst Supreme Court decisions in history, was later cited by Nazi Germany as an indication that their eugenic murders were acceptable.[13]

One *New York Times* article from 1913 provides a historical understanding of what the study of eugenics looked like as it started to gain popularity. First, the article begins by noting that ex-president William H. Taft was elected chairman of the board of the Life Extension Institute, a group formed with the goal of "conserve[ing] human life by the systematic application of modern science." The Institute was set to begin providing the public with free "life-saving knowledge" on hygiene and sanitation. Next, the Institute would retain a large staff of physicians in order to determine the physical condition of policyholders of different life insurance plans. With this, the group surmised that the "simple early discovery of 'slight impairments'" could greatly reduce the death rate among the U.S. population. The Institute also planned to cooperate with "hygiene agencies and movements of all kinds," including the eugenics movement. Finally, the article notes that Metropolitan Life (now MetLife) was the first large insurance company to subscribe to the services of the Institute, paying for physical examinations of 80,000 of its policyholders.[14]

Over time, public opinion towards eugenics and forced sterilization began to shift – specifically during World War II. In 1942, the Supreme Court decided *Skinner v. State of Oklahoma*, in which it stated that by sterilizing only select criminals, prisons were violating the Equal Protection Clause of the Fourteenth Amendment. This decision meant that if the United States intended to sterilize criminals, it could not exempt white-collar criminals from that practice. After *Skinner*, the number of forced sterilizations declined far below their pre-war levels.[15] The decision in

---

[12] See Randall Hansen and Desmond King, "Eugenic Ideas, Political Interests, and Policy Variance: Immigration and Sterilization Policy in Britain and the U.S.," *World Politics* 53, no. 2 (2017): 237.

[13] Philip R. Reilly, "Eugenics and Involuntary Sterilization, 1907–2015," *Annual Review of Genomics and Human Genetics* 16 (2015): 351; Rebecca M. Kluchin, *Fit to Be Tied: Sterilization and Reproductive Rights in America, 1950–1980* (New Brunswick, NJ: Rutgers University Press, 2016), 17; Cohen, *Imbeciles*.

[14] "National Society to Conserve Life: Life Extension Institute Formed to Teach Hygiene and Prevention of Disease," *New York Times*, Dec. 30, 1913.

[15] See Cohen, *Imbeciles; Skinner v. Oklahoma*, 62 S.Ct. 1110, 1112 (1942).

Skinner only ended punitive forced sterilizations of criminals. *Skinner* also did not directly overturn the ruling in *Buck v. Bell* and did not comment on the forced sterilizations of those considered mentally ill or disabled. Forced sterilizations of mentally ill and mentally disabled people continued in large numbers through the early 1960s. Many of these forced sterilizations targeted "social undesirables" and minority ethnic groups. It took until 1981 for the United States to stop the practice of forced sterilization. Current federal law outlaws the use of federal money to perform a sterilization on any mentally incompetent or institutionalized individual.[16]

Today, sterilization is still permitted under federal law, subject to a few requirements: (1) The individual who is subject to being sterilized must give informed consent to the procedure; (2) the individual must be twenty-one at the time they give consent; (3) the individual must not be mentally incompetent; and (4) at least 30 days but not more than 180 days must pass from the time consent is given before the sterilization procedure takes place, unless there is an emergency.[17] In 2013, there were 148 female prisoners in two California prisons sterilized over a four-year period in a program that was said to be voluntary. It was later determined that the prisoners did not give consent to the procedures.[18] This led to the state of California enacting Bill SB1135, which banned sterilization in correctional facilities altogether, unless it is necessary as a life-saving measure.

7.1.1 *Present-Day Views on Eugenics*

In a 2020 article from the *LA Times*, Teresa Watanabe details an email one professor received about a research fund available to faculty members at the School of Public Health at the University of California–Berkeley. The fund, called the Genealogical Eugenic Institute Fund, supports research and education in the field of eugenics. The study of eugenics has been highly criticized after it was used as a justification for the murder of 6 million Jewish people in Adolf Hitler's Nazi Germany, as well as for the forced sterilization of more than 60,000 people in the United States in the early twentieth century.[19] Yet, egregiously, a research fund dedicated to eugenics ideals had continued to exist at UC Berkeley.

The email detailed that the fund was offering an annual payout of about $70,000 per year to support research and education on policies and practices that could "affect the distribution of traits in the human race." Further research found no evidence to show that Berkeley has actually used the money from the fund for genetic research, yet the school had been accepting money for the fund for the past four

---

[16] 42 C.F.R. § 50.209.
[17] 42 C.F.R § 50.203.
[18] Alex Stern and Tony Platt, "Sterilization Abuse in State Prisons: Time to Break with California's Long Eugenic Patterns," *Huffington Post: The Blog*, July 23, 2013.
[19] Teresa Watanabe, "UC Berkeley Is Disavowing Its Eugenic Research Fund after Bioethicist and Other Faculty Call It Out," *LA Times*, Oct. 26, 2020.

decades. As of 2020, the value of the fund was $2.4 million. Since the existence of this fund has come to light, there have been several recommendations of ways that Berkeley might repurpose the funds, including putting the funds to use for financial aid in communities that have been disproportionately harmed by eugenic ideology.[20] This incident is symbolic of how entrenched and mainstream the eugenics movement had become, and also how public opinion has now turned from it.

7.2 THE BIRTH OF EMPLOYEE ASSISTANCE PROGRAMS AND WORKPLACE GENETIC TESTING

Although forced sterilizations in the United States has declined, another type of monitored health program has gained popularity. This program was framed as a way to "help" Americans improve their health and wellness – employee assistance programs. The programs began as a way to aid workers in the new social and economic climate after World War II, with the goal of increasing post-war industrial production. Many programs offered unemployment or disability insurance, counseling, referrals for hospitalization, and assistance for bereaved families of missing soldiers. However, other programs specifically focused on the health of workers with the goal of preventing alcoholism. One program, Alcoholics Anonymous, began in 1939 and slowly spread throughout the midwestern and northeastern United States as employees began to share their experiences with other workers. Soon meetings were held in plants and offices across the country in order to acquaint management and employees with the Alcoholics Anonymous program and to break the stigmas attached to alcoholism in the workplace.[21]

In the 1960s and 1970s, the U.S. military saw an increase in the number of heroin users among its personnel returning from the Vietnam War. This prompted the launch of a large-scale drug testing program of federal employees, especially those in the military.[22] With this, by the mid-1970s, employee assistance programs had stretched far from their anti-alcoholism-based approaches, instead covering many other kinds of substance abuse, mental health, peer counseling, and social work.[23] By 1979, Johnson & Johnson became one of the first private companies to launch a massive corporate worksite wellness program for all employees – the Live for Life program – giving employees access to behavior modification tools and education on topics like nutrition and stress management.[24]

---

[20] Watanabe, "UC Berkeley Is Disavowing Its Eugenic Research Fund."
[21] Dale A. Masi, *The History of Employee Assistance Programs in the United States* (Arlington, VA: Employee Assistance Research Corporation, 2020), 1, 24–25, 28, 31.
[22] Confirm BioSciences, "Workplace Drug Testing Guide," May 4, 2018, www.confirmbiosciences.com/knowledge/workplace/workplace-drug-testing-guide/.
[23] See Masi, *History of Employee Assistance Programs in the United States*, 37.
[24] Andrea Bartz, "This Healthcare Company Is Determined to Have the Healthiest Employees in the World," *Johnson & Johnson: Innovation*, Feb. 25, 2018, www.jnj.com/innovation/how-johnson-johnson-is-improving-workplace-wellness-for-healthiest-employees (accessed May 25, 2021).

Other private companies followed suit, even beginning to test employees' genes in order to determine potential health risks. By 1982, a federal government survey found that 1.6 percent of companies were using genetic testing for employment purposes.[25] This number grew steadily, and by 1997 a similar survey by the American Management Association found that between 6 and 10 percent of employers were conducting genetic tests.[26] However, in 1998, the Ninth Circuit ruled in *Lawrence Berkeley Laboratory* that subjecting employees to genetic testing without their consent violated their constitutional rights.[27] This was the first U.S. Appeals Court decision on genetic privacy in the workplace.[28] Yet in the early 2000s, surveys showed that a fifth of companies still inquired about applicants' family medical histories and a quarter of those relied on that information when taking employment actions.[29]

Advances in genetic research were accelerated by the $3 billion Human Genome Project, which sought to decode the genetic makeup of humans. Among the participants in this research effort were top universities in the United States, the United Kingdom, France, Germany, Japan, and China, making this project a massive effort to understand the functions of genes and proteins.[30] Though the project formally ended in 2003, its large-scale publicity has led to the start of other genome-related research projects, as well as a worldwide increase in individuals interested in knowing the makeup of their own DNA.[31] Many of these researchers take the essentialist view that genetic testing can always be beneficial because it empowers individuals to make crucial decisions about their own health and the health of their future children.[32]

---

[25] See U.S. Congress, OTA, *The Role of Genetic Testing in the Prevention of Occupational Diseases: Survey of the Use of Genetic Testing in the Workplace*, Report, Apr. 1983 (Washington DC: Government Printing Office, 2013), 194; see also Dan Cook, "Large Employers See Health Cost Reductions," *BenefitsPro*, Aug. 13, 2014 (finding that more than 53 percent of companies planned to add or expand their employee wellness and testing programs in 2015 alone).

[26] Rosemary Orthmann, "Three-Fourths of Major Employers Conduct Medical and Drug Tests," *Employment Testing: Law & Policy Reporter* 7 (July 1997): 114.

[27] *Normal-Bloodsaw v. Lawrence Berkeley Laboratory et al.*, 135 F.3d 1260 (9th Cir. 1998); see also *Crummer v. Lewis*, 2018 WL 2222491 (2018) (noting that the constitutional right to information privacy extends to medical information); see *Lowe v. Atlas Logistics Group Retail Servs. Atlanta, LLC*, 102 F. Supp. 3d 1360 (N.D. Ga. 2015) (holding that an employer could not request genetic information with respect to an employee under GINA).

[28] ACLU, "Genetic Discrimination in the Workplace Factsheet," www.aclu.org/other/genetic-discrimination-workplace-factsheet-9 (accessed May 2, 2020).

[29] Louise M. Slaughter, "The Genetic Information Nondiscrimination Act: Why Your Personal Genetics Are Still Vulnerable to Discrimination," *Surgical Clinics of North America* 88, no. 4 (2008): 725–26.

[30] See Leroy Hood and Lee Rowen, "The Human Genome Project: Big Science Transforms Biology and Medicine," *Genome Medicine* 5, no. 9 (2013), www.ncbi.nlm.nih.gov/pmc/articles/PMC4066586/.

[31] See National Human Genome Research Institute, "The Human Genome Project" (2020), www.genome.gov/human-genome-project (accessed May 25, 2021).

[32] See, e.g., Myriad Genetics, "Benefits of Genetic Testing," www.myriad.com/patients-families/genetic-testing-101/benefits-of-genetic-testing/ (accessed May 25, 2021).

7.3 GENETIC DISCRIMINATION IN THE WORKPLACE AND THE PASSING OF GINA

The growth of interest in the human genome was not all positive. By 2008, there had already been as many as five hundred cases of documented genetic discrimination in the workplace.[33] Though the number of complaints remained relatively small, by 2008 the United States was seeing the beginning of a trend towards genetic determinism and the attendant genetic discrimination.[34] The same year, the Genetic Information Nondiscrimination Act (GINA) was passed to protect Americans from being treated unfairly due to differences in their DNA.[35]

GINA is the first federal law to directly address the issue of genetic discrimination. Prior to GINA, Americans had limited protection from both the non-consensual release and the misuse of their health information through the Health Insurance Portability and Accountability Act (HIPAA), which was passed in 1996.[36] Further, federal laws such as the ADA offer some protection to employees against genetic discrimination in the workplace; in 1995, the EEOC clarified that "disability" in the ADA included genetic predisposition to a disease.[37] However, federal courts remain divided about the scope of this federal protection. Specifically, federal appeals courts are split on whether the ADA protects employees who have not yet manifested symptoms of illness.[38]

The passage of GINA in 2008 did help to strengthen protections against genetic discrimination in specific instances. When George W. Bush signed GINA into law, he gave a nod to the Human Genome Project, stating that GINA "was a function of the many achievements in the field of genetics, such as the decoding of the human genome by the Human Genome Project and the creation and increased use of genomic medicine," indicating that the science was growing at such a rate that it effectively required some minor form of protection.[39]

---

[33] See Council for Responsible Genetics, "Genetic Testing, Privacy and Discrimination," *CRG in the Press*, archived Nov. 17, 2015, https://perma.cc/E59R-EQ9Y (accessed May 25, 2021).

[34] Ajunwa, "Genetic Data and Civil Rights," 78.

[35] Genetics Home Reference, "What Is Genetic Discrimination?" *Medline Plus*, last updated July 28, 2021, https://ghr.nlm.nih.gov/primer/testing/discrimination (accessed May 25, 2021).

[36] DHSC, "Health Insurance Portability & Accountability Act," last updated June 13, 2019, www.dhcs.ca.gov/formsandpubs/laws/hipaa/Pages/1.00WhatisHIPAA.aspx (accessed May 25, 2021).

[37] See NCSL, "Genetic Employment Laws," updated Jan. 2008, www.ncsl.org/research/health/genetic-employment-laws.aspx (accessed May 25, 2021).

[38] See *Bragdon v. Abbot*, 118 S. Ct. 2196 (1998) (raising the issue of whether the ADA covers conditions of asymptomatic HIV infections); see also *Lorrillard v. Pons*, 434 U.S. 575, 580–81 (1978) (explaining that administrative and judicial precedent surrounding language in the Rehabilitation Act has long covered cases of asymptomatic HIV and suggesting it was Congress's intention to incorporate these precedential interpretations into other uses of the same language in other statutes).

[39] See Sanger Institute, "The Finished Human Genome: Welcome to the Genomic Age," Sanger Institute, Press Room, Apr. 14, 2003, archived at https://perma.cc/2FX6-HZPW (captured Nov. 17, 2015; accessed May 25, 2021).

GINA was also promulgated to alleviate concerns about genetic testing. Many were fearful that genetic testing outcomes would result in workplace discrimination and the loss of health insurance coverage. GINA sought to allay these fears by forbidding health insurance companies and employers from using the information gained from genetic testing and family medical history to discriminate against individuals. The key provisions of GINA include Title I, which prohibits genetic discrimination in health insurance coverage, and Title II, which prohibits genetic discrimination in employment.[40]

Under Title I, health insurance companies are forbidden from requesting genetic information from their customers and using that information in their decisions on rating and underwriting. Here, GINA puts a figurative wall between health insurance companies and their insured's genetic information. Not only are health insurance companies forbidden from using genetic information, it is a violation of GINA for a health insurance company to even request a genetic test from an insured individual. It is important to note that Title I does not stand on its own as independent law. Title I mostly fills in gaps of other existing federal health insurance laws and does not offer a way to file an action independently on a Title I violation. If a person has a cause of action based on a violation of a provision of Title I, they need to file it based on the appropriate federal health insurance statute that specific provision of Title I applies to.

Title II of GINA (as an anti-employment discrimination law) shares some similarities with other antidiscrimination laws, such as Title VII of the Civil Rights Act of 1964[41] and the ADA of 1990.[42] GINA lacks the former statutes' provision of a disparate impact cause of action. GINA is limited in scope when compared to other anti-discrimination laws, as it solely focuses on discrimination related to health insurance and employment. Under Title II, employers are given six exceptions to the rule against obtaining or requesting genetic information. Employers can obtain genetic information legally from their employees when genetic information is received: (1) unintentionally, (2) *through a voluntary workplace wellness program,* (3) when processing medical leave, (4) through a newspaper or similar information source, (5) through monitoring of occupational toxic substances for employees, and (6) to confirm DNA analysis for law enforcement.[43]

Genetic information is considered unintentionally received through common small talk and everyday discussions among colleagues. If an employee tells their employer about their mother suffering from a heart attack, then the employer just unintentionally received genetic information about that employee due to the genetic link with her mother. GINA addresses only what the employer does with this

---

[40] Pub. L. No. 110-233, 122 Stat. 881 (codified as amended at 29 U.S.C. §§ 216 et seq. (2012); 42 U.S.C. §§ 1182 et seq. (2012)); Ajunwa, "Genetic Data and Civil Rights," 84.

[41] Pub. L. No. 88-352, § 703, 78 Stat. 241, 255 (1964) (codified at 42 U.S.C. § 2000e-2 (2012)).

[42] Pub. L. No. 101-336, 104 Stat. 327 (codified at 42 U.S.C. §§ 12113 et seq. (2012)).

[43] Genetic Information Nondiscrimination Act of 2008 § 202(b), 42 U.S.C. § 2000ff-1(b) (2018).

information. If the employer protects this information and does not use it to discriminate against the employee, then the employer does not violate GINA's protections.

The most notable exception here is that employers may lawfully collect genetic information as part of workplace wellness programs. The only caveat is that the worker's participation should be voluntary. The question of whether a program is voluntary often boils down to how much of a financial incentive an employer can offer an employee to participate in a workplace wellness program before it is considered involuntary, that is, whether it is a true incentive or more like a penalty. While employers are allowed to offer a financial incentive to join workplace wellness programs, they are prohibited from instituting penalties against workers who refuse to join.[44] But consider that a financial incentive may be indistinguishable from a financial penalty. For low-income workers, having their health insurance premium (which can run into thousands of dollars per year) paid if they join can also amount to a severe financial penalty if they refuse to join.

Another issue is the meaning of the phrase *genetic information*. In 2012, *Poore v. Peterbilt Bristol* was the first case to address the question of whether medical information other than the information from an individual's manifested condition could constitute genetic information under GINA. In this case, the court held that the plaintiff's wife's diagnosis of multiple sclerosis was not "genetic information" about the plaintiff himself, and therefore was not sufficient to make a GINA discrimination claim. To make this decision, the court stated that GINA's goal was primarily "to prohibit employers from making a predictive assessment concerning an individual's propensity to get an inheritable genetic disease or disorder based on the occurrence of an inheritable disease or disorder in [a] family member." Therefore, while family history could constitute genetic information, information about Poore's wife could not be used to predict Poore's own propensity to acquire multiple sclerosis and was therefore not genetic information.[45] This case pointed out a hole in GINA, under which information about the manifestation of diseases in *family members* is protected, but the statute never considers whether a spouse is a family member in this context. The *Poore* court also failed to consider that Poore's wife's diagnosis could still be the source of discrimination if the employer failed to hire Poore in order to save on medical benefits for Poore and his family. However, as far as GINA is concerned, an individual's own propensity to manifest the disease remains the controlling element in whether they or their family's genetic information is considered protected.

In 2018, in *Green v. Whataburger*, another plaintiff alleged discrimination and retaliation under GINA based on information about her daughter's surgery "due to the possibility of cancer." The Court held that this information did not constitute a manifested disease or disorder in a family member because Green's daughter had not yet been diagnosed with a condition. However, the Court also suggested that even if

44 Ajunwa, Schultz, and Crawford, "Limitless Worker Surveillance," 766.
45 *Poore v. Peterbilt Bristol, LLC*, 852 F. Supp. 2d 727 (W.D. Va. 2012).

there had been evidence of a manifested disease, the Court would also have to determine whether that information was "taken into account" not only with respect to the daughter but also with respect to the plaintiff herself. In doing so, the Court seemingly suggested that the possible predictive value of the manifested condition would not be sufficient alone, and that it might require an additional burden to plaintiffs, requiring them to show evidence that the information was actually considered by their employer.[46]

Since GINA's passage, many scholars have been quick to criticize it for its limited protections.[47] Employees have had difficulty establishing GINA claims in violation of the privacy and anti-discrimination provisions because of how the GINA exceptions can be used to clear an employer of a GINA violation. One example is *Williams v. Graphic Packaging International*, where an employee was terminated after a cancer diagnosis and alleged inappropriate behavior at work.[48] Here, Williams alleged that he was repeatedly questioned on his cancer test results and was subject to genetic discrimination. The problem with Williams's claim, the court noted, was that he also separately shared to three co-workers that "cancer ran in his family." The GINA claim in Williams's case did not make it past summary judgment because the court noted that Williams voluntarily shared genetic information about his family, an exception to GINA.[49]

Given its limitations, GINA now serves as a sort of "floor" on which states can build their own protections against genetic discrimination. For example, on September 6, 2011, California governor Jerry Brown signed the California Genetic Information Nondiscrimination Act (CalGINA) into law.[50] The law amended and broadened existing anti-discrimination laws in California by including protections in areas such as housing, mortgage lending, education, employment, and public accommodations.[51] In contrast, GINA remains limited to protections from genetic discrimination in employment and health insurance coverage.[52] Moreover, CalGINA allows for the recovery of more money in damages than GINA does.[53]

---

[46] *Green v. Whataburger Rests.*, 2018 WL 6252532 (W.D. Tex. 2018), at 2.

[47] See, e.g., Kathy L. Hudson and Karen Pollitz, "Undermining Genetic Privacy? Employee Wellness Programs and the Law," *New England Journal of Medicine* 377 (2017): 1–3 (arguing that GINA's wellness-program exceptions compromise genetic privacy); Jessica D. Tenenbaum and Kenneth W. Goodman, "Beyond the Genetic Information Nondiscrimination Act: Ethical and Economic Implications of the Exclusion of Disability, Long-Term Care and Life Insurance," *Future Medicine* 14, no. 2. (2017): 153–54 (arguing that there are many related forms of insurance that do not fall within GINA and suggesting the discriminatory outcome of GINA's lack of breadth).

[48] No. 1:16-CV-00102, 2018 WL 2118311, at 1-2 (M.D. Tenn. May 8, 2018).

[49] No. 1:16-CV-00102, 2018 WL 2118311, at 9-10 (M.D. Tenn. May 8, 2018).

[50] See S.B. 559, 2011 Leg., 2011-2012 Sess., (Cal. 2011) (enacted by Chapter 261).

[51] Lisa Hird Chung, "Prohibiting Genetic Discrimination in Calif.," *Law360*, Oct. 6, 2011, www.law360.com/articles/274791.

[52] 42 U.S.C.A. § 2000(ff)(1)(a); Pub. L. 110-233, 122 Stat. 881 (2008).

[53] See Chung, "Prohibiting Genetic Discrimination in Calif."; Pub. L. No. 101-336, 104 Stat. 327 (codified at 42 U.S.C. §§ 12113 et seq. (2012)).

In the employment context, CalGINA amended the California Fair Employment and Housing Act (FEHA), which protects an individual's right to seek, obtain, and hold employment, regardless of that person's race, religion, color, national origin, ancestry, physical disability, mental disability, mental condition, marital status, sex, age, or sexual orientation.[54] CalGINA adds "genetic information" to this list.[55] In practice, this means that employers cannot discriminate against an employee or potential employee based on (1) that individual's genetic tests, (2) the genetic tests of family members of the individual, or (3) the manifestation of a disease or disorder in family members of that individual.[56] Further, employers cannot use knowledge of any request for or receipt of genetic services, or an employee's participation in clinical research that includes genetic services, to discriminate against the employee.[57]

Because of this change to FEHA, an employee in California may recover unlimited monetary damages from their employer if the employer discriminates against them using genetic information. These damages are larger than the federal damages allowed under GINA, which cannot exceed $50,000 for employers with fifteen to one hundred employees and cannot exceed $300,000 for employers with more than five hundred employees.[58]

Though CalGINA is more expansive than federal genetic information law, the state of California has also set some limits. In 2012, California failed to pass the Genetic Information Privacy Act, which would have protected genetic information under the state's constitutional right to privacy.[59] The bill targeted intrinsic privacy harms on the basis of genetic discrimination. A similar bill was introduced in the next legislative term and similarly did not make it out of committee in 2014.[60]

To date, forty-eight states plus Washington DC have enacted laws that prohibit genetic discrimination in health insurance, while thirty-five states have laws prohibiting some types of genetic discrimination in employment.[61] Still, the use of workplace wellness programs is expansive across the United States and is growing due to the Covid-19 pandemic.[62]

---

[54] Cal. Gov't. Code § 12940 et. seq.
[55] S.B. 559, 2011 Leg., 2011–2012 Sess., (Cal. 2011) (enacted by Chapter 261).
[56] Cal. Gov't. Code § 12926(g).
[57] S.B. 559, 2011 Leg., 2011–2012 Sess., (Cal. 2011) (enacted by Chapter 261).
[58] Chung, "Prohibiting Genetic Discrimination in Calif."; Pub. L. No. 101-336, 104 Stat. 327 (codified at 42 U.S.C. §§ 12113 et seq. (2012)).
[59] S.B. 1267, 2011–2012 Reg. Sess. § 56.19(a) (Cal 2012).
[60] See S.B. 222, 2012–2013 Reg. Sess. (Cal. 2013).
[61] Amanda Gammon and Deborah W. Neklason, "Confidentiality and the Risk of Genetic Discrimination: What Surgeons Need to Know," *The Role of Genetic Testing in Surgical Oncology*, special issue of *Surgical Oncology Clinics of North America* 24, no. 4 (2015): 667–81. For individual states' genetic discrimination laws, see NCSL, "Genetics and Health Insurance State Anti-Discrimination Laws," updated Jan. 2008, www.ncsl.org/research/health/genetic-nondiscrimination-in-health-insurance-laws.aspx.
[62] David Burda, "Workplace Wellness Programs and the Coronavirus Pandemic," *4SightHealth*, May 27, 2020, www.4sighthealth.com/workplace-wellness-programs-and-the-coronavirus-pandemic/ (accessed May 25, 2021).

7.4 WORKPLACE GENETIC TESTING AFTER GINA

The promulgation of GINA has not meant a total demise of genetic testing in the workplace. In fact, carve-outs for workplace wellness programs under the ACA mean that employers may still offer voluntary genetic testing in the workplace. Some employers are offering genetic testing services through third-party vendors.

Two such vendors are Genome Medical and Color Health, Inc. Genome Medical boasts that it provides employees with "a personalized clinical action plan" and "refer[s] to specialists as needed." And Color, for example, has a goal of allowing all employers and human resources (HR) leaders to offer genetic testing to employees as an employee benefit. The company has already partnered with many large companies, such as Apple, Salesforce, and Levi's.[63]

In an interesting partnership that began in 2018, Thomas Jefferson University Hospital announced that it was partnering with Color in a pilot project to give its 30,000 employees the ability to access their genetic information. In a detailed press release, the university and the hospital announced that the partnership would include the data processing services of Color, along with two options for employees to access free genetic counseling: Color's board-certified genetic counselors or Jefferson Hospital's Sidney Kimmel Cancer Center. This partnership is a noteworthy match between a private genetic testing company and a university hospital that likely has the capacity to genetically test and screen all of its employees independently.[64]

Both Genome Medical and Color Genomics have privacy policies on their websites that they advertise to their users, discussing the ways they use the genetic data they collect. First, Genome Medical calls this data "Protected Health Information" (PHI) and defines PHI as "information that identifies who you are and relates to your past, present, or future physical or mental health condition, the provision of healthcare to you, or past, present or future payment for the provision of health care to you." Genome Medical notes, however, that "information about you that is in a summary form that does not identify who you are" is *not* in the definition of PHI.[65] Since their privacy policy only protects information that is considered PHI, this essentially limits any privacy protections to data that is *immediately* personally identifiable.

But even Genome Medical's protection of what they term PHI is limited. The policy also states that Genome Medical can make the following categories of uses and disclosures of a person's PHI without that person's authorization: (1) "Treatment, Payment and Health Care Operations" and (2) "Other Types of Use and Disclosures

[63] Color Health, Inc., www.color.com/benefits (updated Nov. 21, 2021); Genome Medical, www .genomemedical.com; Christina Farr, "Apple Is Offering Free Genetic Tests to All Its Silicon Valley Employees," *CNBC*, Dec. 13, 2019.

[64] Jefferson Health, "Jefferson to Offer Free Genetic Testing to Employees," *PR Newswire*, Nov. 14, 2018, www.prnewswire.com/news-releases/jefferson-to-offer-free-genetic-testing-to-employees-300750475 .html (accessed May 26, 2021).

[65] Genome Medical, *Notice of Privacy Practices*, www.genomemedical.com/privacy/?_ga=2.197013676 .1294487464.1585603657-1350403954.1585336333 (accessed May 26, 2021).

(No Authorization Required)." For Treatment, Payment and Health Care Operations, the company explains that "federal and state laws allow us to use and disclose your PHI to provide health care services to you." This can include using PHI to authorize referrals to various healthcare specialists and to review the quality of care provided, or to perform billing and collection activities in connection with care provided to an individual by specialists. Furthermore, Genome Medical can use or disclose an individual's PHI to recommend treatment alternatives, contact users, or remind them of their appointments. Finally, Genome Medical reserves the right to use an individual's PHI to perform "certain business functions" and can disclose the information to their "business associates."[66]

With regard to the second listed category – Other Types of Uses and Disclosures (No Authorization Required) – Genome Medical lists a variety of conditions under which they can disclose an individual's PHI without that individual's authorization, when the conditions set forth by applicable law are met. The list includes public health activities, reports about child and other types of abuse or neglect, reports to governmental agencies for health oversight activities, and law enforcement purposes. In addition to these purposes, Genome Medical's privacy policy also includes a list of scenarios in which they can disclose users' PHI without authorization, as long as they provide written notice to the user and the person "has *the opportunity to agree or object*."[67]

Next, Genome Medical includes a short list of situations that require an individual's authorization before Genome may disclose their PHI. These situations include disclosures of PHI for marketing activities and psychotherapy notes. Importantly, Genome does not immediately inform users that their data has been disclosed. Instead, users have the right to request a list of the disclosures of their information by making a formal request in writing. The site reports that these requests will be answered in sixty days or less. However, some disclosures do not need to be included in their reports, including disclosures already made to the requester; disclosures made for treatment, payment, or healthcare operations; and disclosures made more than six years before the request.[68]

Color Genomics has a privacy policy that looks similar to that of Genome Medical. Instead of protecting PHI, they protect personally identifiable information (PII) and personal and family health information (PFHI). PII is "information that specifically identifies you as an individual ... [which] may include your name, email address, mailing address, phone number, credit card, insurance information ... or other billing information." PFHI includes information about your biological family, such as ancestry, age, biological sex, health conditions, family history of health conditions, medication history, and genetic mutations in you or your family members. Color's

[66] Genome Medical, *Notice of Privacy Practices*.
[67] Genome Medical, *Notice of Privacy Practices*.
[68] Genome Medical, *Notice of Privacy Practices*.

policy states that they can use this information to help improve their services, and to advance genetic research and science. This includes communicating with users, developing new tests, data analysis, publication in Color's research database, and marketing.[69]

Though many of those uses are internal, Color also includes a section about sharing information with third parties, stating that "we may disclose your PII and PHI to others involved in your care, including healthcare providers (your own provider and/or an independent provider who may review your information to determine whether a Test is appropriate for you), genetic counselors … confirmatory laboratories, the health system or clinic where your own provider practices, and other providers that you or your healthcare provider designated to receive your PHI." Further, Color works with third parties to provide its "website, application development, analytics, variant analysis, payment processing, hosting maintenance, support ticketing, transmission of results, distribution and collection of test kits, and other services" and may provide users' information to the extent that "is minimally necessary for them to perform their services."[70]

Moreover, if a user's employer has paid for the user's testing, that user also acknowledges and agrees that their de-identified test results and PFHI may be anonymized and/or aggregated and returned to the employer as a data analytics source. There is no indication of how that policy may be adjusted depending on the size of the workforce, which might impact the identifiability of a person's health information. Yet, many companies have drafted agreements with Color, including GE and Salesforce, and the employees tested by these companies have implicitly agreed to this use of their information.[71] Many companies also offer tests to individuals through a direct-to-consumer testing model, by which they market their products to customers through television, print advertisements, or the internet.[72] These companies have varying privacy policies.

7.5 LEGAL CHALLENGES TO WORKPLACE WELLNESS GENETIC TESTING

There have been several important developments in the legality of workplace wellness programs in recent jurisprudence, specifically with regard to whether the programs are truly "voluntary." Since 2014, there has been a chain of Equal Employment Opportunity Commission (EEOC) challenges to workplace wellness programs. In one complaint, the EEOC alleged that Honeywell International, Inc.,

[69] Color Health, Inc., *Color Privacy Policy*, last updated Nov. 1, 2021, www.color.com/privacy-policy (accessed May 26, 2021).
[70] Color Health, Inc., *Color Privacy Policy*.
[71] Color Health, Inc., *Color Privacy Policy*.
[72] "What Is Direct-to-Consumer Genetic Testing?" *Medline Plus*, https://ghr.nlm.nih.gov/primer/dtcgenetictesting/directtoconsumer (accessed May 26, 2021).

a large technology and manufacturing conglomerate, violated the ADA by effectively requiring participation in medical exams associated with Honeywell's group health plan because the company offered inducements to get employees to participate. This challenge arose without guidance from the EEOC about what constituted a "voluntary medical exam" under the ADA. Instead, the challenge focused on Honeywell's group health plan, which not only provided incentives to participate but also imposed surcharges on employees who chose not to participate.[73]

In response to this behavior, the EEOC sought a temporary restraining order (TRO) to enjoin Honeywell from continuing to offer financial incentives for participation in its program, and similarly to enjoin the company from imposing surcharges on employees when either the employee or the employee's spouse declined to undergo the biometric testing associated with the wellness program. The surcharges were alleged to include penalties such as (1) a $500 surcharge if an employee did not complete the tests; (2) a $1,000 surcharge if the employee did not complete the tobacco screening; (3) a $1,000 surcharge if the employee's spouse did not complete the tobacco screening; and (4) the non-receipt of a payment of $1,500 that would be distributed only to people who completed the test. In its complaint, the EEOC particularly highlighted the fact that, by making some financial incentives contingent upon the participation of an employee's spouse, Honeywell's plan violated GINA. Further, the EEOC argued that the number and dollar amount of possible surcharges here effectively made the program not "voluntary," as Honeywell alleged.[74] Yet, in 2014, the District Court denied the EEOC's motion for a TRO on the grounds that the EEOC had not shown a threat of irreparable harm and did not touch the merits of its claim.

Next, the EEOC sued Flambeau, Inc., a plastics manufacturer in Wisconsin. The complaint alleged that Flambeau violated the ADA by requiring employees to complete a health risk assessment and biometric testing, including blood work, measurements, and the disclosure of medical history. Failure to complete any of these tests would result in the employee's coverage being completely cancelled unless the employee opted to pay for 100 percent of the plan's premiums.[75] The ADA generally bars involuntary medical examinations, but the District Court for the Western District of Wisconsin ruled against the EEOC in *Flambeau*, holding that the ADA's "bona fide benefit plan" exception applies to workplace wellness plans. Effectively, the decision confirmed for employers that there is a safe harbor for issuing health risk assessments and biometric screenings under the ADA in

[73] *EEOC v. Honeywell*, No. 0:14-04517 (2014); Frank Morris, August Emil Huellei, and Adam C. Solander, "Mainstream Wellness Program Challenged in *EEOC v. Honeywell*," *Epstein Becker Green: News*, Nov. 20, 2014, www.ebglaw.com/news/mainstream-wellness-program-challenged-in-eeoc-v-honeywell/ (accessed May 25, 2021).
[74] See *EEOC v. Honeywell*, No. 0:14-04517 (2014); Morris et al., "Mainstream Wellness Program Challenged in *EEOC v. Honeywell*."
[75] Morris, et al., "Mainstream Wellness Program Challenged in *EEOC v. Honeywell*."

some cases.[76] The EEOC appealed the decision of the District Court. However, the Seventh Circuit disposed of the case on procedural grounds, failing to get to the merits of the issue at hand.[77]

Finally, the EEOC sued Orion Energy Systems, alleging that the company's wellness program was unlawful because it required employees to complete a health risk questionnaire and screening, which included blood work.[78] The screenings were not job-related, but failure to undergo screening would result in the employee paying 100 percent of the premium for the employer-provided health insurance, as well as a fifty-dollar monthly penalty. Moreover, the EEOC charged that Orion had fired an employee when she refused to partake in its wellness program.[79] However, the Court in *Orion* rejected the EEOC's complaints, ruling that the wellness plan was lawful under the ADA because it was still an employee's decision to participate, despite the heavy financial consequences for deciding otherwise. The Court noted that "even a strong incentive is still no more than an incentive, it is not a compulsion."[80]

This string of cases suggests that the EEOC is likely to continue challenging workplace wellness programs, especially for voluntariness. The EEOC is not alone in this regard. In fact, employees themselves have begun challenging employers for the voluntariness of workplace wellness programs. In one case, *Ortiz v. City of San Antonio Fire Department*, an employee of a city fire department alleged that the department's mandatory wellness program constituted discrimination and retaliation in violation of Title VII and GINA. The employee had worked for the department for over thirty years when, in 2010, the department initiated a "mandatory wellness program" for all uniformed employees "designed to provide early detection of serious medical conditions and to encourage better health" so that employees could do their jobs more safely and effectively. The tests included a medical history, a complete physical examination, and blood and urine tests, as well as tests for vision, hearing, and lung capacity. They also required chest x-rays and a stress test, both to be completed periodically, usually every five years. If an employee was not certified after these tests, they would be placed on "alternate duty" until they could work with a physician to return to fully duty status.[81]

[76] EEOC v. Flambeau, 14-cv-00638-bbc (2015), http://static.politico.com/e8/bd/e4d94f8c45f39996ca700 fee6bf1/eeoc-versus-flambeau.pdf (accessed May 25, 2021).

[77] Alden Bianchi, "EEOC v. Flambeau, Judicial Restraint, and the Uncertain Future of Employer-Sponsored Wellness Programs," *Mintz: Insight*, Jan. 31, 2017, www.mintz.com/insights-center/ viewpoints/2226/2017-01-eeoc-v-flambeau-judicial-restraint-and-uncertain-future (accessed May 25, 2021).

[78] EEOC v. Orion, No. 1:14-01019 (2014). The final decision is available at https://benefitslink.com/src/ ctop/Orion_EDWis_09192016.pdf (accessed May 25, 2021).

[79] Stephen Miller, "Ruling Is Mixed Bag for EEOC's Effort to Rein in Wellness Programs," *SHRM*, May 17, 2016, www.shrm.org/resourcesandtools/hr-topics/benefits/pages/orion-eeoc-wellness-ruling .aspx (accessed May 25, 2021); Morris et al., "Mainstream Wellness Program Challenged in *EEOC v. Honeywell*."

[80] EEOC v. Orion Energy Systems, Inc., 208 F. SUPP. 3D 989, 1001 (2016).

[81] Ortiz v. City of San Antonio Fire Department, 806 F.3d 822, 822–24 (2015).

In 2012, Mr. Ortiz was placed on alternate duty after failing to comply with the requirements of the wellness program. He then went for testing, and his physician did not administer the mandatory stress test because in that physician's opinion, the test was not necessary. Mr. Ortiz, who had temporarily returned to full duty pending his tests, was then returned to alternate duty. Ortiz sued, claiming that the stress test and questionnaire were in violation of GINA. In order to show disparate impact under Title VII, he also showed evidence that other employees who had refused to answer questions were not removed from full duty. However, the Court dismissed Mr. Ortiz's complaint that the fire department had violated GINA, finding no evidence that anyone had purchased his genetic information or discriminated against him on the basis of his genetic information. Further, the Court found that Ortiz's refusal to comply with a mandatory program designed to ensure that firefighters can perform their jobs safely was a legitimate, non-discriminatory reason to reduce his status. Finally, the Court concluded that the timing of Ortiz's placements on alternate duties showed that the department's motive was ensuring compliance with the wellness program in furtherance of its safety goals and not discriminating against Mr. Ortiz in violation of Title VII.[82] Therefore, the Court rejected Mr. Ortiz's challenges of his employer's wellness programs outright.

In light of decisions such as *Ortiz* and the various EEOC suits that have been brought to challenge workplace wellness programs, the EEOC issued regulations clarifying that an employer may offer incentives for employees to participate in wellness programs that involve sharing medical data, as long as the inducement does not exceed 30 percent of the cost of medical coverage under the plan.[83] While those regulations defined a "voluntary" program as one that does not "penalize" employees for declining participation, they failed to describe what actions would constitute penalties. Indeed, to many employees, the loss of up to 30 percent of the cost of their medical coverage under the plan would likely be seen as a penalty.[84] Because of this lack of clarification, a federal district court vacated these regulations as of January 1, 2019, holding that the EEOC did not adequately explain its decision to permit the 30 percent incentive level it had adopted.[85] Moving forward, it seems that there may be more challenges to similar wellness programs on the horizon.

Aside from litigation specifically surrounding workplace wellness, there have been several cases clarifying the extent to which genetic information can be protected. For example, in a 2019 case, *Darby v. Childvine*, the Southern District of Ohio considered whether a genetic mutation can constitute a "disability" under the ADA. The plaintiff, Sherryl Darby, was hired by Childvine as an administrative

[82] *Ortiz v. City of San Antonio Fire Department*, 827–28.
[83] Genetic Information Nondiscrimination Act, 81 Fed. Reg. 31143, 31158 (May 17, 2016) (codified at 29 C.F.R. § 1635.8(b)(2)(iii)(A) (2018)).
[84] Ajunwa et al., "Limitless Worker Surveillance," 768.
[85] *AARP v. EEOC*, 267 F. Supp. 3d 14, 37 (D.D.C. 2017), amended by 292 F. Supp. 238 (D.D.C. 2017) (staying the effective date of the vacatur order until January 1, 2019).

assistant in August 2016, and underwent a double mastectomy on October 25, 2016. She then received written notice of her termination approximately two weeks after her surgery. Darby filed a complaint, alleging that she was terminated in violation of both federal and state law because of her breast cancer diagnosis. Childvine moved to dismiss, arguing that breast cancer is not a "per se disability." However, through written discovery, Childvine learned that Darby was not diagnosed with breast cancer as alleged in her complaint, but instead tested positive for a gene mutation – BRCA1 – that is associated with an increased risk of cancer. In response to this test, Darby's mastectomy had been elective, to decrease her risk of developing breast cancer. With this new information, Childvine argued that Darby's genetic mutation was not currently limiting a major life activity, but instead increased her likelihood of abnormal cell growth – a major life activity – in the future. Here, the Court found that the ADA does not provide protection based on a future disability, meaning that a genetic mutation by itself is not a protected disability simply because it represents an increased likelihood that a person might develop a condition in the future.[86] As such, the Court dismissed Darby's complaint.

7.5.1 *Workplace Wellness Programs and the ADA*

On May 17, 2016, the EEOC issued a final rule implementing Title I of the ADA as it relates to employer workplace wellness programs. This rule remains current, and it states that employers "may provide limited financial and other incentives in exchange for an employee answering disability-related questions or taking medical examinations as part of a wellness program, whether or not the program is part of a health plan." The central focus of the ADA is to prevent the discrimination of individuals on the basis of disability, and so the ADA generally protects employees from being required to produce medical information but allows health inquiries and medical examinations that are part of a voluntary employee health program, such as a workplace wellness program. Those who wish to be included in workplace wellness programs also cannot be denied access because of their disability, and reasonable accommodations must be made by the employer if it is brought to their attention that an employee has a need due to a disability.[87]

One of the main issues that this final rule sought to clear up was the definition of what makes a workplace wellness program "voluntary" under the ADA. In defining what makes a workplace wellness program voluntary, the EEOC specifically states that an employer cannot require an employee to participate, cannot deny access to health coverage or a specific plan, and cannot take any adverse action or

---

[86] *Darby v. Childvine, Inc.*, 2019 A.D. Cas. (BNA) 447288, 2019 WL 6170743 (S.D. Ohio 2019).

[87] EEOC, "EEOC'S Final Rule on Employer Wellness Programs and Title I of the Americans with Disabilities Act," www.eeoc.gov/regulations/eeocs-final-rule-employer-wellness-programs-and-title-i-americans-disabilities-act (accessed May 25, 2021).

retaliate against an employee who chooses not to participate or fails to reach certain workplace wellness program goals. An employer may offer incentives to encourage participation, but the employer must abide by incentive limits set by the EEOC. The maximum an employer can offer an employee for participating in a workplace wellness program is 30 percent of the regular total cost of their coverage.[88] If an employer offers a higher incentive that does not comply with the 30 percent limit, then that employer's workplace wellness program can be deemed involuntary and against the rules of the ADA.

As stated above, the ADA does allow health inquiries and medical examinations as part of a voluntary employee health program. The ADA further requires that any employee health program be "reasonably designed to promote health or prevent disease." This means that employers cannot require an unreasonable commitment of time from their employees or require unreasonably intrusive procedures in their workplace wellness programs.[89] To offer an allowable workplace wellness program under the ADA, employers also cannot shift or force unreasonable costs on their employees for medical exams. To be considered "reasonably designed," a workplace wellness program must be centered around the health of the worker, not the costs or bottom line of the employer. If an employer seeks medical information from employees in a workplace wellness program but uses the information to try to predict future company health expenses, then that program would not be considered reasonably designed to promote health or prevent disease.

The EEOC final rule did not change the rules or language concerning the confidentiality of employee medical records, but it did add two requirements related to the confidentiality of medical records of employees that participate in workplace wellness programs. First, an entity that is allowed to receive medical records or information of participating employees may not disclose or be likely to disclose the specific identity of a participating individual unless as required to administer a health plan. Second, an employer may not require employees to waive confidentiality rules as a condition for participating in a workplace wellness program or being awarded an incentive, except to the extent allowed by the ADA to administer specific wellness-related activities.[90]

7.6 THE COERCIVE NATURE OF INCENTIVES AND RISK SHIFTING

Many employers have incorporated various incentives to convince employees to participate in workplace wellness programs. From cash bonuses to workplace benefits, employers have rolled out many options to convince their employees to give up private information about their health and after-work activities. In examining the

---

[88] EEOC, "EEOC'S Final Rule on Employer Wellness Programs and Title I of the ADA."
[89] EEOC, "EEOC'S Final Rule on Employer Wellness Programs and Title I of the ADA."
[90] EEOC, "EEOC'S Final Rule on Employer Wellness Programs and Title I of the ADA."

effect of cash bonuses, a study at a Wisconsin hospital asked workers, "What is the lowest reward amount that would make you feel like you had to participate in this year's wellness program?" In examining lower-income employees at the hospital, nearly half (44 percent) of these employees said they would feel that they had to participate for a reward of $200 or less. The percentage of employees who would feel that they had to participate increased with the potential dollar amount, with 56 percent of low-income employees stating that they would feel that they had to participate for a reward that was more than $200. At least 22 percent of the employees surveyed stated that they would feel they had to disclose information about their health if there was any reward offered at all.[91]

7.6.1 *How Employers Shift Risk to Workers*

Scholars have argued that employers have consistently shifted more and more risk to employees since the 1970s.[92] This began in the form of increased job insecurity, as well as a retrenchment in employer-provided health insurance, retirement plans, and other fringe benefits.[93] For example, although Uber connects drivers to consumers, the company has long maintained that its drivers are independent contractors, effectively keeping its drivers at arm's length from the company and relieving the company of ultimate responsibility for these workers. Uber's structure of considering its drivers as independent contractors has allowed Uber to generally avoid providing health care. Uber promotes its "work when you want" platform as a form of workplace wellness while failing to provide anything of substance to drivers other than the ability to earn a wage by driving. If an Uber driver wants health care, they have to work enough hours to be able to pay for the expense themselves or go without proper health insurance, as too many Americans do.

While some risk shifting from employers is obvious, such as the Uber example, other forms of employer risk shifting can be more covert. Some employer risk shifting exists within workplace wellness programs in how they manipulate the user. A dependence on apps that quantify health may frame physical ailments or other health issues as being a result of the user's failings. Users may at first focus solely on the tangible benefits they can get from using the app – such as points. Ultimately, however, the apps are for the benefit of the employer. Although using the app to earn points may not lead to actual long-term health for the employee/user, it enables the employer to perpetually surveil the employees and create risk profiles of

[91] Jennifer Fink, Barbara Zabawa, and Sara Chopp, "Employee Perceptions of Wellness Programs and Incentives," *American Journal of Health Promotion* 34, no. 3 (2020): 258.

[92] Sanford Jacoby, "Risk and the Labor Market: Societal Past as Economic Prologue," in *Sourcebook of Labor Markets*, ed. Ivar Berg and Arne L. Kalleberg (New York: Springer, 2001), 31–60.

[93] Allison Pugh, *The Tumbleweed Society: Working and Caring in an Age of Insecurity* (New York: Oxford University Press, 2015).

them.[94] As employers continue to shift risk, the results can have a profound impact on workers. For example, evidence has shown that a lack of comprehensive access to universal health coverage and social benefits compounds the deleterious effects of precarious work.[95]

7.6.1.1 Employee Experiences Using Workplace Wellness Programs

Although some employees feel they have benefitted from being involved in workplace wellness programs, not all workplace wellness experiences are positive. In a special report from the *Economist*, Leighanne Levansaler, an employee at Workday, discussed the intrusion of workplace wellness into her personal life, stating that "[t]his company knows more about me than my family does."[96] Another employee stated that "tracking apps end up causing more stress." This employee felt that movement tracking technologies could become addictive for the user.[97]

Many employees want to be able to cut off from work as much as possible after their workday or work week is complete, but workplace wellness programs that are based on exercise or other required activity can prevent employees from being able to have their own time. Some employees feel that the goals of workplace wellness are not directed at employees at all, complaining that the goals are on a macro level for the company instead of being on a micro level for the benefit of employees. One employee in a study on workplace wellness opined that "there should be an option to customize the program to fit your personal needs, like set your own goals or small team goals etc. and not just a global company goal." Other employees who participate in workplace wellness programs aren't as concerned about these issues, and a majority of employees in the same study who participated in health tracking programs expressed positive attitudes and said they would recommend health tracking programs to new colleagues. One employee expressed her support for workplace wellness programs by saying, "I would prefer to work for a company that offers health tracking over a company that does not. I find health tracking to be a good way to get employees engaged in the program and with each other."[98]

This study also interviewed employees who chose not to use their workplace health tracking system. Their reasons for opting out of workplace health tracking varied. A slight majority, 51 percent of those who opted out, did so because they

[94] Ann Larson, "My Disturbing Stint on a Corporate Wellness App," *Slate*, Apr. 26, 2021.

[95] Michael Marmot and Ruth Bell, *Health Inequities in a Globalising World of Work Commission on Social Determinants of Health*, ICOH Special Issue (2009).

[96] "There Will Be Little Privacy in the Workplace of the Future," *The Economist*, Special Report, Mar. 28, 2018.

[97] Chia-Fang Chung et al., "Finding the Right Fit: Understanding Health Tracking in Workplace Wellness Programs," *CHI'17: Proceedings of the 2017 ACMSIGCHI Conference on Human Factors in Computing Systems* (2017): 4879.

[98] Chung et al., "Finding the Right Fit," 4857, 4879.

felt that the program was too much of a time commitment. One employee stated that workplace health tracking was "one more thing to do in a busy day." Other employees were more vocally opposed, with one asking, "[W]hy do I have to track ALL THE TIME? It's sickening to have to do that. I only need maybe once a quarter at MOST." A smaller number of employees (16 percent) who opted out of workplace health tracking did so because of technical problems or other uncertainties in the product itself. One employee in this group reasoned that "you had to purchase the product and it was not something I thought I would use after the program." Interestingly, only 5 of the 606 total participants surveyed voiced privacy concerns over workplace health tracking systems. One participant noted, "I feel my stats are personal. I don't need work involved in my personal wellness tracking because it goes beyond my workday. I don't want to feel like my every move is being monitored by work. It just feels uncomfortable." Another voiced a similar concern, stating, "I don't want a 3rd party to have any more data about me than necessary, so I choose against any wearables. I don't like the idea of being monitored."[99] Employers who wish to implement workplace wellness programs face a delicate balancing act – helping improve the overall wellness of employees (thus lowering employee health insurance costs) without being overbearing or too intrusive to those who choose to participate. The psyche of the employee participating in a workplace wellness program is also important, with one grocery store employee describing her workplace wellness app Rocket Health by saying that "at some point, I realized the goal was to make my job kill me slower," and "the 'Rocket Health' program's primary function, then, is to provide the illusion of choice to workers who have no control over the conditions of their labor or to what might become of them after they are no longer useful to employers."[100]

Employee opinions about workplace wellness programs can vary greatly depending on what country the employees are from. A study of Canadian workers and managers provided different viewpoints on workplace wellness programs, with one employee stating that "as long as they are willing to have me there and pay me my salary to do that then that would be fine instead of something else or something above and beyond, but I am sure some people would complain." The worker further said, "[I]f you were being hired to a company that had this program in place and you chose to work there then in my opinion you would have no right to say no, I am not doing that. But to force it on people who already work for you would be difficult, you would need an immense amount of communication, you would almost need counseling to take that on."[101] On the other side of the world, a survey of Australian worksites provided an example of an employee with a much harsher opinion of the

[99] Chung et al., "Finding the Right Fit," 4481–82.
[100] Larson, "My Disturbing Stint on a Corporate Wellness App."
[101] Christina M. Caperchione et al.," How Do Management and Non-Management Employees Perceive Workplace Wellness Programmes? A Qualitative Examination," *Health Education Journal* 75, no. 5 (2015): 561.

value of the workplace wellness program he participates in, stating, "[D]itch it, it has no relevance to me and provided no practical benefits."[102]

7.6.1.2 Employer Attitudes towards Workplace Wellness Programs

Despite any negative worker responses to workplace wellness programs, employers continue to push forward. Major companies such as Johnson & Johnson tout the benefits of their program, with its executive vice president Peter Fasolo stating that "we know that we have one of the healthiest workforces." In its efforts to be the healthcare company with the healthiest employees, Fasolo further stated that "Johnson & Johnson was the first company to be tobacco-free, as well as one of the first to promote employee safe driving and to have a global HIV prevention program." Fasolo noted that Johnson & Johnson's company health statistics consistently beat the national averages from the Centers for Disease Control and Prevention (CDC). In 2016, nationwide, 30 percent of the adult population had hypertension, according to the CDC, compared to just over 9 percent of Johnson & Johnson employees. Fasolo also noted that Johnson & Johnson's annual healthcare costs are a full two to three percentage points lower than most other U.S. corporations. In discussing the earlier days of workplace wellness programs at Johnson & Johnson, Fasolo talked about the rise of health risk assessments for employees, saying that "in the mid-1980s, we were one of the first companies to encourage their employees to sign up for health risk assessments, so we could help them be healthier... fast-forward to today, and 90% of global employees fill out health risk assessments." As a company, Johnson & Johnson looks to continue its workplace wellness programs, with Fasolo pointing out that "we're meeting employees in a twenty-first century manner to help them balance and lead a purpose-driven life."[103]

Other major corporations such as Microsoft have used analytics to help drive employee efficiency. Microsoft implemented a program call MyAnalytics, which claims to provide analytics only to the employees themselves, not to their employer. MyAnalytics puts together data from emails, calendars, and other information to show employees how they use their time so they can make changes if they multitask too much. One Microsoft employee noted that the platform "doesn't have that 'big brother' element. It's designed to be more productive."[104] How much the rest of the Microsoft workforce believes that MyAnalytics information is not shared with their managers is unknown.

Employer attitudes towards workplace wellness programs vary. In Canada, one employer succinctly pointed out his position on the topic: "To me, it is disrespectful

---

[102] Tamara D. Street and Sarah J. Lacey, "Employee Perceptions of Workplace Health Promotion Programs: Comparison of a Tailored, Semi-Tailored, and Standardized Approach," *International Journal of Environmental Research and Public Health* 15, no. 5 (2018): 9.

[103] Bartz, "This Healthcare Company Is Determined to Have the Healthiest Employees in the World."

[104] "There Will be Little Privacy in the Workplace of the Future."

to employees to force them to do something like that. What works is mutual respect, and you don't show respect if you force them to do something." This employer further opined: "I would say that health and fitness is by and large a personal responsibility and it is not up to the organization to get me healthy and fit, it is something I have to look after. Now the organization may help me do that but it is arguable that it is not their responsibility to make sure I am healthy, but it is their responsibility to have adequate resources and not putting on excessive strains or issues, to make sure we have the proper tools and equipment." In a competing viewpoint, a different employer stated that "you spend your life working for your company so I think it is a responsibility to themselves and the employee because if they don't keep their employee healthy then they won't be getting the productivity of the employee, there is a give and take within the relationship."[105]

Some workplace wellness programs are born out of necessity. During the Covid-19 pandemic, many workplace wellness programs put an increasing focus on mental health and emergency services. Supplemental health insurance provider Aflac also added telehealth services such as virtual doctor visits for their customers. Matthew Owensby, the chief human resources director at Aflac, discussed the reasons for these changes, telling CNBC in an interview that "it's partially the convenience factor, but there's also the fear factor: I don't want my employee in high-outbreak cities going to the doctor if I can accomplish the same level of care virtually." He further told CNBC that "your health and wellness can really change medical outcomes if you take care of yourself. These benefit programs will become more standard offerings, versus a 'nice to have.'" The Society of Human Resource Management, a professional human resources membership association, also noted major changes to workplace wellness plans during the Covid-19 pandemic to CNBC in the same report, with its director of data products Liz Supinski stating that "we've seen plans either discontinue physical fitness in favor of broadening mental health or physical fitness options migrate to various online options."[106]

7.7 EEOC PROPOSED NEW RULES IN 2021 FOR WORKPLACE WELLNESS PROGRAMS

On January 7, 2021, the EEOC announced new proposed rules to limit the value of employer incentives for participation in workplace wellness programs that are outside of a group health plan. Shortly after this announcement, on January 20, 2021, the Biden administration withdrew the proposed rules to be reviewed by Charlotte Burrows, the newly appointed EEOC chair. The proposed rules were withdrawn both

[105] Caperchione, "How Do Management and Non-Management Employees Perceive Workplace Wellness Programmes?" 558, 560.
[106] Darla Mercado, "How Workplace Benefits Might Reflect the New Reality of Covid-19," *CNBC*, Oct. 13, 2020.

from the Federal Register and the website of the EEOC. These proposed rules were to apply to both the ADA and GINA, and sought to change the limit on incentives by allowing only minimal incentives to encourage participation in workplace wellness programs.[107] The passing of these proposed rules would result in stricter regulation on employers in terms of the voluntariness of their workplace wellness programs. Workplace wellness programs that don't require medical exams or disability-related medical inquiries would not be governed by these new proposed rules.

If a workplace wellness program is offered under a group health plan, then a safe-harbor provision would be available to avoid violating the ADA or GINA under the proposed rules. Employees that are part of a qualifying group health plan would be able to receive incentives up to 30 percent of their total cost of coverage under the safe-harbor provision. Four factors are listed under the proposed rules to qualify a workplace wellness program as a group health plan: (1) The program is offered only to employees who are part of an employer-sponsored health plan, (2) any incentives must be connected to cost-sharing of coverage, (3) the program is offered by an insurance vendor that has a contract with the health plan, and (4) the program has a specific coverage term under the plan.[108] Until a new final rule is established, the EEOC will continue to follow the guidelines set back in May 2016.

Workplace wellness programs have become a ubiquitous feature of the working world. The prediction is that the Covid-19 pandemic will further entrench them in the workplace. New legal controversies will arise as workplace wellness programs seek to expand into genetic testing of employees. Anti-discrimination laws such as the ADA and GINA have, thus far, not provided comprehensive or robust protection for employees. There will continue to be a need for government to delineate more carefully the margins beyond which the employer cannot quantify the worker, particularly when it comes to sensitive health information. A laissez-faire attitude towards workplace wellness programs or genetic testing in the workplace may inspire more healthcare cost shifting to workers and may encourage employers to limit their risk for greater healthcare costs by embracing eugenics ideals that disadvantage more physically vulnerable workers.

---

[107] Stephen Miller, "EEOC Proposes – Then Suspends – Regulations on Wellness Program Incentives," *SHRM*, Jan. 13, 2021, www.shrm.org/resourcesandtools/hr-topics/benefits/pages/eeoc-proposes-new-limits-on-wellness-program-incentives.aspx (accessed May 25, 2021).
[108] Miller, "EEOC Proposes – Then Suspends – Regulations on Wellness Program Incentives."

8

Telecommuting and Health Surveillance
in the Covid-19 Era

[A]n explosion of numerous and diverse techniques for achieving the subjugation of bodies and the control of populations, marking the beginning of an era of "biopower.

–Michel Foucault

The Covid-19 pandemic has further entrenched the phenomenon of telecommuting for work. Yet, the "work from home" mantra could also be translated as "work anytime." Rather than being freed from work, we now carry it home with us. Traveling alongside the work is the employer's interest to maintain and quantify the maximum productivity of the worker. This chapter details how the Covid-19 era pushes the boundaries of surveillance, both for those who continue to work in the office and for those who now work from home. The chapter also delves into existing law that might delineate the boundaries of worker health surveillance.

8.1 TELECOMMUTING AND COVID: PUSHING THE BOUNDARIES OF WORKER SURVEILLANCE

Telecommuting has been part of American work life since the advent of the internet.[1] The phenomenon has become even more entrenched since the start of the Covid-19 pandemic. The difference is that now the Covid-19 crisis has largely restricted telecommuting to one location – the home. Prior to that, however, the introduction of new technologies to the workplace, such as the telephone, the facsimile machine, the internet, email, or newer messaging applications such as Slack and the even newer video-conferencing applications such as Zoom meant that a significant amount of work was already happening outside the four corners of the physical office. Work

---

[1] Taylor Dever, "The Rise of Telecommuting: Embracing the Virtual Workforce," Jacobson White Paper, 2019, https://jacobsononline.com/uploadfiles/openuptowahemployees.pdf; Kim Parker, Juliana Menasce Horowitz, and Rachel Minkin, "COVID-19 Pandemic Continues to Reshape Work in America," Pew Research Center, Feb. 16, 2022, www.pewresearch.org/social-trends/2022/02/16/covid-19-pandemic-continues-to-reshape-work-in-america/.

had become unbounded by space and time. However, wherever the work was taking place, whether in the office, at home, or in the co-working spaces popularized by Brad Neuberg starting in 2005,[2] the employer retained a business interest in extracting maximum labor from workers. Thus, the unbounded workplace, while bringing with it many advantages, has also wrought new tensions between managers and workers.

With today's technological advances, "people can work remotely from a variety of locations including satellite offices, airports, or hotel rooms,"[3] but three locations are the most common for telecommuting: satellite work centers, neighborhood work centers, and home-based work centers.[4] Despite this expansive definition, the telework arrangement most commonly refers to working from the home. Prior to the Covid-19 crisis, "telecommuting [was] not being predominately used as a substitute for working onsite during the first 40 hours worked per week."[5] Rather, it was primarily a method to expand working hours outside of the traditional nine-to-five.

Pearlson and Saunders extol the advantages of telecommuting, which empowers workers to choose their hours and move beyond the standard nine-to-five office hours. Telecommuting also accords the flexibility of work environment. It offers alternative workspaces and allows for a personalized pace and control over environmental factors such as noise. The flexibility and convenience of telecommuting may operate as an attractive recruiting feature for new employees. They may also help with the retention of existing employees. The Families and Work Institute reports that 70 percent of employees surveyed were willing to change employers and 81 percent were willing to sacrifice advancement to obtain flexible work arrangements. However, Pearlson and Saunders note that "such flexibility is often accompanied by managers' need to make structural changes in the work environment [including adding electronic surveillance] to accommodate the interaction patterns of telecommuters with their managers and group members."[6]

8.2 ADVANTAGES TO TELECOMMUTING

Telecommuting had long been seen as a positive for managers and workers alike, as some researchers have found that "the practice of telecommuting, or alternatively telework, has been heralded as a cure for a variety of organizational and social

---

[2] In 2005, Brad Neuberg first used the term *co-working* to describe the Hat Factory, a work/live loft that he had created in San Francisco.

[3] Wanda J. Orlikowski and Stephen R. Barley, "Technology and Institutions: What Can Research on Information Technology and Research on Organizations Learn from Each Other?" *MIS Quarterly* 25, no. 2 (2001): 155.

[4] Nancy B. Kurland and Terri D. Egan, "Telecommuting: Justice and Control in the Virtual Organization," *Organization Science* 10, no. 4 (1999): 501.

[5] Mary C. Noonan and Jennifer L. Glass, "The Hard Truth about Telecommuting," *Monthly Labor Review*, June 2012 (2012): 40.

[6] Keri E. Pearlson and Carol S. Saunders, "There's No Place Like Home: Managing Telecommuting Paradoxes," *Academy of Management Executive* 15, no. 2 (2001): 118.

ills. It has been lauded as a strategy to help organizations decrease real-estate costs, respond to employees' needs for a healthy work-family balance and aid compliance with the 1990 Americans with Disabilities Act. Telework also has been promoted as a way to reduce air pollution and traffic congestion."[7] Employees who telecommute "report less work and family conflict."[8] They claim to "no longer suffer from the tiredness associated with physical commuting and are removed from many of the distractions of a traditional office."[9] Avoiding interruption is a huge motivator to switch to a telework arrangement for many workers. "Schedule flexibility, freedom from interruptions, and time saved in commuting often emerge as benefits" in the extant literature, and studies have also found "improved productivity, organizational loyalty and belonging, job satisfaction, and employee retention and attraction."[10]

With regard to communication, "teleworkers rely more heavily on scheduled meetings [to] interact with coworkers and managers," and therefore technology support of the avenues that connect a telecommuter to the home office is critical for the success of telework. "[S]eparation, increased ambiguity, and shared interpretive context present significant challenges to individual knowledge sharing,"[11] but when these hurdles are addressed with structured communication systems and tools, benefits emerge. Fritz, Narasimhan, and Rhee found that "increased task predictability was significantly associated with increased satisfaction with office communication for telecommuters ... performance requirements are easier to measure and better defined, possibly making these tasks more portable and therefore suitable for the remote work environment. In addition, the identity of coworkers with whom communication must take place to perform work activities is known and often formalized."[12] Such increased satisfaction from formalization of job requirements, performance standards, and communication ironically results from management's desire to maintain control, but also offers additional benefits.[13] Trust, interpersonal

---

7   Diane E. Bailey and Nancy B. Kurland, "A Review of Telework Research: Findings, New Directions, and Lessons for the Study of Modern Work," *Journal of Organizational Behavior* 23, no. 4 (2002): 383–84 (citing B. Egan, "Feasibility and Cost Benefit Analysis" (1997) (paper presented at the International Telework Association Annual International Conference, Crystal City, VA); Boas Shamir and Ilan Saloman, "Work-At-Home and the Quality of Working Life," *Academy Management Review* 10, no. 3 (1985): 455–64; Karen Matthes, "Telecommuting: Balancing Business and Employee Needs," *HR Focus* 69, no. 3 (1992): 3–17; Susan L. Handy and Patricia L. Mokhtarian, "Planning for Telecommuting: Measurement and Policy Issues," *Journal of the American Planning Society* 61, no. 1 (1995): 99–111; Raymond W. Novaco, Wendy Kliewer, and Alexander Broquet, "Home Environmental Consequences of Commute Travel Impedance," *American Journal of Community Psychology* 19, no. 6 (1991): 881–909.

8   Bailey and Kurland, "Review of Telework Research," 391.

9   N. Ben Fairweather, "Surveillance in Employment: The Case of Teleworking," *Journal of Business Ethics* 22, no. 1 (1999): 40.

10 Bailey and Kurland, "Review of Telework Research," 389.

11 Timothy D. Golden and Sumita Raghuram, "Teleworker Knowledge Sharing and the Role of Altered Relational and Technological Interactions," *Journal of Organizational Behavior* 31, no. 8 (2010): 1079.

12 Mary Beth Watson Fritz, Sridhar Narasimhan, and Hyeun-Suk Rhee, "Communication and Coordination in the Virtual Office," *Journal of Management Information Systems* 14, no. 4 (1998): 20.

13 Kurland and Egan, "Telecommuting," 502.

bonds, and organizational commitment are necessary for teleworkers to engage in knowledge sharing.[14] Therefore, if employers want to promote peak efficiency, they must foster these elements in a company culture that extends beyond the office.

Telecommuting also holds the potential to redefine the relationship between workers and supervisors for the better.[15] Initially, "supervisors demonstrate consideration for employee needs around work-family issues, freedom from distraction, and commute issues when they allow their employees to telecommute." Once a telecommuting practice is in place, "active telecommuters [spend] more time communicating with their supervisors about personal, non-work-related topics than [do] less active telecommuters," enabling the telecommuters to form relationships and understanding with their supervisors. This relationship-building contributes to the fact that "telecommuting programs have the potential to enhance employees' perceptions of the fairness of organizational procedures and interactions. Interestingly, both procedural and interactional justice are linked to positive institutional evaluations, particularly in contexts where potentially negative outcomes may occur."[16] On the employer side, telecommuting may reduce discrimination, as it offers the opportunity to hire more people who are mobility impaired, thus fulfilling the spirit of the Americans with Disabilities Act. Furthermore, telecommuting may allow companies to avoid discrimination against employees on the basis of appearance.[17]

8.2.1 The Downsides of Telecommuting

Despite these stated benefits, there are also downsides to telecommuting. Physical separation of workers means "mutual understandings are difficult to develop, problem solving becomes cumbersome, and misperceptions regarding behavior of others becomes more commonplace. Teleworkers are therefore especially challenged when attempting to co-orient to a particular perspective or approach taken by others, and experience difficulty fully understanding the context of statements and events so as to derive appropriate meanings."[18] Depending on the location of their

---

14 Golden and Raghuram, "Teleworker Knowledge Sharing and the Role of Altered Relational and Technological Interactions," 1073.

15 Donald Tomaskovic-Devey and Barbara J. Risman, "Telecommuting Innovation and Organization: A Contingency Theory of Labor Process Change," *Social Science Quarterly* 74, no. 2 (1993): 368.

16 Kurland and Egan, "Telecommuting," 507, 511.

17 Kurland and Egan, "Telecommuting," 501 (quoting Karen Matthes, "Telecommuting: Balancing Business and Employee Needs," *HR Focus* 69, no. 3 (1992): 3–17) (citing Diana L. Stone and Adrienne Colella, "A Model of Factors Affecting the Treatment of Disabled Individuals in Organizations," *Academy of Management Review* 21 (1996): 352; Margrethe H. Olson, "New Information Technology and Organizational Culture," *Management Information Science Quarterly* 6 (1982): 71; Ilan Salomon and Meira Salomon, "Telecommuting: The Employee's Perspective," *Technology Forecasting and Social Change* 25 (1984): 15).

18 Golden and Raghuram, "Teleworker Knowledge Sharing and the Role of Altered Relational and Technological Interactions," 1064 (citing Susan R. Fussell and Robert M. Krauss, "Coordination of Knowledge in Communication: Effects of Speakers' Assumptions about What Others Know," *Journal*

telework, employees may face social and/or professional isolation.[19] In addition, "the probability of working overtime is higher for telecommuters compared with non-telecommuters. The difference in the probability of working overtime between the two groups is largest when we define overtime as 41 hours or more, and smaller, but still significant, when overtime is defined as working 61 hours or more."[20] While environmental benefits are often cited, environmental impacts of reduced commutes may be offset by trips made for other purposes that would typically be made along the commute route, or by use of the car by another family member. As such, even "[i]f telecommuting ever did reduce congestion noticeably, the excess capacity on the highways would almost certainly be quickly filled by changes in current travel patterns. For example, more people might decide to drive alone instead of using public transportation." Households may relocate farther away from the workplace should they need to commute only a few times a week, at most. The price of office space could continue to drive the growth of telework, while an increase in telework could decrease the cost of office space, in turn reducing the incentive to telecommute.[21] Similarly, "even though telecommuting may reduce car traffic, it does not lead to reduced total energy usage, because more energy is spent on other things."[22]

The outcomes of telecommuting for workers may also vary based on job type. Tomaskovic-Devey and Risman suggest that

> telecommuting tends to be organized very differently for professional and clerical labor forces ... In general, professional telecommuting has been a reorganization of the job that allows increased flexibility and is used to increase the capacity for uninterrupted work. Clerical telecommuting tends to be subcontract or piece rate work done totally at home and with the loss of benefits packages.[23]

As some economic scholars had earlier predicted, "Telecommuting will have profound and permanent effects on many of the social relations which exist in the US economy. It has the potential to change the arrangement of child care and

of Personality and Social Psychology 62 (1992): 378; Robert E. Kraut et al., "Understanding Effects of Proximity on Collaboration: Implications for Technologies to Support Remote Collaborative Work," in *Distributed Work*, eds. Pamela J. Hinds and Sarah Kiesler (2002), 137; Pamela J. Hinds and Diane E. Bailey, "Out of Sight, Out of Sync: Understanding Conflict in Distributed Teams," *Organization Science* 14 (2003): 615; Pamela J. Hinds and Mark Mortensen, "Understanding Conflict in Geographically Distributed Teams: The Moderating Effects of Shared Identity, Shared Context, and Spontaneous Communication," *Organization Science* 16 (2005): 290; Michael F. Schober, "Different Kinds of Conversational Perspective-Taking," in *Social and Cognitive Approaches to Interpersonal Communication*, eds. Susan R. Fussell and Roger J. Kreuz (1998), 145).

[19] Kurland and Egan, "Telecommuting," 502.
[20] Noonan and Glass, "The Hard Truth about Telecommuting," 40, 44.
[21] Ilan Salomon, "Telematics, Travel and Environmental Change: What Can Be Expected of Travel Substitution?" *Built Environment (1978–)* 21, no. 4 (1995): 219.
[22] Tormod K. Lunde, "Will the Internet Move Mountains? Possible Consequences of the Internet for Markets and Societies," *Built Environment (1978–)* 24, no. 2/3 (1998): 180.
[23] Tomaskovic-Devey and Risman, "Telecommuting Innovation and Organization," 368.

educational institutions, revolutionize family relationships, radically alter the wage bargain, shift the distribution of income to the technologically literate, affect marital relations, and foster a social consciousness that is centered in individual independence and freedom."[24] Yet, telecommuting has the tendency to also redefine the employer–worker relationship for the worse, as it could metaphorically invite the employer into the homes of workers. The employer presence in the home, albeit via mechanical managers as surrogates, serves to continue to erode the line between work and home, and to draw back the curtain between professional life and personal life. Technology-driven surveillance methods often allow supervisors to monitor their off-site workers more closely than they would traditionally be able to monitor on-site workers. Although the knowledge of being scrutinized can have productivity benefits, it can also result in low morale. Consider also that health and safety inspection may be required for the telework place and if that place is the worker's home, "there may be an invasion of privacy associated with such inspections, that could be perceived and resented as surveillance."[25]

Another concern involves video-conferencing, which allows a view into the workers' homes. As Fairweather notes, the video camera is poised to capture anyone and anything within its range of vision. Even when an employee takes privacy precautions, other household members may accidentally reveal themselves or private objects to the camera. Thus, a "fear surveillance by the employer may affect the whole household."[26]

8.3 THE COVID-19 ERA AND WORKPLACE SURVEILLANCE

The Covid-19 era and the new worker health surveillance regime that has accompanied it has prompted new questions about worker surveillance and has ushered in new legal controversies regarding employee health testing and screening, masking requirements, and vaccine mandates.

8.3.1 *Covid-19 Testing for Employees*

In August 2020, the U.S. District Court for the Western District of Michigan denied a motion for a preliminary injunction that would enjoin the enforcement of a government order directing all owners of migrant housing camps and all agricultural employers in Michigan to have their workers and residents tested for Covid-19. The basis of the claim for a preliminary injunction to prohibit these Covid-19 tests

[24] J. Patrick Raines and Charles G. Leathers, "Telecommuting: The New Wave of Workplace Technology Will Create a Flood of Change in Social Institutions," *Journal of Economic Issues* 35, no. 2 (2001): 307–13.
[25] Fairweather, "Surveillance in Employment."
[26] Fairweather, "Surveillance in Employment," 46.

was the argument that the individuals tested under this order would be primarily Latinos, as Latino workers predominate the agricultural labor market and migrant housing camps. In denying the motion, the Court noted that although the order would impact a predominantly Latino population, it does not demonstrate discriminatory intent and the plaintiffs were unable to disprove all possible justifications for the order.[27] When the plaintiffs attempted to appeal the denial of their motion for a preliminary injunction, the Court found that they were unlikely to succeed on the merits of their appeal and that the risks of imposing Covid-19 testing in certain agricultural settings were speculative. Similarly, the Court noted that enjoining a testing scheme would pose a significant risk of harm because it would make it more difficult to identify and isolate Covid-19-positive workers, thereby limiting the spread of the virus.[28]

Although there have not been any challenges of Covid-19 testing plans based directly on deterring surveillance and promoting individual privacy rights, this case suggests that courts are likely to uphold Covid-19 testing plans because of the public policy benefit of identifying cases quickly.

Legal scholars Matthew Bodie and Michael McMahon describe the impact of Covid-19 on employers and the legal issues surrounding employer-mandated Covid-19 testing programs. They explain that the U.S. government has largely failed to implement a nationwide plan of prevention and containment for the coronavirus pandemic and that employers in every industry have faced challenges in managing the health of their workforce as a result. In fighting to ascertain comprehensive solutions, employers have turned to testing, tracing, and disclosure plans in order to quickly detect the spread of the virus among their employees if an outbreak occurs. The authors conclude that although these programs are legally feasible, they still require careful planning by employers to protect the privacy of employee health data.[29]

First, the authors note that temperature checks and Covid-19 testing are both considered medical examinations under the Americans with Disabilities Act (ADA), which covers most private employers with fifteen or more employees. The ADA typically forbids employers from requiring employees to undergo medical examinations or making disability-related inquiries of employees, unless the medical examination is both job related and consistent with business necessity. Because of this limitation, the EEOC has stated that exams are job related if the employer has a reasonable belief, based on objective evidence, that an employee's ability to perform essential job functions will be impaired by a medical condition, or that an employee poses a direct threat due to a medical condition – a definition that likely encompasses

---

[27] *Castillo v. Whitmer*, 2020 WL 5029586, No. 1:20-cv-751 (Aug. 21, 2020).

[28] *Castillo v. Whitmer*, 823 Fed. Appx. 413, 413 (6th Cir. 2020).

[29] Bodie and McMahon, "Employee Testing, Tracing, and Disclosure as a Response to the Coronavirus Pandemic."

employee temperature screenings and Covid tests because an employee with Covid-19 would pose a "direct threat" to other workers. Further, the authors explain that coronavirus questionnaires are likely not disability-related inquiries, because of how closely virus symptoms track with the CDC's list of influenza (flu) symptoms, and because having the flu itself is not considered a disability. However, a gray area may form where employers start to inquire about an employee's likelihood of developing serious complications if they were to contract the disease.[30]

8.3.2 *Masking in the Workplace*

One genre of Covid-19 policy that is potentially less severe than testing all employees is requiring employees to wear masks in the workplace. To that end, some states began requiring that all employees wear masks while they work, and some have required masks only for workers in specific industries. Figure 8.1 shows how states have handled workplace mask policies in relation to the Covid-19 pandemic.

8.3.3 *Covid-19 Screening and Temperature Checks*

According to the Equal Employment Opportunity Commission, employers may also ask all employees who are physically entering the workplace whether they have been diagnosed with or tested for Covid-19. The Genetic Information Nondiscrimination Act (GINA) prohibits employers from asking employees medical questions about their family members. However, GINA's protection applies solely to questions specifically about family members, and is indeed narrower than what EEOC guidance allows: Asking an employee only about their contact with family members would limit the information an employer could obtain about an employee's potential exposure to Covid-19, since employers are allowed to ask whether an employee has been in contact with *anyone* who has been diagnosed with the disease or who may have symptoms associated with the disease.[31]

Employers may also measure their employees' body temperature as a precaution, even though this is generally considered a medical examination.[32] In Arizona, Colorado, Kentucky, New Hampshire, and Vermont, all employers are required to check employees' temperature. In other states, such as New Jersey, Washington, and Michigan, specific industries are required to temperature screen all employees.

---

[30] Bodie and McMahon, "Employee Testing, Tracing, and Disclosure as a Response to the Coronavirus Pandemic."

[31] EEOC, "What You Should Know about COVID-19 and the ADA, the Rehabilitation Act, and Other EEO Laws," Sept. 8, 2020, www.eeoc.gov/wysk/what-you-should-know-about-covid-19-and-ada-rehabilitation-act-and-other-eeo-laws.

[32] EEOC, "What You Should Know about COVID-19 and the ADA, the Rehabilitation Act, and Other EEO Laws."

Jurisdiction	Face covering required	Employer required to provide face covering
Federal	No	No
Alabama	Yes	Not specified
Alaska	No	No
Arizona	Yes	Not specified
Arkansas	Yes	Not specified
California	Yes	Not specified
Colorado	Yes	Yes
Connecticut	Yes	Yes
Delaware	Yes	Yes
DC	Yes	Yes
Florida	Yes, for personal care service providers	No
Georgia	Yes, for certain industries	Yes, for certain employers
Hawaii	Yes	Not specified
Idaho	No	No
Illinois	Yes	Yes, for certain employers
Indiana	Yes	Not specified
Iowa	No	No
Kansas	Yes	Not specified
Kentucky	Yes	Yes
Louisiana	Yes	Not specified
Maine	Yes	Not specified
Maryland	Yes	Not specified
Massachusetts	Yes	Not specified
Michigan	Yes	Yes
Minnesota	Yes	Not specified
Mississippi	Yes	Yes
Missouri	No	No
Montana	Yes	Yes
Nebraska	Yes, for personal care service providers	Not specified
Nevada	Yes	Yes, for certain employers
New Hampshire	Yes, for certain industries	No
New Jersey	Yes	Yes
New Mexico	Yes	Yes

FIGURE 8.1 Mask requirements[33]

[33] The current status of state laws surrounding the COVID-19 pandemic as of July 2022 can be found at www.kff.org/coronavirus-covid-19/issue-brief/state-data-and-policy-actions-to-address-coronavirus/.

New York	Yes	Yes
North Carolina	Yes, for certain industries	No
North Dakota	No	No
Ohio	Yes	Not specified
Oklahoma	No	No
Oregon	Yes	Yes
Pennsylvania	Yes	Yes
Rhode Island	Yes	Yes
South Carolina	Yes, for certain industries	Not specified
South Dakota	No	No
Tennessee	No	No
Texas	Yes	Not specified
Utah	Yes	Not specified
Vermont	Yes	Not specified
Virginia	Yes, for certain industries	Yes, for certain employers
Washington	Yes	Yes
West Virginia	Yes	No
Wisconsin	Yes	Not specified
Wyoming	Yes, for certain industries	Yes, for certain employers

FIGURE 8.1 (continued)

In Michigan, these industries include food-selling establishments, pharmacies, manufacturing facilities, meat processing facilities, and casinos.[34] Figure 8.2 shows state policies on temperature and other health screenings.

8.3.4 *Health Surveillance and Covid-19 Issues*

As of 2018, of all organizations using employee monitoring technology, 33 percent were collecting employee medical data.[35] With the onset of the Covid-19 pandemic, this number has likely grown substantially. Health surveillance has seen a massive uptick as employers seek to maintain safe and efficient work operations. In a 1991 report by the Congressional Office of Technology Assessment, researchers found that employees approved of routine medical surveillance in situations where there were known health risks; however, the majority of those surveyed indicated medical

---

[34] Allen Smith, "Temperature Screenings: Review State Laws," *SHRM*, Aug. 31, 2020. In addition, Littler Mendelson has a comprehensive chart of state legislation regarding employee temperature and health screenings, which can be found at www.littler.com/publication-press/publication/wont-hurt-bit-employee-temperature-and-health-screenings-list.

[35] Krouse, "The New Ways Your Boss Is Spying on You."

Jurisdiction	Temperature screening	Other health screenings[36]	URL for additional state information
Federal	Allowed	No guidance	www.eeoc.gov/wysk/what-you-should-know-about-covid-19-and-ada-rehabilitation-act-and-other-eeo-laws#:~:text=Webinar%20Question%201)-,Yes.,cough%2C%20and%20shortness%20of%20breath
Alabama	Recommended	Recommended	www.alabamapublichealth.gov/covid19/assets/cov-sah-businesses.pdf
Alaska	Not required	Recommended	https://dhss.alaska.gov/dph/Epi/id/Pages/COVID-19/default.aspx
Arizona	Required	Required	https://azgovernor.gov/sites/default/files/requirements_for_businesses_0.pdf
Arkansas	Not required	Required for some industries	Dead link
California	Not required	Required	https://covid19.ca.gov/safely-reopening/
Colorado	Required	Required	https://parkco.us/DocumentCenter/View/6758/20-35-Safer-at-Home-DialSecondAmended100820
Connecticut	Recommended	Required for some industries	https://portal.ct.gov/DECD/Content/Coronavirus-Business-Recovery/Safe-Workplace-Rules-for-Essential-Employers
Delaware	Required for some industries	Required for some industries	https://coronavirus.delaware.gov/wp-content/uploads/sites/177/2020/04/High-Risk-Business-List_04.2.20.pdf
DC	Not required	Required for some industries	https://coronavirus.dc.gov/sites/default/files/dc/sites/coronavirus/page_content/attachments/COVID-19_DC_Health_Guidance_for_Retail_08202020.pdf
Florida	Not required	Not required	

FIGURE 8.2 State laws on temperature screenings and other health screenings, as of November 11, 2020[37]

[36] "Other Health Screenings" could refer to checks such as questionnaires about symptoms, making sure employees are wearing masks, and similar screenings that don't involve temperature checks.

[37] This table summarizes data in Littler Mendelson, "This Won't Hurt a Big; Employee Temperature and Health Screenings: List of Statewide Orders," as of Nov. 11, 2020, www.littler.com/publication-press/publication/wont-hurt-bit-employee-temperature-and-health-screenings-list, as well as UR's for individual state policies.

Georgia	Not required	Required	https://gov.georgia.gov/document/2020-executive-order/09302002/download
Hawaii	Not required	Not required	
Idaho	Required for some industries	Required for some industries	https://rebound.idaho.gov/wp-content/uploads/2020/05/stage2-protocols-indoor-gyms-rec-facilities.pdf
Illinois	Recommended for some industries	Recommended	https://dph.illinois.gov/covid19/community-guidance.html
Indiana	Recommended	Required	https://backontrack.in.gov/
Iowa	Not required	Required	https://governor.iowa.gov/sites/default/files/documents/Public%20Health%20Proclamation%20-%202020.11.10.pdf
Kansas	Recommended	Recommended	www.coronavirus.kdheks.gov/248/Business-Employers
Kentucky	Required	Required	https://govsite-assets.s3.amazonaws.com/PuhOvvxS0yUyilXbwvTN_2020-7-10%20-%20Minimum%20Requirements.pdf
Louisiana	Recommended	Recommended	https://govsite-assets.s3.amazonaws.com/PuhOvvxS0yUyilXbwvTN_2020-7-10%20-%20Minimum%20Requirements.pdf
Maine	Not required	Not required	
Maryland	Recommended	Recommended	https://commerce.maryland.gov/Documents/BusinessResource/General-Business-COVID-19-Best-Practices.pdf
Massachusetts	Not required	Required for some industries	www.mass.gov/doc/phase-iii-step-1-restaurants-protocol-summary/download
Michigan	Required for some industries	Required	https://content.govdelivery.com/attachments/MIEOG/2020/09/25/file_attachments/1556012/EO%202020-184%20Emerg%20order%20-%20Worker%20Safeguards.pdf
Minnesota	Recommended	Required	www.health.state.mn.us/diseases/coronavirus/facility hlthscreen.pdf

FIGURE 8.2 (continued)

Mississippi	Not required	Required	https://mcusercontent.com/08cb3e52aa1308600f84d49ea/files/41310415-0838-45f6-b9a9-9fca40b6f508/Executive_Order_1525.pdf
Missouri	Not required	Not required	
Montana	Not required	Required	Dead link
Nebraska	Recommended for some industries	Recommended for some industries	Dead link
Nevada	Not required	Required	https://nvhealthresponse.nv.gov/wp-content/uploads/2020/05/Industry-specific-Guidance-Documents-1.pdf
New Hampshire	Required	Required	www.covid19.nh.gov/best-practices
New Jersey	Required for some industries	Required	Dead link
New Mexico	Recommended for some industries	Required	https://indd.adobe.com/view/3f732e94-0164-424d-9ac6-a0ace27e70c8
New York	Recommended	Required	www.governor.ny.gov/sites/default/files/atoms/files/NYS_BusinessReopeningSafetyPlanTemplate.pdf
North Carolina	Not required	Required	https://files.nc.gov/governor/documents/files/EO169-Phase-3.pdf
North Dakota	Required when state hits "orange" level	Required when state hits "orange" level	www.health.nd.gov/sites/www/files/documents/Files/MSS/coronavirus/Employee_Screening_Tool.pdf
Ohio	Recommended	Required	https://coronavirus.ohio.gov/static/publicorders/revised-business-guidance-sd.pdf
Oklahoma	Not required	Not required	
Oregon	Recommended	Recommended	https://sharedsystems.dhsoha.state.or.us/DHSForms/Served/le2342C.pdf
Pennsylvania	Not required	Required	www.pa.gov/guides/responding-to-covid-19/
Rhode Island	Not required	Required	https://risos-apa-production-public.s3.amazonaws.com/DOH/REG_11203_20201019083149.pdf

FIGURE 8.2 (continued)

South Carolina	Recommended	Required	Dead link
South Dakota	Not required	Recommended	Dead link
Tennessee	Not required	Recommended	Dead link
Texas	Recommended	Recommended	Dead link
Utah	Required for some industries	Not specified	https://coronavirus-download.utah.gov/business/Gyms_Fitness_Centers_Guidelines.pdf
Vermont	Recommended	Required	https://accd.vermont.gov/news/update-new-work-safe-additions-be-smart-stay-safe-order
Virginia	Recommended	Required	www.doli.virginia.gov/wp-content/uploads/2020/07/RIS-filed-RTD-Final-ETS-7.24.2020.pdf
Washington	Not required	Required	Dead link
West Virginia	Recommended for some industries	Recommended for some industries	Dead link
Wisconsin	Not required	Not required	
Wyoming	Not required	Recommended	https://health.wyo.gov/wp-content/uploads/2020/06/WDH-Guidance-for-Employee-Screening-June-15.pdf

FIGURE 8.2 (continued)

surveillance is inappropriate in the absence of known risk.[38] Nonetheless, in recent years employers' use of medical surveillance in risk-free work environments has boomed as employers seek to reduce healthcare costs.

Fitbit, for example, is a product that was originally designed exclusively for corporate wellness programs but that is now available to the general public. The device, which measures steps, heart rate, and calories burned, was subsidized by employers – it was either provided free or "earned through healthy behaviors."[39] The data was sent to an app on an employee's phone, which could then be intercepted by employers or wellness-plan administrators. Because wearable technology data collection is generally not collected in a clinical setting, it may not be protected by HIPAA; thus, employers could have more control over this data than employees may expect.[40] A workplace wellness program may also collect information through medical exams and questionnaires, and in some cases, that information may be sold to third parties for profit.[41]

[38] US Congress OTA, *Medical Monitoring and Screening in the Workplace: Results of a Survey*, 24.
[39] Farr, "Fitbit Has a New Health Tracker, But You Can Only Get It Through Your Employer or Insurer."
[40] Advisory Board, "When Your Employer Gives You a Fitbit, Who Owns the Data?"
[41] Ajunwa, "Workplace Wellness Programs Could Be Putting Your Health Data at Risk. "

Loose privacy restrictions concerning health data are of special concern as cases of Covid-19 rise while employers attempt to reopen operations. New surveillance technologies include apps such as technology developed by PwC, which monitors Bluetooth signals to ensure that individuals maintain social distancing guidelines in the office[42] and provides a portal for mandatory coronavirus testing and self-reporting. Some employee surveillance apps, such as ProtectWell, a joint venture between Microsoft and United Health, allow employers to access all self-reported employee health information and to directly receive employees' Covid-19 test results. Beyond apps, entities from governments to sports teams have implemented mandatory wearable technology that tracks employee movements, sometimes alongside additional health information. Other companies have installed hardware at physical work sites, with common features including infrared temperature and social distancing/PPE compliance monitoring.[43] Although the Covid-19 pandemic certainly qualifies as a workplace health risk factor, experts are concerned that the new invasive technologies developed to monitor the virus may outlast the crisis.[44] Given the fast rollout of these new technologies and lax restrictions concerning employer health data collection, the state of health surveillance in the workplace warrants careful research and reform to protect employees from both employers and third parties.

8.3.5 *Covid-19 Vaccine Mandates*

As Covid-19 vaccines have become available across the country and the world, employers in the United States are trying to determine what is best for their companies in regard to employee vaccination. Mandating vaccines for entire workforces can be tricky in both a practical and a legal sense. Employers who are subject to the protections of the ADA and Title VII of the Civil Rights Act of 1964 must ensure that their vaccination mandates are compliant. The EEOC has confirmed that a Covid-19 vaccination is not in itself a medical exam. The EEOC noted that there are disability-related questions that individuals answer before getting a Covid-19 vaccine that could potentially violate the ADA. When these questions are asked by a third party administering the vaccine, such as a pharmacy, the questions would likely not violate the ADA because the employer is not privy to the answers of their employees. The two main issues that employers must watch out for regarding mandatory Covid-19 vaccinations involve making sure that exemptions are offered for those who are against vaccination because of sincerely held religious beliefs and for those who have medical conditions that would make vaccination dangerous. Employers are

---

[42] Bond, "Your Boss May Soon Track You at Work for Coronavirus Safety."
[43] Public Citizen, *Workplace Privacy after Covid-19* (Washington DC: Public Citizen Digital Rights Program, 2020), 6, 9–10.
[44] Bond, "Your Boss May Soon Track You at Work for Coronavirus Safety."

generally also allowed to ask employees if they have been vaccinated as a measure of workplace health safety under the job-relatedness standard of the ADA.[45]

To be compliant with the ADA, an employer could structure their workplace wellness program to give employees a monetary benefit if they receive a Covid-19 vaccine and show proof. As long as the Covid-19 vaccine provider is not in a contract with the employer and the vaccine provider is a third party, then offering an incentive to an employee to be vaccinated will not violate the ADA. An employer could ask a recently vaccinated employee for proof of their vaccination due to the fact that an individual's vaccination status is not, in itself, a medical exam or inquiry under the ADA.

8.4 DISABILITY IMPLICATIONS OF WORKER SURVEILLANCE

Increased surveillance may disproportionately impact individuals with disabilities. Employee behavior or productivity is measured against an ideal of how an employee should behave or perform, resulting in an ideal that does not account for individual physical or psychological differences or impairments.[46] For example, software such as PwC's facial recognition technology that punishes individuals who often step away from their computer has potentially adverse implications, especially for individuals with physical and/or mental impairments. Individuals are required to provide an acceptable excuse for leaving their desks, a potentially embarrassing or demeaning experience for individuals with physical impairments that require frequent bathroom breaks or medical attention.[47] Individuals with mental differences such as attention-deficit/hyperactivity disorder (ADHD) or anxiety, which affect sustained focus, may need to leave their desks more frequently to manage long work hours while confined in their homes. Removed from the structure of the office environment, some individuals report finding it difficult to manage stress and stay on task.[48] Even software that monitors employee tone and social interaction may adversely affect individuals with social differences such as autism, which can affect one's speech and nonverbal communication patterns.[49] Simple keystroke monitoring, which often picks up personal passwords and information along with work-related data, can be dangerous for those managing their medical records online.

---

[45] Robert S. Nichols et al., "EEOC Says Employers May Mandate COVID-19 Vaccinations – Subject to Limitations," *National Law Review*, Jan. 20, 2021, www.natlawreview.com/article/eeoc-says-employers-may-mandate-covid-19-vaccinations-subject-to-limitations (accessed May 25, 2021).

[46] The social model of disability interprets disability as a result of socially created barriers, as opposed to an individual's impairment or difference. It is widely used by disability scholars and advocates. See Scope, "Social Model of Disability," *Scope.org*, www.scope.org.uk/about-us/social-model-of-disability/ (accessed Oct. 4, 2020).

[47] Webber, "PwC Facial Recognition Tool Criticised for Home Working Privacy Invasion."

[48] Jones, "I Monitor My Staff with Software That Takes Screenshots."

[49] NIEHS, "Autism," last updated Aug. 30, 2021, www.niehs.nih.gov/health/topics/conditions/autism/index.cfm.

The Covid-19 pandemic has made telecommuting a commonplace feature of American work life. Much of the telecommuting carried out during this era is, however, taking place from home. The pandemic has prompted an increase in surveillance across the board – health surveillance for those physically returning to the workplace and productivity surveillance for those working from home. For individuals with cognitive or physical differences, or even simply individuals suffering any personal difficulties in these unprecedented times, this increased surveillance may have deleterious effects. Employers should remain cognizant of how at-home surveillance of employees could create opportunities for unlawful discrimination. Furthermore, employers will need to balance health monitoring and mandates in the workplace with necessary disability accommodations afforded by the American with Disabilities Act. Increased monitoring technology aimed at robotic efficiency, productivity, compliance, and uniformity – which is already known to injure morale[50] – would only serve to add to the distress of workers in the Covid-19 era. This speaks to the continued need for the law to offer bright-line rules that delineate the boundaries of worker surveillance.

---

[50] Debora Jeske and Alecia M. Santuzzi, "Monitoring What and How: Psychological Implications of Electronic Performance Monitoring," *New Technology: Work and Employment* 30, no. 1 (2015): 74.

PART III

Quantified Discrimination

9

Wearable Tech

The Quantified Self at Work[*]

Work has become a stage "where invasive technologies are normalized among captive populations of employees."

–Shoshana Zuboff, *The Age of Surveillance Capitalism*

Wearable technology is perhaps the most invasive form of mechanical manager. These technologies seek to quantify a gamut of worker attributes, including productivity, physical activity, health, emotions, moods, communication style, and so on. Although wearable technologies are often adopted as part of a benevolent approach to aiding worker productivity or even enhancing worker safety, they often serve the additional purpose of worker surveillance and policing worker behavior. Though wearable technologies as a workplace tool hold the technological potential to make work more efficient, the increased capacity of modern-day wearable technologies to enact continuous and discreet worker surveillance also presents them as a socio-technical challenge to worker autonomy and personhood.

Wearable technologies are the best artifacts for illustrating how technological advances are changing the nature of work and reconstituting employer–worker relationships. This is because the form and function of wearable technologies may supercharge Taylorist approaches to management such as close surveillance of workers and the minute quantification of productivity and worker behavior. Compare and contrast the pedometer to the Amazon cage: The pedometer precedes the advent of Taylorist management and could be considered the first iteration of wearable technology. Leonardo da Vinci (1452–1519) invented a mechanical step counter that was worn at the waist and connected to a lever tied to the thigh; walking caused the lever to turn gears that would count the wearer's steps. Several centuries later, Thomas Jefferson commissioned a watchmaker to make a similar device to use to measure

---

[*] Parts of this chapter are adapted from my law review article "Algorithms at Work: Productivity Monitoring Applications and Wearable Technology as the New Data-Centric Research Agenda for Employment and Labor Law," first published in *Saint Louis University Law Journal* 63 (2018).

distances. These early pedometers were solely under the control of their wearers, who determined when to use the device and how to use the information collected. In contrast, wearable technologies under a Taylorist regime have made subjects of their wearers. Worker data is extracted via wearable technology at the behest of the employer, not by the will of the worker. This new subordinate relationship raises questions of data ownership and control. Moreover, within the employment context, this inverted relationship, wherein the technology governs the wearer, also creates new legal controversies around privacy, employment discrimination, worker voice, and – ultimately – worker personhood.

The agency conferred to the worker by early pedometers is in contrast with the dearth of agency reserved for the worker by the Amazon cage. In 2016, Amazon patented a system that would place warehouse workers in metal cages. These cages would then be hoisted on machines that would trundle around the warehouse, allowing the workers to repair broken machinery or clean the warehouse from inside the cages.[1] The patent description maintained that the cages were not meant to confine workers, but to keep them safe.[2] Yet, critics described the system as "an extraordinary illustration of worker alienation" and a "stark moment in the relationship between humans and machines." With these cages, Amazon could fully deploy mechanical managers in the form of a new wearable technology to exact total control over workers. Although this technology has not yet been implemented,[3] the mere existence of a patent application for such technology not only highlights the extent of managerial control over a worker that wearable technology could enable, but also reflects the current state of managerial attitudes towards worker control.

The wearable devices deployed in the workplace today represent an extreme iteration of Taylorism. While Taylor had managers with stopwatches stalking the factory floor, these days wearable technology is deputized as a mechanical manger overseeing workers' productivity, behavior, and emotional response. Another important distinction that places the workplace phenomenon of wearable technologies as a unique iteration of Taylorist principles is the embodiment of managerial control. While in Taylorism the managers remained wholly separate and bodily apart, with wearable technologies, manager control is enacted directly on workers' bodies. Given the direct physical control that some of the wearable technology enables, some have likened it to an earlier labor system – institutionalized slavery – when workers felt the lash of a whip to keep them at pace and correct any work mistakes.

[1]   Kristin Houser, "An Amazon Patent Would Use Cages to Keep Employees 'Safe,'" *Futurism*, Sept. 10, 2018, https://futurism.com/the-byte/amazons-cage-employees.

[2]   Kate Crawford and Vladan Joler, *Anatomy of an AI System*, SHARE Foundation and The AI Now Institute, 2018, https://anatomyof.ai/.

[3]   Matt Day and Benhamin Romano, "Amazon Has Patented a System That Would Put Workers in a Cage, on Top of a Robot," *Seattle Times*, Sept. 7, 2018, www.seattletimes.com/business/amazon/amazon-has-patented-a-system-that-would-put-workers-in-a-cage-on-top-of-a-robot/.

9.1 WEARABLE TECH AND THE QUANTIFIED SELF MOVEMENT

The quantified self movement, which started in 2007 in Silicon Valley, California, is credited to Gary Wolf and Kevin Kelly. As defined by the Quantified Self Institute, which was founded in 2012, "the quantified self (QS) is the term that embodies self-knowledge through self-tracking," with the central conceit that one can find "personal meaning in [one's] personal data."[4] The axiom "The unexamined life is not worth living" is famously attributed to Socrates, who is said to have uttered this at his trial, but the idea that there is value in self-examination and self-evaluation is perhaps as old as time. Other notable figures in history, including Benjamin Franklin, made a practice of logging their life activities to discern avenues for self-improvement.[5] However, as Gina Neff and Dawn Nafus note in *Self Tracking*, "Ubiquitous computing, the idea that computers would one day be a part of bodies and environments, not just offices, arose in the 1980s and has been an important idea within the technology communities."[6] This concept was a necessary precursor to wearable tech.

The rise of wearable tech in the quantified self movement was accompanied by questions regarding its *raison d'etre*. Was it merely "prosthetics of feeling," helping the wearer better intuit their bodily functions as influenced by outside elements? Was it an outsourcing of the task of bodily management to technologies and thus an extension of biomedicalization? Or was it creating "data doubles" – data-manifested shadows of the people who wear them?[7] And if so, what would be the role of these data doubles in society? The concept of data doubles is an interesting one from both a sociological and a legal standpoint. Data doubles may operate as stand-ins for the person; in fact, in an increasingly digitized world, a data double may be the only representation of the person seen by third parties. But what are the societal implications when a data double is taken at face value as an accurate representation? What are the legal implications when a data double can testify in court, for example? Or when data from wearables is deployed as evidence of a person's physical state at a place in time? Would this evidence be refutable, and, if so, how? The central dilemma for a data double is that while it can "talk" – that is, one might ascribe meaning to the data – the data itself offers no explanations. Given the human bias of perceiving automated systems as fair or impartial (as discussed in Chapter 3), will data doubles come to have more legal power than the actual people they represent? These questions provide some inkling that the data generated from the wearables could have applications going beyond merely

---

4   Quantified Self Institute, *What Is Quantified Self?*, https://qsinstitute.com/about/what-is-quantified-self/
5   Franklin describes his "book of virtues" in his autobiography, which is available online at The Electric Ben Franklin, www.ushistory.org/franklin/autobiography/ (accessed Oct. 21, 2020).
6   Gina Neff and Dawn Nafus, *Self-Tracking* (Cambridge, MA: MIT Press, 2016), 27.
7   Minna Ruckenstein, "Visualized and Interacted Life: Personal Analytics and Engagements with Data Doubles," *Societies* 4, no. 1 (2014): 68–84.

self-knowledge. The sociologist Deborah Lupton was among the first to identify that data from self-tracking could serve dual purposes: It could serve to fulfill a self-driven self-improvement imperative, or it could be co-opted by other parties for strictly commercial exploitation and gain, with some gray area existing between these two outcomes.[8]

9.2 WORKPLACE WEARABLE TECH AS TECHNO-SOLUTIONISM

The notion of wearable tracking tech cannot be divorced from a phenomenon that Evgeny Morozov has termed "technosolutionism" – that is, the idea that technology advancements are the solutions to most problems, large or small.[9] Wearable tech devices represent a continuation of the first computer technologies introduced to the workplace that served to both enhance employees' task performance and monitor their actions to ensure productivity levels. Technology was seen as a perfect solution to ensure employees' accountability, as with the increased capabilities in monitoring, employees were less likely to shirk their responsibilities. Wearable technologies are attractive in that because they range in size from a small lapel pin to an exoskeleton, they seem tailor-made to confront any problem. It is no surprise, then, that the quantified self movement that started as a self-improvement ethos was then appropriated by corporations in the next iteration of scientific management. Whereas the members of the quantified self movement tracked their steps or their diet for better health, corporations could now do the same but with a view towards improving productivity and reducing healthcare costs.

9.3 WEARABLE TECH IN THE WORKPLACE

The examples of existing wearable tech reflect the employer's concerns with maximizing profit and minimizing risk. Consider, as another example of wearable technology, the haptic feedback wristband invented by Amazon. The full name for the patent is the Ultrasonic Bracelet and Receiver for Detecting Position in 2D Plane, and the goal of the system is to save time locating items in warehouses and thereby increase productivity. The bracelet would be able to monitor and direct the worker to the correct inventory bins via haptic feedback.[10] But the bracelet can track more than mere productivity: It can also track location and hand movements.[11] According

---

[8] Deborah Lupton, "Self-Tracking Modes: Reflexive Self-Monitoring and Data Practices," Conference paper, Aug. 27, 2014, https://papers.ssrn.com/sol3/papers.cfm?abstract_id=2483549.

[9] Evgeny Morozov, *To Share Everything, Click Here: The Folly of Technological Solutionism* (New York: Public Affairs, 2013).

[10] U.S. Patent No. 9,881,276 (issued Jan. 30, 2018).

[11] Ceylan Yeginsu, "If Workers Slack Off, the Wristband Will Know. (And Amazon Has a Patent for It.)," *New York Times*, Feb. 1, 2018.

to a number of articles, magazines, and the U.S. patent file,[12] the system includes ultrasonic devices installed around the warehouse, the actual wristbands that warehouse workers wear, and a management module that oversees the activity. With an ultrasonic unit, the system tracks where the worker is in relation to a particular inventory bin they are seeking, and the bracelet buzzes when they are heading the wrong direction. By using the device, supervisors would also be able to identify when the workers pause, fidget, or take a bathroom break.[13]

Amazon already holds a reputation for a management style that some allege results in treating workers, especially low-paid laborers, like "human robots" by having them conduct repetitive tasks as fast as possible. By allegedly timing their toilet breaks and using packing timers, the wristband, with its haptic feedback system, has raised further concerns about poor working conditions and the possibility of harsher workplace surveillance.[14] In response to this, Amazon released a statement about its patents for wristband tracking systems in which it characterized concerns as misguided and asserted that the wristbands would improve the process of product retrieval from bins by "free[ing] up [workers'] hands from scanners and their eyes from computer screens."[15]

Amazon has not yet deployed the bracelet device, but the company already makes use of wearable GPS tags to optimize warehouse routes.[16] Other companies such as Intermec Technologies Corporation (Intermec) have also applied for patents on a glove or a wristband that would assist in sorting inventory.[17] Similar to Amazon's patent, Intermec's invention would communicate proximity to inventory bins.[18]

Other companies are following suit. For example, MAD Apparel, Inc., has filed a patent for a vest that can monitor, provide feedback, and make real-time adjustments. Although MAD advertises its vest for personal purposes, the vest has

[12] See Patent 276. See also Thuy Ong, "Amazon Patents Wristbands That Track Warehouse Employees' Hands in Real Time," *The Verge*, Feb. 1, 2018, www.theverge.com/2018/2/1/16958918/amazon-patents-trackable-wristband-warehouse-employees; Solon, "Amazon Patents Wristband That Tracks Warehouse Workers' Movements"; Gunseli Yalcinkaya, "Amazon Patents Wristband to Track Productivity and Direct Warehouse Staff Using Vibrations," *Dezeen*, Feb. 6, 2018, www.dezeen.com/2018/02/06/amazon-patents-wristbands/; Yeginsu, "If Workers Slack Off, the Wristband Will Know."
[13] Yeginsu, "If Workers Slack Off, the Wristband Will Know."
[14] See Solon, "Amazon Patents Wristband That Tracks Warehouse Workers' Movements." See also Yeginsu, "If Workers Slack Off, the Wristband Will Know."
[15] Alan Boyle, "Amazon Wins a Pair of Patents for Wireless Wristbands That Track Warehouse Workers," *GeekWire*, Jan. 30, 2018, www.geekwire.com/2018/amazon-wins-patents-wireless-wristbands-track-warehouse-workers/. See also Ong, "Amazon Patents Wristbands That Track Warehouse Employees' Hands in Real Time."
[16] Yeginsu, "If Workers Slack Off, the Wristband Will Know"; Karen Turner, "Are Performance-Monitoring Wearables an Affront to Workers' Rights?" *Chicago Tribune*, Aug. 7, 2016.
[17] U.S. Patent Application No. 15/145,144, Pub. No. 2016/0247006 (published Aug. 25, 2016) (Intermec Tech. Corp., applicant); U.S. Patent Application No. 13/756,115, Pub. No. 2014/0214631 (published Jul. 31, 2014) (Intermec Tech. Corp., applicant).
[18] Patent 144 Application.

applications for the workplace, especially involving work where physical labor is required.[19] Similarly, Stephan Heath has filed a patent application for an electromagnetic frequency identification device that could be used in different settings, including health care and law enforcement.[20]

Virtual reality technologies, which are usually used in video gaming, are also being applied in industrial settings. The company Immersion Corp. has filed a patent application for a haptic feedback bodysuit that can control the intensity of the haptic feedback. The patent application contains a reference to "work colleagues," meaning the technology is intended for a work environment.[21] Recent healthcare patent applications for wearable technology have the potential to cross over into the workplace. For example, one proposed wearable technology by IBM would work by both detecting and correcting poor posture;[22] other smart exoskeletons that can be adjusted via algorithms would do more than correct gait or prevent falls; they would monitor deviations from a prescribed path and also transmit other biometric data.[23] Others, like Hyundai's proposed exoskeleton, have designated models for the workplace and have been dubbed "wearable robots."[24]

These patent applications with clear workplace intended use and implications demonstrate a continued future for wearables in the workplace and show that Amazon may not be the only company that deploys such technology to improve worker productivity and efficiency. For example, Mike Glenn, the executive vice president of market development and corporate communications at FedEx Corporation, notes that wearable technology is already having a significant impact on FedEx employees – especially those involved in package sorting, pickup, and delivery – who wear ring scanners.[25] In addition, United Parcel Service (UPS) adopted a wearable scanning system in 2012 for its employees who handle packages.[26] The workers

---

[19] U.S. Patent No. 9,498,128 (issued Nov. 22, 2016).

[20] U.S. Patent Application No. 14/998,746, Pub. No. 2016/0189174 (published June 30, 2016) (Stephan Heath, applicant).

[21] U.S. Patent Application No. 15/134,797, Pub. No. 2017/0243453 (published Aug. 24, 2017) (Immersion Corp., applicant).

[22] U.S. Patent Application No. 14/849,152, Pub. No. 2017/0068313 (published Mar. 9, 2017) (Int'l Bus. Mach. Corp., applicant).

[23] See, e.g., U.S. Patent Application No. 15/605,313, Pub. No. 2018/0125738 (published May 10, 2018) (Carnegie Mellon Univ., applicant); Dan Robitzski, "How A.I. Exoskeletons Could Make People Super-Human," *Inverse*, June 22, 2017, www.inverse.com/article/33298-personalized-exoskeletons-carnegie-mellon; Magdalena Petrova, "A Smart Exoskeleton Can Keep the Elderly Safe," *PCWorld*, May 15, 2017.

[24] Hyundai Motor Company, "Hyundai Motor Leads Personal Mobility Revolution with Advanced Wearable Robots," News release, Jan. 4, 2017, www.hyundaiusa.com/about-hyundai/news/Corporate_hyundai_motor_leads_personal_mobility_revolution_with_advanced_wearable_robots-20170104.aspx.

[25] See Timothy L. Fort, Anjanette H. Raymond, and Scott J. Shackelford, "The Angel on Your Shoulder: Prompting Employees to Do the Right Thing through the Use of Wearables," *Northwestern Journal of Technology and Intellectual Property* 14, no. 2 (2016): 145. See also FedEx, "Q&A with Mike Glen, FedEx Services," *Access*, Nov. 2013, http://access.van.fedex.com/qa-mike-glenn-fedex-services/.

[26] Jacques Couret, "UPS Using 'Wearable' Scanning System," *Atlanta Business Chronicle*, Aug. 2, 2012, www.bizjournals.com/atlanta/news/2012/08/02/ups-using-wearable-scanning-system.html.

wear hands-free imagers on a finger and a small terminal on the wrist or hip so they can quickly image barcodes and improve data entry.[27] UPS also has sensors on its delivery trucks to collect data and "track the opening and closing of doors, the engine of the vehicle, and whether a seat belt is buckled."[28] A Canadian startup, Thalmic Labs, invented an armband that lets a wearer control movements on a screen with a flick of the wrist. Moving beyond the consumer space, the company targets workers in industries such as construction, field service, and health care where integration with smart glasses, like Google Glass, can be helpful.[29] In another example of wearables with work applications, XOEye glasses are able to make use of HD video to avoid danger. Furthermore, the XOEye glasses' communication features allow for a worker to be guided by another worker or supervisor via the video transmission.[30]

9.3.1 *Fitbits and Smartwatches*

Fitbit has become a particularly popular wearable technology for the workplace. Holding the top spot in the wearable market, it includes "a GPS monitor, a heart rate monitor, an alarm and can even compile exercise summaries."[31] These days, employees are encouraged and often rewarded for providing their information through such devices. For example, "[a]bout 90% of companies now offer wellness programs, some of which encourage employees to use Fitbit and other devices that measure the quantity and intensity of their workouts and to employ simple visual and motivational tools to track their progress and help sustain their engagement."[32] Appirio, an information technology consulting company, distributed four hundred Fitbits to employees as a part of its corporate wellness program.[33]

---

[27] See Fort, Raymond, and Shackelford, "The Angel on Your Shoulder," 145. See also Couret, "UPS Using 'Wearable' Scanning System."

[28] Andrea Miller, "More Companies Are Using Technology to Monitor Employees, Sparking Privacy Concerns," *ABC News*, Mar. 10, 2018, https://abcnews.go.com/US/companies-technology-monitor-employees-sparking-privacy-concerns/story?id=53388270.

[29] See Hollie Slade, "Hand Gesture Armband Myo Integrates with Google Glass," *Forbes*, Aug. 19, 2014.

[30] Olivia Solon, "Wearable Technology Creeps into the Workplace," *Sydney Morning Herald*, Aug. 7, 2015, www.smh.com.au/business/workplace/wearable-technology-creeps-into-the-workplace-20150807-gitzuh.html.

[31] Alexandra Troiano, "Note: Wearables and Personal Health Data: Putting a Premium on Your Privacy," *Brook. Law Review* 82, no. (2017): 1716. See also Fitbit, *Our Technology*, 2017, www.fitbit.com/technology (last visited Nov. 7, 2018); Fitbit, *SmartTrack*, https://perma.cc/8GYM-46EW (accessed Nov. 7, 2018).

[32] H. James Wilson, "Wearables in the Workplace," *Harvard Business Review*, Sept. 2013, https://hbr.org/2013/09/wearables-in-the-workplace. See also Fort, Raymond, and Shackelford, "The Angel on Your Shoulder," 153; Troiano, "Wearables and Personal Health Data," 1717, 1722 (stating that wellness programs and wearable devices are implemented to increase productivity, and health-related costs can be reduced).

[33] Troiano, "Wearables and Personal Health Data," 1722.

Also, smartwatches that have many of the same capabilities as fitness bands have pedometer technology or GPS functionality that can measure efficiency and improve employee safety. These devices optimize the storage locations of tools and aim to minimize workers' movement – similar to Amazon's haptic wristband – by tracking the steps required to execute particular operations and automatically shutting down machines when employees are in danger. Employees could also use their smartwatches to easily update locations and quantities of inventories, and conduct transactional operations.[34]

9.3.2 *Cap and Helmet*

SmartCap, invented by an Australian company called EdanSafe, detects the wearer's brain activity and delivers data to workers about fatigue levels in real time by reading their brain waves.[35] Once per second, an algorithm analyzes the data collected by the SmartCap to determine the wearer's level of alertness and transmits this information by Bluetooth to the user. Audial and visual alarms are activated when the user's fatigue level increases, and the sensors can tell when the SmartCap is removed. Supervisors can monitor the output and fatigue levels of numerous cap-wearing employees during past shifts using the SmartCap and its accompanying Fatigue Manager Server. The SmartCap was initially developed for use in the mining industry and is currently used by many truck drivers to increase their productive output and physical safety. The company is working on a hardhat version, and a headband version is already being produced.[36]

The DAQRI helmet is a similar product that allows workers to see GPS-guided blueprints via augmented reality vision in real time and spot welds by seeing through walls.[37] In addition to a visor that presents visual overlays of information, such as instructions and warnings, the helmet has "cameras and sensors that can measure, record, and track information about the wearer's surroundings."[38] The helmet is used by companies such as California-based Hyperloop.[39]

---

[34] See Patrick Van den Bossche et al., "Wearable Technology in the Warehouse," *Supply Chain 24/7: Warehouse/DC News*, Feb. 1, 2016, www.supplychain247.com/article/wearable_technology_in_the_warehouse.

[35] See Ben Coxworth, "SmartCap Monitors Workers' Fatigue Levels by Reading Their Brain Waves," *New Atlas*, Jan. 31, 2012, https://newatlas.com/smartcap-measures-fatigue-brain-waves/21271/. See also Natalie Holmes, "Wearable Technology within the Workplace," *Convene*, https://convene.com/catalyst/wearable-technology-within-the-workplace/ (accessed Nov. 8, 2018).

[36] See Turner, "Are Performance-Monitoring Wearables an Affront to Workers' Rights?"; Coxworth, "SmartCap Monitors Workers' Fatigue Levels by Reading Their Brain Waves."

[37] See Turner, "Are Performance-Monitoring Wearables an Affront to Workers' Rights?"

[38] Jeremy P. Brummond and Patrick J. Thornton, "The Legal Side of Jobsite Technology," *Construction Today*, June 22, 2016, www.construction-today.com/sections/columns/2752-the-legal-side-of-jobsite-technology.

[39] See Turner, "Are Performance-Monitoring Wearables an Affront to Workers' Rights?"

9.3.3 *High-Tech Vests*

Similar to the way the Amazon wristband tracks workers' location, high-visibility vests are fitted with GPS to enhance workplace safety by alerting workers when they are entering a hazardous zone on construction sites.[40] This high-tech vest not only reduces danger by tracking workers throughout a geo-fenced jobsite, it also optimizes workflow by allowing managers to track workers' movements.[41]

Another example of wearable technology is the implantation of radio-frequency identification (RFID) microchips under workers' skin to facilitate services. In July 2017, more than fifty out of eighty employees at a River Falls, Wisconsin, technology company called Three Square Market volunteered to have the device implanted under their skin between the thumb and pointer finger.[42] One employee at the company said he readily agreed to embed a microchip into his hand and was satisfied with the experience, as the chip allowed him to easily swipe into secure rooms, log into his computer, and use vending machines. The RFID technology was approved by the Food and Drug Administration in 2004.[43]

Lastly, Hitachi created a device affixed to a lanyard called the Business Microscope.[44] Acting as an advanced employee security badge, the Business Microscope is embedded with "infrared sensors, a microphone sensor, and a wireless communication device," which allow for monitoring of how and when office workers interact with each other by recognizing when two employees wearing the badges are within a certain distance of each other and recording face time and behavioral data.[45] The device tracks everything by sending information to management about how often an employee walks around the office, when they stop to talk to co-workers, and whether they contribute at meetings. The company has provided information regarding the device's capability to detect "who talks to whom, how often, where, and how energetically,"[46] which can provide a better understanding of how frequently different departments interact and improves organizational communication and quantitative evaluation of efficacy, but it has not offered examples of how the device is actually used. Since the Business Microscope was first developed in 2007, Hitachi has collected "over one million days of human behavior and big data."[47]

---

[40] See Holmes, "Wearable Technology within the Workplace."

[41] See Brummond and Thornton, "The Legal Side of Jobsite Technology."

[42] See Miller, "More Companies Are Using Technology to Monitor Employees, Sparking Privacy Concerns." See also Yeginsu, "If Workers Slack Off, the Wristband Will Know."

[43] Miller, "More Companies Are Using Technology to Monitor Employees, Sparking Privacy Concerns."

[44] See Turner, "Are Performance-Monitoring Wearables an Affront to Workers' Rights?"

[45] See Elizabeth A. Brown, "The Fitbit Fault Line: Two Proposals to Protect Health and Fitness Data at Work," *Yale Journal of Health Policy, Law & Ethics* 16, no. 1 (2016): 14.

[46] See Bob Greene, "How Your Boss Can Keep You on a Leash," CNN, Feb. 2, 2014, https://edition.cnn .com/2014/02/02/opinion/greene-corporate-surveillance/index.html?no-st=1529052429.

[47] See Greene, "How Your Boss Can Keep You on a Leash"; Turner, "Are Performance-Monitoring Wearables an Affront to Workers' Rights?"

9.3.4 *Exoskeletons*

In addition to these relatively small wearable devices, exoskeletons, or wearable robotics, are "bionic suits that use springs and counterweights to enhance human power and protect from injuries associated with heavy lifting and repetitive movements."[48] They are comprised of robotics and computers, or "more specifically, motors and sensors and software and novel algorithms that combine the former."[49] Because the most experienced construction workers are in their forties and fifties,[50] and construction work can be strenuous, the use of exoskeletons can benefit both workers and the industry by reducing the physical impact of such work. Ekso Bionics created the Ekso Works Industrial Exoskeleton, which lets a person lift heavy tools as if they weighed nothing at all.[51] Exoskeletons are also suited to help those who have restricted mobility because of paralysis or weakened limbs by allowing them to move in a more sustained way or walk despite spinal injuries. Exoskeletons in the workplace can thus prevent work-related musculoskeletal ailments and improve productivity by reducing absences due to illness and disability, even though they may cause some ethical concerns about dehumanization.[52]

Exoskeletons may also collect user data, such as "location information, usage information, neural input information, vitals data and other private information relating to the user," so that it can be used for product feedback or medical necessity.[53] For example, DARPA's exoskeleton, which is designed to be strong and pro-active, helps the wearer know the precise location and movements of their colleagues, detect and interpret sounds, communicate wirelessly, and monitor their mood as well as mental and physical conditions.[54]

9.3.5 *International Examples of Workplace Wearable Technology*

The expansion of wearable technology into the workplace is not limited to the United States. For instance, Tesco, a British multinational grocery and merchandise

---

[48] JLL, "Wearable Tech: The New Tool for the Modern Construction Workforce," Jones Lang LaSalle: Trends & Insights, Apr. 24, 2017, www.us.jll.com/en/trends-and-insights/workplace/wearable-tech-the-new-tool-for-the-modern-construction-workforce. See also Holmes, "Wearable Technology within the Workplace"; Dov Greenbaum, "Ethical, Legal and Social Concerns Relating to Exoskeletons," *SIGCAS Computers & Society* 45, no. 3 (2015): 234–39.

[49] Greenbaum, "Ethical, Legal and Social Concerns Relating to Exoskeletons," 234.

[50] See Holmes, "Wearable Technology within the Workplace."

[51] See Adam Rogers, "We Try a New Exoskeleton for Construction Workers," *Wired*, Apr. 28, 2015, www.wired.com/2015/04/try-new-exoskeleton-construction-workers/.

[52] Greenbaum, "Ethical, Legal and Social Concerns Relating to Exoskeletons," 234, 236; Isabelle Wildhaber, "The Robots Are Coming: Legalities in the Workplace," *HR Magazine*, June 20, 2016, www.hrmagazine.co.uk/article-details/the-robots-are-coming-legalities-in-the-workplace.

[53] Greenbaum, "Ethical, Legal and Social Concerns Relating to Exoskeletons," 239.

[54] See Ana Viseu, "Simulation and Augmentation: Issues of Wearable Computers," *Ethics & Information Technology* 5, no. 1 (2003): 22.

retailer, has adopted location-tracking wrist computers similar to Amazon's patents for haptic wristbands.[55] It required its workers at a distribution center in Ireland to wear the armbands, officially named Motorola arm-mounted terminals.[56] The band tracked the goods workers gathered; reduced the time spent marking clipboards; and allowed the employers to measure employee productivity by providing data points on the workers' loading, unloading, and scanning speeds.[57] It also allocated tasks to the wearer, forecasted their completion time, and quantified the worker's movements through the facility to provide analytical feedback, verifying the correct order or alerting a worker who performs below expectations. Except for the workers' lunch breaks, any distribution center worker's non-work activity, including the time going to the bathroom or the water fountain, was tracked and marked as decreasing the workers' productivity score.[58]

Moreover, companies are expected to adopt more of these types of wearable devices that improve efficiency by reducing the sequence of movements. According to "Wearables in the Workplace" by H. James Wilson, emerging wearables, most notably Google Glass, will replace the process required to check smartphones for work with simple gestures that take much less time. In addition, Microsoft is developing armbands that project keyboards and displays onto wearers' wrists. Other early prototypes are based on a predictive feedback system of the wearer's movements.[59] Of particular interest to labor scholars may be the implications of XOEye, DAQRI, and their cousins shifting dangerous jobs to untrained, inexperienced, or unskilled workers.

9.4 EMPLOYEE CONCERNS WITH WEARABLE TECH

Although wearable devices can contribute to business productivity, these devices also raise new legal issues.[60] The privacy of the worker is a primary concern, given

---

[55] See Aviva Rutkin, "Wearable Tech Lets Boss Track Your Work, Rest and Play," *New Scientist*, Oct. 15, 2014, www.newscientist.com/article/mg22429913-000-wearabletech-lets-boss-track-your-work-rest-and-play/.

[56] Fort, Raymond, and Shackelford, "The Angel on Your Shoulder," 144; Claire Suddath, "Tesco Monitors Employees with Motorola Armbands," *Bloomberg*, Feb. 13, 2013, www.bloomberg.com/news/articles/2013-02-13/tesco-monitors-employees-with-motorola-armbands.

[57] See Scott R. Peppet, "Regulating the Internet of Things: First Steps toward Managing Discrimination, Privacy, Security, and Consent," *Texas Law Review* 93, no. (2014): 114. See also Suddath, "Tesco Monitors Employees with Motorola Armbands."

[58] See Wilson, "Wearables in the Workplace"; Suddath, "Tesco Monitors Employees with Motorola Armbands."

[59] See Wilson, "Wearables in the Workplace."

[60] See Wilson, "Wearables in the Workplace." See also Suddath, "Tesco Monitors Employees with Motorola Armbands" (from 2007 to 2012, the average number of full-time employees in a Tesco superstore fell nearly 18 percent); Turner, "Are Performance-Monitoring Wearables an Affront to Workers' Rights?" (according to a Rackspace study, workers who integrate wearable technology are 8.5 percent more productive and 3.5 percent more satisfied, and management can get insight about human labor through worker data.).

that these devices are worn in close proximity to the body.[61] In addition, wearable technology may pose challenges to traditional privacy practices and principles such as the Fair Information Practice Principles, which are guidelines concerning fair information practice in an electronic marketplace and for the Internet of Things.[62] Wearable tech may also create opportunities for unlawful discrimination, particularly with regard to the sensitive health information they collect. Furthermore, the data collected by wearable tech may come to play an outsize role in workers' compensation cases.

9.4.1 *Privacy Concerns*

The basic privacy principles include collection limitation, purpose specification, use limitation, accountability, security, notice, choice, and data minimization.[63] As many wearable devices lack input mechanisms and extensively collect, store, and transmit personal data on a cloud, they are at a high risk of challenging basic privacy principles. For example, screenless devices may generate a great amount of invisible data, thus straining the limits of notice and consent.[64]

Furthermore, because of the greater potential for employer surveillance posed by wearables, there is a possibility that the National Labor Relations Act (NLRA) will be challenged. The National Labor Relations Board holds that an employer engages in unlawful surveillance "when it surveils employees engaged in Section 7 activity by observing them in a way that is 'out of the ordinary' and therefore coercive."[65] Since it is difficult for employees to reject using wearable devices in the

---

[61] Janice Phaik Lin Goh, "Privacy, Security, and Wearable Technology," *Landslide* 8, no. (Nov./Dec. 2015): 30, www.americanbar.org/groups/intellectual_property_law/publications/landslide/2015-16/november-december/.

[62] See OECD, "OECD Guidelines Governing the Protection of Privacy and Transborder Flows of Personal Data," 2013, 70–71, www.oecd.org/sti/ieconomy/oecdguidelinesontheprotectionofprivacyandtransborderflowsofpersonaldata.htm; Phaik Lin Goh, "Privacy, Security, and Wearable Technology," 30–31; Christopher Wolf, Jules Polonetsky, and Kelsey Finch, "A Practical Privacy Paradigm for Wearables," Future of Privacy Forum, Jan. 8, 2015, 4, https://fpf.org/wp-content/uploads/FPF-principles-for-wearables-Jan-2015.pdf.

[63] See OECD, "OECD Guidelines," 70–71. See also Phaik Lin Goh, "Privacy, Security, and Wearable Technology," 31; Wolf, Polonetsky, and Finch, "A Practical Privacy Paradigm for Wearables," 4.

[64] See Peppet, "Regulating the Internet of Things," 117. See also Phaik Lin Goh, "Privacy, Security, and Wearable Technology," 32.

[65] Aladdin Gaming, LLC, 345 N.L.R.B. 585, 585–86 (2005), petition for review denied, 515 F.3d 942, 947 (9th Cir. 2008); Clement L. Tsao, Kevin J. Haskins, and Brian D. Hall, "The Rise of Wearable and Smart Technology in the Workplace," Paper presented at the ABA National Symposium on Technology in Labor and Employment, Apr. 5–7, 2017, p. 1; National Labor Relations Act, 29 U.S.C. §157 (2012) (providing that "[e]mployees shall have the right to self-organization, to form, join, or assist labor organizations, to bargain collectively through representatives of their own choosing, and to engage in other concerted activities for the purpose of collective bargaining or other mutual aid or protection.").

employment relationship[66] and employers have the ability to track each employee's precise location and physiological activity, wearable technology could have a chilling effect on protected concerted activity under the NLRA.[67]

However, despite these concerns about privacy for employees' personal information, case law has demonstrated that the law is unlikely to effectively protect employees from privacy intrusions via wearable technology.[68] The Electronic Communications Privacy Act and the Stored Communications Act prohibit the "intentional interception, access and disclosure of wire, oral or electronic communications and data" but contain employer-centric exceptions.[69] Also, legal protection of privacy is weak. While some laws may aim to protect unsuspecting employees or unauthorized gathering of information, case law has shown that few protections exist when an employee consents to information gathering and use within the scope of their employment. The law "generally does not protect employees ... from information that is willingly shared and/or information that is gathered after consent is provided."[70] Regarding this, some states, including California and Texas, have laws protecting employees from equipment tracking without express consent, and the proposal of the Location Privacy Protection Act and other similar bills like the Geolocation Privacy and Surveillance Act (GPS Act) demonstrate that lawmakers are increasingly concerned about location information.[71]

In *United States v. Simons*, the court held that an employee does not have a reasonable expectation of privacy regarding their use of the internet when the employer has policies about internet use. Because the employer's privacy policy in this case stated that it would "audit, inspect, and/or monitor" employees' use of the internet, the employee was found not to have an objectively reasonable expectation of privacy.[72] This conclusion was based on the Supreme Court case of *O'Connor v. Ortega*, in which the Court found that the employee's reasonable expectation of privacy should be analyzed in the employment relationship context.[73] Also, *Seff v. Broward County* shows that the Americans with Disabilities Act (ADA) will not limit employers from requiring employees to submit health and fitness data as part of establishing a "bona fide benefit plan."[74]

---

[66] Adam D. Moore explains that the consent takes the following form: If an employment is to continue, then an employee must agree to such-and-so kinds of surveillance. Moore calls this "thin consent" because it is assumed that jobs are hard to find and the employee needs the job. See Adam D. Moore, "Employee Monitoring and Computer Technology: Evaluative Surveillance v. Privacy," *Business Ethics Quarterly* 10, no. 3 (2000): 701.

[67] See Tsao, Haskins, and Hall, "The Rise of Wearable and Smart Technology in the Workplace," 1.

[68] Phaik Lin Goh, "Privacy, Security, and Wearable Technology," 32.

[69] See Brummond and Thornton, "The Legal Side of Jobsite Technology."

[70] Fort, Raymond, and Shackelford, "The Angel on Your Shoulder," 145, 166.

[71] Cal. Penal Code § 637.7 (West 2018); Tex. Penal Code Ann. § 16.06 (West 2018); Phaik Lin Goh, "Privacy, Security, and Wearable Technology," 33.

[72] 206 F.3d 392, 398 (4th Cir. 2000).

[73] 480 U.S. 709, 717 (1987).

[74] 691 F.3d 1221, 1224 (11th Cir. 2012) (in this case, the employer's wellness program was a term of the county's benefit plan); Brown, "The Fitbit Fault Line," 28.

9.4.2 *Potential for Discrimination*

Wearable technologies can present opportunities for unlawful discrimination on several axes. Another legal issue concerning wearable technology is the potential for discriminatory employer actions in contravention of the ADA and the guidelines of the Equal Employment Opportunity Commission. The ADA prohibits discrimination against a qualified individual in regard to employment on the basis of disability[75] and also prohibits employers from administering medical examinations[76] and other disability inquiries[77] to employees unless the examination or inquiry is job related and consistent with business necessity.[78]

Wearable devices present cause for concern because they are very adept at tracking health data and providing a picture of an employee's health.[79] Managers prohibited from conducting medical examinations on employees can have access to physical data, including health and disability information, about the workers, regardless of the employer's intentions.[80] For example, devices that read heart rates reveal potential medical information.[81] Any employees who might not be reaching productivity standards due to a medical condition or disability could be discriminated against;[82] bosses could potentially abuse the power to monitor by targeting populations of a certain gender, race, or age disproportionally;[83] and it would be very easy for employers to gain access to employees' personal data and use that data without consent in promotion and retention decisions.[84] Furthermore, as some scholars have noted, corporate wellness programs may lead employers to consider data outside work hours, such as sleep patterns or dietary habits, when determining

---

[75] Americans with Disabilities Act, 42 U.S.C. § 12112(a) (2012).

[76] The EEOC's enforcement guidance states that a "medical examination" is any procedure or test "that seeks information about an individual's physical or mental impairments or health." See EEOC, "Enforcement Guidance on Disability-Related Inquiries."

[77] EEOC, "Enforcement Guidance on Disability-Related Inquiries" (stating that a "disability-related inquiry" is a question that "is likely to elicit information about a disability").

[78] Americans with Disabilities Act, 42 U.S.C. § 12112(d)(4)(A) (2012). See also Kevin J. Haskins, "Wearable Technology and Implications for the Americans with Disabilities Act, Genetic Information Nondiscrimination Act, and Health Privacy," ABA *Journal of Labor & Employment Law* 33, no. 1 (2017): 70.

[79] Haskins, "Wearable Technology and Implications for the Americans with Disabilities Act."

[80] See Patience Haggin, "As Wearables in Workplace Spread, So Do Legal Concerns," *Wall Street Journal*, Mar. 13, 2016 ("[I]f a warehouse employee does poorly on tracked activity measures on the job, the employer might need to consider whether the data could indicate a physical disability that would require the employer to make a reasonable accommodation"). See also Haskins, "Wearable Technology and Implications for the Americans with Disabilities Act," 70.

[81] See Turner, "Are Performance-Monitoring Wearables an Affront to Workers' Rights?"

[82] See Haskins, "Wearable Technology and Implications for the Americans with Disabilities Act," 74. See also Turner, "Are Performance-Monitoring Wearables an Affront to Workers' Rights?"; Haggin, "As Wearables in Workplace Spread, So Do Legal Concerns."

[83] See Turner, "Are Performance-Monitoring Wearables an Affront to Workers' Rights?"

[84] See Fort, Raymond, and Shackelford, "The Angel on Your Shoulder," 158.

employee benefits or compensation, potentially discriminating against employees by relying on data entirely outside of the conventional workplace.[85]

Wearable devices such as exoskeletons also have implications for the ADA. The ADA requires employers to provide reasonable accommodations,[86] including acquisition or modification of equipment or devices, to qualified employees with disabilities, unless doing so would pose an undue hardship to the business.[87] Because exoskeletons, unlike other wearable devices discussed above, can be considered a mitigating measure, which is an element that "eliminates or reduces the symptoms or impact of an impairment,"[88] employees using exoskeletons may not be regarded as having a disability. Therefore, there is a concern about defining an employee as disabled and providing reasonable accommodation because while employers cannot ignore the fact that a person is disabled because they use an exoskeleton, they cannot force an employee to use an exoskeleton. It is also unclear whether compensation may be different for employees who use exoskeletons and for those who do not.[89]

Wearable technology that collects employees' health-related information can also implicate the Health Insurance Portability and Accountability Act (HIPAA), which establishes national standards for protecting individually identifiable health information, or protected health information (PHI). However, HIPAA applies to the PHI of "covered entities" and their business associates,[90] and since employees with wearable devices and their employers are not considered "covered entities," such employees are not subject to HIPAA.[91]

9.4.3 *Worker Safety and Workers' Compensation*

Wearable technology such as bionic suits, exoskeletons, and helmets can improve worker performance and safety while also allowing employers to promote biometric analysis beyond mere health and wellness.[92] Better safety and employee performance also lead to reductions in workers' compensation program costs for employers and higher profit margins.[93] Mathiason et al., in a Littler Report on AI

---

[85] Alexander H. Tran, "Note: The Internet of Things and Potential Remedies in Privacy Tort Law," *Columbia Journal of Law and Social Problems* 50, no. 2 (2017): 273.

[86] Americans with Disabilities Act, 42 U.S.C. § 12112(b)(5)(A) (2012); 42 U.S.C. § 12111(9)(b) (2012).

[87] Americans with Disabilities Act, 42 U.S.C. § 12111(10) (2012).

[88] EEOC, "Questions and Answers on the Final Rule Implementing the ADA Amendments Act of 2008."

[89] Greenbaum, "Ethical, Legal and Social Concerns Relating to Exoskeletons," 237–39.

[90] See 45 C.F.R. §160.103 (2014); 45 C.F.R. §162.923 (2012); 45 C.F.R. §164.306 (2013).

[91] See 45 C.F.R. § 160.103 (2014). See also Haskins, "Wearable Technology and Implications for the Americans with Disabilities Act," 76; Phaik Lin Goh, "Privacy, Security, and Wearable Technology," 32–33.

[92] See Michael B. Stack, "Wearable Technology in Workers' Compensation," *Amaxx*, Jul. 27, 2017, http://blog.reduceyourworkerscomp.com/2017/07/wearable-technology-workers-compensation/.

[93] See Garry Mathiason et al., *The Transformation of the Workplace through Robotic Artificial Intelligence, and Automation*, Littler Report, Aug. 4, 2016, § 3.1 ("For example, employers with thousands of

in the workplace, describe that this is realized in two ways: First, as robots replace works that are dangerous, strenuous, or repetitive, workers are likely to suffer less work-related injuries; and second, applications designed to assist workers in performing the physical requirements of their jobs will improve the ability of injured workers to return to work.[94]

Michael B. Stack, an expert in workers' compensation, explains that reduced workers' compensation costs for employers are made possible through real-time reporting of an employee's location; immediate reporting of an employee in distress, which allows summoning of emergency assistance; and measuring the force of impact for diagnosis and treatment of workplace injury.[95] As an example of real-time reporting, wearable technology can caution employees regarding their posture, thereby assisting employees performing sedentary work to make adjustments to reduce injury at the workstation.[96] One major corporation, Target, is using activity- and sleep-tracking devices to promote health habits for employees, and employers are showing greater interest in using wearable technology to prevent occupational injuries.[97] In addition, assistive wearable devices that help employees suffering from severe spinal cord injuries can provide information in relation to post-injury care, progress, and return-to-work issues that contribute to changes in workers' compensation.[98]

Furthermore, employers can use data from wearable devices to defend themselves against an employee's workers' compensation claim. For example, Fitbit "monitors sleep patterns, decides how many hours a user sleeps, and determines the quality and efficiency of that sleep" and a wearer can be compared to the "average" sleeper, so an employer could use that information as evidence of an employee's sleep deprivation at the time of an accident.[99]

---

employees report that reducing the lost-time period by only a few days can result in saving millions of dollars, both in terms of reductions in wage-loss benefits (i.e., 'indemnity' benefits) and medical costs."). See also Greenbaum, "Ethical, Legal and Social Concerns Relating to Exoskeletons," 239 (contending that workers' compensation for employees may be limited in part due to the use of exoskeletons in the workforce); John Rehm, "Exoskeletons and the Workplace," *Worker's Compensation Watch*, Dec. 7, 2015, https://workerscompensationwatch.com/2015/12/07/exoskeletons-and-the-work place/ (positing that the use of exoskeletons could result in fewer workers' compensation claims); Stack, "Wearable Technology in Workers' Compensation"; Turner, "Are Performance-Monitoring Wearables an Affront to Workers' Rights?"

94 See Mathiason et al., *The Transformation of the Workplace through Robotic Artificial Intelligence, and Automation*, § 3.1.

95 See Stack, "Wearable Technology in Workers' Compensation." See also Van den Bossche et al., "Wearable Technology in the Warehouse" ("Employee biometrics could be monitored to identify which operations or situations cause excessive exertion on an operator that could result in future injury").

96 See Stack, "Wearable Technology in Workers' Compensation."

97 William Vogeler, "Technology Is Quickly Reshaping Workers' Compensation Claims," FindLaw: Blogs, Feb. 24, 2017, https://blogs.findlaw.com/technologist/2017/02/technology-is-quickly-reshaping-workers-compensation-claims.html.

98 See Stack, "Wearable Technology in Workers' Compensation."

99 Antigone Peyton, "A Litigator's Guide to the Internet of Things," *Richmond Journal of Law & Technology* 22, no. 3 (2016): 9, 20.

Although no specific lawsuit was found regarding workers' compensation for workplace injury caused by wearable technology, there have been reports of a Canadian law firm – cited by several law reviews and news articles – that used evidence collected by a wearable device in a personal injury case.[100] It is the first known personal injury case in which the plaintiff used activity data from a Fitbit to show the effects of an accident in a legal proceeding.[101] The plaintiff was apparently injured in 2010 and sought to use the Fitbit data in November 2014.[102] The plaintiff was injured when she was working as a personal fitness trainer, and she attempted to use her Fitbit data as evidence of her diminished physical activity resulting from a work-related injury.[103] With the help of an analytic company called Vivametrica that prepared analytical reports from aggregated Fitbit data and a law firm in Calgary, she aimed to show that her "post-injury activity levels were lower than the baseline for someone of the same age and profession."[104] Although not an employment law case, this shows that information from wearable devices could be used as evidence in litigation[105] and could also help to support or disprove disability discrimination, workers' compensation, and harassment claims.[106] It is important to note that prior to the Americans with Disabilities Act Amendments Act (ADAA) becoming law, employers could "account for the ameliorative effects of efforts that employees have undertaken to lessen the negative effect of their conditions when determining whether they were substantially limited in a major life activity …" But passage of the ADAA "changed this paradigm by [defining] an individual's disability without reference to any but the most rudimentary ameliorative measures."[107]

---

[100] See Antigone Peyton, "The Connected State of Things: A Lawyer's Survival Guide in an Internet of Things World," *Catholic University Journal of Labor & Technology* 24, no. 2 (2016): 369, 391. See also Claims and Litigation Management (CLM), "Rise of the Machines: Can and Should Your Fitness Tracker Be Used against You in a Court of Law?" (2017); Kate Crawford, "When Fitbit Is the Expert Witness," *The Atlantic*, Nov. 19, 2014; Parmy Olson, "Fitbit Data Now Being Used in the Courtroom," *Forbes*, Nov. 16, 2014; Turner, "Are Performance-Monitoring Wearables an Affront to Workers' Rights?"

[101] See Peyton, "The Connected State of Things," 391; CLM, "Rise of the Machines," 6.

[102] CLM, "Rise of the Machines," 6.

[103] Peyton, "The Connected State of Things," 391.

[104] Peyton, "The Connected State of Things." See also Crawford, "When Fitbit Is the Expert Witness"; Olson, "Fitbit Data Now Being Used in the Courtroom."

[105] See Nicole Chauriye, "Note: Wearable Devices as Admissible Evidence: Technology Is Killing Our Opportunities to Lie," *Catholic University Journal of Law & Technology* 24, no. 2 (2016): 507, 509–11 (discussing *Commonwealth v. Risley*, a non-employment case in which Fitbit data was used in the courtroom, and the Fitbit data contradicted the statements of an alleged victim). See also Peyton, "The Connected State of Things," 391; CLM, "Rise of the Machines," 6.

[106] See Karla Grossenbacher and Selyn Hong, "Wearable Device Data in Employment Litigation," *Seyfarth Shaw: Employment Law Lookout*, Sept. 29, 2016, www.laborandemploymentlawcounsel .com/2016/09/wearable-device-data-in-employment-litigation/.

[107] Gregory A. Hearing and Marquis W. Heilig, "Recent Developments in Employment Law and Litigation," *Tort Trial & Insurance Practice Law Journal* 45, no. 2 (2010): 322. ("Specifically, the ADAA notes that a vision impairment, properly remedied by eyeglasses or contact lenses, is not a disability.").

Although wearable devices could reduce workers' compensation costs by using the data they collect, employers must also consider the injuries that wearable devices may cause. Wearable products with a heads-up display, such as the DAQRI helmet or Google Glass, are of particular concern because employees may be distracted by images on the displays while operating or driving heavy equipment at workplaces such as construction sites.[108] In addition, robots or exoskeletons that are incompatible with the human body or poorly designed or implemented could damage muscles, tendons, and nerves, especially when performing repetitive tasks.[109] Exoskeletons could also negatively impact workers, particularly those with pre-existing conditions such as chronic obstructive pulmonary disease, because wearing such a device may increase chest pressure.[110] Lawyers explain that workers' compensation and other claims could be brought against employers in the event of an accident involving such devices and advise that employers who intend to implement these wearable devices should consider adjusting their policies and protocols to limit their liability.[111]

9.4.4 *Reasonable Expectation of Privacy for Employees*

A reasonable expectation of privacy is the fulcrum on which employee monitoring cases turn. One problem is that while a reasonable expectation of privacy is well defined for Fourth Amendment cases, it is not as defined within the employment context, and some scholars have argued that workplaces operate as "private governments," with employers exercising near dictatorial power over what privacy rights may be granted to workers.[112] While *Katz v. United States* was the case that introduced the term *reasonable expectation*,[113] that term has been defined as "an objective entitlement founded on broadly based and widely accepted community norms,"[114] and courts have recognized that, in the private sphere, lack

---

[108] See Brummond and Thornton, "The Legal Side of Jobsite Technology."

[109] See Mathiason et al., *The Transformation of the Workplace through Robotic Artificial Intelligence, and Automation*, § 3.1.

[110] Alissa Zingman et al., "Exoskeletons in Construction: Will They Reduce or Create Hazards?" CDC: NIOSH Science Blog, June 15, 2017, https://blogs.cdc.gov/niosh-science-blog/2017/06/15/exoskeletons-in-construction/.

[111] See Mathiason et al., *The Transformation of the Workplace through Robotic Artificial Intelligence, and Automation*, § 3.1 (stating that when determining eligibility for workers' compensation, injuries caused by robots will be treated the same as injuries caused by using other tools used in the workplace such as hammers or computer keyboards). See also Brummond and Thornton, "The Legal Side of Jobsite Technology" (suggesting that employers consider revising their safety policies and protocols).

[112] See Anderson, *Private Government*, 38–39, 41.

[113] 389 U.S. 347, 360 (1967) (Harlan, J., concurring) (note that this case involved government action, and non-governmental employers are not subject to Fourth Amendment restrictions that would be afforded to government employees).

[114] *Gonzales v. Uber Techs., Inc.*, 305 F. Supp.3d 1078, 1091 (N.D. Cal. 2018) (quoting *Hill v. Nat'l Collegiate Athletic Ass'n.*, 865 P.2d 633, 655 (Cal. 1994)).

of notice and consent typically support employees' invasion of privacy claims.[115] Yet, courts have also found that employees do not have a reasonable expectation of privacy when employer-owned equipment or technology is involved, the employer has a legitimate business interest, and the intrusion occurs during normal work hours.[116]

Emerging technologies and their advanced data collection functions challenge the notion that a "reasonable expectation of privacy" continues to hold any well-settled definition. This is especially true for devices such as wearable technologies that continue to collect data even during off-work hours. Consider the 2018 Supreme Court case *Carpenter v. United States*, in which the Court held that accessing cell phone location data without a warrant was a violation of the Fourth Amendment.[117] Although some might argue that any precedents from the *Carpenter* case should be constrained to the Fourth Amendment, the Ninth Circuit reasoned, in *O'Connor v. Ortega*, that the employee's reasonable expectation of privacy should be analyzed in the employment-relationship context.[118] This means that as employees are obliged to interact with emerging technologies in the workplace, which by their operation collect employee data – sometimes without affirmative consent – the question of what constitutes or should constitute a reasonable expectation of privacy for employees remains an important one for legal scholars.

9.5 DATA OWNERSHIP AND CONTROL

The emerging technologies of productivity applications and wearable technology also raise legal questions about the collection and control of employee data. Compounding the problems with data generated by wearable technology at work is the fact that there are no real federal laws to limit the collection of data that is not facially related to the protected category. As my co-authors and I explained in a 2018 article, the applicability of various federal statutes in the context of surveillance is extremely narrow.[119] This gives employers broad license to monitor employees. Furthermore, the sheer volume of data that can legally be obtained from and about employees could make data-generated evidence seem especially persuasive, enhancing biases that may already exist.

---

[115] Matthew E. Swaya and Stacey R. Eisenstein. "Emerging Technology in the Workplace." *Labor Lawyer* 21, no. 1 (2005): 13.

[116] Tsao, Haskins, and Hall, "The Rise of Wearable and Smart Technology in the Workplace," 3. See also *Thygeson v. U.S. Bancorp.*, No. CV–03–467–ST, 2004 WL 2066746, at *21 (D. Or. Sept. 15, 2004) (finding no reasonable expectation of privacy when the employee used his employer's computer and network for personal use, saved personal information in a location that was accessible by his employer, and the employee handbook prohibited personal use of the employer's computer).

[117] 138 S. Ct. 2206, 2221, 2223 (2018).

[118] 280 U.S. 709, 717 (1987).

[119] Ifeoma Ajunwa, Jason Schultz, and Kate Crawford, "Limitless Worker Surveillance," *California Law Review* 105, no. 3 (2018): 748–57.

Workplace wellness programs enjoy the support of the federal government, but they can become a vehicle for the introduction of workplace wearable technologies and their monitoring functions. Employers could use data obtained from wellness programs to run predictive analytics of employee risk of injury. Thus, data from wearables not only will determine workers' compensation but could also influence which workers will remain employed. These risk assessments could include factors such as weight or whether a worker smokes cigarettes, and there would be no federal law to protect workers from that genre of discrimination.[120] Thus, via the use of wearable technology in wellness programs, employers can (absent relevant state laws) discriminate against workers using data that has been collected under the guise of helping employees achieve their personal health goals. Past research has also revealed that employee data collected as part of workplace wellness programs is frequently sold to third parties without the employee's knowledge or consent.[121]

The fight over employee data, however, will not only be about limits on what data can be collected and who controls that data. Rather, particularly for workers' compensation claims, there will also be legal grappling regarding the interpretation of the data. Legal scholars such as Scott R. Peppet ask whether consumers will accept "the possible use of [wearable technology data] by an adversary in court [or] an insurance company when denying a claim."[122] Just as Vivametrica was called upon in the Canadian case to compare personal Fitbit data to some baseline, an employer could compare data from the wearable device against a larger population. As one legal scholar notes, this raises two issues: (1) a comparison not specific to the person or their circumstances and (2) variance among data analysis methods (whether from an outside firm or engineered into the device itself).[123] Though some data may be viewed as admissible, the interpretation for said data might be contested. As the technologist Kate Crawford has noted, this could lead to wildly divergent results whereby someone differently situated from the general population is deemed responsible for their own injury because their patterns stray from a median, or where the use of a different algorithm produced different results. Thus, it seems critical to set the legal standard both for the admissibility of data for workers' compensation claims and for how such data will be interpreted.[124]

Accuracy of the data from wearable technology, however, remains an issue. Fitbit, in particular, has been the focus of class action lawsuits questioning the accuracy of

---

[120] Ajunwa, Crawford, and Schultz, "Limitless Worker Surveillance," 764–67.
[121] See Ifeoma Ajunwa, Kate Crawford, and Joel Ford, "Health and Big Data: An Ethical Framework for Health Information Collection by Corporate Wellness Programs," *Journal of Law, Medicine, and Ethics* 44, no. 3 (2016): 474–80.
[122] Peppet, "Regulating the Internet of Things," 89.
[123] Peyton, "The Connected State of Things," 392–93.
[124] Crawford, "When Fitbit Is the Expert Witness."

features such as sleep and heart rate monitoring.[125] These raise concerns for Fitbit data being introduced in court as evidence for or against workers' compensation claims. Data from wearable technologies may be made even less accurate if device users try to "game" their design flaws. Furthermore, data quality may be affected by the psychological effects of surveillance on workers. As demonstrated by a study, surveillance has the potential to make an individual nervous, which could then skew the data collected.[126] Thus, individuals with adverse results on metrics generated by wearable technology could be reflecting a discomfort with being surveilled. As such, the data wearable technology produces might be favorable to those who are comfortable being surveilled. Wearable data as part of court testimony is challenging because it may not be possible to interrogate the analytical processes behind the data, as those processes might be considered trade secrets.[127] Thus, a belief in data objectivity (the idea that data cannot "lie") goes unquestioned because the information is simply unavailable, though the decision-maker might have the requisite technological knowledge.[128]

Although one could argue that electronic data makes for an unreliable witness, keeping data from wearable devices out of litigation will be nearly impossible in the current legal landscape. As legally there is no expectation of privacy at work, employees cannot prevent data collected from work devices from being used in court. Employers may present wearable technology as a benefit to workers.[129] However, due to the risk of financial penalties to workers and the dearth of precise information, as well as the asymmetrical power relationship between workers and employers, workers may not have a true choice regarding whether to use those devices.[130]

9.6 WEARABLE TECH IN NEW INDUSTRIES: A CASE STUDY IN PROFESSIONAL ATHLETES

As wearable technology for the workplace has exploded over the past decade, so have the number of industries seeking to apply its uses to their own needs. Take, for example, the construction industry. As Terri H. Bui explains in "The Rise of Technology in the Construction Industry," RFID transmitters have been employed

---

[125] See *Brickman v. Fitbit, Inc.*, No. 3:15-cv-02077-JD, 2017 WL 6209307, at *1–3 (N.D. Cal. Dec. 8, 2017) (ongoing class action regarding sleep-tracking accuracy); see also *McLellan v. Fitbit, Inc.*, No. 3:16-cv-00036-JD, 2018 WL 2688781, at *1 (N.D. Cal. June 5, 2018) (ongoing class action regarding heart-rate-monitoring accuracy).

[126] Solon, "Wearable Technology Creeps into the Workplace?"

[127] Peyton, "The Connected State of Things," 398–99.

[128] Crawford, "When Fitbit Is the Expert Witness."

[129] See Ajunwa, Crawford, and Schultz, "Limitless Worker Surveillance," 748; Ajunwa, Crawford, and Ford, "Health and Big Data," 474–80.

[130] See Ajunwa, Crawford, and Ford, "Health and Big Data"; Ajunwa, "Workplace Wellness Programs Could Be Putting Your Health Data at Risk"; Peyton, "The Connected State of Things," 392; Eric Liberatore Unpublished Research Memo.

in wearable devices in order to "[collect] data during construction to increase safety and productivity, and reduce the risks commonly associated with construction." RFID and other cloud-based wearable technology is largely being integrated into forms of personal protective equipment (PPE) that workers already use, such as hard hats and gloves. Bui highlights possible data-based insights employers may glean from this integration. From a worksite management perspective, the technology "allows for closer supervision and monitoring of worksites, including geofencing, location trackers, and safety sensors," which reduces inefficiencies and error rates. From a health perspective, wearable tech may even be employed to reduce risk of workplace injuries by monitoring a worker's "vital signs … like respiration, tempera-ture, heart rate, and intoxication." Bui argues that, on the whole, "with the ability to now track, predict, and prevent injuries through RFID, worker safety is increasing tenfold."[131]

As uses for wearable technology have grown in the construction industry, they also have been growing in the world of sports. Professional sports offers an interest-ing case study on the impacts of wearable tech for both management and employees, as it is an industry marked by high salaries, national interest, and union presence, and employee health directly impacts job performance. As such, since 2019, several legal scholars have taken an interest in the intersection of wearable tech and the legal and privacy concerns of professional athletes. As Anthony Studnicka explains in his article "The Emergence of Wearable Technology and the Legal Implications for Athletes, Teams, Leagues and Other Sports Organizations across Amateur and Professional Athletics," wearable technology in professional sports has been around since 2009, when it was introduced by a European soccer club that monitored player biometrics to understand "the overall workload of players during games." In the present day, wearable technology for athletes takes many forms – from special fabrics to body attachments and smart patches – with the general intent to "help keep athletes safe and healthy." However, Studnicka notes that proliferation of this wearable technology, which collects significant health and performance data, has raised "privacy, medical, contractual, and even gambling issues and concerns" stemming from data ownership.[132] Studnicka emphasizes the need for entities to ensure that data they collect is secure and the importance of regulatory clarity over how collected data is classified; for example, classifying data as "trade secret[s]" as opposed to mere "statistic[s]" would afford both players and consumers greater protection under the law. Ultimately, Studnicka proposes federal legislation to regu-late the growing field of wearable tech, yet argues that such legislation should be

---

[131] Terri H. Bui, "The Rise of Technology in the Construction Industry," *Orange County Lawyer* 61 (Sept. 2019): 38.

[132] Anthony Studnicka, "The Emergence of Wearable Technology and the Legal Implications for Athletes, Teams, Leagues and Other Sports Organizations across Amateur and Professional Athletics," *DePaul Journal of Sports Law* 16, no. 1 (2020): 196–97.

aimed at protecting athletes at the college, high school, and youth levels. Because many professional athletes are already protected by unions, Studnicka believes that "collective bargaining agreements are where it would be most appropriate for these current wearable technology concerns to be addressed."[133]

Sarah M. Brown and Natasha T. Brison, like Studnicka, note that some player unions have already added provisions to their collective bargaining agreements (CBAs) that govern the use of wearable tech. In "Big Data, Big Problems: Analysis of Professional Sports Leagues' CBAs and Their Handling of Athlete Biometric Data," Brown and Brison offer an analysis of "the CBAs of the NFL, NBA, MLB, NHL, and MLS management of wearables and ABD [athletes' biometric data]." Brown and Brison highlight the significance of protecting ABD, as "[w]earable technology enables access to intimate, sensitive data, particularly an athlete's physiological analytics, and without clear delineation of ownership and the athlete's ability to restrict others' access, an athlete's privacy is at risk because the athlete has no control over the data."[134] As sources of legal protection, Brown and Brison suggest that the Genetic Information Nondiscrimination Act (GINA) and HIPAA may govern some ABD, but there are significant loopholes: Wearable tech does not currently collect genetic information as defined under GINA, and it is not clear that ABD falls under HIPAA protection or that HIPAA governs professional sports teams at all. As of 2020, only "three states have enacted statutes aimed at protecting individuals' right to privacy as it relates to their biometric data."[135] Given potentially limited protection under the law, CBA provisions for wearable tech are thus critical to protecting athletes' privacy interests. Brown and Brison offer a comparison of the five major sports unions' CBAs, assessing "each league's controlling provisions for wearables or ABD collection by breaking the language out into eight categories: (1) management, (2) use, (3) ownership, (4) privacy, (5) access, (6) security, (7) commercial use, and (8) definition." At the time of Brown and Brison's writing, only the MLB and NBA directly "[discussed] wearable technology at length in [their] current CBA[s]," only the MLB addressed whether wearable data is private (though the MLS features a blanket statement that all "performance measures" may be made public), and no CBA touched the issue of data ownership.[136] Significantly, according to legal scholar Skyler Berman, the NFL has since passed a new CBA (in March 2020) that directly addresses ABD and wearable technology. However, under this new CBA, biometric data "ownership is not guaranteed and only subject to rights set forth in the NFL Player Contracts."[137]

---

[133] Studnicka, "The Emergence of Wearable Technology and the Legal Implications," 211, 213, 214.
[134] Sarah M. Brown and Natasha T. Brison, "Big Data, Big Problems: Analysis of Professional Sports Leagues' CBAs and Their Handling of Athlete Biometric Data," *Journal of the Legal Aspects of Sport* 42, no. 1 (2020): 63, 65.
[135] Brown and Brison, "Big Data, Big Problems," 66–67.
[136] Brown and Brison, "Big Data, Big Problems," 69–77.
[137] Skyler R. Berman, "Bargaining over Biometrics: How Player Unions Should Protect Athletes in the Age of Wearable Technology," *Brooklyn Law Review* 85, no. 2 (2020): 558.

While Studnicka emphasized that professional sports CBAs *may* offer adequate protection related to issues of athlete wearable data privacy, it is evident based on Brison and Brown's analysis that most currently do not. Brison and Brown suggest a federal statute to "manage ABD collection" for all athletes, which would include "(i) a broad definition for ABD, (ii) classify[ing] ABD as confidential and sensitive, (iii) consideration of the potential risks related to ABD, and (iv) significant fines for noncompliance." As no such law currently exists, however, Brown and Brison emphasize that "each league's players' association should negotiate athlete ownership of ABD to help lessen risk of issues around privacy and commercialization of data." Brown and Brison pose that data ownership is essential to bargaining power and autonomy, allowing athletes to "be the decision-maker for how and if their ABD is commercialized."[138] Analyzing the rights, interests, and state of professional sports CBAs through the lens of wearable tech, Berman comes to a similar conclusion in his recent article "Bargaining over Biometrics: How Player Unions Should Protect Athletes in the Age of Wearable Technology." Berman outlines the inadequacies of existing federal and state laws as sources of athlete privacy protection, and suggests that professional sports organizations position collective bargaining "as the centerpiece tool" to address issues of "biometric data collection and the use of new technologies in surveillance." Berman's proposal "advocate[s] for a players' bill of rights and data ownership structure that is negotiated by the Players Association into league CBAs to ensure that athlete biometric data is protected."[139]

Across the board, it seems legal scholars agree that existing federal and state laws generally offer inadequate protection for employees concerning data insights gleaned from wearable technology. As this new form of invasive surveillance becomes commonplace, professional sports organizations may seek refuge in union protections afforded by their CBAs. Unfortunately, unionism is in a great decline across the country as a whole.[140] As such, many workers face little to no legal protections as wearable technology erodes their autonomy and right to privacy.

9.7 IMPACT OF WEARABLE TECH ON EMPLOYEES

As wearable technology grows as a class to include new forms and new fields of use, so the potential for abuse and misuse at the expense of employees grow with it. In "A Healthy Mistrust: Curbing Biometric Data Misuse in the Workplace," legal scholar Elizabeth A. Brown explores how employers are collecting employees' health data at "skyrocketing rates," thanks to innovations such as wearables, and the consequences of data misuse. Concerning wearables in particular, Brown states

---

[138] Brown and Brison, "Big Data, Big Problems," 78–80.
[139] Berman, "Bargaining over Biometrics," 563, 546.
[140] See Eli Rosenberg, "Workers Are Fired Up. But Union Participation Is Still on the Decline, New Statistics Show," *Washington Post*, Jan. 23, 2020.

that in 2018, "the global market for wearable technology grew nearly 30%." While wearables like the Apple Watch and Omron Heartguide are available to the public at large, many wearables companies – such as Fitbit – "are now catering more expressly to [employer] needs." Fitbit in particular offers a "Fitbit Care division" dedicated to corporate health, providing employees with wearables and incentives to use them, and employers with detailed data on employee use at both the "individual and group" levels. Other wearables specifically targeted towards data collection from women, such as the Owlet band, which "track[s] the wellbeing of fetuses," may exacerbate regular discrimination on the basis of sex.[141] Such wearables, alongside workplace wellness programs that encourage employees to engage in biometric data collection, the normalization of providing biometric data to third parties, the rise of personalized medicine, and incentives from health insurers and data aggregators to glean insights and lower costs, provide employers with increasingly detailed, personal data that is ripe for misuse under the current regulatory regime.[142]

Employer misuse of biometric data, facilitated by the factors discussed above, may result in "consequences [that] range from adverse employment decisions based on monitored data to inaccurate assessment of workers, resulting in a workforce that is decreasingly diverse, inclusive and effective." Brown further argues that such misuse may run rampant given the lack of protection existing laws provide: Antidiscrimination laws do little to protect against "adverse employment action[s] on the basis of [biometric data derived insights]," HIPAA does not cover wearable technology companies and therefore the data they collect, and other privacy laws that don't specifically govern health data "are similarly unhelpful."[143] Brown proposes bolstering health privacy laws, creating new data privacy laws that extend to employees, and divesting health insurance coverage from the employer–employee relationship as potential solutions to "curb employer misuse of biometric data."[144] However, as the current legal regime stands, workers remain vulnerable to wearables collecting and sharing their biometric data with little recourse.

Another potential issue with the use of wearables in the workplace concerns how data collected in the workplace for employer use may be vulnerable to use by third parties, particularly the government. In "Trading Privacy for Promotion? Fourth Amendment Implications of Employers Using Wearable Sensors to Assess Worker Performance," George M. Dery III explores the theoretical legal implications of "a study on a passive monitoring system where employees shared data from wearables, phone applications, and position beacons that provided private information such as weekend phone use, sleep patterns in the bedrooms, and emotional states." The

---

[141] Elizabeth A. Brown, "A Healthy Mistrust: Curbing Biometric Data Misuse in the Workplace," *Stanford Technology Law Review* 23, no. 2 (2020): 252, 264–65, 267.

[142] Brown, "A Healthy Mistrust," 256–71.

[143] Brown, "A Healthy Mistrust," 274, 286, 290–93.

[144] Brown, "A Healthy Mistrust," 294–303.

stated goal of this study was "to examine a 'radically new approach' to employee assessment" by objective measures, "shed[ding] light on behavioral patterns that characterize higher and lower performers"; ultimately, "the researchers were able to successfully link the data collected with the quality of worker performance."[145] Dery sees this study as a sign that employees' Fourth Amendment right to privacy may be in jeopardy in the future.

Under current Fourth Amendment case law, the "thirdparty doctrine" holds that information an individual reveals to a third party, which the third party then reveals to the government, is not subject to Fourth Amendment protections.[146] The Court established an exception to this rule in *Carpenter v. United States*, finding that cell-site location information, although technically provided to a third party, did qualify for Fourth Amendment protections, as government collection of this information "invaded Carpenter's reasonable expectation of privacy in the whole of his physical movements."[147] Dery argues that if in cases concerning passive monitoring, such as in the study he referenced, "the employee would make an initial conscious choice to share his data with his employer … [t]his decision to opt in could cause the Court to find that the employee triggered the Fourth Amendment's traditional third party doctrine … rather than the exception in *Carpenter*." Further, even if *Carpenter* were controlling "in the near term," because an individual's "reasonable expectation of privacy" is central to Fourth Amendment protections, Dery warns that if "passively collected data … become[s] a societal norm," employees may no longer be protected in the future. Thus, the more widespread wearables become, the fewer legal protections the Fourth Amendment may offer. Dery purports that a decision by the Court to allow passive monitoring of employees would not be unprecedented, as the Court has a history of limiting employee rights to privacy in the name of employer and societal interests.[148] Finally, notwithstanding any of the above, Dery argues that because government intrusion of an individual's right to privacy may be allowed if it "has gained consent from someone who possesses 'common authority over [the subject of the search],'" the government may be able to bypass an employee to retrieve data directly from the employer.[149] While these considerations are currently speculative, Dery warns that as employers develop new forms of passive monitoring – such as wearables – employees' right to privacy under the Fourth Amendment may be increasingly undermined.

---

[145] George M. Dery III, "Trading Privacy for Promotion? Fourth Amendment Implications of Employers Using Wearable Sensors to Assess Worker Performance," *Northwestern Journal of Law and Social Policy* 16, no. 1 (2020): 17, 20–21.

[146] Dery, "Trading Privacy for Promotion?" 24 (citing *United States v. Miller*, 425 U.S. 435 (1976)).

[147] Dery, "Trading Privacy for Promotion?" 25–26 (citing *Carpenter v. United States*, 138 S. Ct. 2206, 2211 (2018)).

[148] Dery, "Trading Privacy for Promotion?" 27, 30.

[149] Dery, "Trading Privacy for Promotion?" 39 (quoting *United States v. Matlock*, 415 U.S. 164, 171 (1974)).

Legal scholar Jeffrey M. Hirsch warns that such issues arising from wearable tech may represent only the tip of the iceberg.[150] Hirsch singles out wearables as one of many "technological innovations [that] will provide employers with increased opportunities to pry ever more deeply into workers' personal information and thereby further underscore the lack of privacy protections in the workplace."[151] Hirsch warns that "'wearables' are an early harbinger" of employers stepping closer to monitoring "workers' moods, energy levels, and whether they are likely to engage in certain behaviors," amongst other invasive insights that provide employers with new ways to "monitor and control workers."[152] Concerning the issue of wearables and surveillance technology at large, Hirsch advocates for a general statute, modeled after the European Union's General Data Protection Regulation (GDPR), "that broadly protects certain types of personal information in many different situations," including a "defin[ition of] both the type of information being protected and exceptions." Hirsch also suggests a "just-cause termination law" that may allow employees to effectively refuse to consent to monitoring technology without risking termination.[153]

In "Chipping Away at Workplace Privacy: The Implantation of RFID Microchips and Erosion of Employee Privacy," Wes Turner, like Hirsch, finds that the "private-sector employees must rely on either the common law or a patchwork of statutory protections to protect their privacy interests at work."[154] Further, while "[t]here are a few federal statutory protections against the more egregious privacy violations," such as wiretapping and computer fraud, these protections do little in the face of modern technology. Indeed, "[e]mployment discrimination statutes may provide some protections against discrimination from the *misuse* of the data legally collected but does nothing to hamper the collection of data itself."[155] Turner purports that a major issue with the current regulatory framework is that "legal protections for employee privacy concerns from excessive monitoring are based on 1980s workplaces and technology ... [w]earable technologies, such as Fitbits and smartwatches, leave employees vulnerable to 'adverse employment decisions, discrimination, and invasions of privacy rights.'"[156] Turner argues that the lack of laws protecting workers from employer surveillance is a growing problem in a world where firms are implanting RFID chips in employees' badges; light fixtures; or even, as in the case of one Wisconsin firm, bodies.[157] Turner also argues that "BYOD [bring your own device] policies," wherein employees use their personal technology for work, "show how

---

[150] Hirsch, "Future Work," 928.
[151] Hirsch, "Future Work," 915.
[152] Hirsch, "Future Work," 929–930.
[153] Hirsch, "Future Work," 935–37.
[154] Wes Turner, "Chipping Away at Workplace Privacy: The Implantation of RFID Microchips and Erosion of Employee Privacy," *Washington University Journal of Law & Policy* 61 (2020): 277–81.
[155] Turner, "Chipping Away at Workplace Privacy," 283.
[156] Turner, "Chipping Away at Workplace Privacy," 277.
[157] See Turner, "Chipping Away at Workplace Privacy," 275, 284.

the distinction between work and personal devices can lead to difficult questions of privacy rights" as the distinction between what belongs to employer and employee blurs.[158] To Turner, "[a]n implanted microchip," as developed for surveillance by one technology firm, "is the natural combination of three major workforce trends: increased monitoring and surveillance; decreased expectation of privacy in devices used for work; and wearable technology that tracks health information."[159]

As these trends continue to push surveillance technologies to new extremes, more must be done to protect worker privacy. Turner argues that of many proposals, including federal regulation that limits how work-related activities are defined and wearable products are labeled – a "collectivist approach" that "allows employees to address privacy concerns ... by bargaining over the implantation of new technology" – may be the best way forward.[160] He concludes with the following thought:

> In an employment-at-will regime, employees must assert their privacy rights collectively before the implementation of increased workplace surveillance. Such an approach is the only way to address the 'damned if you do, damned if you don't' conundrum offered by employers: consent or be terminated; it is a structure where an employee cannot resist the erosion of their fundamental privacy rights until they have already been harmed.[161]

The role of collective action in approaching issues brought on by wearables and the seemingly limitless surveillance they enable seems to be a common theme shared by various scholars. Like Turner, scholars studying the role of wearables in professional sports also emphasize the importance of collective bargaining agreements in affirming player rights and privacy protections. However, as explained above, this industry benefits from the existing union infrastructure. How to organize and assert employees' collective rights to govern workplace surveillance seems like a daunting task. In "The Law of Employee Data: Privacy, Property and Governance," Matthew T. Bodie provides a potentially useful framework to approach this issue, examining "a spectrum of potential legal mechanisms that can protect, secure, and reengage employees in their relationship with their data."[162] Bodie offers an "expansive" overview of how data in employment has evolved over time, from Frederick Taylor's observations on employee productivity to Uber and Lyft tracking drivers "as part of a huge algorithm of traffic and transportation that has significant value on its own." Bodie then poses a significant question: "In this world of employee embeddedness within an immersive world of data, how will law react to its construction of the employment relationship?"[163]

---

[158] Turner, "Chipping Away at Workplace Privacy," 288.
[159] Turner, "Chipping Away at Workplace Privacy," 292.
[160] Turner, "Chipping Away at Workplace Privacy," 294–95.
[161] Turner, "Chipping Away at Workplace Privacy," 296.
[162] Matthew T. Bodie, "The Law of Employee Data: Privacy, Property and Governance," *Indiana Law Journal* 97 (2021): 5.
[163] Bodie, "Law of Employee Data," 7–13.

Bodie largely divides existing legal frameworks into issues of privacy law and property rights. Concerning privacy law, he purports that with the exception of certain "clumps of regulatory attention," such as HIPAA, GINA, ADA, and FCRA, "employer practices are largely free from privacy-related oversight ... [and] are allowed to monitor their employees as they wish" with very few exceptions.[164] By and large, employers may use employee data however they see fit, with no limitations on purpose or accuracy. Concerning employee property rights to data – which may fall under copyright, patent, trade secrets, trademark, or publicity protections – Bodie emphasizes that "rights generally end up in the hands of the employer." Work created for or under an employer is generally considered to be their property, and "employers have been more and more aggressive about asserting control over employee information through contract provisions such as covenants not to compete and nondisclosure agreements."[165] The result is a legal regime that largely does not protect employees' privacy or property rights to data.

Bodie presents two paradigms that "used to support the legal infrastructure" but have since collapsed: "the separation of personal information from business-related information, and the ability of the employee to separate herself from the firm." Like Turner, Bodie asserts that "[i]n many fields, the line between one's personal and professional identities has been vigorously smudged," which stands to "substantially [weaken] protections for worker data rights through privacy and intellectual property law."[166] Further, Bodie argues that "existing legal regimes facilitate the disconnection of employees from their data in its collection, aggregation and use," vesting all power and interests to the employer. Bodie offers ride-sharing drivers and professional athletes as two disparate examples of how data insights may decrease worker autonomy (ride-sharing) or empower workers (athletes) depending on the extent to which employees are given input and control in data collection and use. Bodie argues that "[i]f workers can participate in the design of the data program, object when it goes too far, and then better themselves through the program, then data analytics is a positive development."[167]

Ultimately, Bodie proposes three ways to reconceptualize employee data and regulation of the employment relationship. First, he suggests "a hybrid approach to employee data regulation, melding aspects of both privacy law and property law" rooted in ongoing employee data and value rights, and protections against employer misuse. Second, employers would be classified as "information fiduciaries" with "heightened obligations to care for [employee data] and not betray the trust of the owner."[168] Lastly, and in line with suggestions made by other scholars analyzed

---

[164] Bodie, "Law of Employee Data," 18.
[165] Bodie, "Law of Employee Data," 20, 23, 29.
[166] Bodie, "Law of Employee Data," 29, 31–32.
[167] Bodie, "Law of Employee Data," 40, 46.
[168] Bodie, "Law of Employee Data," 46–52.

above, employees would be brought "into the decision-making processes of collecting and using data" through systems of codetermination, employee ownership, or works councils. Though Bodie specifies that the typical union structure is useful for giving employees a seat at the table, it is not necessary. Rather, "[t]he important thread running through [various proposals for employee input in data decisions] is the ability of workers to participate collectively in the management of their collective data."[169]

The advent of wearable tech in the workplace has created the socio-technical phenomenon of workers as the data subjects of their employers. At the surface level, this raises novel legal controversies regarding data ownership and control. At a deeper level, there is an existential crisis regarding how the law should delineate the limits of employer's bodily control over workers. Unlike other measures of surveillance, wearable tech (which is directly attached to the body) impinges on an individual's bodily autonomy and personhood. On one end is wearable tech, such as Fitbits, which may be deemed innocuous because they do not invade the body, and on the other end are RFID chips that some employers are embedding in the skin of employees. But whether a tech remains outside the body or is embedded is ultimately of little import. What is most important is that all wearable tech may have the capability to collect highly sensitive data, including health information. Ownership of this data, and control of its end uses, will continue to be a legal battleground.

[169] Bodie, "Law of Employee Data," 56–59.

10

Quantified Racism[*]

Such findings demonstrate what I call "the New Jim Code": the employment of new technologies that reflect and reproduce existing inequities but that are promoted and perceived as more objective or progressive than the discriminatory systems of a previous era.

–Ruha Benjamin, *Race after Technology*

Racism and the quantification of human beings for the sake of profit maximization have been inextricably linked across time. In *Race after Technology*, scholar Ruha Benjamin fastidiously demonstrates how racial categorization (and attendant subjugation) is embedded in automated systems, in both their design and their programming. As Benjamin notes, while conforming to a colorblind ideology, these technologies nonetheless replicate the historical racial discrimination encoded in their training data and their design. Thus, Benjamin argues, new digital systems are responsible for digital segregation and the creation of digital caste systems in a *de facto* socio-technical phenomenon that she terms "the New Jim Code." This new phenomenon is akin to the *de jure* socio-legal phenomenon of Jim Crowism. Thus, the emerging artificial intelligence (AI) technologies in the workplace used for automated hiring, surveillance, and platform work do not make work more democratic; rather, they help enact racial domination in the workplace.

Although racial quantification is not new, it is both more pronounced and less visible when embedded in automated decision-making technologies. The legal scholar Danielle Citron has described a societal tendency towards "automation bias." This is the notion that AI systems enjoy the perception of impartiality. At the same time, the black box design of automated decision-making systems may mask their inner workings from the outside world. This bias and opacity position AI systems well to insidiously perpetuate systemic racism. Ultimately, this means that automated decision-making processes could serve to further widen the racial divide in the workplace. This chapter offers a survey of the breadth of racial quantification in the workplace.

[*] Parts of this chapter appeared in "Race, Labor, and the Future of Work," published in the *Oxford Handbook of Race and Law in the United States* (Oxford: Oxford University Press, 2022).

Consider that even technologies used to link workers to gig work often nod to a racial hierarchy in which Black workers are solely seen as subordinates. Here is the description of an advertisement for Fiverr, an online marketplace for freelancers: The billboard was bifurcated and each half bore a face. On one side was the face of a white man; on the other was the face of a Black woman. The side with the white face featured this text: "Your project is due ASAP." On the other side, with the face of the Black woman, the text read: "She'll be on it by EOD."[1] Another advertisement was similarly bifurcated. This time, the left half with the white face read: "You're running low on resources." The right half with a Black woman's face read: "She's a source you can rely on."

The implications of these advertisements were clear: The gig economy now affords opportunities for privileged populations (read white managers/supervisors) to take advantage of cheap labor (read Black workers) wherever it may be found in the world, thus creating what Professor Mark Graham has termed "the planetary labor market."[2] The advertisements suggested that those who will benefit from increased access to cheap labor afforded by technological advancements will be white, while those who will provide the cheap labor – the workhorses of automation – will be people of color. Observers have argued that gig economy companies such as Fiverr are a boon to free market capitalism, offering new opportunities to workers in developing countries by connecting them with those in developed countries who are able and willing to pay for their labor. However, there is the question of whether workers in the new world gig economy will receive fair value for their labor or will enjoy the standard labor protections that have been won in the United States.

Although the United States prides itself on projecting a reputation as a land of opportunity, with economic mobility and a ladder to financial security for hard workers from any ethnicity, the truth is that the history of the United States is also one of labor exploitation and exclusion, not to mention more than two centuries of enslavement and indentured servanthood. Despite the end of slavery and the eventual end of the Jim Crow laws that came after it, Black Americans today continue to suffer economic outcomes that are disparate and worse than their white counterparts. As the labor market takes larger strides into automation, and as technological advancements globalize employment opportunities, the preservation of labor protections for racial minorities remains a concern. This chapter describes new ways emerging artificial intelligence (AI) technologies may worsen labor inequalities.

10.1 1865–1871: BLACK CODES, THE THIRTEENTH AMENDMENT EXCEPTION, AND LABOR EXPLOITATION

The demise of slavery did not end the labor exploitation of formerly enslaved people of African descent in the United States. As sociologist W. E. B. Du Bois notes, "[T]he

---

[1] Leila Ettachfini, "Somehow, Fiverr Ads Have Gotten Even More Tone-Deaf," *Vice*, July 24, 2019, www.vice.com/en_us/article/evyy8k/fiverr-ad-white-man-black-woman.

[2] Ettachfini, "Somehow, Fiverr Ads Have Gotten Even More Tone-Deaf."

slave went free; stood a brief moment in the sun; then moved back again toward slavery."[3] Douglas Blackmon, in *Slavery by Another Name*, describes how Redemption[4] was an orchestrated effort coordinated by white merchants, planters, businessmen, and politicians to stymie the social and economic mobility of Black workers.[5] And "[w]hile the Thirteenth Amendment of the U.S. Constitution has been lauded by history books and legal scholars for abolishing slavery, the Amendment has also been read to uphold labor practices that in reality could amount to slavery for a certain segment of the American population – that is, those convicted of a crime."[6] The Thirteenth Amendment, which was meant to abrogate slavery, in actuality, also provided the legal basis for a continued form of slavery via the penal system. The amendment reads, "Neither slavery nor involuntary servitude, *except as a punishment for crime* whereof the party shall have been duly convicted, shall exist within the United States, or any place subject to their jurisdiction."[7]

Southern states seized on the exception in the Thirteenth Amendment as legal cover for the continued labor exploitation of formerly enslaved people of African descent. Starting in 1865, several Southern states passed Black Codes, restrictive state laws similar to some laws that Northern states had already passed to suppress African American economic and political activity. Black Codes were designed to confine newly freed Americans to the plantations of their former owners and force them to work for low wages. Through the charge of vagrancy, for example, Black Codes criminalized, among other things, unemployment. Freedmen and -women could thus be caught up in the dragnet of the penal system and conscripted for low-wage or non-paid work as part of the convict lease system. Characteristic of this era, the Virginia Supreme Court in 1871 held in *Ruffin v. Commonwealth* that a prisoner "during his term of service in the penitentiary … is in a state of penal servitude to the State. He has, as a consequence of his crime, not only forfeited his liberty, but all his personal rights except those which the law in its humanity accords to him. He is for the time being *the slave* of the State."[8]

The Industrial Revolution in the nineteenth century stoked the rise of prison labor, and states started to "lease" inmates to private companies as low-cost labor.

---

[3] W. E. B. Dubois, *Black Reconstruction in America: Toward a History of the Part Which Black Folk Played in the Attempt to Reconstruct Democracy in America, 1860–1880* (1935; Reprint, London: Routledge, 2017).

[4] "By 1873, many white Southerners were calling for 'Redemption' – the return of white supremacy and the removal of rights for blacks – instead of Reconstruction. This political pressure to return to the old order was oftentimes backed up by mob and paramilitary violence, with the Ku Klux Klan, the White League, and the Red Shirts assassinating pro-Reconstruction politicians and terrorizing Southern blacks." See NEH, "Reconstruction vs. Redemption," *National Endowment for the Humanities: News*, Feb. 11, 2014, www.neh.gov/news/reconstruction-vs-redemption.

[5] Blackmon, *Slavery by Another Name*.

[6] Ifeoma Ajunwa and Angela Onwuachi-Willig, "Combatting Discrimination against the Formerly Incarcerated in the Labor Market," *Northwestern University Law Review* 112, no. 6 (2018): 1385–1415.

[7] U.S. Const. amend. XIII, § 1 (emphasis added).

[8] *Ruffin v. Commonwealth*, 62 Va. 790, 796 (1871) (emphasis added).

This convict lease system was most prevalent in the Southern states after the end of slavery. Under the lease system, prisoners were compelled to perform low-paid or unpaid labor on plantations, on railroads, in mines, and at other sites. The goal, of course, was to enable the firm that leased the labor to earn a large profit.[9]

10.2 AUTOMATION AND SURVEILLANCE TECHNOLOGY IN THE WORKPLACE

Today, emerging technologies in the world of work threaten to widen the economic gulf between workers of color and their white counterparts. Enhanced technological capabilities for communication allow for a global gig economy. At the same time, traditional industries have turned to automated processes to streamline human resources functions and to automated surveillance to enhance productivity. There is growing concern that up to half of the labor market will be replaced by automated machines, a phenomenon that would eliminate job opportunities for racial minorities. While the U.S. Bureau of Labor Statistics estimates an overall employment growth of 11.5 million jobs between 2016 and 2026, these jobs likely will be for individuals who have advanced degrees (such as computer scientists or engineers) or individuals whose jobs require creative thinking (such as academic researchers). Jobs that are likely to be automated are those that are mainly routinized or consist of bureaucratic work, such as secretaries, administrative assistants, cashiers, drivers/truck drivers, manufacturing workers, construction workers, retail salespeople, janitors, cooks, and so on.[10] These routinized jobs are most likely to be held by minorities who lack an advanced degree. But much larger than the issue of worker displacement due to automation is how automated work processes impact the experience of workers in the workplace. The widespread displacement of workers is still a projected future, but the introduction of new technologies in the workplace is happening now. Two such areas of automated processes are automated hiring and automated surveillance of workers.

10.2.1 *Automated Hiring and Employment Discrimination*

Although hiring algorithms can help reduce time and costs for human resources staffing and applicant selection, hiring algorithms can also serve to increase inequality. Much of automated hiring involves the precise quantification of applicants with data – including information pulled from social media websites and applications – that goes beyond job fit or job skills.[11] Employers' use of this data reinforces the idea

9   Sharon Dolovich, "State Punishment and Private Prisons," *Duke Law Journal* 55, no. 3 (2005): 451.
10 U.S. Bureau of Labor Statistics, *Labor Force Characteristics by Race and Ethnicity*, 2017, Apr. 2018; Ariane Hegewisch, Chandra Childers, and Heidi Hartmann, "Women, Automation, and the Future of Work," Institute for Women's Policy Research, Report, 2019.
11 Ajunwa, "Paradox of Automation as Anti-Bias Intervention," 1703–4.

that there are those who are "deserving" of being employed – a distinction that goes beyond the question of whether someone is capable of performing the job. This is a distinction similar to the "deserving poor" versus "undeserving poor" divide noted by Professor Khiara Bridges; and as she has pointed out, this genre of distinction tends to stymie the economic mobility of people of color.[12]

Also, automated hiring can increase employment inequality by allowing for the targeting of job advertisements to groups of people who have historically been successful employees in the past. For example, due to algorithmic bias, advertisements for high-income jobs are presented to white men significantly more often than to racial minorities and white women. AI ethics investigators, who describe what they found as "a modern form of Jim Crow,"[13] detailed how a former Facebook feature termed Affinity Groups in essence allowed advertisers to use demographic data to algorithmically target specific audiences for Facebook ads.[14] Notably, a previous page on the Facebook Business section, titled "How to Reach the Hispanic Audience in the United States," claimed that it could allow advertisers to reach up to 26.7 million Facebook users of Hispanic Affinity. From this specific Affinity Group, advertisers could hone in on bilingual users to "refine their audiences."[15] One argument is that the feature is helpful for businesses aiming to increase diversity in their workforce. However, one can easily see how the use of Affinity Groups for ad distribution could also allow for unlawful, yet undetected, employment discrimination.

In a 2016 class action lawsuit filed against Facebook, the plaintiffs alleged that Facebook Business tools both "enable and encourage discrimination by excluding African Americans, Latinos, and Asian Americans – but not white Americans – from receiving advertisements for relevant opportunities."[16] In an amended complaint, the plaintiffs additionally alleged that "Facebook offers a feature that is legally indistinguishable from word-of-mouth hiring, which has long been considered a discriminatory and unlawful employment practice." This second allegation is a reference to Facebook's Lookalike Audiences feature. This feature allows employers and employment agencies to provide a list of their existing workers to Facebook. Their list is then used to generate a list of Facebook users who are demographically the same as the current workers at their organization. The people on the new Lookalike Audience list created by Facebook are then targeted to receive the organization's

[12] Khiara M. Bridges, "The Deserving Poor, the Undeserving Poor, and Class-Based Affirmative Action," *Emory Law Journal* 66, no. 5 (2017): 1049–1114.

[13] Amit Datta, Michael C. Tschantz, and Apunam Datta, "Automated Experiments on Ad Privacy Settings," *Proceedings on Privacy Enhancing Technology* 2015, no. 1 (2015): 92–112.

[14] See Facebook, "About Ad Targeting: Creating a New Audience," *Facebook Business: Advertiser Help*, 2018, www.facebook.com/business/help/717368264947302?helpref=page_content.

[15] See Facebook, "U.S. Hispanic Affinity on Facebook," *Facebook Business*, 2018, www.facebook.com/business/a/us-hispanic-affinity-audience.

[16] *Mobley v. Facebook, Inc.* (first am. compl.), No. 16-cv-06440-EJD, at *1 (N.D. Cal. 2017).

employment ads.[17] This feature (now defunct) would have been certain to replicate historical racial, gender, and other disparities already present in a given labor
market.

As automated decision-making systems are increasingly acting as gatekeepers
to gainful employment, it is critical to consider how they may perpetuate racial
biases in the hiring process. Consider that video interviewing, as the newest iteration of algorithmic hiring, is especially well positioned to reproduce racial employment discrimination. Some video interview algorithms collect data about a client's
workforce in order to create a standard of success by which to measure applicants.
A representative from one automated video interviewing company noted:

> To train the system on what to look for and tailor the test to a specific job, the
> employer's current workers filling the same job – "the entire spectrum, from high
> to low achievers" – sit through the AI assessment … [t]heir responses … are then
> matched with a "benchmark of success" from those workers' past job performance.[18]

This practice is not unique. A 2020 study conducted by Manish Raghavan, Jon
Kleinberg, Solon Barocas, and Karen Levy that analyzed the claims and practices
of various algorithmic hiring companies found that nearly half of the companies
they studied built hiring "assessments based on data from the client's past and current employees."[19] This method of building algorithmic assessments around specific
client data raises serious concerns about the potential for past racial hiring biases –
ingrained in the composition and therefore performance outcomes of a company's
workforce – to become encoded in the predictions of an algorithmic system.

AI justice advocates have raised alarm bells around automated hiring, especially
when used by firms that lack existing diversity.[20] While this algorithmic hiring practice is problematic for many diverse groups, it poses a particular threat to Black
workers. In addition to being underemployed compared to their white counterparts,
consider that Black workers are overrepresented in low-wage service industries
that offer fewer promotion opportunities. In industries where salaried positions are
offered, Black workers are still largely underrepresented at the managerial level, and
are often relegated to frontline positions with no clear path to upward mobility.[21]
Given the unequal distribution of Black talent in low-paying, slow-growth jobs and
industries, therefore, a troubling picture begins to emerge for algorithms built on

[17] See *Bradley v. T-Mobile, Inc.* (first am. class and collective action compl.), No. 17-cv-07232-BLF,
at 21 (N.D. Cal. 2018), www.onlineagediscrimination.com/sites/default/files/documents/og-cwa-
complaint.pdf. See generally, Facebook, "About Lookalike Audiences," *Facebook Business: Advertiser
Help*, www.facebook.com/business/help/164749007013531 (last visited Aug. 10, 2019).
[18] Harwell, "A Face-Scanning Algorithm Increasingly Decides Whether You Deserve the Job."
[19] Raghavan et al., "Mitigating Bias in Algorithmic Hiring: Evaluating Claims and Practices," 469, 472.
[20] Eric Rosenbaum, "Silicon Valley Is Stumped: A.I. Cannot Always Remove Bias from Hiring," *CNBC*,
last updated Apr. 29, 2019.
[21] Bryan Hancock et al., *Race in the Workplace: The Black Experience in the US Private Sector* (New
York: McKinsey & Co., 2019).

existing hiring data. For upwardly mobile jobs, Black talent is statistically less likely to be represented in the benchmark or comparator pool of employees. Thus, when automated decision-making systems are programmed with existing high performers, Black applicants are statistically more likely to face adverse outcomes in the hiring process on the basis of their race.

There are several aspects of video interviewing that make this racialized outcome more likely, despite any anti-bias interventions – such as explicitly removing race as a target variable – that firms may employ. Video interview algorithms consider the content of an individual's response through lingual analysis, taking into account factors such as "a candidate's tone of voice, their use of passive or active words, sentence length and the speed they talk."[22] When racial or ethnic minorities from diverse backgrounds are underrepresented in the training data an algorithm is comparing them to, then any differential in their response that may be attributed to their racial or ethnic identity runs the risk of being penalized by the hiring system that scores them. For example, an algorithm may have difficulty properly scoring the response of a Black candidate whose English dialect adheres more closely to African American Vernacular English (AAVE) as opposed to Standard American English and in turn give the candidate a lower performance score. In such an instance, the algorithm has penalized language as a proxy for race without ever considering race as a factor itself. A 2020 audit of video interview provider HireVue has confirmed that the racial bias of lingual analysis is more than mere speculation. The audit found that HireVue's automated hiring algorithm had trouble scoring answers given by minority candidates who were more likely to structure responses using shorter sentences.[23]

Video interview algorithms analyze not only the content and language of a candidate's answer to an interview question but also the facial expressions a candidate presents while responding. HireVue touted "[a] database of about 25,000 pieces of facial and linguistic information" used to build its assessments. The algorithms assessed facial expressions such as "brow furrowing, brow raising, the amount eyes widen or close, lip tightening, chin raising and smiling."[24] While HireVue announced that it had discontinued use of its facial recognition technology as of 2021, though it continues to use lingual analysis, it is still useful to consider the harm that may come if this technology is deployed more broadly.[25]

Facial recognition technology raises serious concerns of discrimination given the opaque nature of its insights and its potential for racial discrimination. These concerns are rooted in the lived experiences of people of color who have faced AI discrimination on the basis of race in various forms, from soap dispensers to

[22] Ivan Manokha, "How Using Facial Analysis in Job Interviews Could Reinforce Inequality," *PBS News Hour: Making Sen$e*, Oct. 7, 2019.

[23] ORCAA, "Description of Algorithmic Audit: Pre-Built Assessments," Report, Dec. 15, 2020, 5.

[24] Manokha, "How Using Facial Analysis in Job Interviews Could Reinforce Inequality."

[25] Knight, "Job Screening Service Halts Facial Analysis of Applicants."

testing software that are unable to detect their presence.[26] In 2018, Joy Buolamwini and Timnit Gebru examined the performance of facial analysis algorithms across four "intersectional subgroups" of males or females featuring lighter or darker skin. Buolamwini and Gebru found that algorithms designed to identify gender performed better on male faces as opposed to female and on light faces as opposed to dark; darker females were misclassified the most of all groups.[27] This troubling finding suggests that the facial analysis software employed by video interview algorithms may be less accurate when identifying people of color and women. If automated video interview systems have trouble even detecting the presence of applicants with darker skin, how can they then truly glean the facial expressions or emotions of Black applicants?

A 2018 study by Lauren Rhue confirms they cannot. Rhue found that the emotional analysis feature of two facial recognition algorithms "interprets emotions differently based on the person's race." One recognition software interpreted Black individuals as angrier than whites regardless of whether the individual was smiling; the other platform viewed Black individuals as more contemptuous than white individuals when their face featured an "ambiguous" expression, though "[a]s the [individual's] smile widens, the disparity disappears."[28] Thus, not only is facial recognition technology less accurate at identifying traits of women and people with darker skin tones, it is also less accurate at interpreting emotions expressed by individuals with such skin tone. The technology this hiring tool is based on is inherently racist, a problem that is only exacerbated by the underrepresentation of racial minorities in algorithmic training data.

In a 2018 opinion essay for the *New York Times*, Joy Buolamwini succinctly describes the discriminatory potential of automated hiring algorithms with the following example:

> [I]f more white males with generally homogeneous mannerisms have been hired in the past, it's possible that algorithms will be trained to favorably rate predominantly fair-skinned, male candidates while penalizing women and people of color who do not exhibit the same verbal and nonverbal cues.[29]

Biased input data means that machines may be trained to identify and reward the facial and linguistic traits of white, Western, male-presenting candidates. University of Oxford lecturer Ivan Manokha calls on French sociologist Peirre Bourdieu's theory of "symbolic capital" to suggest that these insights are *necessarily* biased. Exalted attributes such as "[e]ase, confidence, self-assurance and linguistic skills" are all a

---

[26] See Taylor Synclair Goethe, "Bigotry Encoded: Racial Bias in Technology," *Reporter*, Mar. 2, 2019, https://reporter.rit.edu/tech/bigotry-encoded-racial-bias-technology; Joy Buolamwini, "When the Robot Doesn't See Dark Skin," *New York Times*, June 21, 2018.

[27] Buolamwini and Gebru, "Gender Shades," 8.

[28] Rhue, "Racial Influence on Automated Perceptions of Emotions," 1.

[29] Buolamwini, "When the Robot Doesn't See Dark Skin."

reflection of one's upbringing and social status; when facial and linguistic technologies code for these traits – which is especially likely considering white elites who historically hold more symbolic capital are likely to be included in the training data set of top performers – algorithms are essentially coding for discrimination.

It is worth restating that the biased nature of these insights cannot simply be coded out with anti-bias measures such as exclusion of the race variable. Black Americans have faced racial discrimination over time that has resulted in decreased opportunities for intergenerational wealth accumulation, and therefore has encoded socio-economic disparity into the fabric of society in the form of the racial wealth gap.[30] This racial wealth gap can have a negative impact on the credentialing of Black Americans and the acquisition of other social, cultural, and symbolic capital. Furthermore, given that property taxes in the United States largely determine educational spending, poor Americans are more likely to face worse educational opportunities.[31] Since Black individuals are more likely to grow up poor and undereducated in America (as a result of historical exclusion), they are also more likely to lack the cultural signals that are determined and valued by white elites of higher socio-economic status. Video interview algorithms that consider facial expressions, tone, sentence structure, and diction by standards set by the cultural capital of the dominant group are therefore coded for bias, based on race.

Indeed, racial disparities can bleed into much of the job search process. Consider the "applicant tracking system" (ATS) technology used by some 98 percent of employers in the Fortune 500, which employs an algorithm to sort through resumes to decide which are worth passing on to hiring managers.[32] Algorithms are often trained to look for certain key words relating to the job in question, requiring that resumes adhere to particular formats so that a proper analysis can be performed. As Cathy O'Neil notes in her 2016 book, the *Weapons of Math Destruction*, knowledge of how to optimize a resume's wording and formatting for ATS technology is often a form of cultural capital held by social elites.[33] Racial minorities who have less access to institutional resources as a by-product of their intersectional societal identities are in turn less likely to know the ins and outs of pandering to resume scanners and other hiring algorithms.

Automated hiring systems may also evince racial bias when they privilege correlations that are, in reality, racially determined. An audit of one resume screening algorithm found that the software favored candidates who were named Jared and played

---

[30] Jane Coaston, "The Intersectionality Wars," *Vox*, last updated May 28, 2019, www.vox.com/the-highlight/2019/5/20/18542843/intersectionality-conservatism-law-race-gender-discrimination.

[31] Linda Darling-Hammond, "Unequal Opportunity: Race and Education," *Brookings Review*, Mar. 1, 1998, www.brookings.edu/articles/unequal-opportunity-race-and-education/.

[32] Regina Borsellino, "Beat the Robots: How to Get Your Resume Past the System and into Human Hands," *The Muse*, www.themuse.com/advice/beat-the-robots-how-to-get-your-resume-past-the-system-into-human-hands (last visited June 3, 2021).

[33] O'Neil, *Weapons of Math Destruction*, 114.

high school lacrosse.[34] These two variables (the name Jared and playing high school lacrosse) are so highly correlated with race that they may stand in as proxy variables for an applicant's race. Algorithms are inherently limited by the data sets they are built on. When hiring algorithms are built on data sets concerning job performance that, for the reasons discussed above, lack racial diversity, the result is a racist algorithm that further disadvantages already historically disadvantaged racial minorities.

10.2.2 *The Racialized Effects of Worker Surveillance*

The history of labor in the United States is rife with instances of invasive worker surveillance. For example, the Ford Corporation in 1914 had a department referred to as the Sociological Department that was comprised of paid private detectives. These detectives spent their time spying on Ford employees to ensure adherence to "Fordliness" and American values such as abstinence from drinking and gambling. Prior to that, the Pinkerton detectives, part of a private security guard company, were sent to spy on union organizers and break up workers' attempts at unionization.[35] In the digital age, it is now digital devices rather than human detectives that can diligently record employee activities and productivity.[36] This perpetual workplace surveillance is usually defended in terms of safety. Factory workers who wear devices to "increase safety" are compelled to record where they were standing, what they were looking at, or if they were doing the correct movements.[37] In addition to corporations being able to use this information to protect themselves from liability when a worker is injured while on the job,[38] employers may also deploy these technologies for harassment or for employment discrimination.[39] Furthermore, corporations may also commodify employee data and make a profit on data collected from workers' behavioral and health practices.[40]

The surveillance of workers has always been racialized. As Professors Devon Carbado and Mitu Gulati write in their canonical article "Working Identity," minority workers are burdened with projecting a "working identity" that mirrors

---

[34] Gershgorn, "Companies Are on the Hook if Their Hiring Algorithms Are Biased."

[35] Ajunwa, Schultz, and Crawford, "Limitless Worker Surveillance."

[36] Paul Attewell, "Big Brother and the Sweatshop: Computer Surveillance in the Automated Office," *Sociological Theory* 5, no. 1 (1987): 87–100.

[37] Mareike Kristzler et al., "Wearable Technology as a Solution for Workplace Safety." *MUM' 15: Proceedings of the 14th International Conference on Mobil and Ubiquitous Multimedia*, Nov. 2015, 213–17.

[38] Ajunwa, Schultz, and Crawford, "Limitless Worker Surveillance."

[39] Ifeoma Ajunwa, "Algorithms at Work: Productivity Monitoring Applications and Wearable Technology as the New Data-Centric Research Agenda for Employment and Labor Law," *St. Louis University Law Journal* 63, no. 1 (2018): 21–53.

[40] Jim Thatcher, David O'Sullivan, and Dillon Mahmoudi, "Data Colonialism through Accumulation by Dispossession: New Metaphors for Daily Data," *Environment and Planning D: Society and Space* 34, no. 6 (2016): 990–1006; Ajunwa, "Workplace Wellness Program Might Be Putting Your Health Data at Risk."

what the employer expects of them. For minority workers, managing stereotypes attached to their race that could result in employment discrimination constitutes additional work.[41] Several studies have shown that there is a disparity regarding the intensity of surveillance for Black workers in comparison to their white counterparts.[42] This disparity has dire economic consequences. Economists Cavounidis and Lang have found that "[while] white workers are hired and retained indefinitely without monitoring, black workers are monitored and fired if a negative signal is received." The authors argue that this heighted surveillance of Black workers leads to greater unemployment. This means that "[t]he fired workers, who return to the pool of job-seekers, lower the average productivity of black job-seekers, perpetuating the cycle of lower wages and discriminatory monitoring." The authors thus conclude that "discrimination can persist even if the productivity of blacks exceeds that of whites."[43]

Consider one recent striking example of selective employee surveillance effectuated by the now easily accessible technology of direct-to-consumer genetic testing. In a case that has been referred to as "the mystery of the devious defecator,"[44] Jack Lowe, a forklift operator, and Dennis Reynolds, a deliveryman, brought suit against their employer Atlas Logistics Group alleging violation of the Genetic Information Non-Discrimination Act (GINA) after the company asked them to take a DNA saliva swab test in 2012 or risk losing their jobs. The compelled DNA tests were part of an investigation the employer was conducting to discover who was defecating on the warehouse grounds. The issue, however, was that the employer had asked Lowe and Reynolds, two African American workers, to take the DNA test, but not their white colleagues.[45] The DNA testing proved that Lowe and Reynolds were not the culprits, and the "devious defecator" was never caught. The judge in the case ruled that the genetic data collection was a violation of GINA, and a jury trial returned a verdict of $1.75 million in punitive damages against Atlas Logistics Group.[46] This story illustrates how some worker protection laws are being reinterpreted to push back against the racialized effects of surveillance.

Employers have a plethora of new, more invasive tools at their disposal to monitor and control worker behaviors. As the employer's technological capacity to surveil workers grows, it is critical to consider how this surveillance may have a disproportionately negative impact on racial minorities. As Alvaro M. Bedoya observes in *The Color of Surveillance*, "[t]here is a myth in this country that in a world where

---

[41] Carbado and Gulati, "Working Identity."
[42] Gillian B. White, "Black Workers Really Do Need to Be Twice as Good," *The Atlantic*, Oct. 7, 2015.
[43] Costas Cavounidis and Kevin Lang, "Discrimination and Worker Evaluation," NBER Working Paper 21612, October 2015.
[44] *Lowe v. Atlas Logistics Group Retail Services (Atlanta) LLC*, 2015 U.S. Dist. LEXIS 178275 (N.D. Ga. 2015).
[45] Gina Kolata, "'Devious Defecator' Case Tests Genetics Law," *New York Times*, May 29, 2015.
[46] CBS News, "Jury Awards Millions in Case of the 'Devious Defecator,'" *CBS News*, June 25, 2015.

everyone is watched, everyone is watched equally."[47] This myth is far from reality: Black and other racial minorities have faced, and continue to face, greater overall levels of surveillance than their white counterparts.

Workplace surveillance is a necessary part of scientific management, the system for organizing and quantifying work popularized in the early twentieth century by the likes of Frederick Taylor and Henry Ford. However, the roots of scientific management go back much deeper than the Industrial Revolution. According to business history scholar Caitlin C. Rosenthal, it was in the 1750s that the origins of scientific management first took hold on slave plantations in the West Indies. Plantation owners developed record-keeping systems to track the productivity of enslaved people, monitoring everything from their food consumption to "how long new mothers breastfed their babies." Thomas Affleck took quantification a step further with his plantation accounting book, in which owners of enslaved people used collected data to set cotton-picking quotas, determine the appropriate level of punishment for enslaved people who fell short, and devise sadistic incentive plans to increase production. The value of an enslaved person was quantified on the basis of "bales per prime hand," a standard unit of measure that allowed plantation owners to calculate their output-to-labor ratio and compare it against other farms.[48] Owners developed such in invasive surveillance in order to extract maximum profit from their laborers – and it is this profit motive that continues to undergird the principles of modern management and workplace surveillance today.

Historians David Roediger and Elizabeth Esch largely concur with Rosenthal's conclusion that the roots of modern management practices date back to the antebellum South. However, they go a step further to assert that modern management not only originated in racism, but that, through the practice of "race management," racial division was a tool actively used to manage workers.[49] As journalist Esperanza Fonseca points out in her analysis of the history of surveillance and racism, at the root of both plantation and modern management is the inherent class structure of capitalism, wherein "one group owns the means of production and is responsible for extracting value from another group."[50] Within this system, the ruling class develops technologies to aid in their pursuit to extract maximum value from their labor source. It was this system that gave rise to the practice of race management – that is, the weaponization of race to increase control over workers in the name of production. Roediger and Esch point to pseudo-scientific data about racial differences in

---

[47] Alvaro M. Bedoya, "The Color of Surveillance," *Slate*, Jan. 18, 2016.

[48] Katie Johnston, "The Messy Link between Slave Owners and Modern Management," *Forbes*, Jan. 16, 2013.

[49] David R. Roediger and Elizabeth D. Esch, *The Production of Difference: Race and the Management of Labor in U.S. History* (New York: Oxford University Press, 2014), 6–8.

[50] Esperanza Fonseca, "Worker Surveillance Is on the Rise, and Has Its Roots in Centuries of Racism," *Truthout*, June 8, 2020, https://truthout.org/articles/worker-surveillance-is-on-the-rise-and-has-its-roots-in-centuries-of-racism/.

work ethic, productivity, and temperament deployed by the managing class well into the early 1900s to account for differences in recruitment, hiring, compensation, and treatment of workers. Shifts in how different racial groups were presented and perceived, aligning with shifting labor supply needs at various points, lend credence to the authors' argument that race is a social construct strategically deployed by the predominately white ruling class to increase the amount of value they can extract from their laborers.[51] It's not merely that racism and capitalism arose at the same time – rather, they constitute a symbiotic system wherein each one ensures the survival of the other.

Re-examining today's systems of modern surveillance with this historical background in mind, one may not be surprised to learn that in the digital age where all workers are being surveilled, Black workers face the highest scrutiny. A 2015 research paper from the National Bureau of Economic Research (NBER) found that due to gaps in employment history, Black workers are more likely to be seen as less skilled than their white counterparts in the eyes of employers and to have their work "scrutinized" to a greater degree than other employees. And as a result of this increased surveillance, the Black worker is more likely to be terminated for observed errors.[52] Thus, increased surveillance creates a feedback loop wherein Black workers become increasingly marginalized in the labor market, limiting their promotion and their total employment opportunities. As Black workers are inordinately surveilled, and thus more of their errors are caught in comparison to white workers who are less surveilled, the more managers feel justified in their increased surveillance of Black workers.

In addition to facing increased surveillance compared to their white counterparts due to prejudiced employer perceptions, Black Americans are also overrepresented in industries where surveillance is simply more prominent overall. Examining the intersection of class status and privacy rights, Michele Gilman observes that low-wage workers, particularly those in the service sector, face far greater levels of surveillance than workers in other industries, from keystroke logging to drug testing to GPS location tracking. He finds also that Black Americans are "disproportionately represented among [these] low-wage workers" – a particularly troubling finding given the negative effects increased surveillance may confer. According to Gilman, various studies suggest that employer surveillance can lead to increased instances of "'stress, high tension, headaches, extreme anxiety, depression, anger, severe fatigue, and musculoskeletal problems'" in workers. Surveillance may also further dampen employee perceptions of worker power and worker voice, important factors that influence job satisfaction.[53] Thus, the oversurveillance of Black workers

[51] Roediger and Esch, *The Production of Difference.*
[52] See White, "Black Workers Really Do Need to Be Twice as Good."
[53] Michele E. Gilman, "The Class Differential in Privacy Law," *Brooklyn Law Review* 77, no. 4 (2012): 1409.

goes beyond creating unequal job promotion outcomes; it can also create serious, life-altering health risks that directly impact Black life outcomes.

Increased employer surveillance in the digital age has enabled worker domination on the whole as employers increasingly consolidate their power.[54] Although employers have the legal and technological power to surveil (and thus dominate) all workers equally, the evidence shows that Black workers face the most scrutiny. This choice results in different job and life outcomes which largely follow the pattern of early twentieth-century race management practices, with the attendant racial disparities in employment outcomes accepted as justification for continued economic subjugation.

10.2.2.1 Race and Productivity Evaluation

There is evidence of racial bias in how productivity is quantified for Black workers. A 2001 study of the personnel data from a large U.S. firm found that, all else equal, Black employees received lower performance ratings than their equally productive white counterparts. Examining the distribution of performance evaluations among white and Black employees in a given year, the researchers found that while supervisors would rate workers of their own race higher than supervisors of another race would, both Black and white managers alike nonetheless rated the performance of Black workers as less than their white counterparts.[55] A 2005 study further validated these first findings, asserting that though white and Black supervisors often disagreed on the *size* of the performance differential between white and Black workers, they nonetheless unanimously found that whites rated higher than Black workers on the whole.[56] These findings are consistent with other studies and suggests that, on the whole, Black workers fall victim to structural racism in the workplace.

Interestingly, the researchers also note that differences in performance ratings account for nearly all pay and job allocation differentials at the firm under study; all else equal, two individuals of different races would receive the same outcome but for a difference in performance evaluations.[57] Although there appear to be systems of procedural justice in the modern workplace, structural racism robs Black individuals of the distributive justice they deserve concerning performance evaluations and the monetary and status awards those evaluations confer.

A 2015 study suggests statistical discrimination may be a major factor in lower productivity evaluations for Black employees. As referenced previously, a research paper by the National Bureau of Economic Research built an economic

---

[54] See Ifeoma Ajunwa, "The 'Black Box' at Work," *Big Data & Society* 7, no. 2 (2020): 4.

[55] See Marta Elvira and Robert Town, "The Effects of Race and Worker Productivity," *Industrial Relations: Journal Economy and Society* 40 (2001): 582.

[56] Joseph M. Stauffer and M. Ronald Buckley, "The Existence and Nature of Racial Bias in Supervisory Ratings," *Journal of Applied Psychology* 90, no. 3 (2005): 589.

[57] See Elvira and Town, "Effects of Race and Worker Productivity," 572.

model to explain why Black Americans experience "lower wages, higher unemployment, longer unemployment duration and shorter employment duration than their apparently similar white counterparts." The model suggests that Black workers' lower productivity evaluations are a by-product of increased surveillance, which itself derives from the perception that Black workers as a class have "lower average skill" than white workers. As result, Black workers are often fired at higher rates than white workers, creating employment gaps that perpetuate skills perceptions.[58]

The tangible effects of this cyclical racism on productivity perceptions of Black workers can be best exemplified through an analysis of the real hourly wages versus wage gaps of white to Black workers from 1979 to 2015 (see Figure 10.1). Since 1979, white hourly wages for the middle 50 percent of workers have increased 11.9 percent; Black median wage growth, however, has seen a marginal 1.8 percent rise, with the Black–white wage gap increasing 32 percent since 1979. The effects of this disproportionate distribution of productivity growth are seen even more acutely for low-wage earners, with the Black–white wage gap increasing nearly 70 percent since 1979.[59] It should be noted that neither white workers nor Black workers saw wage growth as high as the overall productivity growth seen in the United States during this time; however, white workers still received a greater share of this growth than Black workers.[60]

Here the intersectional, complex nature of racism in the workplace reveals itself. Increased surveillance feeds perceptions of lower productivity, which feeds compensation differentials for Black workers. At each step, Black workers face new, compounding forms of racism that manifest in greater inequality over time. While, all else equal, racism accounts for perceptions of productivity differentials between Black and white workers, recent studies also suggest that these perceptions may result in "self-fulling prophecies." A 2017 study suggests that the presence of this racism itself has negative effects on minority worker productivity, "find[ing] that when managers hold negative beliefs, even unconscious ones, about minority workers, minority employees perform much worse than they do with unbiased bosses." While the baseline productivity of minorities studied was equal to non-minority workers in the presence of unbiased managers, minority performance was "in the 79th percentile of worker performance" when they were paired with biased managers. Minority workers were also more likely to be absent and less likely to work late when paired with biased managers. For non-minority workers, there was no observed productivity

[58] Kevin Lang and Costas Cavounidis, "Discrimination and Worker Evaluation," NBER Working Paper 21612, National Bureau of Economic Research, 2015.
[59] See Valerie Wilson, "Black Workers' Wages Have Been Harmed by Both Widening Racial Wage Gaps and the Widening Productivity-Pay Gap," *Economic Policy Institute*, Oct. 25, 2016, Table 1, www.epi.org/publication/black-workers-wages-have-been-harmed-by-both-widening-racial-wage-gaps-and-the-widening-productivity-pay-gap/#epi-toc-2.
[60] See Wilson, "Black Workers' Wages Have Been Harmed," Figure A.

Real hourly wages and wage gaps at the 10th, 50th, and 95th percenties by race, 1979–2015

	10th percentile			50th percentile			95th percentile			Percentile wage ratios	
	White	Black	Black-white wage gap	White	Black	Black-white wage gap	White	Black	Black-white wage gap	White 95th-to-50th	Black 95th-to-50th
1979	$9.24	$8.90	3.6%	$16.89	$13.89	17.7%	$39.08	$30.84	21.1%	2.3	2.2
1989	$8.08	$7.20	10.8%	$16.79	$13.45	19.9%	$42.65	$32.46	23.9%	2.5	2.4
1995	$8.19	$7.60	7.1%	$16.89	$13.24	21.6%	$44.58	$34.07	23.6%	2.6	2.6
2000	$9.23	$8.36	9.4%	$18.15	$14.46	20.3%	$50.03	$35.91	28.2%	2.8	2.5
2007	$9.19	$8.52	7.4%	$19.01	$14.47	23.9%	$54.80	$39.50	27.2%	2.9	2.7
2015	$9.30	$8.20	11.8%	$19.17	$14.14	26.2%	$61.12	$42.07	31.2%	3.2	3.0
Percent change											
1979– 1989	-14.3%	-23.6%	66.4%	-0.6%	-3.2%	10.6%	8.4%	5.0%	11.8%		
1989– 1995	1.3%	-5.3%	-52.0%	0.6%	-1.6%	8.0%	4.3%	4.7%	-1.3%		
1995– 2000	11.3%	9.0%	24.1%	6.9%	8.4%	-6.3%	10.9%	5.1%	16.5%		
2000– 2007	-0.4%	1.8%	-27.7%	4.5%	0.1%	14.9%	8.7%	9.1%	-1.1%		
2007– 2015	-1.2%	-3.8%	37.9%	0.8%	-2.3%	9.0%	10.3%	6.1%	10.4%		
1979– 2015	0.7%	-8.5%	69.3%	11.9%	1.8%	32.4%	36.1%	26.7%	32.3%		

Note: The wage gap is the percent by which black wages lag white wages.

Source: EPI analysis of Current Population Survey (CPS) Outgoing Rotation Group microdata.

Economic Policy Institute

FIGURE 10.1   Real hourly wages and wage gaps at the 10th, 50th, and 95th percentiles by race, 1979–2015 (Table 1 from Wilson, "Black Workers' Wages Have Been Harmed")[61]

difference when working with non-biased versus biased managers.[62] This suggests that worker performance may be tangibly diminished by racism in the workplace.

It is important to qualify that the study discussed above was conducted in France rather than the United States, but even if one argues that France lacks the systemic racism that plagues the United States today, this study shows that minority worker productivity is adversely affected by the mere presence of unconscious or consciously held racial prejudices.[63] Compounding these findings with the systemic racism that is evident in the U.S. employment system, which is exemplified by the racial wage gap and racist productivity evaluation differentials, suggests that Black workers face an increasingly upward battle in the workplace. Not only are Black Americans unfairly perceived as less productive, but these prejudiced perceptions may also cause them to actually become less productive.

[61] Source: Wilson, "Black Workers' Wages Have Been Harmed," Table 1.
[62] Amanda Pallais, "Evidence That Minorities Perform Worse Under Biased Managers," *Harvard Business Review*, Jan. 13, 2017, https://hbr.org/2017/01/evidence-that-minorities-perform-worse-under-biased-managers.
[63] Pallais, "Evidence That Minorities Perform Worse Under Biased Managers."

10.2.2.2 Race and Algorithms of Compensation

While Black Americans are surveilled more in the workplace, they are also quantified as less. Consider this: The National Football League (NFL) has been in the midst of ongoing legal settlements with former players concerning brain injuries sustained during their tenure with the league. In 2015, a jury signed off on a $1 billion, sixty-five-year settlement wherein the NFL agreed to distribute cash payouts to retired players who go on to develop Alzheimer's disease, dementia, Parkinson's disease, or Lou Gehrig's disease as a probable result of play-associated brain trauma. However, former players are required to meet certain thresholds on cognitive tests in order to qualify for a piece of the settlement. The issue: Black players are held to a different standard than their white counterparts. That is, the algorithm the NFL uses to determine payouts employs a different cognitive baseline for Black players' dementia testing, which is predicated on the assumption that "Black men start with lower cognitive skills." This imposed lower cognitive baseline requires that for Black players to qualify for settlement, they must perform significantly worse on cognitive tests than their white counterparts. In practice, this differential standard for Black players – entirely based on faulty racist assumptions – has made it more difficult for Black athletes to receive just compensation for their injuries. According to one metric, only one quarter of some two thousand Black players who sought dementia rewards qualified under this racially biased testing system.[64]

Ultimately, after serious public scrutiny, the NFL agreed to stop the practice of using a different compensation threshold for Black players.[65] However, the NFL did not invent this racist phenomenon of unequal compensation. Take, for example, legal calculations for tort damages. To determine the damages a plaintiff qualifies for in tort claims, juries are often tasked with estimating a plaintiff's potential life earnings absent any injury. In such cases, it is "standard practice" for juries to consider "race- and sex-based data" in their ultimate calculations. In effect, this means that the lives of racial minorities are valued as lesser than their white counterparts. As racial justice advocates Ronen Avraham and Kimberly Yuracko observe, this practice "means that past levels of discrimination are embedded in predictions of the future."[66] The workplace quantification of the Black worker today on the basis of how they have been quantified in the past is incredibly problematic, as that historical quantification reflects generations of prejudice

---

[64] Associated Press, "Judge Approves Potential $1 Billion Settlement to Resolve NFL Concussion Lawsuits," *USA Today*, Apr. 22, 2015; Associated Press, "Black NFL Players Call for End of Algorithm That Assumes Black Men Have Lower Cognitive Abilities," *MarketWatch*, May 14, 2021, www.marketwatch.com/story/retired-black-nfl-players-and-their-families-call-for-race-norming-practice-to-end-01621018741.

[65] Elliot Hannon, "NFL Halts 'Race-Norming' to Calculate Brain Injury Compensation for Former Players," *Slate*, June 3, 2021.

[66] Ronen Avraham and Kimberly Yuracko, "The Use of Race- and Sex-Based Data to Calculate Damages Is a Stain on Our Legal System," *Washington Post*, Apr. 29, 2021.

and exclusion. Such a system is inherently *unfair* "from a social, moral, or anti-discrimination perspective."[67]

10.2.2.3 Race and Wellness Evaluation

Race in the United States has also been inextricably linked to wellness and fitness for work. This has far-reaching implications for Black individuals, particularly considering the resurgence of workplace wellness programs. Health metrics may thus be considered another means of quantifying the worker – with dire results for Black workers. Consider that when an individual visits a doctor, the doctor is presented with a document that reads something like this: "A 21-year-old African American female presented in the emergency department with diabetic ketoacidosis." Known as a patient's history of present illness (HPI), the medical history of a patient almost always leads with a presentation of their race. Why? Because race has long been considered to be a salient factor in medical decision making and deemed "useful for identifying risk factors and treatment options."[68]

This argument, of course, has been scientifically invalidated. Race is a social construct, not a genetic reality – recent studies have empirically shown that "racial categories are weak proxies for genetic diversity and need to be phased out."[69] Arguments that a patient's race may allow doctors to better understand their needs or predisposition to certain illnesses are not only faulty, but also dangerous, as they may "reinforce racial biases" that lead to inadequate care and poor clinical judgment. Interestingly, the practice of labeling a patient by their race is not universal, but rather presents more often in cases when doctors are treating Black Americans; what's more, racial notations are often labeled as a guess on the part of clinical staff rather than a conversation with the patient in question.[70] Misidentifying the racial identity of a patient only exacerbates the reality that racial quantification of Black patients doesn't actually aid doctors in any meaningful way, but rather distracts from proper care with a racial myth.

The results of racial classification can be deadly depending on the algorithm in question. If, for example, an individual is classified as Black or Hispanic in the formula for estimated glomerular filtration rate (eGFR), they may be excluded from consideration for a life-saving kidney transplant. Similarly, formulas for determining if a woman is eligible for a vaginal birth after a caesarean birth are more likely to deny the option to women of color.[71] Interestingly, while the creators of this tool

[67] Joi Ito, "Supposedly 'Fair' Algorithms Can Perpetuate Discrimination," *Wired*, Feb. 5, 2019, www .wired.com/story/ideas-joi-ito-insurance-algorithms/.

[68] Ashley Andreou, "A Tool Doctors Use Every Day Can Perpetuate Medical Racism," *Scientific American*, June 7, 2021.

[69] Megan Gannon, "Race Is a Social Construct, Scientists Argue," *Scientific American*, Feb. 5, 2016.

[70] Andreou, "A Tool Doctors Use Every Day Can Perpetuate Medical Racism."

[71] Andreou, "A Tool Doctors Use Every Day Can Perpetuate Medical Racism."

chose to exclude certain social factors that strongly correlated with outcomes – such as a woman's marital status – they chose to include race.[72] This choice points to how the specter of racial bias in medicine persists despite a plethora of scientific evidence condemning its validity.

Black Americans who are classified by their race are also more likely to fall into the historical trappings of medical racism that have plagued the medical field for generations. From eugenicist sterilizations of the early twentieth century to racist, sadistic medical experiments such as the Tuskegee syphilis study, Black Americans have ample reason to mistrust medical professionals.[73] Black Americans are less likely to be prescribed important antipsychotic drugs due to historical prejudices and more likely to die from breast cancer than their white counterparts, a reality that is likely due in part to inaccurate medical diagnoses due to racist assumptions.[74] When algorithms and other medical evaluation tools explicitly account for the social factor of race alongside other real, medically relevant considerations, the results are necessarily flawed. Physician Darshali Vyas critically observes that "[i]t's not something about being Black that makes people more or less likely to have an outcome of interest. It's the experience of being Black."[75]

At the same time, there is another type of medical racial blind spot: basing medical predictions on white populations without considering how different symptoms or diseases may present in different demographic groups. For example, there has been recent backlash against standard medical textbooks that only teach new doctors how to diagnose white patients without consideration for how different skin types may present illness. Signals such as "blue lips from oxygen deprivation" or "red bumps from rashes" are far from universal, as individuals with different pigmentation will present with different clinical signs of distress.[76] Doctors are taught from a white patient perspective rather than a universal viewpoint.

Furthermore, other key clinical measures are also rooted in the white gaze. Body mass index (BMI), considered by many doctors to be a key measure of an individual's overall health as a ratio of their height to weight, is based on data collected about white males. Many medical justice advocates argue that stereotypes around the typical white male body type are irrelevant for measuring the overall health of the general population.[77] There are observed racial differences in BMI between white and Black populations, with white populations presenting a generally lower

[72] Mary Harris, "The Same Warped, Racist Logic Used by the NFL Is Ubiquitous in Medicine," *Slate*, June 7, 2021.

[73] See Ayah Nuriddin, Graham Mooney, and Alexandre I. R. White, "Reckoning with Histories of Medical Racism and Violence in the USA," *The Lancet* 396, no. 10256 (2020): 949–51.

[74] Andreou, "A Tool Doctors Use Every Day Can Perpetuate Medical Racism."

[75] Harris, "The Same Warped, Racist Logic Used by the NFL Is Ubiquitous in Medicine."

[76] See Mark Wilson, "Medical Textbooks Are Designed to Diagnose White People. This Student Wants to Change That," *Fast Company*, June 16, 2020, www.fastcompany.com/90527795/medical-textbooks-are-designed-to-diagnose-white-people-this-student-wants-to-change-that.

[77] Judith Riddle, "Editor's Spot: Is the BMI Racially Biased?" *Today's Dietitian* 22, no. 8 (2020): 6.

BMI. However, evidence suggests this is as much a measure of social difference as it is genetic. White women are more likely to adhere to diet culture and social ideals of thinness that associate with lower BMIs.[78] This behavior is not necessarily healthy – in fact, it can often be the opposite. On the other hand, Black women, who are considered to have the highest obesity rate in the United States as measured by BMI, are considered unhealthy due to disease risks that are correlated with higher BMIs. Yet, it's not at all clear that weight is the causal factor for these diseases. Across various populations, there is evidence that the correlation between BMI and disease risk is incomplete at best. South Asian populations, for example, experience "'higher incidences of metabolic disorders at a lower BMI'" than other groups.[79]

At first glance, this argument may appear at odds with my previous assertion that considering race as a factor in medical diagnoses and treatment decisions is problematic. However, the issue here is not that race should be *considered*, but that tools such as the BMI should be *discarded*. Rather than an objective measure of health, BMI is merely a tool that has sought to mask stereotypes of the ideal white body in medical language. The critical takeaway is that not only are Black populations being quantified on the basis of their race through medical algorithms, but they are also being harmed by social pseudo-scientific methods of quantification that are designed for the socially defined white body rather than the scientific human body.

Workplace wellness programs bring these health issues into the world of work by setting normative standards for health status and health behaviors. While Black individuals are often mistreated or misdiagnosed, they are also often compared and penalized according to white social norms that set an arbitrary benchmark. As new technologies give employers expanded access to employees' health records, concerns of medical racism playing out as employment discrimination necessarily come to the forefront. For example, in 2011, collegiate football began to mandate that players be tested for the highly racialized sickle cell trait. Drawing on this decision, legal scholar Chika Duru explores possible discriminatory outcomes that may result if the NFL chose to follow the same path and mandate sickle cell disclosure. Duru hypothesizes that if the NFL had information about a player's sickle cell status, it would almost certainly use that information to negotiate for shorter, cheaper contracts. He also hypothesizes that it may be difficult for players to prevail in a disparate impact claim in response to this discrimination.[80]

[78] See Christine A. Vaughan, William P. Sacco, and Jason W. Beckstead, "Racial/Ethnic Differences in Body Mass Index: The Roles of Beliefs about Thinness and Dietary Restriction," *Body Image* 5, no. 3 (2008): 291–98.

[79] Shai I., Jiang R., Manson J. E., et al., "Ethnicity, Obesity, and Risk of Type 2 Diabetes in Women: A 20-Year Follow-up Study," *Diabetes Care* 29 (2006): 1585–90; Pan W. H., Flegal K. M., Chang H. Y., Yeh W. T., Yeh C. J., and Lee W. C., "Body Mass Index and Obesity-Related Metabolic Disorders in Taiwanese and US Whites and Blacks: Implications for Definitions of Overweight and Obesity for Asians," *Am J Clin Nutr.* 79 (2004): 31–39.

[80] See Chika Duru, "Out for Blood: Employment Discrimination, Sickle Cell Trait, and the NFL," *Hastings Race and Poverty Law Journal* 9, no. (2012): 289.

It is worth considering why there is dialogue around the Black-adjacent sickle cell disease, but not other genetic predispositions, such as type 1 diabetes, that also require active management but are more prominent among white demographic groups.[81] The very conversation around the sickle cell trait suggests arbitrary differential treatment on the basis of race. Perhaps, then, it comes as no surprise that racial minorities opt to participate in genetic testing at significantly lower rates than their white counterparts.[82] Black Americans are also more likely "to believe that genetic testing will lead to racial discrimination."[83] As employers increasingly monitor employee health data, it is critical to consider how the well-founded Black mistrust of medical measures and wellness program benchmarks may result in negative outcomes for racial minorities.

10.3 THE GIG ECONOMY AND RACIAL EXPLOITATION

The gig economy represents another arena for worker quantification and exploitation, and racial minorities bear the brunt of its exploitative practices. At companies such as Uber, Deliveroo, TaskRabbit, and Wag, or as Amazon Turkers, workers are paid for piecemeal work such as grocery shopping and tagging photographs. The percentage of workers engaged in alternative work arrangements – defined as temporary help agency workers, on-call workers, contract workers, and independent contractors or freelancers – rose from 10.7 percent in February 2005 to possibly as high as 15.8 percent in late 2015. Workers who provide services through online intermediaries such as Uber or TaskRabbit accounted for 0.5 percent of all workers in 2015.[84]

The attraction of gig economy jobs is that they provide flexible opportunities for work. On the other hand, gig economy work offers little job security and few benefits. Furthermore, these jobs eliminate opportunities for unionization and for the collective bargaining power that comes along with it.[85] The weak regulation of gig economy work can also provide opportunities for racial discrimination to thrive. Niels Van Doorn provides an eye-opening examination of gender and racial exploitation as part of the gig economy. Van Doorn finds that three characteristics of

[81] See Daphne E. Smith-Marsh, "Type 1 Diabetes Risk Factors," *Endocrine Web*, Mar. 1, 2016, www .endocrineweb.com/conditions/type-1-diabetes/type-1-diabetes-risk-factors.

[82] See Kalyn Saulsberry and Sharon F. Terry, "The Need to Build Trust: A Perspective on Disparities in Genetic Testing," *Genetic Testing and Molecular Biomarkers* 17, no. 9 (2013): 647–48.

[83] Richard K. Zimmerman et al., "Racial Differences in Beliefs about Genetic Screening among Patients at Inner-City Neighborhood Health Centers," *Journal of the National Medical Association* 98, no. 3 (2006): 370–77.

[84] Lawrence F. Katz and Alan B. Krueger, "The Rise and Nature of Alternative Work Arrangements in the United States, 1995–2015," *ILR Review* 72, no. 2 (2019): 382–412.

[85] Ileen A. DeVault et al., *On-Demand Platform Workers in New York State: The Challenges for Public Policy*, ILR Worker Institute, 2019, www.ilr.cornell.edu/sites/default/files/OnDemandReport .Reduced.pdf.

platform-mediated labor serve to facilitate exploitation of already vulnerable work-ers. These characteristics include "1) the legal immunity accorded platform inter-mediaries and clients (especially by Section 230 of the Communications Decency Act), 2) the expansion of managerial control over workers, and 3) an expanded fun-gibility and superfluidity of the workforce."[86]

The gig economy that grew out of telecommunications and algorithmic-management advances in developed countries has also gained a foothold in less-developed countries, where is it is transforming the labor market. For example, content moderators now comprise part of the "planetary labor market," where work-ers from less-developed countries compete with other workers around the world to complete mundane tasks such as comparing pictures with mug shots or determin-ing if social media messages are vulgar or hostile. Technology companies in devel-oped countries employ workers in less-developed countries to ensure that apps run smoothly[87] and to moderate the content on apps and social media sites.[88] Thus, for the first time, in lieu of humans migrating to fulfill labor demands, the work itself is displaced to the sources of a cheap supply of labor. This technologically enabled greater access to lower-cost labor represents new challenges for workers' rights around the world.

Although workers may now work for large tech companies from wherever they reside, many of these workers are paid wages that are well below the U.S. mini-mum wage and are relegated to menial jobs.[89] Tech companies employ people from all over world to clean up developed countries' "e-trash," such as inappropri-ate pictures, and to monitor content on their platforms.[90] As anthropologist Mary Gray and computer scientist Siddharth Suri argue, this new planetary labor market obfuscates labor power relationships as it renders invisible the decision-makers con-trolling online behavior and, as a result, could create a global lower class of work-ers with no job security or benefits.[91] Further, joining the global gig economy can have lasting effects with respect to the marginalization of workers. For example, although commercial content moderation is mostly invisible labor, one misstep

---

[86] Niels Van Doorn, "Platform Labor: On the Gendered and Racialized Exploitation of Low-Income Service Work in the 'On-Demand' Economy," *Information, Communication & Society* 20, no. 6 (2017): 898–914.

[87] Mary Gray and Sidharth Suri, *Ghost Work: How to Stop Silicon Valley from Building a New Global Underclass* (Boston: Houghton Mifflin Harcourt, 2019); Mark Graham, "The Rise of the Planetary Labour Market: What It Means and What It Means for the Future of Work," *New Statesmen Tech*, Jan. 29, 2018, https://tech.newstatesman.com/guest-opinion/planetary-labour-market.

[88] Sarah T. Roberts, "Commercial Content Moderation: Digital Laborers' Dirty Work," *Media Studies Publications* 12 (2016): 1–11.

[89] Mark Graham and Mohammad A. Anwar, "The Global Gig Economy: Towards Planetary Labour Market?" *First Monday* 24, no. 4 (2019): 1–31.

[90] Sarah T. Roberts, "Digital Refuse: Canadian Garbage, Commercial Content Moderation and the Global Circulations of Media's Waste," *Media Studies Publications* 10, no. 1 (2016): 1–11.

[91] Gray and Suri, *Ghost Work*.

can result in a worker's dismissal and even blackballing from the gig economy.[92] Without a resume reflecting a traditional work history and without the social networks acquired from traditional workplaces, gig economy workers will struggle to find work outside the gig economy, thus further increasing their marginalization in the labor market.

10.4 INTERSECTIONAL IDENTITIES IN THE FUTURE OF WORK

There is an intersectional dimension to worker quantification. Professor Kimberlé Crenshaw originated the term *intersectionality* to describe the matrix of oppression endured by Black women.[93] Even in the modern civil rights movement, women were often viewed as supporters of their male counterparts – who were the real "fighters for civil liberties" – rather than fellow activists agitating and strategizing alongside the men for equal civil and labor rights. During that era's marches and congregations, Black women were dissuaded from speaking out about the intersection of racial and gender oppression.[94] For example, during the 1968 sanitation workers strike, one prominent slogan was "I *Am* a Man!" – a sentence highlighting that the spotlight was on Black men's labor rights, rather than labor rights for both Black men and Black women. Furthermore, sociologists and historians have noted that protest language posited Black men as providers and dwelled on pay inequity hindering the Black man's ability to provide for his family. This gendered the labor rights language during the civil rights era and left Black women behind in the fight for labor equality.[95]

Current labor trends show not only disparity between racial and ethnic minorities, but also how these labor disparities are further exacerbated when workers have intersectional identities. Whereas men tend to work only one job, women are much more likely to work multiple jobs, and these jobs often pay women less than their male co-workers.[96] Furthermore, Valerie Wilson and Janelle Jones, both of the Economic Policy Institute, have reported that over the past thirty-five years, women's average annual work hours have increased more than 10 percent, while men's

[92] Sarah T. Roberts, "In/visibility," in *Surplus³: Labour and the Digital* (Toronto: Letters & Handshakes, 2016), 30–32.
[93] Kimberlé Crenshaw, "Mapping the Margins: Intersectionality, Identity Politics, and Violence against Women of Color," *Stanford Law Review* 43, no. 6 (1991): 1241–99; Kimberlé Crenshaw, "Demarginalizing the Intersection of Race and Sex: A Black Feminist Critique of Antidiscrimination Doctrine, Feminist Theory and Antiracist Politics," *University of Chicago Legal Forum* 1989, no. 1 (1989): 139–67.
[94] Thomas F. Jackson, *From Civil Rights to Human Rights: Martin Luther King, Jr., and the Struggle for Economic Justice* (Philadelphia: University of Pennsylvania Press, 2009).
[95] Steve Estes, "'I Am a Man!'" Race, Masculinity, and the 1968 Memphis Sanitation Strike," *Labor History* 41, no. 2 (2000): 153–70.
[96] Valerie Wilson, "Women Are More Likely to Work Multiple Jobs Than Men," *Economic Policy Institute*, July 9, 2015, www.epi.org/publication/women-are-more-likely-to-work-multiple-jobs-than-men/.

average annual work hours have increased by only 5 percent.[97] These numbers suggest that not only are women working longer hours than they did before, but that
they are still not getting paid as much as men. (Perhaps this is one reason that more
women than men work multiple jobs.)

Many Black and Hispanic/Latinx female workers work in jobs that are the most
likely to become automated within the next few decades. The U.S. Bureau of Labor
Statistics estimates that over 1.5 million jobs that employ Black women are at risk
due to automation, and that over 2.5 million Hispanic/Latinx women are at risk of
losing their jobs due to automation.[98] Moreover, secretarial and administrative jobs,
which minority women are more likely to have, involve data processing and data
collection, routinized tasks that could be completed by programmed automated
systems. With labor automation threatening to eliminate job opportunities for Black
and Latinx women, large unemployment disparities will likely arise within the next
decade – unless the government takes concrete steps to address the problem.

10.5 SOME PROPOSALS FOR REFORM

Clearly, the issues of emerging technologies and their impacts on racial quantification and subjugation, especially in the workplace, are complex. Even economists
are recognizing that change is necessary. The laissez-faire capitalist approach to
labor market regulation, exemplified by the work of Thomas Sowell and others, has
endured on the assumption that markets alone will correct for discrimination over
time. However, economists are increasingly recognizing and agreeing that government and policymakers ought to take an active – though economically driven – role
in correcting race-based disparities in the labor market.[99]

Several scholars have proposed a rethinking of how data may be deployed to
achieve more ethical outcomes rather than continuing to replicate past injustices.
One such book, *Data Feminism* by Catherine D'Ignazio and Lauren F. Klein,
draws on the intersectional theory of Kimberlé Crenshaw to argue that data science can take a different path than merely supporting the existing problematic
power structures that define the United States today.[100] Taking an intersectional
feminist approach to data would allow for the participation of all affected actors,
such as Black Americans, in the policymaking process, resulting in more equitable

[97] Valerie Wilson and Janelle Jones, "Working Harder or Finding It Harder to Work: Demographic
Trends in Annual Work Hours Show an Increasingly Fractured Workforce," *Economic Policy Institute*,
Feb. 22, 2018, www.epi.org/publication/trends-in-work-hours-and-labor-market-disconnection.

[98] U.S. Bureau of Labor Statistics, "Labor Force Statistics from the Current Population Survey, 2018"
Table 5; Hegewisch, Childers, and Hartmann, *Women, Automation, and the Future of Work*.

[99] Thomas Sowell, *Discrimination and Disparities* (New York: Basic Books, 2019); Jennifer L. Doleac, "A
Review of Thomas Sowell, *Discrimination and Disparities*," *Journal of Economic Literature* 59, no. 2
(2021): 574–89.

[100] See Catherine D'Ignazio and Lauren F. Klein, *Data Feminism* (Cambridge, MA: MIT Press, 2020).

outcomes.[101] Sasha Costanza-Chock's *Design Justice* echoes this call for a participatory model of justice, arguing that structural inequality can be effectively challenged by minority-led, minority-conscious design.[102]

Particularly addressing the issue of inherently biased historical data sets, other scholars have proposed theories of algorithmic intervention to counteract biases. In my 2021 article "The Auditing Imperative for Automated Hiring," I argue that an algorithmic auditing imperative for the workplace would effectively dismantle the "see no evil, hear no evil" approach to Title VII that employers currently adopt.[103] By actively auditing automated hiring algorithms, employers would have direct knowledge if their hiring or evaluation systems were disproportionately harming people of color, creating more equal outcomes and protecting Black workers from the negative effects of biased or incomplete input data.

The legal scholar Anupam Chander has proposed a more far-reaching policy of algorithmic affirmative action which would mandate that algorithms be trained on diverse, complete data sets, monitoring for disparate impact in outcomes and making necessary changes to address any such impact as time goes on.[104] There is some debate over the extent to which altering algorithms on the basis of racially biased outcomes is lawful. Professor Jason Bent argues that a system of algorithmic affirmative action does hold water, both under Title VII of the Civil Rights Act and constitutional equal protection clauses. Drawing on the work of Professor Reva Siegel, Bent argues that an "anti-balkanization" interpretation of anti-discrimination case law – where the Court is less concerned with substantive or formal equality than with ensuring neither side feels classified on the basis of their race – would allow algorithmic affirmative action to survive legal challenges.[105] If the Court were to allow this approach, algorithmic affirmative action may offer a feasible way to mitigate the effects of racial quantification in future algorithmic decisions.

Caroline Criado-Perez's *Invisible Women: Data Bias in a World Designed for Men* is another piece of feminist literature that offers salient policy proposals for issues of race as well, and is aligned in part with Chander's model affirmative action. Much like communities of color, women have been harmed by algorithms and systems of quantification and classification designed for the white male. Criado-Perez argues that collecting more data on women, who have previously been neglected by science and society, for algorithms to use is an important place to start.[106] For racial

---

[101] See Rafaan Daliri-Ngametua, "Book Review: *Data Feminism*," *CUNY Graduate Center: Theory, Research, and Action in Urban Education* 6, no. 1 (2021): 62–64, https://traue.commons.gc.cuny.edu/book-review-data-feminism/ (accessed June 8, 2021).

[102] See Sasha Costanza-Chock, *Design Justice: Community-Led Practices to Build the Worlds We Need* (Cambridge, MA: MIT Press, 2020).

[103] See Ajunwa, "Auditing Imperative for Automated Hiring."

[104] See Anupam Chander, "The Racist Algorithm?" *Michigan Law Review* 115, no. 6 (2017): 1023–45.

[105] See Jason Bent, "Is Algorithmic Affirmative Action Legal?" *Georgetown Law Journal* 108 (2020): 852.

[106] See Lulu Garcia-Navarro, "Caroline Criado-Perez on Data Bias and 'Invisible Women,'" *NPR*, Mar. 17, 2019.

minorities, this approach has equally relevant applications. Collecting data that better represents historically marginalized communities for use in algorithms may lead to more equal outcomes from the outset.

In general, representation and participation are critical themes for reform efforts. The Black American has been quantified according to biased white standards for generations. Challenging this power dynamic requires conscious, active intervention that centers Black voices. This is the path to a future of work that represents just outcomes rather than merely replicates past injustices.

10.5.1 *The Need for Stronger Labor and Social Protections*

As discussed above, the trend towards automation has racial implications. The jobs most in danger of automation are held by racial minorities. Thus, the trend towards automation will most impact minority workers and will likely widen the gulf of inequality as those workers are made redundant in an automated workplace. This means that the idea of a universal basic income (UBI) deserves consideration. As legal scholars such as Cynthia Estlund have noted, there is a pressing need to construct a broader foundation of economic security for all, including for workers who can no longer expect to find steady employment. Professor Estlund has thus argued for a three-prong strategy. This strategy would include a UBI; a federal job guarantee; and a reduction in the number of hours an individual can work, which will increase employment opportunities for a wider range of people.[107]

Other legal scholars, such as Brishen Rogers, however, have argued against a UBI, primarily for its potential to exacerbate racial inequality in the labor market. Professor Rogers notes, "Were a UBI extended to citizens and legal permanent residents but not to irregular migrants and guest workers, employers would have powerful incentives to hire them into the worst jobs and to push to expand the number of such workers in the country, putting downward pressure on overall wages and creating a permanent racialized laboring underclass." As an example, Rogers points to the Gulf Arab states, which grant a form of UBI to their citizens but which have also become "entirely dependent on guest worker labor, and many former guest workers in those countries have alleged that systemic and brutal labor abuses are common."[108]

In addition, Rogers notes that formerly incarcerated citizens are also likely to be left out of any governmental UBI scheme, given the collateral consequences of

---

[107] Cynthia Estlund, "What Should We Do after Work? Automation and Employment Law," *Yale Law Journal* 128, no. 2 (2018): 254–326; Cynthia Estlund, "Three Big Ideas for a Future of Less Work and a Three-Dimensional Alternative," *Law & Contemporary Problems* 82, no. 3 (2019): 1–43.

[108] Brishen Rogers, "Basic Income and the Resilience of Social Democracy," *Comparative Labor Law & Policy Journal* 40, no. 2 (2019): 214–15; Rebecca Falconer, "Qatar's Foreign Domestic Workers Subjected to Slave-Like Conditions," *The Guardian*, Feb. 26, 2014.

conviction that already deny many public benefits to the formerly incarcerated.[109] As Rogers underscores, this omission is likely to have a racial impact: "I find it very difficult to believe that the U.S. Congress will extend a UBI to formerly incarcerated individuals … In the unlikely event that Congress does … many states would devise ways to ensure that those individuals pay back the UBI in some fashion. For example, they could devise special assessments to compensate the state for the costs of their incarceration. In either case, the result would again be to create a pool of easily exploitable laborers – and again, a heavily racialized one." Ultimately, Rogers concludes that a UBI is the least desirable solution. In his view, a better solution would be strengthening labor protections for workers: "If we want to make it easier for workers to leave jobs, a UBI seems like a clear second- (or third-) best solution, compared to reforms that would give workers clear due process rights and real mobility rights."[110]

On one hand, the future of work brings with it technological advances that could enable greater worker productivity. On the other hand, technological advances could allow for greater surveillance, greater quantification, and more opportunities for racial discrimination. Both futures are possible, but governmental action will determine which one will occur. Adequate legal attention to prevent new work technologies from widening the racial divide will enable a future where all workers, regardless of race, can thrive.

---

[109] Michael Pinard, "Collateral Consequences of Criminal Convictions: Confronting Issues of Race and Dignity," *New York University Law Review* 85, no. 2 (2010): 457.

[110] Rogers, "Basic Income and the Resilience of Social Democracy," 214–15.

PART IV

Business Ethics and New Legal Frameworks

11

The Ethical Dimensions of Worker Quantification

[A]utomation cannot be permitted to become a blind monster which grinds out more cars and simultaneously snuffs out the hopes and lives of the people by whom the industry was built ... We too realize that when human values are subordinated to blind economic forces, human beings can become human scrap.

–The Reverend Martin Luther King Jr.[1]

John Rawls's *Theory of Justice* offers a theory of moral justice that has been critically applied to the workplace. Specifically, this theory helps explain why the quantification of workers should be a matter of ethical and legal concern. To understand Rawlsian philosophy, however, one must first acknowledge its roots in social contract theory. In the seventeenth century, philosopher Thomas Hobbes developed social contract theory in response to the political tensions between absolutist regimes and democratic factions that dominated his time. He rationalized the foundations of government as universal to both of these extremes. Hobbes's basic assumption was simple: He believed that human beings were foremost rational and self-interested. Therefore, he argued, individuals would be willing to subject themselves to sovereign political authority to the extent that it allowed them to live in a civil, desirable way. For Hobbes, civil society stood at odds with its default alternative, the "State of Nature." Hobbes saw the State of Nature as wild, brutish, and a threat to individual livelihood. Out of the self-interest of living, individuals would "construct a Social Contract" that would (1) renounce the "rights they had against one another in the State of Nature" and (2) give someone or some institution "the authority and power to enforce the initial contract." Even in circumstances of authoritarian rule, Hobbes argued that it was more important to uphold the existing social contract than risk return to the State of Nature. Hobbes viewed morality as a "conventional" by-product of the original social contract.[2]

---

[1] Dr. Martin Luther King Jr., Address at the Transport Workers Union of America's 11th Constitutional Convention, Apr. 27, 1961.
[2] Celeste Friend, "Social Contract Theory," *Internet Encyclopedia of Philosophy*, https://iep.utm.edu/soc-cont/ (last visited Nov. 10, 2020).

Philosopher John Locke, also in the seventeenth century, operated under a differ-ent assumption. Locke viewed the State of Nature as "a state of perfect and complete liberty to conduct one's life as one best sees fit, free from the interference of others" but a state in which objective morality very much exists. Therefore, according to the rules of nature, all human beings are equal and humans are not to harm others with concern to "life, health, liberty, or possessions": This is the Law of Nature.[3] In a natural state, each man has the right to enforce the Law of Nature. When individu-als enter a social contract, they are explicitly agreeing to give up their individual rights to enforcement, instead investing that power in a public government. Locke emphasized an individual's right to leave a social contract when it is no longer gov-erning in the interests of the people. In contrast, Hobbes viewed the social contract as a critical, untouchable underpinning to all civil society as opposed to an agree-ment that may be modified, rescinded, or renegotiated. These differences largely stemmed from their differing views on the social contract's alternatives. For Locke, humans would continue to balance their interests in the absence of a contract; for Hobbes, such a reality would mean a return to chaos and barbarism.

In the eighteenth century, philosopher Jean-Jacques Rousseau advanced a version of social contract theory that, like Locke's, rested on the assumption that all people are equal, and further that all people are free – therefore, any right to govern must come from some form of agreement, or social contract. Rosseau's normative social con-tract theory finds its origins not from humans seeking to escape the State of Nature, but from humans who already have. Rousseau believed that the social contract origi-nated in a state where civilization had progressed beyond the State of Nature, but in an undesirable way. This is in contrast to Hobbes, who viewed the social contract as inherent to forming civilization rather than as a solution to its perils. Rousseau argued that the social contract would ameliorate this undesirable state of civilization by encoding the wills of all individuals in a society into a "collective ... single body, directed to the good of all considered together." For Rousseau, the sovereign and the people enter into a reciprocal relationship where each is protecting the interests of the whole.[4]

Rawls's theories are rooted in the work of all three of these philosophers. Rather than viewing the State of Nature as the default state of man, Rawls argued that all of man shared what he called the "Original Position." The Original Position, Rawls's "highly abstracted version of the State of Nature," rests on the same assumptions as other social contract theorists: that humans are rational and self-interested. It adds the condition that in this position, humans are also denied any information about their own circumstances or relative societal status, be it age, race, prejudices, and so on. Like Locke, Rawls regards this position as inherently fair; thus, Rawls believed that the Original Position provides the conditions under which principles for a just

3   Friend, "Social Contract Theory."
4   Friend, "Social Contract Theory."

society ought to be chosen. From the Original Position, Rawls purports the rational actor would come to find two Principles of Justice: (1) "there should be as much civil liberty as possible as long as those goods are distributed equally" and (2) "economic inequalities are only justified when the least advantaged member of society is nonetheless better off than she would be under alternative arrangements."[5] These principles essentially guide and constrain how any social contract to govern would be structured.

Rawls's Theory of Justice has salient applications to the employment context. In "The Structure of Rawlsian Theory of Just Work," Lars Lindblom explores Rawlsian theory in the context of business ethics. Lindblom argues that a Rawlsian conception of justice has significant implications for developing social structures. Lindblom divides the implications of Rawlsian theory into two subcategories of justice: domestic justice, or "what institutions there ought to be," and local justice, or "how we ought to act within the constraints of these institutions." An ethical Rawlsian firm would ensure domestic justice through design: It would be free from discrimination, would allow workers to exercise their "basic rights and liberties," and would be structured so as to help society's least advantaged.[6] At the local level, workplace relations would be "based on the idea of fair cooperation," equal rights and liberties, and "the value of reciprocity." To the extent that inequalities did exist within the workplace, they would be a reflection of ability. Workplaces should generally be designed in the best interests of the least advantaged; however, rewards or resources that could be perceived as within the control of any worker – a reflection of their choices – may be distributed based on merit.[7]

This practical justification of meritocracy, all else equal, within Rawlsian justice is significant. Meritocracy in many ways underpins Western society today; yet, we continue to see injustice. This is because the most basic tenets of Rawls's theory have not been universally applied. An equal distribution of civil liberty and a social arrangement designed such that society's least advantaged are best off are prerequisites before any unequal distribution on the basis of choice may be accepted as ethical. Therefore, Lindblom's argument is most useful for understanding how Rawlsian justice may apply to the workplace at its most basic level. The central question is: What would a workplace wherein conditions are tailored to the greatest benefit of the least advantaged workers look like in practice?

Lindblom underscores that such a workplace would be free from unlawful discrimination, allowing workers to exercise liberties with fairness and equality in mind. In my paper "The 'Black Box' at Work," I argue that this means Rawlsian workplaces must allow "for some measure of workplace democracy." Furthermore,

5 Friend, "Social Contract Theory."
6 Lars Lindblom, "The Structure of a Rawlsian Theory of Just Work," *Journal of Business Ethics* 101, (2011): 577–80.
7 Lindblom, "Structure of a Rawlsian Theory of Just Work," 586, 591.

because the concentration of too much power in the hands of employers would necessarily violate Rawls's first principle of justice, I argue that a Rawlsian workplace would also require some measure of worker autonomy, the ethical mandate from which worker privacy rights originate.[8] Workplace design and function must facilitate and protect workers' exercise of civil liberties.

Some scholars argue that the ethical mandates of Rawlsian justice reach far beyond how a workplace is structured or functions. In "Justice at Work: Arguing for Property-Owning Democracy," Nien-hê Hsieh argues that Rawlsian justice extends to mandates concerning the nature of work. Scholars with traditional Rawlsian views on work argue that citizens must have work, while other scholars argue that the nature of that work must allow for worker voice. However, extrapolating his argument from Rawls's favorable treatment of property-owning democracy as opposed to welfare-state capitalism in "A Theory of Justice," Hsieh argues that Rawlsian justice goes further. He highlights two aspects of work under Rawlsian theory: Work is meaningful, and workers are not subjugated to servitude. Central to servitude is arbitrary interference, wherein individuals are subject to and limited by the arbitrary will of others. Hsieh argues that property-owning democracy solves issues of arbitrary interference, as it allows workers to be less dependent on the labor relationship. Further, meaningful work, which "requires the exercise of judgment, initiative, and intellect on the part of workers," is better served by property-owning democracy, as less financial dependency in the labor relationship means more discretion to seek meaningful work. Thus, Hsieh argues, only when taking the *nature* of work into account does Rawls's choice of property-owning democracy over welfare capitalism make sense, as better distribution of productive assets both limits arbitrary interference and allows for adequate opportunities for meaningful work.[9] Therefore, Rawlsian justice requires not only worker autonomy and worker voice and power, but also meaningful work.

For Hsieh, the exercise of worker autonomy, voice, and power does not necessarily mean workplaces must take a democratic structure. In "Rawlsian Justice and Workplace Republicanism," Hsieh instead advocates for organizational design guided by "workplace republicanism," a system by which the managerial level still exists, but in a more limited, controlled way that allows for workers to give input and "contest managerial directives." While workplace republicanism divests firm ownership from workers, therefore limiting worker power more than a worker-controlled democracy would, Hsieh argues that the right to own a firm's "productive assets" is not mandated under Rawls's theory, as it is not sufficiently related to a worker's self-respect. Therefore, while a worker-controlled democracy would satisfy Rawlsian justice, it is not the only workplace structure that can do so. Workplace republicanism

---

[8] Ajunwa, "The 'Black Box' at Work," 4.

[9] Nien-hê Hsieh, "Justice at Work: Arguing for Property-Owning Democracy," *Journal of Social Philosophy* 40, no. 3 (2009): 397, www-users.york.ac.uk/~mpon500/pod/Hsieh.pdf 1, 19.

can also ensure worker voice and autonomy while maintaining the managerial structure that is sometimes critical to efficient management of large firms.[10]

Workplace republicanism may also offer a valuable means by which to mitigate arbitrary interference in the workplace. Under Rawlsian justice, workers maintain the basic right to be protected against and free from "arbitrary interference at work," which may limit workers' pursuit of desirable ends, increase uncertainty, and interfere with an individual's self-worth and self-confidence.[11] Decisions that dictate worker actions, define employment conditions, and indirectly affect the worker are all critical examples of workplace interference; interference is arbitrary if it cannot be justified by a worker's interests. Hsieh argues that workplace democracy may be an adequate tool to hedge arbitrary interference, although not the only such tool; alternative tools, such as workplace exits, may be effective but are also burdensome for the least advantaged. Hsieh argues that workplace republicanism offers the "institutionalized forms of protection" which are critical to mitigating interference.[12] Therefore, it maintains the advantage that worker-controlled democracy has over workplace exits.

In today's global economy, where the firm is already structured around managerial presence, implementing Rawlsian justice as worker-controlled democracy may prove to be a difficult feat. This isn't to say it would be impossible; some companies that identify as worker cooperatives have chosen this approach with great success. For example, the popular Equal Exchange cooperative – which specializes in ethically sourced organic goods – is one of the largest examples of a worker cooperative in the United States today.[13] Equal Exchange employs over 130 "worker-owners" who all own an equal piece of the firm and its profits; the goal is protecting worker-owners and farmers, not caring for the interests of shareholders.[14] Furthermore, some scholars, such as Keith Breen, argue that workplace democracy is much better for affirming worker rights than are republican models.[15] However, for large-scale existing firms that follow the shareholder model, shifting to a worker cooperative seems like an improbability, if not an impossibility. Hsieh's arguments are therefore critical, as they offer a method by which to incorporate the principles of Rawlsian justice within the existing workplace. Instituting checks on managerial control, creating avenues for worker voice, and ensuring protections for individuals against workplace interference is a critical step that any organization can take to become more ethical.

---

[10] Nien-hê Hsieh, "Rawlsian Justice and Workplace Republicanism," *Social Theory and Practice* 31, no. 1 (2005): 116–17, 119.

[11] Hsieh, "Rawlsian Justice and Workplace Republicanism," 124–25.

[12] Hsieh, "Rawlsian Justice and Workplace Republicanism," 123, 131, 134.

[13] Equal Exchange, "About: Our Model," https://equalexchange.coop/about (accessed May 13, 2021).

[14] Equal Exchange, "Worker-Owned," https://equalexchange.coop/worker-owned (accessed May 13, 2021).

[15] See Keith Breen, "Freedom, Republicanism, and Workplace Democracy," *Critical Review International Social and Political Philosophy* 18, no. 4 (2015): 470–85.

Hsieh's work is important, as it draws on not only theories of Rawlsian justice, but also the ethical frameworks of neo-republicanism. To understand what neo-republicanism is and what is means for ethical work, one must look to the work of Philip Pettit, which is essential to the neo-republican canon. In his seminal work *Republicanism: A Theory of Freedom and Government*, Pettit argues for a definition of freedom as "non-domination" as opposed to non-interference or self-mastery. Here, neo-republicanism critically diverges from some conceptions of Rawlsian justice that argue for a freedom as non-interference approach. The advantage of freedom as non-domination is that, according to Pettit, it does not require the dominator to ever take action; rather, domination occurs when a power structure allows one party to exercise arbitrary control or interference over another. Therefore, applied to the workplace, freedom as non-domination offers more protection than other conceptions of freedom that protect individuals from tangible actions but not from non-tangible influence. Defining freedom as non-domination implies that (1) subordination is prohibited, (2) self-mastery or autonomy are pursuable but not required, and (3) republican freedom may transcend politics to apply to all forms of human interaction. In a workplace application, republican freedom in institutions would structurally include "reciprocal power" and "constitutional provision" as well as republican freedom as a social norm that would guide individual interactions beyond mere institutional design.[16]

As I endorse in my 2020 paper "The 'Black Box' at Work," the neo-republican concept of freedom as non-domination does in fact align with Rawlsian justice and is a key component of ethical workplace design.[17] Worker domination means workers are denied effective choice, and therefore voice and power. Thus, neo-republicanism and Rawlsian justice are in convergence, as a workplace must be free from domination in order to satisfy Rawls's basic ethical principles. In "Non-Domination, Contestation and Freedom: The Contribution of Philip Pettit to Learning and Democracy in Organisations," Martyn Griffin, Mark Learmonth, and Carole Elliott explore what freedom as non-domination may look like in practice in the workplace. Griffin et al. define domination as the "capacity to interfere" in an arbitrary way – that is, without consideration of those who interference may affect – such that the interference limits the choices and decision-making abilities of a given group.[18]

To prevent this kind of domination in the workplace, Griffin et al. echo Pettit's call for constitutional provision and reciprocal power. Concerning constitutional provision, the authors argue for a worker-elected work council to represent the interests of employees in the decision-making process, especially as those decisions

---

[16] Philip Pettit, *Republicanism: A Theory of Freedom and Government* (1997; Reprint, Oxford: Clarendon Press, 2002), esp. chap. 2.

[17] See Ajunwa, "The 'Black Box' at Work," 4.

[18] Martyn Griffin, Mark Learmonth, and Carole Elliott, "Non-Domination, Contestation and Freedom: The Contribution of Philip Pettit to Learning and Democracy in Organisations," *Managememt Learning* 46 (2015): 317, 328–29 (accessed via https://dro.dur.ac.uk/12043/1/12043.pdf).

concern employee welfare. Concerning reciprocal power, which is intended to level the playing field between dominators and subjects, Griffin et al. envision an organizational approach wherein resources are equally distributed to minimize the potential for interference. Reciprocal power may take the form of establishing permanent employment contracts for all workers, publishing compensation information for all, distributing training resources equally, considering the input of stakeholders when determining promotions, de-emphasizing status symbols, and compensating workers for participating in democratic endeavors in the workplace.[19]

On the whole, Rawlsian justice in tandem with workplace republicanism seems to offer a picture of what an ethical workplace should look like. Worker voice, worker power, worker autonomy, and meaningful work all seem to play a central role in ethical design. It is necessary to explore these concepts further.

11.1 MEANINGFUL WORK

As Hsieh lays out, meaningful work is a critical component of Rawlsian justice in the workplace. But what does meaningful work actually look like? In *Meaningful Work: Connecting Business Ethics and Organization Studies*, Christopher Michaelson, Michael G. Pratt, Adam M. Grant, and Craig P. Dunn explore developments in organizational understanding of meaningful work, seeking to explain what makes work meaningful, why meaningfulness matters, and how meaningfulness may be cultivated in the workplace through both business ethics and organizational behavior. By a business ethics definition, meaningful work must be "purposeful and significant" and involve "alignment" between an individual and the tasks that they perform, fostering self-respect and identity formation.[20] The authors focus on universal traits of meaningful work, citing work that allows for freedom of association, worker autonomy, personal development, financial well-being, moral growth, and the ability for employees to act in their own self-interest. They also cite the importance of "engag[ing] the worker in both deciding and doing."[21] The authors acknowledge that meaningful work, on the whole, is difficult to define. However, there are certainly "wrong answers," such as work that "fails to help others" and work that "neglects one's responsibility to oneself to try to live a meaningful life." They suggest businesses may enhance meaningfulness at work via corporate social responsibility and by organizational practices with a moral grounding.[22]

Michaelson et al.'s enumeration of qualities of meaningful work that resonate in Rawlsian justice is useful as a starting point for distinguishing meaningful work in

---

[19] Griffin, Learmonth, and Elliott, "Non-Domination, Contestation and Freedom," 317.
[20] Christopher Michaelson et al., "Meaningful Work: Connecting Business Ethics and Organization Studies," *Journal of Business Ethics* 121 (2014): 78–82.
[21] Michaelson et al., "Meaningful Work," 82–83.
[22] Michaelson et al., "Meaningful Work," 84, 87.

the modern day. For example, while Uber drivers may feel their work is meaningful, as it allows for extreme autonomy, many drivers may agree the job itself does little to facilitate personal development, moral growth, or financial security. Uber, if trying to become a more ethical company, would need to address these shortcomings in their employment model. Understanding which elements of meaningful work certain jobs lack is the first step towards ameliorating the problem.

Developing this understanding is more critical than ever as new innovations threaten to upend the nature of work as we know it. New technology is creating new workplaces and new jobs that, if not carefully designed, risk running afoul of ethical workplace principles in the name of efficiency and progress. In *Robots in the Workplace: A Threat to – or Opportunity for – Meaningful Work?*, Jilles Smids, Sven Nyholm, and Hannah Berkers examine one threat of innovation to the ethical workplace through the lens of robotization. Smids et al. argue that innovation, as exemplified by robotization, may either impede the creation of an ethical workplace through meaningful work *or* facilitate it. Intentional design and careful implementation have the power to determine whether the future of work is more Rawlsian than not.

Smids et al. explore the impact of robotization on meaningful work along five dimensions: pursuing a purpose, social relationships, exercising skills and self-development, self-esteem and recognition, and autonomy. Concerning pursuing a purpose, Smids et al. argue that robots may threaten purpose in work if they take over the more complex, skilled tasks that constitute an individual's work or if they take over a majority of the tasks. However, if implemented properly, such that "human workers understand themselves as teaming up with robots," robots in the workplace may enhance a sense of purpose, with robots completing the mundane work in order to free up time for humans to complete more complex, "worthy" tasks.[23]

Robots also have the capacity to change the nature of social interaction in the workplace. As a workforce is increasingly automated, there will be fewer individuals with whom remaining employees can interact, potentially resulting in "isolation" and "a diminished sense of shared agency and purposiveness." Smids et al. argue, however, that if robots are intelligently designed such that "they become seen as team members" that enhance the workspace and facilitate interaction, they may actually improve social work relationships.[24]

Exercising skills and self-development are critical components of meaningful work; if robots supersede humans such that skill development is useless, the personal growth and fulfillment that results from learning skills will never occur. Recent studies suggest this effect of robot interference may already be observable. The authors temper this warning with the suggestion that new, more complex skills

---

[23] Jilles Smids, Sven Nyholm, and Hannah Berkers, "Robots in the Workplace: A Threat to – or Opportunity for – Meaningful Work?" *Philosophy & Technology* 33, no. 3 (2020): 503, 511.

[24] Smids, Nyholm, and Berkers, "Robots in the Workplace," 512.

may replace what robots take over. Humans must still have skills to run and design machines and interpret the data they produce.[25]

Another issue that may arise from robots taking over skilled, difficult tasks is lower self-esteem and self-worth on the part of workers. This issue may be occupation dependent, however, as in certain fields, the use of AI improves individuals' performance and in turn their social standing and self-esteem.[26]

The last aspect of meaningful work Smids et al. address is autonomy. They suggest that robotics may lead to automation that denies workers the opportunity to be creative or employ critical thinking skills. Further, automation may make it more difficult for workers to truly understand their job. These effects "may lead to feelings of alienation and diminished human autonomy." Again, Smids et al. point to organization design as critical to mitigating these negative effects, so that the autonomy and meaning that may result from robots taking over mundane tasks allow workers to focus more on work they find to be of value.[27] Smids et al. ultimately suggest that the future of work hangs in the balance. Applying their argument to automation at large, it seems that new technologies have the power to create more meaningful work in the ethical interest of workers at large. However, this path requires serious thoughtful interventions. As Smids et al. note, there is much room for error. The path towards automation may easily mean a path towards reduced meaning in the workplace. Unfortunately, this latter path already appears to be taking shape.

In "Ethical Implications of the Fourth Industrial Revolution for Business and Society," John Hooker and Tae Wan Kim survey the state of the social contract between businesses and society in light of rapid advancements in automated technologies, and ultimately find that work is not only shifting away from meaning and autonomy, but also in some cases is disappearing altogether. Hooker and Kim level criticism against the gig economy, exemplified by companies such as TaskRabbit, and the sharing economy, featuring companies such as Airbnb, arguing that they have contributed to "a quiet shift" that has seen the full-time employment model morph into an increasingly dominant model of gig or temporary work. Technology, economic incentives, and a cheaper contract-labor market have facilitated this shift away from the traditional employment relationship. While the freedom and flexibility of the gig economy may allow for "self-realization and life satisfaction," Hooker and Kim warn of potential negative ethical implications of the gig economy: unpredictability, economic insecurity, lack of control, and increased inequality.[28] Their warnings aren't abstract. As of 2019, only around 48 percent of Uber drivers self-reported being satisfied with their work, despite an

---

[25] Smids, Nyholm, and Berkers, "Robots in the Workplace," 513.
[26] Smids, Nyholm, and Berkers, "Robots in the Workplace," 513–14.
[27] Smids, Nyholm, and Berkers, "Robots in the Workplace," 514, 515.
[28] John Hooker and Tae Wan Kim, "Ethical Implications of the Fourth Industrial Revolution for Business and Society," in *Business and Society 360*, ed. David M. Wasieleski and James Weber (Bingley, UK: Emerald Publishing, 2019), 35.

overall pay raise for all drivers.[29] Some drivers, frustrated by a lack of autonomy and the rule of Uber's algorithm over their lives, have even turned to self-made hacks to avoid lower fares, such as UberPOOL ride shares, and to increases opportunities for surge premiums.[30]

While I explore this issue at length later in this chapter, it's worth noting what gaming the system says about the ethics of work in the changing technological age. As workers find themselves denied autonomy through traditional structures, they are increasingly looking to take back control. I argue that this is a statement on the inherent value and validity of Rawlsian justice in and of itself. Ethical work is designed to maximize the human rights of a given population in the most egalitarian way. But denying workers these rights does not eradicate their desire or need for fulfillment; instead, it causes workers to live an oppressed existence wherein they seek to take back the resources necessary to respond to their own needs wherever and however they can. Unfortunately, these self-made fixes will always put workers at a disadvantage: The one-sided power dynamic of modern work means that workers are most often helpless to satisfy their self-interests under the yoke of employer domination. It is therefore critical for truly ethical work that workplaces begin the shift towards Rawlsian justice at the institutional level.

Unfortunately, the issue of allowing workers to pursue personal and moral fulfillment becomes even more complicated as work itself begins to go away. In their article, Hooker and Kim also address the issue of unemployment, as AI takes over manufacturing, retailing, and even personal services, displacing thousands of workers. Here, they turn to the issue of inequality and the ethical role of business in mitigating the disaster technology is wreaking in the lives of workers. Hooker and Kim argue that business should be held responsible along the lines of the "responsibility principle," which holds one responsible for fixing the wrongs they create, and by Rawlsian justice, wherein "technological unemployment is justified only if the worst-off group – the unemployed or those who systematically lack opportunities for gainful employment – has reason to accept the societal structure in which massive technological unemployment exists."[31] They further argue that universal basic income (UBI) and market-based wealth redistribution are viable methods by which to ameliorate problems of technological unemployment.

Hooker and Kim argue that a universal basic income is ethically sound on the grounds that it offers financial security while increasing workers' flexibility and therefore opportunities, in turn allowing individuals to live more meaningful lives. Grappling with further obligations of corporations, the authors stop short of arguing they have "natural duties," as they are human inventions. However, they do acknowledge that

[29] Harry Campbell, "Lyft & Uber Driver Survey 2020: Uber Driver Satisfaction Takes a Big Hit," *Ride Share Guy*, Feb. 14, 2021, https://therideshareguy.com/uber-driver-survey/.

[30] "How Uber Drivers Are Gaming the System," Warwick Business School, Aug. 16, 2017, www.wbs.ac.uk/news/how-uber-drivers-are-gaming-the-system/.

[31] Hooker and Kim, "Ethical Implications of the Fourth Industrial Revolution for Business and Society," 35.

UBI is not a full solution in and of itself; living a meaningful life, they argue, is often tied to organizational membership that facilitates development and allows individuals to take part in the communal whole. Because corporations are such organizations in modern society, it may be argued that they are integral to providing a meaningful life. With this in mind, Hooker and Kim ultimately advocate for a view of new, innovative technologies as augmentation that would *enhance* human skill and intelligence, as opposed to automation that would *replace* human skill and intelligence. Hooker and Kim suggest that by augmentation, "as many humans as possible can sustainably obtain opportunities to be part of collective value creation, to contribute to the good of society, and to add meaning to their lives."[32] Work is central to creating meaning in humans' daily lives, and as such cannot merely be done away with.

Hooker and Kim aren't alone in their hesitation in establishing a UBI. While they argue that a UBI may obscure meaningful work, Orlando Lazar, in "Work, Domination, and the False Hope of Universal Basic Income," argues that it may also fail to solve the problems of domination that have given rise to calls for UBI in the first place. For his analysis, Lazar focuses on the "livable UBI," which is intended to replace – rather than supplement – income. Lazar views worker domination through a republican lens; as such, like Hsieh, he cautions that worker exit is not a true solution to workplace injustice – an exit would require savings and self-sufficiency from work. While a UBI could provide such security and allow for a strong exit, Lazar argues it does not fully address the issue of domination. Some employees surely would be able to leverage a UBI to increase their power relative to employers; however, for the majority of workers, instituting a UBI alone would not sufficiently balance out the power differential to prevent worker domination.[33] Workers who quit their jobs would likely find the same conditions elsewhere. For this group, therefore, radical exit would still be necessary, wherein workers would require the means to exit the labor market entirely rather than merely shifting employers. Lazar argues that this sort of UBI is simply not a practical solution.

First, it is not at all clear how much income constitutes a "livable" UBI. For different purposes, such as an anti-poverty tool, Lazar argues, it may be easier to calculate UBI as an objective amount. However, "an anti-domination UBI of this kind would have to provide a subjectively acceptable standard of living, and do so as obviously as possible." According to Lazar, current standards, such as providing income that a "reasonable worker" would deem an acceptable alternative, are insufficient for transforming work. Calculating an "acceptable alternative" would be nearly impossible, and funds required would likely be a large amount that would demand high levels of taxation and generate serious opposition.[34]

---

[32] Hooker and Kim, "Ethical Implications of the Fourth Industrial Revolution for Business and Society," 35.
[33] Orlando Lazar, "Work, Domination, and the False Hope of Universal Basic Income," *Res Publica* 27 (2020): 427–46.
[34] Lazar, "Work, Domination, and the False Hope of Universal Basic Income," 436–37.

Moreover, even if such a UBI were implemented, it would have to be "be protected from electoral and political whims, both to avoid merely exchanging employer domination for state domination, and in order to give workers the credible threat of exit in the first place."[35] If there were a threat a UBI might go away, workers would be unlikely to exit workplaces, defeating the purpose of work-transforming UBI. It would also be an incredible challenge to craft a UBI free from state domination because doing so would require extreme levels of state-administered taxation and create the potential for total state dependency and thus total state power. Thus, "even though a UBI capable of ensuring radical exit would likely be sufficient or near-sufficient for minimizing domination at work, ... this kind of UBI would be more demanding than is often supposed by its proponents." That said, some lesser form of UBI may still be part of a greater strategy to minimize worker domination, as it would likely reduce domination in the aggregate, allow reduced hours, and still increase bargaining power. The caveat is that said UBI must simply be viewed as a *complement* to other, more comprehensive anti-domination strategies.[36]

Lazar's critique of the UBI brings the conversation on business ethics, Rawlsian concepts of justice, and republicanism full circle. He argues that the UBI – a potential solution to problems related to technology-driven unemployment – is an inadequate solution to the issue of worker domination. Thus, he divides the conversation concerning ethical workplace organization into two: the state of work and feasible ethical solutions, and ideations of how work should be and where it should go. With this in mind, it's critical then to consider what feasible ethical solutions may look like. In "Three Big Ideas for a Future of Less Work and a Three-Dimensional Alternative," Cynthia Estlund does just that, exploring three ideas that respond to the gains of automated technology and their potential to reduce work needed from humans: (1) universal basic income (UBI), (2) federal job guarantee (FJG), and (3) reducing hours below the forty-hour week to increase leisure and spread work. Estlund argues that each of these three ideas has its merits and pitfalls.[37]

UBI may increase quality of life but decenter work, which Estlund argues offers unique "social and individual value" that mere income or leisure cannot replicate.[38] This argument mirrors the concerns raised by Hooker and Kim. FJG, conversely, may be too focused on full-time employment, resulting in increased meaningless work and less room for personal preference.[39] Reducing work hours simply does not do enough to address the multiple issues the future of work may face, and further may make certain problems worse.[40] However, from all of these ideas, Estlund selects what she deems the best traits of each to develop a three-dimensional strategy.

---

[35] Lazar, "Work, Domination, and the False Hope of Universal Basic Income," 428.
[36] Lazar, "Work, Domination, and the False Hope of Universal Basic Income," 427.
[37] Estlund, "Three Big Ideas for a Future of Less Work and a Three-Dimensional Alternative," 3, 10.
[38] Estlund, "Three Big Ideas for a Future of Less Work and a Three-Dimensional Alternative," 11.
[39] Estlund, "Three Big Ideas for a Future of Less Work and a Three-Dimensional Alternative," 20.
[40] Estlund, "Three Big Ideas for a Future of Less Work and a Three-Dimensional Alternative," 32.

The first dimension, "expanded universal social benefits and income support," helps decouple aspects of material security from wages without decentering work.[41] The second, "public investments in physical and social infrastructure and the job creation those will entail," would ensure that job creation is meaningful and meets unmet need without going too far.[42] The last dimension, "wider access to paid leaves and respites from work," would allow for more time off subsidized by public funding to avoid putting the burden fully on employers, spreading work while maintaining quality of life.[43]

Estlund's proposal is a useful starting point from which to build a model of ethical work that fits the changing nature of work. Taken in tandem with considerations around the ethical value of workplace republicanism, a clearer picture of what ethical work should and can look like begins to take shape. Obviously, the foremost priority in any system must be the least advantaged. Hsieh and Lindblom's proposals are useful for understanding how firms may structure or restructure themselves to align with ethical principles that promote worker well-being. Estlund's proposal, on the other hand, is useful in ensuring that creating more ethical work is not just left in the hands of employers. Relying on employer restructuring is inherently antithetical to Rawlsian justice and its emphasis on worker autonomy. Therefore, a governmental proposal along the lines of Estlund's three-prong plan would necessarily increase worker satisfaction and bargaining power, in turn forcing employers to create the more ethical workplace that workers desire.

11.2 WORKER POWER AND WORKER VOICE

As touched on above, any solution that seeks to achieve more ethical work must account for the power imbalances that plague the modern workplace. Worker power occupies a unique space in the pursuit of ethical work, as all other facets of a Rawlsian workplace in part hinge on it. Meaningful work, worker autonomy, and worker voice are only assured and secure if workers have the power to advocate and enforce these rights. Unfortunately, as Estlund argues in "Workplace Autocracy in an Era of Fissuring," exercises of worker power are becoming an increasingly scarce reality. Estlund argues that in a time where employers are being held to less and less account for their employees' well-being, they are still increasingly choosing to distance themselves from formal control over their workers, opting for work arrangements that avoid the term *employee* altogether; Estlund quotes David Weil to refer to this trend as the "fissuring of work." Fissuring allows firms to "avoid many of the costs, risks, and liabilities associated with direct employment of people," instead turning to technology or outsourced suppliers who operate in cheaper labor

---

[41] Estlund, "Three Big Ideas for a Future of Less Work and a Three-Dimensional Alternative," 4, 38.
[42] Estlund, "Three Big Ideas for a Future of Less Work and a Three-Dimensional Alternative," 4, 35
[43] Estlund, "Three Big Ideas for a Future of Less Work and a Three-Dimensional Alternative," 4, 37.

markets than the firm itself. By separating work from employment, growing swaths of individuals are being left out of employment law protections and workplace benefits – public protections and private systems the United States has come to rely on. Worker power is thus being squeezed out. Collective bargaining is "complicated" by fissuring because, in the words of Estlund, "[fissuring] erases the very notion of a workplace for some workers, and separates others from the firms with real economic power." Estlund calls for "a serious rethinking of what kind of power workers actually need, and whom their voices need to reach." Estlund states that firms need to be held accountable for their contractors' well-being, not just that of their employees, and that as employers continue to distance themselves from the employee relationship, it may be time for renewed conversations around public initiatives to protect quality of life for workers everywhere.[44]

Furthermore, while some workers are being denied power through changing employment structures, even those who fall under the protection of existing labor laws are being targeted by new employer technologies designed to manipulate wages and "disempower workers *as a class.*" As Brishen Rogers explores in *Worker Surveillance and Class Power*, when employers collect data on the work that their employees do, they are implicitly also collecting data on how to automate the employees' jobs out of existence. Whether this data is actually used to oust employees or not, the simple power to collect it means that workers are necessarily subjugated in the worker–employer power relationship. For example, even if a job cannot be automated, data may be used to "target the specialized skills that give workers bargaining power" and replace them with automated functions that can do the same tasks for cheaper. Rogers gives the example of Uber collecting data on the fastest way to get to a location, replacing the need for a skilled driver who knows the area well and "push[ing] down wages" in the process.[45] In an extreme iteration of Taylorism, other surveillance technology may be used to push workers to work harder, manipulate performance, eradicate loafing, and ensure behavioral compliance. Thus, not only does surveillance technology decimate worker power, but it also uses strengthened employer power to further crush worker autonomy and worker voice.

Significantly, Rogers echoes Estlund's concern that automation can push employees outside of legal protections altogether as employers no longer need to offer employees benefits to ensure "reliable, high-perform[ance]" work.[46] In tandem, these scholars highlight a major problem with technological innovation: It is increasingly acting against workers' interests. The evidence Rogers presents strengthens the call for a legal, political, and ethical framework that ensures these interests are protected; the principles of Rawlsian justice both demand and depend upon it.

---

[44] Cynthia Estlund, "Workplace Autocracy in an Era of Fissuring," *LPE Project*, Apr. 3, 2019, https://lpeproject.org/blog/workplace-autocracy-in-an-era-of-fissuring/.
[45] Brishen Rogers, "Worker Surveillance and Class Power," *LPE Project*, July 11, 2018, https://lpeproject.org/blog/worker-surveillance-and-class-power/.
[46] Rogers, "Worker Surveillance and Class Power."

Some scholars have already started to propose frameworks to fix the current precarious power differential. Existing legal frameworks, such as unionization, for example, have also been proposed as a safeguard for worker power. While unionization might seem like an apt solution, increasing worker power through collective action to exercise worker voice, there remain some roadblocks.

11.3 UNIONIZATION AS WORKER POWER?

Any proposals for unionization as a tool for enacting Rawlsian justice in the workplace must consider how the work landscape has changed in recent decades. Unions are falling behind in the digital age, as work becomes increasingly fissured and the gig economy takes hold. Union advocate Mark Zuckerman of progressive thinktank The Century Foundation argues that unions need to re-strategize workplace organizing, with a new focus on small workplaces and digital presence. Compounding evidence suggests that new union organization is more prominent and more successful in workplaces of less than 250 workers. However, unions continue to focus on larger workplaces, largely – Zuckerman argues – because their "retail organizing" strategy makes it expensive and inefficient to unionize small or geographically isolated workplaces. Zuckerman argues that online organizing and digital marketing can effectively revolutionize the process of unionization. He suggests labor unions follow in the path of political campaigns, using "'big data' to target low-wage workers in specific locations who share traits commonly associated with union support." This strategy, according to Zuckerman, would reduce costs and increase union presence in regions where unionization has typically been difficult. Zuckerman also suggests that online platforms can allow unions to serve members remotely, further reducing costs and increasing access. At a time when "interest in joining a union is at an all-time high," digitization could allow unions to capitalize on this new wave of interest.[47]

Scholars such as Sharon Block and Benjamin Sachs go beyond arguments for digitization, however, arguing that labor law as a whole must be recentered around worker power to increase worker choice. Merely outfitting the antiquated union structure in new clothes will not prevent the pitfalls that led to union decline in the first place. Block and Sachs assert that in revitalizing and reimagining the union, advocates must keep in mind the main goal of unionization: "enabl[ing] workers to build and exercise power." They maintain that any changes to union structuring must contribute to the holistic growth of collective bargaining units and that new organizational structures, such as safety committees and work councils, must be but a part of a "broader *system* of labor representation that extends from the shopfloor, through the economic sector, and to the corporate boardroom." Essentially, they argue that while changes in union structure and worker representation are desirable

---

[47] Mark Zuckerman, "Unions Need to Think Small to Get Big," *The Atlantic*, Feb. 9, 2019.

and possibly inevitable, it is critical that any changes be focused foremost on the worker. According to Block and Sachs, "the point of organizing" and the "point of labor law" are simply ensuring "that workers have the capacity to build and exercise more power than they possess as individuals."[48]

Jack Milroy, another union activist, suggests that, going forward, unions should rely more on popular support and awareness campaigns than the unions of the past did. Milroy suggests that a digital strategy would allow unions to more effectively "[build] an email list of supporters," leveraging public support to increase favorable outcomes.[49] "The list," as Milroy refers to it, is an effective support strategy in the face of restrictive labor laws that limit bargaining power through strikes or certain other forms of collective action. Public support is an increasingly necessary aspect of union bargaining power that digitization makes both more effective and more accessible. Bolstering worker power through public support is a strategic way to effectively expand the bargaining unit for the purposes of power in negotiations. While this strategy surely would not have the same weight as entirely restructured labor law, revitalizing the union through a digital strategy may be an important first step towards recentering worker power.

11.4 A GROWING THREAT: CORPORATE RISK SHIFTING

In the current absence of worker collective power, the phenomenon of "corporate risk shifting" had become an essential feature of the modern workplace and the changing nature of work. In "Melting into Air? Downsizing, Job Stability, and the Future of Work," Sanford M. Jacoby argues that the traditional employment arrangement is "still the norm" in the United States.[50] However, there have been changes within the structure of the employment relationship as employers increasingly shift risk from employers to employees. Jacoby argues that this risk shift "[is] the central dynamic driving today's internal labor markets," and that this shift comes in the form of changes to employer-provided health insurance, pension plans, and pay packages. Though welfare capitalism still generally benefits employers, the increasingly "turbulent [corporate] environment" means "employers are less willing to shoulder as much risk for employees as they did in the past."[51] Significantly, Jacoby's work was published in 2000 – well before the gig economy boom – thus any interpretation of his warnings must take into account changes that have occurred since.

---

[48] Sharon Block and Benjamin Sachs, "Worker Organizations Must Enable Worker Power," *American Compass: A Seat at the Table*, Sept. 22, 2020, https://americancompass.org/articles/worker-organizations-must-enable-worker-power/.

[49] Jack Milroy, "The List Makes Us Strong. Why Unions Need a Digital Strategy," *Medium*, Apr. 29, 2016, https://medium.com/@jack_milroy/the-list-makes-us-strong-why-unions-need-a-digital-strategy-42291213298a.

[50] Sanford M. Jacoby, "Melting into Air? Downsizing, Job Stability, and the Future of Work," *Chicago-Kent Law Review* 76, no. 2 (2000): 1196.

[51] Jacoby, "Melting into Air?" 1225–26.

Jacob S. Hacker agrees with Jacoby's premise but draws more dire conclusions. Exploring causes and implications of a national trend towards declining economic security, Hacker tracks the death of the traditional employer–worker relationship as global trade shocks in the 1970s led to a retraction in corporate benefits such as job security and health insurance in the 1980s, exacerbated by "the philosophy of individualism" encouraged by Ronald Reagan. In the modern day, Hacker argues that "workers must compete for jobs in a 'spot market' that resembles a trading floor, where their pay is determined by their skills and the economy's needs for them at any given moment." This new reality is the culmination of "The Personal Responsibility Crusade" that originated in the 1970s and 1980s. As an example of risk shifting, Hacker observes that taxi drivers once split profits with cab companies in exchange for insurance and fuel costs; now drivers pay their own way, leasing cars from the company out of their own pocket and losing money on slow days.[52]

While these changes have been occurring, families have been more dependent on multiple incomes and thus more vulnerable to layoffs, the percentage of Americans without health insurance has risen 25 percent since the 1980s, and employer-sponsored pensions have been almost universally replaced with 401(k) plans that invite human error. The result, Hacker argues, is newfound "income volatility"; in this troubling trend, "[i]nstability of before-tax family incomes ha[s] skyrocketed" since the 1970s.[53] While he does not advocate for total government takeover of benefits and worker welfare, Hacker suggests these trends must be addressed to reduce the unprecedented financial instability that threatens to crush individuals and families.[54]

The first edition of *The Great Risk Shift* was published in 2006, six years after Jacoby identified trends towards increased worker liability in "Melting into Air?" This is perhaps salient to understand the more dire picture Hacker paints. Hacker suggests that the shift towards increased worker risk has resulted in an overall decline in economic security for American families, thus resulting in potentially perilous effects for both families and the economy at large. While Jacoby argues that the impact of the risk shift may not be as extreme as the rhetoric surrounding it, Hacker disagrees, highlighting income volatility as evidence of the extreme instability to which it contributes.

In "Restoring Retirement Security: The Market Crisis, the 'Great Risk Shift,' and the Challenge for Our Nation," Hacker also notes the impact of the risk shift on retirees and retirement planning, explaining the "peril[ous]" state of retirement security in the United States today, thanks to pension and healthcare risk shifts from employer to worker and rising healthcare costs that have made millions of aging Americans vulnerable.[55] Kim M. Shuey and Angela M. O'Rand, in "New Risks

---

[52] Jacob S. Hacker, *The Great Risk Shift: The New Economic Insecurity and the Decline of the American Dream* (New York: Oxford University Press, 2006).

[53] Hacker, *The Great Risk Shift*, xi.

[54] "Conclusion: Securing the Future," in Hacker, *The Great Risk Shift*, 165–94.

[55] Jacob S. Hacker, "Restoring Retirement Security: The Market Crisis, the 'Great Risk Shift,' and the Challenge for Our Nation," *Elder Law Journal* 19, no. 1 (2011): 3.

for Workers: Pensions, Labor Markets, and Gender," argue that this phenomenon is a reflection of demographic shifts, price competition "eroding" the employer–employee relationship, and an insurer tendency to control the insured to manage risk.[56] As a result, private employer-based pensions – a significant piece of the puzzle of economic security in retirement for middle- and upper-income workers – are going away, replaced in part by defined-contribution plans (such as 401(k) plans) that "greatly increase the degree of risk and responsibility placed on individual workers in retirement planning."[57] Defined-contribution plans are voluntary, are not federally insured, and allow individuals to cash in and out at will, thus "exacerbate[ing] the risk that workers will prematurely use retirement savings, leaving inadequate income upon retirement."[58]

This new system is cause for serious concern, especially as it harms the most vulnerable. Hacker argues that this new system disproportionately hurts low-income workers, to whom the appeal of 401(k) tax benefits is less prominent, a 401(k) is generally less available, and income is less expendable. Those who do have access to and do invest in a 401(k) face challenges in account administration and bear the risks of market fluctuations. Hacker cites increasing wealth depletion paired with rising debt as further evidence that a 401(k) is inadequate to meet the retirement needs of the modern worker. At the same time, healthcare costs are rising while employer-provided health coverage is dwindling. In fact, workplace wellness programs represent a means for further risk shifting. Thus, as retirees are increasingly responsible for saving on their own, rising healthcare costs must be taken into account when considering how much to save – a significant problem considering that future needs are often unpredictable.[59] Shuey and O'Rand extend the conversation further, arguing that risk-averse groups, particularly women, may be disproportionately impacted by this risk shift and are more likely than men to fall victim to pension leakage (failing to reinvest pension funds when changing jobs). Thus, even though defined-contribution plans have increased the total number of pensions in the United States, the nature of these new plans as "dependen[t] on individual prerogatives and capacities to participate means that they pose a serious threat to equality over time."[60]

It's important to consider what implications the corporate risk shift has for Rawlsian justice. Hacker, Shuey, and O'Rand all emphasize that the most vulnerable members of society – those with low incomes and those who are old – assume the most risk via this risk-shifting trend. Consider the Rawlsian tenet that "economic inequalities are only justified when the least advantaged member of society is nonetheless

[56] Kim M. Shuey and Angela M. O'Rand, "New Risks for Workers: Pensions, Labor Markets, and Gender," *American Review of Sociology* 30 (2004): 455.

[57] Hacker, "Restoring Retirement Security," 10.

[58] Hacker, "Restoring Retirement Security," 11

[59] Hacker, "Restoring Retirement Security, "13–15, 18, 21–22, 24–25.

[60] Shuey and O'Rand, "New Risks for Workers," 468, 471.

better off than she would be under alternative arrangements."[61] Clearly, those with low incomes and those who are old are *not* better off under defined-contribution as opposed to defined-benefit plans. A more desirable alternative arrangement would be expanded access of defined-benefit plans for all, or, as Hacker suggests, a three-part solution which would (1) strengthen Social Security as a foundation for retirement planning, (2) fix the 401(k) to adequately supplement Social Security for *all* workers, and (3) directly address the challenge of rising healthcare costs for the aged.[62] Conceptualizing these issues through the lens of Ralwsian justice is a useful framework for both articulating the problem and developing a meaningful solution.

Unfortunately, the nature of work has changed, so the corporate risk shift has continued to become more pronounced over time. The advent of the gig economy has meant that the threat of the corporation to the individual now extends well beyond retirees and low-income individuals. In "Risk Shifts in the Gig Economy: The Normative Case for Insurance Scheme Against the Effects of Precarious Work," Friedmann Bieber and Jakob Moggia argue that a risk shift from employer to worker is also at the heart of the gig economy, emphasizing the problematic implications of this shift for both individuals and society, and proposing potential solutions. Bieber and Moggia argue that the gig economy structure exemplifies risk shifting as an "unstable [form] of employment" that uses the veil of freedom to place almost all risk on the worker that once fell on the employer. They identify five ways in which employers shift risk to workers: (1) use of short-term contracts, (2) flexible work hours, (3) flexible renumeration, (4) flexible scheduling, and (5) reduced insurance coverage. The extent to which firms employ these methods of "risk externalization" varies according to both company values and the nature of their business environment.[63]

Bieber and Moggia argue that this trend has had negative effects for workers, reducing their ability to make long-term plans, such as starting a family, and to commit to activities that require coordination, such as volunteering for a political party. Bieber and Moggia suggest this particular aspect of gig work may be adverse to Rawlsian justice, citing his view that "human life lived according to a plan" is central to a just society.[64] They reject the view that the gig economy offers freedom of choice on the basis of a lack of employment options that mean "many workers have little choice but to accept the flexible employment characteristic of the gig economy."[65] Bieber and Moggia also warn that the gig economy is prone to work relationships characterized by exploitation and domination, as employers have both more power over worker schedules and more information to evaluate productivity.

[61] Friend, "Social Contract Theory."
[62] Hacker, "Restoring Retirement Security," 28.
[63] Friedemann Bieber and Jakob Moggia, "Risk Shifts in the Gig Economy: The Normative Case for an Insurance Scheme against the Effects of Precarious Work," *Journal of Political Philosophy* 29, no. 3 (2020): 5–6.
[64] Bieber and Moggia, "Risk Shifts in the Gig Economy," 7–9.
[65] Bieber and Moggia, "Risk Shifts in the Gig Economy," 10.

Bieber and Moggia also argue that gig work has *"corrosive effects"* on society.[66] It encourages low-skill work through reduced opportunity, reduced incentives, and reduced resources available to invest in training. Gig work is further unsustainable because it results in instability that "undermine[s] the ability of workers to engage in [the] reproductive care and work" necessary to bring up the next generation of workers and possibly is to blame for weakened social cohesion.[67]

Bieber and Moggia suggest that solutions to the problems of the gig economy should (1) "counter the incentives fueling the risk shift and contain the externalization of business risk to the workforce and other third parties" and (2) "seek to alleviate any harmful effects of gig work that remain, in particular its adverse effects on workers."[68] They advocate for a principle of inverse coverage (PIC), "which stipulates that the shorter, more variable, and less predictable a form of employment, the higher should be the contributions to social insurance schemes made by the employer." They acknowledge that this policy would not adequately address the issue of flexible scheduling and thus suggest further policymaking would be necessary to ameliorate the risks of gig work.[69]

Bieber and Moggia bring the gig economy into the risk-shift conversation. While risk shifting began before the gig economy took off, Bieber and Moggia identify the way in which the gig economy has exacerbated the risk assumed by workers beyond 401(k) and insurance plans. The very structure of modern gig work contributes to instability and shifts risk to workers in new ways not previously imagined. Bieber and Moggia importantly touch on the ethical implications of this trend, and how it may necessarily inhibit progress towards a just society.

A lack of stability, reduced opportunities for meaningful work, and the breakdown of the workplace seriously threaten worker voice, freedom as non-domination, and the creation of a just society at large. It's clear the corporate risk shifting is only becoming more pronounced over time. Therefore, it is critical that theories of justice at work, such as Hsieh's workplace republicanism, adapt to offer solutions in light of the changing nature of work.

11.5 GOVERNMENTAL POLICIES FOR ETHICAL WORK

Generally, economists have taken a hands-off approach to labor market discrimination and disparities. However, in a review of Thomas Sowell's *Discrimination and Disparities*, economist Jennifer L. Doleac puts forth a theory of active intervention according to economic principles that may lead to more just outcomes. Doleac suggests that a well-developed understanding of human and market behavior and the nature of

---

[66] Bieber and Moggia, "Risk Shifts in the Gig Economy," 12–13.
[67] Bieber and Moggia, "Risk Shifts in the Gig Economy," 13–15.
[68] Bieber and Moggia, "Risk Shifts in the Gig Economy," 17.
[69] Bieber and Moggia, "Risk Shifts in the Gig Economy," 3, 20.

causal reactions puts economists in a unique position to address market injustice. She argues that economists, drawing on this skillset, can more effectively design targeted policy interventions and test the effects of such interventions for effectiveness and negative outcomes.[70] When it comes to designing more ethical work, Doleac's proposal may be particularly effective. Taking an economic approach to incentivizing firms to create a more ethical workplace may be an effective form of policy intervention, given that already profitable firms have little reason to change. While the government can hardly dictate a moral mandate that companies care more about their workers, it can create policy that gives companies an economic incentive to do so.

11.6 WHEN ALL ELSE FAILS: GAMING THE FUTURE OF WORK

In the absence of government intervention, however, workers have not simply stood by in wait. As technology comes to dominate workplace decisions and interactions, individuals are increasingly trying to find methods to control the systems designed to control them. This, I argue, is an assertion of the basic human right to meaningful work and worker voice. In a world that is increasingly denying workers autonomy and power, some workers are seeking to take it back by force. Whether one calls it cheating, manipulation, or gaming the system, the internet is full of instances of and advice for and from individuals who have managed to exploit workplace tech to liberate their labor from the confines of employer control.

For certain wearable technologies, gaming the technology is relatively straightforward. For example, an article posted on the self-help website LifeHacker enumerates five different ways to fake Fitbit step goals. According to Patrick Allan, individuals may be incentivized to cheat the system to earn insurance discounts for individuals who reach goals and employer fitness incentive programs.[71] To game an app that assigns shifts to Amazon's delivery drivers, some gig workers have turned to bots that "mimic the action of tapping" shift blocks as they appear to increase their odds of getting work for the day.[72]

Some technologies are more difficult to game. Automated interview platforms such as HireVue are notoriously opaque and therefore hard to game, but there are still ways to gain an advantage. Numerous websites provide advice to improve performance in a video interview, including Fast Company's three-step guide to developing a "cheat sheet" that will aid performance in video interviews.[73] It is unclear whether algorithms

---

[70] See Doleac, "A Review of Thomas Sowell's *Discrimination and Disparities*," 574, 586.

[71] Patrick Allan, "Five Ways to Cheat Your Way to 10,000 Fitbit Steps Every Day," *LifeHacker*, Oct. 27, 2016, https://lifehacker.com/five-ways-to-cheat-your-way-to-10-000-fitbit-steps-ever-1788302045.

[72] Annie Palmer, "Amazon Flex Drivers Are Using Bots to Cheat Their Way to Getting More Work," *CNBC*, Feb. 9, 2020, www.cnbc.com/2020/02/09/amazon-flex-drivers-use-bots-to-get-more-work.html.

[73] Stephanie Vozza, "How a Cheat Sheet Can Help You Ace Your Next Video Interview," *Fast Company*, Sept. 12, 2020, www.fastcompany.com/90549127/how-a-cheat-sheet-can-help-you-ace-your-next-video-interview.

Strongly agree	Strongly disagree
Any trouble you have is your own fault.	It bothers you a long time when someone is
It is easy for you to feel what others are	unfair to you.
feeling.	It bothers you when you have to obey a lot of
It is fun to go to events with big crowds.	rules.
It is maddening when the court lets guilty	It is hard to really care about work when the
criminals go free.	job is boring.
When someone treats you badly, you	Many people cannot be trusted.
ignore it.	Other people's feelings are their own
When you are done with your work, you look	business.
for more to do.	People are often mean to you.
When you go someplace, you are	People do a lot of annoying things.
never late.	People do a lot of things that make you
When your friends need help, they call you	angry.
first.	People who talk all the time are annoying.
You agree with people more often than you	People's feelings are sometimes hurt by
argue.	what you say.
You always try not to hurt people's feelings.	Right now, you care more about having fun
You are a friendly person.	than being serious at school or work.
You are always cheerful.	Slow people make you impatient.
You are careful not to offend people.	There are some people you really can't
You are proud of the work you do at school	stand.
or on a job.	There's no use having close friends; they
You are somewhat a of a thrill-seeker.	always let you down.
You avoid arguments as much as possible	When people make mistakes, you correct
You can wait patiently for a long time.	them.
You chat with people you don't know	When you are annoyed with something, you
You could describe yourself as 'tidy'.	say so.
You do not fake being polite.	When you need to, you take it easy
You do things carefully so you don't make	at work.
mistakes.	You are a fairly private person.
You finish your work no matter what	You are more relaxed than strict about
You give direct criticism when you need to.	finishing things on time
You got mostly good grades in high school.	You are not afraid to tell someone off.
You hate to give up if you can't solve a hard	You are not interested in your friends'
problem.	problems.
You have always had good behavior in	You are unsure of what to say when you
school or work.	meet someone.
You have confidence in yourself.	You are unsure of yourself with
You have no big regrets about your past.	new people.
You have no big worries.	You change from feeling happy to sad
You ignore people's small mistakes.	without any reason.
You keep calm when under stress.	You could not deal with difficult people
You know when someone is in a bad mood,	all day.
even if they don't show it.	You criticize people when they deserve it.
You like to be in the middle of a big crowd.	You do not like small talk.
You like to plan things before you	You do not like to meet new people.
do them.	You do not like to take orders.

FIGURE 11.1 Unicru assessment key, posted online (adapted from "Some Answers to the Unicru Personality Test," Timothy Horrigan, Nov. 15, 2011, www.timothyhorrigan .com/documents/unicru-personality-test.answer-key.html#sthash.N7ryuDqp.vtj4c5Nf .dpbs)

You like to talk a lot. You love to be with people. You love to listen to people talk about themselves. You make more sensible choices than careless ones You rarely act without thinking. You think of yourself as being very sensible. You try to sense what others are thinking and feeling. You were absent very few days from high school. You work best at a slow but steady speed. You would rather work on a team than by yourself. Your friends and family approve of the things you do. Your moods are steady from day to day.	You do some things that upset people. You do what you want, no matter what others think. You don't act polite when you don't want to. You don't believe a lot of what people say. You don't care if you offend people. You don't care what people think of you. You don't work hard because it doesn't pay off anyway. You don't worry about making a good impression. You get angry more often that nervous. You get mad at yourself when you make mistakes. You have friends, but don't like them to be too close. You have to give up on some things that you start. You ignore people you don't like. You like to be alone. You like to take frequent breaks when working on something difficult. You look back and feel bad about things you've done. You say whatever is on your mind. You show it when you are in a bad mood. You sometimes thought seriously about quitting high school. You swear when you argue. You would rather not get involved in other people's problems. You'd rather not compete very much. You've done your share of troublemaking. Your stuff is often kind of messy.

FIGURE 11.1 (continued)

can detect such "cheating" or if and when different interview platforms inform employers that candidates were referencing another screen or referring to notes.

In the case of personality job tests, many companies use the same cookie-cutter personality tests, which contain many questions that are straightforward, but some that seemingly have no right answer. One Reddit user asked for advice after repeatedly failing the personality test portion of job interviews, and another user recommended answer keys that are available online, but advised intentionally getting certain questions "wrong" because scoring too high may result in companies voiding a person's scores.[74] As personality and psychometric tests become increasingly

---

[74] ShabbyTester, "How to Answer Pre-Employment Personality Tests," *Reddit: AskReddit*, Feb. 13, 2012, www.reddit.com/r/AskReddit/comments/pneie/how_to_answer_preemployment_personality_tests/.

FIGURE 11.2 Screenshot of supposedly correct target pre-employment assessment answers (source: Tyler Parks, "Target," *Your Job Questionnaire Cheatsheet*, http://onlineapps-answers.blogspot.com/p/target.html, accessed November 24, 2020)

important in the hiring process at all levels, individuals have turned to online resources to improve their chances of success.

Applicants taking the Unicru personality test can refer to the website of Timothy Horrigan, who published a guide on how to pass the Unicru assessment, including advice on the "right" responses for certain questions (see Figure 11.1).[75] Multiple online sources discussing Unicru link back to Horrigan's webpage. Other online communities have sprung up in response to a myriad of other personality tests used by other companies and industries. Job Test Prep offers a range of paid services to prepare candidates for various job personality tests.[76] WikiJob also offers information to help individuals prepare for personality tests, with specific webpages dedicated to

---

[75] Timothy Horrigan, "Some Answers to the Unicru Personality Test," last updated Nov. 15, 2011, www.timothyhorrigan.com/documents/unicru-personality-test.answer-key.html#sthash.N7ryuDqp.vtj4c5Nf.dpbs; Melanie Palen, "Unicru Personality Test Answer Key: Read This, Get Hired," *ToughNickel*, July 24, 2020, https://toughnickel.com/finding-job/Unicru.

[76] See jobtestprep.com (last visited Nov. 21, 2020).

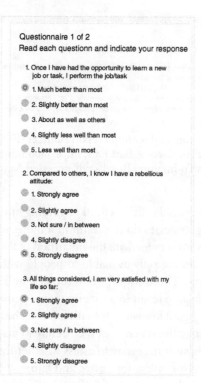

Questionnaire 1 of 2
Read each questionn and indicate your response

1. Once I have had the opportunity to learn a new job or task, I perform the job/task

1. Much better than most
2. Slightly better than most
3. About as well as others
4. Slightly less well than most
5. Less well than most

2. Compared to others, I know I have a rebellious attitude:

1. Strongly agree
2. Slightly agree
3. Not sure / in between
4. Slightly disagree
5. Strongly disagree

3. All things considered, I am very satisfied with my life so far:

1. Strongly agree
2. Slightly agree
3. Not sure / in between
4. Slightly disagree
5. Strongly disagree

FIGURE 11.3 Screenshot of sample correct answers to Walmart assessment (source: "Walmart Assessment Answers," *Facebook*, posted October 4, 2016, www.facebook.com/Walmartassessmentanswers/)

different tests providing detailed information, including whether it is "cheatable" and how to prepare for the assessment (see Figures 11.2 and 11.3).[77]

In addition to these online communities, there are underground communities that provide information such as what are claimed to be screenshots of certain assessments showing the correct responses to lists of questions and answers for certain companies.[78] The Facebook group "Walmart Assessment Answers," for example, offers answers to all sixty-five of Walmart's pre-employment assessment questions.[79] New-wave personality tests, such as Pymetrics, feature complex, variable algorithms that are harder to game; however, online forums have begun to spring up with suggestions of company-specific desirable traits (see Figure 11.4).

[77] WikiJob Team, "The NEO Personality Inventory Test," *WikiJob*, Nov. 10, 2020, www.wikijob.co.uk/content/aptitude-tests/test-types/neo-personality-inventory-test.

[78] Tyler-Parks, "Target," *Your Job Questionnaire Cheatsheet*, blog, Aug. 24, 2011, http://onlineapps-answers.blogspot.com/p/target.html (last visited Nov. 24, 2020).

[79] "Walmart Assessment Answers," *Facebook*, Oct. 4, 2016, www.facebook.com/Walmartassessmentanswers/.

Section 1
For each question in this section, select the most appropriate response.

1. **One of your customers has just said to you, "The service here is terrible." You should say:**
   - ● "What is it about the service that you have not liked?"
   - ○ "Would you like to fill out a complaint form? I can get one for you."
   - ○ "I realize our service is poor today. We are understaffed, so I apologize."
   - ○ "I am really sorry to hear you say that, but we are trying as hard as we can."

FIGURE 11.4 Pymetrics score and recruiter report (source: "How to Interpret Results," *Pymetrics: Predicting Talent Success, Bias Free,* https://about.hyatt.com/content/dam/HyattStories/risehy/HowTo-Interpret-Results.pdf, accessed November 22, 2020)

Whether or not you consider these efforts at gaming ethical conduct, one thing is clear: These gaming strategies do not result in a more just political economy of work. Rather, they may even exacerbate the unfairness of the systems. Consider that these gaming techniques are only available to people with access to the internet who are computer savvy. Those with fewer resources are still left out in the cold. Gaming the system may also result in a cat and mouse game of employers developing more and more stringent assessments to discourage cheating. Such gaming also does nothing to challenge the system that is currently in place.

Ultimately, a reckoning is necessary to assess whether the technological quantification of workers can truly allow for justice and fairness. A Rawlsian approach to justice demands we ask the question of "Who loses?" when workers are deprived of voice and power and are dominated by algorithmic management. The consequences of a total loss of worker autonomy are dire, and include the erosion of personhood and true democracy.

12

Regulating Mechanical Managers[*]

Law for the platform economy is already being written – not via discrete, purposive changes, but rather via the ordinary, uncoordinated but self-interested efforts of information-economy participants and the lawyers and lobbyists they employ.

–Julie Cohen, Professor of Law

This book has examined in detail how *mechanical managers* now proliferate in the workplace and allow for the greater quantification of workers. As the quantification of workers allows for more direct control of workers, there is a risk that employers will not only become private governments, but may also take on the role of dictators. One possible future of work is one in which workers are obliged to trade away both personal privacy and autonomy as part of the employment bargain. This holds dire implications for worker voice, worker power, and worker self-determination. An asymmetrical employment bargain in which workers exchange privacy and dignity for gainful employment could rend the fabric of democracy. This chapter offers proposals for regulating mechanical managers, to restore the balance of power in the workplace.

There are competing schools of thought on how to regulate technology. One school of thought subscribes to the idea of regulation as market driven.[1] For these scholars, the market is the chief regulator, and therefore technologies which have deleterious effects will simply fall out of the market due to disuse.[2] This theory is predicated on the notion that the market is efficient, and that the primary concern of employers, as market players, will be efficiency.[3] Real-world

---

[*] Parts of this chapter appear, in slightly different form, in my previously published law review articles, including "The Auditing Imperative for Automated Hiring," Harvard Journal of Law and Technology 34, no. 2 (2021): 621–700; "The Paradox of Automation as Anti-Bias Intervention," Cardozo Law Review 41, no. 5 (2020): 1671–1742; and "Limitless Worker Surveillance," California Law Review 105, no. 3 (2017): 736–76 (with Professors Jason Schultz and Kate Crawford).
[1] Gary S. Becker, *The Economics of Discrimination*, 2nd ed. (Chicago: University of Chicago Press, 2010). See generally Richard A. Posner, *Economic Analysis of Law*, 2nd ed. (New York: Little Brown, 1977); Gary S. Becker, *The Economic Approach to Human Behavior* (Chicago: University of Chicago Press, 1976).
[2] Richard A. Posner, "Privacy, Secrecy and Reputation," *Buffalo Law Review* 28, no. 1 (1979): 1–55.
[3] Becker, *Economic Approach to Human Behavior*.

findings of the continued occurrence of digital discrimination tend to discredit this theory.[4] Empirical studies show that market actors are significantly influenced by ideology and organizational entrenchment.[5] These factors make unlawful discrimination incredibly resistant to reform, even when it is proven to be inefficient.

If the regulation of quantifying technologies in the workplace cannot simply be left up to the market, the next question is who should be responsible for regulation. Many scholars have called for greater governmental regulation of emerging technologies. As early as 1992, Paul Schwartz, in his article "Data Processing and Government Administration: The Failure of the American Legal Response to the Computer," called for "independent governmental monitoring of data processing systems."[6] Other scholars have followed suit.[7] Although much of the proposed regulatory process focuses on governmental actors, other scholars such as the late Professor Joel Reidenberg have argued for other types of regulation that include industry actors. For example, Reidenberg's *Lex Informatica* regime of regulation envisions a horizontal or peer-to-peer type of regulation among business players, in which the "information flows imposed by technology and communication networks" create their own body of rules.[8] Thus, the norms that arise from the usage of technology ultimately form the body of laws that regulate the same technology. This is a forward-thinking idea for regulation, as it recognizes that the proposed end uses of the technological tools may differ (sometimes widely) from their actual uses.

12.1 CONCURRENT REGULATION

Often the idea of governmental regulation of automated decision-making is pitted against industry or peer regulation as contradictory governance models. My call is for what I term *concurrent regulation*. Governmental regulation of automated decision-making can and should exist alongside industry regulation. In fact, the two should work hand in hand for the best effective regulation. Concurrent regulation should not be seen as an acquiescence to *laissez-faire* economics principles where industry players are left to their own initiative, nor should it be deemed a

---

4   Rebecca Greenfield, "Study Finds Racial Discrimination by Airbnb Hosts," *Bloomberg News*, Nov. 10, 2015, www.bloomberg.com/news/articles/2015-12-10/study-finds-racial-discrimination-by-airbnb-hosts; Rachel Sandler, "EEOC Probing Whether Facebook Has Committed Systemic Racial Discrimination in Hiring," *Forbes*, Mar. 5, 2021, www.forbes.com/sites/rachelsandler/2021/03/05/eeoc-probing-whether-facebook-has-committed-systemic-racial-discrimination-in-hiring/?sh=59025ce7715f.
5   Victor Ray, "Why So Many Organizations Stay White," *Harvard Business Review*, Nov. 19, 2019, https://hbr.org/2019/11/why-so-many-organizations-stay-white.
6   Paul Schwartz, "Data Processing and Government Administration: The Failure of the American Legal Response to the Computer," *Hastings Law Journal* 43, no. 5 (1992): 1321–89.
7   See, as examples, Julie E. Cohen, "Law for the Platform Economy"; Frank Pasquale, "Beyond Innovation and Competition: The Need for Qualified Transparency in Internet Intermediaries," *Northwestern University Law Review* 104, no. 1 (2010): 169–71.
8   See Joel R. Reidenberg, "Lex Informatica: The Formulation of Information Policy Rules Through Technology," *Texas Law Review* 76, no. 3 (1998): 554–55.

governmental abdication of governance responsibilities. Rather, it is a recognition of the limitations of fiat to enact rapid changes when industry standards, which are more mutable, may also be more adroit. For example, industry regulations that focus on design choices and use cases to enable fairness in automated decision-making tools used in the workplace can and should exist *concurrently* with governmental legislation and action to root out unlawful discrimination that results from those systems. In the sections below, I offer some proposals for the concurrent regulation of automated decision-making tools in the workplace.

12.2 REGULATING AUTOMATED HIRING

The problems with the design and use of automated hiring tools are multifold as examined in Chapters 3, 4, and 5. The most concerning of these is perhaps the risk of bias baked into the system that precludes the democratic ideal of equal opportunity in employment. Often when legal scholars raise the topic of bias in automated hiring, a common retort is "Isn't it still better than human decision-making?" First, this conveys the sentiment that bias in algorithmic systems cannot be a novel topic of legal inquiry because it has a pre-existing corollary – bias in human decision-making. Second, it assumes that there is a threshold allowed by law at which unlawful discrimination is acceptable. Third, to posit automated decision-making versus human decision-making is to conjure a false binary – it is to willfully ignore that the human hand remains present in all automated decision-making. When it comes to automated hiring, human discretion remains present in the system from the onset: from the design features, to the choices made for algorithmic specification and training data, and finally during the *ex post* interpretation of the results.

One empirical study concluded that while one purported *raison d'etre* and advertised purpose of automated hiring systems was to reduce hirer bias – "replacing messy human decisions with a neutral technical process" – the reality remained that "algorithmic specification of 'fit' can itself become a vehicle for bias." One prominent slogan used to market automated hiring is "Clone your best people."[9] This slogan indicates that automated hiring can never truly be an anti-bias intervention as many corporations and organizations now seek to use it. Rather, this slogan clearly tells us that the true nature of automated hiring is to serve as a culling machine, to cull those who are "different" and leave only those who match the workers already present in the corporation or organization. This might seem fine in the abstract sense of meeting the "cultural fit" for any given organization. But consider the historical discrimination and the potential gender and racial imbalances already present in any organization, and you begin to grasp the problem. Given the real-world historical biases in how workers are selected, an automated hiring platform that is meant to clone your best people will merely replicate a demographic of workers based on bias for or against certain populations.

[9] Ajunwa and Greene, "Platforms at Work," 77.

This is not to say that human managers may not be biased; the issue is that the reach of an individual manager's bias is limited and may even disappear when that manager is replaced by another. The use of automated hiring platforms, however, serves to entrench bias in perpetuity, as those platforms may continue to deploy flawed algorithmic presumptions and training data tainted by historical bias. Thus, automated hiring platforms present thorny legal problems because (1) the design features of automated hiring platforms may enable them to serve as culling tools that discreetly eliminate applicants from protected categories without retaining a record; (2) automated hiring systems that allow for the deployment of proxies for protected categories, like gender or race, can be used to present discriminatory employment results as fair; (3) intellectual property law, specifically trade secret law, protects automated hiring systems from outside scrutiny and allows discrimination to go undetected; and (4) a worker's lack of control over the portability of applicant data captured by automated hiring systems increases the chance of repeated employment discrimination, thus raising the specter of an algorithmically permanently excluded class of job applicants, meaning that certain applicants might find themselves *algorithmically blackballed.*

But there are several obstacles to deploying litigation to address these issues: (1) at higher levels of automation, it becomes difficult to determine intent to discriminate, which is required for finding liability under the disparate treatment cause of action under Title VII; (2) when bringing suit under the disparate impact cause of action, the design features of automated hiring systems, as well as trade secret claims that may arise, impede the plaintiff's ability to provide the statistical proof required to establish a prima facie case; and (3) litigation remedies in employment anti-discrimination law do not address privacy and discrimination issues associated with the collection of personal and biometric data from job candidates, as enabled by automated video interviewing. This indicates then that employment law, with its emphasis on litigation as redress for employment discrimination, is limited in its capacity to address the full spectrum of identified problems with automated hiring.

The first high-order question is who should bear the legal liability for when an automated hiring algorithm is returning biased results. Is it the business firm that is using the algorithms for its hiring process? Or is it the maker of the algorithmic hiring platform? To regulate automated hiring platforms, the government must view the problem from two vantages: first, from the position of holding accountable the maker of the algorithmic hiring system, and second, from the position of holding the employer accountable.

12.3 HOLDING ACCOUNTABLE THE MAKERS OF AUTOMATED HIRING PLATFORMS

To answer the question of who should bear legal liability, here is some theorization that illuminates the asymmetric power and information relationships present in the triad of job applicant, hiring platform, and employer. Platform authoritarianism makes clear the unequal power relationship between the job applicant and the platform, which allows the platform to dictate how the job applicant may use the platform. The *tertius bifrons* concept reveals the duplicitous relationship between the hiring platform and the job applicant, which then supports the argument for some legal liability to attach to the platform.

12.3.1 *Platform Authoritarianism*

In evaluating certain design policy choices that hiring platform companies make, such as their methods to facilitate the amount of information users can learn about one another and how they are to do so, online platforms may make choices that exacerbate the discrimination in our current society. Thus, makers of platforms cannot be blameless for the discrimination that occurs on them – even if the platform users may be influenced by pre-existing biases. Thus, I theorize *platform authoritarianism* as a socio-technical phenomenon that has transformed the responsibility and liability of platforms. Platform authoritarianism refers to the phenomenon of platforms demanding that users interact with their platforms on terms dictated by the platform makers, sometimes without regard to or in contradiction with the spirit of established laws and business ethics. Some scholars have noted that many online platforms can control "who is matched with whom for various forms of exchange, what information users have about one another during their interactions, and how indicators of reliability and reputation are made salient."[10] This means that, for example, job applicants on hiring platforms must acquiesce to informational data demands from the platforms. The job applicants are also not in control of how their candidacy is presented, but rather must relinquish all control to the platform as quid pro quo for accessing job opportunities. Rejecting platform authoritarianism in favor of a duty of care that the purveyors of online platforms owe to their users is the first step towards returning to a rule of law for algorithms.

12.3.2 *The* Tertius Bifrons

While exercising authoritative control over the content and structure of their users' interactions, hiring platforms also hide their true relationship to job applicants, and this deception can lull applicants into a false sense of trust. I coin the term the *tertius bifrons* – the "two-faced" third – to illustrate the role of the automated hiring platform as an intermediary or broker serving a dual role. According to sociologist Georg Simmel, brokers, as part of a triad, perform the function of brokering information between two separate groups, acting as either *tertius iungens* or *tertius*

---

[10] Karen Levy and Solon Barocas, "Designing against Discrimination in Online Markets," *Berkeley Technology Law Journal* 32, no. 3 (2017): 1183–1237.

gaudens.[11] The *tertius iungens* (the third who joins) orientation is derived from the Latin verb *iungere*, which means to join, unite, or connect. The emphasis of this orientation is on the joining of two parties. Thus, a *tertius iungens* broker will operate with a strategic emphasis on creating friendship and collaboration between two parties, for example, linking disparate parties in one's social network in order to create outcomes that are mutually beneficial for two or more parties. In contrast, the *tertius gaudens* (the third who enjoys) orientation emphasizes the strategic separation of parties. In this sense, a broker would enjoy the benefit of the continued separation between two parties for the broker's own gain.[12]

Moving beyond the two categories of brokerage, organizational theory scholars have noted that brokers may engage in four different brokering strategies. Brokers may:

> (1) coordinate action or information between distant parties who have no immediate prospect for direct introduction or connection, (2) actively maintain and exploit the separation between parties, (3) introduce or facilitate preexisting ties between parties such that the coordinative role of the *tertius iungens* subsequently recedes in importance (brief *iungens*), and (4) introduce or facilitate interaction between parties while maintaining an essential coordinative role over time.[13]

The automated hiring process comprises a triad, with the automated hiring platform as the broker negotiating between the applicant and the employer. I argue that, in this triad, hiring platforms are brokers who perform an "essential coordinative role over time"[14] by continuously parsing resumes received from job applicants before delivering them to employers. The automated hiring platform is the *tertius bifrons* because it is a type of broker that works both in its own interest (to maintain its coordinative role) and in the interest of one of the parties to the triad (the employer), while maintaining the appearance of working for both parties (employer and job applicant).

This categorization rings true in light of the class action allegations against Facebook. Facebook users entrust their information to platforms such as Facebook with the expectation that those platforms will use that information to better the users' experience. However, what has been alleged is that Facebook, by creating "affinity groups" and "lookalike audiences" from its users' information (and especially when such Facebook-provided features are deployed in defiance of anti-discrimination laws),[15]

---

[11] Georg Simmel, *The Sociology of Georg Simmel*, trans. Kurt H. Wolff (New York: Free Press, 1950), 145–69.

[12] David Obstfeld, "Social Networks, the *Tertius Iungens* Orientation, and Involvement in Innovation," *Administrative Science Quarterly* 50, no. 1 (2005): 100–130.

[13] Obstfeld, "Social Networks, the *Tertius Iungens* Orientation, and Involvement in Innovation," 104.

[14] Obstfeld, "Social Networks, the *Tertius Iungens* Orientation, and Involvement in Innovation," 104.

[15] See First Amended Class and Collective Action Complaint at 21, *Bradley v. T-Mobile U.S., Inc.*, No. 17-cv-07232-BLF (N.D. Cal. May 29, 2018), www.onlineagediscrimination.com/ sites/default/files/ documents/og-cwa-complaint.pdf [https://perma.cc/JGU8-DSKT]

has brokered information to employers in a way that benefits both Facebook and the employer, but not necessarily the user.

12.3.3 *The Federal Credit Report Act as Regulatory Mechanism*

Although the Fair Credit Reporting Act (FCRA) is often brought up in the governance of credit reports, it could potentially be leveraged when an employer relies on information from third parties – namely, an applicant tracking system or an algorithmic hiring platform. First, some brief details about the language and intentions of the FCRA. The FCRA, passed in 1970, was initially intended to protect consumers who were being scanned for creditworthiness. The language set forth by the FCRA was applied primarily to the Big Three credit reporting agencies (CRAs) – Equifax, Experian, and TransUnion – all of which would draw up reports about consumers, using their personal information to determine their credit eligibility.[16] The law also protects consumers from unfair background checks and unauthorized collections of their private information, ensuring that consumers are alerted to any information that may adversely affect their ability to obtain either credit or, more recently enforced, employment. Moreover, the law also protects consumers by providing that creditors or employers must disclose "in writing to the consumer who is the subject of the communication, not later than 5 business days after receiving any request from the consumer for such disclosure, the nature and substance of all information in the consumer's file at the time of the request …"[17] Through such provisions, the FCRA gives consumers more control over how their personal information is reported by consumer reporting agencies and used by both banks and employers.

However, since its passage, the FCRA has expanded its bounds such that it no longer only applies to the Big Three credit reporting agencies.[18] Now it also applies to a variety of agencies that collect and sell information that is found outside the workplace and that might be pertinent for applicant-reviewing purposes.[19]

With the advent of many companies whose sole purpose is employment prescreening, a question has arisen regarding the point at which a screening service

---

[16] Kim and Hanson, "People Analytics and the Regulation of Information under the Fair Credit Reporting Act," 26.

[17] See 15 U.S.C. § 1681k(a), 1681a(o)(5)(C)(i).

[18] See Consumer Finance Protection Bureau, *List of Consumer Reporting Companies*, 2020, https://files.consumerfinance.gov/f/201604_cfpb_list-of-consumer-reporting-companies.pdf [https://perma.cc/Y8LW-9JFS].

[19] For example, Checkr (https://Checkr.com [https://perma.cc/9ECB-2RVN]) screens applicants for criminal records and driving records, and also provides employment verifications, international verifications, and drug screenings. Hireright (www.hireright.com [https://perma.cc/6RC7-QJP8]) boasts the industry's broadest collection of on-demand screening applications. First Advantage (www.fadv.com [https://perma.cc/S3YC-ADFW]) provides criminal and pre-employment background checks, as well as drug-testing and tenant screening services.

should be considered a CRA by the FCRA. In essence, how big of a role does a reporting agency have to play in the information collection and reporting process in order to face such substantial government regulation? The language of the FCRA plainly defines the characteristics of entities that can be considered CRAs, as well as the content of reports that can be considered "consumer reports" under the law. A CRA, by definition, is any "person which, for monetary fees, dues, or on a cooperative nonprofit basis, regularly engages in whole or in part in the practice of assembling or evaluating consumer credit information or other information on consumers for the purpose of furnishing consumer reports to third parties."[20] Application screening software companies could be considered CRAs, as they regularly process and evaluate "other information on consumers" for the purpose of providing reports to employers. Furthermore, these companies arguably develop "consumer reports," judging by the legal definition of that term.

The FCRA defines "consumer report[s]" as:

> any written, oral, or other communication of any information by a consumer reporting agency bearing on a consumer's credit worthiness, credit standing, credit capacity, character, general reputation, personal characteristics, or mode of living which is used or expected to be used ... as a factor in establishing the consumer's eligibility for ... credit or insurance ... or ... employment purposes.[21]

The case of Paycor illustrates why the FCRA might be applied to algorithm hiring platforms. Paycor is, for all intents and purposes, a background check access provider, although it also advertises resume-parsing tools and interview-streamlining data reports.[22] The software platform advertises to employers that it takes in applicant information and "intelligently stores that information into the correct fields of the candidate profile, which means errors from manually inputting data are a thing of the past." From these profiles, employers can find employees to fit the requirements of the job descriptions they release.[23] Then Paycor gives employers access to background check software provided by third parties, which Paycor itself entirely oversees.[24] Given these features, I argue that Paycor has enough of a hand in the report-creating process as to have the final reports attributed to itself, making its reports "consumer reports." Paycor acquires sensitive information from third-party background checkers, after overviewing the background screening process, and then relays a report about the screening

---

[20] 15 U.S.C. § 1681a(f).

[21] 15 U.S.C. § 1681a(d)(1)(A)–(B).

[22] See Paycor, "Software & Applicant Tracking System," https://perma.cc/K9UF-YUSV (captured Apr. 23, 2020). Paycor recently acquired Newton. See Paycor, "Announcement: Newton Is Now Paycor Recruiting," https://perma.cc/LF3U-R4ZK (captured May 18, 2020).

[23] See Paycor, "Paycor Recruiting: Find Quality Candidates and Fill Open Positions Fast," last updated Oct. 4, 2019, www.paycor.com/resource-center/recruitment-tools [https://perma.cc/3MS9TVDK].

[24] Paycor, "Recruiting Software & Applicant Tracking System."

to its clients. Further, by parsing resumes and creating new, standardized profiles on applicants for employers to reference, Paycor is certainly changing the nature of the resumes that prospective employees have submitted and is thereby creating its own reports with added information. All of this data, which Paycor relays to employers, can, and likely will, be used to determine employment eligibility. Therefore, under the language of the FCRA, the reports put forth by Paycor qualify as "consumer reports."

Furthermore, the Federal Trade Commission (FTC), the body that oversees the FCRA, has recently held that "[j]ust saying you're not a consumer reporting agency isn't enough." The case, which took place in 2013, dealt with an application available for purchase on iTunes, Filiquarian Publishing, which advertised that it could make "'quick criminal background check[s] for convictions' in specific states." The application had access to "hundreds of thousands of criminal records" and could help employers discover if any of the convictions could be attributed to their applicants. However, Filiquarian also reported in a disclaimer on its site that it was not a consumer reporting agency because its background screening reports were not to be considered screening products for insurance, employment, loans, or credit applications. The FTC took issue with this, finding that Filiquarian provided the exact same information as CRAs, but simply said they didn't use the information for employment purposes, which is not a reasonable excuse from FCRA compliance. Ultimately, the FTC's statement was the following: "Companies offering background screening products for employment or other FCRA purposes ... have to stay in line with the law."[25]

If automated hiring platforms were to be considered consumer reporting agencies under the FCRA, then legal liability should attach for their failure to "follow reasonable procedures to assure the maximum possible accuracy of [their] files," which causes individuals to be denied employment opportunities. For example, in one case, *Thompson v. San Antonio Retail Merchants Ass'n* (SARMA), the Fifth Circuit found that SARMA had erred in its creation of a profile for Thompson, automatically "capturing" the incorrect Social Security number for his profile and erroneously reporting the bad credit history of another man by the same common name. The court ultimately held that under the FCRA, such an oversight by a credit reporting agency as the one presented in *Thompson* was enough to show negligence on the part of the agency.[26]

---

[25] Tony Rodriguez and Jessica Lyon, "Background Screening Reports and the FCRA: Just Saying You're Not a Consumer Reporting Agency Isn't Enough," *Federal Trade Commission*, blog posted Jan. 10, 2013, www.ftc.gov/news-events/blogs/business-blog/2013/01/background-screeningreports-fcra-just-saying-youre-not.

[26] *Thompson v. San Antonio Retail Merchs. Ass'n.*, 682 F.2d 509, 512 (5th Cir. 1982); see also *Spokeo, Inc. v. Robins*, 136 S. Ct. 1540, 1546 (2016) (in which a "people search engine" provided incorrect personal information about a consumer to employers and the Supreme Court ruled that this established concrete injury to the consumer, by damaging his employment prospects).

12.4 HOLDING THE EMPLOYERS ACCOUNTABLE

To engender new regulations or improve extant ones for keeping the employer accountable requires a rethinking of the legal theories for employment discrimination. First, I argue for a revaluation of the burden of proof under the existing causes of action in Title VII (disparate treatment and disparate impact) and for the addition of a third cause of action, *discrimination per se*. I argue also that there is an *auditing imperative* created by the employer's use of automated hiring platforms.

12.4.1 *Discrimination* Per se

Holding employers responsible for the algorithmic bias of the automated hiring platforms the employers use presents a challenging legal problem because of the difficulty of discovering proof and establishing intent. To remedy this, I propose a new burden-shifting theory of liability: *discrimination per se*.[27] Discrimination *per se* would allow for a third cause of action under Title VII.[28] The purpose is to aid plaintiffs who cannot show proof of disparate treatment or who would have difficulty obtaining the means to show statistical proof of disparate impact. Title VII requires intent for liability to attach, or in the absence of intent a clear demonstration of disparate impact with no excuse of business necessity for the disparity.[29] When bringing disparate impact claims, plaintiffs are likely to face three interrelated obstacles: "(1) compiling the requisite statistics to show that the policy has a disparate impact ..., (2) identifying a specific policy or practice that caused the adverse employment decision, and (3) rebutting the employer's defense that the policy is justified by

---

[27] Although my proposed doctrine borrows from tort theory, it is important to note that the National Labor Relations Act characterizes some employer actions as *per se* violations. 29 U.S.C. § 158 (2012). The statute defines *per se* violations of the bargaining obligation as conduct that violates Section 8(a)(5) without need for further inquiry, including unilateral changes involving mandatory subjects of bargaining, even when such changes are made in a context that otherwise indicates good faith bargaining, and even where the changes are partially made in an effort to comply with governmental requirements.
Other *per se* violations include an employer bypassing the union and bargaining directly with employees; insistence to impasse upon permissive subjects of bargaining; and refusing to execute a written agreement embodying the terms of a negotiated contract. See Timothy M. McConville, "Employer Policies May Be *Per se* Violations of the National Labor Relations Act (NLRA)," *National Law Review*, July 12, 2013, www.natlawreview.com/article/employer-policies-may-be-se-violations-national-labor-relations-act-nlra.

[28] Title VII of the Civil Rights Act protects the job applicant against discrimination on the basis of sex, race, color, national origin, and religion. See U.S. Civil Rights Act of 1964 § 7, 42 U.S.C. § 2000e (2012). Plaintiffs must establish that "a respondent uses a particular employment practice that causes a disparate impact on the basis of [a protected characteristic] and the respondent fails to demonstrate that the challenged practice is job related for the position in question and consistent with its business necessity." 42 U.S.C. § 2000e-2(k)(1)(A)(i).

[29] Proving clear intent is necessary when attempting to make a disparate treatment case under Title VII. However, under the disparate impact of clause of action codified in Title VII, the intent is implied from an established pattern. See U.S. Civil Rights Act of 1964 § 7, 42 U.S.C. § 2000e-2(1)(A).

a business necessity."[30] Perhaps the biggest hurdle for plaintiffs is that "courts are inconsistent in addressing the requirement of compiling appropriate statistics to show that a policy has a disparate impact."[31] This makes it rather difficult for plaintiffs to even meet a prima facie showing of disparate impact.

In their essay "Incomprehensible Discrimination," Professors James Grimmelmann and Daniel Westreich make the case that when a plaintiff has met the burden of showing disparate impact, "the defendant's burden to show a business necessity requires it to show not just that its model's scores are not just *correlated* with job performance but *explain* it."[32] This heightened burden acknowledges the information asymmetry that exists between the employer and the employee in the context of automated hiring. My proposed doctrine of *discrimination per se* seeks to further rectify both the information asymmetry and the power imbalance present in automated hiring situations by entirely shifting the burden of proof from plaintiff to defendant.

Per my proposal, a plaintiff can assert that a hiring practice (e.g., the use of proxy variables resulting or *with the potential to result in* adverse impact to protected categories) is so egregious as to amount to discrimination *per se*, and this should shift the burden of proof from the plaintiff to the defendant (employer) to show that its practice is non-discriminatory. I do not set forth a specific rule or standard for how to determine discrimination *per se*; rather, I think this is a question of law that, like other types of American legal doctrines, should be generated through case law. Note also that the discrimination *per se* doctrine does not dictate an automatic win for the plaintiff; rather, it merely reverses the American legal tradition of deference to employers and allows that an employment discrimination plaintiff will at least get a day in court. Note also that it still remains relatively easy for employers to establish business necessity for their practices and therefore defeat any plaintiffs' disparate impact claims.[33]

---

[30] Nicole Buonocore Porter, "Synergistic Solutions: An Integrated Approach to Solving the Caregiver Conundrum for 'Real' Workers," *Stetson Law Review* 39, no. 1 (2010): 808.

[31] See, e.g., Charles A. Sullivan, "Disparate Impact: Looking Past the Desert Palace Mirage," *William & Mary Law Review* 47, no. 3 (2005): 989.

[32] Grimmelmann and Westreich, "Incomprehensible Discrimination," 170 (emphasis in original). See also Margot E. Kaminski, "Binary Governance," *Southern California Law Review* 92 (2019): 1529–1616 (identifying three categories of concerns in regulating algorithmic decision-making: dignitary, justificatory, and instrumental); see also Andrew D. Selbst and Solon Barocas, "The Intuitive Appeal of Explainable Machines," *Fordman Law Review* 87 (2018): 1085–39 (reviewing the rationales behind calls for explanations of algorithmic decision-making). But see Lilian Edwards and Michael Veale, "Slave to the Algorithm? Why a 'Right to an Explanation' Is Probably Not the Remedy You Are Looking for," *Duke Law and Technology Review* 16, no 1 (2017): 17–84 (arguing that a right to an explanation in the EU General Data Protection Regulation [GDPR] is unlikely to present a complete remedy to algorithmic harms).

[33] See Porter, "Synergistic Solutions," 810; it's important to note here that even after a defendant has been able to show business necessity, a plaintiff may nevertheless be able to prevail by showing that there could be an "alternative employment practice" that meets that business necessity." § 703 (k)(1) (A) & C. See also *Jones v. City of Boston*, 845 F.3d 28 (1st Cir. 2016).

The *discrimination per se* cause of action is an answer to the question of whether the liability of corporations could be mitigated by a lack of intent to discriminate or even a lack of awareness that an algorithm is producing biased results.[34] For example, one researcher, Jatinder Singh, has argued that the line of responsibility for problems created by machine learning algorithms is blurred. More specifically, if a machine learning algorithm can operate without being specifically programmed, by *de novo* creating a model from available data, should the blame for any resulting disparate impact lie with the creator of the algorithm, with the entity who chose the training data, or with the algorithm itself – with the last option presuming that the technology is essentially "thinking" on its own? This, Singh argues, is a question that has yet to be addressed by any current legal framework.[35]

In one attempt to surmount this problem, Professor Stephanie Bornstein, in the article "Reckless Discrimination," theorizes a recklessness model of discrimination under Title VII, arguing that an employer should be liable for acts done in reckless negligence, which are consequences of implicit bias and stereotyping in employment decisions. Bornstein explains how employers have made efforts to remove implicit bias from hiring; they have developed "blind interviews over online instant messaging software, application-screening algorithms, pre-commitment to set assessment standards, and more." The author notes that "the ability to prevent and correct for bias and stereotyping in the workplace is more affordable and accessible than ever before." She insists that given the development of technological tools such as predictive algorithms, which employers can utilize to reduce bias in decision-making, an employer that knows about the risks of implicit bias, has evidence that such bias may infect its decision-making, and fails to try to prevent it should be liable for discriminatory intent and reckless action.[36]

Building on Professor Bornstein's line of argumentation, I propose here that the well-established tort principle of *negligence per se* should be the model for creating a new legal framework to answer the question of intent when it comes to discriminatory results obtained by automated hiring platforms. While another legal scholar, Professor Girardeau Spann, has also borrowed from tort doctrine to argue that the invidiousness of racial discrimination in the United States and the undeniable concomitant racial disparities dictate the strict liability standard of *res ipsa loquitur* for racial discrimination claims,[37] and I believe that in some instances such a standard might be warranted, I argue that a discrimination *per se* standard that is modeled on the negligence *per se* standard is more generally applicable (i.e., it would apply to various cases of employment discrimination, not just racially motivated

---

[34] Professor Charles Sullivan has also grappled with these questions. See Sullivan, "Employing AI."

[35] Jatinder Singh et al., "Responsibility & Machine Learning: Part of a Process," Oct. 27, 2016, https://papers.ssrn.com/sol3/papers.cfm?abstract_id=2860048.

[36] Stephanie Bornstein, "Reckless Discrimination," *California Law Review* 105, no. 4 (2017): 1056, 1058, 1110.

[37] See Girardeau A. Spann, "Race Ipsa Loquitor," *Michigan State Law Review* 2018 (2019): 1025–93.

discrimination) and also serves to institute more feasible self-regulation practices. The concept of discrimination *per se* is also in line with Professor Ford's argument that employment discrimination law imposes a duty of care on the employer to ensure that its employment practices are not unlawfully discriminatory.[38] Note that the discrimination *per se* doctrine would work hand in hand with an "auditing imperative" imposed on the employer.[39] The auditing imperative takes into consideration the practical problems associated with proving disparate impact in an algorithmic hiring scenario.

The proto negligence *per se* case involved a Minnesota drug store clerk who sold a deadly poison to a customer at the customer's request. At the time of the sale, the clerk did not label the substance as a "poison," which was required by a state statute for the sales of such substances. Later, the customer who had purchased the substance ingested the chemical, which caused her death. Given these facts, should the clerk have been held legally liable for his actions, which indirectly caused the customer's death? This case, *Osborne v. McMasters*, became one of the earliest cases in the United States to analyze the legal concept of *negligence per se*. Given the facts of the case, the court first found that there could be no "serious doubt of defendant's liability" – as he had known of his duty to label the bottle as poison.[40] In explanation, the court detailed that it was

> well settled … that where a statute or municipal ordinance imposes upon any person a specific duty for the protection or benefit of others, if he neglects to perform that duty he is liable to those for whose protection or benefit it was imposed for any injuries of the character which the statute or ordinance was designed to prevent …[41]

Since the time of *Osborne*, the doctrine of *negligence per se* has become commonly used for violations of laws such as traffic laws, building codes, blood alcohol content limits, and various federal laws.[42] For example, in *Mikula v. Tailors*, an Ohio business invitee was taken to the emergency department after falling down in a snow-covered parking lot at the place of business to which she had been invited.[43]

[38] See, e.g., Richard Thompson Ford, "Bias in the Air: Rethinking Employment Discrimination Law," *Stanford Law Review* 66, no. 6 (2014): 1381–1421 (arguing that employment law imposes a duty of care on employers to avoid decisions that undermine social equality).

[39] I discuss the "auditing imperative" in another article, "Automated Employment Discrimination" (draft manuscript available).

[40] *Osborne v. McMasters*, 41 N.W. 543 (Minn. 1889).

[41] *Osborne v. McMasters*, 41 N.W. 543 (Minn. 1889).

[42] See, e.g., *Williams v. Calhoun*, 333 S.E.2d 408 (Ga. App. 1985) (in which the defendant's failure to stop at a stop sign constituted negligence *per se*); *Lombard v. Colo. Outdoor Educ. Ctr., Inc.*, 187 P.3d 565 (Colo. 2008) (in which an outdoor education teacher fell off a ladder that was in violation of building code restrictions, establishing negligence *per se* on the part of the landowner); *Purchase v. Meyer*, 737 P.2d 661 (Wash. 1987) (in which a cocktail lounge was found negligent *per se* for serving alcohol to a minor).

[43] *Mikula v. Tailors*, 263 NE.2d 316 (Ohio 1970).

Witnesses report having seen her fall after stepping into a hole in the parking lot that was about seven inches deep and had been covered by the snowfall from that day. After careful consideration, the jury determined that

> [a] deep hole in a parking lot which is filled or covered, or both, by a natural accumulation of snow constitutes a condition, the existence of which the owner of the premises is bound, in the exercise of reasonable care, to know. He is also bound to know that a natural accumulation of snow which fills or covers the hole is a condition substantially more dangerous than that normally associated with snow. ... Under such circumstances, the owner's failure to correct the condition constitutes actionable negligence.[44]

Moreover, failure to correct an issue can also lend itself to negligence *per se* claims if the accused individual is found to have violated a statute by their failure to respond to a problem. For example, in *Miller v. Christian*, a landlord was found negligent *per se*, after being placed on notice from a tenant that the building's sewage system had recurring problems. Failure to "fix the immediate problem within a reasonable amount of time" resulted in a backup of the sewage system, which caused the tenant's apartment to flood, ruining much of her personal property.[45] The court in *Miller* found that Allan Christian, the landlord, was liable for the damage to the tenant's property because he had a legal duty to maintain the apartment's sewage system in addition to being legally obligated to keep the premises fit for habitation.[46]

Often, "failure to correct" claims entail a consideration of whether the plaintiff knew of the problem, as it is presumed that a plaintiff with knowledge of an existing problem would be reasonable enough to avoid injury by the issue altogether. In one case, *Walker v. RLI Enterprises*, a tenant in an apartment building sued her landlord after she stepped out the back door of the building and slipped on a sheet of ice. She suffered serious injuries to her ankle. In her suit, the tenant asserted that the landlord was negligent in maintaining the property because she had given him notice of a leaky water faucet by the back door of her apartment. This negligence, the court determined, was negligence *per se* because the landlord had an obligation to maintain the premises under Ohio law.[47]

At trial, however, the landlord argued that "a landlord is only liable where he has 'superior knowledge' of the defect that led to the injury." By this the landlord meant that as the tenant had alerted him of the problem, the tenant then clearly knew as much about the dangerous conditions as he did. He also noted that she had taken no further action to avoid the leaky faucet and could thus be responsible for her own injury. However, the court found this argument unconvincing, holding that such an argument applies only in the context of natural accumulations of ice and snow

---

[44] *Mikula v. Tailors*, 263 NE.2d 316 (Ohio 1970), at 322–23.
[45] *Miller v. Christian*, 958 F.2d 1234 (3d Cir. 1992).
[46] V.I. Code Ann. tit. 29, § 333(b)(1) (2019).
[47] *Walker v. RLI Enters.*, Inc., No. 89325, 2007 WL 4442725, at *1, *2 (Ohio Ct. App. 2007).

because most people have experienced such conditions and know that they should take precautions. Site-specific problems, though, are the responsibility of the landlord to correct, as his knowledge of the issues on the property is likely "superior" to that of his tenants or site visitors.[48]

In the case of automated hiring systems, employers have an obligation not to unlawfully discriminate against applicants, as proscribed by Title VII of the Civil Rights Act and other federal anti-discrimination laws. Furthermore, as I propose later, if self-audits or external audits of hiring algorithms become mandated by law,[49] then it follows that when an employer willfully neglects to audit and correct its automated hiring systems for unlawful bias, a prima facie intent to discriminate could be implied, pursuant to the proposed doctrine of discrimination *per se*. This argument becomes persuasive when one considers that some corporations make use of bespoke internal hiring algorithms, such that no one, except the corporation, has access to the hiring algorithm and its results – meaning then that only the corporation could have "superior knowledge" of any problems of bias.

There are two important arguments against the introduction of the *discrimination per se* doctrine. The first is the difficulty of establishing a standard for when the doctrine might apply; the second is that it imposes too large a burden on the employer. Regarding the first issue, I agree that it will take some work on the part of the courts to establish clear precedents for when the doctrine could apply. But this is true for any new legal doctrine. In fact, even established legal doctrines still face contestation as to when they should or should not apply.[50] Consider that in the context of automated hiring the two legal doctrines currently available to the plaintiff on which to build a case are disparate treatment and disparate impact. The fact is that there are very few cases of disparate treatment because employers are now much too sophisticated to leave the kind of "smoking gun" evidence required. For disparate impact, the problem is that there is wide discrepancy in determining what statistics are enough to show a pattern of disparate impact.[51]

Regarding the second issue of a burden on employers, the fact remains that automated hiring is a cost-saving measure. Employers save significant amounts of money and time by using automated hiring platforms. However, automated hiring

---

[48] *Walker v. RLI Enters.*, Inc., No. 89325, 2007 WL 4442725, *5.

[49] I first discuss the proposal for mandates of self and external audits of hiring algorithms in great detail in: "The Auditing Imperative for Automated Hiring," *Harv. J.L. & Tech.* 34 (2021): 621.

[50] See Laura T. Kessler, "The Attachment Cap: Employment Discrimination Law, Women's Cultural Caregiving, and the Limits of Economic and Liberal Legal Theory," *University of Michigan Journal of Law Reform* 34, no. 3 (2001): 415–16 (noting that because men are not usually primary caregivers, women have a difficult time finding comparisons to prove a disparate impact); Michael Selmi, "Was the Disparate Impact Theory a Mistake?" *UCLA Law Review* 53, no. 3 (2006): 769 (stating that establishing a statistically significant impact might be difficult unless the affected population is sufficiently large and diverse).

[51] William R. Corbett, "Fixing Employment Discrimination Law," *SMU Law Review* 62, no. 1 (2009): 81–116 (noting that courts are inconsistent in applying the disparate impact doctrine).

platforms should not save employers from their duty not to discriminate. Just like an employer holds a responsibility to supervise their human workers for activities that might contravene the law, so, too, does their obligation remain to audit automated hiring systems for bias. This burden neither is heavier than when the intermediary is human, nor does it disappear merely because the intermediary is a set of algorithms. The doctrine of *discrimination per se* is meant to prevent employers from shirking their responsibility.

12.4.2 *The Auditing Imperative*

The auditing imperative for automated hiring systems stems from the affirmative duty of care imposed on an employer. That is, the careful auditing of automated hiring systems represents one means to fulfill that duty of care. Over the last several decades, legal scholars have begun calling for the application of tort law to the framework through which we understand employment discrimination. In his article "Negligent Discrimination," David Benjamin Oppenheimer first noted that the Supreme Court's primary theories of employment discrimination could readily be analogized to intentional tort and strict liability doctrines. Then Oppenheimer elaborates on this analogy, arguing that employment discrimination can most aptly be compared to the tort doctrine of negligence. Oppenheimer shares data showing a swift upward trend towards most white Americans professing a commitment to non-discrimination in employment. Yet Title VII and other statutory prohibitions of race discrimination are still necessary. He explains that this is due to the fact that racism is often an unconscious bias. Furthermore, supporting the principle of non-discrimination in employment does not necessarily mean that all white Americans are also in support of federal enforcement of employment discrimination laws. In fact, based on one study, Oppenheimer suggests that 97 percent of the support for non-discrimination is an "empty gesture," meaning white Americans often do not back up the "support" they suggest in surveys. Similarly, while many white Americans had attested that they were committed to non-discrimination, they were similarly more likely to describe African Americans as being "lazier" and less "honest" than other Americans. Using these studies, Oppenheimer concludes that white Americans are frequently unaware of their own internal racism.[52]

Using this information to fuel his analysis of employment law, Professor Oppenheimer theorizes that a theory of employment discrimination that focuses on intent to discriminate can provide no remedy for most discrimination, because there often is no intent involved. The intent requirement is ultimately based on a false binary: When Congress enacted Title VII, it provided very little guidance on the standard that courts should require for proof of discrimination. The Supreme

---

[52] See David Benjamin Oppenheimer, "Negligent Discrimination," *University of Pennsylvania Law Review* 141, no. 3 (1993): 899, 903, 905, 910, 916.

Court supplemented this with cases that seemingly resolved this issue, dividing discrimination cases into claims that looked like intentional torts, and others that looked more like strict liability.[53]

With this in mind, Professor Oppenheimer provides an analysis of *Griggs v. Duke Power Co.*, the strict liability employment law theory.[54] The case challenged "aptitude tests" given to Black employees in order to transfer out of the "labor department," a department to which only Black employees were hired. The test acted as a clear barrier to Black employees who tried to transfer to other departments, although it was applied universally throughout the department. Here, the Supreme Court discussed the importance of the consequences of the employment practice, not simply the motivation.[55] As such, it found that the employer was strictly liable for its unintended but harmful conduct, without using the words *strict liability*.[56]

Next, Oppenheimer delves into the idea of the intentional tort, which presented itself in the *McDonnell Douglas* case.[57] The case involved a Black man who stated that he had been rejected from a position because of his race, after being a vocal public opponent of the company's past employment practices, which he alleged were racially discriminatory. In this case, the Supreme Court held that in an individual discrimination case, the plaintiff must prove an intent to discriminate by showing, for example, that they were qualified for an open job which remained open after her rejection. After this point, employers can defend themselves by showing that there was a legitimate non-discriminatory reason for their decisions.[58]

Yet, with both of these doctrines previously articulated, the Supreme Court began to articulate a third approach to the adverse impact and strict liability doctrines – the less discriminatory alternative doctrine. In these cases, a plaintiff could prevail if they could show that "other tests or selection devises, without a similarly undesirable racial effect, would also serve the employer's legitimate interest."[59] Professor Oppenheimer argues that this test opened the door for the application of the doctrine of negligence to employment discrimination cases. Ultimately, he explains that "negligence, at its core, is a breach of duty recognized by law for the protection of others." Employers often have this duty – for example, the duty to provide a safe workplace or to protect employees from unfit co-employees or

---

[53] Oppenheimer, "Negligent Discrimination," 919. The paper cites both *McDonnell Douglas Corp. v. Green*, 411 U.S. 792 (1973) (explaining that where an employee challenges a specific employment decision, they must prove it was motivated by an intent to discriminate) and *Griggs v. Duke Power Co.*, 401 U.S. 424 (1971) (explaining that where an employee challenges policies or procedures that have a discriminatory effect, they may rely on strict liability theory rather than having to prove intentional discrimination).

[54] Oppenheimer, "Negligent Discrimination," 920.

[55] See *Griggs v. Duke Power Co.*, 401 U.S. at 428.

[56] Oppenheimer, "Negligent Discrimination," 921.

[57] See Oppenheimer, "Negligent Discrimination."

[58] *McDonnell Douglas Corp. v. Green*, 411 U.S. at 794, 802.

[59] See, e.g., *Grant v. Bethlehem Steel Corp.*, 635 F.2d 1007, 10015 (2d Cir. 1980).

supervisors.[60] Then he argues that the employment relationship is a "special" relationship, such that both employees and employers enter into the employment relationship with care and owe each other certain duties. Here, employers could be responsible for not protecting employees from discriminatory practices.[61]

Professor Richard Thompson Ford similarly mulled over the question of intent as part of employment discrimination. In one article, "Rethinking Rights after the Second Reconstruction," Ford argues for precisely how to fill the gap that Oppenheimer had described – abandoning conceptual disputes over "discrimination" altogether in favor of discussing the employer's affirmative duty to avoid decisions and policies that harm underrepresented or stigmatized groups. Ford begins his argument with the notion of civil rights as the idea that we should protect individuals from potentially oppressive states.[62] Over time, he explains, the law has gradually grown to protect individuals not just from oppressive states but also from oppressive private institutions.[63] By assigning rights to overcome these private actors, he argues that having legal rights does not mean that an individual is specially protected against power. Instead, these rights are a political decision to assign power to a disadvantaged party to stave off subordination. This is the notion that drove change throughout the civil rights era of the American 1960s.[64]

Today, one of these rights is the right not to be discriminated against in employment based on certain prohibited reasons, including race, sex, religion, and so on. Yet, while the law states that employers must not discriminate on certain enumerated bases, it also creates a duty of care, though this duty has been largely undefined. Lacking a definition, the bounds of an employer's duty of care have been debated. Traditionally, the idea has been that employers would be liable only for discrimination they can prevent as institutions but could not be liable for the discrimination they – the entities themselves – did not cause.[65] This meant that employers were simply encouraged to avoid decisions that undermine social equality, but were not actually encouraged to promote social equality.[66]

However, even when employers have reasonable anti-harassment or anti-discrimination policies, employees still may face harassment or discrimination. That injustice is no different for the individual simply because the employer has

---

[60] Oppenheimer, "Negligent Discrimination," 932; see *Hentzel v. Singer Co.*, 188 Cal. Rptr. 159, 164 (Ct. App. 1982) (safe workplace); *Najera v. Southern Pac. Co.*, 13 Cal. Rptr. 146, 148 (Ct. App. 1961) (unfit co-employees and supervisors).

[61] Oppenheimer, "Negligent Discrimination," 932.

[62] Richard Thompson Ford, "Rethinking Rights after the Second Reconstruction," *Yale Law Journal* 132, no. 8 (2014): 2942, 2946.

[63] See *Marsh v. Alabama*, 326 U.S. 501 (1946) (applying constitutional standards to private entities that serve a 'public function'); *Shelley v. Kraemer*, 334 U.S. 1 (1948) (extending constitutional rights to private action).

[64] Ford, "Rethinking Rights after the Second Reconstruction," 2946, 2949.

[65] Ford, "Rethinking Rights after the Second Reconstruction," 2951, 2956.

[66] See Ford, "Bias in the Air," 1381.

an anti-discrimination policy. As such, Ford argues that the law should address the outcomes openly by defining the employer's duty of care. For example, he suggests a policy change that would reward employers who hire members of underrepresented groups, instead of making it "riskier" to hire such people out of a desire to protect the company from liability.[67] Similarly, a manager who discriminates in a workplace where the employer has a reasonable anti-discrimination policy has acted outside the scope of their authority and should be liable for that action independently.[68] In effect, Ford argues for a complete overhaul of the system of anti-discrimination law in favor of policy that hits at the source of discriminatory outcomes.

Following in the footsteps of these legal scholars, I argue that in the age of automated decision-making we now live in, an auditing imperative assigned to the use of automated hiring system is one way to further delineate the employer's affirmative duty of care. This auditing imperative demands certain actions on the part of the employers who use the systems as well as the designers of automated hiring systems. The auditing of automated decision-making systems is an idea that is gaining ground.[69] This is especially true in regard to employment decision-making, as several experts working in the field support the idea of mandated audits for automated hiring systems. One quibble is whether such audits should be internal or external. Meredith Whittaker, former co-founder of the AI Now Institute at New York University and former founder of Google's Open Research group, notes that "AI is not impartial or neutral" and suggests that "in the case of systems meant to automate candidate search and hiring, we need to ask ourselves: What assumptions about worth, ability and potential do these systems reflect and reproduce?

[67] Ford, "Rethinking Rights after the Second Reconstruction," 2957–60.
[68] See Ford, "Bias in the Air," 1417.
[69] Pauline T. Kim, "Auditing Algorithms for Discrimination," *University of Pennsylvania Law Review* 166, no. 1 (2017): 189–203 (proposing the retention of audits of automated decision-making to check for discrimination); Julie E. Cohen, "The Regulatory State in the Information Age," *Theoretical Inquiries Law* 17 (2016): 372–73 ("[P]olicymakers must devise ways of enabling regulators to evaluate algorithmically-embedded controls"); Deven R. Desai and Joshua A. Kroll, "Trust but Verify: A Guide to Algorithms and the Law," *Harvard Journal of Law & Technology* 31, no. (2017): 16–17 (discussing designing algorithmic systems to enable audits by regulators); Citron and Pasquale, "The Scored Society," 24–25 (proposing that the FTC audit consumer scoring systems); Pasquale, "Beyond Innovation and Competition," 169–71 (calling for monitoring of search engines and considering the possibility of the FTC playing that role); W. Nicholson Price II, "Regulating Black-Box Medicine," *Michigan Law Review* 116, no. 3 (2017): 464 (calling for greater FDA and third-party scrutiny of medical algorithms); Schwartz, "Data Processing and Government Administration" (calling for "independent governmental monitoring of data processing systems"); Rory Van Loo, "Helping Buyers Beware: The Need for Supervision of Big Retail," *University of Pennsylvania Law Review* 163 (2015): 1382 (proposing that the FTC monitor Amazon); Shlomit Yanisky-Ravid and Sean K. Hallisey, "Equality and Privacy by Design": A New Model of Artificial Intelligence Data Transparency via Auditing, Certification, and Safe Harbor Regimes," *Fordham Urban Law Journal* 46, art. 5 (2019): 429 (proposing "an auditing regime and a certification program, run either by a governmental body or, in the absence of such entity, by private institutions"); see also Crawford and Schultz, "Big Data and Due Process," 121–24 (considering auditing by public agencies to address predictive privacy).

Who was at the table when these assumptions were encoded?" She also states that because such systems are proprietary and not open to review, we cannot validate their claims of fairness and ensure they are not simply tech-washing and magnifying longstanding patterns of discrimination. Thus, she insists on the need for audits by experts, advocacy groups, and academia.[70] I believe the auditing imperative can be fulfilled in multiple and non-exclusive ways, that is, I advocate for both internal and external audits.

12.4.3 *Internal Audits*

Mandated internal auditing will ensure that companies diligently review the outcomes of automated hiring and correct for any discovered bias. On August 19, 2019, a group of two hundred business executives collaboratively working together as the Business Roundtable released a statement[71] in which they recognized a responsibility beyond merely satisfying shareholders. Rather, the group, which included executives from Walmart, Apple, Pepsi, and others, acknowledged that they must also "invest in their employees, protect the environment and deal fairly and ethically with their suppliers."[72] Given this acknowledgment, I argue that internal audits to check automated hiring systems for bias are a key part of the corporate social responsibility (CSR) of business firms. This is especially necessary when corporations are using machine learning algorithms. Thus, I propose that large corporations and other entities should be required to implement a business system of regular self-audits of their hiring outcomes to check for disparate impact. This system of mandated self-audits would be similar to the mandated self-audits of financial institutions. In an internal audit activity, self-auditing, or self-assessment, a "department, division, team of consultants, or other practitioner(s) [provide] independent, objective assurance and consulting services designed to add value and improve an organization's operations." By evaluating and improving the effectiveness of "governance, risk management and control processes" in a systematic and disciplined way, internal auditing helps an organization reach its objectives.[73]

Standards and best practices already exist for conducting an effective internal audit. As an international professional association, the Institute of Internal Auditors

---

[70] Rosenbaum, "Silicon Valley Is Stumped: Even A.I. Cannot Always Remove Bias from Hiring."
[71] The statement begins, "Americans deserve an economy that allows each person to succeed through hard work and creativity and to lead a life of meaning and dignity. We believe the free-market system is the best means of generating good jobs, a strong and sustainable economy, innovation, a healthy environment and economic opportunity for all." Business Roundtable, Statement on the Purpose of a Corporation, Aug. 2019, https://opportunity.businessroundtable.org/wp-content/uploads/2019/08/BRT-Statement-on-the-Purpose-of-a-Corporation-with-Signatures.pdf.
[72] See David Gelles and David Yaffe Bellany, "Shareholder Value Is No Longer Everything, Top C.E.O.s Say," *New York Times*, Apr. 19, 2019.
[73] Institute of Internal Auditors (IIA), *Standards for the Professional Practice of Internal Auditing* (2016), 23, https://na.theiia.org/standards-guidance/Public%20Documents/IPPF-Standards-2017.pdf.

(IIA) gives guidance on internal auditing.[74] For an internal audit to be considered effective, it should achieve at least one of the ten Core Principles, which include "Demonstrates competence and due professional care" and "Is insightful, proactive, and future-focused."[75] Also, as listed in the Code of Ethics, internal auditors are expected to uphold the following principles: integrity, objectivity, confidentiality, and competency.[76] The quality of the internal audit activity should also be ensured through internal and external assessments, which are public reviews and day-to-day measurement, supervision, and review of the activities and assessment by an independent reviewer from outside of the organization, respectively.[77]

One genre of organization that follow the standards of IIA comprises bank and financial service companies. In banks, internal audits are required not only in terms of financial reporting, but also regarding legal compliance and general effectiveness.[78] The independence of these audits has been constantly emphasized by relevant institutions; the 2001 guidelines of the Basel Committee on Banking Supervision, the principal agency establishing international banking standards, and the guidance issued by a subcommittee of the Federal Reserve System underline that a bank's internal audit must be independent from the everyday internal control process and day-to-day functioning of the bank and that it should have access to all bank activities. In support of this, the manuals of the Federal Deposit Insurance Corporation, Officer of the Comptroller of the Currency, and Federal Financial Institutions Examination Council advocate that internal auditors report "solely and directly" to the audit committee,[79] consisting of outside directors, without reporting to their supervisors, so that the auditing can avoid management interference.

Self-auditing is also conducted and recommended in other types of industries, such as manufacturing sectors, because it helps the businesses meet the requirements of relevant laws. For instance, an occupational safety and health and safety (OSH) self-audit is an "assessment of workplace hazards, controls, programs, and documents performed by a business owner or employee"[80] in compliance with Occupational Safety and Health Administration (OSHA) regulations. Furthermore,

---

[74] IIA, *Standards for the Professional Practice of Internal Auditing*.

[75] See IIA, *Core Principles for the Professional Practice of Internal Auditing*, https://na.theiia.org/standards-guidance/mandatory-guidance/Pages/Core-Principles-for-the-Professional-Practice-of-Internal-Auditing.aspx (last visited June 12, 2018).

[76] See IIA, *Code of Ethics* (Jan. 2009), https://na.theiia.org/standards-guidance/Public%20Documents/IPPF_Code_of_Ethics_01-09.pdf.

[77] IIA, *Standards for the Professional Practice of Internal Auditing*; Matthew Bender, *Banks & Thrifts: Govt Enforce & Receivership* (New York: Matthew Bender Elite Products, 2018), § 5.04.

[78] Federal banking regulators suggest that the internal audit function be conducted according to professional standards. see Michael E. Murphy, "Assuring Responsible Risk Management in Banking: The Corporate Governance Dimension," *Delaware Journal of Corporate Law* 36, no. 1 (2011): 136–37.

[79] Murphy, "Assuring Responsible Risk Management in Banking," 137–39; Gary M. Deutsch, *Risk Assessments for Financial Institutions* (LexisNexis, 2017), § 27A.03.

[80] Samuel C. Yamin et al., "Self-Audit of Lockout/Tagout in Manufacturing Workplaces: A Pilot Study," *American Journal of Industrial Medicine* 60, no. 5 (2017): 504–9.

OSHA allows hiring a consultant within the company to perform self-audits when OSHA is not able to do an inspection immediately.[81]

Others have noted that self-audits can enhance corporate social responsibility (CSR). The four levels of CSR self-audit allow companies to examine their performance in relation to ad hoc policy, standard policy, planned policy, and evaluated and reviewed policy.[82] Furthermore, self-audits allow for strategic and operational business planning through identification of strengths and prevention of problems. This genre of CSR self-audit process requires "proper training of self-auditors, allocation of sufficient time to perform the audit, preparation of audit aids, management support, and an adequate follow-up to audit findings."[83]

There is a question of whether internal audits alone (or even in conjunction with external audits) are adequate for ensuring safe harbor from anti-discrimination laws which other scholars have addressed.[84] I argue that rather than merely serving as a protectionist tool against employment discrimination lawsuits, self-audits would benefit corporations interested in diversifying their personnel. Business scholars have shown that a workplace with diverse employees is ideal for achieving sought-after business goals such as greater innovation.[85] Thus, the self-audits could provide corporations with a tool to discover their blind spots in regard to preconceived notions of qualification and fit and might even help bring other problems of bias in hiring to the attention of the corporation. For example, the audits could shatter misconceptions as to qualifications by surfacing rejected candidates who nonetheless went on to become stellar employees at other companies. Or the audits could reveal a rather shallow pool of diverse qualified applicants, indicating a negative brand image for the company, work climate problems, or the need to establish a sturdier pipeline to the industry for diverse candidates.

12.4.4 *External Audits*

Internal audits are not enough to regulate automated hiring platforms; external audits remain necessary. Dipayan Ghosh, a Harvard fellow and former Facebook

---

[81] See *Martin v. Bally's Park Place Hotel & Casino*, 983 F.2d 1252 (1993); Olivia K. LaBoda, "Dueling Approaches to Dual Purpose Documents: The Reaches of the Work Product Doctrine after Textron," *Suffolk University Law Review* 44, no. 3 (2011): 737.

[82] See Peter Kok et al., "A Corporate Social Responsibility Audit within a Quality Management Framework," *Journal of Business Ethics* 31, no. 4 (2001): 291–93.

[83] See "Self-Audit for Quality Improvement," *Strategic Direction* 18, no. 5 (2002): 17.

[84] See my paper "The Auditing Imperative."

[85] See Katherine W. Phillips, "Commentary: What Is the Real Value of Diversity in Organizations? Questioning Our Assumptions," in *The Diversity Bonus: How Great Teams Pay Off in the Knowledge Economy*, ed. Scott E. Page (Princeton: Princeton University Press, 2017), 223–46 (showing that diverse groups outperform homogenous groups because of both an influx of new ideas and more careful information processing). See also Sheen S. Levine et al., "Ethnic Diversity Deflates Price Bubbles," *PNAS* 11 (52): 18524–29.

privacy and public policy official, has no such confidence in an internal review process given past cases of self-certifying companies revealed to be engaging in practices that were harmful to society and certain populations. According to Ghosh, "The public will have little knowledge as to whether or not the firm really is making biased decisions if it's only the firm itself that has access to its decision-making algorithms to test them for discriminatory outcomes."[86] Ghosh notes that startups do not face enough pressure to use third-party audit firms because doing so is not required by law, costs money, and would "require 'tremendous levels' of compliance beyond what internal audits likely require." However, consider the regulation in other jurisdictions, where, for example, the European General Data Protection Regulation denotes algorithm audits as essential for the public good, particularly for protecting those who are already marginalized citizens.[87] Thus, I argue that there should be federally mandated audits of automated hiring platforms. The next question is who should be in charge of carrying out meaningful third-party audits of automated hiring platforms.

12.5 EXTERNAL AUDITING: THE FAIR AUTOMATED HIRING MARK

Given the proprietary nature of hiring algorithms, one approach that balances intellectual property protection concerns with the need for greater accountability is a certification system that operates on external third-party audits by an independent certifying entity. I take as inspiration for this proposed certification system Professors Ayres and Brown's framework for corporations to certify discrimination-free workplaces that comply with the Employment Non-Discrimination Act (ENDA).[88] The authors propose that

> by entering into the licensing agreement with us, an employer gains the right (but not the obligation) to use the mark and in return promises to abide by the word-for-word strictures of ENDA. Displaying the mark signals to knowing consumers and employees that the company manufacturing the product or providing the service has committed itself not to discriminate on the basis of sexual orientation.[89]

Other legal scholars have also proposed certification systems for algorithms. Notably, Andrew Tutt has proposed an "FDA for algorithms," in which the federal government would establish an agency to oversee different classes of algorithms to

---

[86] Rosenbaum, "Silicon Valley Is Stumped."

[87] Rosenbaum, "Silicon Valley Is Stumped." Ghosh added, "In recruiting – a space in which sensitive and life-changing decisions are made all the time in which we accordingly have established strong civil rights protections ... algorithmic bias [is] especially important to detect and act against."

[88] ENDA is legislation proposed in the U.S. Congress that would prohibit discrimination in hiring and employment on the basis of sexual orientation or gender identity by employers with at least fifteen employees. See generally Ian Ayres and Jennifer Brown, "Mark(et)ing Nondiscrimination: Privatizing ENDA with a Certification Mark," *Michigan Law Review* 104, no. 7 (2006): 1639–1712.

[89] Ayers and Brown, "Mark(et)ing Nondiscrimination," 1641.

ensure that, much like food and medicine marketed for human consumption, those algorithms would pose no harm to those over whom they exercise decision-making power.[90] And in "The Missing Regulatory State," Professor Rory Van Loo makes a compelling case for regulatory monitoring of platforms that employ automated decision-making. He defines regulatory monitoring as "the collection of information that the [government] agency can force a business to provide even without suspecting a particular act of wrongdoing." Professor Van Loo notes that key factors indicating a need for regulatory monitoring include a public interest in preventing harm, information asymmetries, and a lack of faith in self-regulation.[91]

Given that these factors are undeniably present for automated hiring, I argue for either a government agency or a third-party non-governmental agency as an auditing and certifying authority. The governmental agency could be under the aegis of the Equal Employment Opportunity Commission (EEOC). Thus, the commission would audit and certify automated hiring platforms before they can lawfully be deployed in the hiring process. However, given the financial and time burden such a certifying process could exact on governmental resources, a good alternative would be a non-governmental entity, much like, for example, the Leadership in Energy and Environmental Design (LEED) certification system.

LEED was created by the U.S. Green Building Council (USGBC), which was established in 1993 "with a mission to promote sustainability-focused practices in the building industry." Thus, LEED serves as a "green certification program for building design, construction, operations, and maintenance."[92] The LEED certification involves a formal certification letter, as well as plaques and signage for buildings and an electronic badge that may be displayed on a website.[93]

The third-party certification would involve periodic audits of the hiring algorithms to check for disparate impact on vulnerable populations. Thus, this would not be a one-time audit but rather an ongoing process to ensure that the corporations/organizations continue to hew to fair automated hiring practices. In return, the corporation or organization would earn the right to use a Fair Automated Hiring Mark (FAHM) for its online presence and communication materials, and to display on hiring advertisements to attract a more diverse pool of applicants.

I envision that such a third-party certification entity would be composed of multidisciplinary teams of auditors comprising both lawyers and software engineers/data scientists who would audit the hiring algorithms employed by corporations and organizations. This would prevent some of the tunnel-vision problems associated

---

90 Tutt, "An FDA for Algorithms."

91 Rory Van Loo, "The Missing Regulatory State: Monitoring Businesses in an Age of Surveillance," *Vanderbilt Law Review* 72, no. 5 (2019): 1563.

92 See U.S. Green Building Council, *About USGBC*, https://new.usgbc.org/about (accessed Sept. 21, 2019).

93 See U.S. Green Building Council, *Certification*, https://new.usgbc.org/post-certification (accessed Sept. 21, 2019).

with technology created without consideration for legal frameworks and larger societal goals. Furthermore, such a certification system could serve as a feedback mechanism and thus enable the better design of and best practices for automated hiring systems.

12.5.1 *The Pros and Cons of a Governmental Certifying System*

A governmental certification that is federally mandated would provide uniformity in the practice of automated hiring and would also ensure compliance in regards to auditing.[94] However, history has shown that government agencies are vulnerable to regulatory capture,[95] which weighs against the adoption of a governmental certifying system. Regulatory capture refers to the fact[96] that private influence on the workings of such agencies, as well as political shifts, can render such agencies toothless or ineffectual. While there are varying definitions of regulatory capture, "the top officials of federal regulatory agencies are presidential appointees, interest groups, whether they are industries, unions, or consumer or environmental groups that influence the regulatory agencies, and one can think of this influence as a kind of capture."[97]

Examples of regulatory capture abound in American government, including that of the U.S. Securities and Exchange Commission (SEC),[98] the Food and Drug Administration (FDA),[99] and most importantly the EEOC.[100] Most recently, an

---

[94] Some legal scholars have previously argued for governmental oversight based on a taxonomy of the distinct operations of algorithmic systems in a wide range of spheres. See Desai and Kroll, "Trust but Verify," 42–55. My proposed interventions in this chapter focus solely on the employment sphere.

[95] Daniel Carpenter and David Moss define "regulatory capture" as "the result and process by which regulation, in law or application, is consistently or repeatedly directed away from the public interest and towards the interests of the regulated industry, by the action or intent of the industry itself." Daniel Carpenter and David A. Moss, *Preventing Regulatory Capture: Special Interest Influence and How to Limit It* (Cambridge: Cambridge University Press, 2014), 19.

[96] See, e.g., Stavros Gadinis, "The SEC and the Financial Industry: Evidence from Enforcement against Broker Dealers," *Business Law* 67 (2012): 679–728 (highlighting the inherent connection between the public and private enforcement of securities laws); David Freeman Engstrom, "Corralling Capture," *Harvard Journal of Law and Public Policy* 36, no. 1 (2013): 31–39 (arguing that the structural conditions that facilitate regulatory capture naturally move legislatures and agencies together).

[97] Carpenter and Moss, *Preventing Regulatory Capture*, 54.

[98] Other scholars have detailed a revolving door of SEC employees to and from the financial sector and how this has contributed to regulatory capture of the SEC. Stewart L. Brown, "Mutual Funds and the Regulatory Capture of the SEC," *Journal of Business Law* 19, no. 3 (2018): 701–49.

[99] Patrick Radden Keefe, "The Family That Built an Empire of Pain," *New Yorker*, Oct. 30, 2017 (discussing how one family-owned business, through fraud and corruption, co-opted the FDA drug certification system).

[100] Consider that the Trump administration attempted to rescind a pay data collection rule that had been promulgated by the Obama administration to combat the gender pay gap through transparency in pay. See Alexia Fernandez Campbell, "Trump Tried to Sabotage a Plan to Close the Gender Pay Gap: A Judge Wouldn't Have It," *Vox*, Apr. 26, 2019, www.vox.com/2019/4/26/18515920/gender-pay-gap-rule-eeoc.

in-depth investigative report by the *New Yorker* revealed the staggering extent of the regulatory capture of the FDA by Purdue Pharma, a privately held company established by the Sackler family that developed the prescription painkiller OxyContin. The painkiller, which is almost twice as powerful as morphine, has been at the forefront of the current American opioid crisis, as it was extensively marketed for long-term pain relief despite medical evidence of its addictive properties. The FDA, without corroborating evidence from clinical trials, approved a package insert for OxyContin announcing that the drug was safer than competing painkillers – the FDA examiner who approved the package insert, Dr. Curtis Wright, was hired at Purdue Pharma soon after he left the FDA.[101]

In the specific context of employment, the EEOC, which is charged with employment regulation, has also been susceptible to administration change. Consider, for example, that in 2014 President Obama issued an executive order on pay data transparency mandating that private companies with one hundred or more employees and federal contractors with fifty or more employees must disclose pay data broken down by race and gender to the EEOC.[102] This executive order was meant to combat gender gaps in pay.[103] However, in 2017 (after a change in administration) the acting chair of the EEOC (appointed by President Trump) issued a press release announcing an immediate stay of this executive order via memorandum.[104]

12.5.2 *The Pros and Cons of a Third-Party Non-Governmental Certifying System*

A commercial third-party certifying entity with a business reputation to protect would be much less susceptible to regulatory capture. For one thing, when the relationship between the certifying entity and the employer making use of automated hiring systems is voluntary, there is much less impetus for regulatory capture in the first place. Thus, the FAHM mark, rather than representing a mere rubber stamp, would come to serve as a reputable market signal for employers who are truly interested in creating a more diverse workplace. Also of note is that a non-governmental entity would better withstand the sort of vagaries of political shifts, as was demonstrated by 2017 events at the Federal Communications Commission (FCC)[105] and the Federal Trade Commission (FTC) regarding net

[101] Keefe, "The Family That Built an Empire of Pain" (detailing how OxyContin lobbied for the insert to increase its market share of drug sales).

[102] See Bourree Lam, "Obama's New Equal-Pay Rules," *The Atlantic*, Jan. 29, 2016; see also White House, "Fact Sheet: New Steps to Advance Equal Pay on the Seventh Anniversary of the Lilly Ledbetter Fair Pay Act," Jan. 29, 2016, https://obamawhitehouse.archives.gov/the-press-office/2016/01/29/fact-sheet-new-steps-advance-equal-pay-seventh-anniversary-lilly.

[103] See White House, "Fact Sheet: New Steps to Advance Equal Pay."

[104] See Danielle Paquette, "The Trump Administration Just Halted This Obama-Era Rule to Shrink the Gender Wage Gap," *Washington Post*, Aug. 30, 2017.

[105] See Brian Fung, "The House Just Voted to Wipe Away the FCC's Landmark Internet Privacy Protections," *Washington Post*, Mar. 28, 2017; see also Jeff Dunn, "Trump Just Killed Obama's

neutrality[106] as well as at the Environmental Protection Agency (EPA) regarding climate change.[107]

One opposing argument, however, is that even independent third-party certifying agencies are not immune to capture. As such entities will derive an economic benefit from certifications, there is the danger that such an agency could become a mere rubber-stamping entity without adequate legal teeth to enforce any sanctions against the entities it is certifying. However, given that this proposed agency would operate on the trust of job applicants as consumers, and also given the greater information dissemination afforded by the internet, consumers in the form of job applicants are now able to more forcefully make their voices heard regarding algorithmic bias and could still blow the whistle[108] on any misconduct, thus undermining any certifying mark that does not hold true.

12.6 DESIGN MANDATES: THE TEAR-OFF SHEET AND DATA RETENTION

Rethinking and regulating the design choices of automated hiring programs will aid in the pursuit of equal opportunity in employment. Why? First, asking an employer to audit whether their hiring system has had an adverse impact on applicants who are members of a protected class represents a paradox, as employers are typically not allowed to collect that information at the hiring stage. Professor Ignacio Cofone notes this paradox in his article "Algorithmic Discrimination Is an Information Problem," and argues that the true solution is not just to regulate the *use* of the data, but to regulate the *acquisition* of such information.[109]

From an auditing standpoint, neither the use nor the acquisition of this information is as much of a problem as the *lack* of such data. Thus, my proposal is a redesign of automated hiring systems to have a "tear-off sheet" like traditional paper hiring used to have.[110] This was an additional sheet that could be torn away from

Internet-Privacy Rules – Here's What That Means to You," *Business Insider*, Apr. 4, 2017, www .businessinsider.com/trump-fcc-privacy-rules-repeal-explained-2017-4.

[106] See Michael Santorelli and Washington Bytes, "After Net Neutrality: The FTC Is the Sheriff of Tech Again. Is It Up to the Task?" *Forbes*, Dec. 15, 2017 (noting the FTC's stance against net neutrality).

[107] See Brady Dennis and Juliet Ellperin, "How Scott Pruitt Turned the EPA into One of Trump's Most Powerful Tools," *Washington Post*, Dec. 31, 2017; see also Eric Lipton and Danielle Ivory, "Under Trump, EPA Has Slowed Actions against Polluters, and Put Limits on Enforcement Officers," *New York Times*, Dec. 10, 2017.

[108] See Sonia Katyal, "Private Accountability in the Age of Artificial Intelligence," *UCLA Law Review* 66, no. (2019): 58 (in which Professor Katyal makes a powerful argument for the importance of whistle-blowers in rectifying algorithmic bias). Other legal scholars have also made the same argument while noting how trade secret laws might interfere with whistleblowing. See Desai and Kroll, "Trust but Verify," 56–64.

[109] Ignacio N. Cofone, "Algorithmic Discrimination Is an Information Problem," *Hastings Law Journal* 70, no. 6 (2019): 1392.

[110] The U.S. Employment Opportunity Commission noted in an informal discussion letter that "tear-off sheets" are lawful under Title VII because of a legitimate need for the information for affirmative

all paper applications before those applications were passed to the decision-maker. In the case of an automated hiring system, it is a simple method of writing code wherein demographic information (such as age, race, gender) are solicited from the job applicant, but such protected information is separated from the rest of the electronic application and is embargoed, meaning decision-makers cannot access that information until after a hiring decision has been made. The information obtained by this electronic tear-off sheet is crucial to both internal and external audits. That data would allow an employer to continuously check for disparate impact in its hiring practices, and could also prove helpful to the employer in defending against allegations of discrimination *per se*.

Another essential design reconsideration is how automated hiring platforms retain data. As Cathy O'Neil notes in *Weapons of Math Destruction*, applicants who are prevented from fully completing the application – even if, or oftentimes when, such obstacles have a disparate impact on protected categories – are lost to the ether. For example, if a working mother is prevented from completing an automated hiring application because the application required full-time availability for even a part-time job, the automated hiring platform typically retains no proof that there was even an attempt to apply. This crucial information is thus lost and cannot be included in any audits of the system. Allowing for a meaningful audit would require a rethinking of design mandates such that data retention of all completed and attempted applications becomes the default of all automated hiring platforms.

12.7 LABOR LAW AND AUTOMATED HIRING

While internal and external audits could enable litigation by generating data to serve as statistical evidence of disparate impact or by uncovering practices that could be considered discrimination *per se*, collective bargaining as a collaborative exercise between employers and worker unions could also set fair standards for automated hiring and secure applicant data. Notably, collective bargaining could focus on the role of data collection and usage, targeting (1) agreements as to what data will be *digested* by automated hiring systems, that is, setting the standards for probative applicant assessment criteria; (2) agreements as to the *end uses* of such data, that is, contractual agreements as to what the data collected will be used for, as well as data-retention agreements; and (3) agreements as to the control and portability of the data *created* by automated hiring systems.

While there has been much focus on the data input required for automated decision-making, a focus on the data generated by the automated decision-making process is equally as consequential, if not more so. This is because automated hiring

action purposes and/or to track applicant flow. EEOC, Informal Discussion Letter: Title VII/ADA: Pre-Employment Inquiry, Aug. 5, 2002, www.eeoc.gov/foia/eeoc-informal-discussion-letter-78.

systems hold the potential to create indelible portraits of applicants that may be used to classify those individuals.[111] Thus, data submitted by an applicant is deployed not just for one job classification or even presented to just one employer. Rather, applicant data–generated worker profiles may live on past the snapshot in time when the worker applied for a specific position and may come to haunt the worker during an entirely different bid for employment.[112] Thus, in the following sections, I detail the important role of collective bargaining not just for achieving fair standards for the curation of input data, but also for the portability of the output data.

12.7.1 *Data Digested: Probative Evaluation Criteria*

Arguments over standards of fairness and other approaches to algorithmic accountability tend to neglect the role of data in perpetuating discrimination. Yet, as several legal scholars have observed, data is not neutral; rather, it is tainted by structural and institutional bias.[113] Collective bargaining regarding what data may be used for assessment as part of algorithmic hiring systems is one necessary approach to curbing employment discrimination. While hiring criteria is typically not a collective bargaining topic (collective bargaining tends to focus on the conditions of employment for workers who have already been hired) I argue that union leaders should not overlook the importance of securing fair data collection and evaluation standards for their current or future members.[114]

The first task for unions to tackle is negotiating what data may be digested by hiring algorithms. A crucial issue for this negotiation is the determination of what data is probative of "job fitness" and what data may even be considered job-related. Professor Sullivan notes that "the employer's reliance on the algorithm may be job-related, but the algorithm itself is measuring and tracking behavior that has no direct relationship to the job performance."[115] And while some of the information digested by hiring algorithms may be correlated to job success, as other scholars have noted,

---

[111] Professors Rick Bales and Katherine Stone have argued that "[t]he electronic resume produced by A.I. will accompany workers from job to job as they move around the boundaryless workplace." Richard A. Bales and Katherine V. W. Stone, "The Invisible Web at Work: Artificial Intelligence and Electronic Surveillance in the Workplace," *Berkeley Journal of Labor and Employment Law* 41, no. 1 (2020): 1.

[112] Bales and Stone, "The Invisible Web at Work," 1 ("Thus A-I and electronic monitoring produce an invisible electronic web that threatens to invade worker privacy, deter unionization, enable subtle forms of employer blackballing, exacerbate employment discrimination, render unions ineffective, and obliterate the protections of the labor laws.").

[113] See Mike Ananny and Kate Crawford, "Seeing without Knowing: Limitations of the Transparency Ideal and Its Application to Algorithmic Accountability," *New Media & Society* 20, no. 3 (2016): 973–89; Chander, "The Racist Algorithm?" 1041.

[114] There are already some extant incidences of this type of union activity. See Marianne J. Koch and Gregory Hundley, "The Effects of Unionism on Recruitment and Selection Methods," *Industrial Relations* 36, no. 3 (1997): 349–70; see also Anil Verma, "What Do Unions Do to the Workplace? Union Effects on Management and HRM Policies," *Journal of Labor Research* 26 (2005): 415–49.

[115] See Sullivan, "Employing AI," 421.

"if a statistical correlation were sufficient to satisfy the notion of job relatedness, the standard would be a tautology rather than a meaningful legal test."[116]

Rather than rely on flimsy and often irrelevant correlation patterns excavated by the algorithms, I concur with legal scholars[117] who have argued that the Uniform Guidelines on Employee Selection Procedures[118] should apply in negotiating what data will be digested by automated hiring systems. Although these guidelines do not amount to law,[119] they have been accorded deference in case law[120] and have been viewed as authoritative in deciding employment discrimination cases.[121] As Professor Sullivan notes,

> While [the Uniform Guidelines] have been used mainly for the validation of traditional paper-and-pencil tests with a disparate impact, the Guidelines broadly apply to any "selection procedure."[122]

The Uniform Guidelines are useful because they set standards for when selection criteria could be considered valid. Thus, the guidelines provide for "three kinds of validation: criterion, content and construct."[123] The aim of all three types of

---

[116] See Kim, "Data-Driven Discrimination at Work."

[117] See Sullivan, "Employing AI," 420–22; Alan G. King and Marko J. Mrkonich, "'Big Data' and the Risk of Employment Discrimination," *Oklahoma Law Review* 68, no. (2016): 555–84.

[118] Sullivan, "Employing AI," 422 n.108 ("29 C.F.R § 1607.3(A) (2018) ("[T]he hiring, promotion, or other employment or membership opportunities of members of any race, sex, or ethnic group will be considered to be discriminatory and inconsistent with these guidelines, unless the procedure has been validated in accordance with these guidelines"). "Selection procedure" is in turn defined broadly to include "[a]ny measure, combination of measures, or procedure used as a basis for any employment decision," and includes "the full range of assessment techniques from traditional paper and pencil tests, performance tests, training programs, or probationary periods and physical, educational, and work experience requirements through informal or casual interviews and unscored application forms" 29 C.F.R. § 1607.16(Q) (2018).").

[119] See Sullivan, "Employing AI," 422.

[120] The court in *Griggs* concluded that the original EEOC guidelines should be given "great deference." *Griggs v. Duke Power Co.*, 401 U.S. 424, 433–34, (1971). This conclusion was concurred with by the court in *Albemarle Paper Co. v. Moody*, 422 U.S. 405, 430–31 (1975), which further observed that the "Guidelines draw upon and make reference to professional standards of test validation established by the American Psychological Association" and that while the guidelines were "not administrative 'regulations' promulgated pursuant to formal procedures established by the Congress ... they do constitute '[t]he administrative interpretation of the Act by the enforcing agency.'" The Uniform Guidelines replaced the original EEOC guidelines in 1978 and they enjoy broader consensus than the EEOC guidelines, as they represent the collective view of the EEOC and other federal agencies such as the Department of Labor, the Civil Service Commission, and the Department of Justice. Thus, courts have similarly viewed the Guidelines as authoritative. The court in *Gulino* noted that "[t]hirty-five years of using these Guidelines makes them the primary yardstick by which we measure defendants' attempt to validate" a test." *Gulino v. N.Y. State Educ. Dep't*, 460 F.3d 361, 383–84 (2d Cir. 2006).

[121] Per the results of a Lexis Advance search: The courts in more than three hundred cases have applied the Guidelines, including a number of Supreme Court decisions. Sullivan, "Employing AI," n. 106.

[122] Sullivan, "Employing AI," 422 and nn.107–8.

[123] Sullivan, "Employing AI," 423 (citing Ramona L. Paetzold and Steven L. Willborn, *The Statistics of Discrimination*, 2nd ed., §§ 5.13–.17 (2017–18)).

validation is to prompt the employer to provide evidence of a predictive causal relationship between the selection method and the job performance.

Evidence of the validity of a test or other selection procedure by a criterion-related validity study should consist of empirical data demonstrating that the selection procedure is predictive of or significantly correlated with important elements of job performance. Evidence of the validity of a test or other selection procedure by a content validity study should consist of data showing that the content of the selection procedure is representative of important aspects of performance on the job for which the candidates are to be evaluated. Evidence of the validity of a test or other selection procedure through a construct validity study should consist of data showing that the procedure measures the degree to which candidates have identifiable characteristics that have been determined to be important in successful performance in the job for which the candidates are to be evaluated.[124]

As validation generally requires a job analysis, unions can be actively involved in conducting the job analysis and setting the standards to demonstrate that (1) the selection criteria for the hiring algorithm relates to important aspects of the job, (2) the data used actually allows prediction of future job performance based on the selection, and (3) the selected candidates are not the result of some nebulous correlation but rather actually have identifiable characteristics that are causally related to better job performance.

But even after the determination of probative data for job fitness, the problem of biased data still remains. For example, data that may be probative for job fitness, such as test scores, may still bear the taint of past biased decisions. Consider, for example, that racial housing segregation has resulted in a concentration of better-resourced schools in majority-white neighborhoods where students who attend receive better preparation for taking standardized tests. Thus, although performance on standardized tests may be considered probative of job fitness, the use of such criterion could result in disparate impact. In recognition of the historical taint of structural bias on data that could otherwise be probative, some scholars have called for "algorithmic affirmative action," which focuses on transparency about the biases encoded in the data and the correction of the data the algorithms use rather than merely in the design of algorithms.[125] Also, employers could outright reject the use of such biased data.

For example, employers can design games to determine applicants' job performance qualities, such as "social intelligence, goal-orientation fluency, implicit learning, task-switching ability, and conscientiousness," rather than depending on standardized testing. Savage and Bales demonstrate this by showing that these algorithms, which only identify individual personal qualities, can reduce discrimination in evaluating job applicants. Thus, for example, according to some researchers,

---

[124] Sullivan, "Employing AI" (quoting 29 C.F.R. § 1607.5B (2018)) (cross-references omitted in original).
[125] See Chander, "The Racist Algorithm," 1039.

administering algorithm-based video games in the initial hiring process will not only decrease disparate treatment and disparate impact discrimination because they test for individual skill sets, but might also reduce unconscious biases in evaluation of job candidates.[126]

12.8 DATA END USES AND FAIRNESS BY DESIGN

One common retort to addressing bias in algorithms is that machine learning algorithms, which are constantly changing, are ungovernable; however, like previous legal scholars, I argue that design features of hiring platforms could enable anti-discrimination ends, thus bringing them under a rule of law.[127] Thus, I argue that fairness can be part of the design of these algorithmic systems from the onset, especially in establishing data-retention features as a standard. These machine learning algorithms, which have the capacity to derive new models as they learn from large data sets, are constantly re-evaluating the variable inputs to calculations. Some researchers have argued that humans could feasibly lose their agency over algorithms given their extensive potential for calculations and the amount of data they use. To limit this reduction in choice-making power, some have exhorted that humans need to set "checks" on algorithms, ensuring that they can inspect both the data that enters the calculation system and the results that exit. By doing so, humans might reduce the chance that over time algorithms will grow to be unintelligible to humans. For example, IBM's Watson algorithm allows periodic inspections by presenting researchers with the documents it uses to form the basis for its decisions.[128]

Programmers can reduce discriminatory effects of hiring algorithms by complying with key standards of legal fairness in determining design features such that the algorithms will avoid a disparate impact for protected classes and comply with the principles of laws such as the Civil Rights Act of 1964 or the ADEA. Mark MacCarthy in "Standards of Fairness for Disparate Impact Assessment of Big Data Algorithms" explains conditions for algorithms to be certified as fair. According to Professor MacCarthy, algorithms are fair when they meet one of the following conditions (noting that these conditions cannot all be satisfied at once):

---

[126] David D. Savage and Richard Bales, "Video Games in Job Interviews: Using Algorithms to Minimize Discrimination and Unconscious Bias," *ABA Journal of Labor and Employment Law* 32, no. 2 (2017): 222, 224–26.

[127] See Kroll et al., "Accountable Algorithms" (noting that some existing algorithmic systems are largely ungovernable because they were not built with auditing in mind; they note also that there are ways to build for auditing, but that this design logic should exist at the onset).

[128] Marco Tulio Ribeiro, Sameer Singh, and Carlos Guestrin, "'Why Should I Trust You?' Explaining the Predictions of Any Classifier," in *Proceedings of the 2016 Conference*, 1135–44 (New York: Association for Computational Linguistics, 2016).

- Fairness Through Blindness: Algorithms do not contain or use variables that refer directly to a protected status …
- Group Fairness: Algorithms are fair when they treat groups equally.
  - Statistical Parity: Algorithms are fair when they equalize positive acceptance rates across protected groups.
  - Equal Group Error Rates: Algorithms are fair when the rate at which they return false positives and false negatives is the same for all protected groups.
- Individual Fairness: Algorithms are fair when they return the same outcome regardless of an individual's group membership.
  - Predictive Parity: Algorithms are fair when they equalize positive predictive value across groups.
  - Similarity Measures: Algorithms are fair when they classify individuals the same when they have similar characteristics relevant to performing a particular task.[129]

As Professor MacCarthy also notes, there are disputes about statistical concepts of fairness, especially between group fairness and individual fairness, because some believe that anti-discrimination laws aim at practices that disadvantage certain groups, while others think these laws "target arbitrary misclassification of individuals."[130] Those that support group fairness, such as statistical parity[131] and equal group error rates, try to reduce the subordination of disadvantaged groups by allowing for some sacrifice of accuracy.[132]

For instance, King and Mrkonich describe as fair selection algorithms that "[rate] members of the majority and protected groups equally."[133] However, those who advocate for individual fairness aim to promote equal accuracy in classification. To them, algorithms are considered fair "when they make equally accurate predictions about individuals, regardless of group membership."[134] Also, they require that "enforc[ing] similar probabilities of outcomes for two individuals should [be] less than any differences between them"[135] and that "any two individuals who are similar

---

[129] Mark MacCarthy, "Standards of Fairness for Disparate Impact Assessment of Big Data Algorithms," *Cumberland Law Review* 48, no. 1 (2018): 78, 90.

[130] MacCarthy, "Standards of Fairness," 68. See generally Reva B. Siegel, "Equality Talk: Antisubordination and Anticlassification Values in Constitutional Struggles over *Brown*," *Harvard Law Review* 117, no. 5 (2004): 1470–1547 (providing the background for the development of competing theories on equal protection law); Jack M. Balkin and Reva B. Siegel, "The American Civil Rights Tradition: Anticlassification or Antisubordination?" *Miami Law Review* 58, no. 1 (2003): 9–33 (relating the history of the development and application of two distinct anti-discrimination threads in American law).

[131] Proponents of statistical parity argue that it is more desirable because it "equalizes outcomes across protected and non-protected groups." See Cynthia Dwork et al., "Fairness through Awareness," in *ITCS' 12: Proceedings of the 3rd Innovations Theoretical Computer Science Conference*, 214–26 (New York: Association for Computing Machinery, 2012).

[132] MacCarthy, "Standards of Fairness," 68.

[133] King and Mrkonich, "'Big Data' and the Risk of Employment Discrimination," 575–76.

[134] See MacCarthy, "Standards of Fairness," 69.

[135] Kim, "Auditing Algorithms for Discrimination," 195–96.

with respect to a particular task [be] classified similarly."[136] As notions of fairness diverge, organizations must choose which standard to adopt by considering the context of use as well as normative and legal standards.[137]

I argue that important facets of fairness by design for automated hiring systems are record-keeping and data-retention mechanisms that are part of the standard design. As the data from automated hiring systems remain solely in the control of the employer, appropriate record-keeping and data-retention procedures are necessary to enable any disparate impact claims. As it currently stands, job applicants who do not make it past the hiring algorithm are typically lost to the ether.[138] Thus, there is no sure way for plaintiffs to compare percentages of job applicants from protected categories who were hired relative to the number who applied, as required by the EEOC rule,[139] and there is still no clear method to confirm best hiring outcomes against the actual pool of qualified applicants. Determining disparate impact in hiring algorithms is a relatively simple matter of evaluating the outcomes using the EEOC rule. This rule mandates that a selection rate for any race, sex, or ethnic group that is less than four-fifths (80 percent) of the rate for the group with the highest rate will generally be regarded by the federal enforcement agencies as evidence of adverse impact.[140]

Automated hiring systems that do not retain data when an applicant from a protected category is prevented from completing an application or that may not even retain the data of complete but unsuccessful applications thwart the purpose of the EEOC rule. My proposal that corporations be legally required to deploy only automated hiring systems with data-retention mechanisms will ensure that data from failed job applicants are preserved to be later compared against the successful job applicants, with the aim of discovering whether the data evinces disparate impact regarding the population of failed job applicants.

Consider also that responsible record-keeping and data retention are necessary for conducting both internal and external audits. The data for internal audits serves two purposes: first, to alert employers to any disparate impact created by the automated hiring system, thus allowing them to pre-emptively correct any imbalances and avoid costly lawsuits, and second, to alert employers to more structural issues present in their hiring. Such structural issues might include mismatched or non-probative selection criteria, a shallow hiring pool for applicants from protected categories, or technical or accessibility problems present in the automated hiring platform. Thus, the data from internal audits may represent a direct benefit to employers that

---

[136] See Dwork et al., "Fairness through Awareness," 214.

[137] See MacCarthy, "Standards of Fairness," 71.

[138] See O'Neil, *Weapons of Math Destruction*.

[139] See Biddle Consulting Group, *Uniform Guidelines on Employee Selection Procedures*, http://uniform guidelines.com/uniformguidelines.html#18 (accessed Sept. 22, 2019).

[140] See 29 C.F.R § 1607(A) (2018) (noting original language of the EEOC's "four-fifths rule").

is separate from their duty not to discriminate.[141] Such a boon should be counted in any cost–benefit analysis[142] of my proposed record-keeping and data-retention measures.

12.9 DATA CONTROL AND PORTABILITY

Earlier in this chapter, I noted the vast array of information collected by hiring platforms and also the indelibility of the data profiles created by automated hiring systems. These data profiles, some of which are created by third-party automated hiring vendors, contain not just information provided by the job applicant but also data gleaned from online sources (such as social media profiles) and peddled by gray market data brokers.[143] Therefore, such information may include errors or could provide an inaccurate portrait of the applicant as construed from erroneous data.[144] Even if the information contained in the profile is accurate, there is also the issue of "context collapse,"[145] wherein information the applicant provided in the context of

---

[141] See, e.g., Ford, "Bias in the Air" (arguing that employment law imposes a duty of care on employers to refrain from practices that go against equal opportunity in employment); see also Robert Post, "Prejudicial Appearance: The Logic of American Antidiscrimination Law," *California Law Review* 88, no. 1 (2000): 1–40 (arguing that anti-discrimination law aims to achieve positive interventions in social practices as opposed to solely dictating prohibitions). Other professors have also used a "duty of care" framework to propose remedial measures for employment discrimination. See Oppenheimer, "Negligent Discrimination"; Noah D. Zatz, "Managing the Macaw: Third-Party Harassers, Accommodation, and the Disaggregation of Discriminatory Intent," *Columbia Law Review* 109, no. 6 (2009): 1357–1439. I later discuss why the duty not to engage in practices that negate equal opportunity supports my external audit proposal.

[142] Cf. Laurence H. Tribe, "Seven Deadly Sins of Straining the Constitution through a Pseudo-Scientific Sieve," *Hastings Law Journal* 36, no. 2 (1984): 161 (arguing that there is a "pernicious tendency" for cost–benefit analysis to "dwarf soft variables" in constitutional law).

[143] See, e.g., "Web Scraping as a Valuable Instrument for Proactive Hiring," *DataHen*, Apr. 5, 2017, www.datahen.com/web-scraping-valuable-instrument-proactive-hiring/ ("What can recruiters do to use this huge advantage to their benefit? They can scrape or crawl data off of those kind of job portals and run analytics through it. By doing so they are able to determine the likelihood of filling a particular position in a specified location based on historical data patterns. Everything is relevant and important here and can impact the results of the research. Every little nuance, like the day of the week, certain types of jobs should be posted or other kinds of factors that will influence the decision making of the prospective candidate.").

[144] Consider the case of *Thompson v. San Antonio Retail Merchants Association (SARMA)*, where the Fifth Circuit found that SARMA had erred in its creation of a profile for Thompson, automatically "capturing" the incorrect Social Security number for his profile and erroneously reporting the bad credit history of another man by the same common name. *Thompson v. San Antonio Retail Merchs. Ass'n.*, 682 F.2d 509 (1982); see also *Spokeo v. Robins*, 136 S. Ct. 1540, 1546 (2016) (in which a "people search engine" provided incorrect personal information about a consumer to employers and the Supreme Court ruled that this established concrete injury to the consumer, by damaging his employment prospects).

[145] Scholars have used the term *context collapse* to describe the phenomenon when communication that is meant for one particular audience is transported to another (dissimilar) audience without context or translation, resulting in misunderstanding or acrimony. See Alice E. Marwick and Danah Boyd, "I

applying for one specific job position may inappropriately be revived to evaluate the candidate for another job position.

Given these problems, applicant control and agency over both data collection and the portability of any created applicant profiles are crucial matters. Thus, as part of collective bargaining, unions should negotiate with employers regarding how applicant data will be handled. There is some tension here between data retention for the purpose of facilitating audits and applicants' control of their data. But that tension is easily resolved by data anonymization and aggregation. The relevant data for audits here is demographic data. And even then, such demographic data is limited to that which reveals protected characteristics. Unions can negotiate with firms not to retain or trade in applicant profiles that contain not just demographic data but sensitive personal information, as well as evaluations about applicant fitness.

12.10 PREVENTING "ALGORITHMIC BLACKBALLING"

Negotiations regarding the retention of subjective applicant profiles or evaluations are necessary to avoid what I term *algorithmic blackballing*. When applicant profiles are allowed to live on past their shelf life, such profiles may come to haunt the applicant in a different bid for work, whether with the same employer or, if traded, with another employer.[146] Consider this scenario: John applies for work through the hiring platform of a major corporation. This platform creates profiles of all applicants. From those profiles, the employer chooses a subset of applicants to invite for interviews and rejects the rest. However, the corporation still retains the profiles of all job applicants. This data is used internally so that whenever the applicant applies again for a job, even a different job, this applicant profile is revived and is once again the basis for a rejection. This is unfair for various reasons. First, the continued retention and use of applicant profiles misappropriates applicant data – when applicants submit an application, they intend for the information they provide to be used solely for establishing their fitness for the target job position. It is not commonly understood that applicant data submitted at one snapshot in time could be used again, potentially many years later, to determine whether the applicant is fit for another job. Second, retention and reuse of an applicant profile is unfair because it denies the applicant a chance to present herself in a manner that is more competitive for the job. For example, the applicant could have achieved tangible assets such as a new credential, but they also could have attained less quantifiable benefits such as better communication skills.

Tweet Honestly, I Tweet Passionately: Twitter Users, Context Collapse, and the Imagined Audience," *New Media & Society* 13 (2011): 114–33.

[146] Professors Rick Bales and Katherine Stone have argued that "[t]he electronic resume produced by A-I will accompany workers from job to job as they move around the boundaryless workplace." Bales and Stone, "The Invisible Web at Work."

Further exacerbating the problem is that there are no laws prohibiting automated hiring platforms from selling applicant data. This means that applicant data created for one audience, a specific employer, could be transported for the use of a completely different audience, another employer. Thus, an applicant rejected by one employer could also, with no ability to submit amendments to their profile, continue to be rejected by multiple employers. This algorithmic blackballing of applicants thwarts the goals of anti-discrimination law. While an applicant may not be right for a specific job at a specific point in time, using the same information that made that determination and applying it to a different job, even if at the same company, is antithetical to the bedrock legal doctrine of equal opportunity for all job applicants.

12.11 REGULATING WORKER SURVEILLANCE

Even after workers are hired, they are increasingly surveilled by mechanical managers (automated systems) that can enact the surveillance in ways that are simultaneously discreet, intrusive, pervasive, and perpetual. As addressed in Chapters 6, 7, and 8, worker surveillance has now been delegated to indefatigable mechanical managers and such surveillance now controls much of workers' lives, both within and outside the workplace. Workers are surveilled on social media, via productivity monitoring applications, and through the Trojan horse of workplace wellness programs that are presented as benefits to workers but that, in reality, may subsume a vast amount of workers' sensitive health information. The worker surveillance made necessary for the maintenance of public health during the Covid-19 pandemic also raises new legal dilemmas for worker privacy. Below I discuss some potential approaches to regulating worker surveillance and reach the conclusion that what is ultimately necessary is a federal worker bill of rights *coupled with* both information-sensitive and industry-specific regulations. This proposed governance mechanism is in line with my legal philosophy of concurrent regulation wherein governmental regulations can exist alongside business/industry-specific regulation to better address the problem of mechanical managers.

12.11.1 *Information-Sensitive Protection*

A narrow approach to retaining worker privacy would be to focus on protections for specific types of sensitive data, such as data related to worker health.[147] This is relevant in the context of health and wellness programs that serve as sites for the bodily surveillance of workers. An emerging legal issue is the classification of data emerging from wearable devices, particularly devices that are geared towards promoting the health of the worker. Whereas the existing Health Insurance Portability and Accountability Act (HIPAA) protects the portability of health data, defined as

[147] See generally Paul Ohm, "Sensitive Data," *Southern California Law Review* 88, no. 5 (2015): 1125–96.

information that is derived from a healthcare provider (notably, a doctor or health-care insurance provider), wellness programs that are generally not under the auspices of a doctor's office, and increasingly are also not part of a healthcare insurance provider's offerings, may not qualify as being HIPAA-covered entities.

The proposed Employment Health Information Privacy Act (EHIPA) would clarify that information generated through any program (including third-party wellness programs) or device connected to one's employment is considered protected health information under other health privacy laws, such as HIPAA. This clarification of the data from wearable devices as health data operates under the presumption that the classification of health data is not dependent on its genesis; rather, the classification of any data as health data should be predicated on the nature and use of such data. Thus, data from wearable devices that obtain metrics such as heart rate, blood glucose level, and temperature – all of which reveal the health status of any individual and may also be employed in either the diagnosis or treatment plan for disease – should rightfully be considered health data. Similarly, data from wellness programs, such as family medical histories of the sort that would normally be collected in a medical or clinical setting, would also be considered health data under EHIPA. Such a designation would trigger employee consent for the portability of such data, rather than granting wellness programs carte blanche for the control of the data. The EHIPA would also mandate strong rules for employer access to health data collected from fitness devices (even when employer owned) and for vendor control of what happens to data collected from employees as part of a wellness program. For one thing, such data should not be sold without the permission of the employee, and the employee should have the right to request the destruction of the data record once their employment has been terminated.

The EHIPA classification of data from health wellness programs as health data that would enjoy both the protection of HIPAA and enhanced protections in the employment context would bring all information pertinent to the bodily autonomy of workers (with the exception of genetic information, which enjoys even greater protection under GINA) under the same standard and would not allow proxies or end-runs such as those that proliferate in wellness programs.[148] Such a law would also recognize that innovations in physical sensors, such as the Apple Watch, Microsoft Band, or Fitbit, will continue to evolve without the need to revisit privacy rules each and every time those innovations create new data uses.

12.11.2 *Industry-Specific Regulation*

An industry-specific approach to the regulation of worker surveillance recognizes the power differential between employer and employee, while also conceding

---

[148] Nicolas Terry, "Big Data Proxies and Health Privacy Exceptionalism," *Health Matrix* 24, no. 1 (2014): 65–108.

that the employer has a vested interest in monitoring the work activities of the employee. Our proposed Employee Privacy Protection Act (EPPA) would work to curtail workplace surveillance to its appropriate limits – actual work tasks. It would explicitly prohibit limitless surveillance outside the workplace unless such surveillance is directly related and necessary for confirming work activity. Such a boundary could not be breached simply through notice and consent. Much like other worker protection laws, such as minimum wage, overtime, and safe working conditions, this would serve as a general protection for all workers that could not be waived. It would prohibit productivity apps from monitoring employees when they are off duty, notwithstanding any insistence on monitoring as a condition of employment.

Critics of such a proposal may argue, of course, that prohibitions on notice and consent for worker surveillance are antithetical to "freedom to contract" principles and would limit the opportunity for technological innovation to benefit work and the labor economy. However, the fact remains that modern contract law recognizes public policy considerations that may trump intent to contract. For example, we recognize that the preservation of human privacy and dignity entails ensuring that employee privacy does not become an economic good to be exchanged for wages. Furthermore, the proposed law would not chill technological innovations; rather, it would ensure that such innovations would benefit the worker. Technological innovations to maximize productivity would still be available to the worker through third-party products and services – the proposed law merely constrains the ways employers could use such products to surveil workers. This law is compatible with ethical considerations for worker voice and autonomy, as workers would remain free to use productivity applications to study and enhance their productivity or even to call for workplace changes. Thus, the context of the use of such data would shift to one that was more autonomous for the worker. The relinquishment of data autonomy would no longer be considered a condition of employment, and the employer would also no longer be entitled to worker privacy considerations as a benefit to be capriciously withheld or magnanimously granted to the employee. Rather, worker data autonomy would be recognized as an essential human right, a requisite condition for meaningful work and the preservation of democracy.

12.11.3 *Omnibus Bill*

Proposals for omnibus federal information privacy laws are nothing new, although none of those proposals have yet taken root in the United States.[149] Harvard Law

[149] See Sam Han and Scot Ganow, "Model Omnibus Privacy Statute," *University of Dayton Law Review* 35, no. 3 (2010): 345–77; S. Elizabeth Wilborn, "Revisiting the Public/Private Distinction: Employee Monitoring in the Workplace," *Georgia Law Review* 32, no. (1998): 825–88.

School professor Laurence Tribe has even gone as far as calling for a twenty-seventh amendment to the U.S. Constitution to protect employee privacy.[150]

While there is much appeal to this approach as a general panacea for privacy concerns writ large, it still suffers from several weaknesses as a solution to the limitless worker surveillance problem. First, because omnibus approaches intentionally provide broad coverage for all data in all situations, they accede power to standard notice-and-consent mechanisms whereby data collectors and processors seek consent for specific uses of data. In the United States, such an omnibus protection would represent a Pyrrhic victory; as we noted earlier, in the context of at-will employment laws, wherein there is asymmetrical bargaining power between the worker and the employer, standard notice-and-consent mechanisms would merely serve as a sanitizing seal of approval for employer surveillance with no real chance for dispute by the employee.

Arguably, in the consumer context, individuals have some power to forego granting consent to particular requests and can seek marketplace alternatives in data collectors or processors who offer different data practices. However, in the worker context, such consent is essentially a fiction. Moreover, as Paul Schwartz has pointed out, omnibus privacy approaches tend to define privacy at a "lowest common denominator" level because the definition must work for all individuals and for all kinds of data.[151] As noted above, the particular context of employee data, especially data concerning wellness, health, and one's personhood, and data that could be wielded to remove one's access to making a livelihood, demands specific attention and thus is more appropriately considered under a regime with a narrower and more robust approach.[152]

12.12 CURRENT GOVERNMENTAL REGULATORY EFFORTS

In the following sections, I discuss and critique some governmental regulatory efforts that could impact the use of automated decision-making in the workplace. The most notable of those efforts are the proposed federal law – The Algorithmic Accountability Act – and the recent EEOC guidance on how automated video hiring may violate the Americans with Disabilities Act.

12.12.1 *The Algorithmic Accountability Act*

The Algorithmic Accountability Act was originally introduced in 2019 to "study and fix flawed computer algorithms that result in inaccurate, unfair, biased, or

[150] Henry Weinstien, "Amendment on Computer Privacy Urged: Law Professor Tells Conference That the Constitution Should Be Changed to Protect Individual Rights Threatened by Technology," *Los Angeles Times*, Mar. 27, 1991.
[151] Paul M. Schwartz, "Preemption and Privacy," *Yale Law Journal* 118, no. (2009): 902–1021 (arguing there are benefits from a sectoral approach to privacy over an omnibus approach).
[152] See also Helen Nissenbaum, *Privacy in Context: Technology, Policy, and the Integrity of Social Life* (Stanford, CA: Stanford University Press, 2009).

discriminatory decisions impacting Americans."[153] However, the bill stalled out in committee and did not move past the House Subcommittee on Consumer Protection and Commerce and the Senate Committee on Finance.[154] In February 2022, the bill was reintroduced by Senator Ron Wyden, Senator Cory Booker, and Representative Yvette Clarke. The 2022 bill maintained the goals of the 2019 version but was updated with improvements that focused on "clarifying what types of algorithms and companies are covered, ensuring assessments put consumer impacts at the forefront, and providing more details about how reports should be structured."[155]

The Algorithmic Accountability Act of 2022 (AAA) is separated into eleven sections. Sections 1, 10, 11 need not be discussed at length, as Section 1 is simply introducing the short title for the legislation (1:3–5), Section 10 is a requirement that the FTC coordinate with other federal and state regulatory agencies so that future enforcement and regulations for AI and automation are consistent throughout the country (49:20–25), and Section 11 clarifies that the act does not have pre-emption power over state, tribal, city, or local laws and regulations (50:1–3).

Section 2: Definitions (1:6–8:24)

Section 2 introduces several definitions that are relevant to what the act is hoping to address. The crux of the definitions centers around "Augmented Critical Decision Processes" (2:1–5) (ACDPs) and "Augmented Decision Systems" (ADSs) (2:6–13). As the act explains, ACDPs are processes and procedures that utilize ADSs to make a critical decision. Critical Decisions (5:23–7:2), as the act defines, are decisions made by these automated processes that have legal, material, or some other "significant effect on a consumer's life." The act offers a long list of the areas that are encompassed within a consumer's life.

The section continues by introducing the terms *Covered Entity* (2:24–5:22) and *Identifying Information* (7:9–18). A Covered Entity is defined essentially as a company, corporation, or individual that meets a certain financial threshold through their gross income or equity value and develops and/or deploys ACDPs. In the absence of this financial threshold, the act also includes as Covered Entities those companies or individuals who have access to more than 1 million consumers' identifying information, which is defined as sensitive consumer information about a specific consumer, a consumer's household, or a consumer's device.

---

[153] Cory Booker, "Booker, Wyden, Clarke Introduce Bill Requiring Companies to Target Bias in Corporate Algorithms," Press Release, Apr. 10, 2019, www.booker.senate.gov/news/press/booker-wyden-clarke-introduce-bill-requiring-companies-to-target-bias-in-corporate-algorithms.

[154] All Actions: H.R.2231 – 116th Congress (2019–2020), Congress.gov, www.congress.gov/bill/116th-congress/house-bill/2231/all-actions?overview=closed#tabs.

[155] Ron Wyden, "Wyden, Booker and Clarke Introduce Algorithmic Accountability Act to 2022 to Require New Transparency and Accountability for Automated Decision Systems," Press Release, Feb. 3, 2022. www.wyden.senate.gov/news/press-releases/wyden-booker-and-clarke-introduce-algorithmic-accountability-act-of-2022-to-require-new-transparency-and-accountability-for-automated-decision-systems.

Section 3: Regulations and Considerations (9:1–16:14)

Section 3 lays out the regulations that the act requires the FTC to put in place. Most importantly, the act requires the FTC to roll out regulations (9:15–14:7) that would require companies that meet the threshold of a Covered Entity to periodically evaluate and continually document the ways that their ACDPs are making critical decisions that impact consumers. Furthermore, although these evaluations, which the act calls "impact assessments" (10:3–22), are not required to be submitted to the FTC, the bill requires the Covered Entities to annually submit to the FTC a shortened version of the impact assessments and summary reports (11:8–12) that highlight the important portions of the Covered Entities' impact assessment from the previous year. Additionally, even though the act focuses on current and future deployed ACDPs, it requires Covered Entities to maintain the impact assessment documentation at least five years after their ACEPs deployment.

Along with requiring these impact assessments and summary reports, the act also requires Covered Entities to disclose their status as a Covered Entity to other entities who develop ADSs for the Covered Entity (10:23–11:7), consult with internal and external consultants to give feedback and recommendations of the Covered Entities' ACDPs (12:3–14), and attempt to eliminate or reduce foreseeable negative impacts that their ACDPs would have on consumers (12:15–20).

Section 4: Impact Assessment Requirements (16:15–29:8)

As discussed above, Covered Entities are required under the act to perform ongoing evaluations and retain documentation about the impact that their ACDPs have on consumers. The act introduces specific requirements for what must be included within the impact assessments, including:

- Description of any current process being replaced by a new ACDP (16:23–17:15);
- Documentation of any data or other input information used for development, testing, maintaining, or updating (21:22–23:17);
- Testing and evaluation of the privacy risks and privacy-enhancing measures (18:14–19:12);
- Testing and evaluation of the current and historical performance including testing both before and after deployment (19:13–21:3);
- Documentation of significant dates of development and deployment and key points of contact (26:10–22);
- Information about the stakeholder engagement (17:16–18:2);
- Evaluation of the rights of consumers, including the degree to which a consumer may contest, correct, or appeal a decision or opt out of such system or process (23:18–25:6); and
- Identification of likely material negative impacts on consumers and assessment of applicable mitigation strategies (25:7–26:12)

Furthermore, this section requires Covered Entities to train employees who are involved with ACDP development and deployment about the potential and current

negative impacts that their ACDPs have on consumers and how to mitigate or eliminate such impacts. The act seeks to instill in Covered Entities a sense of not being
content with the status quo, but rather to always be evaluating and documenting
ways to make their ACDPs safer and have fewer negative impacts for consumers.
If a Covered Entity finds there is no way to mitigate or eliminate negative impact,
the act requires the Covered Entity to determine whether they should retire these
ACDPs or place limitations on them.

Section 5: Summary Report Requirements (29:9–33:11)
As mentioned, Covered Entities are not required to submit their impact assessments
to the FTC and, instead, must annually submit summary reports. The specific
requirements for summary reports include:

- The critical decision being made and the purpose of (and need for) the ADS or
  ACDP (29:20–30:3);
- The data and other inputs used and their sourcing (31:9–19);
- The performance of the ADS or ACDP (30:9–24);
- Stakeholders consulted (30:4–8);
- The transparency, explainability, and degree to which a consumer may contest,
  correct, or appeal a decision or opt out of such system or process (31:20–32:7);
- Any likely material negative impacts identified, and the steps taken to remedi-
  ate or mitigate, including any publicly stated limitations placed on certain uses
  of the ADS or ACDP (32:8–11);
- Which requirements of impact assessment were and were not completed and
  the rationale for those not completed (32:12–17); and
- Any requests to the Commission for new capabilities, tools, standards, and
  resources to improve any ADS, any ACDP, or the impact assessment process
  (32:18–33:2).

Section 6: Reporting and Creation of a Public Registry (33:12–39:25)
This section of the act sets up a requirement for the FTC to annually publish their
own reports on what they have learned in the past year from the summary reports
that the Covered Entities submitted (33:12–34:5). Additionally, in order to educate
consumers on the information they learn from the Covered Entities' summary
reports, the FTC is required to set up a webpage with a public registry that includes
a subset of that information and allows viewers of the registry to search and sort the
registry and download and print those searched-for or sorted subsets (34:6–39:25).

Section 7: Guidance, Training, and Other Requirements (40:1–41:25)
This section requires the FTC to develop guidance and training information to assist
companies and corporations in better understanding whether they are a Covered
Entity under the act (40:18–41:2). Furthermore, this section requires the FTC to
review the regulations surrounding algorithmic accountability every five years and

share information with the Office of Science and Technology Policy (OSTP) and National Institute of Standards and Technology (NIST) so that regulations and standards are developed consistently (41:16–25).

Section 8: Bureau of Technology (42:1–45:8)
Section 8 establishes a new bureau within the FTC, the Bureau of Technology (42:3–43:2), to be led by the chief technologist (43:3–4). Additionally, the FTC is required to staff the Bureau with fifty experts in various fields to aid and consult the FTC with technology and AI (43:7–44:2). Furthermore, the FTC chair is allowed to hire twenty-five more personnel for the Bureau of Technology's Enforcement Division (44:7–14). Finally, the act requires the FTC to set up cooperation agreements with other federal agencies that also regulate ACDPs and ADSs (44:19–45:8).

Section 9: Enforcement (45:9–49:19)
Finally, Section 9 introduces what will be considered violations of this act and how the FTC is to enforce the regulations within the bill. Specifically, the act:

- Makes violations of the requirements to assess the impact of augmented critical decisions (Sec. 3) an unfair and deceptive practice (45:11–16);
- Requires the FTC to conduct rulemaking as necessary to carry out the act and provides the powers to enforce the act based on the FTC Act (46:11–14); and
- Allows states to bring a civil action on behalf of residents of their states (after required notice to the FTC) based on violations of the requirements to assess the impact of augmented critical decisions (46:15–48:4).

The Algorithmic Accountability Act is primarily consumer facing, so one worry is that it may provide no relief for quantified workers. Yet, I believe it is a crucial first step in regulating mechanical managers and changing the plight of quantified workers. But it is not enough. While the bill may work well to oversee automated decision-making systems such as automated hiring programs, workers will remain quantified by productivity and surveillance applications – the so-called bossware. To counteract the deleterious effects of those kinds of AI systems for workers requires a worker bill of rights that directly addresses the treatment and portability of data demanded from or captured from workers as part of the employment bargain in the digital age.

12.12.2 *EEOC Guidance on Automated Hiring Programs and the ADA*

In 2021, the EEOC announced that it would be launching an initiative to ensure that employers' use of "software, including artificial intelligence (AI), machine learning, and other emerging technologies used in hiring and other employment decisions" complied with the ADA and other laws that the EEOC enforces. Within the announcement, the EEOC stated that it would, among other things, issue "guidance on algorithmic fairness and the use of AI in employment decisions."[156] As part of this initiative, on May 12, 2022, the EEOC released a technical assistance document, titled "The ADA and Use of Software, Algorithms, and AI to Assess Job Applicants and EEs," which "focused on preventing discrimination against job seekers and employees with disabilities." On the same day, the DOJ released a similar document that attempted to make it easier for "people without a legal or technical background" to understand their rights and responsibilities with algorithmic tools and job hiring or employment.[157]

Although the EEOC's document addressed several best practices for both employers and job applicants/employees, it makes it clear that the document does not create a "new policy." Rather, the document simply applies principles that "the ADA's statutory and regulatory provisions" already established. The document approaches this by (1) giving a background of what is being discussed and key definitions for the principles implicated; (2) establishing the basic concepts that the ADA addresses; (3) discussing how algorithmic decision-making tools interact and may violate the ADA; and (4) offering examples of steps that employers and job applicants/employees can take to better comply with the ADA and ensure that they are being fairly assessed by the algorithmic tool, respectively. The background section begins by introducing the definitions of software, algorithms, and AI. Within each of these definitions, the document addresses how an employer may use each of these tools in the hiring or employment settings.[158]

Within the ADA section, the document addresses what a disability is and when an algorithmic tool violates the ADA. Specifically, the document raises the concern about individuals with disabilities not being given reasonable accommodations, being unfairly/discriminatorily screened out by the tools, or having to address "disability-related inquiries and medical examinations." Finally, the EEOC clarifies that just because a third-party vendor creates or manages a tool does not mean that the employer is no longer responsible for it, as "the employer has given [the third party] authority to act on the employer's behalf."[159]

The potential violation section offers several examples to illustrate when an employer's tool violates the ADA. For a reasonable accommodation violation, if the employer utilizes a tool to give a knowledge test but utilizes a keyboard, trackpad, and so on without giving other options, this may be problematic, as it may lead to an

[156] EEOC, "Artificial Intelligence and Algorithmic Fairness Initiative," www.eeoc.gov/artificial-intelligence-and-algorithmic-fairness-initiative (last visited May 18, 2022).
[157] EEOC, "U.S. EEOC and U.S. Department of Justice Warn against Disability Discrimination," *EEOC Newsroom*, Press Release, May 12, 2022, www.eeoc.gov/newsroom/us-eeoc-and-us-department-justice-warn-against-disability-discrimination.
[158] EEOC, "The Americans with Disabilities Act and the Use of Software Algorithms, and Artificial Intelligence to Assess Job Applicants and Employees," EEOC, Guidance, May 12, 2022, www.eeoc.gov/laws/guidance/americans-disabilities-act-and-use-software-algorithms-and-artificial-intelligence.
[159] EEOC, "The Americans with Disabilities Act and the Use of Software Algorithms," question 3.

applicant or employee scoring lower on the test due to their disability and not their actual work qualifications. If this occurs, the employer may be held responsible if they could have addressed the issue with a "promising practice" that did not cause the employer "undue hardship" to create. An example of a screen-out violation was when an employer utilized a chatbot to reject all applicants who indicated they had "significant gaps in their employment history." Unless the employer took steps to prevent potential violations, the chatbot may reject an applicant without considering that their employment history gap was due to a disability. Finally, the document states that an employer might violate the ADA it if utilizes a tool that "poses 'disability-related inquiries' or seeks information that qualifies as a 'medical examination' before giving the candidate a conditional offer of employment." However, a personality test and other similar analyses would not qualify as violative.[160]

The final sections address what employers can do to ensure that they are complicit with the ADA while utilizing algorithmic tools, and what job applicants/employees can do to ensure they are being treated fairly by such tools. For the employer, the focus is on ensuring that their staff is properly trained to quickly process requests for reasonable accommodations and to evaluate job candidates and employees by "alternative means" if the current process may be unfair. Additionally, the EEOC makes it clear that the employer must ensure that any third parties used have taken the steps to make their tool "accessible to individuals with as many different kinds of disabilities as possible." If the employer is the one reviewing the data from the tools, the employer should implement promising practices that ensure applicants and employees are being evaluated solely on whether they are "able to perform the essential functions of the job."[161]

The EEOC encourages employees and job applicants to be proactive. If such employees/applicants believe that they have an ADA disability that could be negatively evaluated by an algorithmic tool, they should ask the employer for details about the tool. If the individual believes that the tool will not allow them to "compete on equal footing," they may want to ask the employer for a reasonable accommodation. If an individual is unable to take proactive measures, they should notify the employer as soon as they are aware of the problem; or if they think their rights have been violated, they can reach out to the EEOC to consider filing a charge of discrimination.[162]

12.13 IMAGINING A WORKER BILL OF RIGHTS FOR THE DIGITAL AGE

Many are familiar with posters in workplaces announcing the minimum wage owed workers and declaring other rights, such as work breaks and other rights accorded to workers. Missing from these posters is any mention of data rights or

---

[160] EEOC, "The Americans with Disabilities Act and the Use of Software Algorithms," questions 6, 9, and 13.

[161] EEOC, "The Americans with Disabilities Act and the Use of Software Algorithms," question 14.

[162] EEOC, "The Americans with Disabilities Act and the Use of Software Algorithms," question 15.

the rights of the worker to be free from unreasonable surveillance. It is high time we imagined a worker bill of rights for the digital age. What could such a bill of rights include?

12.13.1 *The Model Digital Worker Bill of Rights*

- The affirmation of the worker's personhood as separate from their data doubles, thus retaining the voice of the worker to make amendments to their record, offer context, request revision, or contest data-driven findings
- The right of the worker to have access to the data profile(s) created for employment applications or maintained by a current employer
- The right of the worker to be free from extraction of data that is not relevant or necessary for their job position or to carrying out work tasks
- The right of the worker to demand that sensitive health information either directly shared with the employer or inadvertently acquired through surveillance should receive the highest level of care for safeguarding against data breaches
- The right of the worker to request a hard delete of their data upon termination
- The right of the worker to be free from unreasonable surveillance; the reasonableness of work monitoring/surveillance will be judged by the norms of the work industry and may also be subject to collective bargaining agreements between worker unions and employers
- The right of the worker to benefit economically from the captured capital of the data extracted from them – such data may not be sold or ported for other purposes without their express consent

12.14 A ROLE FOR UNIONS AND WORKER DATA

With the understanding that data derived about workers could also benefit said workers, I believe that there is a role for unions to play. The future of work looks very different when workers are empowered through their own data. For example, the AFL-CIO released a report in 2019 in which the organization suggested ways for individual unions to use AI to empower their workers.[163] Furthermore, they emphasized that "unions must understand members not only as workers, but whole and complex people" and, to achieve that, the AFL-CIO suggested unions create "an advisory task force aimed at deploying the most sophisticated data collection, analysis and experimental techniques to understand what working people want and to suggest how we retool to meet those needs and desires." The AFL-CIO took this action themselves when, in January 2021, they launched the Technology Institute,

---

[163] AFL-CIO, *Commission on the Future of Work and Unions*, Report, Sept. 13, 2019, https://aflcio.org/reports/afl-cio-commission-future-work-and-unions.

which will "serve as the labor movement's think tank, to help us solve issues created by technology in collective bargaining and in any place it arises."[164]

Apart from the AFL-CIO, most major unions such as the Teamsters, United Food and Commercial Workers (UFCW), and Service Employees International Union (SEIU) (as seen on their websites) have not taken proactive action to harness the data of their members for the collective good. The UFCW website mentions AI and automation as something that labor organizations can use to their advantage but does not give any suggestions as to how.[165] Most union actions regarding automated decision-making have been reactive (how best to handle employers introducing and utilizing automation) rather than focused on proactive measures.

This lack of proactive strategies is criticized by scholars who believe that unions could make better use of automated decision-making and digital data. For example, Mark Zuckerman has suggested that organizations could use "virtual organizing" to "innovate and experiment with a new platform that is faster, homegrown, and simplified for workers to gain influence at work."[166] The platform would work by "adopt[ing] technology already widely used in social networking sites, such as survey and mapping software and other tools that could be adapted to virtual labor organizing" to give unions various scenarios or tactics that a company may use during an election, such as "audience meetings, 'canned messages' against the union, the hiring of consultants, threats, and disciplinary action." Zuckerman argues that if organizations began using virtual organizing, it "could transform how the nation's top labor unions deploy their organizing capabilities."

As has been demonstrated in this chapter, the regulation of mechanical managers in the workplace cannot merely take a one-track approach. What is necessary is *concurrent* regulation in which top-down mandates are supplemented by industry-level measures. Furthermore, labor law can have an important role to play, with unions becoming critical to preserving the freedom of workers when it comes to data collection in the workplace. The overwhelming message remains that concerted regulation is urgently necessary to preserve the personhood and dignity of the quantified worker.

---

[164] AFL-CIO, "AFL-CIO Launches Technology Institute," Press Release, Jan. 11, 2021, https://aflcio.org/press/releases/afl-cio-launches-technology-institute.

[165] UFCW, *Keeping Jobs Safe from Automation and Artificial Intelligence Technology*, www.ufcw.org/better/technology-and-the-future-of-work/ (last visited Mar. 3, 2022).

[166] Mark Zuckerman, Richard D. Kahlenberg, and Moshe Marvit, *Virtual Labor Organizing: Could Technology Help Reduce Income Inequality?* The Century Foundation, Issue Brief, June 9, 2015, p. 5, https://tcf.org/content/report/virtual-labor-organizing/?agreed=1&agreed=1&session=1.

Conclusion:
Imagining a Better Future for Workers

There is a future of work in which we all become digital serfs. We toil away in crowded open-floor offices with no privacy or in cavernous warehouses. Workplaces, optimized for the greatest level of surveillance, closely resemble the panoptical ideal, in which worker surveillance is omnipresent and indefatigable. In this future, the surveillants are not human; rather, they are mechanical managers. They take screenshots of our computer screen every ten seconds; they use productivity applications to log each keystroke and parse each email message; and they require wristbands, fitness trackers, or chips embedded under the skin. They are the exoskeletons monitoring the worker's every move.

In this future of work, we are all quantified by our data. As workers, we become synonymous with our data doubles. We lose all of our personhood and voice, and our digital doubles speak for us. All of our interactions, within the workplace and without, become data that is used to quantify our personalities, quantify our work ethic, quantify our trustworthiness, and so on. We are at the mercy of mechanical managers. From the beginning, with the automated interview and automated onboarding, to the automated productivity checks and the automated dismissal, we are judged by algorithmic systems. We have no right to explanations and no venue to contest automated decisions. It is a bleak future.

But a different, better, future of work is possible. One in which we, as workers, are empowered by our data, not ruled by it. Worker personhood and human dignity are retained as paramount and separate from the representations of digital data. Rather than being quantified by automated decision-making systems, these systems exist to enable workers to reach their highest potential. It will not be enough to merely declare a stance against worker quantification. Achieving true worker autonomy necessitates concrete changes in our legal regime. It requires a reconsideration of our ethical values concerning workers. One might start with a Rawlsian approach to the adoption of new technologies in the workplace. This approach prompts the first-order question of "Who loses?" – a question that encourages us to ponder who is disadvantaged by the AI technologies of work. Only by focusing on the least well off can we be attuned to the oppressive potential of these technologies. The liberty of all depends on this consideration. As Dr. Martin Luther King Jr., a great champion of human rights, once noted, "The society that performs miracles with machinery has the capacity to make some miracles for men – if it values men as highly as it values machines."[1]

The Declaration of Independence presaged a break from colonialism but it was the Constitution and, furthermore, the Bill of Rights that solidified democracy as the new order in the United States of America. Similarly, emerging AI technologies serve as harbingers for an upcoming economic societal upheaval, one that threatens to tilt power further in the balance of employers, thus threatening our democracy. Awareness of this shifting landscape dictates decisive preventative action. First, we must envision a future in which workers' labor and employment rights are respected, workers' dignity and autonomy are valued, and technology is deployed to enhance the lives of workers rather than to control them. To achieve this requires concrete changes to employment law doctrine, such as a rethinking of the traditional deference accorded to employers and the adoption of the proposed discrimination per se cause of action, allowing workers to more easily bring suit when confronted with automated systems that have a disparate impact on minority workers. It requires a worker's bill of rights that clearly delineates limits for worker surveillance and the use of the data derived from workers. It requires the mandated audits of automated hiring systems and design initiatives for them that have the goal of inclusion as its primary objective. It requires a reconsideration of the privacy and discrimination risks that arise from workplace wellness programs, wearable technology, and the laissez-faire approach to trading worker health data.

On the side of workers, one could envision a coalescence around worker unions that deploy worker data for the greater good of union members. Real-time worker data is wielded as worker power for better working conditions, as a bargaining chip for better pay, and to safeguard other work benefits. One could also preview employers compensating workers for their data when such data is used for new work innovations or deployed to build AI technologies that render those workers redundant. There is also a possible future where the idea of a universal basic income that ensures human welfare is not subsumed by corporate greed.

As it stands, we are set on a course towards a disastrous future of work where the worker is quantified in all aspects. The worker loses all individuality, all trace of personhood. Rather, she becomes a set of binaries, fit or unfit, to be plugged into the computerized workplace. She is merely a cog in the machine – fungible and disposable. Yet, a different future of work still exists. We have to course correct for a better future of work by adopting a more worker protective legal regime.

---

[1] Dr. Martin Luther King Jr., Address at the Transport Workers Union of America's 11th Constitutional Convention, Apr. 27, 1961.

Bibliography

PUBLISHED SOURCES

Abril, Patricia Sanchez, et al. "Blurred Boundaries: Social Media Privacy and the Twenty-First- Century Employee." *American Business Law Journal* 49, no. 1 (2012): 63–124.

ACLU. "Genetic Discrimination in the Workplace Factsheet." www.aclu.org/other/genetic-discrimination-workplace-factsheet-9 (accessed May 2, 2020).

ACLU of Rhode Island. "ACLU and CVS/Pharmacy Resolve Discrimination Complaint." *ACLU RI News*, July 19, 2011. www.riaclu.org/news/post/aclu-and-cvs-pharmacy-resolve-discrimination-complaint.

ADA National Network. "What Is the Americans with Disabilities Act (ADA)?" https://adata.org/learn-about-ada (accessed Mar. 17, 2021).

Advisory Board. "When Your Employer Gives You a Fitbit, Who Owns the Data?" Advisory Board: Daily Briefing, Feb. 20, 2019. www.advisory.com/daily-briefing/2019/02/20/employee-wearables.

AFL-CIO. "AFL-CIO Launches Technology Institute." Press Release, Jan. 11, 2021, https://aflcio.org/press/releases/afl-cio-launches-technology-institute.

AFL-CIO. *Commission on the Future of Work and Unions.* Report, Sept. 13, 2019. https://aflcio.org/reports/afl-cio-commission-future-work-and-unions.

Ajunwa, Ifeoma. "Algorithms at Work: Productivity Monitoring Applications and Wearable Technology as the New Data-Centric Research Agenda for Employment and Labor Law." *Saint Louis University Law Journal* 63, no. 1 (2018): 21–53.

Ajunwa, Ifeoma. "The Auditing Imperative for Automated Hiring." *Harvard Journal of Law and Technology* 34, no. 2 (2021): 621–700.

Ajunwa, Ifeoma. "Automated Employment Discrimination." *Harvard Journal on Law and Technology* 34, no. 2 (2021): 621–99.

Ajunwa, Ifeoma. "Automated Video Interviewing as the New Phrenology." *Berkeley Technology Law Journal* 36, no. 3 (2021): 1173–225.

Ajunwa, Ifeoma. "The 'Black Box' at Work." *Big Data & Society* 7, no. 2 (2020): 1–6.

Ajunwa, Ifeoma. "Genetic Data and Civil Rights." *Harvard Civil Rights-Civil Liberties Law Review* 51, no. 1 (2016): 75–114.

Ajunwa, Ifeoma. "Genetic Testing Meets Big Data: Torts and Contract Law Issues." *Ohio State Law Journal* 75, no. 6 (2014): 1225–62. https://papers.ssrn.com/sol3/papers.cfm?abstract_id=2460891.

Ajunwa, Ifeoma. "Facebook Users Aren't the Reason Facebook Is in Trouble Now." *Washington Post*, Mar. 23, 2018. www.washingtonpost.com/news/posteverything/wp/2018/03/23/facebook-users-arent-the-reason-facebook-is-in-trouble-now/.

Ajunwa, Ifeoma. "The Paradox of Automation as Anti-Bias Intervention." *Cardozo Law Review* 41, no. 5 (2020): 1671–742.

Ajumwa, Ifeoma. "Race, Labor, and the Future of Work." In *Oxford Handbook of Race and Law in the United States*, edited by Emily Houh, Khiara Bridges, and Devon Carbado. New York: Oxford University Press, 2022: 1–18.

Ajunwa, Ifeoma. "Workplace Wellness Programs Could Be Putting Your Health Data at Risk." *Harvard Business Review*, Jan. 19, 2017. https://hbr.org/2017/01/workplace-wellness-programs-could-be-putting-your-health-data-at-risk.

Ajunwa, Ifeoma, et al. "Limitless Worker Surveillance." *California Law Review* 105, no. 3 (2017): 736–76.

Ajunwa, Ifeoma, and Angela Onwuachi-Willig. "Combatting Discrimination against the Formerly Incarcerated in the Labor Market." *Northwestern University Law Review* 112, no. 6 (2018): 1385–415.

Ajunwa, Ifeoma, and Daniel Green. "Platforms at Work: Automated Hiring Platforms and Other New Intermediaries in the Organization of Work." *Work and Labor in the Digital Age* 33 (2019): 61–91.

Ajunwa, Ifeoma, Jason Schultz, and Kate Crawford. "Limitless Worker Surveillance." *California Law Review* 105, no. 3 (2017): 736–76.

Ajunwa, Ifeoma, Kate Crawford, and Joel Ford. "Health and Big Data: An Ethical Framework for Health Information Collection by Corporate Wellness Programs." *Journal of Law, Medicine, and Ethics* 44, no. 3 (2016): 474–80.

Alaka, Aida Marie. "Corporate Reorganizations, Job Layoffs, and Age Discrimination: Has *Smith v. City of Jackson* Substantially Expanded the Rights of Older Workers Under the ADEA?" *Albany Law Review* 70, no. 1 (2006): 143–80.

Allan, Patrick. "Five Ways to Cheat Your Way to 10,000 Fitbit Steps Every Day." *LifeHacker*, Oct. 27, 2016. https://lifehacker.com/five-ways-to-cheat-your-way-to-10-000-fitbit-steps-ever-1788302045.

Alon-Shenker, Pnina. "Legal Barriers to Age Discrimination in Hiring Complaints." *Dalhousie University Law Journal* 39, no. 1 (2016): 289–325.

American Diabetes Association. *The History of a Wonderful Thing We Call Insulin*, July 1, 2019. www.diabetes.org/blog/history-wonderful-thing-we-call-insulin (accessed May 26, 2021).

American Management Association (AMA). "The Latest on Workplace Monitoring and Surveillance." Apr. 8, 2019. www.amanet.org/articles/the-latest-on-workplace-monitoring-and-surveillance/.

American Management Association (AMA). *Workplace Testing and Monitoring*. Briarcliff Manor, New York: American Management Association, 1998.

American Psychological Association (APA). *Diagnostic and Statistical Manual of Mental Disorders (DSM-5)*. Washington DC: American Psychological Association, 2015.

American Psychological Association (APA). "DSM History." www.psychiatry.org/psychia trists/practice/dsm/history-of-the-dsm (accessed May 10, 2021).

American Psychological Association (APA). "Highlights of Changes from DSM-IV-TR to DSM-5." https://psychiatry.msu.edu/_files/docs/Changes-From-DSM-IV-TR-to-DSM-5.pdf (accessed May 10, 2021).

American Social Project. *Who Built America?* Vol. 1, *To 1877*. New York: Worth Publishing, 2000.

American Social Project. *Who Built America?* Vol. 2, *Since 1877*. New York: Worth Publishing, 2000.

Ananny, Mike, and Kate Crawford. "Seeing without Knowing: Limitations of the Transparency Ideal and Its Application to Algorithmic Accountability." *New Media & Society* 20, no. 3 (2016): 973–89.

Anderko, Laura, et al. "Promoting Prevention through the Affordable Care Act: Workplace Wellness." *Preventing Chronic Disease* 9, no. 12 (2012): E175. https://pubmed.ncbi.nlm.nih .gov/23237245/.

Anderson, Elizabeth. *Private Government: How Employers Rule Our Lives (and Why We Don't Talk about It)*. Princeton: Princeton University Press, 2017.

Andreou, Ashley. "A Tool Doctors Use Every Day Can Perpetuate Medical Racism." *Scientific American*, June 7, 2021. www.scientificamerican.com/article/a-tool-doctors-use-every-day-can-perpetuate-medical-racism/.

Angwin, Julia, Noam Schelber, and Ariana Tobin. "Facebook Job Ads Raise Concerns about Age Discrimination." *New York Times*, Dec. 20, 2017. www.nytimes.com/2017/12/20/busi ness/facebook-job-ads.html.

Argyris, Chris. *Personality and the Organization: The Conflict between the System and the Individual*. New York: Harper, 1957.

Article 19. Emotional Entanglement: China's Emotion Recognition Market and Its Implications for Human Rights. [Report], January 2021.

Arvey, Richard D., and James E. Campion. "The Employment Interview: A Summary and Review of Recent Research." *Personnel Psychology* 35, no. 2 (1982): 281–322.

Ashley, Kevin, Karl Branting, Howard Margolis, and Cass R. Sunstein. "Legal Reasoning and Artificial Intelligence: How Computers 'Think' Like Lawyers." *University of Chicago Law School Roundtable* 8, no. 1 (2001): 1–27.

Associated Press. "Black NFL Players Call for End of Algorithm That Assumes Black Men Have Lower Cognitive Abilities." *MarketWatch*, May 14, 2021. www.marketwatch.com/story/ retired-black-nfl-players-and-their-families-call-for-race-norming-practice-to-end-01621018741.

Associated Press. "Judge Approves Potential $1 Billion Settlement to Resolve NFL Concussion Lawsuits." *USA Today*, Apr. 22, 2015. www.usatoday.com/story/sports/nfl/2015/04/22/nfl-concussion-lawsuit-settlement-judge-1-billion/26192827/.

Atlassian. "Building Equitable, Balanced Teams and a Sense of Belonging." www.atlassian .com/belonging [https://perma.cc/3949-T3ZN] (accessed Mar. 2, 2020).

Atlassian. "Company Values." www.atlassian.com/company/values [https://perma.cc/WS37-QL4Q] (accessed Mar. 2, 2020).

Attewell, Paul. "Big Brother and the Sweatshop: Computer Surveillance in the Automated Office." *Sociological Theory* 5, no. 1 (1987): 97–100.

Autor, David H., and David Scarborough. "Does Job Testing Harm Minority Workers? Evidence from Retail Establishments. *Quarterly Journal of Economics* 123, no. 1 (2008): 219–77.

Avraham, Ronen, and Kimberly Yuracko. "The Use of Race- and Sex-Based Data to Calculate Damages Is a Stain on Our Legal System." *Washington Post*, Apr. 29, 2021. www.washington post.com/opinions/2021/04/29/race-sex-based-data-legal-damages/.

Ayres, Ian, and Jennifer Gerarda Brown. "Mark(et)ing Nondiscrimination: Privatizing ENDA with a Certification Mark." *Michigan Law Review* 104, no. 7 (2006): 1639–1712.

Ayres, Ian, and Peter Siegelman. "The Q-Word as Red Herring: Why Disparate Impact Liability Does Not Induce Hiring Quotas." *Texas Law Review* 74, no. 1 (1996): 1487–1526.

Baez, H. Beau. "Personality Test in Employment Selection: Use with Caution." *Cornell HR Review*, Jan. 26, 2013. https://digitalcommons.ilr.cornell.edu/chrr/59/.

Bailey, Diane E., and Nancy B. Kurland. "A Review of Telework Research: Findings, New Directions, and Lessons for the Study of Modern Work." *Journal of Organizational Behavior* 23, no. 4 (2002): 383–400.

Bales, Richard A., and Katherine V. W. Stone. "The Invisible Web at Work: Artificial Intelligence and Electronic Surveillance in the Workplace." *Berkeley Journal of Labor and Employment Law* 41, no. 1 (2020): 1–60.

Balkin, Jack M., and Reva B. Siegel. The American Civil Rights Tradition: Anticlassification or Antisubordination?" *Miami Law Review* 58, no. 1 (2003): 9–33.

Ballaban, Michael. "When Henry Ford's Benevolent Secret Police Ruled His Workers." *Jalopnik*, Mar. 23, 2014. https://jalopnik.com/when-henry-fords-benevolent-secret-police-ruled-his-wo-1549625731.

Ballman, Donna. "10 New (and Legal) Ways Your Employer Is Spying on You." *Business Insider*, Sept. 29, 2013. www.businessinsider.com/10-new-and-legal-ways-your-employer-is-spying-on-you-2013-9.

Barber, Linda. "E-recruitment Development." Institute for Employment Studies, HR Network Paper MP63, Mar. 2006. www.employment-studies.co.uk/system/files/resources/files/mp63.pdf.

Barenberg, Mark. "The Political Economy of the Wagner Act: Power, Symbol, and Workplace Cooperation." *Harvard Law Review* 106, no. 7 (1993): 1381–1496.

Bariso, Justin. "This Company's Approach to Remote Work Is the Worst I've Ever Seen." *Inc.*, Sept. 16, 2020. www.inc.com/justin-bariso/this-companys-approach-to-remote-work-is-worst-ive-ever-seen-emotional-intelligence.html.

Barnes, Patricia. "Artificial Intelligence Poses New Threat to Equal Employment Opportunity." *Forbes*, Nov. 10, 2019. www.forbes.com/sites/patriciagbarnes/2019/11/10/artificial-intelligence-poses-new-threat-to-equal-employment-opportunity/?sh=6e0a33036488.

Barocas, Solon, and Andrew D. Selbst. "Big Data's Disparate Impact." *California Law Review* 104, no. 3 (2016): 671–732.

Barrett, Lisa Feldman. "Are Emotions Natural Kinds?" *Perspectives on Psychological Science* 1, no. 1 (2006): 28–58.

Barrett, Lisa Feldman, et al. "Emotional Expressions Reconsidered: Challenges to Inferring Emotions from Human Facial Movements." *Psychological Science in the Public Interest* 20, no. 1 (2019): 1–68. https://journals.sagepub.com/doi/10.1177/1529100619832930.

Bartz, Andrea. "This Healthcare Company Is Determined to Have the Healthiest Employees in the World." *Johnson & Johnson: Innovation*, Feb. 25, 2018. www.jnj.com/innovation/how-johnson-johnson-is-improving-workplace-wellness-for-healthiest-employees (accessed May 25, 2021).

Bassett, Debra Lyn. "Silencing Our Elders." *Nevada Law Review* 15, no. 2 (2015): 519–36.

Becker, Gary S. *The Economic Approach to Human Behavior*. Chicago: University of Chicago Press, 1976.

Becker, Gary S. *The Economics of Discrimination*, 2nd ed. Chicago: University of Chicago Press, 2010.

Bedoya, Alvaro M. "The Color of Surveillance." *Slate*, Jan. 18, 2016. https://slate.com/technology/2016/01/what-the-fbis-surveillance-of-martin-luther-king-says-about-modern-spying.html.

Bell, Alexander Graham. Memoir upon the Formation of a Deaf Variety of the Human Race. 1883. Paper Presented to the National Academy of Sciences at New Haven, Nov. 13, 1882.

Bender, Matthew. *Banks & Thrifts: Government Enforcement & Receivership*. New York: Matthew Bender Elite Products, 2018.

Beniger, James. *The Control Revolution: Technological and Economic Origins of the Information Society*. Cambridge, MA: Harvard University Press, 1989.

Bensinger, Greg. "So Far, under California's New Privacy Law, Firms Are Disclosing Too Little Data – or Far Too Much." *Washington Post*, Jan. 21, 2020. www.washingtonpost.com/technology/2020/01/21/ccpa-transparency/.

Bent, Jason. "Is Algorithmic Affirmative Action Legal?" *Georgetown Law Journal* 108, no. 4 (2020): 803–53.

Berman, Skyler R. "Bargaining Over Biometrics: How Player Unions Should Protect Athletes in the Age of Wearable Technology." *Brooklyn Law Review* 85, no. 2 (2020): 543–70.

Bertrand, Marianne, and Sendhill Mullainathan. "Are Emily and Greg More Employable than Lakisha and Jamal? A Field Experiment on Labor Market Discrimination." *American Economic Review* 94, no. 4 (2004): 991–1013.

Bianchi, Alden. "*EEOC v. Flambeau*, Judicial Restraint, and the Uncertain Future of Employer-Sponsored Wellness Programs." *Mintz Insight*, Jan. 31, 2017. www.mintz.com/insights-center/viewpoints/2226/2017-01-eeoc-v-flambeau-judicial-restraint-and-uncertain-future (accessed May 25, 2021).

Biddle Consulting Group. *Uniform Guidelines on Employee Selection Procedures*. http://uniformguidelines.com/uniformguidelines.html#18 (accessed Sept. 22, 2019).

Bieber, Friedemann, and Jakob Moggia. "Risk Shifts in the Gig Economy: The Normative Case for an Insurance Scheme against the Effects of Precarious Work." *Journal of Political Philosophy* 29, no. 3 (2021): 271–304.

Blackmon, Douglas A. *Slavery by Another Name: The Re-Enslavement of Black Americans from the Civil War to World War II*. New York: Doubleday, 2008.

Blau, Peter M. *The Dynamics of Bureaucracy: A Study of Interpersonal Relations in Two Government Agencies*. Chicago: University of Chicago Press, 1955.

Block, Sharon, and Benjamin Sachs. "Worker Organizations Must Enable Worker Power." *American Compass: A Seat at the Table*, Sept. 22, 2020. https://americancompass.org/articles/worker-organizations-must-enable-worker-power/.

Bloy, Marjorie. "The Repeal of the Combination Acts (1824)." *The Web of English History*, last updated Jan. 12, 2016, www.historyhome.co.uk/c-eight/l-pool/combacts.htm.

Bodie, Matthew T. "The Law of Employee Data: Privacy, Property and Governance." *Indiana Law Journal* 97, no. 2 (2021): 1–68.

Bodie, Matthew T., et al. "The Law and Policy of People Analytics." *University of Colorado Law Review* 88, no. 4 (2017): 961–1042.

Bodie, Matthew, and Michael McMahon. "Employee Testing, Tracing, and Disclosure as a Response to the Coronavirus Pandemic." *Washington University Journal of Law and Policy* 64, no. 1 (2021): 31–61.

Bogen, Miranda. "All the Ways Algorithms Can Introduce Bias." *Harvard Business Review*, May 6, 2019. https://hbr.org/2019/05/all-the-ways-hiring-algorithms-can-introduce-bias.

Bond, Shannon. "Your Boss May Soon Track You at Work for Coronavirus Safety." *NPR: The Coronavirus Crisis*, May 8, 2020. www.npr.org/2020/05/08/852896051/your-boss-may-soon-track-you-at-work-for-coronavirus-safety.

Booker, Cory. "Booker, Wyden, Clarke Introduce Bill Requiring Companies to Target Bias in Corporate Algorithms." Press Release, Apr. 10, 2019. www.booker.senate.gov/news/press/booker-wyden-clarke-introduce-bill-requiring-companies-to-target-bias-in-corporate-algorithms.

Bornstein, Stephanie. "Antidiscriminatory Algorithms." *Alabama Law Review* 70, no. 2 (2018): 519–72.

Bornstein, Stephanie. "Reckless Discrimination." *California Law Review* 105, no. 4 (2017): 1055–110.

Borsellino, Regina. "Beat the Robots: How to Get Your Resume Past the System and into Human Hands." *The Muse*. www.themuse.com/advice/beat-the-robots-how-to-get-your-resume-past-the-system-into-human-hands (accessed June 3, 2021).

Boyd, Danah, and Kate Crawford. "Critical Questions for Data: Provocations for a Cultural, Technological, and Scholarly Phenomenon." *Information, Communication & Society* 15, no. 5 (2012): 662–679.

Boyle, Alan. "Amazon Wins a Pair of Patents for Wireless Wristbands That Track Warehouse Workers." *GeekWire*, Jan. 30, 2018. www.geekwire.com/2018/amazon-wins-patents-wireless-wristbands-track-warehouse-workers/ [https://perma.cc/XN4M-LUQS].

Bradley, Keith. *Slavery and Society at Rome*. Cambridge: Cambridge University Press, 1994.

Breen, Keith. "Freedom, Republicanism, and Workplace Democracy." *Critical Review of International Social and Political Philosophy* 18, no. 4 (2015): 470–85.

Bridges, Khiara M. "The Deserving Poor, the Undeserving Poor, and Class-Based Affirmative Action." *Emory Law Journal* 66, no. 5 (2017): 1049–114.

Bright, David S., et al. *Principles of Management*. OpenStax, 2019. https://opentextbc.ca/principlesofmanagementopenstax/ (accessed Nov. 11, 2021).

Brocklehurst, Michael. "Power, Identity and New Technology Homework: Implications for 'New Forms' of Organizing." *Organization Studies* 22, no. 3 (2001): 445–66.

Broich, John. "2017 Isn't '1984' – It's Stranger Than Orwell Imagined." *The Independent*, Feb. 1, 2017. www.independent.co.uk/news/world/politics/2017-isn-t-1984-it-s-stranger-than-orwell-imagined-a7555341.html.

Brown, Elizabeth A. "The Fitbit Fault Line: Two Proposals to Protect Health and Fitness Data at Work." *Yale Journal of Health Policy, Law & Ethics* 16, no. 1 (2016): 1–49.

Brown, Elizabeth A. "A Healthy Mistrust: Curbing Biometric Data Misuse in the Workplace." *Stanford Technology Law Review* 23, no. 2 (2020): 252–98.

Brown, Lauren. "'Gut Feeling' Still the Most Common Deciding Factor in Hiring, Survey Shows." *People Management*, July 11, 2018. www.peoplemanagement.co.uk/news/articles/gut-feeling-most-common-deciding-factor-in-hiring-survey-shows.

Brown, Sarah M., and Natasha T. Brison. "Big Data, Big Problems: Analysis of Professional Sports Leagues' CBAs and Their Handling of Athlete Biometric Data." *Journal of Legal Aspects of Sport* 30, no. 1 (2020): 63–81.

Brown, Stewart L. "Mutual Funds and the Regulatory Capture of the SEC." *Journal of Business Law* 19, no. 3 (2018): 701–49.

Brummond Jeremy P., and Patrick J. Thornton. "The Legal Side of Jobsite Technology." *Construction Today*, June 22, 2016. www.construction-today.com/sections/columns/2752-the-legal-side-of-jobsite-technology [https://perma.cc/P5AX-9GRT].

Bui, Terri H. "The Rise of Technology in the Construction Industry." *Orange County Lawyer* 61, no. 9 (Sept. 2019): 37–39.

Buolamwini, Joy. "When the Robot Doesn't See Dark Skin." *New York Times*, June 21, 2018. www.nytimes.com/2018/06/21/opinion/facial-analysis-technology-bias.html.

Buolamwini, Joy, and Timnit Gebru. "Gender Shades: Intersectional Accuracy Disparities in Commercial Gender Classification." *Proceedings of Machine Learning Research* 81, no. 1 (2018): 1–15.

Burawoy, Michael. *Manufacturing Consent: Changes in the Labor Process under Monopoly Capitalism*. Chicago: University of Chicago Press, 1979.

Burda, David. "Workplace Wellness Programs and the Coronavirus Pandemic." *4SightHealth*, May 27, 2020. www.4sighthealth.com/workplace-wellness-programs-and-the-coronavirus-pandemic/ (accessed May 25, 2021).

Bushnell, Sarah Terrill. *The Truth about Henry Ford*. Chicago: Reilly & Lee Co., 1922.

Business Roundtable. "Statement on the Purpose of a Corporation," Aug. 2019. https://s3.amazonaws.com/brt.org/BRT-StatementonthePurposeofaCorporationJuly2021.pdf.

Cable, Daniel M., and Timothy A. Judge. "Interviewers' Perceptions of Person–Organization Fit and Organizational Selection Decisions." *Journal of Applied Psychology* 82, no. 4 (1997): 546–61.

Campbell, Alexia Fernandez. "Trump Tried to Sabotage a Plan to Close the Gender Pay Gap. A Judge Wouldn't Have It." *Vox*, Apr. 26, 2019. www.vox.com/2019/4/26/18515920/gender-pay-gap-rule-eeoc.

Campbell, Harry. "Lyft & Uber Driver Survey 2020: Uber Driver Satisfaction Takes a Big Hit." *Ride Share Guy*, Feb. 14, 2021. https://therideshareguy.com/uber-driver-survey/.

Caperchione, Christina M., et al. "How Do Management and Non-Management Employees Perceive Workplace Wellness Programmes? A Qualitative Examination." *Health Education Journal* 75, no. 5 (2015): 553–64.

Cappelli, Peter. *The Future of the Office*. Philadelphia: Wharton School Press, 2021.

Carbado, Devon W. "Racial Naturalization." *American Quarterly* 57, no. 3 (2005): 633–58.

Carbado, Devon W., and Mitu Gulati. "Working Identity." *Cornell Law Review* 85, no. 5 (2005): 1259–1308.

Carpenter, Daniel, and David A. Moss, eds. *Preventing Regulatory Capture: Special Interest Influence and How to Limit It*. Cambridge: Cambridge University Press, 2014.

Cavounidis, Costas, and Kevin Lang. "Discrimination and Worker Evaluation." National Bureau of Economic Research, Working Paper 21612, October 2015. www.nber.org/papers/w21612.

CB Media. "Factories during the Industrial Revolution." IndustrialRevolution.com, 2010. https://industrialrevolution.org.uk/factories-industrial-revolution/.

CBS News. "Jury Awards Millions in Case of the 'Devious Defecator.'" *CBS News*, June 25, 2015. www.cbsnews.com/news/jury-awards-millions-in-case-of-the-devious-defecator/.

Chander, Anupam. "The Racist Algorithm?" *Michigan Law Review* 115, no. 6 (2017): 1023–45.

Chauriye, Nicole. "Wearable Devices as Admissible Evidence: Technology Is Killing Our Opportunities to Lie." *Catholic University of Law and Technology* 24, no. 2 (2016): 495–528.

Checkr. Home Page. Feb. 2020. https://Checkr.com [https://perma.cc/9ECB-2RVN].

Chen, Angela. "The AI Hiring Industry Is Under Scrutiny – But It'll Be Hard to Fix." *MIT Technology Review*, Nov. 7, 2019. www.technologyreview.com/2019/11/07/75194/hirevue-ai-automated-hiring-discrimination-ftc-epic-bias/.

Cherry, Kendra. "The Origins of Psychology." *VeryWellMind*, June 25, 2020. www.verywellmind.com/a-brief-history-of-psychology-through-the-years-2795245.

Chua, Amy, and Jed Rubenfeld. *The Triple Package: How Three Unlikely Traits Explain the Rise and Fall of Cultural Groups in America*. New York: Penguin Book Publishing, 2014.

Chung, Chia-Fang, et al. "Finding the Right Fit: Understanding Health Tracking in Workplace Wellness Programs." In *CHI'17: Proceedings of the 2017 ACM SIGCHI Conference on Human Factors in Computing Systems*, May 6–11, 2017. New York: Association of Computing Machinery, 2017.

Chung, Christine Sgarlata. "From Lily Bart to the Boom-Boom Room: How Wall Street's Social and Cultural Response to Women Has Shaped Securities Regulation." *Harvard Journal of Law & Gender* 33, no. 1 (2010): 175–245.

Chung, Lisa Hird. "Prohibiting Genetic Discrimination in Calif." *Law360*, Oct. 6, 2011. www.law360.com/articles/274791.

Citron, Danielle Keats, and Frank A. Pasquale. "The Scored Society: Due Process for Automated Predictions." *Washington Law Review* 89, no. 1 (2014): 1–33.

Claims and Litigation Management (CLM). "Rise of the Machines: Can and Should Your Fitness Tracker Be Used against You in a Court of Law?" Session 2B, CLM 2017 National Management & Professional Liability Conference, July 26–28, 2017.

Clemont, Kevin M., and Stewart J. Schwab. "How Employment Discrimination Plaintiffs Fare in Federal Court." *Journal of Empirical Legal Studies* 1, no. 2 (2004): 429–58.

Clever Control. *Frequently Asked Questions.* https://clevercontrol.com/faq (accessed Oct. 2, 2020).

CLIC Faculty. "Professor Woodrow Hartzog Calls for a Ban on Facial Recognition Technology in New Publication." *Northeastern: CLIC*, Apr. 14, 2020. www.northeastern .edu/clic/2020/04/.

Coaston, Jane. "The Intersectionality Wars." *Vox*, last updated May 28, 2019. www.vox .com/the-highlight/2019/5/20/18542843/intersectionality-conservatism-law-race-gender-discrimination.

Cofone, Ignacio N. "Algorithmic Discrimination Is an Information Problem." *Hastings Law Journal* 70, no. 6 (2019): 1389–1443.

Cohen, Adam. *Imbeciles: The Supreme Court, American Eugenics, and the Sterilization of Carrie Buck.* New York: Penguin, 2016.

Cohen, Julie E. "Law for the Platform Economy." *UC Davis Law Review* 51, no. 1 (2017): 133–204.

Cohen, Julie E. "The Regulatory State in the Information Age." *Theoretical Inquiries in Law* 17, no. 2 (2016): 369–414.

Cohen, Julie E. "The Surveillance-Innovation Complex: The Irony of the Participatory Turn." In *The Participatory Condition of the Digital Age*, edited by Darin Barney et al., 207–28. Minneapolis: University of Minnesota Press, 2016.

Colker, Ruth. "The Americans with Disabilities Act: A Windfall for Defendants." *Harvard Civil Rights-Civil Liberties Law Review* 34, no. 1 (1999): 99–139.

Color Health, Inc. *Color Privacy Policy.* Last updated Nov. 1, 2021. www.color.com/privacy-policy.

Color Health, Inc. Home Page. www.color.com/ (accessed May 26, 2021).

Confirm Biosciences. "Workplace Drug Testing Guide," May 4, 2018. www.confirmbiosci ences.com/knowledge/workplace/workplace-drug-testing-guide/.

Consumer Finance Protection Bureau. *List Of Consumer Reporting Companies*, 2020. https:// Files.consumerfinance.gov/F/201604_Cfpb_List-Of-Consumer-Reporting-Companies.pdf [https://perma.cc/Y8LW-9JFS].

Cook, Dan. "Large Employers See Health Cost Reductions." *BenefitsPro*, Aug. 13, 2014. www.benefitspro.com/2014/08/13/large-employers-see-health-cost-reductions/?slret urn=20211120163334.

Copeland, Rob, and Bradley Hope. "The World's Largest Hedge Fund Is Building an Algorithmic Model from Its Employees' Brains." *Wall Street Journal*, Dec. 22, 2016. www .wsj.com/articles/the-worlds-largest-hedge-fund-is-building-an-algorithmic-model-of-its-founders-brain-1482423694.

Corbett, William R. "Fixing Employment Discrimination Law." *SMU Law Review* 62, no. 1 (2009): 81–116.

Costanza-Chock, Sasha. *Design Justice: Community-Led Practices to Build the Worlds We Need.* Cambridge, MA: MIT Press, 2020.

Council for Responsible Genetics. "Genetic Testing, Privacy and Discrimination." *CRG in the Press.* Archived Nov. 17, 2015, https://perma.cc/E59R-EQ9Y (accessed May 25, 2021).

Couret, Jacques. "UPS Using 'Wearable' Scanning System." *Atlanta Business Chronicle*, Aug. 2, 2012. www.bizjournals.com/atlanta/news/2012/08/02/ups-using-wearable-scanning-system.html [http://perma.cc/8B27-MEN9].

Coxworth, Ben. "SmartCap Monitors Workers' Fatigue Levels by Reading Their Brain Waves." *New Atlas*, Jan. 31, 2012. https://newatlas.com/smartcap-measures-fatigue-brain-waves/21271/ [https://perma.cc/X7RM-66GE].

Crain, Marion. "Building Solidarity through Expansion of NLRA Coverage: A Blueprint for Worker Empowerment." *Minneapolis Law Review* 74, no. 1 (1990): 953–1021.

Craver, Charles. "Privacy Issues Affecting Employers, Employees, and Labor Organizations." *Louisiana Law Review* 66, no. 4 (2006): 1057–77.

Crawford, Kate. *Atlas of AI: Power, Politics, and the Planetary Costs of Artificial Intelligence.* New Haven, CT: Yale University Press, 2021.

Crawford, Kate. "Time to Regulate AI That Interprets Human Emotions." *Nature*, Apr. 6, 2021. www.nature.com/articles/d41586-021-00868-5.

Crawford, Kate. "When Fitbit Is the Expert Witness." *The Atlantic*, Nov. 19, 2014. www.theatlantic.com/technology/archive/2014/11/when-fitbit-is-the-expert-witness/382936/ [https://perma.cc/3NXD-UWUT].

Crawford, Kate, and Jason Schultz. "Big Data and Due Process: Toward a Framework to Redress Predictive Privacy Harms." *Boston College Law Review* 55, no. 1 (2014): 93–128.

Crawford, Kate, and Vladan Joler. *Anatomy of an AI System.* SHARE Foundation and The AI Now Institute, 2018. https://anatomyof.ai/.

Crenshaw, Kimberlé. "Demarginalizing the Intersection of Race and Sex: A Black Feminist Critique of Antidiscrimination Doctrine, Feminist Theory and Antiracist Politics." *University of Chicago Legal Forum* 1989, no. 1 (1989): 139–67.

Crenshaw, Kimberlé. "Mapping the Margins: Intersectionality, Identity Politics, and Violence against Women of Color." *Stanford Law Review* 43, no. 6 (1991): 1241–99.

Crozier, Michael. *The Bureaucratic Phenomenon.* London: Tavistock, 1964.

Cupcea, George. "Timekeeping in the Roman Army." *The Hour Glass*, July 7, 2018. www.thehourglass.com/cultural-perspectives/timekeeping-in-the-roman-army/.

Cyphers, Bennett, and Karen Gullo. "Inside the Invasive, Secretive 'Bossware' Tracking Workers." *Electronic Frontier Foundation: Deeplinks Blog*, June 30, 2020. www.eff.org/deeplinks/2020/06/inside-invasive-secretive-bossware-tracking-workers.

D'Ignazio, Catherine, and Lauren F. Klein. *Data Feminism.* Cambridge, MA: MIT Press, 2020.

Daliri-Ngametua, Rafaan. "Book Review: *Data Feminism.*" *CUNY Graduate Center: Theory, Research, and Action in Urban Education* 6, no. 1 (2021): 62–64. https://traue.commons.gc.cuny.edu/book-review-data-feminism/ (accessed June 8, 2021).

Dallas, Mary Elizabeth. "Smokers Cost Employers More than Nonsmokers." *WebMD*, June 4, 2013. www.webmd.com/smoking-cessation/news/20130604/smokers-cost-employers-thousands-more-than-nonsmokers.

Darling-Hammond, Linda. "Unequal Opportunity: Race and Education." *Brookings Review*, Mar. 1, 1998. www.brookings.edu/articles/unequal-opportunity-race-and-education/.

Dassbach, Carl H. A. "The Origins of Fordism: The Introduction of Mass Production and the Five-Dollar Wage." *Critical Sociology* 18, no. 1 (1991): 77–90.

Dastin, Jeffrey. "Amazon Scraps Secret AI Recruiting Tool that Showed Bias against Women." *Reuters*, October 19, 2018. www.reuters.com/article/us-amazon-com-jobs-automation-insight/amazon-scraps-secret-ai-recruiting-tool-that-showed-bias-against-women-idUSKCN1MK08G.

Datta, Amit, Michael C. Tschantz, and Apunam Datta. "Automated Experiments on Ad Privacy Setting." *Proceedings on Privacy Enhancing Technologies* 2015, no. 1 (2015): 92–112.

Davies, Alun C. "The Industrial Revolution and Time Keeping." *Open University*, last updated Aug. 30, 2019. www.open.edu/openlearn/history-the-arts/history/history-science-technology-and-medicine/history-technology/the-industrial-revolution-and-time.

Davies, W. R. "Peace-Time Routine in the Roman Army." PhD thesis, Durham University, 1967. On file with the Durham University e-Theses database: http://etheses.dur.ac.uk/8075/.

Day, Matt, and Benhamin Romano. "Amazon Has Patented a System That Would Put Workers in a Cage, on Top of a Robot." *Seattle Times*, Sept. 7, 2018. www.seattletimes.com/business/amazon/amazon-has-patented-a-system-that-would-put-workers-in-a-cage-on-top-of-a-robot/.

Dembe, Allard E. "How Historical Factors Have Affected the Application of Workers Compensation Data to Public Health." *Journal of Public Health Policy* 31, no. 2 (2010): 227–43.

Dennis, Brady, and Juliet Ellperin. "How Scott Pruitt Turned the EPA into One of Trump's Most Powerful Tools." *Washington Post*, Dec. 31, 2017. www.washingtonpost.com/national/health-science/under-scott-pruitt-a-year-of-tumult-and-transformation-at-epa/2017/12/26/f93d1262-e017-11e7-8679-a9728984779c_story.html.

DePauw, Rhett. "A Brief History of Time Management." *Exaktime*, Oct. 11, 2017. www.exaktime.com/blog/brief-history-time-management/.

Dery, George M., III. "Trading Privacy for Promotion? Fourth Amendment Implications of Employers Using Wearable Sensors to Assess Worker Performance." *Northwestern Law Journal of Law and Social Policy* 16, no. 1 (2020): 17–46.

Desai, Deven R., and Joshua A. Kroll. "Trust but Verify: A Guide to Algorithms and the Law." *Harvard Journal of Law & Technology* 31, no. 1 (2017): 1–64.

DeSaulles, Martin, and David Horner. "The Portable Panopticon: Morality and Mobile Technologies." *Journal of Information, Communication, and Ethics in Society* 9, no. 3 (2011): 206–16.

Desmond, Matthew. "In Order to Understand the Brutality of American Capitalism, You Have to Start on the Plantation." *New York Times Magazine*, Aug. 14, 2019. www.nytimes.com/interactive/2019/08/14/magazine/slavery-capitalism.html.

Deutsch, Gary M. *Risk Assessments for Financial Institutions*. New York: LexisNexis, 2017.

DeVault, Ileen A., Maria Figueroa, Fred B. Kotler, Michael Maffie, and John Wu. *On-Demand Platform Workers in New York State: The Challenges for Public Policy*. ILR Worker Institute, 2019. www.ilr.cornell.edu/sites/default/files/OnDemandReport.Reduced.pdf.

Dever, Taylor. "The Rise of Telecommuting: Embracing the Virtual Workforce." Jacobson White Paper, 2019. https://jacobsononline.com/uploadfiles/openuptowahemployees.pdf.

DHCS. "Health Insurance Portability & Accountability Act." Last modified June 13, 2019. www.dhcs.ca.gov/formsandpubs/laws/hipaa/Pages/1.00WhatisHIPAA.aspx (accessed May 25, 2021).

Dickson, Peter R., and Philippa K. Wells. "The Dubious Origins of the Sherman Antitrust Act: The Mouse That Roared." *Journal of Public Policy and Marketing* 20, no. 1 (2001): 3–14.

Dinerstein, Robert D. "The Americans with Disabilities Act of 1990: Progeny of the Civil Rights Act of 1964." *Human Rights Magazine* 31, no. 3 (July 1, 2004). www.americanbar.org/groups/crsj/publications/human_rights_magazine_home/human_rights_vol31_2004/summer2004/irr_hr_summer04_disable/.

Dixon, Lauren. "The Pros and Cons of Hiring for 'Cultural Fit.'" *Chief Learning Office: Talent Economy*, Dec. 6, 2017. www.chieflearningofficer.com/2017/12/06/pros-cons-hiring-cultural-fit.

Doleac, Jennifer L. "A Review of Thomas Sowell's *Discrimination and Disparities*." *Journal of Economic Literature* 59, no. 2 (2021): 574–89.

Dolovich, Sharon. "State Punishment and Private Prisons." *Duke Law Journal* 55, no. 3 (2005): 437–546.

Dubois, W. E. B. *Black Reconstruction in America: Toward a History of the Part Which Black Folk Played in the Attempt to Reconstruct Democracy in America, 1860–1880*. 1935. Reprint, London: Routledge, 2017.

Dunn, Jeff. "Trump Just Killed Obama's Internet-Privacy Rules: Here's What That Means for You." *Business Insider*, Apr. 4, 2017. www.businessinsider.com/trump-fcc-privacy-rules-repeal-explained-2017-4.

Durán, Juan I., Rainer Reisenzein, and José-Miguel Fernández-Dols. "Coherence between Emotions and Facial Expressions: A Research Synthesis." In *The Science of Facial*

Expression, edited by James A. Russell and José-Miguel Fernández-Dols, 107–29. New York: Oxford University Press, 2017.

Duru, Chika. "Out for Blood: Employment Discrimination, Sickle Cell Trait, and the NFL." *Hastings Law and Poverty Law Journal* 9, no. 2 (2012): 265–90.

Dutton, Jane E., and Jane Webster. "Patterns of Interest around Issues." *Academy of Management Journal* 31, no. 3 (1988): 663–75.

Dwork, Cynthia, Moritz Hardt, Toniann Pitassi, Omer Reingold, and Rich Zemel. "Fairness Through Awareness." In *ITCS' 12: Proceedings of the 3rd Innovations in Theoretical Computer Science Conference*, pp. 214–26. New York: Association for Computing Machinery, 2012.

"Economic Boom." In *The USA: A Nation of Contrasts 1910–1929*. BBC: Bitesize, www.bbc .co.uk/bitesize/guides/zw9wb82/revision/2 (last visited Jan. 5, 2021).

Edwards, Lilian, and Michael Veale. "Slave to the Algorithm? Why a 'Right to an Explanation' Is Probably Not the Remedy You Are Looking For." *Duke Law and Technology Review* 16, no. 1 (2017): 18–84.

Edwards, Richard. *Contested Terrain: The Transformation of the Workplace in the Twentieth Century*. New York: Basic Books, 1979.

EEOC. "The Americans with Disabilities Act and the Use of Software Algorithms, and Artificial Intelligence to Assess Job Applicants and Employees." EEOC, Guidance, May 12, 2022. www.eeoc.gov/laws/guidance/americans-disabilities-act-and-use-software-algorithms-and-artificial-intelligence.

EEOC. "Artificial Intelligence and Algorithmic Fairness Initiative." www.eeoc.gov/artificial-intelligence-and-algorithmic-fairness-initiative (accessed May 18, 2022).

EEOC. "Best Buy and EEOC Reach Agreement to Resolve Discrimination Charge." *U.S. EEOC Newsroom*, July 6, 2018. www.eeoc.gov/newsroom/best-buy-and-eeoc-reach-agreement-resolve-discrimination-charge.

EEOC. "CVS Caremark Corporation and EEOC Reach Agreement to Resolve Discrimination Charge." *U.S. EEOC Newsroom*, July 6, 2018. www.eeoc.gov/newsroom/cvs-caremark-corporation-and-eeoc-reach-agreement-resolve-discrimination-charge.

EEOC. "EEOC Sues Party City for Disability Discrimination." *U.S. EEOC Newsroom*, Sept. 19, 2018. www.eeoc.gov/newsroom/eeoc-sues-party-city-disability-discrimination.

EEOC. "EEOC'S Final Rule on Employer Wellness Programs and Title I of the Americans with Disabilities Act." U.S. Equal Employment Opportunity Commission: Regulations. www.eeoc.gov/regulations/eeocs-final-rule-employer-wellness-programs-and-title-i-americans-disabilities-act (accessed May 25, 2021).

EEOC. "Enforcement Guidance on Disability-Related Inquiries and Medical Examinations of Employees under the ADA," *U.S. EEOC Newsroom*," July 26, 2000. www.eeoc.gov/laws/guidance/enforcement-guidance-disability-related-inquiries-and-medical-examina tions-employees.

EEOC. "Enforcement Guidance on Disability-Related Inquiries and Medical Examinations of Employees under the Americans with Disabilities Act." U.S. Equal Employment Opportunity Commission, Notice 915.002, 2000. www.eeoc.gov/policy/docs/guidance-inquiries.html [https://perma.cc/6H5R-QLJ5].

EEOC. "Enforcement Guidances and Related Documents." U.S. Equal Employment Opportunity Commission, www.eeoc.gov/enforcement-guidances-and-related-documents (last visited May 10, 2021).

EEOC. "Fact Sheet: Disability Discrimination." U.S. Equal Employment Opportunity Commission, Jan. 15, 1997. www.eeoc.gov/laws/guidance/fact-sheet-disability-discrimination.

EEOC. "Fact Sheet: Immigrants' Employment Rights Under Federal Anti-Discrimination Laws." *EEOC Guidance*, Apr. 27, 2010. www.eeoc.gov/laws/guidance/fact-sheet-immigrants-employment-rights-under-federal-anti-discrimination-laws.

EEOC. "Informal Discussion Letter: Title VII/ADA: Pre-Employment Inquiry," Aug. 5, 2002. www.eeoc.gov/foia/eeoc-informal-discussion-letter-78.

EEOC. "Notice Concerning the Americans with Disabilities Act (ADA) Amendments Act of 2008." EEOC Notice, Mar. 25, 2011. www.eeoc.gov/statutes/notice-concerning-americans-disabilities-act-ada-amendments-act-2008.

EEOC. "Overview." www.eeoc.gov/overview (accessed May 10, 2021).

EEOC. "Party City to Pay $155,000 to Settle EEOC Disability Discrimination Lawsuit." *U.S. EEOC Newsroom*, Apr. 22, 2019. www.eeoc.gov/newsroom/party-city-pay-155000-settle-eeoc-disability-discrimination-lawsuit.

EEOC. "Questions and Answers on the Final Rule Implementing the ADA Amendments Act of 2008." U.S. Equal Employment Opportunity Commission: Laws/Guidance. www.eeoc.gov/laws/regulations/ada_qa_final_rule.cfm [https://perma.cc/K7KN-CZZC] (accessed Nov. 8, 2018).

EEOC. "Questions and Answers: Enforcement Guidance on Disability Related Inquiries and Medical Examinations under the Americans with Disabilities Act." U.S. Equal Employment Opportunity Commission, July 27, 2000. www.eeoc.gov/laws/guidance/questions-and-answers-enforcement-guidance-disability-related-inquiries-and-medical.

EEOC. "Randstad US Sued by EEOC for Disability Discrimination." *EEOC Newsroom*, May 13, 2011. www.eeoc.gov/newsroom/randstad-us-sued-eeoc-disability-discrimination.

EEOC. "Randstad US, LP to Pay 60,000 to Settle EEOC Disability Bias Suit." *EEOC Newsroom*, May 10, 212. www.eeoc.gov/newsroom/randstad-us-lp-pay-60000-settle-eeoc-disability-bias-suit.

EEOC. "Subway Franchisee Sued by EEOC for Disability Discrimination." *EEOC Newsroom*, [Press Release], Sept. 23, 2020. www.eeoc.gov/newsroom/subway-franchisee-sued-eeoc-disability-discrimination.

EEOC. "Subway Franchisee to Pay $28,700 to Settle EEOC Disability Discrimination Suit." *EEOC Newsroom*, [Press Release], Mar. 26, 2021. www.eeoc.gov/newsroom/subway-franchisee-pay-28700-settle-eeoc-disability-discrimination-suit.

EEOC. "Systemic Enforcement at the EEOC." www.eeoc.gov/systemic-enforcement-eeoc (accessed May 10, 2021).

EEOC. "Target Corporation to Pay $2.8 Million to Resolve EEOC Discrimination Finding." *U.S. EEOC Newsroom*, Aug. 24, 2015. www.eeoc.gov/newsroom/target-corporation-pay-28-million-resolve-eeoc-discrimination-finding.

EEOC. "U.S. EEOC and U.S. Department of Justice Warn against Disability Discrimination." *EEOC Newsroom*, Press Release, May 12, 2022, www.eeoc.gov/newsroom/us-eeoc-and-us-department-justice-warn-against-disability-discrimination.

EEOC. "What You Should Know about COVID-19 and the ADA, the Rehabilitation Act, and Other EEO Laws." U.S. Equal Employment Opportunity Commission, Sept. 8, 2020. www.eeoc.gov/wysk/what-you-should-know-about-covid-19-and-ada-rehabilitation-act-and-other-eeo-laws.

Efron, Louis, "How A.I. Is About to Disrupt Corporate Recruiting." *Forbes*, July 12, 2016. www.forbes.com/sites/louisefron/2016/07/12/how-a-i-is-about-to-disrupt-corporate-recruiting/#75ae172d3ba2.

Eisenberg, Theodore. "Litigation Models and Trial Outcomes in Civil Rights and Prisoner Cases." *Georgetown Law Journal* 77, no. 4 (1989): 1567–1602.

Ella, V. John. "Employee Monitoring and Workplace Privacy Law." Paper presented at the 2016 National Symposium on Technology in Labor and Employment Law. American Bar Association: Labor and Employment Law Section. www.americanbar.org/content/dam/aba/events/labor_law/2016/04/tech/papers/monitoring_ella.authcheckdam.pdf (accessed Nov. 24, 2020).

Elmes, Michael B., et. al. "Panoptic Empowerment and Reflective Conformity in Enterprise Systems-Enabled Organizations." *Information and Organization* 15, no. 1 (2005): 1–37.

Elvira, Marta, and Robert Town. "The Effects of Race and Worker Productivity." *Industrial Relations: A Journal of Economy and Society* 40, no. 4 (2002): 571–90.

Engler, Alex. "For Some Employment Algorithms, Disability Discrimination by Default." *Brookings Institute blog*, Oct. 31, 2019. www.brookings.edu/blog/techtank/2019/10/31/for-some-employment-algorithms-disability-discrimination-by-default/.

Engstrom, David Freeman. "Corralling Capture." *Harvard Journal of Law & Public Policy* 36, no. 1 (2013): 31–39.

Enlyft. "Companies Using HireVue." https://enlyft.com/tech/products/hirevue#:~:text=We%20have%20data%20on%20733,and%20%3E1000M%20dollars%20in%20revenue (accessed Apr. 22, 2021).

Equal Exchange. "About: Our Model." https://equalexchange.coop/about (accessed May 13, 2021).

Equal Exchange. "Worker-Owned." https://equalexchange.coop/worker-owned (accessed May 13, 2021).

Estes, Steve. "I Am a Man!" Race, Masculinity, and the 1968 Memphis Sanitation Strike." *Labor History* 41, no. 2 (2000): 153–70.

Estlund, Cynthia L. "The Ossification of American Labor Law." *Columbia Law Review* 102, no. 6 (2002): 1527–1612.

Estlund, Cynthia. "Three Big Ideas for a Future of Less Work and a Three-Dimensional Alternative." *Law and Contemporary Problems* 82, no. 3 (2019): 1–43.

Estlund, Cynthia. "What Should We Do after Work? Automation and Employment Law." *Yale Law Journal* 128, no. 2 (2018): 254–326.

Estlund, Cynthia L. *Working Together: How Workplace Bonds Strengthen a Diverse Democracy*. New York: Oxford University Press, 2003.

Estlund, Cynthia. "Workplace Autocracy in an Era of Fissuring." *LPE Project*, Apr. 3, 2019. https://lpeproject.org/blog/workplace-autocracy-in-an-era-of-fissuring/.

Ettachfini, Leila. "Somehow, Fiverr Ads Have Gotten Even More Tone-Deaf." *Vice*, July 24, 2019. www.vice.com/en_us/article/evyy8k/fiverr-ad-white-man-black-woman.

Eubanks, Virginia. *Automating Inequality: How High-Tech Tools Profile, Police, and Punish the Poor*. New York: St. Martin's Press, 2018.

Facebook Business. "About Ad Targeting: Creating a New Audience." Facebook Business: Advertiser Help (2018). www.facebook.com/business/help/717368264947302?helpref=page_content.

Facebook Business. "About Lookalike Audiences." Facebook Business: Advertiser Help. www.facebook.com/business/help/164749007013531 (last visited Aug. 10, 2019).

Facebook Business. "U.S. Hispanic Affinity on Facebook." Facebook Business: Ad Targeting, 2018. www.facebook.com/business/a/us-hispanic-affinity-audience.

Fairweather, N. Ben. "Surveillance in Employment: The Case of Teleworking." *Journal of Business Ethics* 22, no. 1 (1999): 39–49.

Falconer, Rebecca. "Qatar's Foreign Domestic Workers Subjected to Slave-Like Conditions." *The Guardian*, Feb. 26, 2014. www.theguardian.com/global-development/2014/feb/26/qatar-foreign-workers-slave-conditions.

Farr, Christina. "Apple Is Offering Free Genetic Tests to All Its Silicon Valley Employees." *CNBC*, Dec. 13, 2019. www.cnbc.com/2019/12/13/apple-teams-with-color-to-offer-free-dna-tests-to-employees.html (accessed May 26, 2021).

Farr, Christina. "Fitbit Has a New Health Tracker, But You Can Only Get It through Your Employer or Insurer." *CNBC: High Tech Matters*, Feb. 8, 2019. www.cnbc.com/2019/02/08/fitbit-releases-insprire-for-employers.html.

Fast, Scott L. "Breach of Employee Confidentiality: Moving toward a Common-Law Tort Remedy." *University of Pennsylvania Law Review* 142, no. 1 (1993): 431–70.

Fayol, Henri. *General and Industrial Management*. London: Pitman & Sons, 1949.

Federal Trade Commission (FTC). "The Antitrust Laws." In *Guide to Antitrust Laws*. www.ftc.gov/tips-advice/competition-guidance/guide-antitrust-laws/antitrust-laws (accessed Jan. 4, 2021).

FedEx. "Q&A with Mike Glen, FedEx Services." *Access*, Nov. 2013. http://access.van.fedex.com/qa-mike-glenn-fedex-services/ [http://perma.cc/7CXE-PZJ6].

Feinberg, Ashely. "This Wearable Abacus Is Basically the World's Oldest Smart Ring." *Gizmodo*, Mar. 17, 2014. www.gizmodo.com.au/2014/03/this-wearable-abacus-is-basically-the-worlds-oldest-smart-ring/.

Feldman, Michael, Sorelle Friedler, John Moeller, Carlos Scheidegger, and Suresh Venkatasubramanian. "Certifying and Removing Disparate Impact." *2015 ACM SIGKDD Conference on Knowledge Discovery and Data Mining* no. 3 (2015): 1–28.

Feloni, Richard. "Consumer-Goods Giant Unilever Has Been Hiring Employees Using Brain Games and Artificial Intelligence – and It's a Huge Success." *Business Insider*, June 28, 2017. www.businessinsider.com/unilever-artificial-intelligence-hiring-process-2017-6.

Feloni, Richard. "I Tried the Software That Uses AI to Scan Applicants for Companies Like Goldman Sachs and Unilever Before Meeting Them – and It's Not as Creepy as It Sounds." *Business Insider*, Aug. 23, 2017. www.businessinsider.com/hirevue-ai-powered-job-interview-platform-2017-8.

Fink, Jennifer, Barbara Zabawa, and Sara Chopp. "Employee Perceptions of Wellness Programs and Incentives." *American Journal of Health Promotion* 34, no. 3 (2020): 257–60.

First Advantage. Home Page. Feb. 2020. www.fadv.com [https://perma.cc/S3YC-ADFW].

Firth-Godbehere, Rich. "Silicon Valley Thinks Everyone Feels the Same Six Emotions." *NEXT*, Sept. 5, 2018. https://howwegettonext.com/silicon-valley-thinks-everyone-feels-the-same-six-emotions-38354a0ef3d7.

Fischer, Judith D. "Public Policy and the Tyranny of the Bottom Line in the Termination of Older Workers." *South Carolina Law Review* 53, no. 2 (2002): 211–47.

Fisher, Phllips. "Collection of Biometric Data Raises Privacy Concerns for Employees and Compliance Issues for Employers." *Fisher Phillips: Insights*, Mar. 15, 2018. www.fisherphillips.com/Employment-Privacy-Blog/collection-of-biometric-data-raises-privacy-concerns.

Fisk, Catherine, and Adam Barry. "Contingent Loyalty and Restricted Exit: Commentary on the Restatement of Employment Law." *Employee Rights and Employment Policy Journal* 16, no 2 (2012): 413–64.

Fitbit. "Our Technology" 2017. www.fitbit.com/technology [https://perma.cc/87R3-EMG9] (accessed Nov. 7, 2018).

Fitbit. "SmartTrack." https://perma.cc/8GYM-46EW (accessed Nov. 7, 2018).

Fonseca, Esperanza. "Worker Surveillance Is on the Rise, and Has Its Roots in Centuries of Racism." *Truthout*, June 8, 2020. https://truthout.org/articles/worker-surveillance-is-on-the-rise-and-has-its-roots-in-centuries-of-racism/.

Ford, Richard Thompson. "Bias in the Air: Rethinking Employment Discrimination Law." *Stanford Law Review* 66, no. 6 (2014): 1381–1421.

Ford, Richard Thompson. "Rethinking Rights after the Second Reconstruction." *Yale Law Journal* 123, no. 8 (2014): 2574–3152.

Foreman, Michael L. "*Gross v. FBL Financial Services* – Oh So Gross!" *University of Memphis Law Review* 40, no. 4 (2010): 681–704.

Fort, Timothy L., Anjanette H. Raymond, and Scott J. Shackelford. "The Angel on Your Shoulder: Prompting Employees to Do the Right Thing through the Use of Wearables." *Northwestern Journal of Technology and Intellectual Property* 14, no. 2 (2016): 139–70.

Foucault, Michael. *Discipline and Punish: The Birth of the Prison.* New York: Random House, 1977.

Foucault, Michael. "The Subject and Power." *Critical Inquiry* 8, no. 4 (1982): 777–95.

Freedman, Max. "Spying on Your Employees? Better Understand the Law First." *Business News Daily,* updated Dec. 23, 2020. www.businessnewsdaily.com/6685-employee-mon itoring-privacy.html.

Freeman, Joshua. "The History of Labor in the U.S." U.S. Dept. of State: FPC Briefing, June 17, 2020. https://2017-2021.state.gov/briefings-foreign-press-centers/the-history-of-labor-in-the-u-s/index.html.

Frey, Carl Benedikt, and Michael A. Osborne. "The Future of Employment: How Susceptible Are Jobs to Computerisation?" *Technological Forecasting and Social Change* 114(C) (2017): 254–80.

Friend, Celeste. "Social Contract Theory." *Internet Encyclopedia of Philosophy.* https://iep .utm.edu/soc-cont/ (accessed Nov. 10, 2020).

Fritz, Mary Beth Watson, Sridhar Narasimhan, and Hyeun-Suk Rhee. "Communication and Coordination in the Virtual Office." *Journal of Management Information Systems* 14, no. 4 (1998): 7–28.

Fruchterman, Jim, and Joan Mellea. "Expanding Employment Success for People with Disabilities." *Benetech,* Nov. 2018. https://benetech.org/about/resources/expanding-employment-success-for-people-with-disabilities-2/.

FTC. "Privacy Online: Fair Information Practices in the Electronic Marketplace." Report to Congress, May 2000. www.ftc.gov/sites/default/files/documents/reports/privacy-online-fair-information-practices-electronic-marketplace-federal-trade-commission-report/ privacy2000.pdf.

Fukuyama, Francis. "The Calvinist Manifesto." *New York Times,* Mar. 13, 2005. www.nytimes .com/2005/03/13/books/review/the-calvinist-manifesto.html.

Fung, Brian. "The House Just Voted to Wipe Away the FCC's Landmark Internet Privacy Protections." *Washington Post,* Mar. 28, 2017. www.washingtonpost.com/news/the-switch/ wp/2017/03/28/the-house-just-voted-to-wipe-out-the-fccs-landmark-internet-privacy-protections/.

Gadinis, Stavros. "The SEC and the Financial Industry: Evidence from Enforcement against Broker Dealers." *Business Lawyer* 67, no. 3 (2012): 679–728.

Galor, Oded, and David N. Weil. "Population, Technology, and Growth: From Malthusian Stagnation to the Demographic Transition and Beyond." *American Economic Review* 90, no. 4 (2000): 806–28.

Galton, Sir Francis. Inquiries into Human Faculty and Its Development. London: MacMillan, 1883.

Gammon, Amanda, and Deborah W. Neklason. "Confidentiality and the Risk of Genetic Discrimination: What Surgeons Need to Know." *The Role of Genetic Testing in Surgical Oncology, special issue of Surgical Oncology Clinics of North America* 24, no. 4 (2015): 667–81.

Gannon, Megan. "Race Is a Social Construct, Scientists Argue." *Scientific American,* Feb. 5, 2016. www.scientificamerican.com/article/race-is-a-social-construct-scientists-argue/.

Garcia-Navarro, Lulu. "Caroline Criado-Perez on Data Bias And 'Invisible Women.'" *NPR,* Mar. 17, 2019. www.npr.org/2019/03/17/704209639/caroline-criado-perez-on-data-bias-and-invisible-women.

Gartner. "Gartner HR Survey Shows 86% of Organizations Are Conducting Virtual Interviews to Hire Candidates during Coronavirus Pandemic." Gartner Newsroom, Press Release, Apr. 30, 2020. www.gartner.com/en/newsroom/press-releases/2020-04-30-gartner-hr-survey-shows-86—of-organizations-are-cond.

Geffe, Jeremiah K. "License to Sniff: The Need to Regulate Privately Owned Drug-Sniffing Dogs." *Journal of Gender Race & Justice* 19, no. 1 (2016): 167–94.

Gelles, David, and David Yaffe Bellany. "Shareholder Value Is No Longer Everything, Top C.E.O.s Say." *New York Times*, Apr. 19, 2019. www.nytimes.com/2019/08/19/business/business-roundtable-ceos-corporations.html.

Genetics Home Reference. "What Is Genetic Discrimination?" *Medline Plus*, last updated July 28, 2021. https://ghr.nlm.nih.gov/primer/testing/discrimination (accessed May 25, 2021).

Genome Medical. "Notice of Privacy Practices." www.genomemedical.com/privacy/?_ga=2.197013676.1294487464.1585603657-1350403954.1585336333 (accessed May 26, 2021).

Gershgorn, Dave. "Companies Are on the Hook if Their Hiring Algorithms Are Biased." *Quartz*, Oct. 22, 2018. https://qz.com/1427621/companies-are-on-the-hook-if-their-hiring-algorithms-are-biased/.

Gerwirtz, David. "Volume, Velocity, and Variety: Understanding the Three V's of Big Data." *ZDNet*, Mar. 21, 2018. www.zdnet.com/article/volume-velocity-and-variety-understanding-the-three-vs-of-big-data.

Ghaffary, Shirin, and Jason Del Rey. "Amazon Employees Fear HR Is Targeting Minority and Activism Groups in Email Monitoring Program." *Vox*, Sept. 24, 2020. www.vox.com/recode/2020/9/24/21455196/amazon-employees-listservs-minorities-underrepresented-groups-worker-dissent-unionization.

Giang, Vivian. "The Potential Hidden Bias in Automated Hiring Systems." *Fast Company*, May 8, 2018. www.fastcompany.com/40566971/the-potential-hidden-bias-in-automated-hiring-systems.

Giang, Vivian. "This Is the Latest Way Employers Mask Age Bias, Lawyers Say." *Fortune*, May 4, 2015. http://fortune.com/2015/05/04/digital-native-employers-bias/.

Gibby, Robert E., and Michael J. Zickar. "A History of the Early Days of Personality Testing in American Industry: An Obsession with Adjustment." *History of Psychology* 11, no. 3 (2008): 164–84. www.researchgate.net/publication/23562101_A_history_of_the_early_days_of_personality_testing_in_American_industry_An_obsession_with_adjustment.

Gilman, Greg. "Bill Maher Rips 'Shallow' American Culture for Allowing 'Ageism' to Impact Politics." *The Wrap*, Nov. 9, 2014. https://perma.cc/U4M3-YHC6.

Gilman, Michele E. "The Class Differential in Privacy Law." *Brooklyn Law Review* 77, no. 4 (2012): 1389–1445.

Goering, Sara. "Eugenics." In *Stanford Encyclopedia of Philosophy* (Fall 2014). https://plato.stanford.edu/cgi-bin/encyclopedia/archinfo.cgi?entry=eugenics.

Goethe, Taylor Synclair. "Bigotry Encoded: Racial Bias in Technology." *Reporter*, Mar. 2, 2019. https://reporter.rit.edu/tech/bigotry-encoded-racial-bias-technology.

Gold, Michael Evan. "Disparate Impact under the Age Discrimination in Employment Act of 1967." *Berkeley Journal of Employment and Labor Law* 25, no. 1 (2004): 186.

Goldberg, Amir, and Sameer B. Srivastava. "Should You Hire for Cultural Fit or Adaptability?" *re:Work*, Dec. 6, 2016. https://rework.withgooogle.com/glob/hire-for-cultural-fit-or-adaptability/.

Goldberg, Amir, V. Govind Manian, Sameer B. Srivastava, William Monroe, and Christopher Potts. "Fitting in or Standing out? The Tradeoffs of Structural and Cultural Embeddedness." *American Sociological Review* 81, no. 6 (2016): 1190–222.

Golden, Timothy D., and Sumita Raghuram. "Teleworker Knowledge Sharing and the Role of Altered Relational and Technological Interactions." *Organizational Behavior* 31, no. 8 (2010): 1061–85.

Goldhill, Olivia. "Centuries before Myers-Briggs, Workplace Personalities Were Assessed Using Skull Measurements." *Quartz at Work*, Dec. 29, 2017. https://qz.com/work/1168283/centuries-before-myers-briggs-workplace-personalities-were-assessed-using-phrenology/.

Gosselin, Peter, and Ariana Tobin. "Cutting 'Old Heads' at IBM." *ProPublica*, Mar. 22, 2018. https://features.propublica.org/ibm/ibm-age-discrimination-american-workers/.

Graham, Mark. "The Rise of the Planetary Labour Market: What It Means and What It Means for the Future of Work." *New Statemen: Tech*, Jan. 29, 2018. https://tech.newstatesman.com/guest-opinion/planetary-labour-market.

Graham, Mark, and Mohammad A. Anwar. "The Global Gig Economy: Towards Planetary Labour Market?" *First Monday* 24, no. 4 (2019): 213–34.

Gray, Mary L., and Siddharth Suri. *Ghost Work: How to Stop Silicon Valley from Building a New Global Underclass*. Boston: Houghton Mifflin Harcourt, 2019.

Green, Andy. "A Practical Software Approach to Insider Threats." *Varonis: Inside Out Security Blog*, June 17, 2020. www.varonis.com/blog/a-practical-software-approach-to-insider-threats/.

Greenbaum, Dov. "Ethical, Legal and Social Concerns Relating to Exoskeletons." *SIGCAS Computers & Society* 45, no. 3 (2015): 234–39.

Greenbaum, Joan. *Windows on the Workplace: Technology, Jobs, and the Organization of Office Work*. 2nd ed. New York: Monthly Review Press, 2004.

Greene, Bob. "How Your Boss Can Keep You on a Leash." *CNN*, Feb. 2, 2014. https://edition.cnn.com/2014/02/02/opinion/greene-corporate-surveillance/index.html?no-st=1529052429 [https://perma.cc/8WM6-EJFE].

Greenfield, Kent. "The Unjustified Absence of Federal Fraud Protection in the Labor Market." *Yale Law Journal* 107, no. 3 (1997): 715–89.

Greenfield, Rebecca. "Study Finds Racial Discrimination by Airbnb Hosts." *Bloomberg News*, Nov. 10, 2015. www.bloomberg.com/news/articles/2015-12-10/study-finds-racial-discrimination-by-airbnb-hosts.

Griffin, Emma, *Liberty's Dawn: A People's History of the Industrial Revolution*. New Haven, CT: Yale University Press, 2014.

Griffin, Martyn, Mark Learmonth, and Carole Elliott. "Non-Domination, Contestation and Freedom: The Contribution of Philip Pettit to Learning and Democracy in Organisations." *Management Learning* 46, no. 3 (2015): 317–36. https://dro.dur.ac.uk/12043/1/12043.pdf.

Grimmelmann, James, and Daniel Westreich. "Incomprehensible Discrimination." *California Law Review Online* 7, no. 1 (2017): 164–78.

Grint, Keith, and Steve Woolgar. *The Machine at Work: Technology, Work, and Organization*. Cambridge: Polity Press, 1997.

Gross, James A. "Worker Rights as Human Rights: Wagner Act Values and Moral Choices." *Journal of Labor and Employment Law* 4, no. 3 (2002): 479–92.

Grossenbacher, Karla, and Selyn Hong. "Wearable Device Data in Employment Litigation." *Seyfarth Shaw: Employment Law Lookout*, Sept. 29, 2016. www.laborandemploymentlawcounsel.com/2016/09/wearable-device-data-in-employment-litigation/ [https://perma.cc/3D99-BXDV].

Guion, Robert M., and Richard F. Gottier. "Validity of Personality Measures in Personnel Selection." *Personnel Psychology* 18, no. 2 (1965): 135–64.

Guo, Anhong, et al. "Toward Fairness in AI for People with Disabilities: A Research Roadmap." *ACM SIGACCESS Accessibility and Computing* 125, no. 2 (October 2019). https://doi.org/10.1145/3386296.3386298.

Habermas, Jürgen. *Knowledge and Human Interests*. Translated by Jeremy J. Shapiro. Boston: Beacon Press, 1971.

Habermas, Jürgen. *Theory and Practice*. Translated by John Viertel. Boston: Beacon Press, 1971.

Hacker, Jacob S. *The Great Risk Shift: The New Economic Insecurity and the Decline of the American Dream*. Oxford: Oxford University Press, 2006.

Hacker, Jacob S. "Restoring Retirement Security: The Market Crisis, the 'Great Risk Shift,' and the Challenge for Our Nation." *Elder Law Journal* 19, no. 1 (2011): 1–47.

Hackett, Robert. "Psst, Your Company Is Watching You Now." *Fortune*, Mar. 13, 2017. http://fortune.com/2017/03/13/company-employee-surveillance-laws-technology/.

Haggin, Patience. "As Wearables in Workplace Spread, So Do Legal Concerns." *Wall Street Journal*, Mar. 13, 2016. www.wsj.com/articles/as-wearables-in-workplace-spread-so-do-legal-concerns-1457921550?ns=prod/accounts-wsj [https://perma.cc/3DNA-XRKG].

Hall, Margaux J. "A Fiduciary Theory of Health Entitlements." *Cardozo Law Review* 35, no. 5 (2014): 1729–80. http://cardozolawreview.com/wp-content/uploads/2018/08/HALL.35.5.pdf.

Han, Sam, and Scot Ganow. "Model Omnibus Privacy Statute." *University of Dayton Law Review* 35, no. 3 (2010): 345–77.

Hancock, Bryan, Monne Williams, James Manyika, Lareina Yee, and Jackie Wong. *Race in the Workplace: The Black Experience in the US Private Sector*. McKinsey & Co., 2019.

Handy, Susan L., and Patricia L. Mokhtarian. "Planning for Telecommuting: Measurement and Policy Issues." *Journal of the American Planning Society* 61, no. 1 (1995): 99–111.

Hannon, Elliot. "NFL Halts 'Race-Norming' to Calculate Brain Injury Compensation for Former Players." *Slate*, June 3, 2021. https://slate.com/news-and-politics/2021/06/nfl-race-norming-brain-injury-compensation-black-players.html.

Hansen, Randall, and Desmond King. "Eugenic Ideas, Political Interests, and Policy Variance: Immigration and Sterilization Policy in Britain and the U.S." *World Politics* 53, no. 2 (2001): 237–64.

Harbert, Tam. "Watching the Workers." *SHRM*, Mar. 16, 2019. www.shrm.org/hr-today/news/all-things-work/pages/watching-the-workers.aspx.

Harper, Michael. "Reforming the Age Discrimination in Employment Act: Proposals and Prospects." *Employee Rights and Employment Policy Journal* 16, no. 1 (2012): 13–49.

Harris, Mary. "The Same Warped, Racist Logic Used by the NFL Is Ubiquitous in Medicine." *Slate*, June 7, 2021. https://slate.com/technology/2021/06/race-norming-nfl-medicine-racism-discrimination.html.

Hart, Melissa. "Procedural Extremism: The Supreme Court's 2008–2009 Labor and Employment Cases." *Employee Rights and Employment Policy Journal* 13, no. 1 (2009): 253–84.

Harwell, Drew. "A Face-Scanning Algorithm Increasingly Decides Whether You Deserve the Job." *Washington Post*, Nov. 6, 2019. www.washingtonpost.com/technology/2019/10/22/ai-hiring-face-scanning-algorithm-increasingly-decides-whether-you-deserve-job/.

Hasday, Jill Elaine. "The Principle and the Practice of Women's 'Full Capacity': A Case Study of Sex-Segregated Public Education." *Michigan Law Review* 101, no. 3 (2002): 755–810.

Haskins, Kevin J. "Wearable Technology and Implications for the Americans with Disabilities Act, Genetic Information Nondiscrimination Act, and Health Privacy." *ABA Journal of Labor & Employment Law* 33, no. 1 (2017): 69–78.

Hearing, Gregory A., and Marquis W. Heilig. "Recent Developments in Employment Law and Litigation." *Tort Trial & Insurance Practice Law Journal* 45, no. 2 (2010): 319–28.

Hegewisch, Ariane, Chandra Childers, and Heidi Hartmann. *Women, Automation, and the Future of Work*. Institute for Women's Policy Research, Report, 2019.

Heilweil, Rebecca. "Illinois Says You Should Know if AI Is Grading Your Online Job Interviews." *Vox*, Jan. 1, 2020. www.vox.com/recode/2020/1/1/21043000/artificial-intelligence-job-applications-illinios-video-interivew-act.

Held, David. *Introduction to Critical Theory: Horkheimer to Habermas*. Berkeley: University of California Press, 1980.

Hern, Alex. "Shirking from Home? Staff Feel the Heat as Bosses Ramp Up Remote Surveillance." *The Guardian*, Sept. 27, 2020. www.theguardian.com/world/2020/sep/27/shirking-from-home-staff-feel-the-heat-as-bosses-ramp-up-remote-surveillance.

Herzberg, Frederick. *Work and the Nature of Man*. Cleveland, OH: World Publishing Co., 1966.

Hill, Stephen. *The Tragedy of Technology: Human Liberation versus Domination in the Late Twentieth Century*. London: Pluto Press, 1988.

HireRight. Home Page. www.hireright.com [https://perma.cc/6RC7-QJP8].

HireVue. "Hirevue Leads the Industry with Commitment to Transparent and Ethical Use of AI in Hiring." HireVue Press Release, Jan. 12, 2021. www.hirevue.com/press-release/hire vue-leads-the-industry-with-commitment-to-transparent-and-ethical-use-of-ai-in-hiring.

HireVue. "HireVue Privacy Notice." www.hirevue.com/privacy#what-info-does-hirevue-col lect (last updated Jan. 20, 2021).

HireVue. "HireVue Ranked a Fastest Growing Company on Deloitte's 2018 Technology Fast 500." Press Release, Nov. 15, 2018. www.hirevue.com/press-release/deloitte-2018-technology-fast-500-hirevue-ranked-fastest-growing-company.

HireVue. "Our Science: Meet the IO Psychology Team." www.hirevue.com/our-science (accessed Apr. 22, 2021).

Hirsch, Jeffrey M. "Future Work." *University of Illinois Law Review* 2020, no. 3 (2020): 889–958.

History.com Editors. "The Homestead Strike." *The History Channel Online*, last updated Apr. 28, 2018. www.history.com/topics/homestead-strike.

Holdren, Nate. "Incentivizing Safety and Discrimination: Employment Risks under Workmen's Compensation in the Early Twentieth Century United States." *Enterprise and Society* 15, no. 1 (2014): 31–67.

Holmes, Natalie. "Wearable Technology within the Workplace." *Convene*. https://convene .com/catalyst/wearable-technology-within-the-workplace/ [https://perma.cc/W4LH-UA3S] (accessed Nov. 8, 2018).

Holtom, Brooks, and David Allen. "Better Ways to Predict Who's Going to Quit." *Harvard Business Review*, Aug. 16, 2019. https://hbr.org/2019/08/better-ways-to-predict-whos-going-to-quit.

Hood, Leroy, and Lee Rowen. "The Human Genome Project: Big Science Transforms Biology and Medicine." *Genome Medicine* 5, no. 9 (2013). www.ncbi.nlm.nih.gov/pmc/articles/PMC4066586/.

Hooker, John, and Tae Wan Kim. "Ethical Implications of the Fourth Industrial Revolution for Business and Society." In *Business and Society 360: Business Ethics*, edited by David M. Wasieleski and James Weber, 35–63 (Bingley, UK: Emerald Publishing Ltd., 2019). https://static1.squarespace.com/static/592ee286d482e908d35b8494/t/5bcf14ce8165f5 dee7250232/1540297934941/Ethical+Implications+of+the+4th+Industrial+Revolution+for +Business+and+Society2.pdf.

Horrigan, Timothy. "Some Answers to the Unicru Personality Test." Last updated Nov. 15, 2011. www.timothyhorrigan.com/documents/unicru-personality-test.answer-key.html#sthash .N7ryuDqp.vtj4c5Nf.dpbs.

Houser, Kristin. "An Amazon Patent Would Use Cages to Keep Employees 'Safe.'" *Futurism: The Byte*, Sept. 10, 2018. https://futurism.com/the-byte/amazons-cage-employees.

Hovenkamp, Herbert. "Labor Conspiracies in American Law, 1880–1930." *Texas Law Review* 66, no. 1 (1988): 919–65.

Hsieh, Nien-hê. "Justice at Work: Arguing for Property-Owning Democracy." *Journal of Social Philosophy* 40, no. 3 (2009): 397–411. www-users.york.ac.uk/~mpon500/pod/Hsieh.pdf.

Hsieh, Nien-hê. "Rawlsian Justice and Workplace Republicanism." *Social Theory and Practice* 31, no. 1 (2005): 115–42.

Hubstaff. "Time Reporting." https://hubstaff.com/time-report (accessed Oct. 2, 2020).

Hudson, Kathy L., and Karen Pollitz. "Undermining Genetic Privacy? Employee Wellness Programs and the Law." *New England Journal of Medicine* 377, no. 1 (2017): 1–3.

Hyundai Motor Company. "Hyundai Motor Leads Personal Mobility Revolution with Advanced Wearable Robots." Hyundai: News Release, Jan. 4, 2017. www.hyundai.com/worldwide/en/company/newsroom/hyundai-motor-leads-personal-mobility-revolution-with-advanced-wearable-robots-0000006597.

Institute of Internal Auditors. *Code of Ethics* (Jan. 2009). https://na.theiia.org/standards-guidance/Public%20Documents/IPPF_Code_of_Ethics_01-09.pdf.

Institute of Internal Auditors. *Core Principles for the Professional Practice of Internal Auditing.* https://na.theiia.org/standards-guidance/mandatory-guidance/Pages/Core-Principles-for-the-Professional-Practice-of-Internal-Auditing.aspx (accessed June 12, 2018).

Institute of Internal Auditors. *Standards for the Professional Practice of Internal Auditing* 23 (2016). https://na.theiia.org/standards-guidance/Public%20Documents/IPPF-Standards-2017.pdf.

Issacs, Jennifer. "Proving Title VII Discrimination in 2019." ABA. www.americanbar.org/groups/young_lawyers/projects/no-limits/proving-title-vii-discrimination-in-2019/ (accessed Mar. 12, 2021).

Isson, Jean Paul, and Jesse S. Harriot. *People Analytics in the Era of Big Data.* Hoboken, NJ: Wiley, 2016.

Ito, Joi. "Supposedly 'Fair' Algorithms Can Perpetuate Discrimination." *Wired*, Feb. 5, 2019. www.wired.com/story/ideas-joi-ito-insurance-algorithms/.

Jackson, Susan E., and Jane E. Dutton. "Discerning Threats and Opportunities." *Administrative Quarterly* 33, no. 3 (1988): 370–87.

Jackson, Thomas F. *From Civil Rights to Human Rights: Martin Luther King, Jr., and the Struggle for Economic Justice.* Philadelphia: University of Pennsylvania Press, 2009.

Jackson-Gibson, Adele. "The Racist and Problematic History of the Body Mass Index." *Good Housekeeping*, Feb. 23, 2021. www.goodhousekeeping.com/health/diet-nutrition/a35047103/bmi-racist-history/.

Jacobson, Louis. "Does the 8-Hour Day and the 40-Hour Week Come from Henry Ford, or Labor Unions?" *PolitiFact*, Sept. 9, 2015. www.politifact.com/truth-o-meter/statements/2015/sep/09/viral-image/does-8-hour-day-and-40-hour-come-henry-ford-or-lab/.

Jacoby, Sanford M. "Melting into Air? Downsizing, Job Stability, and the Future of Work." *Chicago-Kent Law Review* 76, no. 2 (2000): 1195–1234.

Jacoby, Sanford. "Risk and the Labor Market: Societal Past as Economic Prologue." In *Sourcebook of Labor Markets: Evolving Structures and Processes*, edited by Ivar Berg and Arne L. Kalleberg, 31–60. New York: Springer, 2001.

Jaffe, Ina. "Older Workers Find Age Discrimination Built Right into Some Job Websites." *NPR: All Things Considered*, Mar. 28, 2017. www.npr.org/2017/03/28/521771515/older-work ers-find-age-discrimination-built-right-into-some-job-sites.

Jayaweera, Neville, and Sarath Amunugama. *Rethinking Development Communication.* Singapore: Asian Mass Communication Research and Information Centre, 1987.

Jedreski, Matthew, Jeffrey S. Bosley, and K. C. Halm. "Illinois Becomes First State to Regulate Employers' Use of Artificial Intelligence to Evaluate Video Interviews." Davis Wright Tremaine LLP website, Sep. 3, 2019. www.dwt.com/blogs/artificial-intelligence-law-advisor/2019/09/illinois-becomes-first-state-to-regulate-employers.

Jefferson Health. "Jefferson to Offer Free Genetic Testing to Employees." *PR Newswire*, Nov. 14, 2018. www.prnewswire.com/news-releases/jefferson-to-offer-free-genetic-testing-to-employees-300750475.html (accessed May 26, 2021).

Jeske, Debora, and Alecia M. Santuzzi. "Monitoring What and How: Psychological Implications of Electronic Performance Monitoring." *New Technology, Work and Employment* 30, no. 1 (2015): 62–78.

JLL. "Wearable Tech: The New Tool for the Modern Construction Workforce." *Jones Lang LaSalle: Trends & Insights*, Apr. 24, 2017. www.us.jll.com/en/trends-and-insights/workplace/wearable-tech-the-new-tool-for-the-modern-construction-workforce.

JobTestPrep. "How It Works." jobtestprep.com/how-it-works (accessed Nov. 21, 2020).

Jobvite. "Jobvite Recruiter Nation Report 2016: The Annual Recruiting Survey." www.jobvite.com/wp-content/uploads/2016/09/RecruiterNation2016.pdf.

Johnston, Katie. "The Messy Link b Slave Owners and Modern Management." *Forbes*, Jan. 16, 2013. www.forbes.com/sites/hbsworkingknowledge/2013/01/16/the-messy-link-between-slave-owners-and-modern-management/?sh=4fad5033317f.

Jolly-Ryan, Jennifer. "Have a Job to Get a Job: Disparate Treatment and Disparate Impact of the 'Currently Employed' Requirement." *Michigan Journal of Race and Law* 18, no. 1 (2012): 189–212.

Jones, Lora. "I Monitor My Staff with Software That Takes Screenshots." *BBC News*, Sept. 29, 2020. www.bbc.com/news/business-54289152.

Kahn, Jeremy. "HireVue Drops Facial Monitoring Amid A.I. Algorithm Audit." *Fortune*, Jan. 19, 2021. https://fortune.com/2021/01/19/hirevue-drops-facial-monitoring-amid-a-i-algorithm-audit/.

Kaminski, Margot E. "Binary Governance: Lessons from the GDPR's Approach to Algorithmic Accountability." *Southern California Law Review* 92, no. 6 (2019): 1529–1616.

Kanigel, Robert. "Taylor-Made: How the World's First Efficiency Expert Refashioned Modern Life in His Own Image." *The Sciences* 37, no. 3 (May 1997): 18–23.

Kaplan, Robert M., and Dennis P. Saccuzzo. *Psychological Testing: Principles, Applications, and Issues*. 8th ed. Belmont, CA: Wadsworth Cengage, 2012.

Kaplinsky, Raphael. *Automation: The Technology and Society*. London: Addison-Wesley Longman Ltd., 1984.

Karlis, Nicole. "Time to Rethink How We Talk about Older People." *Salon*, Mar. 31, 2018. www.salon.com/2018/03/31/time-to-rethink-how-we-talk-about-the-elderly/.

Katyal, Sonia. "Private Accountability in the Age of Artificial Intelligence." *UCLA Law Review* 66, no. 1 (2019): 54–141.

Katz, Lawrence F., and Alan B. Krueger. "The Rise and Nature of Alternative Work Arrangements in the United States, 1995–2015." *ILR Review* 72, no. 2 (2019): 382–412.

Keefe, Patrick Radden. "The Family That Built an Empire of Pain." *New Yorker*, Oct. 30, 2017. www.newyorker.com/magazine/2017/10/30/the-family-that-built-an-empire-of-pain.

Kellogg, Katherine C., Melissa A. Valentine, and Angèle Christin. "Algorithms at Work: The New Contested Terrain of Control." *Academy of Management Annals* 14, no. 1 (2020): 366–410.

Kennedy, Gavin. "Of Pins and Things." Adam Smith Institute of Economics, May 28, 2012. www.adamsmith.org/blog/economics/of-pins-and-things.

Kessler, Laura T. "The Attachment Gap: Employment Discrimination Law, Women's Cultural Caregiving, and the Limits of Economic and Liberal Legal Theory." *University of Michigan Journal of Law Reform* 34, no. 3 (2001): 371–468.

Kim, Pauline. "Auditing Algorithms for Discrimination." *University of Pennsylvania Law Review Online* 166, no. 1 (2017): 189–203.

Kim, Pauline T. "Data-Driven Discrimination at Work." *William and Mary Law Review* 58, no. 3 (2017): 857–936.

Kim, Pauline T., and Erika Hanson. "People Analytics and the Regulation of Information under the Fair Credit Reporting Act." *St. Louis University Law Journal* 61, no. 1 (2016): 17–33.

King, Alan G., and Marko J. Mrkonich. "'Big Data' and the Risk of Employment Discrimination." *Oklahoma Law Review* 68, no. 3 (2016): 555–84.

King, Gilbert. "How the Ford Motor Company Won the Battle and Lost Ground." *Smithsonian Magazine*, Apr. 30, 2013. www.smithsonianmag.com/history/how-the-ford-motor-company-won-a-battle-and-lost-ground-45814533/.

Kingsley, Charles. *Health and Education*. New York: Macmillan, 1887.

Kluchin, Rebecca M. *Fit to Be Tied: Sterilization and Reproductive Rights in America, 1950–1980*. New Brunswick, NJ: Rutgers University Press, 2016.

Knight, Will. "Job Screening Service Halts Facial Analysis of Applicants." *Wired*, Jan. 12, 2021. www.wired.com/story/job-screening-service-halts-facial-analysis-applicants/.

Knouse, Laura E., et al. "Adult ADHD Symptoms and Five Factor Model Traits in a Clinical Sample: A Structural Equation Modeling Approach." *Journal of Nervous Mental Disease* 201, no. 10 (Oct. 2014): 848–54.

Koch, Marianne J., and Gregory Hundley. "The Effects of Unionism on Recruitment and Selection Methods." *Industrial Relations: A Journal of Economy and Society* 36, no. 3 (1997): 349–70.

Kok, Peter, Ton van der Wiele, Richard McKenna, and Alan Brown. "A Corporate Social Responsibility Audit within a Quality Management Framework." *Journal of Business Ethics* 31, no. 4 (2001): 285–97.

Kolata, Gina. "'Devious Defecator' Case Tests Genetics Law." *New York Times*, May 29, 2015. www.nytimes.com/2015/06/02/health/devious-defecator-case-tests-genetics-law.html.

Kritzler, Mareike, Martin Bächman, Anders Tenfält, and Florian Michahelles. "Wearable Technology as a Solution for Workplace Safety." *MUM' 15: Proceedings of the 14th Internatoinal Conference on Mobil and Ubiquitous Multimedia*, Nov. 2015, 213–17.

Kroll, Joshua A., et al. "Accountable Algorithms." *University of Pennsylvania Law Review* 165, no. 3 (2017): 633–705.

Kropp, Brian. "5 Changes HR Leaders Can Expect to Manage in 2019." *Gartner: Insights*, Jan. 24, 2019. www.gartner.com/smarterwithgartner/5-changes-hr-leaders-can-expect-to-manage-in-2019/.

Kropp, Brian. "The Future of Employee Monitoring." *Gartner: Insights*, May 3, 2019. www.gartner.com/smarterwithgartner/the-future-of-employee-monitoring/.

Krouse, Sarah. "The News Ways Your Boss Is Spying on You." *Wall Street Journal*, July 19, 2019. www.wsj.com/articles/the-new-ways-your-boss-is-spying-on-you-11563528604.

Kurland, Nancy B., and Terri D. Egan. "Telecommuting: Justice and Control in the Virtual Organization." *Organization Science* 10, no. 4 (1999): 500–513.

LaBoda, Olivia K. "Dueling Approaches to Dual Purpose Documents: The Reaches of the Work Product Doctrine after Textron." *Suffolk University Law Review* 44, no. 3 (2011): 727–68.

Lam, Bourree. "Obama's New Equal-Pay Rules." *The Atlantic*, Jan. 29, 2016. www.theatlantic.com/business/archive/2016/01/eeoc-pay-discrimination-obama/433926/.

Lang, Kevin, and Costas Cavounidis. "Discrimination and Worker Evaluation." NBER Working Paper 21612. National Bureau of Economic Research, 2015.

Larson, Ann. "My Disturbing Stint on a Corporate Wellness App." *Slate*, Apr. 26, 2021. https://slate.com/human-interest/2021/04/corporate-wellness-grocery-store-work-dangers.html (accessed May 25, 2021).

Lawrence III, Charles R.,. "The Id, the Ego, and Equal Protection: Reckoning with Unconscious Racism." *Stanford Law Review* 39, no. 2 (1987): 317–88.

Lazar, Orlando. "Work, Domination, and the False Hope of Universal Basic Income." *Res Publica* 27, no. 3 (2021): 427–46.

Leclercq-Vandelannoitte, Aurélie, et al. "Mobile Information Systems and Organizational Control: Beyond the Panopticon Metaphor?" *European Journal of Information Systems* 23, no. 5 (2014): 543–57.

Lee, Alex. "An AI to Stop Hiring Bias Could Be Bad News for Disabled People." *Wired*, Nov. 26, 2019. www.wired.co.uk/article/ai-hiring-bias-disabled-people.

Leonard, Thomas C. "Progressive Era Origins of the Regulatory State and the Economist as Expert." *History of Political Economy* 47, no. 5 (2015): 49–76.

Levenson, Alec, and Gillian Pillans. *Strategic Workforce Analytics*. Corporate Research Forum Report, Nov. 2017. https://cdn2.hubspot.net/hubfs/2950977/strategic-workforce-analytics-report.pdf?__hssc=172100604.1.1.

Levin-Waldman, Oren. "Taylorism, Efficiency, and the Minimum Wage: Implications for a High Road Economy." Global Institute for Sustainable Prosperity, Working Paper No. 105, Feb. 2015. www.global-isp.org/wp-content/uploads/WP-105.pdf.

Levine, Sheen S., et al. "Ethnic Diversity Deflates Price Bubble.," *PNAS* 11, no. 52 (2014): 18524–29.

Levy, Karen, and Solon Barocas. "Designing against Discrimination in Online Markets." *Berkeley Technology Law Journal* 32, no. 3 (2017): 1183–1238.

Levy, Karen, and Solon Barocas. "Refractive Surveillance: Monitoring Customers to Manage Workers." *International Journal of Communication* 12, no. 0 (2018): 1166–88.

Lewis, C. M. "Labor Has Opposed Taft-Hartley for Decades. Here's Why It's Time to Repeal It." *Strike Wave*, Apr. 3, 2019. www.thestrikewave.com/original-content/2019/4/3/labor-has-opposed-taft-hartley-for-decades-heres-why-its-time-to-repeal-it.

Lewis, David. *The Public Image of Henry Ford: An American Folk Hero and His Company*. Detroit: Wayne State University Press, 1976.

Lewis, Jackson. "Illinois Biometric Information Privacy Act FAQs (2021)." www.jacksonlewis.com/sites/default/files/docs/IllinoisBIPAFAQs.pdf.

Liberman, Matt. "Inside the Lack of Racial Diversity in Lacrosse." *The Daily Orange* [Syracuse University], Apr. 22, 2019. http://dailyorange.com/2019/04/inside-lack-racial-diversity-lacrosse/.

Library of Congress (LOC). "Taylorism and Economic Efficiency in the 1920s." In *Coolidge-Consumerism Collection*, Aug. 14, 1995. http://lcweb2.loc.gov:8081/ammem/amrlhtml/intaylor.html.

Lindblom, Lars. "The Structure of a Rawlsian Theory of Just Work." *Journal of Business Ethics* 101, no. 4 (2011): 577–99.

Lipton, Eric, and Danielle Ivory. "Under Trump, EPA Has Slowed Actions against Polluters, and Put Limits on Enforcement Officers." *New York Times*, Dec. 10, 2017. www.nytimes.com/2017/12/10/us/politics/pollution-epa-regulations.html.

"Lochner Era." Cornell Law School, Legal Information Institute www.law.cornell.edu/wex/lochner_era (accessed Jan. 4, 2020).

"*Lochner v. New York*." *Oyez*. www.oyez.org/cases/1900-1940/198us45 (accessed Jan. 4, 2021).

Loehr, Anne. "How to Predict Which of Your Employees Are about to Quit." *Fast Company*, Mar. 10, 2018. www.fastcompany.com/40538396/how-to-predict-which-of-your-employees-are-about-to-quit.

Lohr, Steven. "Big Data, Trying to Build Better Workers." *New York Times*, Apr. 20, 2013. www.nytimes.com/2013/04/21/technology/big-data-trying-to-build-better-workers.html.

Loizides, Georgios Paris. "Deconstructing Fordism: Legacies of the Ford Sociological Department." PhD diss., Western Michigan University, 2004.

Ludwig, Sarah. "Credit Scores in America Perpetuate Racial Injustice: Here's How." *The Guardian*, October 13, 2015. www.theguardian.com/commentisfree/2015/oct/13/your-credit-score-is-racist-heres-why.

Lunde, Tormod K. "Will the Internet Move Mountains? Possible Consequences of the Internet for Markets and Societies." *Built Environment* 24, no. 2/3 (1978–): 169–81.

Lung, Shirley. "Overwork and Overtime." *Indiana Law Review* 39, no. 1 (2005): 51–86.

Lupton, Deborah. "Self-Tracking Modes: Reflexive Self-Monitoring and Data Practices." Conference Paper, Aug. 27, 2014. https://papers.ssrn.com/sol3/papers.cfm?abstract_id=2483549.

Lyon, David. *Electronic Eye: The Rise of Surveillance Society*. Minneapolis: University of Minnesota Press, 1994.

Lyon, David. "An Electronic Panopticon? A Sociological Critique of Surveillance Society." *Sociological Review* 41, no. 4 (1993): 653–78.

Lyons, Rich. "Lose Those Cultural Fit Tests: Instead Screen New Hires for 'Enculturability.'" *Forbes*, June 7, 2017. www.forbes.com/sites/richlyons/2017/06/07/lose-those-cultural-fit-tests-instead-screen-new-hires-for-enculturability/#450b9e6b63a8.

MacCarthy, Mark. "Standards of Fairness for Disparate Impact Assessment of Big Data Algorithms." *Cumberland Law Review* 48, no. 1 (2018): 67–144.

Mae, John F. "Frederick W. Taylor: American Inventor and Engineer." *Encyclopedia Britannica*, www.britannica.com/biography/Frederick-W-Taylor (accessed Nov. 11, 2021).

Maltby, Lewis. "Electronic Monitoring in the Workplace: Common Law & Federal Statutory Protection." National Workrights Institute: Privacy. www.workrights.org/nwi_privacy_comp_ElecMonitoringCommonLaw.html.

Mann, Gideon, and Cathy O'Neal. "Hiring Algorithms Are Not Neutral." *Harvard Business Review*, Dec. 9, 2016. https://hbr.org/2016/12/hiring-algorithms-are-not-neutral.

Manokha, Ivan. "How Using Facial Analysis in Job Interviews Could Reinforce Inequality." *PBS News Hour: Making Sen$e*, Oct. 7, 2019. www.pbs.org/newshour/economy/making-sense/how-using-facial-recognition-in-job-interviews-could-reinforce-inequality.

Marglin, Stephen. "What Do Bosses Do? The Origins and Function of Hierarchy in Capitalist Production." *Review of Radical Political Economy* 6, no. 2 (1974): 60–112.

Marglin, Stephen "What Do Bosses Do? Pt. II." *Review of Radical Political Economy* 7, no. 1 (1975): 20–37.

Marmot, Michael, and Ruth Bell, Health Inequities in a Globalising World of Work Commission on Social Determinants of Health. *ICOH: Commission on Social Determinants of Health* (2009).

Marshall, Gordon. "Panopticon." A Dictionary of Sociology. Encyclopedia.com, Nov. 29, 2022, www.encyclopedia.com/literature-and-arts/art-and-architecture/architecture/panopticon.

Martin, Natasha T. "Immunity for Hire: How the Same-Actor Doctrine Sustains Discrimination in the Contemporary Workplace." *Connecticut Law Review* 40, no. 4 (2008): 1117–74.

Martin, Whitney. "The Problem with Using Personality Tests for Hiring." *Harvard Business Review*, Aug. 27, 2014. https://hbr.org/2014/08/the-problem-with-using-personality-tests-for-hiring.

Marwick, Alice E., and Danah Boyd. "I Tweet Honestly, I Tweet Passionately: Twitter Users, Context Collapse, and the Imagined Audience." *New Media & Society* 13, no. 1 (2011): 114–33.

Masi, Dale A. *The History of Employee Assistance Programs in the United States*. The Employee Assistance Research Foundation, 2020.

Matheny, Ken, and Marion Crain. "Disloyal Workers and 'Un-American' Labor Law." *North Carolina Law Review* 82, no. 5 (2004): 1705–57.

Mathiason, Garry, et al. *The Transformation of the Workplace Through Robotic Artificial Intelligence, and Automation*. Littler Report, Aug. 4, 2016. www.littler.com/publication-press/publication/transformation-workplace-through-robotics-artificial-intelligence-and.

Matsuda, Mari J. "Voices of America: Accent, Antidiscrimination Law, and a Jurisprudence for the Last Reconstruction." *Yale Law Journal* 100, no. 5 (1991): 1329–1407.

Matthes, Karen. "Telecommuting: Balancing Business and Employee Needs." *HR Focus* 69, no. 3 (1992).

Maurer, Roy. "Use of Video for Recruiting Continues to Grow." *SHRM*, Aug. 21, 2015. www.shrm.org/resourcesandtools/hr-topics/talent-acquisition/pages/use-video-recruiting-grow.aspx.

Mayo, Elton. *The Social Problems of an Industrial Civilization.* Cambridge, MA: Harvard University, Graduate School of Business Administration, 1945.

Mayson, Sandra G. "Bias In, Bias Out." *Yale Law Journal* 128, no. 8 (2019): 2122–473.

McCann, Laurie A. "The Age Discrimination in Employment Act at 50: When Will It Become a 'Real' Civil Rights Statute?" *American Bar Association Journal of Law and Employment Law* 33, no. 1 (2017): 89–104.

McConville, Timothy M. "Employer Policies May Be per se Violations of the National Labor Relations Act (NLRA)." *National Review*, July 12, 2013. www.natlawreview.com/article/employer-policies-may-be-se-violations-national-labor-relations-act-nlra.

McCrae, Robert R., and Oliver P. John. "An Introduction to the Five-Factor Model and Its Applications. *Journal of Personality* 60, no. 2 (1992): 175–215. http://psych.colorado .edu/~carey/courses/psyc5112/readings/psnbig5_mccrae03.pdf.

McGregor, Douglas. *The Human Side of Enterprise.* New York: McGraw Hill, 1960.

Melson-Silimon, Arturia, et. al. "Personality Testing and the Americans with Disabilities Act: Cause for Concern as Normal and Abnormal Personality Models Are Integrated." *Industrial and Organizational Psychology* 12, no. 2 (2019): 119–32.

Mercado, Darla. "How Workplace Benefits Might Reflect the New Reality of Covid-19." *CNBC*, Oct. 13, 2020. www.cnbc.com/2020/10/13/how-workplace-benefits-might-reflect-the-new-reality-of-covid-19.html (accessed May 25, 2021).

Meredith, Jeff, et al. "AI Identifying Steady Workers." *Chicago Tribune*, July 16, 2001. www .chicagotribune.com/news/ct-xpm-2001-07-16-0107160013-story.html.

Michaelson, Christopher, Michael G. Pratt, Adam M. Grant, and Craig P. Dunn. "Meaningful Work: Connecting Business Ethics and Organization Studies." *Journal of Business Ethics* 121, no. 1 (2014): 77–90.

Miller, Alex P. "Want Less-Biased Decisions? Use Algorithms." *Harvard Business Review*, July 26, 2018. https://hbr.org/2018/07/want-less-biased-decisions-use-algorithms.

Miller, Andrea. "More Companies Are Using Technology to Monitor Employees, Sparking Privacy Concerns." *ABC News*, Mar. 10, 2018. https://abcnews.go.com/US/companies-tech nology-monitor-employees-sparking-privacy-concerns/story?id=53388270 [https://perma.cc/ HHP2-R9DK].

Miller, Stephen. "EEOC Proposes – Then Suspends – Regulations on Wellness Program Incentives." *SHRM*, Jan. 13, 2021. www.shrm.org/resourcesandtools/hr-topics/benefits/ pages/eeoc-proposes-new-limits-on-wellness-program-incentives.aspx (accessed May 25, 2021).

Miller, Stephen. "Ruling Is Mixed Bag for EEOC's Effort to Rein in Wellness Programs." *SHRM*, Sept. 28, 2016. www.shrm.org/resourcesandtools/hr-topics/benefits/pages/orion-eeoc-wellness-ruling.aspx (accessed May 25, 2021).

Milroy, Jack. "The List Makes Us Strong. Why Unions Need a Digital Strategy." *Medium*, Apr. 29, 2016. https://medium.com/@jack_milroy/the-list-makes-us-strong-why-unions-need-a-digital-strategy-42291213298a.

"Mob Law at Homestead: Provoked by an Attack of Pinkerton Detectives." *New York Times*, July 7, 1892. https://timesmachine.nytimes.com/timesmachine/1892/07/07/104139908.pdf.

Moore, Adam D. "Employee Monitoring and Computer Technology: Evaluative Surveillance v. Privacy." *Business Ethics Quarterly* 10, no. 3 (2000): 697–709.

Moore, Phoebe V. "Electronic Performance Monitoring." *PhoebeVMoore blog*, Oct. 29, 2019. https://phoebevmoore.wordpress.com/2019/10/29/electronic-performance-monitoring/.

Morn, Frank. *The Eye That Never Sleeps: A History of the Pinkerton National Detective Agency.* Bloomington: Indiana University Press, 1982.

Morozov, Evgeny. *To Save Everything, Click Here: The Folly of Technological Solutionism.* New York: Public Affairs, 2013.

Morris, Frank C., Jr., August Emil Huellei, and Adam C. Solander. "Mainstream Wellness Program Challenged in *EEOC v. Honeywell*." *Epstein Becker Green: Insights*, Nov. 20, 2014. www.ebglaw.com/news/mainstream-wellness-program-challenged-in-eeoc-v-honeywell/ (accessed May 25, 2021).

Morse, Minna Scherlinder. "Facing a Bumpy History." *Smithsonian Magazine*, Oct. 1997. www.smithsonianmag.com/history/facing-a-bumpy-history-144497373/.

Murphy, Michael E. "Assuring Responsible Risk Management in Banking: The Corporate Governance Dimension." *Delaware Journal of Corporate Law* 36, no. 1 (2011): 121–64.

MyNameStats.com. "First Names: Jared." www.mynamestats.com/First-Names/J/JA/JARED/index.html (last visited May 9, 2022).

Myriad Genetics. "Benefits of Genetic Testing." www.myriad.com/patients-families/genetic-testing-101/benefits-of-genetic-testing/ (accessed May 25, 2021).

Nahill, Bill. "*Commonwealth v. Hunt*." *American Legal History*, Mar. 12, 2013. http://moglen .law.columbia.edu/twiki/bin/view/AmLegalHist/BillNahillWikiProject.

National Conference of State Legislatures (NCSL). "Genetic Employment Laws." Updated Jan. 2008. www.ncsl.org/research/health/genetic-employment-laws.aspx (accessed May 25, 2021).

National Conference of State Legislatures (NCSL). "Genetics and Health Insurance State Anti-Discrimination Laws." Updated Jan. 2008. www.ncsl.org/research/health/genetic-nondiscrimination-in-health-insurance-laws.aspx.

National Human Genome Research Institute. "The Human Genome Project" (last updated Dec. 22, 2020). www.genome.gov/human-genome-project (accessed May 25, 2021).

"National Society to Conserve Life: Life Extension Institute Formed to Teach Hygiene and Prevention of Disease." *New York Times*, Dec. 30, 1913. Available at ProQuest Historical Newspapers.

Nazari, Tourang. "More Responsible Use of Workforce Data Required to Strengthen Employee Trust and Unlock Growth, According to Accenture Report." *Accenture Newsroom*, Jan. 21, 2019. https://newsroom.accenture.com/news/more-responsible-use-of-workforce-data-required-to-strengthen-employee-trust-and-unlock-growth-according-to-accenture-report.htm.

Neff, Gina, and Dawn Nafus. *Self-Tracking*. Cambridge, MA: MIT Press, 2016.

NEH. "Reconstruction vs. Redemption." *National Endowment for the Humanities: News*, Feb. 11, 2014. www.neh.gov/news/reconstruction-vs-redemption.

Nelles, Walter. "*Commonwealth v. Hunt*." *Columbia Law Review* 32, no. 7 (1932): 1128–69.

Neumark, David, Ian Burn, and Patrick Button. "Age Discrimination and Hiring of Older Workers." Federal Reserve Bank of San Francisco, Economic Letter, Feb. 27, 2017. www.frbsf .org/economic-research/publications/economic-letter/2017/february/age-discrimination-and-hiring-older-workers/.

Newman, Mark. *The HireVue Story*. Vimeo, posted Apr. 26, 2013. https://vimeo.com/64921188.

Nichols, Robert S., et al. "EEOC Says Employers May Mandate Covid-19 Vaccinations – Subject to Limitations." *National Law Review*, Jan. 20, 2021. www.natlawreview.com/article/eeoc-says-employers-may-mandate-covid-19-vaccinations-subject-to-limitations (accessed May 25, 2021).

NIEHS. "Autism." Last updated Aug. 30, 2021. www.niehs.nih.gov/health/topics/conditions/autism/index.cfm.

"1919 Steel Strike." *Encyclopedia of Cleveland History*. https://case.edu/ech/articles/n/1919-steel-strike (accessed Jan. 5, 2021).

Nissenbaum, Helen. *Privacy in Context: Technology, Policy, and the Integrity of Social Life*. Stanford, CA: Stanford University Press, 2009.

NLRB. "1947 Taft-Hartley Substantive Provisions." www.nlrb.gov/about-nlrb/who-we-are/our-history/1947-taft-hartley-substantive-provisions (accessed Jan. 6, 2021).

Noble, Safiya Umoja. *Algorithms of Oppression: How Search Engines Reinforce Racism.* New York: New York University Press, 2018.

Noonan, Mary C., and Jennifer L. Glass. "The Hard Truth about Telecommuting." *Monthly Labor Review,* United States Department of Labor, Bureau of Labor Statistics: June 2012, 38–45.

Novaco, Raymond W., Wendy Kliewer, and Alexander Broquet. "Home Environmental Consequences of Commute Travel Impedance." *American Journal of Community Psychology* 19, no. 6 (1991): 881–909.

Nuriddin, Ayah, Graham Mooney, and Alexandre I. R. White. "Reckoning with Histories of Medical Racism and Violence in the USA." *The Lancet* 396, no. 10256 (2020): 949–51.

O'Connor, Austin. "Bias towards Older Workers on the Rise as Age Discrimination Goes Online." *The Milwaukee Independent,* January 10, 2018. www.milwaukeeindependent.com/syndicated/bias-toward-older-workers-on-the-rise-as-age-discrimination-goes-online/.

O'Neil, Cathy. "Personality Tests Are Failing American Workers." *Bloomberg,* January 18, 2018. www.bloomberg.com/opinion/articles/2018-01-18/personality-tests-are-failing-american-workers.

O'Neil, Cathy. *Weapons of Math Destruction: How Big Data Increases Inequality and Threatens Democracy.* New York: Crown Publishing, 2016.

O'Neill, Heather. "Video Interviewing Cuts Costs, but Bias Worries Linger." *Workforce,* Oct. 5, 2011. www.workforce.com/news/video-interviewing-cuts-costs-but-bias-worries-linger.

O'Rourke, Kevin Hjortshøj. "Luddites, the Industrial Revolution, and the Demographic Transition." *Journal of Economic Growth* 18, no. 4 (2013): 373–409.

Obstfeld, David. "Social Networks, the Tertius Iungens Orientation, and Involvement in Innovation." *Administrative Science Quarterly* 50, no. 1 (2005): 100–130.

OECD. "OECD Guidelines Governing the Protection of Privacy and Transborder Flows of Personal Data." *Updated* 2013. www.oecd.org/sti/ieconomy/oecdguidelinesontheprotectionofprivacyandtransborderflowsofpersonaldata.htm [https://perma.cc/YX8E-JJRX].

Ohm, Paul. "Sensitive Data." *Southern California Law Review* 88, no. 5 (2015): 1125–96.

Olson, Parmy. "Fitbit Data Now Being Used in the Courtroom." *Forbes,* Nov. 16, 2014. www.forbes.com/sites/parmyolson/2014/11/16/fitbit-data-court-room-personal-injury-claim/#19c35e5d7379 [https://perma.cc/AZ6L-AQTU].

Ong, Thuy. "Amazon Patents Wristbands That Track Warehouse Employees' Hands in Real Time." *The Verge,* Feb. 1, 2018. www.theverge.com/2018/2/1/16958918/amazon-patents-trackable-wristband-warehouse-employees [https://perma.cc/8FYU-4RNR].

Onion, Rebecca. "Tracking a Slave Trader through His Expense Reports." *Slate,* Apr. 7, 2014. https://slate.com/human-interest/2014/04/slave-trader-ledger-william-james-smith-accounting-book.html.

Onwuachi-Willig, Angela, and Jacob Willig-Onwuachi. "A House Divided: The Invisibility of the Multiracial Family." *Harvard Civil Rights-Civil Liberties Law Review* 44, no. 1 (2009): 231–53.

Opacity. "Worcester State Hospital." *Opacity: Urban Ruins,* 2018. https://opacity.us/site56_worcester_state_hospital.htm

Oppenheimer, David Benjamin. "Negligent Discrimination." *University of Pennsylvania Law Review* 141, no. 3 (1993): 899–972.

ORCAA (O'Neill Risk Assessment and Algorithmic Auditing). "Description of Algorithmic Audit: Pre-Built Assessments." Report, Dec. 15, 2020. https://techinquiry.org/HireVue-ORCAA.pdf.

Orlikowski, Wanda J., and Stephen R. Barley. "Technology and Institutions: What Can Research on Information Technology and Research on Organizations Learn from Each Other?" *MIS Quarterly* 25, no. 2 (2001): 145–65.

Orth, John V. "English Combination Acts of the Eighteenth Century." *Law and History Review* 5, no. 1 (1987): 175–211.

Oswal, Nilam. "The Latest Recruitment Technology Trends and How to Really Use Them." *PC World*, Feb. 9, 2018. www.pcworld.idg.com.au/article/633219/latest-recruitment-technology-trends-how-really-use-them/.

Oswald, Fred. "Can a Personality Test Determine if You're a Good Fit for a Job? *Speaking of Psychology* (blog), interview with Fred Oswald PhD, episode 150, July 2021. www.apa.org/research/action/speaking-of-psychology/personality-tests.

Palen, Melanie. "Unicru Personality Test Answer Key: Read This, Get Hired." *ToughNickel*, July 24, 2020. https://toughnickel.com/finding-job/Unicru.

Pallais, Amanda. "Evidence That Minorities Perform Worse under Biased Managers." *Harvard Business Review*, Jan. 13, 2017. https://hbr.org/2017/01/evidence-that-minorities-perform-worse-under-biased-managers.

Palmer, Annie. "Amazon Flex Drivers Are Using Bots to Cheat Their Way to Getting More Work." *CNBC*, Feb. 9, 2020. www.cnbc.com/2020/02/09/amazon-flex-drivers-use-bots-to-get-more-work.html.

Paquette, Danielle. "The Trump Administration Just Halted This Obama-Era Rule to Shrink the Gender Wage Gap." *Washington Post*, Aug. 30, 2017. www.washingtonpost.com/news/wonk/wp/2017/08/30/the-trump-administration-just-halted-this-obama-era-rule-to-shrink-the-gender-wage-gap/.

Parker, Kim, Juliana Menasce Horowitz, and Rachel Minkin. "Covid-19 Pandemic Continues to Reshape Work in America." Pew Research Center, Feb. 16, 2022. www.pewresearch.org/social-trends/2022/02/16/covid-19-pandemic-continues-to-reshape-work-in-america/.

Parker, Wendy. "Lessons in Losing: Race Discrimination in Employment." *Notre Dame Law Review* 81, no. 3 (2006): 889–954.

Parry, Jim, Simon Robinson, and Nick Watson. *Sport and Spirituality: An Introduction*. New York: Routledge, 2007.

Pascale, Richard. "The Paradox of 'Corporate Culture': Reconciling Ourselves to Socialization." *California Management Review* 27, no. 2 (1985): 26–47.

Pasquale, Frank. "Beyond Innovation and Competition: The Need for Qualified Transparency in Internet Intermediaries." *Northwestern University School of Law* 104, no. 1 (2010): 105–73.

Pasquale, Frank. *The Black Box Society: The Secret Algorithms That Control Money and Information*. Cambridge, MA: Harvard University Press, 2015.

Paycor. "Announcement: Newton Is Now Paycor Recruiting." https://perma.cc/LF3U-R4ZK (captured May 18, 2020).

Paycor. "Paycor Recruiting: Find Quality Candidates and Fill Open Positions Fast." Last updated Oct. 4, 2019. www.paycor.com/resource-center/recruitment-tools [https://perma.cc/3MS9TVDK].

Paycor. "Paycor Recruiting Software & Applicant Tracking System." https://perma.cc/K9UF-YUSV (captured Apr. 23, 2020).

Pearlson, Keri E., and Carol S. Saunders. "There's No Place Like Home: Managing Telecommuting Paradoxes." *Academy of Management Perspectives* 15, no. 2 (2001): 117–28.

Peppet, Scott R. "Regulating the Internet of Things: First Steps toward Managing Discrimination, Privacy, Security, and Consent." *Texas Law Review* 93, no. 1 (2014): 85–176.

Perea, Juan F. "Doctrines of Delusion: How the History of the G.I. Bill and Other Inconvenient Truths Undermine the Supreme Court's Affirmative Action Jurisprudence." *University of Pittsburgh Law Review* 75, no. 1 (2014): 583–651.

Petrova, Magdalena. "A Smart Exoskeleton Can Keep the Elderly Safe." *Computer World*, May 15, 2017. www.computerworld.com/article/3196823/a-smart-exoskeleton-can-keep-the-elderly-safe.amp.html.

Pettit, Philip. *Republicanism: A Theory of Freedom and Government*. 1997; Reprint, Oxford: Clarendon Press, 2002.

Peyton, Antigone. "The Connected State of Things: A Lawyer's Survival Guide in an Internet of Things World." *Catholic University Journal of Law and Technology* 24, no. 2 (2016): 369–400.

Peyton, Antigone. "A Litigator's Guide to the Internet of Things." *Richmond Journal of Law and Technology* 22, no. 3 (2016): 1–20.

Phaik Lin Goh, Janice. "Privacy, Security, and Wearable Technology." *Landslide* 8, no. 2 (Nov./Dec. 2015): 1–8. www.americanbar.org/groups/intellectual_property_law/publications/landslide/2015-16/november-december/.

Phillips, Katherine W. "Commentary: What Is the Real Value of Diversity in Organizations? Questioning Our Assumptions." In *The Diversity Bonus: How Great Teams Pay Off in the Knowledge Economy*, edited by Scott E. Page. Princeton: Princeton University Press, 2017, 223–46.

Pierce, Benjamin A. *Genetics: A Conceptual Approach*. 7th ed. New York: Macmillan, 2020.

Pinard, Michael. "Collateral Consequences of Criminal Convictions: Confronting Issues of Race and Dignity." *New York University Law Review* 85, no. 2 (2010): 457–534.

Pinkerton.com. "Our History: Our Roots Trace Back to 1850." Pinkerton Consulting and Investigations website, 2018. www.pinkerton.com/our-difference/history.

Porter, Nicole Buoncore. "Synergistic Solutions: An Integrated Approach to Solving the Caregiver Conundrum for 'Real' Workers." *Stetson Law Review* 39, no. 1 (2010): 777–860.

Posner, Richard A. *Economic Analysis of Law*, 2nd ed. New York: Little Brown, 1977.

Posner, Richard A. "Privacy, Secrecy and Reputation." *Buffalo Law Review* 28, no. 1 (1979): 1–55.

Post, Robert. "Prejudicial Appearance: The Logic of American Antidiscrimination Law." *California Law Review* 88, no. 1 (2000): 1–40.

Poster, Mark. *The Mode of Information: Poststructuralism and Social Context*. Chicago: University of Chicago Press, 1990.

Potuzak, Melissa, et al. "Categorical vs Dimensional Classifications of Psychotic Disorders." *Comprehensive Psychiatry* 53, no. 8 (Nov. 2012): 1118–29. www.ncbi.nlm.nih.gov/pmc/articles/PMC3488145/.

Prenkert, Jamie Darin. "Bizarro Statutory Stare Decisis." *Berkeley Journal of Employment and Labor Law* 28, no. 1 (2007): 217–68.

Press, Joshua S. "Crying Havoc over the Outsourcing of Soldiers and Democracy's Slipping Grip on the Dogs of War." *Northwestern University Law Review* 103, no. 33 (2008): 109–20. www.law.northwestern.edu/lawreview/colloquy/2008/33/.

Price, W. Nicholson, II. "Regulating Black-Box Medicine." *Michigan Law Review* 116, no. 3 (2017): 421–74.

Privacy Rights Clearinghouse. "California Privacy Rights Act: An Overview." Dec. 10, 2020. https://privacyrights.org/resources/california-privacy-rights-act-overview.

Pruitt, Jeff. "3 Ways to Know if an Employee Is a Culture Fit." *Inc.com*, Aug. 12, 2016. www.inc.com/jeff-pruitt/3-ways-to-know-if-an-employee-is-a-culture-fit.html.

Public Citizen. *Workplace Privacy after Covid-19*. Digital Rights Program, Aug. 13, 2020. www.citizen.org/wp-content/uploads/Workplace-Privacy-after-Covid-19-final.pdf.

Pugh, Allison. *The Tumbleweed Society: Working and Caring in an Age of Insecurity*. New York: Oxford University Press, 2015.

Pustilnik, Amanda C. "Violence on the Brain: A Critique of Neuroscience in Criminal Law." *Wake Forest Law Review* 44, no. 1 (2009):183–237.

Quantified Self Institute. *What Is Quantified Self?* https://qsinstitute.com/about/what-is-quantified-self/.

Raczkowski, Christopher. "From Modernity's Detection to Modernist Detectives: Narrative Vision in the Work of Allan Pinkerton and Dashiell Hammett." *MFS Modern Fiction Studies* 49, no. 4 (2003): 629–59.

Rafferty, John P. "The Rise of the Machines: Pros and Cons of the Industrial Revolution." *Encyclopedia Britannica*, 2018. www.britannica.com/story/the-rise-of-the-machines-pros-and-cons-of-the-industrial-revolution.

Raghavan, Manish, Jon Kleinberg, Solon Barocas, and Karen Levy. "Mitigating Bias in Algorithmic Hiring: Evaluating Claims and Practices." *FAT*' 20: Proceedings of the 2020 Conference on Fairness, Accountability, and Transparency*, Jan. 2020, 469–81.

Raines, J. Patrick, and Charles G. Leathers. "Telecommuting: The New Wave of Workplace Technology Will Create a Flood of Change in Social Institutions." *Journal of Economic Issues* 35, no. 2 (2001): 307–13.

Raub, McKenzie. "Bots, Bias and Big Data: Artificial Intelligence, Algorithmic Bias and Disparate Impact Liability in Hiring Practices." *Arkansas Law Review* 71, no. 2 (2018): 529–70.

Ray, Victor. "Why So Many Organizations Stay White." *Harvard Business Review*, Nov. 19, 2019. https://hbr.org/2019/11/why-so-many-organizations-stay-white.

Rehm, John. "Exoskeletons and the Workplace." *Worker's Compensation Watch*, Dec. 7, 2015. https://workerscompensationwatch.com/2015/12/07/exoskeletons-and-the-workplace/ [https://perma.cc/L73A-4MYJ].

Reidenberg, Joel R. "Lex Informatica: The Formulation of Information Policy Rules through Technology." *Texas Law Review* 76, no. 3(1998): 553–93.

Reilly, Philip R. "Eugenics and Involuntary Sterilization, 1907–2015." *Annual Review of Genomics and Human Genetics* 16, no. 1 (2015): 351–68.

Rhue, Lauren. "Racial Influence on Automated Perceptions of Emotions." *SSRN: Race, AI, and Emotions*, Nov. 9, 2018. https://papers.ssrn.com/sol3/papers.cfm?abstract_id=3281765.

Ribeiro, Marco Tulio, Sameer Singh, and Carlos Guestrin. "'Why Should I Trust You?' Explaining the Predictions of Any Classifier." In *Proceedings of the 2016 Conference of the North American Chapter of the Association for Computational Linguistics*, 1135–44. New York: Association for Computing Machinery, 2016.

Rice, Ralph S. "The Wagner Act: It's Legislative History and It's Relation to National Defense." *Ohio State University Law Journal* 8, no. 1 (1941): 17–73.

Riddle, Judith. "Editor's Spot: Is the BMI Racially Biased?" *Today's Dietician* 22, no. 8 (2020): 6.

"Riot at Homestead." *Chicago Tribune*, July 6, 1892. https://chicagotribune.newspapers.com/search/?ymd=1892-07-06.

Roberts, Laura Morgan, and Darryl D. Roberts. "Testing the Limits of Antidiscrimination Law: The Business, Legal, and Ethical Ramifications of Cultural Profiling at Work." *Duke Journal of Gender Law & Policy* 14, no. 1 (2007): 369–405.

Roberts, Sarah T. "Commercial Content Moderation: Digital Laborers' Dirty Work." In *Intersectional Internet: Race, Sex, Class, and Culture*, edited by S. U. Noble & B. Tynes. *Media Studies Publications* (2016): 1–11.

Roberts, Sarah T. "Digital Refuse: Canadian Garbage, Commercial Content Moderation and the Global Circulations of Media's Waste." *Journal of Mobile Media* 10, no. 1 (2016): 1–18.

Roberts, Sarah T. "In/visibility." In *Surplus3: Labour and the Digital*, 30–32. Letters & Handshakes, 2016.

Robey, Daniel. "Computers and Management Structure: Some Empirical Findings Re-examined." *Human Relations* 30, no. 11 (1977): 963–76.

Robitzski, Dan. "How A.I. Exoskeletons Could Make People Super-Human." *Inverse*, June 22, 2017. www.inverse.com/article/33298-personalized-exoskeletons-carnegie-mellon.

Rodder, A. "Technologies of Control: The Construction of the Modern Worker." MS thesis, University of Oslo, 2016. www.semanticscholar.org/paper/Technologies-of-Control%3A-The-Construction-of-the-Rodder/813b851fda76c6e8dcd41c61e29ca55fe447fa30.

Rodriguez, Tony, and Jessica Lyon. "Background Screening Reports and the FCRA: Just Saying You're Not a Consumer Reporting Agency Isn't Enough." *Federal Trade Commission*, blog, posted Jan. 10, 2013. www.ftc.gov/news-events/blogs/business-blog/2013/01/background-screeningreports-fcra-just-saying-youre-not [https://perma.cc/9YEN-QXKH].

Roediger, David R., and Elizabeth D. Esch. *The Production of Difference: Race and the Management of Labor in U.S. History*. New York: Oxford University Press, 2014.

Roethlisberger, Fritz Jules. *Management and Morale*. Cambridge, MA: Harvard University Press, 1941.

Roethlisberger, Fritz Jules, and William J. Dickson. *Management and the Worker: An Account of a Research Program Conducted by the Western Electric Company, Hawthorne Works, Chicago*. Cambridge, MA: Harvard University Press, 1939.

Rogers, Adam. "We Try a New Exoskeleton for Construction Workers." *Wired*, Apr. 28, 2015. www.wired.com/2015/04/try-new-exoskeleton-construction-workers/ [https://perma.cc/PLQ7-4NVK].

Rogers, Brishen. "Basic Income and the Resilience of Social Democracy." *Comparative Labor Law & Policy Journal* 40, no. 2 (2019): 199–221.

Rogers, Brishen. "Worker Surveillance and Class Power." *LPE Project*, July 11, 2018. https://lpeproject.org/blog/worker-surveillance-and-class-power/.

Rosenbaum, Eric. "Silicon Valley Is Stumped: Even A.I. Cannot Always Remove Bias from Hiring." *CNBC*, May 30, 2018. www.cnbc.com/2018/05/30/silicon-valley-is-stumped-even-a-i-cannot-remove-bias-from-hiring.html.

Rosenberg, Eli. "Workers Are Fired Up. But Union Participation Is Still on the Decline, New Statistics Show." *Washington Post*, Jan. 23, 2020. www.washingtonpost.com/business/2020/01/22/workers-are-fired-up-union-participation-is-still-decline-new-statistics-show/.

Rosenblat, Alex, Tamara Kneese, and Danah Boyd. *Workplace Surveillance*. Open Society Foundations: Data and Society Working Paper. Oct. 8, 2014.

Rosenthal, Caitlin. *Accounting for Slavery: Masters and Management*. Cambridge, MA: Harvard University Press, 2018.

Ross, Andrew S. "In Silicon Valley, Age Can Be a Curse." *SF Gate*, Aug. 20, 2013. www.sfgate.com/bu~siness/bottomline/article/In-Silicon-Valley-age-can-be-a-curse-4742365.php.

Ruckenstein, Minna. "Visualized and Interacted Life: Personal Analytics and Engagements with Data Doubles." *Societies* 4, no. 1 (2014): 68–84.

Rutkin, Aviva. "Wearable Tech Lets Boss Track Your Work, Rest and Play." *New Scientist*, Oct. 15, 2014, www.newscientist.com/article/mg22429913-000-wearabletech-lets-boss-track-your-work-rest-and-play/ [https://perma.cc/U4PW-KYYX].

Sales, Francesca. "What Is Cultural Fit?" *Tech Target: Search CIO*, Sept. 2014. https://searchcio.techtarget.com/definition/Cultural-fit.

Salomon, Ilan. "Telematics, Travel and Environmental Change: What Can Be Expected of Travel Substitution?" *Built Environment* 21, no. 4 (1978): 214–22.

Sandberg, Sheryl. "Managing Unconscious Bias." *Meta Newsroom*, July 28, 2015. https://newsroom.fb.com/news/2015/07/managing-unconscious-bias.

Sandler, Rachel. "EEOC Probing Whether Facebook Has Committed Systemic Racial Discrimination in Hiring." *Forbes*, Mar. 5, 2021. www.forbes.com/sites/rachelsandler/2021/03/05/eeoc-probing-whether-facebook-has-committed-systemic-racial-discrimination-in-hiring/?sh=59025ce7715f.

Sanger Institute. "The Finished Human Genome: Welcome to the Genomic Age." Sanger Institute, Press Office, Apr. 14, 2003. https://perma.cc/2FX6-HZPW (captured Nov. 17, 2015; accessed May 25, 2021).

Santorelli, Michael, and Washington Bytes. "After Net Neutrality: The FTC Is the Sheriff of Tech Again. Is It up to the Task?" *Forbes*, Dec. 15, 2017. www.forbes.com/sites/washington bytes/2017/12/15/the-game-is-on-the-ftc-tech-regulation-post-net-neutrality/.

Sanzaro, Karen. "Big Data: FTC Issues Report Cautioning That Use of Big Data May Violate Federal Consumer Protection Laws or Raise Ethical Considerations." Alston & Bird: Privacy, Cyber, & Data Strategy Blog, Jan. 19, 2016. www.alstonprivacy.com/big-data-ftc-issues-report-cautioning-that-use-of-big-data-may-violate-federal-consumer-protection-laws-or-raise-ethical-considerations/.

Saulsberry, Kalyn, and Sharon F. Terry. "The Need to Build Trust: A Perspective on Disparities in Genetic Testing." *Genetic Testing and Molecular Biomarkers* 17, no. 9 (2013): 647–48.

Savage, David D., and Richard Bales. "Video Games in Job Interviews: Using Algorithms to Minimize Discrimination and Unconscious Bias." *ABA Journal of Labor and Employment Law* 32, no. 2 (2017): 211–28.

Saval, Nikil. *Cubed: A Secret History of the Workplace.* New York: Doubleday, 2014.

Scheiber, Noam. "The Brutal Ageism of Tech." *The New Republic*, Mar. 23, 2014. https://newrepublic.com/article/I17088/silicons-valleys-brutal-ageism.

Schlag, Pierre. "Commentary: Law & Phrenology." *Harvard Law Review* 110, no. 4 (1997): 877–921.

Schmidt, Lars. "The End of Culture Fit." *Forbes*, Mar. 21, 2017. www.forbes.com/sites/larsschmidt/2017/03/21/the-end-of-culture-fit/#70fbdb72638a.

Schumpeter, Joseph A. *History of Economic Analysis.* 1954. Reprint, London: Routledge, 1994.

Schwartz, Justin. "Voice without Say: Why Capital-Manage Firms Aren't (Genuinely) Participatory." *Fordham Journal of Corporate and Financial Law* 18, no. 4 (2013): 963–1020.

Schwartz, Paul M. "Data Processing and Government Administration: The Failure of the American Legal Response to the Computer." *Hastings Law Journal* 43, no. 5 (1992): 1321–89.

Schwartz, Paul M. "Preemption and Privacy." *Yale Law Journal* 118, no. 5 (2009): 902–1021.

"Scientific Management." *The Economist*, Feb. 9. 2009. www.economist.com/news/2009/02/09/scientific-management.

Scope. "Social Model of Disability." Scope.org. www.scope.org.uk/about-us/social-model-of-disability/ (accessed Oct. 4, 2020).

Selbst, Andrew D., and Solon Barocas. "The Intuitive Appeal of Explainable Machines." *Fordham Law Review* 87, no. 3 (2018): 1085–1139.

"Self-Audit for Quality Improvement." *Strategic Direction* 18, no. 5 (2002): 17–19.

Selinger, Evan, and Woodrow Hartzog. "The Inconsentability of Facial Surveillance." *Loyola Law Review* 66, no. 1 (2019): 101–22.

Selmi, Michael. "Was the Disparate Impact Theory a Mistake?" *UCLA Law Review* 53, no. 3 (2006): 701–82.

Selmi, Michael. "Why Are Employment Discrimination Cases So Hard to Win?" *Louisiana Law Review* 61, no. 3 (2001): 555–75.

Sening, Yvonne Koontz. "Heads or Tails: The Employee Polygraph Protection Act." *Catholic University Law Review* 39, no. 1 (1989): 235–68.

Sewell, Graham. "The Discipline of Teams: The Control of Team-Based Industrial Work Through Electronic and Peer Surveillance." *Administrative Science Quarterly* 43, no. 2 (1998): 397–428.

ShabbyTester. "How To Answer Pre-Employment Personality Tests." *Reddit: AskReddit,* posted Feb. 13, 2012. www.reddit.com/r/AskReddit/comments/pneie/how_to_answer_pre employment_personality_tests/.

Shamir, Boas, and Ilan Saloman. "Work-at-Home and the Quality of Working Life." *Academy of Management* 10, no. 3 (1985): 455–64.

Shang, Ellen. "Employee Privacy in the US Is at Stake as Corporate Surveillance Technology Monitors Workers' Every Move." *CNBC,* Apr. 15, 2019. www.cnbc.com/2019/04/15/ employee-privacy-is-at-stake-as-surveillance-tech-monitors-workers.html.

Shawl, William Frank. "The Repeal of the Combination Acts 1824–1825." MA thesis, Montana State University, 1954. https://scholarworks.umt.edu/cgi/viewcontent.cgi?article =9663&context=etd.

Shell, Ellen Ruppel. "The Employer-Surveillance State." *The Atlantic,* Oct. 15, 2018. www .theatlantic.com/business/archive/2018/10/employee-surveillance/568159/.

Shellenbarger, Sue. "Work at Home? Your Employer May Be Watching." *Wall Street Journal,* July 30, 2008. www.wsj.com/articles/SB121737022605394845.

Shellenbarger, Sue. "'Working from Home' without Slacking Off." *Wall Street Journal,* July 11, 2012. www.wsj.com/articles/SB10001424052702303684004577508953483021234.

Shestakofsky, Benjamin J. "Working Algorithm, Software Automation and the Future of Work." *Work and Occupations* 44, no. 4 (2017): 376–423.

SHRM. *What Is the Function of the National Labor Relations Act (NLRA)?* www.shrm.org/ resourcesandtools/tools-and-samples/hr-qa/pages/nlrafunction.aspx (accessed Jan. 5, 2021).

Shuey, Kim M., and Angela M. O'Rand. "New Risks for Workers: Pensions, Labor Markets, and Gender." *Annual Review of Sociology* 30, no. 1 (2004): 453–77.

Sia, Siew Kien, et al. "Enterprise Resource Planning (ERP) as a Technology of Power: Empowerment or Panoptic Control?" *ACM SIGMIS Database: The Database for Advances Information Systems* 33, no. 1 (2002): 23–37.

Siegel, Eric. *Predictive Analytics: The Power to Predict Who Will Click, Buy, Lie, or Die.* Hoboken, NJ: Wiley, 2013.

Siegel, Reva B. "Equality Talk: Antisubordination and Anticlassification Values in Constitutional Struggles over *Brown.*" *Harvard Law Review* 117, no. 5 (2004): 1470–1547.

Silverman, Rachel Emma. "Bosses Tap Outside Firms to Predict Which Workers Might Get Sick." *Wall Street Journal,* Feb. 17, 2016. www.wsj.com/articles/bosses-harness-big-data-to-predict-which-workers-might-get-sick-1455664940.

Silverman, Rachel E., and Nikki Waller. "The Algorithm That Tells the Boss Who Might Quit." *Wall Street Journal,* Mar. 13, 2015. www.wsj.com/articles/the-algorithm-that-tells-the-boss-who-might-quit-1426287935.

Simmel, Georg. *The Sociology of Georg Simmel,* edited and translated by Kurt H. Wolff. New York: Free Press, 1950.

Simonite, Tom. "This Call May Be Monitored for Tone and Emotion." *Wired,* Mar. 19, 2018. www.wired.com/story/this-call-may-be-monitored-for-tone-and-emotion/.

Singh, Jatinder, et al. "Responsibility & Machine Learning: Part of a Process," Oct. 27, 2016. https://papers.ssrn.com/sol3/papers.cfm?abstract_id=2860048.

Sink, Jessica, and Richard A. Bales. "Born in the Bandwidth: 'Digital Native' as Pretext for Age Discrimination." *American Bar Association Journal of Law and Employment Law* 31, no. 3 (2016): 521–36.

Sklansky, David A. "The Private Police." *UCLA Law Review* 46, no. 4 (1999): 1165–1287.

Slade, Hollie. "Hand Gesture Armband Myo Integrates with Google Glass." *Forbes,* Aug. 19, 2014. www.forbes.com/sites/hollieslade/2014/08/19/hand-gesture-armband-myo-integrates-with-google-glass/#39309793608c [https://perma.cc/QZ95-HYSZ].

Slaughter, Louise M. "The Genetic Information Nondiscrimination Act: Why Your Personal Genetics Are Still Vulnerable to Discrimination." *Surgical Clinics of North America* 88, no. 4 (2008): 723–38.

Smallwood, Stephanie E. *Saltwater Slavery: A Middle Passage from Africa to American Diaspora*. Cambridge, MA: Harvard University Press, 2008.

Smids, Jilles, Sven Nyholm, and Hannah Berkers. "Robots in the Workplace: A Threat to – or Opportunity for – Meaningful Work?" *Philosophy and Technology* 33, no. 3 (2020): 503–22.

Smith, Aaron, and Monica Anderson. *Automation for Everyday Life*. Pew Research Center, Oct. 4, 2017. http://assets.pewresearch.org/wp-content/uploads/sites/14/2017/10/03151500/PI_2017.10.04_Automation_FINAL.pdf.

Smith, Allen. "Temperature Screenings: Review State Laws." *SHRM.org*, Aug. 31, 2020. www.shrm.org/resourcesandtools/legal-and-compliance/employment-law/pages/corona virus-temperature-screening-review.aspx.

Smith, Robert Michael. *From Blackjacks to Briefcases: A History of Commercialized Strikebreaking and Unionbusting in the United States*. Athens: Ohio University Press, 2003.

Smith-Marsh, Daphne E. "Type 1 Diabetes Risk Factors." *Endocrine Web*, Mar. 1, 2016. www .endocrineweb.com/conditions/type-1-diabetes/type-1-diabetes-risk-factors (last updated Mar. 3, 2016).

Snustad, D. Peter, and Michael J. Simmons. *Principles of Genetics*. 6th ed. Hoboken, NJ: John Wiley & Sons, 2011.

Solon, Olivia. "Amazon Patents Wristband That Tracks Warehouse Workers' Movements." *The Guardian*, Jan. 31, 2018. www.theguardian.com/technology/2018/jan/31/amazon-warehouse-wristband-tracking.

Solon, Olivia. "Big Brother Isn't Just Watching: Workplace Surveillance Can Track Your Every Move." *The Guardian*, Nov. 6, 2017. www.theguardian.com/world/2017/nov/06/workplace-surveillance-big-brother-technology.

Solon, Olivia. "Wearable Technology Creeps into the Workplace." *Sydney Morning Herald*, Aug. 7, 2015. www.smh.com.au/business/workplace/wearable-technology-creeps-into-the-workplace-20150807-gitzuh.html.

Sowell, Thomas. *Discrimination and Disparities*. New York: Basic Books, 2019.

Spann, Giradeau A. "Race Ipsa Loquitor." *Michigan State Law Review* 2018, no. 1 (2018): 1025–93.

Sperino, Sandra F. "Disparate Impact of Negative Impact: Future of Non-Intentional Discrimination Claims Brought by the Elderly." *Elder Law Journal* 13, no. 2 (2005): 339–86.

Sprague, Robert D. "From Taylorism to the Omnipticon: Expanding Employee Surveillance Beyond the Workplace." *Journal of Computer & Information Law* 25, no. 1 (2007): 1–35.

Stack, Michael B. "Wearable Technology in Workers' Compensation." *Amaxx*, July 27, 2017. http://blog.reduceyourworkerscomp.com/2017/07/wearable-technology-workers-compen sation/ [https://perma.cc/KW6G-8SZK?type=image].

Stark, Luke. "Facial Recognition Is the Plutonium of AI." *XRDS: Crossroads* 25, no. 3 (2019): 50–55.

Starnes, Cynthia. "Divorce and the Displaced Homemaker: A Discourse on Playing with Dolls, Partnership Buyouts and Dissociation Under No-Fault." *University of Chicago Law Review* 60, no. 1 (1993): 67–139.

Stauffer, Joseph M., and M. Ronald Buckley. "The Existence and Nature of Racial Bias in Supervisory Ratings." *Journal of Applied Psychology* 90, no. 3 (2005): 596–91.

Steadman, Phillip. "Samuel Bentham's Panopticon." *Journal of Bentham Studies* 14, no. 1 (2012): 1–30.

Steele, Chandra. "The Quantified Employee: How Companies Use Tech to Track Workers." *PC Mag*, Feb. 14, 2020. www.pcmag.com/news/the-quantified-employee-how-companies-use-tech-to-track-workers.

Stephens, Bret. "Opinion: The Secrets of Jewish Genius." *New York Times*, Dec. 27, 2019. www.nytimes.com/2019/12/27/opinion/jewish-culture-genius-iq.html.

Stern, Alex, and Tony Platt. "Sterilization Abuse in State Prisons: Time to Break with California's Long Eugenic Patterns." *Huffington Post: The Blog*, July 23, 2013. www.huff post.com/entry/sterilization-california-prisons_b_3631287 (accessed May 26, 2021).

Street, Tamara D., and Sarah J. Lacey. "Employee Perceptions of Workplace Health Promotion Programs: Comparison of a Tailored, Semi-Tailored, and Standardized Approach." *International Journal of Environmental Research and Public Health* 15, no. 5 (2018): 1–17.

Studnicka, Anthony. "The Emergence of Wearable Technology and the Legal Implications for Athletes, Teams, Leagues and Other Sports Organizations across Amateur and Professional Athletics." *DePaul Journal of Sports Law* 16, no. 1 (2020): 195–224.

Suddath, Claire. "Tesco Monitors Employees with Motorola Armbands." *Bloomberg*, Feb. 13, 2013. www.bloomberg.com/news/articles/2013-02-13/tesco-monitors-employees-with-motorola-armbands [http://perma.cc/G925-8BR9].

Suemo, Jemimah. "2019 Employee Monitoring Software Industry Trends." *Worktime*, Oct. 21, 2019. www.worktime.com/2019-employee-monitoring-software-industry-trends.

Suk, Julie C. "Discrimination at Will: Job Security Protections and Equal Employment Opportunity in Conflict." *Stanford Law Review* 60, no.1 (2007): 73–113.

Sullivan, Bob. "Online Job Sites May Block Older Workers." *CNBC*, Mar. 13, 2017. www.cnbc.com/2017/03/10/online-job-sites-may-block-older-workers.html.

Sullivan, Charles A. "Disparate Impact: Looking Past the Desert Palace Mirage." *William and Mary Law Review* 47, no. 3 (2005): 911–1002.

Sullivan, Charles A. "Employing AI." *Villanova Law Review* 63, no. 3 (2018): 395–429.

Summers, Clyde W. "Employment at Will in the United States: The Divine Right of Employers." *University of Pennsylvania Journal of Labor and Employment Law* 3, no. 1 (2000): 65–86.

Surden, Harry. "Computable Contracts." *University of California at Davis Law Review* 46, no. 1 (2012): 629–700.

Surden, Harry. "Machine Learning and Law." *Washington Law Review* 89, no. 1 (2014): 87–115.

Susser, Daniel. "Notice After Notice-and-Consent: Why Privacy Disclosures Are Valuable Even if Consent Frameworks Aren't." *Journal of Information Policy* 9, no. 1 (2019): 37–62.

Swaya, Matthew E., and Stacey R. Eisenstein. "Emerging Technology in the Workplace." *Labor Lawyer* 21, no. 1 (2005): 1–17.

Taylor, Frederick Winslow. "A Piece-Rate System." Paper presented to American Society of Mechanical Engineers, June 1895. http://wps.prenhall.com/wps/media/objects/107/109902/ch17_a3_d2.pdf.

Taylor, Frederick Winslow. *The Principles of Scientific Management*. New York: Harper & Bros., 1911.

Tenenbaum, Jessica D., and Kenneth W. Goodman. "Beyond the Genetic Information Nondiscrimination Act: Ethical and Economic Implications of the Exclusion of Disability, Long-Term Care and Life Insurance." *Future Medicine* 14, no. 2 (2017): 153–54.

Terry, Nicolas. "Big Data Proxies and Health Privacy Exceptionalism." *Health Matrix* 24, no. 1 (2014): 65–108.

Thatcher, Jim, David O'Sullivan, and Dillon Mahmoudi. "Data Colonialism through Accumulation by Dispossession: New Metaphors for Daily Data." *Environment and Planning D: Society and Space* 34, no. 5 (2016): 990–1006.

"There Will Be Little Privacy in the Workplace of the Future." *The Economist*, Special Report, Mar. 28, 2018. https://perma.cc/343W-P69Y (captured Aug. 25, 2018; accessed May 25, 2021).

Thompson, Edward Palmer. *The Making of the English Working Class.* New York: Vintage Books, 1963.

Thompson, Mary. "Goldman Sachs Is Making a Change to the Way It Hires." *CNBC*, June 23, 2016. www.cnbc.com/2016/06/23/goldman-sachs-is-making-a-change-to-the-way-it-hires.html.

Tinwalla, Abdi, and Joseph Richard Ciccone. "ADA and Medical Examinations." *Journal of the American Academy of Psychiatry and Law* 34, no. 2 (2006): 255–57.

Tolson, Franita. "The Boundaries of Litigating Unconscious Discrimination: Firm-Based Remedies in Response to a Hostile Judiciary." *Delaware Journal of Corporate Law* 33, no. 2 (2008): 347–421.

Tomaskovic-Devey, Donald, and Barbara J. Risman. "Telecommuting Innovation and Organization: A Contingency Theory of Labor Process Change." *Social Science Quarterly* 74, no. 2 (1993): 367–85.

Townley, Barbara. "Foucault, Power/Knowledge, and Its Relevance for Human Resource Management." *Academy of Management Review* 18, no. 3 (1993): 518–45.

Tribe, Laurence H. "Seven Deadly Sins of Straining the Constitution through a Pseudo-Scientific Sieve." *Hastings Law Journal* 36, no. 2 (1985): 155–72.

Tran, Alexander H. "Note: The Internet of Things and Potential Remedies in Privacy Tort Law." *Columbia Journal of Law & Social Problems* 50, no. 2 (2017): 263–98.

Troiano, Alexandra. "Note: Wearables and Personal Health Data: Putting a Premium on Your Privacy." *Brooklyn Law Review* 82, no. 4 (2017): 1715–53.

Trueman, C. N. "Factories in the Industrial Revolution." *The History Learning Site*, last updated Mar. 31, 2015. www.historylearningsite.co.uk/britain-1700-to-1900/industrial-revolution/factories-in-the-industrial-revolution/.

Tsao, Clement L., Kevin J. Haskins, and Brian D. Hall. "The Rise of Wearable and Smart Technology in the Workplace." Paper presented at the ABA National Symposium on Technology in Labor and Employment, Apr. 5–7, 2017.

Turner, Karen. "Are Performance-Monitoring Wearables an Affront to Workers' Rights?" *Chicago Tribune*, Aug. 7, 2016. www.chicagotribune.com/bluesky/technology/ct-wearables-workers-rights-wp-bsi-20160807-story.html.

Turner, Wes. "Chipping Away at Workplace Privacy: The Implantation of RFID Microchips and Erosion of Employee Privacy." *Washington University Journal of Law & Policy* 61, no. 1 (2020): 275–97.

Tutt, Andrew. "An FDA for Algorithms." *Administrative Law Review* 69, no. 1 (2017): 83–123.

Tyler-Parks. "Applying Online." *Your Job Questionnaire Cheatsheet*, Aug. 24, 2011. http://onlineapps-answers.blogspot.com/2011/ (accessed Nov. 24, 2020).

Tyler-Parks. "Target." *Your Job Questionnaire Cheatsheet*, http://onlineapps-answers.blogspot.com/p/target.html (accessed Nov. 24, 2020).

UFCW. *Keeping Jobs Safe from Automation and Artificial Intelligence Technology.* www.ufcw.org/better/technology-and-the-future-of-work/ (accessed Mar. 3, 2022).

Urick, Lyndall F. *The Elements of Administration.* New York: Harper, 1944.

U.S. Bureau of Labor Statistics. *Labor Force Characteristics by Race and Ethnicity,* 2017. Apr. 2018. www.bls.gov/opub/reports/race-and-ethnicity/2017/home.htm.

U.S. Bureau of Labor Statistics. *Labor Force Statistics from the Current Population Survey,* 2018. Table 5, Employment Status of the Civilian Non-Institutional Population by Sex, Age and Race. www.bls.gov/cps/cpsaat05.htm.

U.S. Congress, Office of Technology Assessment (OTA). *Medical Monitoring and Screening in the Workplace: Results of a Survey.* Background Paper, OTA-BP-BA-67. Washington DC: Government Printing Office, 1991.

U.S. Congress, Office of Technology Assessment (OTA). The Role of Genetic Testing in the Prevention of Occupational Diseases: Survey of the Use of Genetic Testing in the Workplace. Report, Apr. 1983. Washington DC: Government Printing Office, 2013.

U.S. Department of Labor. "US Labor Department Settles Charges of Hiring Discrimination with Federal Contractor Leprino Foods." U.S. Department of Labor Newsroom, July 19, 2012. www.dol.gov/newsroom/releases/ofccp/ofccp20120719

U.S. GAO. "In-Car Location-Based Services." GAO-14-81, Dec. 2013. www.gao.gov/assets/gao-14-81.pdf

U.S. Green Building Council (USGBC). *About USGBC.* https://new.usgbc.org/about (accessed Sept. 21, 2019).

U.S. Green Building Council (USGBC). *Certification.* https://new.usgbc.org/post-certification (last visited Sept. 21, 2019). This URL redirects to a page "Promote your LEED project" at the URL www.usgbc.org/leed/tools/project-promotion.

U.S. House of Representatives. "Employment of Pinkerton Detectives." Report No. 2447, Feb. 7, 1893. In *The Reports of Committees of the House of Representatives for the Second Session of the Fifty-Second Congress, 1892–93.* Washington DC: Government Printing Office, 1893.

U.S. House of Representatives. Investigation of Taylor System of Shop Management. Hearings before the Committee on Labor of the House of Representatives, 62nd Congress, 1st session on House Resolution 90. Vol. 1. Washington DC: Government Printing Office, 1911.

U.S. House of Representatives. *Investigation of the Employment of Pinkerton Detectives in Connection with the Labor Troubles at Homestead, Pa.* 52nd Congress, 1st session, Mis. Doc. No. 335. Washington DC: Government Printing Office, 1892.

U.S. House of Representatives. Proposed Amendments to the National Labor Relations Act: Hearings before the [House] Committee on Labor, 76th Congress, 3rd session. Vol. 9 [Feb. 1–Mar. 4, 1940]. Washington DC: Government Printing Office, 1940.

U.S. House of Representatives. The Taylor and Other Systems of Shop Management. Hearings before Special Committee of the House of Representatives to Investigate the Taylor and Other Systems of House Management under Authority of H. Res. 90. Vol. 1 [Oct.–Nov. 1911]. Washington DC: Government Printing Office, 1912.

U.S. House of Representatives. The Taylor and Other Systems of Shop Management. Hearings before Special Committee of the House of Representatives to Investigate the Taylor and Other Systems of House Management under Authority of H. Res. 90. Vol. 2 [Jan. 1912]. Washington DC: Government Printing Office, 1912.

U.S. House of Representatives. The Taylor and Other Systems of Shop Management. Hearings before Special Committee of the House of Representatives to Investigate the Taylor and Other Systems of House Management under Authority of H. Res. 90. Vol. 3 [Jan.–Aug. 1912]. Washington DC: Government Printing Office, 1912.

Van Buren, Harry J., III. "Fairness and the Main Management Theories of the Twentieth Century: A Historical Review, 1900–1965." *Journal of Business Ethics* 82, no. 3 (2008): 633–44.

Van den Bossche, Patrick, et al. "Wearable Technology in the Warehouse." *Supply Chain 24/7: Warehouse/DC News,* Feb. 1, 2016. www.supplychain247.com/article/wearable_technology_in_the_warehouse [https://perma.cc/T3N5-SG43].

Van Doorn, Niels. "Platform Labor: On the Gendered and Racialized Exploitation of Low-Income Service Work in the 'On-Demand' Economy." *Information, Communication & Society* 20, no. 6 (2017): 898–914.

Van Loo, Rory. "Helping Buyers Beware: The Need for Supervision of Big Retail." *University of Pennsylvania Law Review* 163, no. 5 (2015): 1311–92.

Van Loo, Rory. "The Missing Regulatory State: Monitoring Businesses in an Age of Surveillance." *Vanderbilt Law Review* 72, no. 5 (2019): 1563–1631.

van Wyhe, John. "Overview." *The History of Phrenology on The Web*. www.historyofphrenol ogy.org.uk/overview.htm (last updated 2011).

van Wyhe, John. "Ridiculing Phrenology: 'This Persecuted Science.'" *The History of Phrenology on The Web*. www.historyofphrenology.org.uk/ridicule.htm (last updated 2011).

Vaughan, Christine A., William P. Sacco, and Jason W. Beckstead. "Racial/Ethnic Differences in Body Mass Index: The Roles of Beliefs about Thinness and Dietary Restriction." *Body Image* 5, no. 3 (2008): 291–98.

Veblen, Thorstein. *The Theory of Business Enterprise*. New Brunswick, NJ: Transaction Books, 1904.

Verma, Anil. "What Do Unions Do to the Workplace? Union Effects on Management and HRM Policies." *Journal of Labor Research* 26, no. 3 (2005): 415–49.

VidCruiter. "Where Did Video Hiring Come from and Where Is It Going?" https://vidcruiter .com/video-interviewing/history-of-video-interview/ (accessed Nov. 6, 2021).

Villadsen, Kaspar. "Managing the Employee's Soul: Foucault Applied to Modern Management Technologies." *Cadernos EBAPE BR* 5, no. 1 (2007): 1–10.

Viseu, Ana. "Simulation and Augmentation: Issues of Wearable Computers." *Ethics & Information Technology* 5, no. 1 (2003): 17–26.

Vogeler, William. "Technology Is Quickly Reshaping Workers' Compensation Claims." *FindLaw blog*, Feb. 24, 2017. https://blogs.findlaw.com/technologist/2017/02/technology-is-quickly-reshaping-workers-compensation-claims.html [https://perma.cc/E72X-AWKJ].

Vozza, Stephanie. "How a Cheat Sheet Can Help You Ace Your Next Video Interview." *Fast Company*, Sept. 12, 2020. www.fastcompany.com/90549127/how-a-cheat-sheet-can-help-you-ace-your-next-video-interview.

Vroom, Victor H. *Work and Motivation*. New York: Wiley, 1964.

Waddell, Kaveh. "Why Bosses Can Track Their Employees 24/7." *The Atlantic*, Jan. 6, 2017. www.theatlantic.com/technology/archive/2017/01/employer-gps-tracking/512294/ (accessed Sept. 13, 2018).

Wagner, Steven. "How Did the Taft-Hartley Act Come About?" *History News Network*, George Washington University, https://historynewsnetwork.org/article/1036 (accessed Jan. 6, 2020).

"Walmart Assessment Answers." *Facebook*, Oct. 4, 2016, www.facebook.com/Walmart assessmentanswers/.

Warwick Business School. "How Uber Drivers Are Gaming the System." *Warwick Business School*, Aug. 16, 2017. www.wbs.ac.uk/news/how-uber-drivers-are-gaming-the-system/.

Watanabe, Teresa. "UC Berkeley Is Disavowing Its Eugenic Research Fund after Bioethicist and Other Faculty Call It Out." *Los Angeles Times*, Oct. 26, 2020. www.latimes.com/california/story/2020-10-26/uc-berkeley-disavows-eugenics-research-fund (accessed May 25, 2021).

Watson, Nick, et al. "The Development of Muscular Christianity in Victorian Britain and Beyond." *Journal of Religion & Society* 7, no. 1 (2005): 1–21.

Wax, Amy, and Larry Alexander. "Opinion: Paying the Price for Breakdown of the Country's Bourgeois Culture." *Philadelphia Inquirer*, Aug. 9, 2017. www.inquirer.com/philly/opinion/commentary/paying-the-price-for-breakdown-of-the-countrys-bourgeois-culture-20170809.html.

"Web Scraping as a Valuable Instrument for Proactive Hiring." *DataHen*, Apr. 5, 2017. www .datahen.com/web-scraping-valuable-instrument-proactive-hiring/.

Webber, Ashleigh. "PwC Facial Recognition Tool Criticised for Home Working Privacy Invasion." *Personnel Today*, June 16, 2020. www.personneltoday.com/hr/pwc-facial-recognition-tool-criticised-for-home-working-privacy-invasion/.

Weber, Lauren, and Elizabeth Dwoskin. "Are Workplace Personality Tests Fair?" *Wall Street Journal*, Sept. 29, 2014. www.wsj.com/articles/are-workplace-personality-tests-fair-1412044257.

Weber, Max. *The Theory of Social and Economic Organization*. Translated by A. M. Henderson & Talcott Parsons, edited by Talcott Parsons. Oxford: Oxford University Press, 1947.

Weinstein, Henry. "Amendment on Computer Privacy Urged: Law Professor Tells Conference That the Constitution Should Be Changed to Protect Individual Rights Threatened by Technology. *Los Angeles Times*, Mar. 27, 1991. www.latimes.com/archives/la-xpm-1991-03-27-mn-938-story.html.

Weller, Chris. "Employees at a Dozen Fortune 500 Companies Wear Digital Badges That Watch and Listen to Their Every Move." *Business Insider*, Oct. 20, 2016. www.businessinsider.com/humanyze-badges-watch-and-listen-employees-2016-10.

"What Is Direct-to-Consumer Genetic Testing?" *Medline Plus*. https://ghr.nlm.nih.gov/primer/dtcgenetictesting/directtoconsumer (accessed May 26, 2021).

White House. "Fact Sheet: New Steps to Advance Equal Pay on the Seventh Anniversary of the Lilly Ledbetter Fair Pay Act." Jan. 29, 2016. https://obamawhitehouse.archives.gov/the-press-office/2016/01/29/fact-sheet-new-steps-advance-equal-pay-seventh-anniversary-lilly.

White, Gillian B. "Black Workers Really Do Need to Be Twice as Good." *The Atlantic*, Oct. 7, 2015. www.theatlantic.com/business/archive/2015/10/why-black-workers-really-do-need-to-be-twice-as-good/409276/.

Whyte, William H. *Money and Motivation: Analysis of Incentives in Industry*. New York: Harper & Row, 1955.

Whyte, William H. *The Organization Man*. New York: Simon & Schuster, 1956.

Wijngaards, Indy, et al. "Worker Well-Being: What It Is, and How It Should Be Measured." *Applied Research in Quality of Life* (2021). https://link.springer.com/article/10.1007/s11482-021-09930-w.

WikiJob Team. "The NEO Personality Inventory Test." *WikiJob*, Nov. 10, 2020. www.wikijob.co.uk/content/aptitude-tests/test-types/neo-personality-inventory-test.

Wilborn, Elizabeth. "Revisiting the Public/Private Distinction: Employee Monitoring in the Workplace." *Georgia Law Review* 32, no. 2 (1998): 825–88.

Wildhaber, Isabelle. "The Robots Are Coming: Legalities in the Workplace." *HR Magazine*, June 20, 2016. www.hrmagazine.co.uk/article-details/the-robots-are-coming-legalities-in-the-workplace [https://perma.cc/VMP9-Z2QX].

Willcocks, Leslie P. "Foucault, Power/Knowledge and Information Systems: Reconstructing the Present." In *Social Theory and Philosophy for Information Systems*, edited by John Mingers and Leslie P. Willcocks, 238–98. New York: John Wiley & Sons, 2004.

Willcocks, Leslie P. "Michel Foucault in the Social Study of ICTs: Critique and Reappraisal." *Social Science Computer Review* 24, no. 3 (2006): 274–95.

Wilmot, Michael P., and Deniz S. Ones. "A Century of Research on Conscientiousness at Work." *PNAS* 116, no. 46 (Nov. 12, 2019): 23004–23010. www.pnas.org/content/116/46/23004.short.

Wilson, H. James. "Wearables in the Workplace." *Harvard Business Review*, Sept. 2013. https://hbr.org/2013/09/wearables-in-the-workplace [https://perma.cc/UJJ7-BW9L].

Wilson, Mark. "Medical Textbooks Are Designed to Diagnose White People. This Student Wants to Change That." *Fast Company*, July 16, 2020. www.fastcompany.com/90527795/medical-textbooks-are-designed-to-diagnose-white-people-this-student-wants-to-change-that.

Wilson, Valerie. "Black Workers' Wages Have Been Harmed by Both Widening Racial Wage Gaps and the Widening Productivity-Pay Gap." *Economic Policy Institute*, Oct. 25, 2016. www.epi.org/publication/black-workers-wages-have-been-harmed-by-both-widening-racial-wage-gaps-and-the-widening-productivity-pay-gap/#epi-toc-2.

Wilson, Valerie. "Women Are More Likely to Work Multiple Jobs Than Men." *Economic Policy Institute*, July 9, 2015. www.epi.org/publication/women-are-more-likely-to-work-multiple-jobs-than-men/.

Wilson, Valerie, and Janelle Jones. "Working Harder or Finding It Harder to Work: Demographic Trends in Annual Work Hours Show an Increasingly Fractured Workforce." *Economic Policy Institute*, Feb. 22, 2018. www.epi.org/publication/trends-in-work-hours-and-labor-market-disconnection.

Winick, Erin. "Lawyer-Bots Are Shaking Up Jobs." *MIT Technology Review*, Dec. 12, 2017. www.technologyreview.com/s/609556/lawyer-bots-are-shaking-up-jobs.

Withers, Rachel. "Should Robots Be Conducting Job Interviews?" *Slate*, Oct. 5, 2020. https://slate.com/technology/2020/10/artificial-intelligence-job-interviews.html.

Wolf, Christopher, Jules Polonetsky, and Kelsey Finch. "A Practical Privacy Paradigm for Wearables." Future of Privacy Forum, Jan. 8, 2015. https://fpf.org/wp-content/uploads/FPF-principles-for-wearables-Jan-2015.pdf [https://perma.cc/W8R9-8HRW].

Woodfill, David. "Brown & Brown Settles Suit over Nigerian Accent." *East Valley Tribune*, Oct. 7, 2011. www.eastvalleytribune.com/news/brown-brown-settles-suit-over-nigerian-accent/article_f41851cd-f3ab-537b-9d60-74127f44a6ba.html.

Workman, Michael. "A Field Study of Corporate Employee Monitoring: Attitudes, Absenteeism, and the Moderating Influences of Procedural Justice Perceptions." *Information and Organization* 19, no. 4 (2009): 218–32.

Wrege, Charles D., and Richard M. Hodgetts. "Frederick W. Taylor's 1899 Pig Iron Observations: Examining Fact, Fiction, and Lessons for the New Millennium." *Academy of Management Journal* 43, no. 6 (2020): 1283–91.

Wu, Chi Chi. "Data Gatherers Evading the FCRA May Find Themselves Still in Hot Water." *National Consumer Law Center Digital Library*, June 14, 2019. https://library.nclc.org/data-gatherers-evading-fcra-may-find-themselves-still-hot-water.

Wyden, Ron. "Wyden, Booker and Clarke Introduce Algorithmic Accountability Act of 2022 to Require New Transparency and Accountability for Automated Decision Systems." Wyden.Senate.gov, Press Release, Feb. 3, 2022. www.wyden.senate.gov/news/press-releases/wyden-booker-and-clarke-introduce-algorithmic-accountability-act-of-2022-to-require-new-transparency-and-accountability-for-automated-decision-systems.

Yalcinkaya, Gunseli. "Amazon Patents Wristband to Track Productivity and Direct Warehouse Staff Using Vibrations." *Dezeen*, Feb. 6, 2018. www.dezeen.com/2018/02/06/amazon-patents-wristbands/ [https://perma.cc/8Q8S-89MY].

Yamin, Samuel C., David L. Parker, Min Xi, and Rodney Stanley. "Self-Audit of Lockout/Tagout in Manufacturing Workplaces: A Pilot Study." *American Journal of Industrial Medicine* 60, no. 5 (2017): 504–9.

Yanisky-Ravid, Shlomit, and Sean K. Hallisey. "'Equality and Privacy by Design': A New Model of Artificial Intelligence Data Transparency via Auditing, Certification, and Safe Harbor Regimes." *Fordham Urban Law Journal* 46, no. 5 (2019): 428–86.

Yeginsu, Ceylan. "If Workers Slack Off, the Wristband Will Know. (And Amazon Has a Patent for It.)" *New York Times*, Feb. 1, 2018. www.nytimes.com/2018/02/01/technology/amazon-wristband-tracking-privacy.html.

YMCA. *Our History: 1800–1899*. YMCA.net, www.ymca.net/history/1800-1860s.html (accessed May 25, 2021).

Youngman, Julie Furr. "The Use and Abuse of Pre-Employment Personality Tests." *Business Horizons* 60, no. 3 (2017): 261–69.

Zatz, Noah D. "Managing the Macaw: Third-Party Harassers, Accommodation, and the Disaggregation of Discriminatory Intent." *Columbia Law Review* 109, no. 6 (2009): 1357–1439.

Zerzan, John. "Unionism and Taylorism: Labor Cooperation with the 'Modernization' of Production." *Fifth Estate* 278 (Nov. 1976). www.fifthestate.org/archive/278-november-1976/unionism-and-taylorism/.

Zickuhr, Kathryn. *Workplace Surveillance Is Becoming the New Normal for U.S. Workers.* Washington Center for Equitable Growth report, Aug. 18, 2021. https://equitablegrowth.org/research-paper/workplace-surveillance-is-becoming-the-new-normal-for-u-s-workers/.

Zimmer, Michael J. "The New Discrimination Law: Price Waterhouse Is Dead, Whither McDonnell Douglas?" *Emory Law Journal* 53, no. 2 (2004): 1887–1950.

Zimmerman, Richard K., et al. "Racial Differences in Beliefs about Genetic Screening among Patients at Inner-City Neighborhood Health Centers." *Journal of the National Medical Association* 98, no. 3 (2006): 370–77.

Zingman, Alissa, et al. "Exoskeletons in Construction: Will They Reduce or Create Hazards?" *CDC: NIOSH Science Blog*, June 15, 2017. https://blogs.cdc.gov/niosh-science-blog/2017/06/15/exoskeletons-in-construction/.

Zuboff, Shoshana. *In the Age of the Smart Machine: The Future of Work and Power.* New York: Basic Books, 1988.

Zuboff, Shoshana, and James Maxmim. *The Support Economy: Why Corporations Are Failing Individuals and the Next Episode of Capitalism.* New York: Penguin Books, 2002.

Zuckerman, Mark. "Unions Need to Think Small to Get Big." *The Atlantic*, Feb. 9, 2019. www.theatlantic.com/ideas/archive/2019/02/how-online-organizing-can-revolutionize-unions/582343/AFL-CIO.

Zuckerman, Mark, Richard D. Kahlenberg, and Moshe Marvit. *Virtual Labor Organizing: Could Technology Help Reduce Income Inequality.* The Century Foundation, Issue Brief, June 9, 2015. https://tcf.org/content/report/virtual-labor-organizing/?agreed=1&agreed=1&session=1.

Zumoff, Jacob A. "Politics and the 1920s Writings of Dashiell Hammett." *American Studies* 52, no. 1 (2012): 77–98.

ARCHIVAL SOURCES

Correspondence of American Federation of Labor President William Green on Microfilm No. 5402, Cornell University Library: Kheel Center for Labor-Management Documentation and Archives.

Frederick Winslow Taylor Collection (SCW.001), Stevens Institute of Technology Digital Collections: Samuel C. Williams Library, https://stevensarchives.contentdm.oclc.org/digital/collection/p4100coll1 (last accessed Nov. 11, 2021).

Slave Ship Manifests filed at New Orleans, 1807–1860, National Archives: African American Heritage, www.archives.gov/research/african-americans/slave-ship-manifests.html (last accessed Nov. 11, 2021).

LAWSUITS

AARP v. EEOC, 267 F. Supp. 3d 14, 37 (D.D.C. 2017).

Aladdin Gaming, LLC, 345 N.L.R.B. 585, 585–86 (2005), petition for review denied, 515 F.3d 942, 947 (9th Cir. 2008).

Albemarle Paper Co. v. Moody, 422 U.S. 405, 430–31 (1975).
Bethlehem Steel Co. v. NLRB, 120 F.2d 641, 646 (D.C. Cir. 1941).
Boumkepor v. Wal-Mart Stores East, 2020 WL 4569587, 3:18-CV-30093-KAR (Aug. 7, 2020).
Boyd v. City of Wilmington, 943 F. Supp. 585, 587 (E.D.N.C. 1996).
Bradley v. T-Mobile U.S., Inc., No. 17-cv-07232-BLF (N.D. Cal. May 29, 2018).
Bragdon v. Abbot, 118 S. Ct. 2196 (1998).
Brickman v. Fitbit, Inc., No. 3:15-cv-02077-JD, 2017 WL 6209307, at *1–3 (N.D. Cal. Dec. 8, 2017).
Buck v. Bell, 47 S.Ct. 584 (1927).
Castillo v. Whitmer, 823 Fed. Appx. 413, 413 (6th Cir. 2020).
CoCommonwealth v. Hunt, 45 Mass. 111, 122 (1842).
Connally v. General Constr. Co., 269 U.S. 385, 391 (1926).
Cramblett v. McHugh, No. 3:10-CV-54-PK, 2012 WL 7681280 (D. Or. Nov. 19, 2012).
Crummer v. Lewis, 2018 WL 2222491 (2018) (noting that the constitutional right to information privacy extends to medical information).
Darby v. Childvine, Inc., 2019 A.D. Cas. (BNA) 447288, 2019 WL 6170743 (S.D. Ohio 2019).
Dodge v. Ford Motor Co., 204 Mich. 459 (1919).
EEOC v. Flambeau, 14-cv-00638-bbc (2015), http://static.politico.com/e8/bd/e4d94f8c45f 39996ca700fee6bf1/eeoc-versus-flambeau.pdf (last visited May 25, 2021).
EEOC v. Honeywell, No. 0:14-04517 (2014).
EEOC v. Orion Energy Systems, Inc., 208 F. Supp. 3d 989, 1001 (2016).
EEOC v. Orion, No. 1:14-01019 (2014).
EEOC v. Randstad, Civil Action No. 1:11-cv-01303-WDQ).
Eugene Scalia v. KP Poultry, Inc., No. CV 19-3546-TJH, 2020 WL 6694315 (Nov. 6, 2020).
Fafnir Bearing Co. v. NLRB, 362 F.2d 716 (2d Cir. 1966).
Fragante v. Honolulu, 888 F.2d 591, 599 (9th Cir. 1989).
Fredenburg v. Contra Costa Cnty. Dep't of Health Servs. 172 F.3d 1176, 1182 (9th Cir. 1999).
Gerardi v. City of Bridgeport, 294 Conn. 461 (2010).
Gladden v. Bolden, 802 F. Supp. 2d 209 (D.D.C. 2011).
Gonzales v. Uber Techs., Inc., 305 F. Supp.3d 1078, 1091 (N.D. Cal. 2018) (quoting Hill v. Nat'l Collegiate Athletic Ass'n., 865 P.2d 633, 655 (Cal. 1994)).
Grant v. Bethlehem Steel Corp., 635 F.2d 1007, 10015 (2d Cir. 1980).
Green v. Whataburger Rests., 2018 WL 6252532 (W.D. Tex. 2018).
Griffin v. Steeltek, Inc., 160 F.3d 591 (10th Cir. 1998).
Griggs v. Duke Power Co., 401 U.S. 424, 433–34, (1971).
Gross v. FBL Fin. Servs., 557 U.S. 167 (2009).
Gulino v. N.Y. State Educ. Dep't, 460 F.3d 361, 383–84 (2d Cir. 2006).
Harrison v. Benchmark Elecs. Huntsville, Inc., 593 F.3d 1206, 1211-12 (11th Cir. 2010),
Hentzel v. Singer Co., 188 Cal. Rptr. 159, 164 (Ct. App. 1982));
Hodgson v. Approved Personnel Serv., Inc., 529 F. 2d 760 (4th Cir. 1975).
Hosler v. Smithfield Packing Co., 2010 U.S. Dist. LEXIS 101776 (E.D.N.C. 2010).
Jones v. City of Boston, 845 F.3d 28 (1st Cir. 2016).
Karraker v. Rent-a-Center, Inc., 411 F.3d 831, 836 (7th Cir. 2005).
Kroll v. White Lake Ambulance Authority, 691 F.3d 809, 816-817 (6th Cir. 2012).
Larry P. v. Riles, 793 F.2d 969, 972 (9th Cir. 1984).
Lemon v. Williamson County Schools, 2019 WL 4598201, 1 (Sept. 23, 2019).
Lewis v. Smithfield Packing Co., 2010 U.S. Dist. LEXIS 87883, 13-18 (E.D.N.C. 2010).
Lochner v. New York, 198 U.S. 45 (1905).
Lombard v. Colo. Outdoor Educ. Ctr., Inc., 187 P.3d 565 (Colo. 2008).
Lorrillard v. Pons, 434 U.S. 575, 580-81 (1978).

Lowe v. Atlas Logistics Group Retail Services (Atlanta) LLC, 2015 U.S. Dist. LEXIS 178275 (N.D. Ga. 2015).

Lowe v. Atlas Logistics Group Retail Servs. Atlanta, LLC, 102 F. Supp. 3d 1360 (N.D. Ga. 2015).

Marsh v. Alabama, 326 U.S. 501 (1946).

Martin v. Bally's Park Place Hotel & Casino, 983 F.2d 1252 (1993).

McDonnell Douglas Corp. v. Green, 411 U.S. 792 (1973).

McLellan v. Fitbit, Inc., No. 3:16-cv-00036-JD, 2018 WL 2688781, at *1 (N.D. Cal. June 5, 2018).

Mikula v. Tailors, 263 NE.2d 316 (Ohio 1970).

Miller v. Christian, 958 F.2d 1234 (3d Cir. 1992).

Mobley v. Facebook, Inc., No. 16-cv-06440-EJD, at *1 (N.D. Cal. 2017).

Murdock v. Washington, 193 F.3d 510, 512 (7th Cir. 1999).

Murphy v. NCRNC, LLC., 2020 L.R.R.M. BNA 278, XX (July 27, 2020).

Murray v. Mayo Clinic, 934 F.3d 1101, 1105 (9th Cir. 2019), cert. denied, 140 S. Ct. 2720 (2020).

Najera v. Southern Pac. Co., 13 Cal. Rptr. 146, 148 (Ct. App. 1961).

Natay v. Murray Sch. Dist., 119 Fed. Appx. 259 (10th Cir. 2005).

NLRB v. Ford Motor Co., 114 F.2d 905 (6th Cir. 1940).

NLRB v. Gate City Cotton Mills, 167 F.2d 647, 649 (1948).

NLRB v. Otis Elevator Co., 208 F.2d 176 (2d Cir. 1953).

NLRB v. Pennsylvania Greyhound Lines, 303 U.S. 261 (1938).

Normal-Bloodsaw v. Lawrence Berkeley Laboratory et al., 135 F.3d 1260 (9th Cir. 1998).

Opinion of Justices, 358 Mass. 827 (1970).

Opinion of the Justices, 356 Mass. 756, 758 (1969).

Ortiz v. City of San Antonio Fire Department, 806 F.3d 822, 822 (2015).

Osborne v. McMasters, 41 N.W. 543 (Minn. 1889).

Poore v. Peterbilt Bristol, LLC, 852 F. Supp. 2d 727 (W.D. Va. 2012).

Purchase v. Meyer, 737 P.2d 661 (Wash. 1987).

Reid v. Google, Inc., 50 Cal. 4th 512 (2008).

Republic Aviation v. NRLB, 324 U.S. 793 (1945).

Ruffin v. Commonwealth, 62 Va. 790 (1871).

Sandel v. Fairfield Indus., No. 4:13-CV-1596, 2015 U.S. Dist. LEXIS 161555, at *5–6 (S.D. Tex. June 25, 2015).

Shelley v. Kraemer, 334 U.S. 1 (1948).

Skinner v. Oklahoma, 62 S.Ct. 1110, 1112 (1942).

Spokeo, Inc. v. Robins, 136 S. Ct. 1540 (2016).

Thompson v. San Antonio Retail Merchants Association (SARMA), 682 F.2d 509 (1982).

Thygeson v. U.S. Bancorp., No. CV–03–467–ST, 2004 WL 2066746, at *21 (D. Or. Sept. 15, 2004).

United States v. Equifax, Inc., 557 F.2d 456 (5th Cir. 1977).

Villarreal v. R.J. Reynolds Tobacco Co., 839 F.3d 958, 961 (11th Cir. 2016).

Walker v. RLI Enters., Inc., No. 89325, 2007 WL 4442725 (Ohio Ct. App. 2007).

West Coast Hotel Co. v. Parrish, 300 U.S. 379 (1936).

Wheeler v. Jackson Nat'l Life Ins. Co., 159 F. Supp. 3d 828, 860 (M.D. Tenn. 2016).

Williams v. Calhoun, 333 S.E.2d 408 (Ga. App. 1985).

LAWS AND STATUTES

§ 1681(a)(d)(2)(i).

§ 703 (k)(1)(A) & C.

138 S. Ct. 2206, 2206 (2018).

15 U.S.C. § 1 (1982).
15 U.S.C. § 1681a (2018).
15 U.S.C. § 1681a(d).
15 U.S.C. § 1681a(d)(1) (2018).
15 U.S.C. § 1681a(d)(1)(A)–(B) (2018).
15 U.S.C. § 1681a(f) (2018).
15 U.S.C. § 1681a(o)(5)(C)(i) (2018).
15 U.S.C. § 1681k.
15 U.S.C. § 1681k(a) (2018).
198 U.S. 45 (1905).
20 U.S.C. § 1412(5)(C).
206 F.3d 392, 398 (4th Cir. 2000)
280 U.S. 709, 717 (1987).
29 C.F.R § 1607.5(A) (2018).
29 C.F.R. § 1607.14.
29 C.F.R. § 1607.4.
29 C.F.R. § 1607.5B (2018)).
29 C.F.R. § 1630.14(d).
29 C.F.R. § 1910.1020.
29 U.S.C. § 157 (2012).
29 U.S.C. § 158 (2012).
29 U.S.C. § 158 (2018).
29 U.S.C. § 207(a)(1) (2000)).
29 U.S.C. § 623(a), (b), (e) (2012).
29 U.S.C. § 623(f)(1).
29 U.S.C. §§ 621; 631(a)-b) (2012).
31 U.S.C. § 231-32 (1970).
389 U.S. 347, 360 (1967) (Harlan, J., concurring).
42 C.F.R § 50.203.
42 C.F.R. § 50.209.
42 U.S.C. § 12112.
42 U.S.C. § 12112(b)(7).
42 U.S.C. § 2000e.
42 U.S.C. § 2000ff-1(b) (2018).
42 U.S.C. §§ 1182 et seq. (2012).
42 U.S.C. §§ 12112(d)(2)(B), (d)(4)(A).
42 U.S.C.A. § 2000(ff)(1)(a).
45 C.F.R § 162.923 (2012).
45 C.F.R. § 160.103 (2014).
45 C.F.R. §160.103 (2014).
45 C.F.R. §164.306 (2013).
48 Code of Federal Regulations, 37.109 (2010).
480 U.S. 709, 717 (1987).
5 U.S.C. § 3108 (1970).
691 F.3d 1221, 1224 (11th Cir. 2012).
AB-25 (Cal. 2019. California Consumer Privacy Act of 2018 (accessed via https://leginfo.legis
    lature.ca.gov/faces/billTextClient.xhtml?bill_id=201920200AB25).
Algorithmic Accountability Act. HR 6580 (2022).
All Actions: HR 2231 – 116th Congress (2019–2020). www.congress.gov/bill/116th-congress/
    house-bill/2231/all-actions?overview=closed#tabs.

Americans with Disabilities Act of 1990, 42 U.S.C. § 12112(b)(6) (1990).

Americans with Disabilities Act, 42 U.S.C. § 12112(a) (2012).

Article 19, Emotional Entanglement: China's Emotion Recognition Market and Its Implications for Human Rights 15 (2021).

Cal. Gov't. Code § 12926(g).

Cal. Gov't. Code § 12940 et. seq.

Cal. Penal Code § 637.7 (West 2018).

Cal. Penal Code § 653n.

Capture of Use of Biometric Identifier Act, 50 Tex. Bus. & Com. Code Ann. § 503.001.

Civil Rights Act of 1964, 42 U.S.C. § 2000e-2(a)(1) (1964).

Conn. Gen. Stat. § 31-48b (amend. 2012).

Emancipation Proclamation, 12 Stat. 1268 (1863).

Fair Labor Standards Act, 29 U.S.C. §§ 201–19 (2012).

G.A. Res. 217 (III) A, Universal Declaration of Human Rights, art. 23(1) (Dec. 10, 1948) ("Everyone has the right to work, to free choice of employment, to just and favourable conditions of work and to protection against unemployment.").

Genetic Information Nondiscrimination Act of 2008 § 202(b).

Genetic Information Nondiscrimination Act, 81 Fed. Reg. 31143, 31158 (May 17, 2016) (codi-fied at 29 C.F.R. § 1635.8(b)(2)(iii)(A) (2018).

H.B. 1493, 2017 Sess., 65th Leg. (Wash. 1999).

Labor Management Relations (Taft-Hartley) Act.

National Labor Relations Act of 1935, 29 U.S.C. §§ 151-69 (1988).

National Labor Relations Act, 29 U.S.C. § 157 (2012).

No. 1:16-CV-00102, 2018 WL 2118311, at 1-2 (M.D. Tenn. May 8, 2018).

Pub. L. No. 101-336, 104 Stat. 327 (codified at 42 U.S.C. §§ 12113 et seq. (2012)).

Pub. L. No. 110-233, 122 Stat. 881 (codified as amended at 29 U.S.C. §§ 216 et seq. (2012).

Pub. L. No. 80-101, ch. 120, § 101, 61 Stat. 136, 137-38 (1947) (codified at 29 U.S.C. § 152 (1988).

Pub. L. No. 88-352, § 703, 78 Stat. 241, 255 (1964) (codified at 42 U.S.C. § 2000e-2 (2012)).

Pub. L. No. 89-554, 80 Stat. 416 (1966).

Pub. L. No. 90-202, 81 Stat. 602 (2012).

Restatement (Second) Of Agency § 2 (1958).

Restatement (Third) Of Agency § 7.07(3)(A) (2006).

Restatement Of Employment Law § 7.05(A) (2015).

RI Gen. Laws 1956 § 28-6.12-1 (2005).

S.B. 1267, 2011-2012 Reg. Sess. § 56.19(a) (Cal 2012).

S.B. 222, 2012-2013 Reg. Sess. (Cal. 2013).

S.B. 559, 2011 Leg., 2011-2012 Sess., (Cal. 2011) (enacted by Chapter 261).

Tex. Penal Code Ann. § 16.06 (West 2018).

U.S. Civil Rights Act of 1964 § 7, 42 U.S.C. § 2000e (2012).

V.I. Code Ann. tit. 29, § 333(b)(1) (2019).

W. Va. Code § 21-3-20.

PATENT DOCUMENTS

U.S. Patent Application No. 14/849,152, Pub. No. 2017/0068313 (published Mar. 9, 2017) (Int'l Bus. Mach. Corp., applicant).

U.S. Patent Application No. 14/998,746, Pub. No. 2016/0189174 (published June 30, 2016) (Stephan Heath, applicant).

U.S. Patent Application No. 15/134,797, Pub. No. 2017/0243453 (published Aug. 24, 2017) (Immersion Corp., applicant).

U.S. Patent Application No. 15/145,144, Pub. No. 2016/0247006 (published Aug. 25, 2016) (Intermec Tech. Corp., applicant); U.S. Patent Application No. 13/756,115, Pub. No. 2014/0214631 (published Jul. 31, 2014) (Intermec Tech. Corp., applicant).

U.S. Patent Application No. 15/605,313, Pub. No. 2018/0125738 (published May 10, 2018) (Carnegie Mellon Univ., applicant).

U.S. Patent No. 9,498,128 (issued Nov. 22, 2016).

U.S. Patent No. 9,881,276 (issued Jan. 30, 2018).

Index

quantified racism (cont.)
  Black Codes, 294–96
  against Black workers
    African American Vernacular English and, 299
    automated hiring bias and discrimination against, 298–99, 301
    productivity evaluation of, 306–308
    wellness evaluation of, disparities in, 310–11
    workplace surveillance of, 303–306
  compensation assessment, by race, 309–310
    in professional sports, 309–310
  conceptual approach to, 293–94
  through employment discrimination, 296–302
    African American Vernacular English and, 299
    with automated video interviewing, 298
    symbolic capital theory, 300–301
  in gig economy, 293–94, 313–15
  intersectional identities and, 315–16
    feminist approaches to, 316–17
  labor exploitation and, 294–96
  laissez-faire capitalist approaches to, 316
  against Latinx workers, 316
  "New Jim Code," 293
  productivity evaluation and, by race, 306–308
    wage gaps as result of, 307, 308
  racial exploitation and, 313–15
  reform proposals for, 316–19
    algorithmic affirmative action, 317
    for labor protections, 318–19
    for social protections, 318–19
  Thirteenth Amendment Exception and, 294–96
    prison labor and, 295–96
  wellness evaluation and, by race, 310–13
    against Black workers, 310–11
    for medical diagnoses, 311–12
  workplace surveillance and, 296
    of Black workers, 303, 305–306
    Fordism and, 302
    racialized effects of, 302–306
quantified self movement, 265–66
quantified worker
  conceptual description of, 1–2
  historical development of, 3–4
  methodological approach to, 4–5

Race after Technology (Benjamin), 293
racial exploitation, 313–15
racism. *See also* bias; discrimination; quantified racism; slave trade; slavery
  Black Codes, 294–96
  Ku Klux Klan and, 295
  white supremacy and, 295

radio-frequency identification (RFID)
  microchips, 186–87
  wearable technology and, 271
Raghavan, Manish, 298
Railroad Labor Act, U.S. (1926), 60
Railroad Labor Board, 60
Raub, McKenzie, 153–54
Raushenbush, Carl, 65–66
Rawls, John, 323–25
Reagan, Ronald, 339
reciprocal power, 328–29
Reed, Hudson, 56
reentry organizations, 3
refractive surveillance, 174
Rehabilitation Act, U.S. (1973), 106–107
Reidenberg, Joel, 163, 350
relationship-building, through telecommuting, 246
Republicanism (Pettit), 328
republicanism, in workplace, 327, 328
responsibility principle, 332
Restatement of Employment Law, U.S., 178
Reusskamp, Harry J., 56
Reynolds, Dennis, 303
RFID chips. *See* radio-frequency identification microchips
Rhue, Lauren, 149, 300
right to unionize. *See also* labor unions
  worker surveillance and, 202–14
    historical development of, 179–80
    under National Labor Relations Act, 202–214
risk shifting
  by corporations, ethics of worker quantification and, 338–42
  gig economy and, 341–42
  Personal Responsibility Crusade and, 339
  Principle of Inverse Coverage, 342
  in workplace wellness programs, 236–41
  from employers to workers, 237–38
robotics, meaningful work and, 330–31
Robots in the Workplace (Berkers, Nyholm, and Smids), 330
Roediger, David, 304–305
Rogers, Brishen, 318–19, 336
Roman Empire, quantification of workers during, 16
Rosenthal, Caitlin C., 304
Rousseau, Jean-Jacques, 215–19, 324
Rubenfeld, Ned, 75
Rucker, Edward, 42–43

Sachs, Benjamin, 337–38
salary compensation, 277–80
  quantified racism as influence on, 309–310
  in professional sports, 309–310

Printed in the USA
CPSIA information can be obtained
at www.ICGtesting.com
LVHW020105010923
756929LV00001B/12

9 781316 636954